HINDU DHARMA

The Universal Way of Life

VOICE OF THE GURU

PŪJYAŚRĪ CHANDRAŚEKHARENDRA SARASVATĪ SVĀMĪ

HINDU DHARMA

The Universal Way of Life

ॐ

1996

BHARATIYA VIDYA BHAVAN
Kulapati Munshi Marg
Mumbai - 400 007

First Edition : June, 1995
Second Revised Edition : October, 1995
Third Edition : August, 1996

ISBN 81-7276-055-8

Price : Rs 600.00

Typesetting : Turbo Computer Services

PRINTED IN INDIA

By Atul Goradia at Siddhi Printers, 13/14 Bhabha Building, 13th Khetwadi Lane, Mumbai - 400 004, and published by S. Ramakrishnan, Executive Secretary, Bharatiya Vidya Bhavan, Kulapati Munshi Marg, Mumbai - 400 007.

Śrī Śankara Bhagavatpāda (509-477 B.C.).

Śhri Chandraśekharendra Sarasvati Svāmi (1894-1994)

गुरुर्ब्रह्मा गुरुर्विष्णुः गुरुर्देवो महेश्वरः ।
गुरुः साक्षात् परं ब्रह्म तस्मै श्री गुरवे नमः ॥

Gururbrahmā Gururviṣṇuḥ Gururdevo Maheśvaraḥ
Guruḥ sākṣāt Param Brahma tasmai Śrī Gurave namaḥ

(The guru is Brahmā, the guru is Viṣṇu, the guru is Maheśvara. Obeisance to the guru who, verily, is the Parabrahman.)

Dedicated to the
Seers, Sages and Saints
of India and the World
who have held aloft the ideal
Vasudhaiva Kutumbakam
(The World is One Family)

PUBLISHER'S NOTE

This book comprises the discourses originally delivered in Tamil by Pūjyaśrī Chandraśekharendra Sarasvatī Svāmī and included in Volumes I & II of *Deivattin Kural,* compiled by Rā. Gaṇapati, and published by Vānadi Padippakam, Madras.
The translation is by R.G.K.

Foreword

"Man is no different from animals," says Śrī Śankara Bhagavatpāda in his *Sūtrabhāṣya*. "Paśvādibhiścāviśeṣāt."

Texts tell us: "Human beings and animals have the same urges. They eat and sleep and copulate and, besides, the feelings of fear are common to both. What, then, is the difference between the two? It is adherence to dharma that distinguishes human beings from animals. Without dharma to guide him man would be no better than an animal."

"Āhāranidrābhayamaithunam ca sāmānyametat paśubhirnarāṇām
Dharmo hi teṣāmadhiko viśeṣaḥ dharmeṇa hīnā paśubhissamānāḥ"

The Lord says in the Bhagavadgītā: "When a man thinks of the objects of sense, attachment to them is born; from attachment arises desire; and from desire arises anger. Anger causes delusion and from delusion springs loss of memory; loss of memory leads to the destruction of the sense of discrimination; and because of the destruction of his sense of discrimination man perishes."

Dhyāyato viṣayān puṁsaḥ saṅgasteṣū'pajāyate
Saṅgāt saṁjāyate kāmaḥ kāmāt krodho'bhijāyate

Krodhād bhavati saṁmohaḥ saṁmohāt smṛtivibhramaḥ
Smṛtibhraṁśād buddhināśo buddhināśāt praṇaśyati

Commenting on these two ślokas of the Gītā, Svāmī Chinmayānanda says that evil develops from our wrong thinking or false imagination like a tree developing from the seed. Thought has the power to create as well as to destroy. Rightly harnessed, it can be used for constructive purposes; if misused it will be the cause of our utter destruction. When our mind constantly dwells on a "sense-object", an attachment is created for that object. When we keep thinking of this object with increasing intensity, our attachment to it becomes crystallized as burning desire for the same. But as obstacles arise to the fulfilment of this desire, the force that at first caused the desire now turns into anger.

Svāmī Chinmayānanda further observes that anyone whose intellect is in the grip of anger becomes deluded and loses his sense of discrimination since he is also deprived of his memory. A man who is the victim of anger is capable of doing anything, forgetful of himself and his relationship with other people. Śrī Śankarāchārya observes in this connection that a deluded fool will fight even with revered persons like his own parents and preceptors, forgetting his indebtedness to them.

Says Socrates: "The noblest of all investigations... is what man should be and what he should pursue." And Samuel Taylor Coleridge observes: "If man is not rising upward to be an angel, he is sinking downward to be a devil. He cannot stop at the beast."

It is perhaps because of his understanding of the instincts of man and the need for human actions to be inspired by dharma that the famous poet Nīlakaṇṭha Dīkṣita said: "If, even after being born a man, one does not have any sense of discrimination, it would be better for such a one to be born an animal since animals are not subject to the law that controls the senses."

Our rishis knew that "all except God will perish". Man with his capacity for discrimination must be able to grasp the truth that the Ātman is not different from the Brahman. The Ātman has neither a beginning nor an end. Every individual goes through a succession of births and, determined by his karma, either sinks further and further down or rises further and further up. But in life after life the Ātman remains untainted.

There is a difference of opinion even among the learned as to the meaning of the word "dharma". The word is derived from "dhṛ" to uphold, sustain or nourish. The seers often use it in close association with "ṛta" and "satya". Śrī Vidyāraṇya defines ṛta as the mental perception and realisation of God. The *Taittirīya Upanishad* also uses it with "satya" and "dharma". It exhorts students to speak the truth and practise dharma ("Satyam vada"; "Dharmam chara"). According to Śankara Bhagavatpāda, satya means speaking the truth and dharma means translating it (satya) into action.

"Satyamiti yathāśāstrārthatā sa eva anuṣṭhīyamānaḥ dharmanāmā bhavati."

In this connection, the explanation given by Śrī K. Bālasubrahmania Aiyar is relevant: "An analysis of the significance of these three words (ṛta, satya and dharma) brings out clearly to us the fundamental basis of dharma as the ideal for an individual. While ṛta denotes the mental perception and realization of truth and satya denotes the exact true expression in words of the truth as perceived by the mind, dharma is the observance, in the conduct of life, of truth. In fact, dharma is the way of life which translates into action the truth perceived by the man of insight as expressed by him truly. In short, ṛta is truth in thought, satya is truth in words and dharma is truth in deed."

To right-thinking people "dharma" and "satya" are interchangeable words and their goal is — as it has always been — to rise higher so as to realise Him who alone is the Truth. For them there is no pursuit higher than that of practising truth in thought, word and deed.

"Bhūtahitam" is Śrī Śankarāchārya's answer to the question (that he himself raised), "Kim satyam?" It means that truth (or truthfulness) is what is spoken for the well-being of all living beings. To the question, "Ko dharmaḥ?", his answer is "Abhimato yaḥ śiṣṭānām nija kulīnām." It means that dharma is that which is determined by the elders and by learned people.

Of the four purushārthas or aims of life, dharma is always mentioned first, artha second, kāma third and moksha last. The four stanzas of the Mahābhārata that together go by the name of "Bhārata-Sāvitrī" contain these profound truths: Dharma is eternal but neither happiness nor sorrow is eternal; the Ātman is everlasting but not that which embodies it; and from dharma arise artha and kāma. They also contain Vedavyāsa's lamentation: "With uplifted arms I cry but no one listens to me, 'From dharma spring artha and kāma. Why is dharma then not practised?'"

Śrī Śankara Bhagavatpāda observes that even the wise and the learned, even men who have a vision of the exceedingly subtle Ātman, are overpowered by tamas and do not understand it even though clearly explained in various texts.

The Reality is perceived by one who has śraddhā or faith which, according to the saints, is acceptance of the truth as proclaimed by the scriptures and as taught by the guru. By following the reasoning of the śāstras and the path shown by the guru the bonds of avidyā are broken and one becomes aware of the Ātman. One's own experience obtained through one-pointed meditation of the Truth is another means to achieve the same goal. These moments are indeed blessed, the moments during which the Truth dawns on us as we receive instruction from our guru and as we gain wisdom that is supported by the authority of the scriptures. Yes, these indeed are moments of bliss when the senses are quietened and the mind is firmly fixed on the Ātman. Thus dharma, to be precise Veda Dharma, has been and is essential for man to become a real man.

According to Śrī Chandraśekharendra Sarasvatī, the Mahāsvāmī, dharma is our only protection. In this book, the Great Āchārya recounts all that we need to know about dharma and presents in an integrated form the various systems of thought that have flourished in this country. "The Vedas," Śrī Mahāsvāmī affirms, "represent the lofty principle that it is the One Truth that is envisaged as all that we perceive."

The discourses that make up this book are remarkable for their simple and enchanting style. The most complex of ideas are explained with such lucidity as to make them comprehensible to the ordinary reader. Śrī Mahāsvāmī deals not only with the wisdom of the Samhitā part of the Vedas and with other scriptural matters, he takes in his stride even modern scientific concepts like those of time and space. It is all at once so wide-ranging and so profound that we bow our heads in reverence to the Great Master of our time, the Sage of Kāmakoṭi Pīṭha. His approach shows that he has no doubts in his mind, no hesitation in affirming the truths contained in the Vedas and the śāstras:

"The point to be noted is that if you believe in the śāstras, you must believe in them fully. If you are an atheist, you could of course reject all the śāstras. But to make a show of being very clever and twist the śāstras as you like, accepting some parts and rejecting and changing some others, is an offence more grave than that of being an atheist. To think that Mother Veda should dance to your tune is also a great offence. Learning the Vedas with such an attitude is tantamount to ridiculing them.

"I am not angry with the reformists, nor do I suspect their intentions. They go wrong because of their ignorance and thoughtlessness. If they wish to pull down the fence so as to go to the other side, they must think of the possibility of the few still remaining there crossing over to this side."

The Great Āchārya has commanded us to protect the old dhārmic traditions and keep them alive :

"All old dhārmic traditions must be protected and kept alive. Śrī Śankara Bhagavatpāda has commanded us to do so. I bear his name; so it is my duty to remind you of his command. Whether or not you will heed his command, I should like to impress upon you that the śāstric customs have the purpose of ensuring the good of all mankind."

I am aware of the alarm sounded by Vedavyāsa, but I still sincerely believe that the words of the Great Master of our time shall rekindle the lamp of wisdom and lead us from darkness unto light. It is my great privilege to write the Foreword to this book. The translator has done a service to people like us who believe in the *saha-chintan* and the words of the Yajurveda:

"Vayam rāṣṭre jāgryāma purohitāḥ.

Let us be awake and alert to the noble cause of the nation, to the India of the Ṛgveda — our svadeśa from the Himavān to the ocean. There is need for a fresh commitment on the part of its people to the ideal expressed by the time-honoured saying, *"Jananī janmabhūmiśca svargādapi garīyasī."*

P.S. MISHRA
Judge
High Court of Madras

Madras,
March 13, 1995

(*Since writing this, Śrī Mishra has been appointed Chief Justice of Andhra Pradesh.)*

Preface

When India was straining at the leash during the unique "Weaponless War" conceived, planned and led by Mahātmā Gāndhī to win freedom, some of the finest flowers of Indian manhood and womanhood were forced to languish in prison for long years. During his ninth incarceration, this time in the Ahmednagar Fort Prison (August 9, 1942 to July 15, 1945), Paṇḍit Jawāharlāl Nehru, one of the best among them, embarked upon a voyage of *"Discovery of India"*. He "discovered" for himself and for us, the common people, an India that is "a myth and an idea, a dream and a vision and yet very real and pervasive."

Nehru, with the poetic touch so characteristic of him, looked upon India as "a lady with a glorious past, whose deep eyes had seen so much of life's passion and joy and folly and looked deep down into wisdom's well." It is this "wisdom's well" that is represented by our Vedic heritage, the "living words", as Gurudeva Rabīndranāth Tagore put it, "that have issued from the Illuminated Consciousness of our great ones."

This offering of *Hindu Dharma : The Universal Way of Life* deals with another kind of discovery of India, a discovery in the spiritual realm, made by Jagadguru Śrī Chandraśekharendra Sarasvatī Svāmigal, the 68th Śankarāchārya of Kānchi Kāmakoṭi Pīṭha. The Sage of Kānchi was spiritually supreme, intellectually pre-eminent. He was verily an *akshayapātra* -- inexhaustible reservoir -- of the spiritual wisdom of India dating back to the beginning of Time, and of Vedic Dharma. So was he with regard to modern knowledge, current affairs and contemporary men and matters.

In a special eassy in the *Bhavan's Journal,* this true sanātanī hailed Gāndhiji, a staunch Hindu and a secularist nonpareil, as one of the "greatest redeemers of Hinduism". Hailing Gāndhījī's services to Hinduism, he said: "From the time Gāndhījī came into the arena, he augmented his political movements by his spiritual researches and devotion. Almost all the features of Hinduism that were discarded as weeds by the previous reform movements were clearly explained by Gāndhījī as being of indispensable utility. His views on *Rāmanāma,* the Rāmāyaṇa, varṇa dharma, āhāraniyama and his definition of God are such that the most faithful Hindu cannot but profit spiritually by digesting them."

During one of the satsangas some members of the Bhavan's family were privileged to have with him, this remarkable advaitin said that Jawāharlāl Nehru was "an advaitin at heart."

II

The Mahāsvāmī will shine for ever as one of the greatest exemplars of sanātana dharma, the Universal Way of Life. This sanātanī extraordinary personified in himself all that is best and noblest in Hinduism. He always stressed that Hinduism is the latter-day name given to mankind's earliest religion -- sanātana dharma. It is beginningless (anādi), endless (ananta) and hence eternal (sanātana), because it is in consonance with Nature's Laws.

To drive home the eternal or the sanātana aspect of our religion, the Mahāsvāmī used to narrate a telling episode : "There was a palm-tree round which a creeper entwined itself. The creeper grew fast and within months it entwined the entire tree. 'This palm has not grown a bit all these months,' said the creeper laughing. The palm-tree retorted: 'I have seen tens of thousand creepers in my life. Each creeper before you said the same thing as you have now said. I do not know what to say to you.' Our religion is like this tree in relation to other faiths."

We were fortunate to have lived in the times, and to have had frequent *darshans,* of one with such "Illuminated Consciousness", whose nearly 100-year-long Pilgrimage on Earth ended on January 8, 1994. He was a realised soul, and whenever he spoke, he spoke in the accents of the Vedic seers — precise, profound and authentic — words that found a permanent lodgement in the hearts of his listeners.

The Mahāsvāmī's words of distilled wisdom, as compiled by his ardent devotee Śrī Rā. Gaṇapati, run into six volumes covering more than 6,500 pages. Śri Rā. Gaṇapati and Śri A. Tirunāvukkaraśu of Vānadi Padippakam, the publisher, deserve our eternal gratitude for their invaluable efforts to preserve for posterity the Sage of Kānchi's words of wisdom.

Being in Tamil, these volumes, with their precious content, remain a closed book to tens of thousands of devotees in India and abroad who do not know that language but are athirst and ever-yearning for the Mahāsvāmī's spiritual ambrosia.

The English versions of selected discourses, which have so far appeared in book-form, touch but a fringe of what the Mahāsvāmī has said about sanātana dharma. The Bhavan, too, has had the privilege of contributing its humble mite in this direction — we have published *Aspects of Our Religion, The Vedas, Adi Śankara : His Life and Times, The Guru Tradition* and *Kanchi Mahaswami on Poets and Poetry.*

This volume of nearly 900 pages has been rendered into English from the Tamil by R.G.K. It is a monumental effort reflecting enormous, dedicated and unremitting labour over a long period of time. In translation, the transformation is normally from gold to lead but R.G.K. has ensured that the sheen of the original is retained. He has also spared no pains to explain obscure points of legend, purānic allusions and scriptural references covering both *Śruti* and *Smṛti.*

We are thankful to Justice Śri P.S. Mishra, at present Chief Justice of Andhra Pradesh, for his illuminating Foreword and Śri A. Kuppuswāmi for his learned Introduction.

III

The Bhavan has been the blessed recipient of the Mahāsvāmī's grace right from its inception in 1938. He has been one of the Bhavan's greatest guides and philosophers. He very closely watched with a benign concern the landmark projects of the Bhavan like the monumental 11-volume *History and Culture of the Indian People* covering nearly 5,000 years from the Vedic Age to the Modern Age. This is the only comprehensive history of India written by Indians — a team of 100 eminent scholars, each a specialist in his chosen field. They laboured on it for 32 years under the inspiration and guidance of Kulapati Munshi, with the doyen of Indian historians Dr Romesh Chandra Majumdar as General Editor. The Jagadguru then observed : "Distinguished historians like K.M. Munshi are engaged in writing afresh our history without any bias".

Commending Kulapati Munshi's ceaseless efforts through the Bhavan for the revival of Sanskrit, of India's ages-old traditions and the resuscitation of ethical and spiritual values embedded in sanātana dharma, the Mahāsvāmī remarked : "Munshi is not an old-fashioned sanātanist like me. He is a reformist and a friend and follower of Gāndhiji. And he was a member of the Nehru Cabinet. So he cannot be included among the 'reactionaries'!......"

During the Bhavan's Silver Jubilee in 1962, the Mahāsvāmī sent the following benediction:

> "The Bhāratīya Vidyā Bhavan has made the people of Bhārata Varṣa in general and the intellectuals in particular evince interest in the various aspects of our culture and progress.
>
> "May we pray: Give fresh vigour to the Bhavan, a unique institution, in directing its attention more and more, with greater and greater fulfilment, to the dissemination of moral principles and devotion."

He also sent along with it a cash "donation" of Rs 1,000. Kulapati Munshi shed copious tears of joy and exclaimed in ecstasy: "This is the holiest of holy *prasads*. This is invaluable, inestimable and much more than several thousand crores of rupees. Nothing, nothing, can surpass divine grace."

IV

The Mahāsvāmī brings out the essentials of sanātana dharma in a language that is at once simple and clear. Commendable indeed is the cogency of the narrative. We are left in no doubt about any aspect of our eternal Dharma.

As will be seen in this volume, the Mahāsvāmī's approach is catholic. He avers : "The goal of all religions is to lead people to the Paramātman according to the different attitudes of the devotees concerned. Our forefathers were well aware that all religions are different paths to realise the one and only Paramātman."

More than a century ago, in 1893, did not Svāmi Vivekānanda thunder at the World Parliament of Religions in Chicago that "Mankind ought to be taught that religions are but the varied expressions of THE RELIGION, which is Oneness, so that each may choose the path that suits him best"?

The Discovery of India by Jawāharlāl Nehru, the Political Monarch of Modern India and Free India's first Prime Minister (1947-1964), inspired the people of India, particularly its youth, to regain our political freedom. This was true also of the people, particularly the young, of many nations of South-East Asia and Africa then under foreign domination.

The eminent historian, parliamentarian and author of several scholarly volumes such as the Bhavan's publications : *The Fundamental Unity of India* (first published in London in 1914 with a Foreword by the Rt Hon'ble J. Ramsay MacDonald, first Labour Prime Minister of Britain, 1929 (he was also P.M. during 1929-35) and *Hindu Civilization,* Dr Radha Kumud Mookerji, has pointed out the uniqueness of the Vedas, especially the Ṛgveda, thus:

> "The Vedas, and especially the primordial work known as the Ṛgveda, represent not merely the *dawn* of culture, but also its *zenith.* Indian thought is seen at its highest in the Ṛgveda... On the one hand it is the *first book of India and also of mankind.* At the same time, it shows the highest point of human wisdom. We see in it the whole process of evolution, from its beginning to its completion."

Ekam sad viprā bahudhā vadanti (The truth is One, the wise speak of it in different ways).

This volume *Hindu Dharma : The Universal Way of Life* is in the nature of a discovery of Vedic India, Immortal India, by Pūjyaśrī Chandraśekharendra Sarasvatī, the Moral Monarch of this century. Sooner than later, this is bound to immensely inspire not only the people and youth of India but also the people and youth of the world over to restore and retain values, purity and sanity in personal and public life. This is our hope and prayer, nay conviction.

Vedo'khilo dharmamūlam; Dharmo rakshati rakshitaḥ – the Vedas are the root of all Dharma; Dharma protected, protects.

S. RAMAKRISHNAN
General Editor

Bhāratîya Vidyā Bhavan,
Bombay

101st Mahāsvāmi Jayanti,
June 12, 1995

Introduction

The word "Introduction", used with reference to a publication, signifies "the preliminary matter" prefixed to it. Does the present work, comprising as it does the discourses on Hindu Dharma, or more properly Veda Dharma, delivered by the greatest spiritual luminary of the century (that is the Sage of Kānchi), and translated into English by a seasoned writer, need an Introduction? For days this was the question that revolved in my mind following the request made by Śrī R.G.K. that I should write an Introduction to this translation. (Śrī R.G.K., a good friend of mine, was formerly Assistant Editor of *The Illustrated Weekly of India.)*

I felt that I was not qualified for the job of writing the Introduction. I was reminded of the short Introduction I had written to *The Guru Tradition* which also incorporates the discourses of the Sage of Kānchi and which is also translated by Śrī R.G.K. — this book was published in 1991. I should like to quote a sentence from it: "It is only the devotion to the sacred feet of the Great Guru of Kānchi, implanted in my heart in my boyhood days and nurtured during the past six decades and more, combined with the persistent desire of the translator (an esteemed friend), that has emboldened me to pen this short piece which is but an apology for an Introduction."

As desired by the translator, I have gone through the entire typescript of *Hindu Dharma* and this gives me the courage to write a few lines by way of a preliminary note.

The lectures delivered decades ago in Tamil by His Holiness the Sage of Kānchi on diverse aspects of our Dharma, on our ancient culture and our arts and on a variety of other subjects have been brought out in six volumes by Vānadi Padippakam, a well-known publishing house of Madras. But until now ardent followers of Hindu Dharma, who do not know Tamil, have not had access to these discourses given by the incomparable preceptor of our time, discourses that are as extensive and educative as they are enlightening and enchanting. Śrī R.G.K. deserves the thanks of people living outside Tamil Nadu, both in India and abroad, for throwing open to them the treasure-house of the upanyāsas of the Great Āchārya.

Translating any work from one language into another is an arduous task, especially so if the work translated consists of the spoken word. I know for a fact that the translator of this book has toiled for months on end and tried his best to maintain fidelity to the original.

It is my earnest hope that middle-aged people and youngsters — particularly teachers and students — belonging to regions outside Tamil Nadu will get copies of *Hindu Dharma* and benefit by reading the same. I should like to make a humble request to the publishers to take such steps as would bring the book within easy reach of all, especially teachers and students.

May the Divine World Mother and the Sage of Kānchi, who remains shining as the all-pervading "cit", grant long life and health to Śrī R.G.K. to enable him to bring out further English translations of the Great Āchārya's discourses.

A. KUPPUSWAMI

Kānchipuram,
March 10, 1995

Translator's Note

More than 20 years ago, I said in an article in *The Illustrated Weekly of India* that "Hindus know less about their religion than Christians and Muslims know about *theirs*". Wanting to verify the statement, my editor Sardar Khushwant Singh asked my colleagues (most of them were Hindus), in schoolmasterly fashion, to name any four Upanishads. For moments there was silence and it was a Muslim lady member of the staff who eventually responded to the editor's question by "reeling off" the names of six or seven Upanishads.

Why are "educated" Hindus ignorant about their religion? Is it their education itself that has alienated them from their religious and cultural moorings? If so it must be one of the tragic ironies of the Indian condition. The Paramaguru[1] himself speaks of our ignorance of the basic texts of our religion (Chapter 1, Part Five): "We must be proud of the fact that our country has produced more men who have found inner bliss than all other countries put together. It is a matter of shame that we are ignorant of the śāstras that they have bequeathed to us, the śāstras that taught them how to scale the heights of bliss. Many are ignorant about the scripture that is the very source of our religion—they do not know even its name... Our education follows the Western pattern. We want to speak like the white man, dress like him and ape him in the matter of manners and customs..."

The fact is that during the past two or three centuries Hindus have gone through a process of de-Hinduization which in some respects is tantamount to de-Indianization. Various other reasons are given as to why Hindus do not have a clear idea of their religion. One is that it is not a religion in the sense the term is usually understood. Another is that it is not easily reduced to a catechism. A third reason is that, unlike other faiths, it encompasses all life and activity, individual, social and national, and all spheres of knowledge. Hindu Dharma is an organic part of the Hindu. It imposes on him a discipline that is inward as well as outward and it is a process of refinement and inner growth. Above all it is a quest, the quest for knowing oneself, for being oneself.

Hindu Dharma, it must be remembered, is but a convenient term for what should ideally be known as Veda Dharma or Sanātana Dharma, the immemorial religion. Indeed, it might be claimed with truth, that this Dharma is more than a religion, that it is an entire civilization, the story of man from the very beginnings of time to find an answer to the problems of life, the story of that greatest of all

[1] Pūjyaśrī Chandraśekharendra Sarasvatī Svāmī, also respectfully referred to as Mahāsvāmī, *Mahā-Periyavāl* (in Tamil), the Great Āchārya, the Sage of Kānchi, ...

adventures, that of the human spirit trying to discover its true identity. "From our total reactions to Nature," says J.W.N. Sullivan, "science selects a small part only as being relevant to its purpose..." Everything is relevant to Hinduism because its "purpose" is to know the Truth in its entirety, not fractions of truth that may have their own purposes but not the Great Purpose of knitting together everything to arrive at the ultimate knowledge. It needs a master to speak about such a religion. We must consider ourselves blessed that we had such a master living in our own time, I mean the Sage of Kānchi, Pūjyaśrī Chandraśekharendra Sarasvatī Svāmī, to teach us our Dharma. He was no ordinary master, but a Master of Masters.

This Great Master's discourses on Hindu Dharma, included in Volumes I and II of *Deivattin Kural,* are divided into 22 parts (there are two appendices in addition) in this book. There is, however, nothing rigid about this arrangement and we have here a single great stream that takes us through the variegated landscape that has come to be called Hinduism. To vary the imagery, it is a vast canvas on which the Paramaguru portrays the Hindu religion and it is a luminous canvas and there is nothing garish about the colours he dabs on it.

The Great Āchārya does not lecture from a high pedestal. Out of his compassion for us he speaks the language that everybody understands. (We must here acknowledge our profound indebtedness to Śrī Rā. Gaṇapati, the compiler of *Deivattin Kural,* and Śrī A. Tirunāvukkaraśu, the publisher, for having preserved the Sage of Kānchi's light of knowledge and wisdom for posterity.)

Throughout these discourses we recognise the Great Svāmī's synaptic vision. He sees connections where others see only differences. Is this not the special quality of a *seer,* the special quality of a mystic, who refuses to see things in compartments? Indeed, during the long decades during which Śrī Chandraśekharendra Sarasvatī Svāmī was the Śankarācharya of Kānchi Kāmakoṭi Pīṭha he was a great unifying force, a great civilizing influence. The manner in which he braids together the karmakāṇḍa and jñānakāṇḍa of the Vedas is indeed masterly. So too the way he presents the message of the Vedas or the essence of the Upanishads. Here we have something like the architectonics of great music or of a great monument like the Kailāsanātha temple of Ellora or the Bṛhadīśvara temple of Tañjāvūr. The Paramaguru takes all branches of knowledge in his stride, linguistics, astronomy, history, physics. He combines ancient wisdom with modern concepts like those of time and space -- he is aware, though, that some of these concepts are not new to our own scientific tradition. All the same, it must be noted that he does not speak what is convenient for today but what is true for all time.

It is difficult to summarise the ideas of our religion or to present the teachings of our Master in a few words. But it is necessary to underline certain points. For instance, the message of the Vedas on which Hindu Dharma is founded. "The Vedas hold out," declares the Paramaguru, "the ideal of liberation here itself. That is their glory. Other religions hold before people the ideal of salvation after a man's departure for another world." To repeat, the ultimate teaching of the Vedic religion is liberation here and now. After all, what is the purpose of any religion? Our Āchārya answers the question: "If an individual owing allegiance to a religion does not become a jñānin with inward experience of the truth of the Supreme Being, what does it matter whether that religion does exist or does not?"

"That thou art," is the great truth proclaimed by the Vedas. But how are you to realise the truth of "That"? Our Master's answer is: "Now itself when we are deeply involved in worldly affairs." In fact he tells us the practical means of becoming a jīvanmukta, or how to be liberated in this life itself. After all, he was a jīvanmukta himself and he speaks of truths not from a vacuum but from actual experience. That reminds one of the special feature of Hindu Dharma which is that it contains the practical steps to liberation; in other words Hinduism leads one to the Light in gradual stages. Critics call this Dharma ritual-ridden without realising that the rituals have a higher purpose, that of disciplining you, cleansing your consciousness, and preparing you for the inward journey. In a word, chitta-śuddhi is the means to a higher end. From work we must go to worklessness. The Paramaguru's genius for synthesizing ideas is demonstrated in the way he weaves together karma, bhakti, yoga and jñāna.

In our Vedic religion, individual salvation is not—as is often alleged—pursued to the neglect of collective well-being. "The principle on which the Vedic religion is founded," observes the Sage of Kānchi, "is that a man must not live for himself alone but serve all mankind." Well, varṇa dharma in its true form is a system according to which the collective welfare of society is ensured. As expounded by the Paramaguru, we see it to be radically different from what we are taught about it in school. Critics call caste a hierarchic and exploitative arrangement. But, actually, the system is one in which the duties of each jāti are interlinked with those of others. In this way society is knit together, leaving no room in it for jealousies and rivalries to arise. One point must be specially noted: the Great Āchārya lays stress again and again on the fact that no jāti is inferior to another jāti or superior to it.

In the varṇa dharma, as explained by our Master, the Brahmin does not lord it over other communities. Why do we need Brahmins at all? To preserve the Vedic dharma, to keep alive the sound of the Vedas which is important for the well-being not only of all Hindus but of all mankind. This duty can be performed only on a hereditary basis by one class of people. The Great Āchārya goes to the extent of saying that we do not need a class of people called Brahmins if they do not serve other communities, indeed mankind itself, by truly practising the ancient Vedic dharma. To paraphrase, if a separate class called Brahmins must exist—*and it must exist*—it is not for the sake of this class itself but for the ultimate good of mankind. The Paramaguru makes an impassioned plea to Brahmins to return to their dharma. He also points out that in varṇa dharma, in its ideal form, there are no differences among the jātis economically speaking -- all of them live a simple life, performing their duties and being devoted to the Lord.

It is varṇa dharma that has sustained Hindus or Indian civilization for all these millennia, observes the Paramaguru. And all our immense achievements in metaphysics and philosophy, in literature, in music, in the arts and sciences must be attributed to it. Above all, it is varṇa dharma that has made it possible for this land to produce so many great men and women, so many saintly men, who have been the source of inspiration for people all these centuries. Now this system has all but broken up and with it we see the decay of the nation.

There are so many other matters on which the Sage of Kānchi speaks -- for example, conducting an upanayana or a marriage meaningfully. He speaks with eloquence about our ideals of marriage and condemns dowry, describing it as an evil that undermines our society. There are, then, moving discourses on philanthropy, love and so on in which we see the Great Master as one who is concerned about the happiness of all, as one whose heart goes out to the poor and the suffering. His short discourses like "Outward Karma—Inward Meditation" or "Karma--the Starting Point of Yoga" encapsulate his philosophy with power and beauty. And the message of Advaita runs like a golden thread all through the book.

Altogether in these discourses we come face to face with a Great Being who is beyond time and space and we experience the "oceanic feeling", a term (originally French) coined by Romain Rolland and made familiar by Sigmund Freud. To us the Sage of Kānchi means an ocean of wisdom and an ocean of compassion. To think of him is to sanctify ourselves however unregenerate we may be.

I must now, in all humility, pay obeisance to Pūjyaśrī Jayendra Sarasvatī Svāmī and Pūjyaśrī Śankara Vijayendra Sarasvatī Svāmī and seek their blessings.

Śrī Meṭṭūr Svāmigal, gentle, devout and learned, has been a source of inspiration to me in my work.

I am thankful to Śrī P.S. Mishra, Chief Justice of Andhra Pradesh, for his learned Foreword.

The venerable Śrī A. Kuppuswāmi, who is a spry 84 and who served his Master, the Sage of Kānchi, with devotion for almost a lifetime, read the typescript of this book running into more than 1,000 pages and made valuable suggestions. I have always relied on him for advice and I am grateful to him for his Introduction, although I feel I don't deserve a bit the appreciative references he has made to me.

I am indebted to Śrī V. Śivarāmakrishṇan, Associate Editor of *Bhavan's*

Journal, for reading the proofs. With his practised eye he detected a number of errors -- he also suggested a number of improvements. I must add that Śrī Sivarāmakrishnan has himself written a book based on the Sage of Kānchi's discourses on Sanskrit and Tamil poets and their works.

The Kamākshi Sevā Samithi lost one of its stalwarts in the death of its Secretary, Śrī V. Krishnamurthi. For most of us the Samithi meant Śrī Krishnamurthi and Śrī Krishnamurthi meant the Samithi. Members of the Samithi and devotees of the Sage of Kānchi were distraught by his passing but they find consolation in the thought that he must still be serving the lotus feet of his Master.

Śrī P.N. Krishnaswami, Chairman of the Samithi, brought me cheer whenever I felt depressed about the progress of the book. I look upon him as a model of devotion to the Lord and service to fellow-men. So many others belonging to the Samithi have helped me in my work like Śrī R.S. Mani, Śrī V. Narāyanaswāmi, Captain N. Swāmināthan, Śrī B. Ramani and Śrī A.G. Rāmarathnam.

Dr W. R. Antarkar, a distinguished Sanskrit scholar, has laid me under a deep debt of gratitude by giving the once-over to the Sanskrit part of the main text. But he is not to be held responsible for mistakes, if any, that still remain uncorrected. I must also thank Śrī L.N. Subrahmanya Ghanapāṭhi, Dr R. Krishnamurthi Śāstrigal, Śrī S. Lakshmīnārāyaṇan, Śrīmatī (Dr) Viśalākshī Śivarāmakrishṇan and Śrī V. Rāmanāthan for their assistance.

Thanks are particularly due to Śiromaṇi R. Naṭarājan, of *Manjari* fame, for his help in preparing the Tamiḷ Glossary. He checked the notes I had made and added copious notes of his own. Owing to pressure on space all the material provided by him could not be incorporated. I also owe a debt of gratitude to Śrīmatī Bhavāni Vānchināthan, a gifted Tamil teacher, for "double-checking" the glossary, and to Śrīmatī Sarojā Krishṇan for her help.

Mrs Margaret Da'Costa converted my typescript into computer format in record time. I am thankful to her as well as to Kumārī Sandhyā Gaṇapathy: this dedicated young lady worked day and night for nearly three months to carry out my corrections. Śrī R. Gaṇapathy gave his daughter a helping hand. There were also inputs by Śrī R. S. Maṇi and Śrī N.Rāmamoorthy.

I must thank Śrī S Rāmakrishṇan, Executive Secretary of Bhāratīya Vidyā Bhavan, for the readiness with which he agreed to publish *Hindu Dharma* and for his unfailing courtesy, encouragement and cooperation. I must also acknowledge the help received from other officials of the organisation like Śrī A.P. Vāsudevan, Śrī C.K. Venkaṭarāman and Śrī P.V. Śankarankuṭṭy.

I am grateful to Śrī Atul Goradia of Siddhi Printers for the fine job of work he has done in printing this book. He remained unfazed by all the problems encountered in the course of the production of this work.

In all humility I place *Hindu Dharma* as an offering at the sacred lotus feet of Pūjyaśrī Chandraśekharendra Sarasvatī Svāmī. As one who has miles to go to become a jñānin, I can look upon the Mahāguru only in the form I knew him before he attained videhamukti. The dvaita-bhava, it is said, is the appropriate attitude in which one expresses one's devotion to one's guru. Our Great Master is the Infinite dissolved in the Infinite. But do we not separate the Infinite from the Infinite to meditate on It and to worship It as the Saguṇa Brahman? It is thus that I adore the lotus feet of the Mahāguru. As the Upanishads proclaim, "Pūrṇasya pūrnamādāya pūrṇamevāvaśiṣyate."

"CHINNAVAN"

Bombay,
May 19, 1995

Translator's Note — Third Edition

The Paramaguru has spoken illuminatingly on sound and its creative power. He believed that sound, or voice, was not destroyed, that it remained in space. The very meaning of what we call "akṣara" (a letter of the alphabet) is "imperishable". We believe that the words spoken by the Paramaguru are imperishable , that his voice is present in space or ākāśa.

India is today plunged in adharma — it is indeed unmaking itself. If it is to regain its true nature and is to be restored to the ancient values that made it a great civilization, its people must try to retain that voice — the voice of the Paramaguru — in their hṛdayākāśa and act according to the message contained in it. By the grace of the Great Guru, *Hindu Dharma—The Universal Way of Life* is going into its third edition and we feel happy that our own humble efforts in spreading this message have been rewarded with some measure of success.

The Index has been enlarged, but it is perhaps still not exhaustive. It took the translator more than three months to prepare it. It was a laborious job, like peeling cumminseeds, to translate a Malayalam saying. It would have taken longer but for the fact that three young friends of the translator's, Śrī K. Bālakrishṇan, Śrī S. Krishṇan and Śrī S. Hariharan, came to his help.

The translator also wishes to express his gratitude to Śrī K. Ranganāthan for his generous encouragement.

"CHINNAVAN"

Mumbai,
August 15, 1996

Key to Pronunciation

ā	(आ)	as in ācārya, vidyā, rājā
ī	(ई)	as in Īśvara, Sītā, Pārvatī
ū	(ऊ)	as in pūjya, dūra, vibhūti
ṛ	(ऋ)	as in Kṛṣṇa, Ṛgveda, gṛhastha
l	(-)	as in klpta
ṁ	(-)	as in saṁskāra, Mīmāṁsā
ḥ	(:)	as in namaḥ, guruḥ, Rāmaḥ
kh	(ख)	as in khadga, śākhā, duḥkha
gh	(घ)	as in ghṛta, ghanapāṭhin, Māghā
ṅ	(ङ)	as in liṅga, paṅkti
c	(च)	as in caraṇa, ācāra, vacana
ch	(छ)	as in Chandas, Chāndogya
jh	(झ)	as in jhankāra
ñ	(ञ)	as in jñāna, Kāñcī
ṭ	(ट)	as in ṭīkā, ghaṭikā, Jaṭādhara
ṭh	(ठ)	as in pāṭha, maṭha, Kaṭhopaniṣad
ḍ	(ड)	as in ḍamaruka, paṇḍita, nāḍi
ḍh	(ढ)	as in ḍhakka
ṇ	(ण)	as in Kṛṣṇa, vīṇa, bāṇa
th	(थ)	as in ratha, kathā, manthana
dh	(ध)	as in dhana, madhu, Rādhā
ph	(फ)	as in phala, kapha
bh	(भ)	as in bhāsa, abhaya, lābha
ś	(श)	as in śānti, Śiva, Śakti
ṣ	(ष)	as in Kṛṣṇa, bhāṣa, Upaniṣad
kṣ	(क्ष)	as in kṣamā, Lakṣmī, Kṣatriya
ṟṟ	(-)	as in *arangeṟṟam, kuṟṟam* (Tamil words)
ḷ	(ळ)	as in *aruḷ* (Tamil word), Kāḷī, Vaḷḷuvar

For the Reader's Attention

Sanskrit words are not italicised; but titles of Sanskrit works are, except those of well-known classics like the Rāmāyaṇa, the Mahābhārata, the Bhagavadgītā (or the Gītā for short).

No uniform style is adopted in the use of Sanskrit words; they occur either in their stem form or in the nominative singular.

"Brahmin" is used instead of "Brāhmaṇa"; "Śankara" instead of "Śaṁkara" or "Śaṅkara", the last-mentioned being the correct form; and the anglicized "Sanskrit" instead of "Saṁskṛtam".

The term "Self" in this translation denotes the "Ātman" -- this is in keeping with the generally accepted usage. "Jivātman" is referred to as the "individual self".

"Devas" are referred to as "celestials" in order to distinguish them from gods like Śiva, Rāma, Kṛṣṇa, Gaṇapati and so on.

What may be called "Hindī-ised" Sanskrit words like *"bhajan"* and *"paṇḍit"* are italicised.

"Ātmic" and "śāstric", though admittedly hybrid derivatives, are used as a matter of convenience. "Ātmaic" (Ātmanic?) and "śāstraic" are perhaps less euphonic

"Ācārya" with a capital "A", unless otherwise indicated, means Ādi Śankara or Śrī Śankara Bhagavatpāda.

"Maṭha" with a capital "M" refers to the Kāñcī Maṭha.

"Paramaguru", meaning the "Supreme Guru", refers to Śrī Candraśekharendra Sarasvatī Svāmī.

Words put in square brackets and intended to explain a term or passage in the main text are added either by the compiler of the discourses or by the translator. But simple meanings of words in the main text are given in round brackets.

In "Notes & References", some notes appear with "Ra. Ga": it means these are by Śrī Rā. Gaṇapati, the compiler. The translator wishes to own responsiblity for errors, if any, in the rest of the "Notes & References."

Words in the main text marked with a superior "S" (for instance, "Adhyāya^S", "Dīkṣā^S") are included in the Sanskrit Glossary. Similarly, words marked with a superior "T" (for example, "Āṇḍāḷ^T", "Vaḷḷuvar^T") are included in the Tamiḷ Glossary.

For the quotations from the Upaniṣads, used in the main text or reproduced in "Notes & References", the translator has relied mostly on *Ekādaśopaniṣadaḥ* printed at the Nirṇayasāgara Yantrālaya and published by Bā. Rā. Ghāṇekar.

The Guru Tradition, referred to in "Notes & References", comprises discourses by the Paramaguru and is published by the Bharatīya Vidyā Bhavan.

In the main text as well as in the notes there are references to places in Tamiḷ Nāḍu. It must be noted that the names of the districts mentioned may not all of them be correct since they keep changing.

CONTENTS

Contents

PART THIRTEEN: NYĀYA

PART FOURTEEN: PURĀNAS

PART TWENTY-ONE: FROM WORK TO WORKLESSNESS

PART TWENTY-TWO: DHARMAS COMMON TO ALL

Contents

Cover Photograph : Pūjyaśrī Candraśekharendra Sarasvatī Svāmī

Part One

RELIGION IN GENERAL

Chapter 1

Dharma Alone Protects

The *pīpal*[1] and the *neem*[2] are the royal children of Mother Nature's kingdom of trees. As the new year[3] approaches they shed their leaves, sprout tender green shoots again not long after. It is all the work of Mother Nature.

The custom of marrying the *pīpal* to the *neem* and of installing the idols of Vināyaka[4] and Nāgarāja[5] under them goes back to the dim past. After the winter months these trees will be bare and Vināyaka and Nāgarāja will remain exposed to the sun. This is the time when we may sit under the open sky and bask in the sun because it is now neither too warm nor too cold. When it rains or when the sun beats down harshly on us, we need to shield ourselves with an umbrella. And when it is bitterly cold we cannot sit in the open and gaze at the sky. But now, when the leaves fall[6] and the warmth of the sun is comforting (it is believed that with Śivarātri[7] the cold season bids you goodbye with the chant, "Śiva, Śiva"), we may sit in the open, by day or at night, to gaze upon the sky. To proclaim the beneficial nature of this season as it were — when the *pīpal* and the *neem* are shorn of their leaves — Mother Nature worships the gods under the trees (Vināyaka and Nāgarāja) with the rays of the gentle sun.

Nāgarāja may also be called Subrahmaṇya[8]. Indeed to the Telugu-speaking people the name "Subbarāyuḍu" denotes both Subrahmaṇya and the snake. The Tamiḷ-speaking people worship snakes on Ṣaṣṭī[9], a custom that has existed from time immemorial. Mother Nature's concern for Vighneśvara and Subrahmaṇya, the children of Pārvatī and Parameśvara, is an expression of her love for all of us who too are but the offspring of the same primordial couple.

There is a fullness about this love. As I said just now, when it is neither too warm nor too cold, Vighneśvara and Nāgarāja are exposed to the sun. But, as the sun gets warmer with the advance of spring, Mother Nature protects these deities from the heat. How? The trees now burgeon and form a green umbrella over Vināyaka and Nāgarāja. The shedding of leaves, the burgeoning again, all this is a part of the natural process and according to the immutable law of the universe which has been in force from the very beginning of time.

There is a law governing the behaviour of everything in this universe. All must submit to it for the world to function properly. Otherwise things will go awry and end up in chaos. It is the will of the Lord that all his creation, all his creatures, should live in happiness. That is why he has ordained a dharma, a law, for each one of them. It is compliance with this dharma that ensures all-round harmony. While Īśvara protects his children from rain and sun, he also provides them, when needed, with the warmth of the gentle sun. His love for his children is expressed in the scheme ordered by him for the functioning of Nature and the law he has laid down for trees is a part of it.

To be worthy of Īśvara's love we must possess certain qualities, certain virtues. If there is a law that applies to trees, there must be one that applies to us also. We shall deserve the Lord's love and compassion only by living in accordance with this law and by working for the well-being of all mankind. What is called dharma is this law, the law governing the conduct of man. Īśvara has endowed man with intelligence, but it is by using this very intelligence that human beings keep violating their dharma. If it is asked why they do so, all we can say in answer is that it is but the sport of the Lord. Man goes seeking this and that, believing that they will make him happy, and all the while he keeps violating his dharma. But he will discover sooner or later that it is dharma alone that gives him happiness in the end.

There is something that somehow turns people all over the world towards dharma. It is this something that inspires human beings everywhere to go beyond their material needs and do things that appear strange. How? One man reads the Bible, cross in hand; another smears ashes all over his body; and a third man wears the Vaiṣṇava mark. From generation to generation mankind has been practising such customs even without deriving any perceptible material benefit. What is the reason for this?

Man first earned the means for his daily upkeep. But he soon discovered that meeting the needs of the present would not be enough. So he tried to earn more and save for his future needs also. The question, however, arose as to what precisely constituted his "future". As he reflected on it, it became clear that his "future" on this earth would not be endless, that he would not live a thousand years or ten thousand. So he concerned himself with earning enough to see him through his life and at the same time leaving enough for his children.

What happened to a man after his death was the question that worried him next. The great men who emerged from time to time in various climes came to believe that the entity called man did not cease to exist even after his body perished. The truth dawned on them that the money and property acquired for the upkeep of a man's body served no purpose after his passing. As a next step they formed a view of what a human being must do in this life to ensure for himself a happy state in afterlife. Religious leaders in different countries taught different ways to achieve this. The cross, the *namāz,* the sacred ashes, the sacred earth came to be adopted in this manner by people belonging to different religious persuasions[10].

"You must look upon the world as belonging to the Lord, and it is your duty to so conduct yourself as to conform to this belief. This constitutes the dharma of humanity. Acts dictated solely by selfish interests will push one into unrighteousness. A man must learn to be less and less selfish in his thoughts and actions; he must always remember the Lord and must ever be conscious that he is the master of all this world." This view is the basis on which all religions have evolved.

No religion teaches us to live according to our whims and fancies; no religion asks us to acquire wealth and property for our personal needs alone. If a man believes that he alone is important, that he is all, he will live only for himself. That is why all religions speak of an entity called God and teach man to efface his ego or I-feeling. "Child," they tell him, "you are nothing before that Power, the author of this universe. It is he — that Power — who has endowed you with intelligence. Your intelligence, your intellect, must guide you on the path of dharma, righteousness. For this purpose you must look up to this Power for support." The great importance attached to bhakti or devotion in all religions is founded on this belief, the need for divine support for virtuous conduct.

Ordinarily it is not easy to develop faith in, or devotion to, God expressed in abstract terms. For the common people devotion must take the form of practical steps. That is how ritual originated. Sandhyāvandana[S], *namāz* and other forms of prayer are examples of such ritual. The religions teach people their duties, how they must conduct themselves in this world, and how they must devote themselves to God in the very midst of their worldly life.

"Love everyone." "Live a life of sacrifice." "Serve mankind." Such are the teachings of the various religions. If a man lives according to these tenets, it is believed that his soul will reach God after it departs from his body. Those who subscribe to Advaita or non-dualism declare that the soul will become one with the Godhead. According to another system of belief, after reaching the Lord, the soul will serve him and ever remain happy as the recipient of his compassion. There is no need to quarrel over the nature of the final state. "By following one path or another we attain the Lord. And that will be the end of all our sorrows, all our frustrations and all our failures in this world. There will now be nothing but bliss, full and everlasting." No more than this do we need to know for the present.

If the Paramātman is to draw us unto himself we must, without fail, perform our duties to him as well as to the world. It is these duties that constitute what is called dharma. Dharma it is that serves us when we dwell in our body and when we cease to dwell in it. It serves us in life and afterlife. When we are in this world we must do that which would take us to a desirable state after we depart from it. We take an insurance policy so that our relatives will be able to take care of themselves when we are gone. But is it not far more important to ensure that we will be happy in our afterlife? Dharma is afterlife insurance. But in this life too it is dharma that gives us peace and happiness.

There need be no doubt or confusion about the dharma we ought to follow. We are all steeped in the dharma that our great men have pursued from generation to generation. They have inwardly realised eternal beatitude and we know for certain that they lived without any care, unlike people in our own generation who are always discontented and are embroiled in agitations and demonstrations of all kinds. All we need to do is to follow the dharma that they practised. If we tried to create a new dharma for ourselves it might mean trouble and all the time we would be torn by doubts as to whether it would bring us good or whether it would give rise to evil. It is best for us to follow the dharma practised by the great men of the past, the dharma of our forefathers.

Man is subject to all kinds of hardships and misfortunes. To remind ourselves of this, we eat the bitter flowers of the *neem* on New Year's Day — that is on the very first day of the year we accept the bitternesses of life. During the *Poṅgal*[11] ceremony, which is celebrated almost towards the close of the year, we have sugarcane to chew. If we have only sweetness in the beginning we may have to experience bitterness towards the end. We must not have any aversion for the bitter but welcome it as the medicine administered by Mother Nature or by dharma. If we do so, in due course, we will learn to regard any experience, even if it be unpleasant, as a sweet one.

Great indeed were the misfortunes suffered by Śrī Rāma during his exile in the forest. To a son going on a long journey the mother gives food to take with him. Kausalyā does the same when her son Rāma leaves for the forest, but she does so after much thought, for she wants the food to last during all the fourteen years of his exile. And what is that food? Kausalyā gives Rāma the eternal sustenance of dharma. "Rāghava," she says to him, "it is dharma alone that will protect you, and this dharma is what you yourself protect with courage and steadfastness." It is the escort of dharma that the mother provides her son sent out from his kingdom.

Yam pālayasi dharmam tvam dhṛtya ca niyamena ca
Sa vai Rāghava-śārdūla dharmastvāmabhirakṣatu

Dharma Alone Protects

It was dharma that brought victory to Rāma after all his struggle. If a man treads the path of dharma he will win universal respect. If he slips into adharma, unrighteousness, even his brother will turn a foe. The Rāmāyaṇa illustrates this truth. Śrī Rāma was regarded with respect by the vānaras[12]. What about Rāvaṇa? Even his brother Vibhīṣaṇa forsook him.

Dharma — and dharma alone — is our protecting shield. How did Rāvaṇa with his ten heads perish and how did Śrī Rāmacandra rise with his head held high as Vijayarāghava (the victorious Rāghava)? It was all the doing of dharma.

One's religion is nothing but the dharma practised by one's forefathers. May all adhere to their dharma with unwavering faith and courage and be rewarded with everlasting bliss.

Notes & References

1 *Pīpal,* aśvattha, *Ficus religiosa.*

2 *Neem,* nimba, *Melia azadirachta.*

3 The Tamil New Year's Day falls in mid-April.

4 Vināyaka, "exalted leader" or "one without a leader", is another name of Ganeśa, Gaṇapati or Vighneśvara.

5 Nāgarājā, king of snakes.

6 The leaves of many species of trees, especially in Peninsular India, fall after the cold season.

7 Śivarātri is celebrated in February-March.

8 Subrahmaṇya is Kārtikeya or Kumāra — also known as "Muruga" or "Kanda" (Skanda) in the South.

9 Ṣaṣṭī, the sixth day of the lunar fortnight, is sacred to Subrahmaṇya.

10 "*Namāz*" is a Persian word denoting Islamic prayer; the sacred ashes worn by Hindus is "vibhūti", or "bhasma"; "the sacred earth" is a literal translation of the Tamil "*Tiruman*" which is worn by Vaiṣṇavas on the forehead and body. (See Tamiḷ Glossary.)

11 Makara Saṁkrānti is observed as *Poṅgal* in Tamiḷ Nāḍu. It is the day on which the sun turns from the tropic of Capricorn. (The day traditionally observed as Makara Saṁkrānti or *Pongal,* however, is more than three weeks after the winter solstice.)

12 This term is usually translated into English as monkeys or apes. But here the reference is to monkeys who were almost human or were even godly like Hanumān.

Chapter 2

Pāpa and Puṇya

Nobody wants to be known as a sinner, but all the same we keep transgressing the bounds of morality and disobeying the divine law. We wish to enjoy the fruits of virtue without being morally good and without doing anything meritorious.

Arjuna says to Bhagavān Kṛṣṇa: "No man wants to commit sin. Even so, Kṛṣṇa, he does evil again and again. What is it that drives him so?" The Lord replies "It is desire. Yes, it is desire, Arjuna[1]."

We try to gain the object of our desire with no thought of right or wrong (dharma or adharma). Is fire put out by ghee being poured into it? No, it rises higher and higher. Likewise, when we gratify one desire, another, much worse, crops up. Are we to take it, then, that it would be better if our desires were not satisfied? No. Unfulfilled desire causes anger, so too failure to obtain the object we hanker after. Like a rubber ball thrown against the wall such an unsatisfied desire comes back to us in the form of anger and goads us into committing sin. Kṛṣṇa speaks of such anger as being next only to desire (as an evil).

Only by banishing desire from our hearts may we remain free from sin. How is it done? We cannot but be performing our works. Even when we are physically inactive, our mind remains active. All our mental and bodily activity revolves round our desires. And these desires thrust us deeper and deeper into sin. Is it, then, possible to remain without doing any work? Human nature being what it is, the answer is "No".

"It is difficult to quell one's thinking nor is it easy to remain without doing anything", says Tāyumānavasvāmigal[T]. We may stop doing work with the body, but how do we keep the mind quiet? The mind is never still. Apart from being unstill itself, it incites the body to action.

We are unable either to efface our desires or to cease from all action. Does it then mean that liberation is beyond us? Is there no way out of the problem? Yes, there is. It is not necessary that we should altogether stop our actions in our present immature predicament. But, instead of working for our selfish ends, we ought to be engaged in such work as would bring benefits to the world as well as to our inward life. The more we are involved in such work, the less we shall be drawn by desire. This will to some extent keep us away from sin and at the same time enable us to do more meritorious work. We must learn the habit of doing work without any selfish motive. Work done without any desire for the fruits thereof is puṇya or virtuous action.

We sin in four different ways. With our body we do evil; with our tongue we speak untruth; with our mind we think evil; and with our money we do so much that is wicked. We must learn to turn these very four means of evil into instruments of virtue.

We must serve others with our body and circumambulate the Lord and prostrate ourselves before him. In this way we earn merit. How do we use our tongue to add to our stock of virtue? By muttering, by repeating, the names of the Lord. You will perhaps excuse yourself saying: "All our time is spent in earning our livelihood. How can we then think of God or repeat his names?" A householder has a family to maintain; but is he all the time working for it? How much time does he waste in gossip, in amusements, in speaking ill of others, in reading the papers? Can't he spare a few moments to remember the Lord? He need not set apart a particular hour of the day for his japa[S]. He may think of God even on the bus or the train as he goes to his office or any other place. Not a *paisa* is he going to take with him finally after his lifelong pursuit of money. The Lord's name (Bhagavannāma) is the only current coin in the other world.

The mind is the abode of Īśvara but we make a rubbish can of it. We must cleanse it, install the Lord in it and be at peace with ourselves. We must devote at least five minutes every day to meditation and resolve to do so even if the world crashes around us. There is nothing else that will give us a helping hand when the whole cosmos is dissolved.

It is by helping the poor and by spreading the glory of the Lord that we will earn merit.

Pāpa, sinful action, is two-pronged in its evil power. The first incites us to wrong-doing *now*. The second goads us into doing evil *tomorrow*. For instance, if you take snuff now you suffer now. But tomorrow also you will have the yearning to take the same. This is what is called the vāsanā[2] that comes of habit. An effort must be made not only to reduce such vāsanā but also to cultivate the vāsanā of virtue by doing good deeds.

It is bad vāsanā that drags us again and again into wrong-doing. Unfortunately, we do not seem to harbour any fear on that score. People like us, indeed even those known to have sinned much, have become devotees of the Lord and obtained light and wisdom. How is Īśvara qualified to be called great if he is not compassionate, and does not protect sinners also? It is because of sinners like us that he has come to have the title of "Patitapāvana" [he who sanctifies or lifts up the fallen with his grace]. It is we who have brought him such a distinction.

"Come to me, your only refuge. I shall free you from all sins. Have no fear (sarvapāpebhyo mokṣayiṣyāmi mā śucaḥ)[3]." The assurance that Śrī Kṛṣṇa gives to free us from sin is absolute. So let us learn to be courageous. To tie up an object you wind a string round it again and again. If it is to be untied you will have to do the unwinding in a similar manner. To eradicate the vāsanā of sinning you must develop the vāsanā of doing good to an equal degree. In between there ought to be neither haste nor anger. With haste and anger the thread you keep unwinding will get tangled again. Īśvara will come to our help if we have patience, if we have faith in him and if we are rooted in dharma.

The goal of all religions is to wean away man — his mind, his speech and his body — from sensual pleasure and lead him towards the Lord. Great men have appeared from time to time and established their religions with the goal of releasing people from attachment to their senses, for it is our senses that impel us to sin. "Transitory is the joy derived from sinful action, from sensual pleasure. Bliss is union with the Paramātman." Such is the teaching of all religions and their goal is to free man from worldly existence by leading him towards the Lord.

Notes & References

[1] Arjuna uvāca:

Atha kena prayukto 'yaṁ pāpaṁ carati pūruṣaḥ
Anicchannapi Vārṣṇeya balādiva niyojitaḥ?

Śrī Bhagavān uvāca:

Kāma eṣa krodha eṣa rajo-guṇa-samudbhavaḥ
Mahāśano mahāpāpmā viddhyenam iha vairiṇam.

— Bhagavadgītā, 3. 36-37

[2] The word "vāsanā" is from the root *vas* "to dwell in". It means that which sticks to a cloth, for instance, a smell. There is thus the "smell" of earlier births adhering to the subtle body. Vāsanā is the latent memory of past experience, the impression left on the mind by past actions.

[3] *Sarvadharmān parityajya mām ekaṁ śaraṇaṁ vraja*
Ahaṁ tvā sarva-pāpebhyo mokṣayiṣyāmi mā śucaḥ.

— Bhagavadgītā, 18.66

Chapter 3

The Purpose of Religion

Religion is the means of realising dharma, artha, kāma and mokṣa. These four are called puruṣārthas.

In Tamiḷ, dharma is called "*aram*"; artha is known as "*poruḷ*"; and kāma and mokṣa are called "*inbam*" and "*vīḍu*"[1] respectively. "Artha" occurs in the term "puruṣārthas", but it is itself one of the puruṣārthas. What a man wants for himself in his life — the aims of a man's life — are the puruṣārthas. What does a man want to have? He wants to live happily without lacking for anything. There are two types of happiness : the first is ephemeral; and the second is everlasting and not subject to diminution. Kāma or *inbam* is ephemeral happiness and denotes worldly pleasure, worldly desires. Mokṣa or *vīḍu* is everlasting happiness, not transient pleasure. It is because people are ignorant about such happiness, how elevated and enduring it is, that they hanker after the trivial and momentary joys of kāma.

Our true quest must be for the fourth artha, that is *vīḍu* or mokṣa. The majority of people today yearn for the third artha that is kāma. When you eat you are happy. When you are appointed a judge of the high court you feel elated. You are delighted when presented with a welcome address by some institution, aren't you?. Such types of happiness are not enduring. The means by which such happiness is earned is *poruḷ*. *Poruḷ* may be corn, money, house. It is this *poruḷ* that is the way to happiness. But the pleasure gained from material possession is momentary and you keep constantly hungering for more.

Mokṣa is the state of supreme bliss and there is no quest beyond it. We keep going from place to place and suffer hardships of all kinds. Our destination is our home. A prisoner goes to his *vīḍu* or his home after he is released. But the word *vīḍu* also means release or liberation. Since we are now imprisoned in our body, we commit the grave mistake of believing that we *are* the body. The body is in fact our gaol. Our real home is the bliss called mokṣa. We must find release from the gaol that is our body and dwell in our true home. God has sentenced us to gaol (that is he has imprisoned us in our body) for our sins. If we practise virtue he will condone our sins and release us from the prison of our body before the expiry of the sentence. We must desist from committing sinful acts so that our term of imprisonment is not extended and endeavour to free ourselves and arrive in our true home, our true home that is the Lord. This home is bliss that passeth understanding, bliss that is not bound by the limitations of time, space and matter.

Lastly, I speak of the first puruṣārtha, dharma. Dharma denotes beneficent action, good or virtuous deeds. The word has come to mean giving, charity. "Give me *dharmam*. Do *dharmam*, mother," cries the beggar[2]. We speak of "dāna-dharma" [as a portmanteau word]. The commandments relating to charity are called "*ara-kaṭṭaḷai*" in Tamiḷ. Looked at in this way, giving away our artha or *poruḷ* will be seen to be dharma. But how do we, in the first place, acquire the goods to be given away in charity? The charity practised in our former birth -- by giving away our artha — it is that brings us rewards in this birth. The very purpose of owning material goods is the practice of dharma. Just as material possessions are a means of pleasure, so is dharma a means of material possession. It is not charity alone that yields rewards in the form of material goods; all dharma will bring their own material rewards.

If we practise dharma without expecting any reward — in the belief that Īśvara gives us what he wills — and in a spirit of dedication, the impurities tainting our being will be removed and we will obtain the bliss that is exalted. The pursuit of dharma that brings in its wake material rewards will itself become the means of attaining the *Paramporuḷ*[3]. Thus we see that dharma, while being an instrument for making material gain and through it of pleasure, becomes the means of liberation also if it is practised unselfishly. Through it we acquire material goods and are helped to keep up the practice of dharma. This means that artha itself becomes a basis of dharma. It is kāma or desire alone that neither fulfils itself nor becomes an instrument of fulfilling some other purpose. It is like the water poured on burning sands. Worse, it is an instrument that destroys everything— dhārmic thoughts, material possessions, liberation itself.

All the same it is difficult, to start with, to be without any desire altogether. Religion serves to rein in desire little by little and take a man, step by step, from petty ephemeral pleasure to the ultimate bliss. First we are taught the meaning and implications of dharma and how to practise it, then we are instructed in the right manner in which material goods are to be acquired so as to practise this dharma; and, thirdly, we are taught the proper manner in which desires may be satisfied. It is a process of gaining maturity and wisdom to forsake petty pleasure for the ultimate bliss of mokṣa.

Mokṣa is release from all attachments. It is a state in which the Self remains ever in untrammelled freedom and blessedness. The chief purpose of religion is to teach us how this supreme state may be attained.

We know for certain that ordinarily people do not achieve eternal happiness. The purpose of any religion is to lead them towards such happiness. Everlasting blessedness is obtained only by forsaking the quest for petty pleasures. The dictates of dharma help us to abandon the pursuit of sensual enjoyments and endeavour for eternal bliss. They are also essential to create a social order that has the same high purpose, the liberation of all. Religion, with its goal of liberation, lays down the tenets of dharma. That is why the great understand the word dharma itself to mean religion.

Notes

1 "*Vīḍu*" also means "home".

2 This cry is more commonly heard in Tamiḷ Nāḍu and Keraḷa.

3 "*Paramporuḷ*" is the supreme *poruḷ*, which means the Supreme Reality (Paramārtha). *Poruḷ* or artha here becomes indirectly a means of attaining the *Paramporuḷ*.

Chapter 4
Man and Beast

Animals grow transversely. That is why they are called "tiryak" in Sanskrit. Man who grows upright ought to have, unlike beasts, a high ideal before him. He will then obtain more happiness than all other creatures. But what do we see in reality? Man experiences greater sorrow than all other creatures. Animals do not know so much desire, so much sorrow and so much humiliation as do humans. More important, they are innocent of sin. It is we humans who keep sinning and suffering as a consequence.

In one sense it seems to me that Īśvara has not endowed us with the same advantages that he has endowed animals with. We are not fitted with weapons of defence. If a cow feels threatened it has horns to defend itself. The tiger has its claws. We have neither horns nor claws. Sheep have hair to protect them from the cold of winter, so too other animals. But man is not similarly equipped. So he cannot repulse an attack; nor can he run fast like the horse which has no horns but is fleet - footed. Against all these handicaps, man has the advantage of being more intelligent than all other creatures.

In order to protect himself from the cold of winter, man removes the hair (fur) of animals and weaves it into rugs. When he wants to travel fast he yokes a horse to his cart. God has furnished man with this kind of skill; though he has neither claws nor horns to defend himself, a human being can forge weapons on his own. With the strength of his intelligence he remains the master of all other creatures and also rules over the entire world of inert matter.

All species of animals have their own habitats. Some types of bear that are native to the cold climes do not thrive in our country. The elephant is a denizen of the forests of India and some other countries of South-East Asia and Africa, but it does not flourish in a cold climate. But man inhabits the entire earth. He uses his brains to make any part of this planet fit for him to live.

But, even with his superior intelligence, man suffers. All hardships stem from the fact of birth. How can one save oneself from being born again? But, then, what is the cause of our birth? The wrongs committed by us are the cause of our birth and we have taken this body of flesh and blood to suffer punishment for the same. Suppose a certain number of whiplashes are to be administered according to the law. If the body perishes after ten lashes, we take another birth to suffer the remaining strokes. The sins we commit in satisfying our desires are the cause of our being born again and again. If there is no "doing", there will be no birth also. Anger is responsible for much of the evil we do and desire is at the root of it. It is of the utmost importance that we banish desire from our hearts. But it is not possible to remain without any action after having cultivated so many attachments. If the attachments were done away with we would cease to sin.

What is the cause of desire? Desire arises from the belief that there is something other than ourselves and our being attached to it. In truth it is the one Śivam[1] that manifests itself as everything.

The cow sees its reflection in the mirror and charges it imagining it to be another cow. If a man sees his own image thus, does he think that there is another person in the mirror? He is not perturbed by his image because he knows that it is himself. Similarly, all that we see is one and the same thing. Desire springs from our belief in the existence of a second entity, and it causes anger which, in turn, plunges us in sin. A new birth becomes inevitable now. If we are enlightened enough to perceive that all objects are one, there will be no ground for desire. There must be an object other than ourselves, a second entity, to be desired. No desire means no anger and no sin. In this state there will be neither any "doing" nor any birth. And, finally, there will be no sorrow.

How do we obtain such enlightenment or jñāna? Our body is sustained by our mother's milk. It is Ambā who nourishes us with the milk of jñāna. She is indeed the personification of jñāna. We will be rewarded with the light of wisdom if we firmly hold her lotus feet and dissolve ourselves in her. One who does so becomes God.

The first step in this process of enlightenment is to make a man truly a man, by ensuring that he does not live on an animal level. The second step is to raise him to the heights of divinity. All religions have this goal. They may represent different systems of thought and philosophy. But their concern ought to be that man is not condemned as he is today to a life of desire and anger. All religions speak in one voice that man must be rendered good and that he must be invested with the qualities of love, humility, serenity and the spirit of sacrifice.

Note

[1] "Śivam" is the Supreme Reality according to the Śaiva Siddhānta. See Part Seven of *The Guru Tradition*. Also see the passage on "Śivo'dvaita" in Chapter 33, Part Five.

Chapter 5

Devotion Common to all Faiths

All religious traditions have one purpose, to elevate man by freeing him from his cares and worries. A human being has worries that are not shared by other creatures. But it must be noted that all religious systems proclaim that man can not only free himself from his cares, if he makes an effort, but that he can also attain the enlightenment that is not within the reach of other creatures. They speak in one voice that he will be rid of his cares if he goes for refuge to the Great Power that rules all worldly activities. Devotion or bhakti is a feature common to all religious schools—Advaita (non-dualism), Dvaita (dualism), Viśiṣṭādvaita (qualified non-dualism), Śaiva Siddhānta, Christianity, Islam and so on. The Buddha did not speak of devotion but it seems his followers cannot regard their master without bhakti. They have deified the Buddha and created images of him that are bigger than those sculpted for any deity. In very recent times a number of jñānins have laid stress on inquiry into the Self as the sole means of liberation. But they are themselves worshipped as God by their followers. Bhakti is an inborn characteristic of man; it is indeed an organic part of him.

Devotion in the Advaita system implies adopting an attitude of non-difference between the worshipper and the worshipped; that is the devotee must look upon Iśvara as not being different from himself. It might be asked: "The devotee who worships the omnipotent and omniscient Lord has only very limited strength and knowledge. How can the two of them be the same?" But the question also arises: "Does God regard us as being different from himself? If there are objects, entities, different from God how did they originate? If they came into existence as entities separate from him how can he hold sway over them?"

If we think on these lines it will become clear that the one and only Paramātman exists in various forms: if the ocean stands for Iśvara we have in contrast the pond, the well and the little quantity of water contained in a spoon and so on that stand for diverse living beings. The water in all is the same. There may be differences in the strengths of the various entities. But if you go to the base, the ground or root, you will discover that they are the same. If we go to the root we will become one with the root. This is liberation according to Advaita. Merely to talk about non-dualistic liberation is nothing more than an intellectual exercise and will serve no purpose. The truth of such liberation must become an inward reality. In other words the quest must culminate in actual experience and it can be had only with the grace of Īśvara. Great sages proclaim that it is only with the blessings of that Power which keeps us in a constant whirl of action that the whirl itself will stop and that we will have the Advaitic urge to seek the ground. "Īśvarānugrahādeva puṁsām Advaitavāsanā."

Even in the initial stages when we feel that Īśvara and his devotee are separate, we must try to cultivate the awareness, albeit to a small degree, that the Paramātman who appears as Īśvara is the same as the Paramātman that has become "us". If such be our approach, our love for the Lord will become more intense. After all, is there anything or anyone we love more than ourselves?

Īśvara awards us the fruits of our actions. If we become more and more devoted to him, as recipients of his grace, we will get closer and closer to him. He will himself reveal to us who he is and what he is and there will be no need for us to inquire about him or into him. In response to our devotion he will deign to reveal his true nature to us. He declares so in the Gītā: "Bhaktyā māṁ abhijānāti yāvān yaścāsmi...." (By devotion he comes to know who in truth I am...)[1.]

Countless are the attributes of Īśvara that bespeak his surpassing beauty and auspicious qualities. Devotees find constant delight in contemplating them. But for the jñānin, the enlightened one, the ideal is the Godhead that has no attributes and it is in this Godhead that he is finally absorbed. Saguṇopāsanā (worship of Īśvara with attributes) is the first step towards this end. For it our religion has evolved the concept of "iṣṭadevatā" ("the deity of one's choice", "the deity one likes").

What is special about sanātana dharma[S] or Hinduism as it has come to be called? Alone among all religions it reveals the one and only Godhead in many different divine forms, with manifold aspects. The devotee worships the Lord in a form suited to his mental make-up and is thus helped to come closer to the Lord with his love and devotion. These different forms are not the creation of anyone's imagination. The Paramātman has revealed himself in these forms to great men and they have had close contact, so to speak, with the deities so revealed. They have also shown us how we too may come face to face with these divinities, given us the mantras to accomplish this and also prescribed the manner in which the divine forms, whose vision they have had, are to be adored.

Bhakti or devotion is common to all religions whatever the manner of worship they teach. It is not exclusive to our faith in which different deities are reverenced.

Reference

[1] *Bhaktyā mām abhijānāti yāvān yaśeāsmi tattvataḥ*
Tato māṁ tattvato jñātvā viśate tadanantaram

— Bhagavadgītā, 18.55

Chapter 6

The Unity of Religions

All religions have one common ideal, worship of the Lord, and all of them proclaim that there is but one God. This one God accepts your devotion irrespective of the manner of your worship, whether it is according to this or that religion. So there is no need to abandon the religion of your birth and embrace another.

The temple, the church, the mosque, the vihāra may be different from one another. The idol or the symbol in them may not also be the same and the rites performed in them may be different. But the Paramātman who grants grace to the worshipper, whatever be his faith, is the same. The different religions have taken shape according to the customs peculiar to the countries in which they originated and according to the differences in the mental outlook of the people inhabiting them. The goal of all religions is to lead people to the same Paramātman according to the different attitudes of the devotees concerned. So there is no need for people to change over to another faith. Converts demean not only the religion of their birth but also the one to which they convert. Indeed they do demean God.

"A man leaves the religion of his birth because he thinks there is something wanting in it," so you may think. "Why does the *Svāmigaḷ*[T] say then that the convert demeans the new religion that he embraces?" I will tell you why. Is it not because they think that God is not the same in all religions that people embrace a new faith? By doing so, they see God in a reduced form, don't they? They presumably believe that the God of the religion of their birth is useless and jump across to another faith. But do they believe that the God of their new religion is a universal Lord? No. No. If they did there would be no need for any change of faith. Why do people embrace a new faith? Is it not because they believe that continuance in the religion of their birth would mean a denial of the blessings of the God of the new faith to which they are attracted? This means that they place limitations on their new religion as well as on its God. When they convert to a new religion, apparently out of respect for it, they indeed dishonour it.

One big difference between Hinduism and other faiths is that it does not proclaim that it alone shows the path to liberation. Our Vedic religion alone has not practised conversion and the reason for it is that our forefathers were well aware that all religions are nothing but different paths to realise the one and only Paramātman. The Vedas proclaim: "The wise speak of the One Truth by different names[1]." Śrī Kṛṣṇa says in the Gītā: "In whatever way or form a man worships me, I increase his faith and make him firm and steady in that worship."[2] And says one of the Āzhvārs[T]: "*Avaravar tamatamadu tarivari vahaivahai avaravar iraiyavar*"[3]. This is the reason why Hindus have not practised—like adherents of other religions — proselytisation and religious persecution. Nor have they waged anything like the crusades or *jehāds*[4].

Our long history is sufficient proof of this. All historians accept the fact of our religious tolerance. They observe that, when an empire like Śrivijaya[5] was established in the East, people there accepted our culture and our way of life willingly, not because they were imposed on them by force. They further remark that Hinduism spread through trade and not through force.

In my opinion the Vedic religion was once prevalent all over the world. Certain ruins and relics found in various regions of the planet attest to this fact. Even historians who disagree with my view concede that in the past people in many lands accepted Indian culture and the Indian way of life willingly and not on account of any force on our part.

All religions that practise conversion employ a certain ritual. For instance, there is baptism in Christianity. Hinduism has more ritual than any other religion, yet its canonical texts do not contain any rite for conversion. No better proof is needed for the fact that we have at no time either encouraged conversion or practised it.

When a passenger arrives at a station by train he is besieged by the driver of the horse-cart, by the *rikṣāvāla,* by the cabbie, and so on. He hires the vehicle in which he likes to be driven to his destination. It cannot be said with reason that those who ply the different vehicles are guilty of competing with one another for the fare. After all it is their livelihood. But it makes no sense for the adherents of various faiths to vie with one another to take a man to the one and only destination that is God.

There is a bridge across a river, consisting of a number of arches, each of them built to the same design and measurement. To the man sitting next to a particular arch it would appear to be bigger than the other arches. So is the case with people belonging to a particular religion. They feel that their religion alone is great and want others to join it. There is in fact no such need for anyone to leave the religion of his birth for another.

That the beliefs and customs of the various religions are different cannot be a cause for complaint. Nor is there any need to make all of them similar. The important thing is for the followers of the various faiths to live in harmony with one another. The goal must be unity, not uniformity.

Notes & References

[1] *"Ekam sad viprā bahudhā vadanti."*

[2] *Ye yathā mām prapadyante tāmstathaiva bhajāmyaham*
Mama vartmā'nuvartante manuṣyāḥ Pārtha sarvaśaḥ

— Bhagavadgītā, 4.11

[3] How a man prays depends on the level of his understanding of the Lord.

[4] Crusades were Christian expeditions to recover Jerusalem, etc, from Muslims. *Jehād* is a religious war waged by Muslims.

[5] The Śrīvijaya empire, comprising Sumātra and some other islands of Indonesia, flourished for several centuries attaining its peak of glory in the 7th century A.D.

Chapter 7

Qualities of Religious Teachers

Today students of philosophy and seekers all over the world accept Advaita or non-dualism as the supreme system of thought. Since you call me a teacher of Advaita you will naturally expect me to say that it is because of the excellence of this Vedāntic system that it has so many followers.

But, on reflection, the question arises as to whether all people do indeed subscribe to non-dualism. The world over people follow so many different religions, subscribe to so many different philosophical systems. People belonging to the same country go from one faith to another. During the time of the Buddha many adherents of the Vedic religion embraced his system. In later centuries many Hindus became converts to Christianity or Islam. Jainas have become Vaiṣṇavas with the name of "Puṣṭimārgins". During the time of Śrī Rāmānuja[S] a number of people went over to the Viśiṣṭādvaita (qualified non-dualism) fold. Similarly, Śrī Madhva's[S] school of Dvaita or dualism also gained many adherents. When Ādi Śankara held sway, non-Vedic religions like Buddhism and Jainism suffered a decline. Those following the path of karma then — the karma mārga is a part of the Vedic religion — returned to Advaita which indeed is a wholly Vedic system.

Why did religions that had flourished at one time go under later? Do people really follow a religion or subscribe to a philosophical system after making a proper inquiry into the same? Perhaps only thinking people embrace a religion after an assessment of its doctrines. The same cannot be said about the generality of people who follow any faith. If it is claimed that the common people accept a religion for its concepts, they must be able to speak about them and tell us how these doctrines are superior to those of other religions. The fact is that the vast majority of the followers of any faith know precious little about the beliefs or doctrines on which it is founded.

I believe that the growth or expansion of a religion is in no way related to its doctrines. The common people do not worry about questions of philosophy. A great man of exemplary character and qualities appears on the scene — a great man of compassion who creates serenity all round — and people are drawn to him. They become converts to his religion in the firm belief that the doctrines preached by him, whatever they be, must be good. On the other hand, a religion will decline and decay if its spokesmen, however eloquent they are in expounding its concepts, are found to be guilty of lapses in character and conduct. It is difficult to give an answer to the question why people flock to religions that have contradictory beliefs. But, if we examine the history of some religions— how at one time people gloried in them and how these faiths later perished — we shall be able to know the reason. At the same time, it would be possible for us to find out how in the first place they attracted such a large following. If you find out how a religion declined you will be able to know how it had first grown and prospered.

The decay of a religion in any country could be attributed to the lack of character of its leaders and of the people constituting the establishment responsible for its growth.

When we listen to the story of the Buddha, when we see again and again his images that seem to exude the milk of human kindness, compassion and tranquillity spring in our own hearts and we feel respectful towards him. People must have been attracted to him thus during his time. How, in later times, there was a moral decline in the Buddhist monastic establishments will be seen from the *Mattavilāsam*[1] written by Mahendra Pallava. This work shows how Buddhism came to be on the decline and demonstrates that the rise or fall of a religion is dependent on the quality and character of its spokesmen.

After the Buddha came Ādi Śankara to whom people were drawn for his incomparable goodness and greatness. Later appeared Rāmānuja and Madhva who, in their personal lives, stood out as men of lofty character. They too were able to gather round them a large following and extend the sway of their respective systems. Recently came Gāndhījī as a man of peace and sacrifice. Millions of people accepted his teachings which indeed came to constitute a separate religion, "Gāndhīsm". If a system owes its growth to the excellence of the philosophical principles on which it is based, Gāndhīsm ought to be at the peak of its glory today. But what do we see in reality? The Gāndhian way of life as practised now is all too obvious to need any comment.

The question here is not about the religions that try to draw people to themselves either through force or the lure of money. It is but natural for ignorant people to become converts to a new religion through rites like baptism after receiving various inducements and "social rewards". It was in this manner, they say, that Christianity extended its influence during times of famine. It is also said that Islam was propagated with the sword, that masses of people were forced to join it by force of arms. Here again there is proof of the fact that the common people do not adopt a religion for the sake of any principle or out of any interest in its philosophical system. There is one more matter to consider. The padres [Christian missionaries] converted mainly people living in the *ceris* [that is people on the outskirts of a village or town]. Their usual procedure was to tell these poor folk that they were kept suppressed in the religion of their birth and offer them inducements in the form of free education and medical treatment and the promise of a better status.

Not all, however, fell to such lures. However much they seemed to be suppressed in the religion of their birth, many of them refused to be converted, ignoring the advantages held out. Why? One reason was their good-naturedness and the second reason was respect for the great men who have appeared in our religion from time to time. They told themselves: "Let us continue to remain in the religion of our forefathers, the religion that has produced so many great men."

We must not censure those who convert people to their faith. They believe that their religion represents the highest truth. That is why they practise conversion by compulsion or by placing various temptations before people belonging to other faiths. Let us take it that they try to bring others into their fold because they believe that that is the only means of a man's salvation. Let us also presume that they believe that there is nothing wrong in carrying out conversion either by force or through the offer of inducements because they think that they are doing it for the well-being of the people they seek to convert.

If religions that resort neither to force nor to money power have grown, it is solely because of the noble qualities of their teachers. Outward guise alone is not what constitutes the qualities of the representative or spokesman of a religion. Whatever the persuasion to which he belongs he must be utterly selfless, bear ill-will towards none, in addition to being morally blameless. He must live an austere life, and must be calm and compassionate by nature. Such a man will be able to help those who come to him by removing their shortcomings and dispelling the evil in them.

Producing men of such noble qualities from amongst us is the way to make our religion flourish. It is not necessary to carry on propaganda against other religions. The need is for representatives, for preceptors, capable of providing an example through their very life of the teachings of our religion. It is through such men that, age after age, sanātana dharma has been sustained as a living force. Hereafter too it will be through them that it will continue to remain a living force.

If a militant proselytiser appears on the scene, I shall not be able to gather a force to combat him. Nor can I spend crores and crores like those religious propagandists who build schools and hospitals to entice people into their faith. Even if I were able to do so, conversions carried out in such a manner would be neither true nor enduring. Suppose a group comes up that has more muscle and money power; it will undo my work with its superior force and greater monetary strength. We should not, therefore, depend on such outward forces to promote our religion but instead rely on our Ātmic strength to raise ourselves. In this manner our religion will flourish without any need for aggressive propaganda or the offer of inducements.

At present many intellectuals abroad talk in glowing terms of Advaita, may be because of its lofty character as a philosophical system. They come to the school of Vedānta after examining it and after being inwardly convinced of its truth. But the common people need the example of a great soul, a great life [not abstract principles].

A man of peace and compassion, a man of wisdom and self-sacrifice, must arise from our midst.

Note

1 *Mattavilāsam* is a "prahasana" or farcical comedy. Its author, Mahendravarman I, gave up Jainism under the influence of Apparsvāmigal to become a Śaiva again.

Part Two

THE VEDIC RELIGION : INTRODUCTORY

Chapter 1

The Religion without a Name

We speak of the "Hindu religion", but the religion denoted by the term did not in fact have such a name originally. According to some, the word "Hindu" means "love"; according to some others a Hindu is one who disapproves of hiṁsā or violence. This may be an ingenious way of explaining the word.

In none of our ancient śāstras does the term "Hindu religion" occur. The name "Hindu" was given us by foreigners. People from the West came to our land across the Sindhu river which they called "Indus" or "Hind" and the land adjacent to it by the name "India". The religion of this land came to be called "Hindu". The name of a neighbouring country is sometimes applied to the land adjacent to it. Let me tell you an interesting story in this connection.

In the North people readily give alms to anybody calling himself a *bairāgi*[1]. The *bairāgis* have a grievance against Southerners because they do not follow the same practice. "*Illai po po kahe Telungi*" is one of their ditties. "Telugus do not give us alms but drive us away" : this is the meaning of the line. Actually, Telugus do not say "*po, po*" but "*vellu, vellu*" for "go, go". "*Po*" is a Tamiḷ word. Then how would you explain the line quoted above? During their journey to the South, the *bairagis* had first to pass through the Telugu country (Āndhra); so they thought that the land further south also belonged to the Telugus.

There is the same logic behind the Telugus themselves referring to Tamiḷ Nāḍu as "Arava Nāḍu" from the fact that a small area south of Āndhra Prades̀ is called "Arva". Similarly, foreigners who came to the land of the Sindhu called all Bhārata beyond also by the same name.

However it be, "Hinduism" was not the name of our religion in the distant past. Nor was it known as "Vaidīka Mata" (Vedic religion) or as "sanātana dharma" (the ancient or timeless religion). Our basic texts do not refer to our faith by any name. When I thought about it I felt that there was something deficient about our religion.

One day, many years ago, someone came and said to me: "Rāmu is here." At once I asked somewhat absent-mindedly : "Which Rāmu ?" Immediately came the reply : "Are there many Rāmus ?" Only then did it occur to me that my question, "Which Rāmu?", had sprung from my memory of the past. There were four people in my place bearing the name of "Rāmu". So, to tell them apart, we called them "Dark Rāmu", "Fair Rāmu", "Tall Rāmu" and "Short Rāmu". When there is only one Rāmu around there is no need to give him a distinguishing label.

It dawned on me at once why our religion had no name. When there are a number of religions they have to be identified by different names. But when there is only one, where is the problem of identifying it?

All religions barring our own were established by single individuals. "Buddhism" means the religion founded by Gautama Buddha. Jainism was founded by the Jina called Mahāvīra. So has Christianity its origin in Jesus Christ. Our religion predating all these had spread all over the world. Since there was no other religion to speak about then it was not necessary to give it a name. When I recognised this fact I felt at once that there was no need to be ashamed of the fact that our religion had no name in the past. On the contrary, I felt proud about it.

If ours is a primeval religion, the question arises as to who established it. All inquiries into this question have failed to yield an answer. Was it Vyāsa, who composed the *Brahmasūtra,* the founder of our religion? Or was it Kṛṣṇa Paramātman who gave us the Bhagavadgitā? But both Vyāsa and Kṛṣṇa state that the Vedas existed before them. If that be the case, are we to point to the ṛṣis, the seers, who gave us the Vedic mantras, as the founders of our religion? But they themselves declare: "We did not create the Vedas." When we chant a mantra we touch our head with our hand mentioning the name of one seer or another. But the sages themselves say: "It is true that the mantras became manifest to the world through us. That is why we are mentioned as the 'mantra ṛṣis'. But the mantras were not composed by us but revealed to us. When we sat meditating with our minds under control, the mantras were perceived by us in space. Indeed we *saw* them (hence the term mantra-draṣṭas). We did not compose them." [The seers are not "mantra-kartās".]

All sounds originate in space. From them arose creation. According to science, the cosmos was produced from the vibrations in space. By virtue of their austerities the sages had the gift of seeing the mantras in space, the mantras that liberate men from this creation. The Vedas are apauruṣeya (not the work of any human author) and are the very breath of the Paramātman in his form as space. The sages saw them and made a gift of them to the world.

If we know this truth, we have reason to be proud of the fact that we do not know who founded our religion. In fact we must feel happy that we have the great good fortune to be heirs to a religion that is eternal, a religion containing the Vedas which are the very breath of the Paramātman[2].

Note & Reference

1 *"Bairāgi"* is from "vairāgin" meaning one without "rāga" or without passion. The word is also applied to a religious mendicant.

2 There is more on this subject in Parts Three and Five.

Chapter 2

The Universal Religion

In the dim past what we call Hinduism today was prevalent all over the world. Archaeological studies reveal the existence of relics of our Vedic religion in many countries. For instance, excavations have brought up the text of a treaty between Rameses II and the Hittites dating back to the 14th century B.C. In this, the Vedic gods Mitra and Varuṇa are mentioned as witnesses to the pact. There is a connection between the name of Rameses and that of our Rāma.

About 75 per cent of the names of places in Madagascar have a Sanskritic origin.

In the Western Hemisphere too there is evidence of Hinduism having once flourished there. In Mexico a festival is celebrated at the same time as our Navarātri; it is called "Rāma-Sītā". Wherever the earth is dug up images of Gaṇapati are discovered here[1]. The Aztecs had inhabited Mexico before the Spaniards conquered that land. "Aztecs" must be a distorted form of "Astikas". In Peru, during the time of the holy equinox [vernal?] worship was conducted in the sun temple. The people of this land were called Incas: "Ina" is one of the Sanskrit names of the sun god. Don't we call Rāma "Inakula-tilaka[2]?"

There is a book containing photographs of the aborigines of Australia dancing in the nude *(The Native Tribes of Central Australia,* by Spencer Killan, pages 128 & 129). A close look at the pictures, captioned "Śiva Dance", shows that the dancers have a third eye drawn on the forehead[3].

In a virgin forest in Borneo which, it is said, had not been penetrated by any human being until recently, explorers have found a sacrificial post with an inscription in a script akin to our Grantha[S] characters. Historians know it as the inscription of Mūlavarman of Kotei[4]. Mention is made in it of a sacrifice, the king who performed it, the place where the yupa[S] was installed. That the king gave away kalpavṛkṣas[S] as a gift to Brahmins is also stated in this inscription. All such details were discovered by Europeans, the very people who ridicule our religion.

Now something occurs to me in this context, something that you may find amusing. You know that the Sagaras[5] went on digging the earth down to the nether world in search of their sacrificial horse. An ocean came into being in this way and it was called sāgara after the king Sagara.

The Sagaras, at last, found the horse near the hermitage of Kapila Maharṣi. Thinking that he must be the man who had stolen the animal and hidden it in the nether world they laid violent hands on him. Whereupon the sage reduced them to ashes with a mere glance of his eye. Such is the story according to the Rāmāyaṇa. America, which is at the antipodes, may be taken to be Pātāla or the nether world. Kapilāraṇya (the forest in which Kapila had his hermitage), we may further take it, was situated there. It is likely that Kapilāraṇya changed to California in the same manner as Madurai is sometimes altered to "Marudai". Also noteworthy is the fact that there is a Horse Island near California as well as an Ash Island.

Another idea occurs to me about Sagara and sāgara. Geologists believe that ages ago the Sahara desert was an ocean. It seems to me that Sahara is derived from sāgara.

Some historians try to explain the evidence pointing to the worldwide prevalence of our religion in the past to the exchange of cultural and religious ideas between India and other countries established through travels. I myself believe that there was one common religion or dharma throughout and that the signs and symbols that we find of this today are the creation of the original inhabitants of the lands concerned.

The view put forward by some students of history about the discovery of the remnants of our religion in other countries — these relating to what is considered the historical period of the past two or three thousand years — is that Indians went to these lands, destroyed the old native civilizations there and imposed Hindu culture in their place. Alternatively, they claim, Indians thrust their culture into the native ways of life in such a way that it became totally absorbed in them.

The fact, however, is that evidence is to be found in many countries of their Vedic connection dating back to 4,000 years or more. That is, with the dawn of civilisation itself, aspects of the Vedic dharma existed in these lands. It was only subsequently that the inhabitants of these regions came to have a religion of their own.

Greece had an ancient religion and had big temples where various deities were worshipped. The Hellenic religion had Vedic elements in it. The same was the case with the Semitic religions of the pre-Christian era in the region associated with Jesus. The aborigines of Mexico had a religion of their own. They shared the Vedic view of the divine in the forces of nature and worshipped them as deities. There was a good deal of ritual in all such religions.

Now none of these religions, including that of Greece, survives. The Greek civilization had once attained to the heights of glory. Now Christianity flourishes in Greece. Buddhism has spread in Central Asia and in East Asia up to Japan. According to anthropologists, religions in their original form exist only in areas like the forests of Africa. But even these ancient faiths contain Vedic elements.

Religious and philosophical truths are often explained through parables, stories, so that ignorant people can understand them easily. Since metaphysical concepts are difficult to grasp, either they have to be told in the form of a story or they have to be given the form of a ritual, that is they must find expression as religious acts. For the common people the performance of a rite is a means of finding the truth present in it in the form of a symbol. I do not, however, agree with the view that all rituals are nothing but symbolic in their significance and that there is no need to perform them so long as their inner meaning is understood.

Ritual as ritual has its own place and efficacy. Similarly, I would not say that stories from the Purāṇas are nothing but illustrations or explanations of certain truths or doctrines. As stories they are of a high order and I believe that they really happened. But, at the same time, they demonstrate the meaning of certain truths. As for rites, their performance brings us benefits. But, in due course, as we learn to appreciate their inner meaning we shall become purified in mind. This is the stage when we shall no more yearn for any benefits from their performance and will be rewarded with supreme well-being (that is, liberation).

It is likely, though, that, with the passage of time, some stories or rites will become far removed from their inner meaning. Or, it may be, the inner meaning will be altogether forgotten. So it must be that, when new religions took shape abroad, after the lapse of thousands of years — religions not connected with the Vedic faith that is the root — the original Vedic concepts became transformed or distorted.

You must be familiar with the story of Adam and Eve which belongs to the Hebrew tradition. It occurs in the Genesis of the Old Testament and speaks of the Tree of Knowledge and God's commandment that its fruit shall not be eaten. Adam at first did not eat it but Eve did. After that Adam too ate the forbidden fruit.

Here an Upaniṣadic concept has taken the form of a biblical story. But because of the change in time and place the original idea has become distorted — or even obliterated.

The Upaniṣadic story[6] speaks of two birds perched on the branch of a pippala[7] tree. One eats the fruit of the tree while the other merely watches its companion without eating. The pippala tree stands for the body. The first bird represents a being that regards himself as the jīvātman or individual self and the fruit it eats signifies sensual pleasure. In the same body (symbolised by the tree) the second bird is to be understood as the Paramātman. He is the support of all beings but he does not know sensual pleasure. Since he does not eat the fruit he naturally does not have the same experience as the jīvātman (the first bird). The Upaniṣad speaks with poetic beauty of the two birds. He who eats the fruit is the individual self, jīva, and he who does not eat is the Supreme Reality, the one who knows himself to be the Ātman.

It is this jīva that has come to be called "Eve"[8] in the Hebrew religious tradition. "Ji" changes to "i" according to a rule of grammar and "ja" to "ya". We have the example of "Yamunā" becoming "Jamunā" or of "Yogīndra" being changed to "Jogīnder". In the biblical story "jīva" is "Eve" and "Ātmā" (or "Ātman") is "Adam". "Pippala" has in the same way changed to "apple". The Tree of Knowledge is our "bodhi-vṛkṣa". "Bodha" means "knowledge". It is well known that the Buddha attained enlightenment under the bodhi tree. But the *pīpal* (pippala) was known as the bodhi tree even before his time.

The Upaniṣadic ideas transplanted into a distant land underwent a change after the lapse of centuries. Thus we see in the biblical story that the Ātman (Adam) that can never be subject to sensual pleasure also eats the fruit of the Tree of Knowledge. While our bodhi tree stands for enlightenment, the enlightenment that banishes all sensual pleasure, the biblical tree affords worldly pleasure. These differences notwithstanding there is sufficient evidence here that, once upon a time, the Vedic religion was prevalent in the land of the Hebrews.

Let me give you another example to strengthen the view that however much a custom or a concept changes with the passage of time and with its acceptance by people of another land, it will still retain elements pointing to its original source. Our *Tiruppāvai*[T] and *Tiruvembāvai*[T] are not as ancient as the Vedas. Scholars ascribe them to an age not later than 1,500 years ago. However it be, the authors of these Tamiḻ hymns, Āṇḍāḷ[T] and Māṇikkavācakar[T], belong to an age much later than that of the Vedas and epics. After their time Hindu empires arose across the seas. Even the Coḷa kings extended their sway beyond the shores of the country. More worthy of note than our naval expeditions was the great expansion in our sea trade and the increase with it of our foreign contacts. As a result, people abroad were drawn to the Hindu religion and culture. Among the regions that developed such contacts, South-East Asia was the most important. Islands like Bāli in the Indonesian archipelago became wholly Hindu. People in Siam (Thailand), Indochina[9] and the Philippines came under the influence of Hindu culture. Śrīvijaya was one of the great empires of South-East Asia.

[Here the Paramaguru briefly touches upon the stages representing the emergence of various religions.] In primeval times the Vedic religion was prevalent everywhere: this was the first stage. In the second stage new religions emerged in various parts of the world. In the third stage these decayed and their place was taken by Buddhism, Christianity or Islam. In the subsequent stage the Hindu civilization became a living force outside the shores of India also, particularly in South-East Asia. This was the period during which great temples reminding us of those of Tamiḷ Nāḍu arose with the spread of our religion and culture: Angkor-vat in Cambodia; Borobudur in Jāva, Indonesia; Prambanan, also in Jāva. Now it was that our *Tiruppāvai* and *Tiruvembāvai* made their passage to Thailand.

Even today a big festival is held in Thailand in December- January, corresponding to the Tamiḷ *Mārgazhi,* the same month during which we read the *Tiruppāvai* and *Tiruvembāvai* with devotion. As part of the celebrations a dolotsava (swing festival) is held. A remarkable feature of this is that, in the ceremony meant for Viṣṇu, a man with the make-up of Śiva is seated on the swing. This seems to be in keeping with the fact that the *Tiruppāvai* and *Tiruvembāvai* contribute to the unification of Vaiṣṇavism and Śaivism.

If you ask the people of Thailand about the *Pāvai*[10] poems, they will not be able to speak about them. It might seem then that there is no basis for connecting the Thai festival with the *Pāvai* works merely because it is held in the month corresponding to the Tamiḷ *Mārgazhi.* But the point to note is that the people of that country themselves call it "*Triyampāvai-Trippāvai.*"

Those who read the Bible today are likely to be ignorant about the Upaniṣads, but they are sure to know the story that can be traced back to them, that of Adam and Eve. The Thais now must be likewise ignorant about the *Pāvais* but, all the same, they hold in the month of Dhanus[11] every year a celebration called "*Triyampāvai-Trippāvai.*" As part of it they also have a swing festival in which figures a man dressed as Śiva. Here the distortions in the observance of a rite have occurred during historical times — one of the distortions is that of Śiva being substituted for Viṣṇu. Also during this period the Thais have forgotten the *Pāvais* but, significantly enough, they still conduct a festival named after them. Keeping these facts before you, take your mind back to three or four thousand years ago and imagine how a religion or a culture would have changed after its passage to foreign lands.

It is in this context that you must consider the Vedic tradition. For all the changes and distortions that it has undergone in other countries during the past millennia its presence there is still proclaimed through elements to be found in the religions that supplanted it.

How are we to understand the presence of Hindu ideas or concepts in the religious beliefs of people said to belong to prehistoric times? It does not seem right to claim that in the distant past our religion or culture was propagated in other countries through an armed invasion or through trade, that is at a time when civilization itself had not taken shape there. That is why I feel that there is no question of anything having been taken from this land and introduced into another country. The fact, according to me, is that in the beginning the Vedic religion was prevalent all over the world. Later, over the centuries, it must have gone through a process of change and taken different forms. These forms came to be called the original religions of these various lands which in the subsequent period — during historical times — came under Buddhism, Christianity or Islam as the case may be.

Notes & References

1 Baron Humboldt quoted in Har Bilās Sārda's *Hindu Superiority.*

2 "Inakula-tilaka", ornament of the solar dynasty. For the correct meaning of the word "tilaka", see Sanskrit Glossary.

3 Signifying the third eye of Śiva.

4 Kotei or Kutei district is in East Borneo.

5 Sagaras are the 60,000 children of Sagara of the solar race. It was their descendant Bhagīratha who performed austerities and brought the Gangā from the heavens to redeem his ancestors who had been reduced to ashes.

6 The story is told in the *Muṇḍakopaniṣad.*

7 "Pippala" is the *pīpal* or *Ficus religiosa.*

8 The meaning of the original Hebrew word is indeed "life".

9 Now it consists of Vietnam, Cambodia and Laos.

10 *Pāvai* poems or works mean the *Tiruppāvai* and *Tiruvembāvai.*

11 Dhanus, solar month, same as *Mārgazhi* in Tamiḷ.

Chapter 3

Distinctive Features of Sanātana Dharma

Our religion has a number of unique or distinctive features. One of them is what is called the theory of karma, though this theory is common to religions like Buddhism which are offshoots of Hinduism.

What is the karma doctrine? For every action there is an equal and opposite reaction. There is an ineluctable law of physics governing cause and effect, action and reaction. This law pertaining to physical phenomena our forefathers applied to human life. The cosmos includes not only sentient beings endowed with consciousness but also countless insentient objects. Together they constitute worldly life. The laws, the dharma, proper to the first order must apply to the second also. According to the karma theory, every action of a man has an effect corresponding to it. Based on this belief our religion declares that, if a man commits a sin, he shall pay the penalty for it. Also if his act is a virtuous one, he shall reap the benefits thereof.

Our religion further asserts that one is born again and again so as to experience the consequences of one's good and bad actions. "Do good." "Do not do evil," such are the exhortations of all religions. But Hinduism (and its offshoots) alone lay stress on the cause-and-effect connection. No religion originating in countries outside India subscribes to the cause-and-effect connection, nor to the reincarnation theory as one of its articles of faith. Indeed religions originating abroad hold beliefs contrary to this theory and strongly oppose the view that man is born again and again in order to exhaust his karma. They believe that a man has only one birth, that when his soul departs on his death it dwells somewhere awaiting the day of judgement. On this day God makes an assessment of his good and bad actions and, on the basis of it, rewards him with eternal paradise or sentences him to eternal damnation.

Some years ago, a well-known writer from Europe came to see me—nowadays you see many white men coming to the Maṭha[1]. This gentleman told me that the Bible stated more than once that God is love. He could not reconcile this with the belief that God condemns a sinner to eternal damnation without affording him an opportunity for redemption. On this point a padre had told him: "It is true that there is an eternal hell. But it is eternally vacant."

The padre's statement is difficult to accept. Let us suppose that the Lord in his compassion does not condemn a sinner to hell. Where then does he send his soul? Since, according to Christianity, there is no rebirth the sinner is not made to be born again. So he too must be rewarded with heaven (as much as the virtuous man). This means that we may merrily keep sinning without any fear of punishment. After all, God will reward all of us with heaven. This belief implies that there is no need for morality and truthfulness.

According to our religion too, Īśvara who decides our fate after death on the basis of our karma is infinitely merciful. But, at the same time, he does not plunge the world in adharma, in unrighteousness -- that is not how his compassion manifests itself. What does he do then? He gives us another birth, another opportunity to reap the fruits of our good and bad actions. The joys of heaven and the torments of hell truly belong to this world itself. The sorrow and happiness that are our lot in our present birth are in proportion to the virtuous and evil deeds of our past birth. Those who sinned much suffer much now and, similarly, those who did much good enjoy much happiness now. The majority is made up of people who know more sorrow than happiness and of people who experience sorrow and happiness almost in equal measure. There are indeed very few blessed with utter happiness. It is evident from this that most of us must have done more evil than good in our past birth.

In his mercy the Lord gives us every time a fresh opportunity to wash away our sins. The guru, the śāstras, and the temples are all his gifts to wipe away our inner impurities. That Īśvara, in his compassion, places his trust even in a sinner confident that he will raise himself through his own efforts and gives him a fresh opportunity in the form of another birth to advance himself inwardly — is not such a belief better than that he should dismiss a sinner as good-for-nothing and yet reward him with heaven? If a man sincerely believes, in a spirit of surrender, that there is nothing that he can do on his own and that everything is the Lord's doing, he will be redeemed and elevated. But it is one thing for God to bless a man who goes to him for refuge forsaking his own efforts to raise himself and quite another to bless him thinking him to be not fit to make any exertions on his own to advance inwardly. So long as we believe in such a thing as human endeavour we should think that Īśvara's supreme compassion lies in trusting a man to go forward spiritually through his own efforts. It is in this way that the Lord's true grace is manifested.

That God does not condemn anyone to eternal punishment in hell is the personal opinion of a particular padre. It cannot be said that all religions like Christianity which believe that a man has only one birth agree with this view. They believe that God awards a man hell or paradise according to the good or evil he has done in one single birth. Since sinners who deserve to be condemned to hell predominate, the day of judgement has come to be known by the terrible name of doomsday. Here we have a concept according to which the Lord's compassion seems to be circumscribed.

There is strong evidence to support the reincarnation theory. A lady from the West came to see me one day and asked me if there was any proof of reincarnation. I did not have any discussion with her on the subject. Instead, I asked her to visit the local obstetric hospital and find out all about the children born there. There was a learned man who knew English where we were camping then. I asked him to accompany the lady. Later, on their return from the hospital, I asked the woman about her impressions of the new-born children. She said that she had found one child plump and lusty, another skinny; one beautiful and another ungainly. One child was born in a comfortable ward [that is to a well-to-do mother] and another to a poor mother.

"Leave aside the question of God consigning a man to eternal hell after his death," I said to the foreign lady. "We are not witness to such a phenomenon. But now you have seen with your own eyes how differently the children are born in the hospital that you visited. How would you account for the differences? Why should one child be born rich and another poor? Why should one be healthy and another sickly? And why should one be good-looking and another unpretty?

"If you accept the doctrine that men are born only once, you cannot but form the impression that God is neither compassionate nor impartial — think of all the differences at birth — and that he functions erratically and unwisely. How are we to be devoted to such a God and have the faith that he will look on us with mercy? How are we to account for the differences between one being and another if we do not accept the doctrine that our life now is determined by the good and the bad we did in our past births." The lady from the West accepted my explanation.

Such an explanation is not, however, good enough for people in modern times. They demand scientific proof of reincarnation. Parapsychologists have done considerable research in the subject and their findings are in favour of the theory of rebirth. During the studies conducted in various parts of the world they encountered people who remembered their past lives. The latter recalled places and people they had seen in their previous birth — places and people that have nothing to do with them now. The parapsychologists verified these facts and to their amazement found them to be true. The cases investigated by them were numerous. Most of us are wholly unaware of our past lives, but some do remember them. According to the researchers the majority of such people had been victims of accidents or murder in their previous lives.

The doctrine of the incarnations of the Lord — avatāras — is another unique feature of our religion. The Reality (Sadvastu) is one. That It manifests itself as countless beings is one of our cardinal tenets. It follows that it is this one and only Reality that transforms itself again and again into all those beings that are subject to birth and death. Also it is the same Reality that is manifested as Īśvara to protect this world of sentient beings and insentient objects. Unlike humans he is not subject to the law of karma. It is to live out his karma — to experience the fruits of his actions — that man is born again and again. But in birth after birth, instead of washing away his old karma, he adds more and more to the mud sticking to him.

If the Lord descends to earth again and again it is to lift up man and show him the righteous path. When unrighteousness gains the upper hand and righteousness declines, he descends to earth to destroy unrighteousness and to establish righteousness again — and to protect the virtuous and destroy the wicked. Śrī Kṛṣṇa Paramātman declares so in the Gītā[2].

Īśvara is to be known in different states. That the Lord is all — that all is the Lord — is a state that we cannot easily comprehend. Then there is a state mentioned in the "vibhūti[3] yoga" of the Gītā according to which the Lord dwells in the highest of each category, in the "most excellent" of things[4]. To create the heights of excellence in human life he sends messengers to earth in the guise of preceptors (acāryas), men of wisdom and enlightenment (jñānins), yogins and devotees. This is another state in which God is to be known. Not satisfied with the previous states, he assumes yet another state: he descends to earth as an avatāra. The word "avataraṇa" itself means "descent". Īśvara is "parātpara", that is "higher than the highest", "beyond what is beyond everything". Yet he descends to earth by being born in our midst to re-establish dharma.

Siddhānta Śaivas[5] do not subscribe to the view of Śiva having avatāras. Nor do they agree with the belief that Ādi Śankara and Jñānasaṁbandhar[T] were incarnations of Śiva and Muruga (Subrahmaṇya) respectively. Their view is that if Īśvara dwells in a human womb, in a body of flesh, he makes himself impure. According to Advaitins even all those who inhabit the human womb made up of flesh are in substance nothing but the Brahman. They see nothing improper in the Lord coming down to earth.

All Vaiṣṇavas, without exception, accept the doctrine of divine avatāras. Philosophically speaking, there are many points of agreement between Vaiṣṇavas and Śaivas though the former are not altogether in agreement with the view that it is the Brahman itself that is expressed as the individual self. When we speak of the avatāras, we generally mean the ten incarnations of Viṣṇu. Vaiṣṇavas adhere to the doctrine of avatāras because they believe that

Viṣṇu descends to earth to uplift humanity. Indeed it is because of his boundless compassion that he makes himself small [or reduces himself] to any degree. In truth, however, the Lord is neither reduced nor tainted a bit in any of his incarnations because, though in outward guise he looks a mortal, he knows himself to be what in reality he is.

Altogether the Vedic dharma that is Hinduism accepts the concept of incarnations of the Lord. Śaivas too are one with Vaiṣṇavas in believing in the ten incarnations of Viṣṇu.

That the one and only Paramātman who has neither a form nor attributes is manifested as different forms with attributes is another special feature of our religion. We worship idols representing these forms of deities. For this reason others label us polytheists. Their view is utterly wrong. Because we worship the one God, the one Reality, in many different forms it does not mean that we believe in many gods. It is equally absurd to call us idolaters who hold that the idol we worship is God. Hindus with a proper understanding of their religion do not think that the idol alone is God. The idol is meant for the worshipper to offer one-pointed devotion and he adores it with the conviction that the Lord who is present everywhere is present in it also. We see that practitioners of other religions also have symbols for worship and meditation. So it is wholly unjust to believe that Hindus alone worship idols -- to regard them with scorn as idolaters is not right.

That ours is the only religion that does not proclaim that its followers have an exclusive right to salvation is a matter of pride for us Hindus. Our catholic outlook is revealed in our scriptures which declare that whatever the religious path followed by people they will finally attain the same Paramātman. That is why there is no place for conversion in Hinduism.

Christianity has it that, if a man does not follow the teachings of Jesus Christ, he shall be condemned to hell. Islam says the same about those who do not follow the teachings of the Prophet Mohammed. We must not be angry with the adherents of either religion on that score. Let us take it that Christians and Muslims alike believe that followers of other religions do not have the same sense of fulfilment as they have. So let us presume that it is with good intentions that they want to bring others into their fold (Christianity or Islam as the case may be) out of a desire to help them.

Let us also assume that if they resort to means that seem undesirable, it is to achieve what they think to be a good objective, luring others into their faith. It was thus that they carried out conversions in the past, by force of arms. Islam, particularly, expanded its sway in this way. It is often said that Christianity spread with the help of money power. But Christians also used their army to gain adherents, though with the force of arms was associated the philanthropic work of the missionaries. White men had the advantage of money that the Muslims of the Arabian desert did not possess[6]. Christian missionaries built schools, hospitals and so on to induce the poor to embrace their faith.

We may not approve of people being forced into a religion or of conversions carried out by temptations placed before them. But we need not for that reason doubt that those who spread their religion in this fashion really believe that their work will bring general well-being.

We cannot, however, help asking whether their belief is right. People who do not follow either Christ or the Prophet, are they really condemned to hell? A little thinking should show that the belief that the followers of Christianity or Islam have an exclusive right to salvation cannot be sustained. It is only some 2,000 years since Jesus was born and only about 1,400 years or so since the birth of the Prophet[7]. What happened to all the people born before them since creation? Are we to believe that they must have passed into hell? We are also compelled to infer that even the forefathers of the founders of Christianity and Islam would not have earned paradise.

If, like Hindus, all those who lived before Christ or the Prophet had believed in rebirth, we could concede that they would have been saved: they would have been born again and again until the arrival of Christ or the Prophet and then afforded the opportunity of following their teachings. But if we accept the logic of Christianity and Islam, according to which religions there is no rebirth, we shall have to conclude that hundreds of millions of people for countless generations must have been consigned to eternal hell.

The question arises as to whether God is so merciless as to keep despatching people for ages together to the hell from which there is no escape. Were he compassionate would he not have sent, during all this time, a messenger of his or a teacher to show humanity the way to liberation? Why should we worship a God who has no mercy? Or, for that matter, why should there be any religion at all?

The countries are many and they have different climates and grow different crops. Also each part of the world has evolved a different culture. But the Vedas encompassed lands all over this planet from the very beginning. Later other religions emerged in keeping with the changing attitudes of the nations concerned. That is why aspects of the Vedic tradition are in evidence not only in the religions now in force but in what we know of those preceding them. But in India alone has Hinduism survived as a full-fledged living faith.

It must also be added that this primeval religion has regarded — and still regards — with respect the religions that arose subsequent to it. The Hindu view is this: "Other religions must have evolved according to the degree of maturity of the people among whom they originated. They will bring well-being to their adherents." "Live and let live" has been and continues to be the ideal of our religion. It has given birth to religions like Buddhism and Jainism and they [particularly Buddhism] have been propagated abroad for the Ātmic advancement of the people there.

I have spoken about the special characteristics of Hinduism from the philosophical and theological points of view. But it has also another important feature which is also distinctive — the sociological.

All religions have their own philosophical and theological systems. Also all of them deal with individual life and conduct and, to a limited extent, with social life. "Look upon your neighbour as your brother." "Regard your adversary as your friend." "Treat others in the same way as you would like to be treated yourself." "Be kind to all creatures." "Speak the truth." "Practise non-violence." These injunctions and rules of conduct relate to social life up to a point— and only up to a point. To religions other than Hinduism social life or the structure of society is not a major concern. Hinduism alone has a sturdy sociological foundation, and its special feature, "varṇāśrama dharma", is an expression of it.

Varṇa dharma is one and āśrama dharma is another (together they make up varṇśrama dharma). Āśrama dharma deals with the conduct of an individual during different stages of his life. In the first stage, as a brahmacārin[S], he devotes himself to studies in a gurukula[S]. In the second stage, as a youth, he takes a wife, settles down in life and begets children. In the third, as he ages further, he becomes a forest recluse and, without much attachment to wordly life, engages himself in Vedic karma. In the fourth stage, he forsakes even Vedic works, renounces the world utterly to become a sannyāsin and turns his mind towards the Paramātman. These four stages of life or āśramas are called brahmacarya, gārhasthya, vānaprastha and sannyāsa.

Varṇa dharma is an "arrangement" governing all society. It is very much a target of attack today and is usually spoken of as the division of society into "jātis". But "varṇa" and "jāti" are in fact different. There are only four varṇas but the jātis are numerous. For instance, in the same varṇa there are Ayyars, Ayyangārs, Raos, etc — these are jātis. Mudaliars, Pillais, Reddiars and Naikkars are jātis belonging to another varṇa. In the Yajurveda (third aṣṭaka, fourth praśna) and in the Dharmaśāstra a number of jātis are mentioned — but you do not meet with them today.

Critics of varṇa dharma brand it as "a blot on our religion" and as "a vicious system which divides people into high and low". But, if you look at it impartially, you will realise that it is a unique instrument to bring about orderly and harmonious social life[8].

Notes & References

1 Obviously the Paramaguru states this with a touch of irony.

2 *Yadā-yadā hi dharmasya glānir bhavati Bhārata*
Abhyutthānam adharmasya tadātmānam sṛjāmyaham

Paritrāṇāya sādhūnām vināśāya ca duskṛtām
Dharma-saṁsthāpanārthāya sambhavāmi yuge yuge

— Bhagavadgītā, 4. 7 & 8.

3 "Vibhūti yoga", Chapter 10 of the Bhagavadgītā.

4 Some scholars express this idea by describing God as the "quintessence of essences".

5 Siddhānta Śaivas", followers of the Śaiva Śiddhanta, that developed in the South about the 11th century. One of its chief exponents was Meykandar, 13th century, author of *Śivajñānabodham.*

6 The situation in this respect has changed now with the boom in petrodollars in West Asia.

7 Prophet Mohammed -- A.D. 570-632.

8 Aspects of varṇa dharma are dealt with in detail in Parts Three and Twenty.

Chapter 4

The Vedas, the Root of All

Our religion consists of two major divisions, Śaivism and Vaiṣṇavism. The doubt arises as to whether we are speaking here of two separate faiths or of a single one.

Christianity too has two major divisions but people belonging to both conduct worship in the name of the same God. In Buddhism we have the Hīnayāna and Mahāyāna[1] streams but they do not make two separate faiths since both are based on the teachings of the same founder, the Buddha.

Do Śaivas and Vaiṣṇavas worship the same god? No. However it be with ordinary Vaiṣṇavas, their ācāryas or teachers never go anywhere near a Śiva temple. Their god is Viṣṇu, never Śiva. In the opinion of the worshippers of Viṣṇu, Śiva is also one of his (Viṣṇu's) devotees. There are extremists among Śaivas also according to whom Viṣṇu is not a god but a devotee of Śiva. How then can the two groups be said to belong to the same religion?

Are they to be regarded as belonging to the same faith by virtue of their having a common scripture? The divisions [sects] of Christianity have one common scripture, the Bible; so too is the Qur'ān the common holy book for all divisions of Islam. Is such the case with Śaivas and Vaiṣṇavas? Śaivas have the *Tirumurai*[T] as their religious text, while Vaiṣṇavas have the *Nālāyira-Divyaprabandham*[T] as their sacred work[2]. For Śaivas and Vaiṣṇavas thus the deities as well as the scriptures are different. How can it be claimed that both belong to the same religion?

Though divided into Śaivas and Vaiṣṇavas, we have been saved by the fact that the white man brought us together under a common name, "Hindu". But for this, what would have been our fate? In village after village, we would have been fragmented into separate religious groups — Śaivas, Vaiṣṇavas, Śāktas[3], worshippers of Muruga[4], Gaṇapati, Ayyappa[5], and so on. Further, in these places followers of religions like Christianity and Islam would have predominated. Now two regions of our subcontinent have become Pākistān[6]. Had we not been brought together with the label of Hindu, the entire subcontinent would have become Pākistān. The very same men who created Pākistān through their evil designs and sowed the seeds of differences among us with their theory of two races — Āryans and Dravīḍians — unwittingly did us a good turn by calling us Hindu, thereby bringing into being a country called "India."

So are we one religion or are we divided into two *faiths*? The belief that Śaivas and Vaiṣṇavas have separate deities and religious works does not represent the truth. Though the present outlook of the two groups suggests that they represent different faiths, the truth will be revealed if we examine their prime scriptures. The saints who composed the *Tirumurai* of the Śaivas and the *Nālāyira-Divyaprabandham* of the Vaiṣṇavas never claimed that these works of theirs were the prime religious texts of the respective sects. Nor did they regard themselves as founders of any religion. Vaiṣṇavism existed before the ĀzhvārsT and so too there was Śaivism before the Nāyanmārs*T*.

The original scripture of both sects is constituted by the Vedas. Śaivas describe Īśvara thus[7]:

Vedamoḍārangamāyinānai
Vedanāthan, Vedagītan, āraṇan kān

Similarly, the Vaiṣṇava texts proclaim, "*Vedam Tamizh śeyta Māran Śaṭhakopan*[8]*.*" If we pay close attention to their utterances, we will discover that the Vedas are the prime scripture of both sects. The *Tevāram* and the *Nālāyira-Divyaprabandham* are of the utmost importance to them (to the Śaivas and Vaiṣṇavas respectively); but the Vedas are the basis of both. The great saint-poets who composed the Śaiva and Vaiṣṇava hymns sing the glories of the Vedas throughout. Whenever they describe a temple, they go into raptures, saying, "Here the air is filled with the sound of the Vedas and pervaded with the smoke of the sacrificial fire. Here the six Angas[9] of the Vedas flourish." In the songs of these hymnodists veneration of the Vedas finds as much place as devotion to the Lord.

The Vedas reveal the One Truth to us in the form of many deities. The worship of each of these divine beings is like a *ghat* on the river called the Vedas. ŚekkizhārT says the same thing[10]: *"Veda neri tazhaittonga mihu Śaivatturai viḷaṅga."*

Apart from Śaivism and Vaiṣṇavism, there are a number of sectarian systems like Śāktam, Gāṇapatyam, Kaumāram, and Sauram (worship of Śakti, Gaṇapati, Kumara or Subrahmaṇya and the Sun God)[11]. The adoration of these deities is founded in the Vedas according to the texts relating to them: "Our deity is extolled in the Vedas," each system contains such a declaration.

Thus we find that there is but one scripture as the source common to the different sects and schools of thought in the Hindu religion.

This source includes the Upaniṣads. On ten of them (Daśopaniṣad) the great teachers of the Śaiva, Vaiṣṇava, and Smārta traditions have written commentaries. The Upaniṣadic texts proclaim that the Brahman is the one and only Godhead. In the *Kaṭhopaniṣad* it is called Viṣṇu; in the *Māṇḍūkyopaniṣad* it is called Śivam. All the deities mentioned in the Saṁhitās of the Vedas — Mitra, Varuṇa, Agni, Indra and so on — are different names of the same Truth. So it is said in the Vedas: "Ekam sad viprā bahudhā vadanti."

It emerges that for all the divisions in our religion there is but one scripture — a scripture common to all — and one Godhead which is known by many names. The Vedas are the common scripture and the Godhead common to all is the Brahman. Thus we can say with finality, and without any room for doubt, that all of us belong to the same religion.

The Vedas that constitute the scripture common to all and which reveal the Godhead that is common to us also teach us how to lead our life, and — this is important — they do us the ultimate good by showing us in the end the way to become that very Godhead ourselves. They are our refuge both here and the hereafter and are the source and root of all our different traditions, all our systems of thought. All sects, all schools of our religion, have their origin in them. The root is one but the branches are many.

The Vedas are the source not only of the various divisions of Hinduism, all the religions of the world may be traced back to them. It is our bounden duty to preserve them for all time to come with their glory undiminished.

Notes & References

1 "Hīnayāna" ("Lesser Vehicle", "Lower Way") is a school of Buddhism which teaches the attainment of salvation for oneself alone, that is it is fit for a select few. "Mahāyāna" ("Greater Vechicle" or "Higher Way") teaches the salvation of all. (The definitions given here are too brief and perhaps over-simplified.) Hīnayāna is the earlier school and claims to represent the teachings of the Buddha in a "purer" form. Mahāyāna is usually ascribed to Nāgārjuna,

2 The Paramaguru is referring here to the Śaivas and Vaiṣṇavas of Tamiḷ Nāḍu.

3, 4 & 5 "Śāktas" are worshippers of Śakti, the Supreme Goddess. "Muruga" is Subrahmaṇya or Kārtikeya. Tamils are particularly devoted to him. "Ayyappa" is "Śāstā" or "Hariharaputra". He represents the oneness of Śiva and Viṣṇu.

6 This discourse was given before Bāṅgladeś came into being.

7 "Behold, Īśvara in his form of the Vedas and the six Angas."

8 "Nammāzhvar (Māran or Śaṭhakopan) who created the Tamiḷ Veda."

9 Parts Six to Eleven deal with the six Angas.

10 "For the Vedas to flourish and for Śaivism to prosper."

11 Ādi Śankara instituted the six religious systems (Ṣanmata) -- worship of Śiva, Viṣṇu, Śakti, Gaṇapati, Kumāra and Sūrya.

Chapter 5

The Vedas in their Original Form

It is sad that people keep fighting over this language or that. It seems that it would be better for us to be voiceless than keep quarrelling in this manner. Language is but a tool, a tool to convey our thoughts and feelings, to make ourselves understood. It cannot be the same in all countries. Each community, each region or country, has its own tongue. So it is absurd to quarrel over claims that one's language is superior to another's. We could at best say that "we know that language" or "we do not know it". But to talk of "my language" and "your language" is not right. It is also wrong to give greater importance to one's mother tongue than to God or religion. I would go to the extent of saying that we have no need even for Sanskrit, considered merely as a language, as a language *per se*. But our Vedas and śāstras, which are basic to our religion, are in that language and, since they must be preserved, Sanskrit too must be kept alive.

After composing his *Kural*[T], Tiruvaḷḷuvar[T] went to Madurai for its *araṅgeṟṟam*[T]. There, in the city, was the pond of the golden lotuses and the seat of the learned (the *Samgapalagai*). The poet placed his work on this seat. At once all the learned men seated on the *Samgapalagai* fell into the pond but the book remained on it. It was thus that the *Kural* was presented to the public. Many distinguished poets and savants have sung the praises of this work and its content. In *Tiruvaḷḷuvar-Mālai* which contains these praises one poet says:

Āriyamum centamizhum ārāynditaninidu
Śiriyadu tenronraiceppariḍāl—Āriyam
Vedam udaittu Tamizh Tiruvaḷḷuvanār
Odu Kuraṭpāvuḍaittu.

"I thought about the question, which is superior, Sanskrit or Tamiḷ. Sanskrit and Tamiḷ are equal in their greatness. We cannot say that the one is superior to the other. The reason is that the Vedas are in Sanskrit and now in Tamiḷ we have the *Kural*. If there were nothing equal to the Vedas in Tamiḷ, Sanskrit should have been said to be superior. Now the *Kural* is present in Tamiḷ as the equal of the Vedas. Both languages — Sanskrit and Tamiḷ — are now seen to be equally great."

Why is Sanskrit considered a great language? In his praise of the *Tirukkural* here the poet gives the answer: it is because the Vedas are in that language.

Some do not seem to attach any special significance to the fact that the Vedas are in Sanskrit[1]. They think that these sacred texts could be known through translations.

Nowadays a number of books are translated from one language into another and in this process the original form or character is changed or distorted. The words spoken by a great man on a particular subject may not be fully understood today. But if they are preserved in the original in the same language, there is the possibility of their meaning being fully grasped at some future date. You use a beautiful word to convey an idea in your language, but its equivalent may not be found in any other tongue. Also, it may become necessary to express the same in a roundabout way.

There is also the possibility that the opinion expressed first, in its original context, may not come through effectively in a translation. We must consider the further disadvantage of the translation being circumscribed by the mental make-up of the translator, the limitations of his knowledge and understanding of the subject dealt with. The translation done by one may not seem right to another. When there are a number of translations of the same work, it would be hard to choose the right one. We shall then be compelled to go back to the original.

This is the reason why I insist that the Vedas must be preserved in their original form. They are the source of the philosophical systems associated with the great ācāryas. These masters evolved their doctrines from their own individual viewpoints, without making any modifications in the Vedas to suit them; nor did they establish any religions of their own outside the Vedic tradition. The source, the root, of their systems of thought is one and the same — the Vedas. It is because this source has remained unchanged in its original character that thinkers and teachers have, from time to time, been able to draw inspiration and strength from it to present new viewpoints. But these view-points have not meant the creation of new religions. The reason is that all of them — all these systems -- belong to the larger system called the Vedic religion.

Note

[1] In a later discourse (Appendix 1), the Paramaguru reveals that the language of the Vedas is "Chandas" which predates "classical" Sanskrit.

Part Three

THE VEDIC RELIGION AND VARNA DHARMA

Chapter 1

Division of Labour

The proper functioning of society is dependent on a number of factors. Meeting the needs of man entails many types of physical as well as intellectual work. It is totally wrong to claim that one kind of work is inferior to another kind or superior to it.

We need rice, all of us, don't we? Also salt, clothing, books, and so on. Would it be possible — or practicable — for each one of us to grow rice or wheat, to make salt or to produce clothing and books? The tiller grows crops not only for himself but for the entire community. The weaver weaves for all of us. Some carry on trade for the sake of the entire society. And some wage war on behalf of all of us to defend the country.

What about the Ātmic well-being of mankind? Well, some people are charged with the caring of such well-being: they practise meditation, perform pūjā, conduct sacrifices and carry out the ordinances of the śāstras that are meant for the good of all mankind. Our dharmaśāstras have cut out an ideal path of happiness for us by creating a system which is to the advantage of all and in which different sections of people are allotted different occupations.

How has this allotment been made? Is it according to the capacity of each? If so there is the risk of everyone having an excessive idea of his own ability. If work is assigned according to the predilection of each individual, everyone will claim that he is suited for jobs that are "prestigious" and, in the end, no one will come forward to do other jobs. How should a system be devised in which people fill vocations in a manner that ensures the smooth functioning of all society? It must be one that works not only for the present but for all time. This is not possible if everyone competes with everybody else for every kind of job. It is as an answer to such problems that varṇa dharma in which vocations are hereditarily determined came into existence.

The principle behind this arrangement is that a man must do the work handed down to him from his forefathers — whatever such work be -- with the conviction that it has been ordained by Īśvara and that it is for the good of the world. The work he does in this spirit itself becomes a means of his inward advancement.

The religious observances meant to free people from worldly existence vary according to their callings. We cannot expect a man who does hard physical work to observe fasts. Those who do intellectual work do not need much bodily nourishment. They are enjoined to perform many a rite and to observe a number of fasts so that they will learn not to take pride in their body. There would be no room for disputes and misunderstandings among the various sections of people if they realised that the differences in the observance of religious practices are in keeping with the different vocations.

If we keep performing the rites prescribed even without understanding their meaning, it will stand us in good stead in later life when we do come to understand the meaning. It would indeed be commendable if each one of us carried out the duties prescribed and helped others to carry out theirs. "Why do you pursue that vocation, that dharma? Why don't you do the work that I do? Or shall I take up your dharma, your duties?" We must not give room for such feelings of rivalry or become victims of the competitive spirit. When a man thinks of abandoning his dharma — the duties allotted to him by birth — you must persuade him not to do so and impress upon him that he must remain loyal to his dharma since it serves not only him individually but all others.

As I said earlier there is no gradation among people doing various kinds of work: the man who does one type of job is neither inferior to the man doing another kind of job nor superior to him. It is to ensure that society functions properly that the śāstras have divided jobs into a number of categories and assigned them to different groups of people.

If we are guided only by our likes and dislikes in the choice of our occupation — or if we are engaged in work according to our sweet will — the common purpose of society will suffer. You see today that everyone is intent on filling his pockets with other people's money. If there were no principle to guide us in the fulfilment of the common good, the only concern of people would be that of finding such work as can bring them a lot of cash. There is no place for any division of labour in all this and so also no concern for the well-being of mankind in general.

If everyone does his hereditary work and performs the rites that his forefathers performed, there will be no cause for feelings of rivalry or jealousy. There is the further advantage that life in the community will go on smoothly without any hindrance to the common work and, at the same time, each individual will feel pure inwardly. All this must be taken into account if, in the name of carrying out reforms, society is not "deformed".

The government has the obligation to provide food, clothing and housing to all irrespective of the work they do. Jealousies and rivalries will develop if people hunger for things beyond these essentials. All the trouble today arises from the fact that the satisfaction gained from money is greater than that gained from anything else. This attitude must change. With maturity of outlook a man will come to realise that the fulfilment he obtains from doing the work allotted to him properly is itself his God[1]

You see such a variety of eatables in front of you. The rāgas (musical modes) you listen to are numerous. And many and varied are the types of work essential to the smooth functioning of society. You add salt to your *rasam* to give it the right flavour[2]. But if you add it to a sweet drink the result will be rasābhāsa (the drink will not be palatable). Similarly there would be rasābhāsa if the svara (musical note) of one rāga were used in another [the music so produced would be unaesthetic, not pleasing to the ear]. People today are lacking in taste. While narrating a moving incident from a purāṇic story the Bhāgavatar[1] tells cheap jokes which the audience relishes immensely. When there are so many delectable things to eat, people smoke tobacco which is injurious to health. These are all instances of rasābhāsa on a small scale. The rasābhāsa on a big scale is the confusion created in the varṇa system [making a mess of it], a system that has contributed so much to the welfare of our people through its enunciation of different codes of conduct for different sections of the community.

Notes

[1] This is more or less a literal translation of the original. The Paramaguru means here more than what is conveyed by the statement "Work is worship". We may further elaborate his idea thus: A man who carries out the duties assigned to him by the śāstras will come face to face with God. He will be freed from worldly bondage if he remains true to his svadharma or "own duty".

[2] In this passage the Paramaguru plays on the word "rāga" which means [apart from a "musical mode"] "flavour", "mood", "quintessence", "taste", "the substance of aesthetic experience". "*Rasam*" is derived from "rasa" and is used here for the well-known South Indian culinary item, one variety of which is known to Englishmen as "mulligatawny". "Rasābhasa" is difficult to translate. "Ābhāsa" literally means "reflection", "back-shining". In common usage "rasābhāsa" means "an improper rasa", "contrary to good taste". In the South ābhāsa has come to mean anything that is "vulgar" or "indecent".

[3] "Bhāgavatar", strictly speaking, means a devotee of Bhagavān, the Lord. In the South the term also denotes a musician. ("Bhāgavatar" is the honorific Tamil plural of "Bhāgavata"). Here the word means particularly a musician who is also a story-teller, what is called a "kīrtankār" in Mahārāṣṭra.

Chapter 2

What is Varṇa Dharma?

In the old days the kitchen fireplace was fuelled with dried wood, cowdung and so on. On rainy days it was difficult to light it. But if only a few sparks were produced they could be fanned into a flame so as to set the wood or cowdung on fire. Our sanātana dharma[S] has not entirely perished. A few sparks of it are present in the life of a small number of great men still living in our midst. It is my ardent wish to keep blowing on them with a view to propagating our ancient religion in its true character.

Our reformers want to do away with varṇa dharma so as to make Hinduism no different from other faiths.

In this context, I must ask you: What is religion? Religion is like a therapeutic system meant to cure the ills contracted by the Self. The physician alone knows about the disease afflicting the patient and how it is to be treated. Our sanātana dharma is the medicine prescribed by our sages and creators of the dharmaśāstras who never sought anything for themselves and who, in their utter selflessness, were concerned only about the good of mankind.

In other countries other physicians have prescribed medicines in the form of their own religious systems. Would your doctor like to be told that he should treat you in the same way as another doctor treats his patient? There are several systems of medicine. In one there is a strict diet regimen, in another there is not much strictness about the patient's food. In one system the medicines administered taste sweet; in another they taste bitter. To be restored to health we have to follow strictly any one method of treatment, not insist on a combination of the various therapies.

Other religions lay down only such duties as are common to all their followers. In the Vedic religion there are two types of dharma, the one being common to all and the other to individual varṇas. The duties common to all Hindus, the universal code of conduct, have the name of "sāmānya dharma"[1]. Non-violence, truthfulness, cleanliness, control of the senses, non-acquisitiveness (one must not possess material goods in excess of what is needed for one's bare requirements, not even a straw must one own in excess), devotion to Īśvara, trust in one's parents, love for all creatures — these form part of the sāmānya dharma. Then each varṇa has its own special code of conduct or "viśeṣa dharma" determined by its hereditary vocation

If the special duties (viśeṣa dharma) of the various varṇas were made common to all (that is made part of the sāmānya dharma) a situation would arise in which no one would observe any dharma. To illustrate, I shall give you an example. Abstaining from meat was laid down as a common dharma in Buddhism. But what do we see today in countries where that religion has a wide following? There almost all Buddhists eat meat. In contrast to this is what obtains in our religion. Our seers and authors of the dharmaśāstras had a profound understanding of human nature. They made abstention from meat applicable to a limited number of people. But others follow the example of these few, on days of fasting, on special occasions like the death anniversaries of their parents, on days sacred to the gods.

The religions that flourished once upon a time in other countries — religions that had one common code of conduct for all its adherents —have become extinct. In Europe the Hellenic religion is gone. So too in West Asia the prehistoric Hebrew faiths no longer exist. And in the East only a residue remains of Confucianism, Shintoism, etc. Religions like Buddhism, Christianity and Islam too have but one code of conduct for all their adherents. Their followers in various countries now find less and less inner satisfaction. The number of people who have lost faith in their religion is on the increase in all these lands. They become either atheists or turn to the yoga, bhakti or jñāna schools of Hinduism.

It is difficult to say how long people will continue to owe allegiance to the religions that arose in various countries during historical times. I say this not because I happen to be a representative of Hindus nor is it my wish to speak in demeaning terms about other religions. My wish is indeed that people following different religions ought to continue to remain in their respective folds and find spiritual fulfilment in them. I do not invite others to embrace my faith. In fact I believe that to do so is contrary to the basic tenets of my religion. Nothing occurs in this world as an accident. People with different levels of maturity are born in different religions: so it is ordained by the Lord. I believe that a man grows inwardly by practising the tenets of the religion of his birth.

If I speak about what I feel to be the worthy features of Hinduism -- features that are not found in other religions — it is neither to speak ill of the latter nor to invite their followers to our side. Non-Hindus attack these unique aspects of our religion without taking the trouble of understanding them and some Hindus themselves are influenced by their views. That is why I am constrained to speak about the distinctive doctrines of our religion. Acceptance of concepts like karma, the Lord's incarnations, etc, will in no way weaken their [of non-Hindus] attachment to the basic beliefs of their own religions. What is the fundamental concept of any religion, its living principle? It is faith in the

Lord and devotion to him. For others to view these special concepts of Hinduism sympathetically does not mean that their faith in God or devotion to him will be affected in any way.

I say all this not because I think that other religions are in any trouble nor because I have reason to be happy if indeed they are. I echoed the views of distinguished students of religion like Toynbee, Paul Brunton and Köstler. I merely repeated their view that lack of faith in religion — indeed atheism — is growing day by day everywhere and that all religions are struggling for their survival.

This trend is seen to be on the rise in our own country. But foreigners who have made a study of religious beliefs all over the world are unanimous in their view that in comparison with other countries things are better here. "The religious urge has not yet reached a lamentable state in your country," they tell us. Sādhakas, seekers, keep coming to India in large numbers. A little thought should show without a shadow of doubt that if religious feeling is on the decline and atheism on the rise in India it is due to the fact that we have become increasingly lax in observing varṇa dharma and have come to believe that all Hindus should be made into one without any distinction of caste.

When a religion divides its followers in many ways, we think that there will be no unity or integrity among them. It also seems to us that such a religion will fall apart as a result of internal squabbles. Since the time of Alexander, India has been invaded by wave after wave of foreigners belonging to other faiths. Considering the divisions in our religion and the series of foreign invasions, Hinduism should have ended up in smoke. But what we actually see is different. Religions which have no distinctions of caste and which prescribe the same duties and rites for all their followers have disappeared in the flow of time. Similar systems still surviving today are faced with danger, as is attested to by the intellectuals amongst their own followers. But Hinduism with its many divisions is still breathing. We must try to understand the secret of its survival without being carried away by emotions.

We have practised varṇa dharma for millennia and it has continued to be a living force. What is its secret? Or think of this. It is the special duty of Brahmins to preserve the mantras[S]. But have they ever been in a majority? No. Have they enjoyed the power of arms? No. Have they had at least money power, the advantage gained from wealth? The answer again is "No". (Brahmins acquiring the habit of accumulating money is a recent phenomenon. It is of course quite undesirable.) How or why did other castes accept the divisions laid down in the śāstras created by the Brahmins who did not have the strength derived either from money or from arms or from numbers?

A great man like the Buddha or the Jina arose to proclaim: "We do not need the Vedas, nor do we need the sacrifices prescribed by them. Let us have one uniform dharma for all people. We do not need Sanskrit either. Let us write our new śāstras in Pāli or some other Prākṛt, in a language understood by the common people." It is true that some people were persuaded to embrace these new religions, Buddhism and Jainism, but the attraction of these faiths was momentary and the two gradually declined. The old Vedic religion emerged again with new vigour.

A great man has sung thus: "It is indeed a wonder that life remains in this body with its nine apertures (nava-dvara or nine gates). If it departs it is no matter to be wondered at." Likewise, it would not have beeen a matter for surprise if Hinduism had perished with all its divisions and with its constant exposure to attack from outside. It is indeed a miracle that it is not dead.

If some faiths in India itself and outside have declined and if our religion alone has survived for ten thousand years, does it not mean that it has something that is lacking in others? This something is the varṇa system. Our present-day reformers argue that the varṇa division is responsible for the disintegration of our society. The fact is it is precisely this division, varṇa dharma, that has sustained it and kept it intact. It follows that this dharma has features that are superior in character to concepts like equality, features that are vital to the very well-being of people. Our society is divided on the basis of it, but it must be noted that this division has helped our religion to preserve itself successfully against all onslaughts.

Reference

[1] Part Twenty-two is devoted to this.

Chapter 3

Unity in Diversity

Talking of the varṇa system I am reminded of the early days of aviation. In the beginning the airship [dirigible balloon] was filled with one gas bag. It was discovered that the vessel would collapse even if it sprang just one leak. So it was fitted with a number of smaller gas bags and kept afloat without much danger of its crashing. The principle of different duties and vocations for different sections of society is similar to what kept the old type of airship from collapsing. In the varṇa system we have an example of unity in diversity.

Fastening together a large number of individual firesticks is not easy: the bundle is loosened quickly and the sticks will give way. The removal of even one stick will make the bundle loose and, with each stick giving way, you will be left with separate sticks. Try to tie together a handful of sticks at a time instead of all the sticks together. A number of such small sheaves may be easily fastened together into a strong and secure larger bundle. Even if it becomes loose, none of the smaller bundles will come away. This is not the case with the large bundle bound up of individual sticks. A bundle made up of a number of smaller sets will remain well secured.

To keep a vast community bound together in a single uniform structure is well-nigh an impossible task. Because of its unmanageable size it is not easily sustained in a disciplined manner. This is the reason why — to revert to the example of the fuelsticks — the community was divided into jātis [similar to the smaller bundles in the analogy of the firesticks] and each jāti assigned a particular vocation. Each varṇa was divided into a number of jātis [smaller bundles], with each jāti having a headman with the authority to punish offenders. Today criminals are sentenced to prison or punished in other ways. But the incidence of crime is on the increase since all such types of punishment have no deterrent effect. In the jāti system the guilty took the punishment to heart. So much so that, until the turn of the century, people lived more or less honourably and there was little incidence of crime. The police and the magistrates did not have much work to do.

What was the punishment meted out to offenders by the village or jāti headman? Excommunication. Whether it was a cobbler or a barber — anyone belonging to any one of the jātis now included among the "backward" or "depressed" classes — he would feel deeply stung if he were thrown out of his jāti: no punishment was harsher or more humiliating than excommunication.

What do we learn from all this? No jāti thought poorly of itself or of another jāti. Members of each jāti considered themselves the supreme authority in managing their affairs. This naturally gave them a sense of contentment and satisfaction. What would have happened if some jātis were regarded as "low" and some others as "high"? Feelings of inferiority would have arisen among some sections of the community and perhaps, apart from Brahmins and Kṣatriyas, no jāti would have had any sense of pride in itself. If each jāti had no respect for itself no one would have taken excommunication to heart. When the entire society was divided into small groups called jātis, not only did one jāti have affection for another, each also trusted the other. There was indeed a feeling of kinship among all members of the community. This was the reason why the threat of excommunication was dreaded.

Now some sections of the community remain attached to their jātis for the only reason that they enjoy certain privileges as members belonging to the "backward" classes. But they take no true pride in belonging to their respective jātis. In the old days these sections "enjoyed "no special privileges but we know it to be a fact that, until some three or four generations ago, they were proud of belonging to their jātis. We must add that this was not because — as is the case today — of rivalries and jealousies among the various groups. There were indeed no quarrels, no rivalries, based on differences of jāti. Apart from pride, there was a sense of fulfilment among members of each jāti in pursuing the vocation inherited from their forefathers and in observing the rites proper to it.

Nowadays trouble-makers defy even the police. But in the past, in the system of jātis, there was no opposition to the decisions of the headman. The police are, after all, part of an outward system of discipline and law enforcement. But in jāti rule the discipline was internal since there was a sense of kinship among the members of each jāti. So in the jāti set-up crime was controlled more effectively than in today's system of resorting to weapons or the constabulary. Though divided according to jātis and the occupations and customs pertaining to each of them, society remained united. It was a system that ensured harmony.

Chapter 4
Divided by Work but still of One Heart

I spoke about the different jātis, the work allotted to each of them and the rites and customs prescribed for each. What I said was not entirely correct. The vocation is not for jāti; it is jāti for the vocation. On what basis did the Vedic religion divide the fuelsticks [that is the jātis] into small bundles? It fixed one jāti for one vocation. In the West economists talk of division of labour but they are unable to translate their ideas into practice. Any society has to depend on the proper execution of a variety of jobs.

It is from this social necessity that the concept of division of labour arose. But who is to decide the number of people for each type of work? Who is to determine the proportions for society to function in a balanced manner? In the West they had no answer to these questions. Everybody there competes with everybody else for comfortable jobs and everywhere you find greed and bitterness resulting from such rivalries. And, as a consequence of all this, there are lapses from discipline and morality.

In our country we based the division of labour on a hereditary system and, until it worked, people had a happy, peaceful and contented life. Today even a multimillionaire is neither contented nor happy. Then even a cobbler led a life without cares. What sort of progress have we achieved today by inflaming evil desires in all hearts and pushing everyone into the slough of discontent? Not satisfied with such "progress" there is talk everywhere that we must go forward rapidly in this manner.

Greed and covetousness were unknown during the centuries when varṇa dharma flourished. People were bound together in small well-knit groups and they discovered that there was happiness in their being together. Besides they had faith in religion, fear of God and devotion, and a feeling of pride in their own family deities and in the modes of worshipping them. In this way they found fullness in their lives without any need to suffer the hunger and disquiet of seeking external objects. All society experienced a sense of well-being.

Though divided into a number of groups people were all one in their devotion to the Lord; and though they had their own separate family deities, they were brought together in the big temple that was for the entire village or town. This temple and its festivals had a central place in their life and they remained united as the children of the deity enshrined in it. When there was a car festival (rathotsava) the Brahmins and the people living on the outskirts of the village [the so-called backward classes] stood shoulder to shoulder and pulled the chariot together. We wonder whether those days of peace and harmony will ever return. Neither jealousy nor bitterness was known then and people did not trade charges against one another. Everyone did his job, carried out his duties, in a spirit of humility and with a sense of contentment.

Considering all this, would it be correct to say that Hinduism faced all its challenges *in spite of the divisions in society?* No, no. Such a view would be totally wrong. The fact is that our religion has survived as a living force for ages together *because of these very divisions.* Other great religions which had but one uniform dharma for all have gone under. And there is the fear that existing religions of the same type might suffer a similar fate. What has sustained Hinduism as an eternal religion? We must go back to the analogy of the fuelsticks. Like a number of small bundles of sticks bound together strong and secure — instead of all the individual sticks being fastened together — Hindu society is a well-knit union of a number of small groups which are themselves bound up separately as jātis, the cementing factor being devotion to the Lord.

Religions that had a common code of duties and conduct could not withstand attacks from within and without. In India there were many sets of religious beliefs that were contained in, or integrated together with, a common larger system. If new systems of beliefs or dharmas arose from within or if there were inroads by external religious systems, a process of rejection and assimilation took place: what was not wanted was rejected and what was fit to be accepted was absorbed. Buddhism and Jainism sprang from different aspects of the Vedic religion, so Hinduism (later) was able to digest them and was able to accommodate many other sets of beliefs or to make them its own. There was no need for it to treat other systems as adversaries or to carry on a struggle against them.

After the advent of Islam we adopted only some of its customs but not any of its religious concepts. The Moghul influence was felt to some extent in our dress, music, architecture and painting. Even such impressions of the Muslim impact did not survive for long as independent factors but were dissolved in the flow of our Vedic culture. Also the Islamic impact was largely confined to the North; the South did not come much under it and stuck mostly to its own traditional path.

Later, with the coming of the Europeans, faith in the Vedic religion began to decline all over India, in North as well as South. How did this change occur? Why do all political leaders today keep excoriating the varṇa system, giving it the name of "casteism"? And how has the view gained ground everywhere that the division of jātis has greatly hindered the progress of the nation? And why does the mere mention of the word jāti invite a gaol sentence?

I shall tell you later, as best I can, about who is responsible for this state of affairs. For the present let us try to find out why some people want to do away with varṇa dharma. To them it seems an iniquitous system in which some jātis occupy a high status while some others are pushed down to low depths. They want all to be raised to the same uniform high level.

Is such a step possible or practicable? To find an answer, all that we have to do is to examine conditions in countries where there is no caste. If there were no distinctions of high and low in these lands, we should see no class conflicts there. But in reality what do we see? People in these countries are divided into "advantaged" and "disadvantaged" classes who are constantly fighting between themselves. A true understanding of our religion will show that in reality there are no differences in status based on caste among our people. But let us for argument's sake presume that there are; our duty then is to make sure that the feelings of differences are removed, not get rid of varṇa dharma itself.

One more point must be considered. Even if you concede that the social divisions have caused bitterness among the different sections here, what about the same in other countries? Can the existence of such ill-will in other lands be denied? The differences there, based on wealth and status, cause bitterness and resentment among the underprivileged and poorer sections. In America, it is claimed that all people have enough food, clothing and housing. They say that even a domestic servant there owns a car. It is reasonable to infer from this that the Americans are a contented people. But what is the reality there? The man who has only one car is envious of another who has two. Similarly, the fact that one person has a bank balance of a hundred million dollars is cause for heart-burning for another with a bank balance of only a million. Those who have sufficient means to live confortably quarrel with people better off over rights and privileges. Does this not mean that even in a country like the United States there are conflicts between the higher and lower classes of society?

The story is not different in the communist countries[1]. Though everyone is said to be paid the same wages there, they have officers and clerks who do not enjoy the same status. As a result of the order enforced by the state, there may not be any outward signs of quarrel among the different cadres, but jealousy and feelings of rivalry must, all the same, exist in the hearts of people. In the higher echelons of power there must be greater rivalry in the communist lands than elsewhere. The dictator of today is replaced by another tomorrow. Is it possible to accord the same status to all in order to prevent the growth of antagonisms? Feelings of high and low will somehow persist, so too the competitive urge.

It seems to me that better than the distinctions prevailing in the West — distinctions that give rise to jealousies and social discord — are the differences mistakenly attributed to the hereditary system of vocations. In the old days this arrangement ensured peace in the land with everyone living a contented life. There was neither envy nor hatred and everyone readily accepted his lot.

The different types of work are meant for the good of the people in general. It is wrong to believe that one job belongs to an "inferior" category and another to a "superior" type. There is no more efficacious medicine for inner purity than doing one's work, whatever it be, without any desire for reward and doing it to perfection. I must add that even wrong notions about work (one job being better than another or worse) is better than the disparities and differences to be met with in other countries. We are [or were] free from the spirit of rivalry and bitterness that vitiate social life there.

Divided we have remained united, and nurtured our civilization. Other civilizations have gone under because the people of the countries concerned, though seemingly united, were in fact divided. In our case though there were differences in the matter of work there was unity of hearts and that is how our culture and civilization flourished. In other countries the fact that there were no distinctions based on vocations (anyone could do any work) itself gave rise to rivalries and eventually to disunity. They were not able to withstand the onslaught of other civilizations.

It is not practicable to make all people one, nor can everyone occupy the same high position. At the same time it is also unwise to keep people divided into classes that are like water-tight compartments.

The dharmaśāstras have shown us a middle way that avoids the pitfalls of the two extremes. I have come as a representative of this way and that is why I speak for it: that there ought to be distinctions among various sections of people in the performance of rites but that there must be unity of hearts. There should be no confusion between the two.

Though we are divided outwardly in the matter of work,with unity of hearts there will be peace. That was the tradition for ages together in this land — there was oneness of hearts. If every member of society does his duty, does his work, unselfishly and with the conviction that he is doing it for the good of all, considerations of high and low will not enter his mind. If people carry out the duties common to them, however adverse the circumstances be, and if every individual performs the duties that are special to him, no one will have cause for suffering at any time.

Note

[1] This discourse was given many years before the collapse of communism in the Soviet Union and Eastern Europe.

Chapter 5

Why only in this Country

The question arises: "What about countries other than India? And what about the religions practised there? They do not have a system of jātis nor do they have in force any division of labour based on heredity. Why should we alone have such an arrangement?"

It will be conceded that even such countries as do not have any social division based on vocations have produced wise men who have contributed to the growth of knowledge and also statesmen, administrators, warriors, agriculturists, traders and labourers. But if you look at the matter impartially — and not necessarily as a proud patriot — you will realise that no other country has had such a great civilization as we have had. It is true that great civilizations flourished in other lands too, but they did not last thousands of years like ours. To say this is not to blow our own trumpet. From the time of Alexander until today — when we seem to have fallen into an abyss from the heights of glory — foreigners have been filled with wonder for the Hindu civilization.

Other countries, it is true, have given birth to great men, to men of God, to philanthropists, to men of sacrifice. But if you take a census of all nations, you will see that no other nation would have given birth, generation after generation for thousands of years in an uninterrupted manner, to such a large number of great men, saintly men, wise men, philosophers, devotees and philanthropists. They will outnumber all such men produced in other countries put together. Foreigners refer to India as the "land of saints", as "the land of sages". They express their profound admiration for our Vedānta, for our metaphysics, and all our ancient works.

The whole world acknowledges our unparalleled contributions to art, sculpture, music, poetry, astronomy, mathematics, medicine. It never ceases to wonder at our great works of philosophy and literature like the Upaniṣads, the Bhagavadgītā, the Rāmāyaṇa, the *Śākuntalam,* etc. Scholars abroad are of the opinion that there are hardly any devotional works outside India like the Tamiḷ *Tevāram*[T] and *Divyaprabandham*[T]. They note the *Kural,* in the same language, to be an astonishingly profound and lucid ethical work that is yet so brief. Foreigners come to our land, leaving their home and hearth, to find out all about our gopurams, our sculptures, our dances like Bharatanāṭyam all of which have cast a spell over them. Europeans enslaved us, ascribed all kinds of faults to us and held us in bondage with their policy of divide and rule. But, all the same, out of admiration for our culture they have sought out our śāstras, our ancient texts, conducted research into them and translated them into their own languages.

To what special factors are we to attribute the existence of such a great and unique civilization? In looking for an answer you will discover that there was something in our social structure that was not shared by other countries, that is varṇa dharma. According to our reformers all our ills are due to the caste system. But it is this land with this unique system — varṇāśrama — that has excelled all other nations in metaphysics, in the arts, in social values and in wisdom. Stability in society and peace go hand in hand. Without them, without an atmosphere conducive to creative work, no arts, no philosophy, no culture could have flourished generation after generation. Philosophers and sages and geniuses in the field of arts would not have otherwise been thrown up in such amazingly large numbers.

The religions that governed life in other countries did not evolve a social structure capable of creating this kind of stability. One might say that the question of creating a sociological foundation was overlooked in them. They did not lay down rules for orderly social life and had but general interdictions and injunctions like "Do not steal"; "Do not tell lies"; "Do not commit adultery"; "Live a life of sacrifice". In Buddhism and Christianity the institutionalised system is meant only for the monks. Unlike in Hinduism in none of these religions was attention directed towards weaving together the entire society into a fabric in which one member formed a support to another.

One does not deny that there was scientific advancement in other nations. They had a system of defence and they carried on trade and commerce. But the spirit of rivalry vitiated all walks of life in these lands. No community had an occupation entirely to itself. Everyone could compete with everyone else for every kind of job. In our country people had their own hereditary callings and they were assured of their livelihood. This meant peace and stability in society. We must remember that it was because our people were bound together in the unique varṇa system that they excelled in culture and character, not to mention the fact that the stability afforded by the system facilitated the birth of countless numbers of individuals who exemplified all that is noble in mankind. In contrast, in the absence of a similar institution, jealousy and rivalry became disturbing factors in the life of other countries.

Our nation should have witnessed many a revolution if, as claimed by our social reformers, the people were kept suppressed in the varṇa system. However, the term "social revolution" was new to us until recently. It is only after reading about the French Revolution, the American Revolution and the Soviet Revolution that we have known that compulsions would arise for great masses of people to be plunged in unrest. The common people in other countries were again and again involved thus in revolutionary movements. But we note— and this is important — that no revolution has achieved anything of permanent value. If there is an upsurge today there is another fifty or a hundred years later. We have to conclude from this that people abroad have remained discontented most of the time.

Today's situation is all too obvious to be stated. The whole world is in turmoil. Indiscipline, strikes, social upsets and savage orgies of violence have become the order of the day. It is only in a country like the Soviet Union where there is a dictatorship that comes down heavily on those who voice any opposition to it that there is hardly any unrest. However, it is said that the volcano of unrest might erupt any time there[1]. Now and then an intellectual or writer escapes from that land to tell us about the tyranny from which people suffer there. Obviously in the Soviet Union too people are not happy and contented.

India has seldom had an autocracy or dictatorship of this type. It would not have taken the strides it did in the sciences and arts had it been a slave country or a country ruled by despots. People here never lamented before others that they were kept suppressed. All our works of knowledge and wisdom, all our arts and all our temples would not have been possible if the mind was not enabled to unfold itself in an atmosphere of freedom. It would also be preposterous to suggest that a majority of the common people were victims of superstition and delusion and lived in fear of priestcraft. You could speak thus of the tribes living in the forests of Africa or South America. In these places the priest was like a king. He would be fearsome even to look at and he was able to impress his tribesmen that he could do anything with his utterances (his mantra - like formulae). He had also the power to punish people. Such was not the case in our country. People here were fairly knowledgeable irrespective of the jātis to which they belonged and they were devoted and advanced in matters pertaining to the Self.

If you go through the Purāṇas (including the Tamiḻ *Periyapurāṇam*[T]) you will learn that there were great men in all jātis. Imperial rulers like Candragupta and ministers like Śekkizhār[T] belonged to the fourth varṇa. Our priests had no authority to punish anyone. According to the canonical texts the priest must be a man of spotless character and, if he commits a wrong, he must punish himself. If a white man happens to come into physical contact with a Negro, the latter is taken to task. But if a priest in our country comes into similar contact with an untouchable, it is he (the priest) who is enjoined to have a bath. Let us leave aside for the moment the question of untouchability. The point to note is that it was not by inspiring fear, by the threat of punishment or by suppression, that such customs were practised. A civilization like ours that is glorified all over the world could not have flourished if some sections of the people were suppressed or were victims of deception. It is only when the dharmaśāstras are advantageous to all that there will be no cause for any section of the people to revolt.

When the ancient varṇa system was in force, our civilization grew steadily without giving any cause for revolt or discontent among the people. But, that apart, look at the state of India after it broke with the old system of division of labour and took to the new path adopted by other countries on the pretext of "progress" and "equality". Everywhere you see immorality, dishonesty, corruption and prostitution. Agitations, strikes, demonstrations, *hartals,* curfew, etc, have become the order of the day. Is it not obvious from this that there is much discontent among the people? In matters of trade we have come to such a pass that we are the target of attack and ridicule of other nations for our dishonest practices. The time is past when everyone had nothing but praise for India. Even a small country like Pākistān drags us into war. Does this not show that our spiritual strength has diminished so much?

How did we lose our inner vitality? By giving up what have we become weak? What was it that nurtured our civilization and kept it growing for thousands of years? By parting with what have we descended so low as to be ashamed of calling ourselves heirs to this civilization? The fact is that, so long as we practised varṇa dharma that is unique to our country, our civilization stood like a rock arousing the admiration of all the world. But after this dharma began to decline we have been on the descent day by day.

Why should this country alone practise varṇa dharma? Because this dharma is necessary if we want to sustain a civilization that can promote the growth of philosophy, nourish our arts and culture, inspire us more and more in our inward search and help us in the realisation of the Godhead. If the varṇa system is followed at least in this country, it will be an example to the rest of the world.

If there is no varṇa dharma, it means at once the growth of social disharmony, the rise of jealousies and discontent among the people. Men will compete with one another for the jobs they like or are convenient to them. There will be competition for education on the same lines. Since all will not succeed in their efforts or in their desire or ambition being satisfied, the result will be hatred and resentment everywhere. Look at what is happening now in India. When educated unemployment is on the increase, it is suggested that admissions to colleges must be restricted, that there are too many engineers already in the country and that some engineering colleges must be closed down. Here we see that the theory of throwing open everything to everybody does not work; imposing some restrictions on people is seen to be inevitable. In the old days a man's work, whatever it was, became second nature to him and he had a sense of pride in it as an "asset", a legacy that had come to him from his forefathers, indeed a prized family "possession". He also did his job efficiently and sincerely. Money was a secondary consideration then. Since everything was done on the basis of trust and with a high degree of personal involvement — the worker was always conscious that he was doing *his work* — there were no problems. The whole society prospered.

No civilization can flourish in the absence of a system that brings fulfilment to all. Varṇa dharma brought fulfilment and satisfaction to all.

Is it possible to bring varṇa dharma back to life? Whether we fail in doing all we can in reviving the system or whether we abandon our efforts finding them to be futile, we must at least recognise that it is this system that for thousands of years brought well-being to all communities of our religion and to our country and through them to the whole world outside. Again, we must at least have the good sense not to find fault with such a system.

Note

[1] These words spoken many years before the break-up of the Soviet Union have proved prophetic.

Chapter 6

Who is Responsible for the Decay of Varṇa Dharma?

Politicians and intellectuals alike say that jāti is part of an uncivilized system. Why? Who is responsible for the disintegration of so worthy an arrangement as varṇa dharma?

These are questions that I raised earlier and I shall try to answer them. The wrong ideas that have developed about varṇa dharma must be ascribed to the Brahmins themselves. They are indeed responsible for the decay of an ages-old system that contributed not only to our Ātmic advancement but also to the well-being of the nation as well as of all mankind.

The Brahmin relinquished the duties of his birth — the study of the Vedas and performance of the rites laid down in the Vedic tradition. He left his birthplace, the village, for the town. He cropped his hair and started dressing in European style. Giving up the Vedas, he took to the mundane learning of the West. He fell to the lure of jobs offered by his white master and aped him in dress, manners and attitudes. He threw to the winds the noble dharma he had inherited from the Vedic seers through his forefathers and abandoned all for a mess of pottage. He was drawn to everything Western, science, life-style, entertainment.

The canonical texts have it that the Brahmin must have no love for money, that he must not accumulate wealth. So long as he followed his dharma, as prescribed by the śāstras, and so long as he chanted the Vedas and performed sacrifices, he brought good to the world, and all other castes respected him and treated him with affection. In fact they looked upon him as a guide and model.

Others now observed how the Brahmin had changed, how his life-style had become different with all its glitter and show and how he went about with all the pretence of having risen on the scale of civilization. The Brahmin had been an ideal for them in all that is noble, but now he strayed from the path of dharma; and following his example they too gave up their traditional vocations that had brought them happiness and contentment and left their native village to settle in towns. Like the Brahmin they became keen to learn English and secure jobs in the government.

For thousands of years the Brahmin had been engaged in Ātmic pursuit and intellectual work. In the beginning all his mental faculties were employed for the welfare of society and not in the least for his own selfish advancement. Because of this very spirit of self-sacrifice, his intelligence became sharp like a razor constantly kept honed. Now the welfare of society is no longer the goal of his efforts and his intelligence has naturally dimmed due to his selfishness and interest in things worldly. He had been blessed with a bright intellect and he had the grace of the Lord to carry out the duties of his birth. Now, after forsaking his dharma, it is natural that his intellectual keenness should become blunted.

Due to sheer momentum the bicycle keeps going some distance even after you stop pedalling. Similarly, though the Brahmin seeks knowledge of mundane subjects instead of inner light, he retains yet a little intellectual brightness as a result of the "pedalling" done by his forefathers. It is because of this that he has been able to achieve remarkable progress in Western learning also. He has acquired expert knowledge in the practices of the West, in its law and its industries. Indeed he has gained such insights into these subjects and mastered their finer points so remarkably well that he can give lessons to the white man himself in them.

A question that arises in this context is how Vedic studies which had not suffered much even during Muslim rule received a severe set-back with the advent of the European. One reason is the impact of the new sciences and the machines that came with the white man. Granted that many a truth was revealed through these sciences — and this was all to the good up to a point. But we must remember that the knowledge of a subject *per se* is one thing and how we use it in practice is another.

The introduction of steam power and electricity made many types of work easier but it also meant comforts hitherto unthought of to gratify the senses. If you keep pandering to the senses more and more new desires are engendered. This will mean the production of an increasing number of objects of pleasure. The more we try to obtain sensual pleasure the more we will cause injury to our innermost being. The new pleasures that could be had with scientific development and the introduction of machines were an irresistible lure for the Brahmin as they were to other communities. Another undesirable product of the sciences brought by the white man was rationalism which undermined people's faith in religion and persuaded some to believe that the religious truths that are based on faith and are inwardly experienced are nothing but deception. The man who did not give up his duties even during Muslim rule now abandoned them for the new-found pleasures and comforts. He dressed more smartly than the Englishman, smoked cigarettes and even learned to dance like his white master. Those who thus became proficient in the arts of the white man were rewarded with jobs.

Now occurred the biggest tragedy.

Up till now all members of society had their hereditary jobs to do and they did not have to worry about their livelihood. Now, with the example of the Brahmin before them, members of other castes also gave up their traditional occupations for the jobs made available by the British in the banks, railways, collectorates, etc. With the introduction of machinery our handicrafts fell into decay and many of our artisans had to look for other means of livelihood. In the absence of any demarcation in the matter of work and workers, there arose competition for jobs for the first time in the country. It was a disastrous development and it generated jealousy, ill-will, disputes and a host of other evils among people who had hitherto lived in harmony.

Ill feelings developed between Brahmins and non-Brahmins also. How? Brahmins formed only a small percentage of the population. But they were able to occupy top positions in the new order owing to their intelligence which, as I said before, was the result of the "pedalling" done by their forefathers. They excelled in all walks of life — in administration, in academics, in law, in medicine, engineering and so on. The white man made his own calculations about developing animosity between Brahmins and non-Brahmins and realised that by fuelling it he could strengthen his hold on the country. He fabricated the Āryan-Dravīḍian theory of races and the seeds of differences were sown among children born of the same mother. It was a design that proved effective in a climate already made unhealthy by rivary for jobs.

As if to exacerbate this ill-will, the Brahmin took one more disastrous step. On the one hand he gave up the dharma of his caste and joined hands with the British in condemning the old order by branding it a barbarous one in which one man exploited another. But, on the other hand, though he spoke the language of equality, he kept aloof from other castes thinking himself to be superior to them. If in the past he had not mixed physically with members of other castes, it did not mean that he had placed himself on a high pedestal. We must remember that there was a reason for his not coming into physical contact with other castes. There have to be differences between the jātis based on food, work and surroundings. The photographer needs a dark room to develop his films. To shoot a film, on the contrary, powerful lights are needed. Those who work in a factory canteen have to be scrupulously clean; but those who dust machinery wear soiled clothes. This does not mean that the waiter in a canteen is superior to the factory hand who dusts machines. The man who takes the utmost care to keep himself intellectually bright, without any thought of himself, observes fasts, while the soldier, who has to be strong and tough, eats meat.

Why should there be bad feelings between the two, between the Brahmin and the Kṣatriya? Does the Brahmin have to come into physical contact with the Kṣatriya to prove that he does not bear any ill-will towards him? If he interdined with the Kṣatriya he would be tempted to taste meat and such a temptation might eventually drag him into doing things that militate against his own duty. Each community has its own duties, customs and food habits. If all jātis mixed together on the pretext of equality without regard to their individual ways of life, all work would suffer and society itself would be plunged in confusion.

It was with a definite purpose in view that the village was divided into different quarters: the agrahāra[S] (the Brahmin quarter), the agriculturists' quarter and so on. Such a division was possible in rural life but not in the new urban way of living. With urbanisation and industrialisation it became necessary for people belonging to various jātis to work together on the same shift, sit together in the same canteen to eat the same kind of food. The Brahmin for whom it is obligatory to observe fasts and vows and to perform various rites was now seen to be no different from others. Office and college timings were a hindrance to the carrying out of these rites. So the Brahmin threw them to the winds. He had so far taken care to perform these rites with the good of others in mind. Like a trustee, he had protected dharma for the sake of society and made its fruits available to all.

All that belonged to the past. Now the Brahmin came forward proclaiming that all were equal and that he was one with the rest. All the same he became the cause of heart-burning among others and -- ironically enough -- in becoming one with them he also competed with them for jobs. That apart, though he talked of equality, he still thought himself to be superior to others, in spite of the fact that he was not a bit more careful than they about the performance of religious duties. Was this not enough to earn him more hatred?

The Brahmin spoiled himself and spoiled others. By abandoning his dharma he became a bad example to others. Now, after he had divested himself of his dharma, there was nothing to give him distinction, to mark him out from others. As a matter of fact, even by strictly adhering to his dharma the Brahmin is not entitled to feel superior to others. He must always remain humble in the belief that "everyone performs a function in society; I perform mine". If at all others respected him in the past and accorded him a high place in society it was in consideration of his selfless work, his life of austerity, discipline and purity. Now he had descended to such depths as to merit their most abrasive criticism.

Who is Responsible for the Decay of Varṇa Dharma?

It is my decided opinion that the Brahmin is responsible for the ruin of Hindu society. Some people have found an explanation for it. The Brahmin, if he is to be true to his dharma, has to spend all his time in learning and chanting the Vedas, in performing sacrifices, in preserving the śāstras, etc. What will he do for a living? If he goes in search of money or material he will not be able to attend to his lifetime mission — and this mission is not accomplished on a part-time basis. And if he takes up some other work for his livelihood, he is likely to become lax in the pursuit of his dharma. It would be like taking medicine without the necessary diet regimen: the benign power gained by the Brahmin from his Vedic learning will be reduced and there will be a corresponding diminution in the good accruing to mankind from his work.

This is one reason why Brahmins alone are permitted by the śāstras to beg for their living. In the past they received help from the kings — grants of lands, for instance — in consideration of the fact that the dharma practised by them benefited all people. But the śāstras also have it that the Brahmins must not accept more charity than what is needed for their bare sustenance. If they received anything in excess, they would be tempted to seek sensual pleasures and thereby an impediment would be placed to their inner advancement. There is also the danger of their becoming submissive to the donor and of their twisting the śāstras to the latter's liking. It was with a full awareness of these dangers that in the old days the Brahmins practised their dharma under the patronage of the rājās (accepting charity to the minimum and not subjecting themselves to any influence detrimental to their dharma).

The argument of those who have found an excuse for the conduct of latter-day Brahmins goes thus. "Brahmins ceased to receive gifts from rulers after the inception of British rule. How can you expect them to live without any income? Force of circumstances made them take to English education and thereafter to seek jobs with the government. It is unjust to find fault with them on that score."

There is possibly some force in this argument but it does not fully justify the change that has come over Brahmins. Before the British, the Moghuls ruled us and before them a succession of sultanates. During these periods a few *paṇḍits* must have found a place in the *darbār*. But all other Brahmins adhered to their dharma, did they not, without any support from any ruler? The phenomenon of the Brahmin quarter becoming deserted, the village being ruined, the pāṭhaśālā (the Vedic school) becoming forlorn and the lands (granted to Brahmins) turning into mere certificates is not more than a hundred years old. Did not Vedic dharma flourish until a generation ago?

The Vedic religion prospered in the past not only because of the patronage extended to the Brahmins by the Hindu rulers. People belonging to all varṇas then were anxious that it should not become weak and perish. They saw to it that the Brahmin community did not weaken and contributed generously to its upkeep and to the nurturing of the Vedic tradition. Today you see hundreds of Vedic schools deserted. There are few Brahmin boys willing to study the scriptures. Who had raised the funds for the Vedic institutions? [In Tamiḷ Nāḍu] the Nāṭṭukoṭṭai Nagarattārs, Komuṭṭi Ceṭṭis and Veḷḷāḷas[1]. The work done by Nagarattārs for our temples is indeed remarkable. Throughout Tamiḷ Nāḍu, if they built a temple they also built a Vedic school along with it in the belief that the Vedas constituted the "root" of the temple. This root, they felt, was essential to the living presence of the deity in the temple and for the pūjā conducted there. Similarly, the big landowners among the Veḷḷāḷas made lavish donations to the Vedic schools.

If the Brahmin had not been tempted by the European life-style and if he were willing to live austerely according to the dictates of the śāstras, other castes would have come forward to help him. It is not that the others deserted him. He himself ran away from his dharma, from his agrahāra[S], from his village and from the Vedic school because of his new appetite for the life of luxury made possible with the new technology of the West. He forgot his high ideals and paid scant respect to the principle that the body's requirements are not more than what it takes — in physical terms — to help the well-being of the Self. All told the argument that the Brahmin was compelled to abandon his dharma because he was denied his daily bread does not hold water. We cannot but admit that the Brahmin became greedy, that he yearned far more than what he needed for his sustenance.

Let us concede that the Brahmin left his village because he could not feed himself there and came to a city like Maḍrās. But did he find contentment here? What do we see today in actual practice? Suppose a Brahmin receives a salary of Rs 1,000 in Maḍrās today. If he gets a job in Delhi with double the salary he runs off there. When he goes to Delhi he would abandon totally the dharma he was able to practise at least to a small extent in Maḍrās. Later, if he were offered $ 4,000 a month in America he would leave his motherland for that country, lured by the prospect of earning a fortune. There, in the United States, he would become totally alienated from his religion, from his dharma, from all his traditions. The Brahmin is willing to do anything, go to any extent, for the sake of money. For instance, he would join the army if there were the promise of more income in it. If necessary he would even take to eating meat and to drinking. The usual excuse trotted out for the Brahmin deserting his dharma does not wash.

I will go one step further. Let us suppose that, following the import of Western technology, other communities also became averse to observing their respective dhārmic traditions. Let us also assume that, with their thinking and feelings influenced by the Āryan-Dravīḍian theory concocted by the English, these castes decided not to support the Brahmins any longer. Let us further assume that to feed himself (for the sake of a handful of rice) the Brahmin had to leave hearth and home and work in an office somewhere far away from his native village. Were he true to his dharma he would tell himself: "I will continue to adhere to my dharma come what may, even at the risk of death". With this resolve he could have made a determined effort to pursue Vedic learning and keep up his traditional practices.

There is no point, however, in suggesting what people belonging to the generation that has gone by should have done. I would urge the present generation to perform the duties that the past generation neglected to perform. To repeat, you must not forsake your dharma even on pain of death. Are we going to remain deathless? As it is we accumulate money and, worse, suffer humiliation and earn the jealousy of others and finally we die losing caste by not remaining true to our dharma.

Is it not better then to starve and yet be attached firmly to our dharma so long as there is breath in us? Is not such loyalty to our dharma a matter of pride? Why should we care about how others see us, whether they honour us or speak ill of us? So long as we do not compete with them for jobs they will have no cause for jealousy or resentment. Let them call us backward or stupid or think that we are not capable of keeping abreast of the times. Are we not now already their butt of ridicule? Let us be true to our dharma in the face of the mockery of others, even in the face of death. Is not such a lot preferable to suffering the slings of scorn and criticism earned by forsaking our dharma for the sake of filling our belly? People nowadays die for their motherland; they lay down their lives for their mother tongue. They do not need a big cause like the freedom of the country to be roused to action: they court death, immolate themselves, even for a cause that may seem trivial like the merger of a part of their district in another. Was there any demonstration of faith like this, such willingness to die for a cause or a belief, when the British came here with their life-style? At that time did we protect our dharma with courage, in the belief that even death was a small price to pay for it?

The Lord himself has declared in the Gītā that it is better to die abiding by one's dharma than prosper through another man's dharma ("nidhanam śreyaḥ")[2]. Brahmins who had seen no reason to change their life-style during the long Muslim period of our history changed it during British rule. Why? New sciences and machinery came with the white man. The motor car and electricity had their own impact on life here. Brahmins were drawn to comforts and conveniences not thought of before. This could be a reason for their change of life, but not a justification.

The Brahmin is not to regard his body as a means for the enjoyment of sensual pleasures but as an instrument for the observance of such rites as are necessary to protect the Vedas — and the Vedas have to be protected for the welfare of mankind. The basic dharma is that to the body of the Brahmin nothing must be added that incites his sensual appetite. It was a fundamental mistake on the part of the Brahmin to have forgotten the spirit of sacrifice that imbues his dharma and become a victim of the pleasures and comforts easily obtained from the new gadgets and instruments. There is pride in adhering to one's dharma even when one is faced with adverse circumstances. Brahmins (during British rule) committed a grave mistake by not doing so and we are suffering the consequences. See the ill-will in the country today among children of the same mother. We have created suffering for others also. At first Brahmins were denied admission to colleges and refused jobs. Now things have come to such a pass that other communities also suffer the same fate.

All was well so long as man, using his own innate resources, lived a simple life without the help of machines. With more and more factories and increasing machine power, life itself has become complicated. The situation today is such that everyone is facing difficulties in getting admission to college or in getting a job.

People ask me: "What is the remedy today? Do you expect all Brahmins to leave their new life-style and return to Vedic learning?" Whether or not I expect them to do so and whether or not such a step seems possible, I must ask them to do so (to return to their Vedic dharma). Where is the need for a guru-pīṭha or a seat on which an ācārya is installed if I am to keep my mouth shut and watch idly as the dharma that is the source of everything is being endangered? Even if it seems not possible (Brahmins returning to the dharma of their birth) it must be shown to be possible in practice: that is the purpose of the institutions called maṭhas[S]. They must harness all their energies towards the attainment of this goal.

During the years of the freedom struggle some people wondered whether the white man would quit because of satyagraha. Many things in this world regarded as not being within the realm of possibility have been shown to be possible. It is not for me to say that this (the return of all Brahmins to the Vedic dharma) is not possible; to take such a view would be contrary to our very dharma. It is up to you to make it possible in practice or not to make it possible. All I can do is to keep reminding you of the message of the dharmaśāstras.

Note & Reference

[1] Non-Brahmin jātis of Tamiḷ Nāḍu.

[2] *Śreyān svadharmo viguṇaḥ para-dharmāt svanuṣṭhitāt*
Svadharme nidhanaṁ śreyaḥ para-dharmo bhayāvahaḥ.

—Bhagavadgītā, 3.35.

Chapter 7

The Least Expected of Brahmins

Whether or not the present Hindu society changes and whether or not it can be changed, it is essential to have a class of people whose very life-breath is Vedic learning. I do not speak thus because I am worried about the existence of a caste called Brahmins. Nothing is to be gained if there is such a caste and it serves only its own selfish interests. If a caste called Brahmins must exist, it must be for the good of mankind. The purpose of the Vedas, the purpose of the sound of the Vedas, is the well-being of the world. That is the reason why I feel that, hereafter at least, there ought not to be even a single Brahmin who does not chant the Vedas. The only remedy for all the ills of the world, all its troubles, is the return of all Brahmins to the Vedic dharma.

In this context I should like to tell you the least expected of Brahmins. I am prepared to ignore the fact that they have neither the courage nor the spirit of sacrifice necessary to come back to their dharma. But they can at least make their children take to it. In the next generation there must not be a single Brahmin who is not conversant with the Vedas. You must work for this goal and make sure that your sons learn these sacred texts.

If you are averse to making your sons mere Vaidīkas[1] and are anxious that they too should lead a life of comfort like you (what you think to be a life of comfort), I am prepared to come one step further down to make the following suggestion. You would not perhaps like your children to take up Vedic learning as a lifelong vocation and would like to give them an education on modern lines so as to prepare them for office or factory work or to make them doctors, engineers, and so on. I am prepared to go with you so far. But I would ask you to perform the upanayana[2] of your son when he is eight years old. He must then be put in a Veda class held for one hour in the evening after school hours. He must be taught the Vedas in this manner for ten years.

This is the least Brahmins can do to preserve the Vedic tradition. Arrangements to impart Vedic learning to children must be made in every Brahmin household. I know that there are not enough teachers, a sad reflection on the state of our dharma. Considering this and the likely economic condition of parents I would suggest that Veda classes may be conducted for all children together of a locality or neighbourhood. Children of poor families may be taught on a cooperative basis.

Step by step in this way the boys will be able to memorise the mantra part[3] of the Vedas and also learn the prayoga[S] to conduct rites like upākarma[S]. I speak here about "prayoga", the conduct or procedure of rites, because in the absence of purohitas (priests) in the future everyone should be able to perform Vedic rites himself.

The sound of the Vedas must pervade the world for all time to come. Everyone must sincerely work towards achieving this end. It is your duty to ensure the good not only of the Brahmin community, not only of all the castes of India, but of all the countless creatures of earth. It is a duty imposed on you by Īśvara — it is a divine duty.

It is important that we perform this duty we owe to the people of the present. But it is equally important that we perform it so as to be saved from committing a crime against future generations. "As it is nobody cares for the Vedas," you are likely to tell me. "Who is going to care for them in the coming years? What purpose is served by all the efforts we take now to keep up their study?" I do not share this view. When the wheel keeps turning, that part of it which is now down has necessarily to come up. Modern civilization with its frenzied pace is bound to have its fall after attaining its peak. We have been carried away by the supposed comforts made possible by advanced technology. But one day we will realise that they do not give us any feeling of fullness and that we have indeed created only discomforts for ourselves through them.

The example of America is enough to drive home this point. People there are believed to have attained the acme of luxury and yet feel empty within. They are anxious to dispel the disquiet created by modern comforts. Americans who have some degree of awareness have been drawn towards Vedānta, yoga, devotional music and so on. Others want to forget sensual enjoyment somehow. They swallow all kinds of tranquillizers and are immersed in a deep stupor.

This fate may overtake our country also. We are always tempted by the feeling that there is some worldly pleasure yet to be savoured and we know no rest until we have done so. After draining pleasures to the dregs we will discover the impermanence of it all. That is the moment when we will turn to matters of the Self, to the quest of enduring bliss. When we realise the peace and harmony that society derived from Vedic practices, we will be keen to take to the path shown by them. If we of this generation create a break in the chain of Vedic study[4] kept up for ages, from generation to generation, we shall be committing the unforgivable crime of denying our descendants the opportunity of learning the Vedas.

"There are so many books dealing with the Vedic mantras and sacrifices, volume after volume produced by Indian and foreign scholars," the suggestion is likely to be made. "Surely future generations can read them and learn the Vedas thus."

Before I speak about this I have to answer another important question, a question that goes to the very heart of the Vedic tradition. It is this : "What do you mean by saying that the sound of the Vedas protects the world? The mantras are certain sounds expressed in the form of words. These words have their own profound meaning. Could we not learn the mantras and their meaning from books? Why should there be a class of people specially devoted to the chanting of the Vedas? If the meaning of these scriptures is to be preserved there is no cause for worry since there are books to serve such a purpose. There is no need for an exclusive caste functioning on a hereditary basis and charged with the duty of preserving these texts. But the question of the meaning of the Vedas apart, why should there be a class of people whose duty it is to chant the Vedic hymns and preserve their sound in the form it has come to us from time immemorial?" This question must be answered.

Notes & References

1 "Vaidīka" is one learned in the Vedas. That the term has come to have a pejorative sense even among Brahmins shows the sorry state of the community.

2 For a detailed account of upanayana, see Part Seventeen. Also *The Guru Tradition*.

3 The mantra part of the Vedas is constituted by the Saṁhitās. This is dealt with in a subsequent chapter.

4 We must remember that the Vedas are handed down orally from generation to generation. This precisely is the theme of the succeeding passages.

Chapter 8

Preserving the Vedas : Why it is a Lifetime Mission

[This chapter contains an illuminating exposition of the physics and metaphysics of sound.]

"If the division of labour on a hereditary basis is good for all society, what specifically is the benefit gained from the vocation of Brahmins, that is preserving the Vedas?" is a question frequently asked.

The potter makes pots for you; the washerman launders your clothes; the weaver weaves cloth for you to wear; the cowherd brings you your milk; the peasant tills the land to grow rice for you to cook and eat. Everyone does some work or other essential in the life of everybody else. The rice (or wheat) grown by the tiller sustains us all. The cloth woven by the weaver is indispensable to our modesty, it is also needed to keep us warm in the cold season. We drink the milk brought by the cowherd and also use it to make buttermilk; we cook our food in the pot made by the potter. We find thus that all jātis provide commodities useful to all society. What is the Brahmin's contribution in this context? What vocation is assigned to him by the śāstras which are the basis of varṇa dharma?

The Brahmin has to learn the Vedas by listening to his teacher chanting them: this is adhyayana. If adhyayana is chanting the Vedas, adhyāpana is teaching the same. The śāstras have charged the Brahmin with the additional duty of performing various rites including Vedic sacrifices.

The Vedas contain lofty truths. People in modern times may not be averse to the idea that these truths are worthy of being cherished. Society requires knowledge, arts, etc. The Vedas are a storehouse of knowledge. So the idea that we must have a special class of people to propagate the truths contained in the Vedas may seem reasonable enough. According to the śāstras, however, such a special class is needed to preserve the sound of these scriptures. This class is constituted by the Brahmins and they perform their function on a hereditary basis. The idea that propagating the truths of the Vedas will help mankind may be acceptable to many, but not the belief that a small group of people can contribute to the good of the world by preserving the sound of the Vedas. The community stands to lose if the peasant does not till the land and the potter, weaver, carpenter, etc, do not do their respective jobs. But would you say the same thing about the work of the Brahmin? What difference would it make to society if he ceased intoning the Vedas?

To understand the questions raised above we must first try to find out the nature of the Vedas. No purpose is served by approaching the subject entirely on an intellectual level. We must accept the words of great men who know the Vedas deep in their hearts. "How can we do that, sir?" some people might protest. "We are rationalists and we can be convinced of a truth or statement only on the basis of reason or direct knowledge."

What do we do then? How can anyone claim, as a matter of right, that all subjects ought to be brought within the ken of human reasoning? Man is but one among countless creatures. Take for instance the experiments conducted by a physicist in his laboratory. Does a cow understand them? If the scientist formulates certain laws on the basis of his experiments, does the cow say that "these laws of physics do not exist"? But how are humans ignorant of physics to know about such laws? They trust the statements made by people proficient in the subject.

To illustrate, take the example of any common appliance. Let us assume that you are told that it works on the basis of certain principles of science. Don't you accept these principles by observing how the appliance works? In the same way we must have faith in what great men say about the Vedas, great men who live strictly adhering to the śāstras. We must also place our faith in our scripture on the basis of the fruits or benefits yielded by them, the benefits we directly perceive. One such "fruit" is still there for all of us to see. It is Hinduism itself, the religion that has withstood the challenges of all these millennia. Our religion has produced more great men than any other faith. People have been rewarded with the highest inner well-being [the highest bliss] as a result of their faith in the Vedic tradition. There is no insistence on their part that everything on earth must be brought within the realm of reason or direct perception.

"The sages transcended the frontiers of human knowledge and became one with the Universal Reality. It is through them that the world received the Vedic mantras," this is one of the basic concepts of our religion. If you do not accept that human beings can obtain such Ātmic power as exemplified by these seers, any further talk on the subject would be futile. One could point to you great men whom you can see for yourself, great men who have perfected themselves and acquired powers not shared by the common people. But if you think of them to be cheats or fraudulent men, any further talk would again be useless. In our present state of limited understanding, the argument that denies the existence of anything beyond the range of human reason and comprehension itself betrays the height of irrationalism.

You have come here to listen to me instead of going to a political meeting where you can hear interesting speeches. So I believe that few of you here are full-fledged rationalists. You may not therefore refuse to listen to me if I speak to you about why the Vedas should be preserved according to the time-honoured tradition. But it is also likely that even if some of you happen to be rationalists, you may still be willing to listen to me thinking that there may be some point in what the *Svāmiyār*[T] has to say.

Some people are at a loss to understand why the sound of the Vedas is given so much importance[1]. How does sound originate or how is it caused? Where there is vibration, where there is movement or motion, there is sound. This is strictly according to rational science. Speech is constituted of vibrations of many kinds. We hear sounds with our ears. But there are sounds that are converted into electric waves and these we cannot hear. We know this from the working of the radio and the telephone. All that we hear or perceive otherwise are indeed electric waves. Science has come to the point of recognising all to be electric waves — the man who sees and listens, his brain, all are electric waves.

There are countless numbers of inert objects in the world — land masses and mountains, rivers and oceans, and so on. Also there are sentient creatures of many kinds. All of them must have been created out of something. During creation this something must have vibrated in many different ways and given rise to all that we see today. If all movements are sound, there must have existed numerous different kinds of sound before creation. In this creation one is sustained by another. In the process of mutual sustenance, different movements and sounds must be produced. It is not necessary that vibrations should form a part only of gross activities. Science has discovered that even our thinking process is a kind of electric current or energy. Each thought process is a form of electric current or energy and it must produce a vibration and a sound. This kind of sound being very subtle we do not hear it with our ears. Just as there are bacteria which we do not see with our naked eye, there are many sounds that our ears do not pick up. According to science any physical or mental movement must produce a sound.

The idea that each movement produces its own sound may be put differently thus: to create a particular sound a particular movement must be produced. Take the case of a vidvān[2] singing. If you want to sing like him or create *birqas*[3] like him, you will have to produce the same vibrations that he creates in his throat.

Sound and vibration (or motion) go together. The vibrations produce either a gross object or a mental state. We come to the conclusion that creation is a product of sound. This ancient concept is substantiated by science itself.

Creation, the many things connected with it, thoughts and movements and the sounds associated with them fill space. What happens to the sound produced by the clapping of our hands? It remains in space. Good as well as bad actions produce their own sounds as well as movements associated with them. Conversely, the creation of these types of movements will result in good as well as evil. To produce good thoughts in people, good movements must be created: the sounds corresponding to them must be produced. If we can generate such sounds, good thoughts will permeate the minds of men. What more is needed for the good of mankind than such good thoughts? The mantras of the Vedas are sounds that have the power to inspire good thoughts in people.

One more thing. We need food for our sustenance. And to grow food there must be rain. The formation of clouds and their precipitation are dependent on certain vibrations. Rainfall depends on the production of particular sounds which, in turn, create particular vibrations. The same applies to all our needs in life. It is true that unnecessary and evil objects are also produced by sound. But the one and only goal of the sound of the Vedas is the creation of well-being throughout the world.

But are sounds and vibrations spontaneously produced? No. If vibrations arise on their own they will be erratic and confusing and not related to one another. But what do we see in the cosmos? There is a certain orderliness about it and one thing in it is linked to another. What do we infer from this? That a Great Intelligence has formulated this scheme that we see, that it has created it from its own vibrations.

The Vedas are sounds emanating from the vibrations of this Great Intelligence, the Great Gnosis. That is why we believe that the mantras of the Vedas originate from the Paramātman himself. We must take special care of such sounds to ensure the good of the world. Yes, the Vedic mantras are sequences of sounds that are meant for the good of the world.

Doubts are expressed on this point. People argue : "We hear the mantras of the Vedas distinctly. But we do not hear the sounds in space, the sounds of creation. How can the two be the same?"

What exists in the cosmos is present in the individual being. The belief that the "microcosm" inheres the "'macrocosm" is not in keeping with our commonsense view of things. But all people, including atheists, will agree that there are "instruments" in our body in the form of the senses that can grasp what exists in the macrocosm. The sun in the macrocosm is felt by our body as heat. We perceive the flower in our garden through its scent. We savour the sweet taste of sugarcane with our tongue. With our eyes we learn that one object is red, that another is yellow.

Unless the macrocosm and the microcosm are constituted of the same substance[4] the one will not be able to be aware of the other. Indeed the very conduct of life will not be possible otherwise. If we go one step further, the truth will dawn on us that it is not merely that the macrocosm and the microcosm are constituted of the same substance but that it is the same substance that becomes the macrocosm and the microcosm. The yogins know this truth directly from their experience.

Whatever is present in space is also present in the individual being. These elements exist in the human body in a form that is accessible to the senses. The sounds a person makes in his throat have their source in space in a form not audible to us. The radio transforms electrical waves into sound waves. If a man can grasp the sounds in space and make them audible, he will be able to create with them what is needed for the good of the world. Yoga is the science that accomplishes such a task. Through yogic practice (perfection) one can become aware of what is in the macrocosm and draw it into the microcosm. I shall not be able to give you proof of this in a form acceptable to human reason. Yoga transcends our limited reason and understanding. The purpose of the Vedas is to speak about matters that are beyond the comprehension of the human mind.

You must have faith in the words of great men or else, to know the truth of such matters, you must practise yoga strictly observing its rules. It may not be practicable for all those who ask questions or harbour doubts about the Vedas to practise yoga in this manner. Even if you are prepared to accept the words of a true yogin, how are you, in the first place, to be convinced that he is indeed a true yogin and not a fraud? Altogether it means that you must have faith in someone, in something. Later such faith will be strengthened from your own observations, inference and experience. There is no point in speaking to people who have either no faith or refuse to develop it through their own experience.

There is a state in which the macrocosm and the microcosm are perceived as one. Great men there are who have reached such a state and are capable of transforming what is subtle in the one into what is gross in the other. I am speaking here to those who believe in such a possibility.

When we look at this universe and the complex manner in which it functions, we realise that there must be a Great Wisdom that has created it and sustains it. It is from this Great Wisdom, that is the Paramātman, that all that we see are born and it is from It that all the sounds that we hear have emanated. First came the universe of sound and then the universe that we observe. Most of the former still exists in space. All that exists in the outer universe is present in the human body also. The space that exists outside us exists also in our heart.

The yogins have experience of this hṛdayākāśa , this heart-sky or this heart-space, when they are in samādhi (absorbed in the Infinite)[5]. In this state of theirs all differences between the outward and the inward vanish and the two become one. The yogins can now grasp the sounds of space and bestow the same on mankind. These successions of sounds that bring benefits to the world are indeed the mantras of the Vedas.

These mantras are not the creation of anyone. Though each of them is in the name of a ṛṣi or seer, in reality it is not his creation. When we say that a certain mantra has a certain sage associated with it, all that we mean is that it was he who first "saw" it existing without a beginning in space, and revealed it to the world. The very word "ṛṣi" means "mantra-draṣṭā" (one who saw — discovered — the mantra), not "mantra-kartā" (i.e. not one who created the mantra). Our life is dependent on how our breathing functions. In the same way the cosmos functions in accordance with the vibrations of the Vedic sounds— so the Vedic mantras are the very breath of the Supreme Being. We must thus conclude that, without the Vedas, there is no Brahman: To put it differently, the Vedas are self-existent like the Paramātman.

The mantras of the Vedas are remarkable in that they bring blessings to the world in the form of sound — even if their meaning is not understood. Of course, they are pregnant with meaning and represent the lofty principle that it is the One Truth that is manifested as all that we perceive. They also confer blessings on us by taking the form of deities appropriate to the different sounds (of the mantras).

Sound does not bring any benefits, any fruits, by itself. Īśvara alone is the bestower of benefits. However, instead of making the fruits available to us directly, he appoints deities to distribute them in the same manner as the king or president of a country appoints officials to carry out his dictates. The mantras represent various deities in the form of sound. If we attain perfection (siddhi) by constant chanting and meditation of a mantra, it should be possible for us to see the deity invoked in his physical form. The deities also arise if we make offerings into the sacrificial fire reciting specific mantras. If a sacrifice is conducted in this manner, the deities give us their special blessings. We do not pay taxes directly to the king or president. In the same way, we pay taxes in the form of sacrifices and Vedic chanting to the aides of the Paramātman for the sake of the welfare of the world. The sounds of the mantras constitute their form.

The Vedas have won the admiration of Western scholars for their poetic beauty. They bring us face to face with many deities -- they bring us also their grace. Above all, through the Upaniṣads they teach us the great truths relating to the Self. The Vedas are thus known for the profundity of the truths contained in them, but their sound is no less important. Indeed their sound has its own significance and power. All mantras, it must be noted, have power, not only Vedic mantras.

The sound of some mantras have greater value than their meaning. Their syllables chanted in a particular manner create a special energy, but their meaning has no special significance. Take the mantra recited to cure a man stung by a scorpion. The words, the syllables, constituting the mantra have no special meaning. Indeed, they say, the meaning is not to be told. But by chanting the mantra, vibrations are caused in space and one stung by a scorpion will be cured: the potency of the syllables of the mantra is such. The efficacy of sounds varies with the different mantras. Evil is caused by reciting certain mantras or formulae: this is called "abhicāra" [understood as black magic in the West]. In all this the clarity with which the syllables are enunciated is important. There was the practice of knocking off the teeth of those who practised *billi sūnyam* (a form of black magic). The black magician, if toothless, will not be able to articulate the mantras properly and so his spells will not have the intended effect. If the syllables of the spells are not clearly and properly enunciated, they will not give us the desired benefit. It we appreciate the fact that sounds have such power, the question of the language of the mantras loses its importance. It would be meaningless then to demand that the mantras must be expressed in some other language [that we understand]. It would be equally meaningless to wonder whether the mantras of the śrāddha[S] ceremony should be rendered into English, Tamiḷ or some other language so that our departed parents would understand them better.

The Vedic mantras do good to all creatures in this world and the hereafter: we must have implicit faith in this belief. It is not proper to ask whether what we ourselves cannot hear with our ears will be heard by the seers. There is such a thing as the divine power of seeing and hearing. Our sight is dependent on the lens in our eyes. Were this lens different what we observe would also be different. Through the intense practice of yoga we can obtain the divine power of seeing and hearing.

We must not inquire into the Vedas with our limited powers of perception and with our limited capacity to reason and comprehend. The Vedas speak to us about what is beyond the reach of our eyes and ears and reasoning — that is their very purpose. There are things that we comprehend through direct perception. We do not need the help of the Vedas to know about them. What cannot be proved by reasoning and what is beyond the reach of our intellect — these the seers have gifted us in the form of the Vedas with their divine perception. How do we learn about the affairs of other countries? We are not eyewitnesses to them but we depend on newspaper reports of these affairs. There is another kind of newspaper which tells us about matters that cannot be known through any worldly means and this newspaper is constituted of the Vedic mantras that are the gift of the seers.

We have to accept the Vedas in faith. Develop a little faith in them and experience for yourself the fruits yielded by them. In due course you will be convinced about the truths told about them.

Even today we see how mantras are efficacious though what we see is more often their power to do evil rather than good. The very word "māntrikam" inspires dread in us. If mantras have the power to do evil, they must also have the power to do good. We do hear reports of how mantras are beneficent, for instance how the mantras invoking the god Varuṇa produce rains.

It may be that sometimes the "Varuṇa japa"[6] does not succeed in bringing rains. But this is no reason why all mantras should be rejected outright as of no value. Sick people die even after the regular administration of medicine. For this reason do we condemn medical science as worthless? We have an explanation for the patient's failure to recover: his illness had reached such an advanced stage that no medicine could be of any avail. Similarly, no mantra is of any help when it has to contend against the working of powerful karma. There is also another reason. If you are not strict about your diet, the medicine taken may not work. Similarly, if we are lax in the observance of certain rules, the mantras will not produce the desired result.

Yoga is a science. In a scientific laboratory, certain rules have to be observed in the conduct of experiments. If the electrician refuses to wear gloves or to stand on a wooden stool during his work, what will happen? So too, anyone practising yoga has to follow the rules governing it. To return to Varuṇa japa. If the japa is not always successful, it is because — as I have found out through inquiries— of the failure of those performing the rite to observe the rule of "alavaṇa" [taking food without salt].

In Tiruvānaikkā (near Tirucirāpaḷḷi) people have seen with their own eyes a tree bare of foliage putting forth green shoots under the spell of mantras. The sthalavṛkṣa here [the tree sacred to a place or temple] is the white jambu[S]. That is why the place (Tiruvānaikkā) is also called Jambukeśvaram. Once the tree was dead except for one branch or so. Then the Ceṭṭiārs—the trustees of the temple—had an Ekādaśa-Rudrābhiṣeka[7] conducted for it. And, behold, by the power of the mantras the tree put forth fresh leaves.

Each sound has a specific impact on the outward world. Experiments were once conducted by a lakeside by producing a certain pattern of svaras on an instrument. It was observed that as a result of the vibrations so created the light on the water shone as particles. Later these particles took a specific shape. From such scientific proof it is possible to believe that we can perceive the form of a deity through chanting the appropriate Veda mantraṣ. It is not that sound is transformed into light alone in the outward world. It is pervasive in many ways and produces various kinds of impacts. The sound of the Vedic mantras pervading the atmosphere is extremely beneficial. There are ways in which sound is to be produced to make it advantageous to us. Some notes are to be raised, some lowered and some to be uttered in an even manner. The Vedas have to be chanted in this way. The three different ways of chanting are "udātta", "anudātta" and "svarita"[S]. The sound and svara together will turn the powers of the cosmos favourable to us.

The question that now occurs is why there should be a separate caste committed to Vedic learning and Vedic practices even if it is conceded that Vedic mantras have the power to do good.

In answering this question we must first remember that the Vedas are not to be read from the written text. They have to be memorised by constant listening and repeated chanting. The learner then becomes a teacher himself and in this manner the process goes on from generation to generation. Maintaining such a tradition of learning and teaching is a whole-time occupation. Neither the teacher nor the taught may take up any other work.

We must also remember that the Brahmin is expected to master subjects other than the Vedas also, like the arts and crafts and the various sciences (śāstras). He has in fact to learn the vocations of other jātis (but he must not take up any for his own livelihood). It is the responsibility of the Brahmin to promote knowledge and culture. He is expected to learn the hereditary skills of all jātis, including the art of warfare, and pass on these skills to the respective jātis to help them earn their livelihood. The Brahmin's calling is adhyayana and adhyāpana (learning and teaching the Vedas). According to the śāstras he must live in a modest dwelling, observe strict rules and vows so as to gain mastery of the mantras. He must eat only as much as is needed to keep body and soul together. All temptations to make money and enjoy sensual pleasures he must sternly resist. All his actions must be inspired by the spirit of sacrifice and he must pass his days sustaining the Vedic tradition and practices for the good of mankind.

It is the duty of other jātis to see that the Brahmin does not die of starvation. They must provide him with the bare necessities of life and such materials as are needed for the performance of sacrifices. Wages are paid to those who do other jobs or a price is paid for what they produce. The Brahmin works for the whole community and serves it by chanting mantras, by performing sacrifices and by leading a life according to the dictates of religion. That is why he must be provided with his upkeep. The canonical texts do not say that we must build him a palace or that he must be given gifts of gold. The Brahmin must be provided with the wherewithal for the proper performance of sacrifices. In his personal life he must eschew all show and luxury. It is by taming his senses—by burning away all desire—that he gains mastery over the mantras.

I have said more than once that the Vedas are to be learned by constant listening, that they are not to be learned from the written text. Let me tell you why. The sound of the Vedas must pervade the world. This is of paramount importance, not that the text itself should be maintained in print. Indeed the Vedas must not be kept in book form. If the printed text is available all the time, we are likely to neglect the habit of memorising the hymns and chanting them. There is not the slightest doubt about this. "After all it is in the book. When the need arises we can always refer to it. Why should we waste our time in memorising the mantras?" Thus an attitude of indifference will develop among those charged with the duty of maintaining the Vedic tradition.

Nowadays we have what is called the *"pañcāngāran"* (*pañcāngakkāran*), that is the "almanac-man". We understand his job to be that of officiating at the rites performed by members of the fourth varṇa. But from the term "almanac-man" we know that this is not his main duty. The *pañcāngakkāran* or almanac-man is truly one who determines the five "angas" or components of the almanac. Each day has five angas: tithi, vāra, nakṣatra, yoga and karaṇa[8]. To find out whether or not a particular day is auspicious or whether a certain work or function may be performed on a particular day, all these five factors have to be taken into account. Today astronomers in Greenwich observe the sun, the moon and the stars to fix the timings of sunrise and sunset. Three or four generations ago, every village had an almanac-man who was an expert in such matters. He could predict eclipses, their exact timings, with the precision of present-day astronomers. He inscribed the five angas relating to the day on a palm-leaf and took it round from house to house to help people in their worldly and religious duties. In the past he had also another name, "*Kuṭṭai Cuvaḍī*" (meaning "Shortened Palm-leaf").

How have the present-day almanac-men forgotten their great science? With the advent of the printing press the almanac could be printed for a whole year and made available to all people. There was no longer any need for the old type of almanac-man — he is now one only in name. It is sad that the science relating to pañcānga, an important part of astronomy, is now on the verge of extinction.

The Vedas would have suffered a similar fate had we stuck to a system of learning them from written or printed texts. Their sound would not have then filled the world and created all-round well-being.

Our forefathers realised that to put anything in writing was not the best way of preserving it since it bred indifference to the subject so preserved. One who recited the Vedas from the written text ("likhita-pāṭhaka") was looked down upon as an "adhama" (one belonging to the lowest order among those chanting the Vedas). In Tamiḷ the Vedas are known as the "unwritten old text" *(ezhutākiḷavi).* In Sanskrit the Vedas are also called "Śruti", which means "that which is heard", that is to say not to be learned from any written text. Since listening to the Vedas as they were chanted and then memorising them was the practice, preserving the Vedic tradition came to be a full-time vocation. The teacher taught pāda by pāda (foot by foot) and the student repeated each pāda twice[9]. In this way the sound of the Vedas filled the whole place. It was thus that the study of our scripture, with all its recensions which are like the expanse of a great ocean, was maintained in the oral tradition until the turn of the century. This treasure, this timeless crop that sustains our inner being, has come to us through the ages as ordained by the Lord. There can be no greater sin than that of neglecting this treasure and allowing it to perish.

If the Vedic tradition becomes extinct there is no need for a separate caste called Brahmins. Nowadays the cry is often heard, "Brahmin, get out". But do we hear cries like, "Potter, get out" or "Washerman, go away"? If the potter and the washerman leave the village they will be brought back by force and retained. Why so? Because the community needs their services.

So long as the Brahmin possessed sattva-guṇa[S] (the quality of goodness and purity) and so long as he kept the Vedic tradition going and lived a simple life, others recognised his value for society. They regarded him with affection and respect and placed their trust in him. They realised that if society was not afflicted by famine and disease (as is the case today), it was because the sound of the Vedas pervaded everywhere and the performance of Vedic rites created a healthy atmosphere around and brought its own blessings.

This was not the only way in which the Brahmin served society. His personal example was itself a source of inspiration to people. They saw how he curbed his sensual appetites, how he lived a life of peace, how he was compassionate to all creatures, how he meditated on the Lord, how he performed a variety of rites strictly adhering to śāstric rules and without any expectation of rewards. They saw a whole caste living a life of selflessness and sacrifice. Naturally, they too were drawn to the qualities exemplified by its members. They emulated their example, observed fasts and vows to the extent permitted by the nature of their occupations. It is preposterous to accuse the Brahmin of having kept other jātis suppressed. There is a special way of life that the scriptures have prescribed for him and in remaining true to it he becomes a personal example for others desirous of raising themselves.

It is equally preposterous to suggest that others were kept down because they were denied the right to learn the Vedas. I have already spoken to you that preserving the Vedic tradition is a hereditary and lifelong vocation. Any calling must be pursued on a hereditary basis. Otherwise, there is the risk of society being torn asunder by jealousies and rivalries. The maintenance of the Vedic tradition is a calling by itself. There will be confusion and chaos in the system of division of labour if people whose vocations are different are allowed to pursue one common tradition. Also, as a consequence, will not the social structure be disturbed? Every vocation has as high a place on the social scale as any other. Why should anyone nurse the idea that the pursuit of the Vedic dharma belongs to a plane higher than all other types of work?

Some castes are not permitted to learn the Vedas but there is no bar on their learning the truths contained in them. This is all that is needed for their Ātmic advancement. We need only one class of people charged with the mission of keeping the sound of the Vedas alive in the world. The ideas contained in them for spiritual uplift are open to all. The songs of non-Brahmin saints like Appar[T] and Nammāzhvār[T] are replete with Vedic and Vedāntic thoughts.

Were it true that Brahmins had monopolised Ātmic knowledge and devotion and kept others downtrodden, how would you explain the rise among the non-Brahmin jātis of so many great saints, not only the examples just mentioned above, Appar and Nammāzhvār, but a number of other Nāyanmārs[T] and Āzhvārs[T]? The Nāyanmārs included men belonging even to jātis regarded as "low". Where do you find men of inner enlightenment like Tāyumānavar[T] and Paṭṭiṇattār? Apart from the fact that there were among non-Brahmins men worthy of being lauded by Brahmins for their enlightenment and devotion, there were individuals from the fourth varṇa who established empires and gave new life and vigour to the Vedic dharma. That Brahmins exploited other castes is a recently invented myth.

I do not claim that Brahmins are free from faults or are not guilty of lapses. Nobody is free from faults. But on the whole the Brahmin has done good to society and has been a guide to all its members. That is why he was enabled to live with dignity all these centuries.

When other communities now see that the Brahmin no longer serves society in any manner, they raise the cry, "Brahmin, get out". If they do not serve society and if all they do is to join others in the scramble for money, where is the need for a separate caste called Brahmins? It occurs to me that, if the caste called Brahmins serves no purpose to society, I shall be the first to seek its destruction. Nothing has any right to exist if it has no utility value. There is no need for a caste called Brahmins if the world does not stand to benefit from it.

Now there are "toll-gates" located in many places but often without any "gate". In the past a toll used to be collected from people crossing the boundary marked by these "gates". Later such a system was discontinued and no purpose was served by the gate. Nothing exists without a purpose. Now, if the Brahmin without Vedic learning has become as purposeless as the toll-gate without any toll actually charged, with what reason or justice can we say that he must not be thrown out?

The Brahmin today deserves to be reproved, if he expects to be treated with any special respect. Criticism, however, should be just. The Brahmin must be faulted for abandoning his dharma, but the dharma itself, the Vedic dharma, is another matter. It is not proper to find fault with this dharma itself and it is the duty of others to help the Brahmin practise it. The Vedic dharma must be sustained so as to ensure the well-being of the world. Other jātis must support the principle that there must be a caste whose hereditary calling it is to maintain the Vedic tradition. If they themselves have lost faith in the Vedic dharma, they cannot find fault with the Brahmin for having forsaken it. If they believe that the Vedic dharma is not wanted, then it would mean (according to their own logic) that the Brahmin is not committing any offence by giving up his hereditary vocation. It also follows that for the sake of his livelihood he will have to take up some other job, competing with others for the same. So to hold that there is no need for the Vedic dharma and that, at the same time, the Brahmin should not do any work other than the pursuit of that dharma does not stand to reason. On the one hand, it is proclaimed that the Vedic dharma is all wrong and must cease to exist but, on the other, the man whose duty it is to practise that dharma is hated for trying to do some other work. Is this just? It is part of humanity to see that not even a dog or a jackal goes hungry and it is a dharma common to all religions. Even those who maintain that we do not need any religion speak for compassion and the spirit of sacrifice in all our actions. So it is not just to insist that a man must not pursue his hereditary vocation and that he must not, at the same time, do any other work but die of starvation.

Others can help greatly by making the Brahmin true to himself as the upholder of the Vedic dharma. I have heard it said that in the old days some Brahmins would go to the untouchable quarter and tell people there: "You and we, let us become one." Whereupon the untouchables would reply: "No, no. You keep doing your work. That is for the good of both of us. Don't come here again." They would prevent the Brahmins from approaching them again by breaking their pots in front of them, the pots which were their only asset. Though people then were divided in the matter of work and did not mix together, they had affection for one another and believed that each did his work for the common good.

Even today the common people are not non-believers, nor have they lost faith in the Vedas. I feel that they will continue to have respect for the Vedic dharma and that the propaganda of hate [against Brahmins and the Vedas] is all to be attributed to political reasons. People, I repeat, do have faith in the Vedas, in Vedic rites and customs and if the Brahmin becomes a little better [that is by being true to his vocation] all hatred will vanish. As I said before, instead of expecting respect from others, he must remain true to his dharma even at the risk of his life. It is my belief that society will not allow him to suffer such an extreme fate. But my stand is that, even if it does, he must not forsake his dharma. Whatever the attitude of others, whether they help him or whether they run him down, the Brahmin must uphold the Vedic tradition for the well-being of all.

What I have spoken for the Brahmin community applies in principle to others also. The duties about which I have to speak to them (non-Brahmins) are many. They too are eager to know about them and I am confident that, if things are properly explained, they will pursue faithfully their respective dharmas. I must, however, be qualified to give them advice. It is generally believed that I have a special relationship with the Brahmin community. In the Maṭha a number of Vedic rites are performed. So, rightly or wrongly, the impression has gained ground that I have much to do with the caste whose duty it is to uphold the Vedic dharma. That being the case, a question will arise in the minds of people belonging to other communities if I speak to them on matters of dharma, even if it is assumed that they will listen to me with affection and respect. The question is this: "Brahmins are so much dependent on his[10] support. Yet we don't see them acting on his advice and correcting themselves. So why should he come to speak to us of our duties?"

As a matter of fact, both are same to me, Brahmins and non-Brahmins. I am indeed more dissatisfied with Brahmins than with the others because they have abandoned the Vedic dharma, the dharma that confers the highest inner well-being on all. Even so, since it is believed that Brahmins are specially attached to me, I keep admonishing them to go back to the Vedic dharma with all their heart, with all their strength. If Brahmins observe in practice a fraction of what is expected of them, then alone shall I be qualified to remind other communities of their duties. Brahmins must try as best they can to keep up the Vedic tradition. That is how they will help me to speak to other communities of their duties.

All mankind, all creatures of earth, must live in happiness. Everybody must practise his allotted dharma for the good of all with the realisation that there is no question of any work being "higher" than any other or "lower". Preserving the sound of the Vedas must remain the duty of one class so as to ensure plenty in this world as well as to create universal Ātmic uplift. To revert to the question I put to you first. Leaving aside the vocation of the Vedic dharma, let us assume that the hereditary system is beneficial in respect of all types of work. But why should the preservation of the Vedic dharma be the lifelong vocation of one class? It is now established, as I conclude, that however it may be with the other vocations, whether or not they exist, whether or not there is a mix-up in them, the pursuit of the Vedic dharma must remain a separate calling.

(See also the chapter entitled, "Can a New Brahmin Caste be Created?" in Part Nineteen; and Part Twenty, "Varṇa Dharma and Universal Well-being").

Notes & References

1 See Chapter 7, Part Five.

2 A Carṇāṭic musician is usually referred to as a vidvān (f. "viduṣī").

3 *Birqa* is a fast and intricate passage in Carṇāṭic music.

4 The Paramaguru's holistic philosophy is reminiscent of Mach's Principle (Ernst Mach was a German physicist— it is after him that units of supersonic sound are named). Commenting on the principle Arthur Köstler says in his *The Roots of Coincidence*: "Firstly there is the unity in things whereby each thing is at one with itself, consists of itself, and coheres with itself. Secondly, there is the unity whereby one creature is united with the others, and all parts of the world constitute one world." Mach's Principle is stated in simple terms thus: "The whole is constituted of the parts and the part is constituted of the whole."

5 The transcendent space becomes the immanent space in the heart.

6 A rite in which Varuṇa, the god of the seas and water, is propitiated during times of drought.

7 Ekādaśa Rudrābhiṣeka is a ceremony in which the Śivaliṅga is bathed to the chanting of the Śrī Rudra hymn (of the Taittirīya Saṁhitā) eleven times.

8 Tithi is the day according to the lunar fortnight. Vāra is the day of the week and nakṣatra the astersim conjoining a given day. According to Mahāmahopādhyāya P.V. Kāṇe "Yoga is calculated from the sum of the longitudes of the sun and the moon (or it is the time during which the sun and the moon together accomplish 13 degrees and 20 minutes in space".) Half a tithi is a karaṇa. There are two kinds of karaṇas : cāra (or moving) and sthira (immovable).

9 This is dealt with again in Part Four.

10 That is the Paramaguru's.

Chapter 9

Is Cutting off the Head a Cure for Headache?

Today everybody—from the top leader down to the man in the street—is asking: Why should there be caste? With a little thinking, you will realise that the division of society into various jātis is for the good of all. It serves in two ways. While, on the one hand, it contributes to the progress of the entire community, on the other, it helps each individual to become pure of mind and obtain ultimate liberation.

You do not have to accept this view because it comes from me or because it is that of the śāstras. You may think that people like me are reactionaries opposed to progress. But consider the opinion of a man whose goal, all will agree, was the advancement of this nation. This man was determined to do away with all differences among the people, eradicate superstition and elevate the "backward classes" to the level of the rest of society. This man was Gāndhījī who extolled the varṇāśrama system and whole-heartedly accepted it. I mention this because I thought, if not anything else, at least the views of Gāndhījī would persuade you to accept the fact that the varṇa system has good features.

Gāndhījī has written an essay entitled, "My Varṇaśrama Dharma"[1]. In it he says[2]: "Varṇaśrama is a system that has happened on its own. It is natural and inherent in a man's birth. It is a natural law that Hinduism has systematised into a science. This system makes a fourfold division of labour and lays down the duties of each section but not its rights. For any individual to think himself to be superior to others and look down upon another as inferior to himself is against the very spirit of Hindu culture. In the varṇāśrama system each individual learns to discipline himself and the energies of society are prevented from being frittered away. I keep fighting against untouchability because I consider it an evil but I support varṇāśrama as healthy for society and believe that it is not the product of a narrow mind. This arrangement gives the labourer the same status as it does a great thinker." Gāndhījī supported varṇāśrama with greater ardour than sanātanists[S].

It would be pointed out that Gāndhījī's actions were such as to suggest that he was opposed to differences in society based on rites and customs. He supported even intercaste marriage. How is all this to be reconciled with the fact that he upheld varṇāśrama? Gāndhījī thought that, though varṇa dharma was a worthy system, it had broken down and that it was not possible to revive it. What was the use of keeping the remains after the essence had been extracted from a thing, he asked. So he thought that retaining the outward differences in society was not justified after the principles on which these differences were founded were no longer in force.

I do not think like him. Varṇāśrama is the backbone of our religion. If it is to be abandoned on the pretext that it is beyond repair, we do not require either a maṭha or a man to preside over it. For any individual to run an institution labelling himself as its head [that is as the head of any maṭha] after the root of all dharma is gone, is tantamount to exploiting society. If the old system of caste is in reality extinct, there is no need for a maṭha and it should be disbanded. But I nurse the belief that such a thing has not happened yet. Nor do I think that caste will before long inevitably cease to exist. I am also confident that, if we are awake to the problem at least now and mobilise all our strength and resources to take the necessary steps, we shall be able to impart the varṇa system new life and vigour.

No matter how the varṇa system has become muddled with reference to other vocations, Vedic learning which is the life-breath of all occupations still survives in the pāṭhaśālās here and there. In these schools the scriptures are taught strictly in the traditional way. There is enthusiastic support for the efforts taken to spread Vedic learning. Students join the pāṭhaśālās in fairly large numbers. There is a small group committed to the cause of the Vedic tradition and to its continuance. My duty is the creation of more and more such groups and to work for their growth. If Vedic learning flourishes, a way will open up to counteract the evil consequences of the muddle created in the other varṇas. And if Brahmins become an example and a guide—if not all of them, at least a few—by remaining true to their old way of life, others will return to their hereditary duties.

Since Gāndhījī believed that varṇāśrama dharma could neither be mended nor revived in its true form, he wanted it to be totally scrapped. I think otherwise. Though [the flame of] varṇa dharma has become dim it is not totally extinguished and I feel that there are some sparks still left which could be fanned into a bright flame again. We must learn the lesson from our history during the past fifty years that our society will have to pay dearly if it gives up varṇa dharma. You will learn this lesson from the fate suffered by the great civilizations that flourished in the rest of the world where such a system did not obtain.

The disintegration of the old system of hereditary vocations must be attributed to the introduction of machinery and the establishment of big factories. There is not much scope for machines in a simple life. The old varṇa system could be saved if people live a simple life and are occupied with the old handicrafts and cottage industries. Gāndhījī spoke untiringly of his ideal that all work must be done by human power. He was against monstrous machines and urged people to live a simple life, eschewing all luxury. In this respect his views are in conformity with the ideals of varṇa dharma.

Today the various schemes introduced by the government together with the changed outlook of the people militate against the ideal of a simple life and the system of handicrafts. But, ironically enough, politicians and others keep singing the praises of Gāndhījī unceasingly without translating his ideas into action. Gāndhījī was a reformer who ardently wished the good of society and worked in the cause of egalitarianism. He was not a hard-nosed sanātanist who tenaciously clung to the canonical texts merely because they were old. People had faith in one like him. I thought that the views of such a man on varṇāśrama should make a deep impression on you.

Why are people generally opposed to caste? Because they believe that caste is responsible for the differences and disparities in society and the quarrels arising from them. I have told you so often that in reality no jāti is inferior to another or superior to it. However, critics of varṇa dharma argue that, whether or not in reality it has caused differences in society, an impression has gained ground that it has. As you can see for yourself, they add, "There are quarrels arising out of them. We want to do away with the system of jātis because we don't want these fights to go on indefinitely and divide society."

To speak thus, however, is to suggest that we must cut off the head to cure a headache. If the old dharma suffers from a headache in the form of quarrels in society, it is our duty to restore it to health. How? We must speak to the people concerned about the true principles of varṇa dharma in a friendly and peaceful manner and yet persistently and remove the misunderstandings from their minds — the misunderstandings that cause quarrels. This is the mode of treatment to keep the old system of varṇa healthy. It is preposterous to suggest that, because of the disputes, the dharma that is the root and source of our society should itself be done away with.

If there is something that is the cause of a dispute, it does not stand to reason to destroy this something itself. We cannot conduct the affairs of the world in this manner. There will naturally be people for and against any question. Such differences are inevitable. Today there are two issues which have been the cause of a great deal of conflict. These are language and ideology. It would be absurd to argue that we want neither any language nor any ideology because they are the cause of conflict.

Nowhere else in the world today do we witness the sort of clashes that we face in our own country on the question of language. The caste quarrels are not of the same scale as these — the frenzy aroused by language is so intense. The Tamiḷ and the Telugu keep quarrelling with one another, so too the Bengāḷi and the Bihāri, the Kannaḍiga and the Mahārāsṭrian. Then there is the English vs Hindī controversy. People indeed come to blows on the language issue. How would you solve this problem? Would you suggest universal dumbness as a solution, that is abolition of all speech, all tongues?

Disputes concerning political ideology, about the type of government wanted, are far too numerous. There is the big divide between communism and capitalism: it has been the cause of trouble throughout the world. Without any world war actually breaking out, thousands of people have perished in the clash of ideologies. Apart from the struggle between capitalism and communism you see other kinds of unrest in various parts of the world: monarchy giving way to republicanism; the rise of dictatorial governments. Large numbers of people become victims in these ideological wars. Although everybody claims that he is for democracy, at heart there are so many differences between one man and another on the question of political ideology and hence all the quarrels.

Would it be right to argue that all ideologies must be scrapped merely because they lead to quarrels? Any government is constituted on some ideological basis or other, is it not? No ideology would mean no government— is it not so? Are we then to abolish the institution of governments and be like animals [in the absence of an authority to enforce law and order]? If languages are not wanted because they are the cause of trouble and if governments are not wanted because they lead to ideological wars, it follows logically that religions and jātis also are not wanted since they too create disputes. Going a step further we may ask : Is it not because we human beings exist that we keep quarrelling among ourselves? So should we .... [the Paramaguru just smiles without completing the sentence].

Though there is a vociferous campaign carried on against caste, jāti crops up as a crucial factor in elections. It is on the basis of caste that all parties conduct their electioneering. The cry, "We don't want any jāti", seems really to mean, "we don't want a particular jāti".

Maintaining the system of jātis on a nominal basis is not justified if each of the jātis does not have a special social responsibility to discharge. To assign a vocation to each group or jāti on a hereditary basis is for the good of all society. It is particularly important that this country has a section of people whose lifetime work is to keep chanting the Vedas, the Vedas which bring happiness to all living creatures through the loftiness of their sound and the profundity of the truths contained in them. Performance of the rites that form part of the Vedic tradition is as much a duty of this section as that of learning the mantras.

Modernists think that it is the varṇa system that is responsible for quarrels in society over questions of "high" and "low" among the various jātis. On the contrary, I think it is precisely for the purpose of ridding society of feelings of differences in status that we need the caste system. "If we are born in this jāti, well, it is the will of Īśvara. Our vocation has also been handed down to us in the same manner. Let us stick to it and do good to society as best we can. If somebody else finds that he has some other vocation, it is also according to the will of the Lord. Let each one of us do the work allotted to us in a spirit of dedication to Īśvara." If such an attitude develops there will be no room to think or feel that one kind of work is better than another kind or worse.

We must try to cultivate this outlook and inculcate it in everybody. We must set an example through our own life — there is no better way of making people understand the true spirit of the system of jātis. Then even our "oral propaganda" will not be necessary. If there is ill-will in society, it is because the concept of varṇa dharma is not properly understood. We must resolve right now to practise this dharma in its true spirit so that there will be no cause for society to be riven by bitterness.

With the decay of jāti dharma, livelihood has become a major problem for everybody. The obsession with money is a natural consequence of this worry. Until 70 or 75 years ago, nobody had any problem about his means of sustenance. The worry or concern then was about one's duty. If obtaining the means of livelihood were the only goal of life, the less well-off would be jealous of those who are affluent and occupy high places in society. It would also lead to misunderstandings and quarrels. If each man is concerned only about his duty and about doing it well, questions of status will not arise. But if money and status are the objectives, it will naturally mean that the man who has more money or occupies a higher place is superior to the man who is less prosperous and occupies a lower position. The point is such differences do not exist in true varṇa dharma. Even if the social order of jātis were abolished and together with it the quarrels among the various communities came to an end, society would have to face another problem, that is class conflict. We see this phenomenon all over the world today.

Our society must be one in which there are no differences of high and low. All will then live in harmony as the children of Īśvara without fighting among themselves. They will live as a united family helping one another and spreading a sense of peace and happiness everywhere. I ask you to follow the old dharma so that we may achieve such an ideal society. If we take a small step now towards such a goal, Īśvara will give us a helping hand for us to go further ahead. I keep praying to him.

References

[1] Actually this is a collection of the Mahātmā's writings on the subject. The Paramaguru must be quoting Gāndhijī from memory.

[2] "Varṇāśrama is, in my opinion, inherent in human nature, and Hinduism has simply reduced it to a science. It does attach to birth... The divisions define duties, they confer no privileges. It is, I hold, against the genius of Hinduism to arrogate to oneself a higher status or to assign to another a lower... Varṇāśrama is self-restraint and conservation and economy of energy...

"I have often shown the distinction between varṇāśrama and untouchability. I have defended the one as a rational, scientific fact and condemned the other as an excrescence and unmitigated evil... I do regard varṇāśrama as healthy division of work based on birth... Varṇāśrama, in my opinion, was not conceived in any narrow spirit. On the contrary, it gave the labourer, the Śūdra, the same status as the thinker, the Brahmin. It provided for the accentuation of merit and elimination of demerit, and it transformed human ambition from the general worldly sphere to the permanent and the spiritual. The aim of the Brahmin and Śūdra was common — mokṣa or Self-realisation, not realisation of fame, riches and power."

—from *My Varṇāśrama Dharma* by M.K. Gandhi.

Chapter 10

My Work

I could live in solitude in some village somewhere, performing pūjā and meditating. For the conduct of the Maṭha it is not at all necessary to have so much money as I receive from people in the cities. In my opinion the maṭhas ought to have only the minimum of strength in terms of money and men. A large entourage and a battalion of hangers-on are not essential to their maintenance. A maṭha's financial support and strength are nothing but the quality of the individual presiding over it.

If I leave my life of solitude and come to the city it is not because you give me a lot of money. You have great affection and devotion for me and you are so glad that I am present here at your request. You wanted me to come here and you are happy that I am in your midst. This is your business. But I have my own business, my own work, in coming to this city[1]. What is it?

I have come with the hope of making some arrangement according to which Brahmins will not give up the Vedic dharma and will continue to practise it without a break. The purpose of my being here is to ask you to prepare a scheme for the promotion of the Vedic dharma which is the source and root of all our systems of thought and ways of life; the scheme must ensure that the dharma does not become extinct in this generation itself. The Vedas which know no origin should be kept shining for ever in their original authentic form. The Brahmin must be a servant who will keep holding up this light, this torch, to illumine all the world. This is a duty he cannot but perform not only for today but for the generations to come.

"Brāhmaṇya" or Brahminhood did not come into being for Brahmins to lord it over others or for their own individual advancement. Its purpose is that the Brahmin should serve as a peon to hold up the Vedic lamp and show the path of Vedic dharma to mankind. If I come to the cities it is to urge the Brahmin community there not to extinguish this lamp, for to put out this light would be to plunge the whole world in darkness for all time.

In the towns and cities people come to listen to me in their thousands. So I am able to talk directly to a large number of people. It is with this idea in mind that I come to the big towns though it means some detriment to the observance of the rites associated with the Maṭha.

You spend a lot of money on constructing *paṇḍāls* in locality after locality for people to gather and listen to me. You come to hear my discourses in the midst of all your problems. However, my conscience does not permit me to give an entertaining talk without speaking to you about what is wrong with your way of life and perhaps causing you hurt thereby. It would serve no purpose if I take all your money but fail to tell you about what is good for you and the world. That is why I keep asking you again and again to protect the Vedic tradition and to practise the ancient dharmas. Whether or not I will succeed, I have come here to urge you again and again to do it.

You honour me with a "shower" of gold coins and celebrate with much pomp the day of my installation on the Pīṭha[2]. You do so because of your great affection for me. You appoint committees, collect money and toil day and night for the purpose. But how are we to be sure that the ācāryas who will succeed to the Pīṭha in the future will also be similarly honoured? If the Vedic dharma becomes extinct why should there be a maṭha at all or a maṭhādhipati (head of the maṭha)? So I tell you: "I see that you are so enthusiastic about honouring me with a shower of gold coins to celebrate the day of my ascending the Pīṭha. Why don't you have the same enthusiasm to work for the preservation of the Vedic dharma? Why don't you appoint committees for the purpose, draw up schemes, raise funds?

"It does not matter if you are unable to create conditions in which Brahmins henceforth will make the pursuit of the Vedic dharma their lifelong vocation. All I ask you is the minimum you can do, make arrangements to impart to your children the Vedic mantras, to teach them the scripture for at least one hour a day from the time they are eight years old until they are eighteen. Teach them also the prayoga[s] (the conduct of rites). Do this on a cooperative basis in each locality. If you succeed in this you will have truly honoured me with a shower of gold coins."

Nothing is achieved without effort. If we take up some work for our own sake we are ready to suffer any amount of hardship. There is a university in a distant land and you are told that if you take a degree from it you will get a very attractive job. What do you to then? You get the syllabus from that institution by post at once, manage to go and study there. Must we abandon our dharma on the plea that its pursuit involves a great deal of trouble? If there is trouble it means the benefits yielded will be proportionately greater — also it should be a matter of greater pride.

I have come to give you trouble in this fashion. I wonder why I should not stay here and keep giving you trouble until you agree to complete the arrangements to carry out my suggestion. After all, I have to stay somewhere, so why not here?

It gives me joy that more and more *bhajans* are conducted in the towns than before, that work connected with temples is on the increase and that purāṇic discourses are given more often than before. But we must remember that the Vedas constitute the basis of all these. If our scripture suffers a decline, how long will the activities based on it survive? The Vedas must be handed down from father to son, from one generation to the next. It is because we have forgotten this tradition that our religion itself has become shaky. All the trouble in the world, all the suffering and all the evil must be attributed to the fact that the Brahmin has forsaken his dharma, the Vedic dharma.

I am not worried about the system of jātis being destroyed, but I am worried about the setback to the welfare of mankind. I am also extremely concerned about the fact that, if the Vedic tradition which has been maintained like a chain from generation to generation is broken, it may not be possible to create the tradition all over again.

The good arising in a subtle form from the sound of the Vedas and the performance of sacrifices is not the only benefit that constitutes "lokakṣema" or the welfare of mankind. From Vedānta are derived lofty truths that can bring Ātmic uplift to people belonging to all countries. How did foreigners come to have an interest in our Vedānta? When they came to India they discovered here a class of people engaged in the practice of the Vedic dharma as a lifetime calling. They were curious to find out in what way the Vedas were great that an entire class of people should have dedicated themselves to them all their life. They conducted research into these scriptures and discovered many truths including those pointing to the unity of the various cultures of the world.

The Vedas bring universal good. This is not all. In the beginning, in my opinion, the Vedic culture was prevalent throughout the world. Others also, it is likely, will arrive at the same view on a thorough inquiry into the subject. The fact that there is something common to all mankind should be a source of universal happiness and it should also contribute to a sense of harmony among the various religions. Apart from this, I feel that people belonging to any faith may raise themselves inwardly through an understanding of the truths of the Vedic religion.

If a separate class of people ready to sacrifice everything for the cause of the Vedic tradition did not exist, how would you expect people of other countries to become interested in this tradition? If we ourselves discard something that is our own, thinking it to be useless, how can we expect others to take an interest in it? Because of our neglect we have been guilty of denying others the benefits to be earned from the Vedas. It is the responsibility of the present generation to ensure the continuance of the Vedic tradition not only for the happiness of people belonging to all castes in this country but for people throughout the world. Without this task accomplished, no purpose is going to be served by honouring me with a shower of gold coins.

Why then did I agree to the kanakābhiṣeka[3]? Had I not agreed to it, would you have gathered in such large numbers to listen to me?

To dispel the hatred, anger and bitterness that vitiate our social life people whose duty it is to sustain the Vedic dharma must remain true to it and set an example to others by living a life of virtue and tranquillity. The benefits that come from such a life may not be immediately perceptible. What happens when there is a *hartāl*? All shops are closed and people have to suffer much inconvenience. Think of what will happen when the work of preserving the Vedic dharma comes to a stop? The ill effects suffered by society will not be felt immediately but over a period. People then will realise the advantage of having an exclusive class that is devoted to Vedic learning as a lifelong mission. If alone you (Brahmins) do not fail in your duty, one day all the present hatred in society will be wiped away and happiness will reign instead.

In the hoary past it was in the Tamiḷ country that Manu lived. It was here that Vedic learning, Ātmic enlightenment and devotion attained their heights of glory. "Draviḍeṣu bhūriśaḥ," they say. We had not only saints like Tāyumānavar and Paṭṭinattār in Tamiḷ Nāḍu, but also great men belonging to other religions like Vedanāyagam Piḷḷai[T] and Mastān Sāhib[T] who became Vedāntins because of the special quality of the Tamiḷ soil.

The original home of the Vedas is this land. It is believed that, as the age of Kali comes to a close, Kalki (the tenth incarnation of Viṣṇu) will be born in the Tirunelveli region of the Drāviḍa land with the mission of protecting the Vedas. He will be born the son of a Brahmin who will be steadfast in performing the duties of his birth — so it is mentioned in the Purāṇas. In a land like this there ought not to be any opposition to the Vedic dharma. I have come here, to this city [Maḍrās], to remind you that Brahmins hold the key to the Vedas, to the continuance of the Vedic tradition.

Our religion places on its followers more restraints than any other faith does on its, but these are meant to elevate man to his true state, to take him to his true destination. There are restraints to be observed by the individual as well as by the community. Any restraint is like the embankment of a lake or a river. If the embankments are damaged, or if they are swept away, the whole area will be devastated. Today there are no restraints at all in the life of the individual or of society, no restraints in a religion that once imposed the maximum number of restrictions on its followers.

I go from place to place and keep giving discourses. I do so to keep Brahmins under some check or restraint because they are expected to be pathfinders for the rest of the entire society. There is a general belief that Brahmins are more attached to me than are others — whether or not Brahmins themselves think so or I think so. So, if I first succeed a little in binding them to their dharma, I will have the strength to teach others *their* dharma.

In brief, what do I ask of Brahmins? Before giving up his mortal frame, the Ācārya composed five stanzas that contain the essence of his teachings. I keep telling Brahmins today what the Ācārya says right at the start: "Vedo nityam adhīyatām." The same exhortation is made by the saint-poetess Auvvaiyār[T]. It reads almost like a Tamiḷ translation of the words of the Ācārya — *"Odāmal orunāḷum irukkaveṇḍām"*. What the Ācārya says in a positive manner ("You must chant the Vedas every day"), Auvvaiyār puts in a negative way ("Not a single day should you pass without chanting the Vedas"). In Tamiḷ the Vedas are called "*Ottu*". The *Tirukkural*[T] has also the same term. The place where the Vedas worshipped Īśvara is known as Vedapurī: in Tamiḷ it is "Tiruvottūr" ("Tiru-Ottu-ūr"). Vedic chanting has survived up till now from the time of Brahmā's creation. I keep visiting places to give people trouble and make them spend money during these visits. I do so only to impress upon them that the chanting of the Vedas must go on for ever.

So many thousands of you are gathered here. It is my hope that my words will have made an impact on at least ten or twenty of my listeners and that these ten or twenty will remember them and try to act according to them.

It was only after people emigrated to the big towns and cities that they found themselves compelled to lead a life contrary to the teachings of their dharma. It is in urban centres that you see some of the worst aspects of modern civilization. That is why I had decided not to come to such places, preferring to stay in the villages. But people from these urban centres insisted that I should visit them and, though I was touched by their affection, I was at first reluctant to accede to their request. I told them: "I shall come if you agree to return to our old way of life, even if it be to a small extent. You need not take lessons in the Vedas all at once. But, as a beginning, you must adopt the external symbols of our Vedic dharma. The peon wears a uniform, doesn't he? The Brahmin must wear the pañcakacchā[S] and śikhā[S]. These are not symbols proclaiming his superiority; on the contrary, they denote that he is a servant of all other communities, a servant of the Vedas. You must wear these symbols if you want me to come to your city."

It was in vain that I had laid down these conditions. Perhaps there was no desire on the part of the Brahmins I had spoken to to change their style of dress or their outlook or perhaps they did not have the courage to do it. But they requested me again and again that I should visit them. Eventually, I reconciled myself to accepting their invitation even though they had not acted on my words. "They still have some respect and affection for me," I told myself. "I will agree to their request. and see whether my purpose will be served if I go into their midst and speak to them directly again. After all, what is the Maṭha for? It is meant for the welfare of the people, to cure them of their ills and turn them to the right path. It is my duty to speak to them again and again—whether or not they like it—about how in my opinion they have gone wrong."

Thus I started visiting the towns again. When people welcome me in great joy, honour me wherever I go, decorate the roads with bunting, how can I wound their feelings by speaking about what is wrong with them? Everybody has problems in life. The world is plunged in turmoil and people face all sorts of hardships. In the midst of all this they come to me hoping to forget their problems. Is it then right for me to remind them of their faults? Or am I to keep everybody happy by turning my religious discourse into an entertaining performance?

Am I to speak to people about what is good for them, what is good for society, or am I to make them happy for the moment by making my talk a *kacceri*-like[4] performance? But there are musicians for *kacceris* and why should I be invited to perform something similar? If I were to give a *kacceri*-like performance for the sake of money, I would have to make the listeners happy for the time being. But my purpose is not money. If more money comes, it is spent in feeding more than the usual number of people, in holding assemblies of the learned, etc. The affairs of the Maṭha could be managed with the smaller amounts received in the villages. However, an effort must be made, all the same, to speak to the entire community of people about what is good for them, for their life. Is this not the very purpose of the Maṭha?

Thinking on these lines, I came to this conclusion: "It is up to them (the people I am to address in the towns) to listen to me and act on my advice. Whether or not they like it, I will speak to them about their duties, about what they should do for spiritual uplift as well as for the happiness of mankind." I can do no more than speak to them about their duty. I have no authority to punish them if they fail in this. Even in political parties which believe in the oneness and equality of all, disciplinary action is taken against erring members — some are expelled like untouchables. I have no authority to excommunicate anyone for any of their offences. Nor do I ask for myself such authority to be exercised over men. The only right I ask for is to have the ears of people. I cannot but do what I can do—that is why I am here.

Sufficient it would be even if a single individual somewhere paid heed to my words and acted according to them. He would be the starting point in the direction of the desired growth. Have not movements that do not have an iota of justification behind them grown with just ten people to start with? For a good cause also it would be enough if ten people joined together initially.

I keep speaking in the hope of finding such people. You must not feel unhappy thinking that I am very much dissatisfied with you. I am not unaware of the complexities and problems of modern life. If one is trapped in it, I know how difficult it is to be freed from it. In the midst of all this, you make arrangements in a big way for kumbhābhiṣekas[S], *bhajans,* discourses, etc. I am happy about it all. I feel also encouraged by it to speak to you about that which is the very basis, the very life-breath, of these activities of yours. It is that of fostering the Vedic dharma.

Though there is much room for offences against the śāstras in the present way of life and though there is cause for worry about the future, I am reassured by certain signs that promise our well-being. Instead of lamenting that "all is lost", the proper thing to do is to promote the good aspects in present-day life and to speak about what still needs to be done. In this way those who have taken the wrong path will sooner or later see the light and turn to the path of wisdom.

All this gives me the confidence to speak about the old ways of life and the old customs. I do not claim that all that is old is necessarily good. At the same time, I feel that nothing should be rejected merely because it is old. An object (or idea) is to be judged not on the basis of whether it is old or new; it is to be accepted or rejected after finding out how useful it is. Let us accept what is good in the new and reject what is bad in the old. Likewise, let us reject what is bad in the new and accept what is good in the old. Kālidāsa says the same thing[5].

You have invited me with much affection and treated me with much honour. So I feel reluctant to tell you about what is bad in your present way of life. I have dealt with many subjects—about devotion, jñāna, culture, and so on. True, they are edifying topics. But they are all like the branches, flowers and fruits supported by something deeper, supported by the root constituted by the Vedas. Nothing grows without this root, without the Vedic tradition being nourished. It is pointless to speak about other matters after leaving out this vital subject. The preservation of the Vedic dharma is the basic service we render to our religion, and while on the subject, we have necessarily to dwell on the drawbacks in the present way of life. After speaking to you about other matters, after mixing with you, I have become friends with you and I feel I could take the liberty of talking to you about your duties and responsibilities. I am taking up the topic of the Vedas since I feel I need not be as reluctant as I was before in telling you about what is wrong with your way of life.

The very purpose of my visit is this. But is it proper for me to speak about it right at the start? Since you have done your job by honouring me and pleasing me, I feel I can now do my job by speaking about the importance of sustaining the Vedic way of life. I have given you so much trouble for this purpose and put you to a lot of expense. As if this were not enough, I am asking you, like Vinoba Bhāve, for "saṁpatti-dāna"[6].

Every Brahmin must learn the Vedas and teach his sons the same. Necessary though this is, there is something even more important to be done as a matter of priority: it is to make sure that the schools that teach the Vedas (the pāṭhaśālās) which are gasping for breath as it were are not closed down but given new life. For this purpose both teachers and taught must be given monetary help. More Vedic schools must also be established not only to teach the mantras but also their meaning and to conduct examinations. During the years of study the students must be given a stipend. On passing their examinations they must be given substantial cash awards, the amount depending upon their marks. You have to do all this to maintain the Vedic dharma[7]. Naturally, you need capital for it.

Trusts have been created for this purpose. A number of people have made gifts of land (bhūdāna) — like Vinoba Bhāve I too have received bhūdāna. Now ceilings on landownings have come into force. It is difficult to foresee how the rights of landowners will be affected in the future. That is why I am asking for sampatti-dāna.

Everyone of you must put one rupee in a piggybox every month on the day on which your janma-nakṣatra[8] falls. Think of me as you do it for, after all, it is I who am asking you to do it. After twelve months you must send the Rs 12 so collected to the Veda Rakṣana Nidhi. On your janma-nakṣatra, the Maṭha will send you prasāda[S] (vibhuti[S] — sacred ashes—*kumkum,* mantrākṣata[S]). You will be the recipient of the blessings of Candramaulīśvara[9] if you contribute to the Veda Rakṣana Nidhi year after year.

You pay taxes and spend so much on so many things. Take this contribution to the Veda Rakṣana Nidhi as a tax imposed by me: pay one rupee every month for my sake. If everyone agreed to do so, it would mean great support to the task of preserving the Vedic dharma. The maintenance of the Vedic tradition is uppermost in my mind and it is a duty we have to carry out for the good of future generations.

If you ask me why the Vedic dharma must be perpetuated, the answer is that the sound of Vedic mantras and the conduct of Vedic rites like sacrifices will bring universal material and spiritual well-being. Second, if people in every country of the world are to know that the Vedic religion was once a universal religion and, if unity and peace are to be achieved on the basis of such awareness, there must be a class of people in our country who will devote themselves solely to Vedic learning. I maintain that fostering the Vedic dharma is of the utmost importance because it will bring prosperity and inward tranquillity to people not only in our country but all over the world.

There should not be even a single Brahmin in the next generation who will not be able to chant the Vedas. We need the Brahmin not to exercise authority over others, but to carry out the duty of protecting the primordial dharma—and this not only for the unity of our land but for the oneness of the whole world.

How can we claim that a small group of people in this country (dedicated to maintaining the Vedic tradition) can create happiness throughout the world? Well, take the case of a powerhouse. Only four or five work in it but the entire town receives light. If these four or five people do not work, the whole town will be plunged in darkness. In the same way only a few people are required to keep the auspicious world lamp of the Vedas burning. My mission here is to protect somehow the seed capital necessary for it. For the sake of this, I agreed to all the festivities you conducted in my honour. The chant of "Jaya-Jaya Śankara, Hara-Hara Śankara" heard during these festivities brought so many people here to listen to my discourses. Those who conducted the festival in my honour must pay heed to what I wish to say. You exert yourself in many ways in the cause of so many things. Why not exert yourself a little for my sake also? You do so much for yourself: you go to your office; you have your own pastime; and you conduct all kinds of businesses. For my sake do this job of protecting the Vedic dharma.

Why should I speak differentiating between you and me ["For your sake" and "my sake"]. My work is also your work. Maintaining the Vedic tradition is the one job that ensures the supreme good of all. Doing this duty means well-being for you—and I shall be earning a name as a result!

Notes & References

1 This discourse was given in Maḍrās.

2 The reference is to the 50th anniversary of the Paramaguru's installation as the Śankarācārya of Kāñcī Kāmakoti Pīṭha in 1907

3 "Kanakābhiṣeka" literally means "showering", "sprinkling" or bathing someone (usually a revered person like an ācārya) with flowers or coins made of gold or small pieces of the same metal.

4 The term *"kacceri"* (from the Hindī *kachari,* meaning lawcourt) is used in the South for a music or dance recital.

[5] The Paramaguru refers to this verse from Kālidāsa's *Mālavikāgnimitram :*

Purāṇamityeva na sādhusarvam
Na cāpikāvyam navamityavadyam
Santaḥ parikṣānyatarad bhajante
Mūḍhaḥ parapratyayaneya buddhiḥ

[6] Gift of wealth. Vinoba Bhāve, the Gāndhian, started his movement first with *bhoodan,* then he enlarged it to include *sampattidān* and *shramdān.*

[7] See Appendix 2.

[8] "Janma-nakṣatra" is the asterism under which one is born. It occurs every month (or in a 27-day cycle).

[9] Candramaulīśvara (Śiva) is the tutelary deity of Kāñci Kāmakoṭi Pīṭha.

Part Four

THE ŚĀSTRAS AND MODERN LIFE

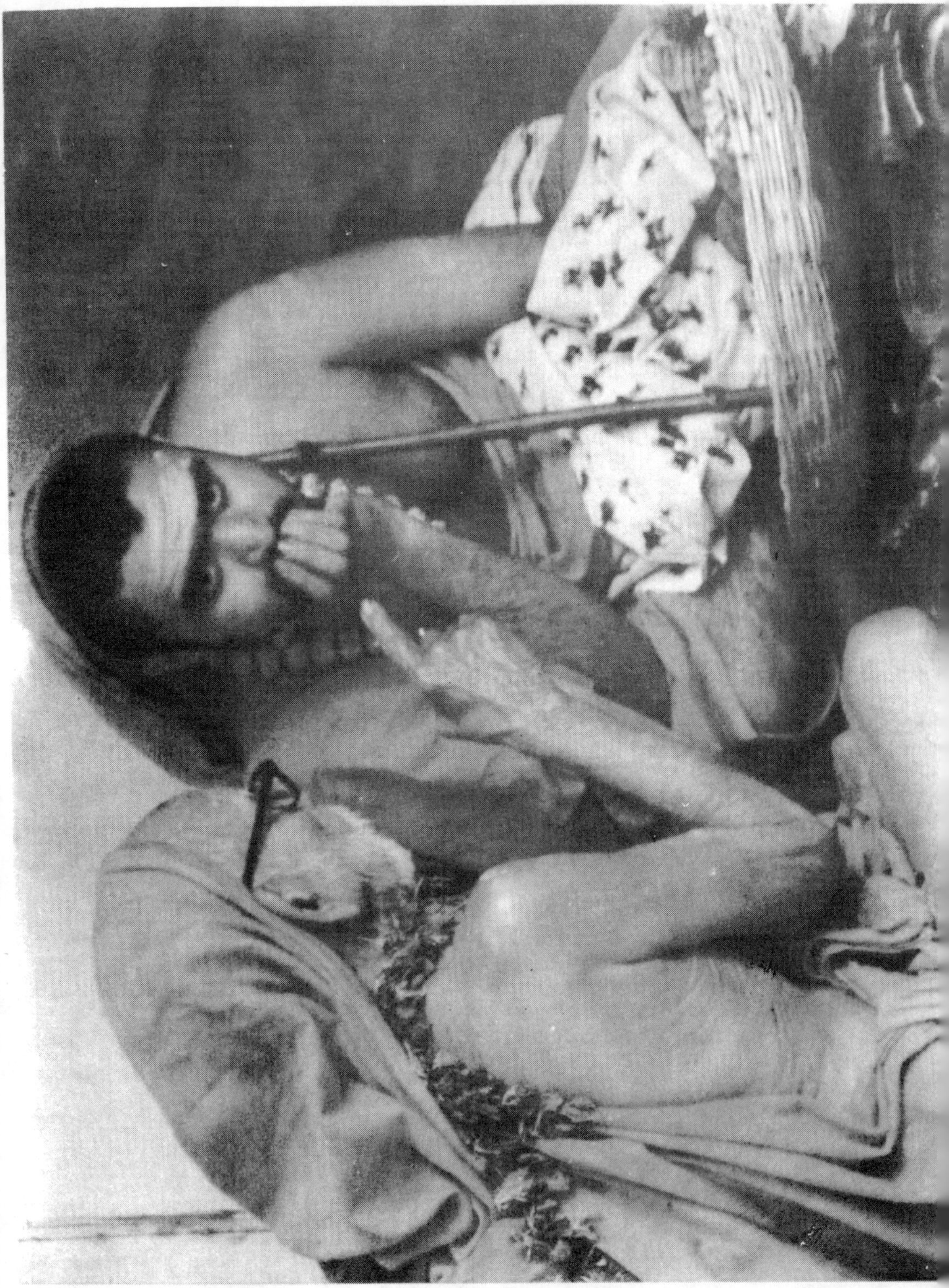

Chapter 1

The Cure for the Disease called Modern Civilization

People are caught between two groups holding opposing views. On the one side they feel the pull of individuals like us who maintain that they must take to the path shown by the śāstras; on the other they find themselves drawn in the opposite direction by the reformers who want these śāstras to be changed. From a youthful age people nowadays are used to reading reports extolling the changes that go by the name of reforms. It is all due to the influence of modern education. All this notwithstanding, people have not altogether given up the old customs. A fraction of the dharmas laid down in the śāstras and followed for ages is still to be seen in our domestic and social life. On the one hand, there is the habit formed by custom and, on the other, the habit now being learned through the new system of education.

It is universally recognised that contentment is lacking in the modern way of life. People do not dispute the fact that the peace that once existed in the previous generations no longer obtains today. They have more money now — or that at any rate is the belief. But are they yet free from poverty? The claim is made that everything is in abundance, that we grow more food than what is needed. Yet there is anxiety everywhere about the supply of essentials.

In the place of the old thatched hut or modest tiled house now stands a multistorey building. Then we had just four or five utensils to cook, a basket made of palm-fronds, containers made of gourd shells. Now the house is crammed with all sorts of articles and gadgets that are part of today's "civilized" life. People enjoy new comforts and make new acquisitions, yet they are not as happy and contented as were their forefathers.

Even now there are people who at heart long for a life of peace lived according to the old tradition. But they do not have the courage to give up either the trammels of modern life or the feeling of pride in the changes effected under the reformist movement. They are in an awkward predicament because they are not fully committed either to the traditional way of life or to the new. Let me tell you how people cannot decide for themselves — how they are neither here nor there. In most homes you will see Gāndhījī's portrait and mine. Now Gāndhījī advocated widow marriage — and I ask people to wear a śikhā[S]. Those who respect Gāndhījī do not, however, have the courage to marry widows nor do they have the courage to wear a śikhā. Poor people, they have no moorings and keep swinging between one set of beliefs and another. We must have the courage of our convictions and unflinching faith in the śāstras.

If we start making small compromises in our adherence to the śāstras, it will eventually mean following only such scriptural practices as we find convenient in our everyday life. Some people tell me with all good intentions: "The dharmaśāstras are the creation of ṛṣis. You are like a ṛṣi. You must make changes in the śāstras in keeping with the times." Their view is that just as we remove weeds from the fields we must change our customs and duties according to our times. If I take out some rites and observances from the śāstras now, thinking them to be "weeds", later another man will turn up and remove some more for the same reason. At this rate, a time will come when we will not be able to distinguish the weed from the crop and the entire field will become barren.

It is important to realise that if we are to remain true to the śāstras it is not because they represent the views of the seers but because they contain the rules founded on the Vedas which are nothing but what Īśvara has ordained. That is the reason why we must follow them. It is my duty to see that the śāstras are preserved as they are. I have no authority to change them.

We must not give up the śāstric way of life thinking it to be difficult to follow. If we are not carried away by the glitter of modern mundane life, if we reduce our wants and do not run after money, there will be no need to abandon the customs and rites laid down by our canonical texts. If we are not obsessed with making money there will be plenty of time to think of the Lord. And peace, contentment and happiness will reign.

Money is not essential to the performance of the rites enjoined by the śāstras, nor is pomp and circumstance essential to worship. Even dried tulasī[S] and bilvā[S] leaves are enough to perform pūjā. The rice we cook for ourselves will do as the naivedya. "Marriage also is a śāstric ceremony. We spend a lot of money on it. What about such expenses?" it is asked. All the lavish display we see at weddings today are unnecessary and do not have the sanction of the scriptures[1]. Specifically, the dowry that forms such a substantial part of the marriage expenses has no scriptural sanction at all[2]. If money were important to the performance of the rites enjoined by our canonical texts it would mean that our religion is meant for rich people. In truth it is not so.

Of the four aims of life — dharma, material acquisitions, desire and liberation — we seek gratification of kāma alone (in the form of pleasure, love, etc). And to have our desires satisfied we keep struggling to acquire material things. Our efforts must be directed towards obtaining liberation through the practice of dharma. All that we need to do for this ideal is to resolve to live a simple life. There should then be no compulsion to run after money and other material goods. It would naturally become easier for us to practise dharma and reap the ultimate fruit, that is eternal bliss.

Reference

[1] & [2] See Part Eighteen.

Chapter 2
Religion and Society

While adherence to the tenets of our religion entails certain inconveniences in our workaday life, following the rules of the dharmaśāstras, people feel, creates difficulties in social life. On this pretext reformers want to change the śāstras.

Unfortunately, they are not aware either of the truths on which the dharmaśāstras are founded or their ultimate purpose. By "social life" they — the reformers — do not have in mind anything relating to the Self. They take into account the political order that keeps changing every now and then, the sciences, trade and commerce, fashion, etc. If our worldly existence alone were the objective of social life, the rules pertaining to it would also be subject to change. But our scriptures do not view social life as having such an objective alone. They (the śāstras) are meant for the Self, for the Ātman, and their goal is our release from worldly existence. That which has to do with mundane life is subject to change but not the truths relating to the Self. The injunctions of the śāstras have the purpose of establishing changing society on the foundation of the unchanging Truth; they cannot be subject to change themselves.

If our goal were but a comfortable and happy life in this world, matters concerning social life could be changed now and again. But ours is an exalted goal and it concerns the Self. The rules of worldly life are in keeping with this high purpose and they cannot be changed according to our convenience. The śāstras do not regard happiness in this world as of paramount importance. They teach us how we may experience joy in the other world even by suffering many kinds of hardships or discomforts here. So it is not right to seek changes in them to suit our worldly existence.

The views of the reformers must have been shaped by our present system of education and so it is no use blaming them. In other countries no contradiction exists between their religion and their system of education. Unfortunately, the schools established by the British in India had nothing to do with our religion. People were compelled to take to Western education for the sake of their livelihood. Soon a situation arose in which they came to be steeped from childhood itself in an alien system of instruction. They had therefore no way of developing acquaintance with, or faith in, our ancient śāstras. And, since they were kept ignorant of their scriptures and their underlying purpose, they persuaded themselves to take the view that the śāstras could be changed according to their convenience.

Our youngsters are exposed to criticism of our religion and our sacred texts from a tender age. They are told that the Purāṇas are a tissue of lies, that the śāstras help the growth of superstition. How can they have any attachment to our faith, to its rites and traditions?

Faith in religion and God must be inculcated in people from their childhood. They must get to know about great men who lived and continue to live an exemplary life true to the tenets of our religion. Faith in the works of the seers must be instilled in them, works based on the experience of the seers themselves, experience beyond a life of sensation, and pointing the way to spiritual uplift. They must also be helped to believe that the ṛṣis formulated the śāstraś in such a way as to make worldly happiness and social life subservient to the advancement of the Self. Only then will people recognize that the rules of religion have a far higher purpose than the comforts and conveniences of temporal life.

Chapter 3

Neither too Much Ease nor too Many Comforts

Now people want to live in comfort and to be provided with all sorts of amenities. There is no end to their unseemly desires. In America, it is said, everybody has a bungalow, car, radio, telephone, etc. But are people there contented ? No. There is more discontent in that country than in our own. There the incidence of crime is more than anywhere else. It is all right that every American has a car. But today's car is not good enough for them tomorrow. More and more new models keep coming in the market and each new model offers more comfort than the previous one. This means that the American citizen is compelled to earn more with the appearance of each new car. A time may come when aircraft will be used in the U.S. for people to fly from house to house.

Similarly, we see such a progression all over the world in the matter of housing. First there was the hovel or the hut; then came the dwelling with the tiled roof; afterwards houses with cement and concrete walls. The flooring also changed over the years. First the floor was wiped with cowdung; then it was plastered and cemented; the mosaic flooring came later; and the search is on for smoother and shinier surfaces. It is the same case with clothing — better and finer fabrics are being made every day. Although we are already living in comfort we are all the time using our ingenuity to discover objects and gadgets that will make our life still easier. However, all the time we are likely to have the feeling of uneasiness with all the comforts we already possess and this means there will be no end to our yearnings. Not knowing any contentment or peace of mind we are compelled to earn more and more. It is like thinking that fire can be extinguished by pouring petrol on it; we keep discovering newer and newer objects but in the process we keep further inflaming our longing for ease and comfort.

This truth was known to our sages, to our forefathers. They taught us that we ought not to seek more than our bare needs. In recent times Gāndhījī impressed upon people the same lesson.

In this century, people seek ostentatious living in the name of progress. So long as the hunger for new comforts continues neither the individual nor society will have contentment. There will always be feelings of rivalry, jealousy and heart-burning among people. In the varṇāśrama dharma, the Brahmin and non-Brahmin are equal economically speaking. In spite of the caste differences, the same simple living is enjoined on all. The ideal of equality can be achieved only if all people live a simple life. In this order every individual experiences contentment and inner happiness and no one has cause of envying others their prosperity.

No man, whatever his vocation, should have either too much money or too many comforts. Above all what is important is *that* for which all these are intended but *that* which cannot be truly obtained through them: contentment and a sense of fullness within. Only when there is inner satisfaction can one meditate on the Lord. And only in the mind of a man who has such contentment is the Ultimate Truth realised as a reality. When a person has too many comforts he will be incapable of going beyond the stage of sensual pleasures. If he is addicted to enjoyments, without any need for physical exertion, he will do injury to his mind, and his inner being. Hard work and the capacity to suffer discomforts are essential for those who yearn for Ātmic uplift. They will then learn to realise that there is comfort in discomfort and in hard work.

Chapter 4

Śāstra or Conscience?

The goal of dharma is universal welfare. The great men who produced the works on Dharmaśāstra did not have a trace of self-interest in them and had nothing but the thought of the happiness of all creatures. These treatises are the authority on which dharma is founded. You find the form of things, the image, with your eyes; you perceive sound with your ears; you know dharma with the help of Dharmaśāstra[1].

The Vedas (Śruti) are the root of all dharma. After Śruti comes Smṛti. The latter consists of the "notes" based on Śruti[2]. It is the same as Dharmaśāstra. Another guide for dharma is the example of great men. The Purāṇas provide an answer to how great men conducted themselves. Then there is śiṣṭācāra to guide us, the life of virtuous people of noble character. Not everybody's conduct can be a guide to us. The individual whose life is an example for the practice of dharma must have faith in the śāstras and must live in accordance with their ordinances. Besides, he must be free from desire and anger. The conduct of such men is śiṣṭācāra. Another authority or guide is what we know through our conscience in a state of transparency.

In matters of the Self, of dharma and religion, the Vedas are in the forefront as our guide. Next come the dharmaśāstras. Third is the conduct of the great sages of the past. Fourth is the example of the virtuous people of our own times. Conscience comes last in determining dharma.

Now everything has become topsyturvy. People give importance first to their conscience and last to the Vedas. We must consult our conscience only as a last resort when we have no other means of knowing what is dharma with reference to our actions. Why is conscience called one's "manaḥsākṣī"? Conscience is fit to be only a witness (sākṣī), not to be a judge. A witness often gives false evidence. The mind, however, does not tell an untruth— indeed it knows the truth of all things. "There is no deceit that is hidden from the heart (mind)," says Auvvai[T]. Conscience may be regarded as a witness. But nowadays it is brought in as a judge also in dhārmic matters. As a witness it will give us a true report of what it sees or has seen. But on the basis of it we cannot give a decision on what is just with any degree of finality. "What I think is right," everybody would try to satisfy himself thus about his actions if he were to be guided only by his conscience. How can this be justified as the verdict of dharma?

We often hear people say, "I will act according to what my conscience tells me." This is not a right attitude. All at once your conscience cannot be given the place of a judge. It is only when there is no other way open to you that you may tell your mind: "You have seen everything as a witness. Now tell me your opinion." The mind belongs to each one of us as individuals. So it cannot be detached from our selfish interests. The place it has in one's personal affairs cannot be given to it in matters of religion. On questions of dharma the opinion of sages alone is valid, sages who were concerned with universal welfare and who transcended the state of the individual concerned with his own mind [or with himself].

Reference

[1] & [2] See Part Fifteen.

Part Five

THE VEDAS

Chapter 1

The Basic Texts of Hinduism: Our Ignorance of Them

There are books aplenty in the world dealing with a vast variety of subjects. The adherents of each religion single out one book for special veneration, believing that it shows them the way to salvation. The followers of some faiths even build temples in honour of their holy scriptures. The Sikhs, for instance, do so; they venerate their sacred book, calling it the "Granth Sāhib" [and enshrine it in temples].

Thus the followers of each religion have come to have a work showing them the way to their spiritual uplift. Such books are believed to enshrine the utterances and commandments of God conveyed through the founders of the respective faiths. For this reason they are called revealed texts. We call the same "apauruṣeya" (not the work of a human author). What men do of their own accord is "pauruṣeya" and what the Paramātman reveals, using man as a mere instrument, is "apauruṣeya".

What is the authoritative text of our Vedic religion? People of other faiths are clear about what their sacred books are. Buddhists have the Tripiṭaka, Pārsis (Zoroastrians) the Zend-Avesta, Christians the Bible, and Muslims the Qur'ān. What work is basic to our religion, common to Śaivas, Vaiṣṇavas, Dvaidins (dualists), Advaitins (non-dualists) and the followers of various other (Hindu) traditions? Most of us find the answer difficult. Why?

There is an important reason. People born in other religions are taught their sacred texts in school. Or they receive instruction [at home] in their respective faiths for two or three years, and then have what is called "secular" education. So even at a youthful age they are fairly conversant with the religion into which they are born. We Hindus receive no religious instruction at all. How has this affected us? Whenever adherents of other faiths go seeking converts, we become a convenient target for them. How is it that people belonging to other religions do not leave their faith to embrace another in any considerable numbers? The reason is that they learn about the tenets of their religion in childhood itself and remain firmly attached to it. In contrast, we are not taught even the elements of our religion in our early years. Worse, we speak ill of our scriptures and have no qualms about even destroying them.

Our education follows the Western pattern. We want to speak like the white man, dress like him and ape him in the matter of manners and customs. We remain so even after our having won independence. In fact, though we keep speaking all the time about our culture, about svadeśī and so on, we are today more Westernised than before. Remaining a paradeśī (alien) at heart we keep talking of svadeśī. Religion has been the backbone of our nation's life from time immemorial. If we wish to remain svadeśī, both inwardly and outwardly, we must receive religious instruction from childhood itself. The secular state is of no help in this matter because, in the secular set-up, education continues to be imparted to our children on the Western pattern, and the children are taught that our śāstras are all superstition. The result is that most of us do not know what the sacred text is that is common to all Hindus.

Our Ātma-vidyā (science of the Self) is extolled by people all over the world. (In our country learning even subjects that are apparently mundane like political economy, economics, dance, etc, has a transcendent purpose.) Foreigners come to India in search of our śāstras and translate them into their own languages. If we want to be respected by the world we must gain more and more knowledge in such śāstras as have won the admiration of all the world. We cannot earn more esteem than others for achievements in fields like science and technology. We feel proud if one or two Indians win the Nobel prize but the rest of the world hardly takes any notice of it. Its attitude may be expressed thus: "The strides we have taken in science and technology do not give us satisfaction. So we go to the Hindus seeking things that are beyond. But they themselves seem to forsake the philosophical and metaphysical quest for our science and technology." We must be proud of the fact that our country has produced more men who have found inner bliss than all other countries put together have. It is a matter of shame that we are ignorant of the śāstras that they have bequeathed to us, the śāstras that taught them how to scale the heights of bliss.

Many Hindus are ignorant of the scripture that is the very source of their religion—they do not know even its name. "What does it matter if we don't know?" they ask. "What do we gain by knowing it?"

Though we are heirs to a great civilization, a civilization that is universally admired, we are ignorant of its springs. "Who cares about our culture? Money is all that we need," such is the attitude of our people and they keep flying from continent to continent in search of a fortune. Some of them come to me and tell me : "People abroad ask us about our religion, about the Vedas, about the Upaniṣads. They want to know all about the Gītā and yoga, about our temples and Purāṇas and about so many other things. We find it difficult to answer their questions. In fact we seem to know less than what they already know about these matters. We are indeed ashamed of ourselves. So would you please briefly put together the concepts of our religion and philosophy?"

What does this mean? We are proud of living as foreigners in our own land, but the foreigners themselves think poorly of us for being so. We are inheritors of the world's oldest religion and culture; yet we have no concern for them ourselves. How would you then expect foreigners to have any respect for us?

Perhaps it would not have mattered much if we were an unlettered people. Others would have thought us to be ignorant, not anything worse. But what is the reality today? We read and write and talk a great deal. Science and technology, politics, cinema, fiction—these are our interests. Yet foreigners think poorly of us because we ignore what is unique to our land, the śāstras relating to the Self.

There are so many books on our religion but we seem to have no need for any of them. All our reading consists of foreign literature. We know all the works of Milton and Wordsworth, but know precious little of the poetry of Bhavabhūti[S] and Oṭṭakkūttar[T]. We are acquainted with the history of the Louis dynasty and of the Tsars, but we know nothing of the solar and lunar dynasties of our own country. Why, we do not know even the names of the seers of the various gotras[S]. We are thoroughly acquainted with things that are of no relevance to us, but of the subjects that have aroused the wonder of the world we are ignorant, ignorant even of the names of the śāstras on which they are founded. Even if men learned in the scriptures come forward to speak about them we refuse to listen to them. It causes me great pain that our country and countrymen have descended to such abysmal depths of ignorance.

The reason for this sorry state of affairs is that we are not as anxious to know about our culture as we are to find out how much it would fetch us in terms of money. Indeed the true purpose of earning money and other activities of ours must be to know this culture fully, live in consonance with its spirit and experience a sense of fulfilment. Why should we care to know about our religion? A question like this is absurd. Religion itself is the purpose of all our actions—it is its own purpose. There need be no purpose for religion although the performance of religious rites brings us great benefits such as tranquillity of mind, affection for all and, finally, liberation. Unmindful of all this, we want to know whether it would fetch us money. If we were truly interested in religion and truly attached to it, we would never be worried about the purpose served by it.

"Brāhmaṇena niṣkāraṇo dharmaḥ ṣaḍango Vedādhyeyo jñeyaśca," so say the śāstras. It means that a Brahmin must learn the Vedas and śāstras not because there is any reason for it, not because there is any purpose served by the same. It is only in our childhood that we learn a subject without asking questions about how useful it is. A schoolgoing child does not ask : "Why should I learn history or geography?"

Our religious texts must be taught early in life. When a child grows up and goes to college, he believes his studies will perhaps prove useful to him. If he reads for a B.L. or LL.B. degree, it is to become a lawyer. Similarly, if he reads for an L.T. (or B.Ed.) degree or an M.B.B.S., it is to become a teacher or a doctor. If you ask a teenager to study our religious texts, he would retort : "Why should I learn them? How will it help me in my career?" So religious texts should be taught in childhood itself, that is, before the youngster is old enough to question you about their utility [or harbour doubts about the same]. Only then will he develop an interest in our religion and śāstras. Do we pay our children for their being interested in sports, music or cinema? Similarly, they must be made to take an interest in religion also and such interest must be created in the same way as in sports and entertainment. If children take to sports and entertainment which afford only temporary pleasure, they are bound to take to religion which will confer on them everlasting happiness. The present sorry state of affairs is due to our basic education being flawed.

Today we have come to such a pass that people ask whether a knowledge of religion is of help in their upkeep. This is a matter of shame. The śāstras admonish : "Do not ask whether Vedic education will provide you with food. We eat and live but to learn the Vedas." Your approach must be based on this principle. A child born in a faith which has such high ideals is cut off from all opportunities of religious instruction at his very birth. Our concern is imparting him worldly knowledge from the very start. Our children must be brought up properly and faith in God inculcated in them early in life.

We spend so much on our youngsters — but what do we spend on their religious instruction? A father spends thousands on his son's upanayana[S]. But if he were to spend one-tenth of the sum towards achieving what constitutes the very purpose of the upanayana ceremony—making the child a good brahmacārin[S] — faith in our religion would be kept alive. To repeat, far better would it be to spend money on achieving the goal of upanayana than on the upanayana ceremony itself[1]. The child must be given religious instruction by a private tutor and taught the duties of the brahmacārin. Why should teachers conversant with such matters be denied an income? If religion is taught in childhood itself, people will be free from doubts as they grow up and the teacher too will be benefited. Today the situation is so lamentable that most of us do not know even the name of the text that forms the foundation and authority of our religion.

The fact that our people are not taught religion at an early age is one reason why there are so many differences among them. One man is a theist and another an atheist. One performs religious rites without devotion while another is devoted but does not perform any rites. The differences and disputes are many. As for the doubts harboured by people about our religion there is no end. If our religion were taught in childhood itself there would be unanimity of views and freedom from doubts. We know it for a fact that there are not so many doubting people among followers of other religions as there are among ours: the reason is that, unlike us, they are better informed about the concepts of their respective religions.

What is *the* book of our religion? A definite answer even to this question seems to be a difficult task for people these days. However, if we follow the truths of that book which is the basic work of our religion there will be universal uplift.

Followers of most religions point to a single book as their sacred text even if the matters mentioned in it are dealt with in other works of theirs also. A man may write one book today, tomorrow a second man will come up to write another. There may be good as well as bad points about them and it would be difficult to determine the value of each. So is it not to our advantage if a single book is accepted for all time as our basic religious text? That is why every religion treats such a single book as its prime scripture.

What are the works that tell us all about our religion? The libraries are chock-full of books on Hinduism; indeed there are hundreds of thousands of them. The subjects that come under our religion are also numerous. It all seems to cause confusion. But we must remember that there are a few texts that constitute a common basis for all the other numerous works.

By practising the tenets of our religion many have had the beatific experience and remained in tranquil samādhi[S], without knowing death and oblivious of the outside world. We see such men even today. There are books from which we learn about Sadāśiva Brahmendra[S], Paṭṭinattār[T], and similar realised souls. Other religious systems have not produced as many realised souls as has our own faith. Is it possible that a religion that has been a source of inspiration for such a large number of great men should have no authoritative texts?

Note

1 The upanayana ceremony has become an expensive affair today without its true purpose being understood.

Chapter 2

Why Religion?

Why do we need religion? Why do we listen to a religious teacher? We do so hoping to have our problems solved and our faults corrected. We do not seek a preceptor when we are not in trouble or when we feel that there is nothing lacking in us. The more we are besieged by troubles the more often we go to worship in temples or seek the *darshan* and advice of great men.

We approach great men, saintly persons, hoping to find a remedy for our suffering and to have our doubts cleared. When we are harassed by difficulties, we try to find solace in books or in listening to the advice of men of wisdom and virtue. Or we go on pilgrimage and bathe in sacred ponds or rivers. Thus we hope to find mental peace by and by. Those who know utter tranquillity remain in bliss. It does not matter to them in the least whether they are stabbed or injured otherwise, whether they are honoured or maligned.

Great men arise in all jātis, great men who experience inner peace. What is religion? It is that which shows the way to śānti, the peace that passeth understanding. Religion is known as "mata" or "dharma". Dharma is the means to attain the ultimate good that is liberation—and it is the same as "mata".

The pursuit of dharma is first meant for happiness and well-being in this world. When it is practised, without desiring happiness here, it will lead to liberation. Yes, this is dharma; this is mata.

"Dharma" which is the term used by the śāstras for religion denotes all the moral and religious principles that constitute the means to obtain fullness of life. We have many a work that teaches us this dharma, but we remain ignorant of them. Since they deal with matters that are the very basis of dharma, they are called "dharma-pramāṇas." "Pramāṇa" is that which establishes the truth or rightness of a thing (or belief). We have fourteen basic śāstras that pertain to dharma, that is canonical texts that deal with what has come to be known as Hinduism and what has been handed down to us from the time of the primordial Vedas. These treatises tell us about the doctrines and practices of dharma.

Angāni Vedāścatvāro mīmāṁsā-nyāyavistaraḥ
Purāṇam dharmaśāstram ca vidyā hyetāścaturdaśa

—Manusmṛti

Purāṇa-nyāya-mīmāṁsā-dharmaśāstrāṅgamiśritaḥ
Vedāḥ sthānāni vidyānām dharmasya ca caturdaśa

—Yājñavalkyasmṛti

The term "caturdaśa" occurs in both verses. It means "fourteen". We learn from these two stanzas that we have fourteen authoritative works on dharma embracing all aspects of our religion.

"Vid" means "to know". From it is derived "vidyā" which means a work that imparts knowledge, that sheds light on the truths of religion. That there are fourteen treatises on vidyā is mentioned in the above two stanzas: "vidyā hyetāścaturdaśa" and "vidyānām dharmasya ca caturdaśa". The fourteen are not only śāstras that impart knowledge but also treatises on moral principles. That is why they are called "vidyāsthānas" and "dharmasthānas" : "sthānāni vidyānām dharmasya ca caturdaśa". Though "vid" means to know, the word does not connote every type of knowledge. The "vid" in "vidyā" means knowledge of truth. The English words "wit" and "wisdom" are derived from this root. And it is from the same root that we have "Veda", which term may be said to mean literally the "Book of Knowledge". As sources of knowledge the fourteen śāstras are called "vidyāsthānas", that is they are "abodes of knowledge or learning". The dharmasthānas ("abodes of dharma") are also the abodes of vidyā.

Chapter 3

The Fourteen Abodes of Knowledge

The fourteen "abodes" of knowledge are: the four Vedas; the six Aṅgas or limbs of the Vedas; Mīmāṁsā, Nyāya, the Purāṇas and Dharmaśāstra. You must have seen at least references to the Vedas and the six Angas. The Tamiḷ work *Tevāram*[T] says[1]: "*Vedamoḍāraṅgamāyinānai*". According to this devotional work Īśvara is the form of the four Vedas and the six Angas.

The fourteen dharma-pramāṇas (authorities of dharma) are called "caturdaśa-vidyā". The well-known poetic work *Naiṣadham* mentions that Nala was conversant with these fourteen branches of learning. The poet (Śrīharṣa[S]) plays on the word "caturdaśa": he says that "Nala accorded caturdaśa to the caturdaśa-vidyā", meaning he gave the fourteen branches of learning four daśas[2]: reading, understanding what is read, living according to the teachings contained in what is read, and making others also live in accordance with them.

Caturdaśatvam kṛtavān kutaḥ svayam
Na vedmi vidyāsu caturdaśasvapi

—Naiṣadham, 1.4

All religious knowledge is encompassed by these fourteen branches of learning.

There are yet four more vidyās. If you add these to the fourteen already mentioned, you will have eighteen vidyās—aṣṭādaśa-vidyā which are all-inclusive. Of them, the fourteen already mentioned are directly concerned with dharma. The remaining four — Āyurveda, Arthaśāstra, Dhanurveda and Gāndharvaveda[3] —do not directly deal with dharma. They are not dharmasthānas (abodes of dharma) but they qualify to be vidyāsthānas (abodes of knowledge). The first fourteen, as already mentioned, are both dharmasthānas and vidyāsthānas (abodes of dharma as well as abodes of knowledge).

The dharmasthānas and vidyāsthānas are together commonly known as the śāstras. The word "śāstra" means an order or commandment. We speak of a royal "śāsana", meaning a royal "edict". There is a chapter in the Mahābhārata in which Bhīṣma expounds the ordinances of dharma to Yudhiṣṭhira and it is called "Anuśāsana-parva". Aiyanār is called "Śāstā" because he keeps the hosts of Śiva under his control (through his orders). Works on śāstras incorporate the ordinances that are calculated to keep us disciplined and ensure that we tread the right path.

While all the fourteen śāstras are basic and authoritative texts, the Vedas are their crown. Just as Buddhism, Zoroastrianism (Zarathustrianism), Christianity and Islam have the Tripīṭaka, the Zend-Avesta, the Bible and the Qur'ān respectively as their scriptures, we have the Vedas as our prime scripture.

Of the fourteen branches of learning the first four (the four Vedas) form the basis for the subsequent ten. Together they constitute the complete corpus of śāstras on which our religion is founded.

Notes & References

[1] See notes appended to Chapter 4, Part Two

[2] The poet puns on the word "caturdaśa" : it means both "fourteen" and "four stages". See also *The Guru Tradition,* page 184.

[3] The science of life or medicine; political economy; military science, and music.

Chapter 4

Past Glory and Present Shame

The fourteen branches of learning were taught in our country from the remote past until the inception of British rule. Let me tell you something interesting about them. You must have read about the Chinese pilgrims Fa-hsien and Hsüan Tsang. The former visited India early in the fifth century A.D. and the latter in the seventh century A.D. They have both recorded impressions of their travels here and given particularly glowing accounts of the big universities of Nālandā and Takṣaśilā[1]. We learn about these institutions from archaeological investigations also. They were at the peak of their glory when Buddhism flourished in the country. It is noteworthy that the syllabuses of both these universities included the caturdaśa-vidyā. Of course Buddhist religious texts were also taught, but only after the students had learned the fourteen Hindu śāstras. The reason : acquaintance with Vedic learning was a help to any religious community in acquiring knowledge and in character building. The Buddhists thus believed that education to be called education must include a course in the Hindu caturdaśa-vidyā.

In the South also these śāstras were taught at gaṭikāsthānas[2] and other institutions established by the rājās of Tamiḷ Nāḍu. In the copper-plate inscriptions, dated 868 A.D., there is a reference to an educational institution at Bāhur, between Cuddalore and Poṇḍicerri, where it is stated that the fourteen vidyās were taught. Similarly, there was a school at Eṇṇāyiram, between Vizhupuram and Tiṇḍivanam, where the ancient śāstras were part of the syllabus as evidenced by an inscription of Rājendra Coḷa (11th century). There are many more similar examples.

Nowadays considerable research is conducted into Tamiḷ history. It has inspired stories and novels. However, nobody seems to have dealt with the information that I have gained from my own historical inquiries — that the Tamiḷ rulers supported the Vedas and śāstras in a big way. There is much talk about the need for impartiality in all matters and about the importance of having a scientific outlook, but we do not see any evidence of it in practice. The Buddhists were opposed to the Vedas, but they believed that an acquaintance with the fourteen Hindu śāstras was necessary to nurture the intelligence and shape the moral character of the students learning in their institutions. But people here who claim to have faith in our religion (it does not matter that they do nothing to promote our śāstras) maintain silence about the work done by Tamiḷ kings in the past in the cause of Vedic learning.

We have come to such a pass that, if we are asked about our vidyās, we can do no better than keep silent. Indeed we do not even know what is meant by "vidyā". In all likelihood we think it to be jugglery, witchcraft or magic. Vidyā and kalā are the same. Kalā means knowledge that waxes like the moon. Now most people think that "kalā"[3] means only dance.

We must no longer be ignorant of our śāstras or indifferent to them and we must try to be true to ourselves. That is why I want to speak briefly about the fourteen—or eighteen—branches of learning. You must at least learn their names.

Śikṣā, Vyākaraṇa, Mīmāṁsā, and Nyāya[4] are among the fourteen śāstras. You may find these subjects somewhat tiresome and think that they do not serve the Self in any way. But I ask you, what about all your daily activities? How do they help the Self? You take so much time to read the newspaper which has a whole page or two on sports. What purpose does it serve in your daily life? Or, for that matter, in your inward growth?

One day, some years ago, I happened to be in a certain town. It was noontime and, as I went out, I saw a big crowd in front of a shop. The radio was blaring out the news and I was told that the crowd had gathered to listen to it. I asked a passer-by what was so exciting about the news. He said that a cricket match was being played somewhere, some thousands of miles away across the seas in a far-off continent, and that the latest score was being announced.

The fact is that people are prepared to spend their time, money and energy on things they fancy but are of no practical value to them. Now I ask you to take an interest in our śāstras. They are certainly more useful than cricket and such other things. They may not seem to bring you any direct spiritual benefit. While their ultimate purpose is to take us to the path of enlightenment, they are essential to our knowledge and to making us mature.

Knowledge is a treasure and it is a gift of the Lord. If you sharpen it with good education and the spirit of inquiry, the Ultimate Reality will be revealed to you in a flash. Man alone is the recipient of the divine blessing called speech. If it is used wisely he will have an abundance of good will. That is why so many śāstras relating to speech like Vyākaraṇa, Nirukta, Śikṣā have been developed. Everyone of you must have at least a basic knowledge of these subjects.

Notes & References

[1] & [2] For a detailed account of Nālandā, Takṣaśilā and the ghaṭikāsthānas, see *The Guru Tradition*. Ghaṭikāsthānas are Vedic schools or universities which flourished in India in ancient and medieval times.

[3] According to the Paramaguru, the English word "school" (or, for that matter, the French "ecole") is derived from "kalā".

[4] These subjects are dealt with separately in Parts Six, Seven, Twelve and Thirteen.

Chapter 5

The Root of our Religion

The Vedas — Ṛgveda, Yajurveda, Sāmaveda and Atharvaveda— are the first four of the pramāṇas (authoritative texts) of our religion and also the most important. Of the remaining ten, six are Angas[1] of the Vedas and four are Upāngas[2].

Man possesses a number of angas or limbs. In the same way the Vedas personified— the Vedapuruṣa — has six limbs. (It must be noted that the Vedas are also spoken of as Vedamātā, Mother Veda.) The four Upāngas, though not integral to the Vedas, are supporting limbs of the Vedapuruṣa. The Angas, as already stated, are six in number— Sikṣā, Vyākaraṇa, Chandas, Nirukta, Jyotiṣa and Kalpa. The four Upāngas are Mīmāṁsā, Nyāya, Purāṇa and Dharmaśāstra.

The Vedas are of fundamental importance; the Angas and Upāngas derive their importance from them. Āyurveda, Arthaśāstra, Dhanurveda and Gāndharvaveda are called Upavedas, subsidiary Vedas. Their connection with the prime scripture is thus obvious.

The Vedas must be learned along with the Angas and Upāngas. Such a thorough study of the scriptures is called "Sa-Anga-Upānga-adhyayana" (study of the Vedas with the Angas and Upāngas). The term "sāṅgopāṅga", which has come into popular usage, is derived from this. If a speaker deals with a subject thoroughly, whether it be politics or something else, we use the word "sāṅgopāṅga" in describing his performance. The term refers to the ancient caturdaśa-vidyā (the six Angas plus the four Upāngas). We have totally forgotten the old system of education but our culture is so steeped in it that we still use the term (sāṅgopāṅga) to refer to any full-scale treatment or exposition of a subject. The inference is clear. That for centuries the Vedas, together with their Angas and Upāngas, formed such an intimate part of life in the Tamiḷ land that a term associated with this tradition, "sāṅgopāṅga", is still used by the common people there[3]. But the irony of it is that today we do not know even the names of these old śāstras.

The Vedas form the core of our religion and are the direct authority for our dharma and for all our religious practices. They are our Bible, our Qur'ān, our Granth Sāhib. But, of course, the Vedas are far far older than these scriptures of other faiths. All of them originate from truths found in the Vedas. The very word "Veda" connotes what is authoritative. There is a practice of referring to the Bible, the Qur'ān and other scriptures as the "Christian Veda", "Mohammedan Veda", "Pārsi Veda", "Sikh Veda" and so on. Christians in India refer to the Bible as "Satya-Veda".

It is rather difficult to speak about the Vedas as a topic. One does not know where to begin and how to conclude. It is a bewildering task. The magnitude of our scripture is such— and such is its glory.

"Pramāṇam Vedāśca," says the *Āpastamba Dharmasūtra.* The Vedas are indeed the source of all dharmas as well as the authority on which they are founded. A book that has been cherished by the great men of the Tamiḷ country from the earliest times is *Manu-dharma-nūl (Manusmṛti).* Throughout India, Manu's dharmaśāstra is held in the highest esteem. In Tamiḷ Nāḍu there was a king who earned the name of "Manu-nīti-kaṇḍa-Coḷa[T]" for the exemplary manner in which he administered justice. Once a calf got crushed under the wheel of the chariot ridden by his son. The king was so fair and strict that, when the aggrieved cow, the mother of the calf, sought justice, he ordered his son to be crushed to death under the wheel of the same chariot. For us "Manu-nīti-śāstra" *(Manusmṛti)* is the authority on dharma. But does it claim that it is the authority for all dharma? No. "Vedo'khilo dharmamūlam," says Manu, i.e. the Vedas constitute the root of all dharma. They prescribe the dharma for all time, he says.

We must obey the dictates of the Vedas. When we are asked to accept a statement without questioning it, it is customary to remark : "Is that the word of the Vedas?" This confirms the fact that the common people believe that the word of the Vedas, or their injunction, must be obeyed without being questioned. The "Vedavāk" (the word or pronouncement of the Vedas) has been our inviolable law for thousands of years.

References

[1] & [2] These are dealt with in detail in Parts Six to Fifteen.

[3] See Appendix 1.

Chapter 6
Eternal

It is not possible to tell the age of the Vedas. If we say that an object is "anādi"[1] it means that nothing existed before it. Any book, it is reasonable to presume, must be the work of one or more people. The Old Testament contains the sayings of several Prophets. The New Testament contains the story of Jesus Christ as well as his sermons. The Qu'rān incorporates the teachings of the Prophet Mohammed. The founders of such religions are all historical personalities and their teachings did not exist before them. Are the Vedas similarly the work of one or more teachers? And may we take it that these preceptors lived in different periods of history? Ten thousand years ago or a hundred thousand or a million years ago? If the Vedas were created during any of these periods they cannot be claimed to be "anādi". Even if they were created a million years ago, it obviously means that there was a time when they did not exist.

Questions like the above are justified if the Vedas are regarded as the work of mortals. And, if they are, it is wrong to claim that they are "anādi". We think that the Vedas are the creation of the ṛṣis, seers who were mortals. So it is said, at any rate, in the textbooks of history we are taught.

Also consider the fact that the Vedas consist of many "sūktas". Jñānasaṁbandhar's *Tevāram*[T] consists of a number of *patigams*[T]. And just as each *patigam* has ten stanzas, each sūkta consists of a certain number of mantras. "Su + ukta" = "sūkta". The prefix "su" denotes "good" as in "suguṇa" or "sulocana". "Ukta" means "spoken" or "what is spoken". "Sūkta" means "well spoken", a "good word" or a "good utterance" (or "well uttered").

When we chant the Vedas in the manner prescribed by the śāstras, we mention the name of the seer connected with each sūkta, its metre and the deity invoked. Since there are many mantras associated with various seers we think that they were composed by them. We also refer to the ancestry of the seer concerned, his gotra[S], etc. For instance, "Agastyo Maitrāvaruṇiḥ", that is Agastya, the son of Mitra-Varuṇa. Here is another : "Madhucchanda Vaiśvāmitraḥ", the sage Madhucchanda descended from the Viśvāmitra gotra. Like this there are mantras in the names of many sages. If the mantra connected with the name of Agastya were composed by him it could not have existed during the time of Mitra-Varuṇa; similarly that in the name of Madhucchanda could not have existed during the time of Viśvāmitra. If this is true, how can you claim that the Vedas are "anādi"?

Since the mantras are associated with the names of sages, we make the wrong inference that they must have been composed by them. But it is not so as a matter of fact. "Apauruṣeya" means not the work of any man. Were the Vedas composed by one or more human beings, even if they were ṛṣis, they would be called "pauruṣeya". But since they are called "apauruṣeya" it follows that even the seers could not have *created* them. If they were composed by the seers they (the latter) would be called "mantra-kartās" which means "those who 'created' the mantras". But, as a matter of fact, the ṛṣis are called "mantra-drasṭās," those who "saw" them.

When we say that Columbus discovered America we do not mean that he created that continent: we mean that he merely made the continent known to the world. In the same way the laws attributed to Newton, Einstein and so on were not created by them. If an object thrown up falls to earth it is not because Newton said so. Scientists like Newton perceived the laws of nature and revealed them to the world. Similarly, the seers discovered the mantras and made a gift of them to the world. These mantras had existed before the time of their fathers, grandfathers, great-grandfathers... But they had remained unknown to the world. The seers now revealed them to mankind. So it became customary to mention their names at the time of intoning them.

The publisher of a book is not necessarily its author. The man who releases a film need not be its producer. The seers disclosed the mantras to the world but they did not create them. Though the mantras had existed before them they performed the noble service of revealing them to us. So it is appropriate on our part to pay them obeisance by mentioning their names while chanting the same.

Do we know anything about the existence of the mantras before they were "seen" by the ṛṣis? If they are eternal does it mean that they manifested themselves at the time of creation? Were they present before man's appearance on earth? How did they come into being?

If we take it that the Vedas appeared with creation, it would mean that the Paramātman created them along with the world. Did he write them down and leave them somewhere to be discovered by the seers later? If so, they cannot be claimed to be anādi. We have an idea of when Brahmā created the present world.

There are fixed periods for the four yugas or eons, Kṛta, Tretā, Dvāpara and Kali. The four yugas together are called a caturyuga. A thousand caturyugas make one daytime of Brahmā and another equally long period is his night. According to this reckoning Brahmā is now more than fifty years old. Any religious ceremony is to be commenced with a saṁkalpa[S] ("resolve") in which an account is given of the time and place of its performance in such and such a year of Brahmā, in such and such a month, in such and such a fortnight (waxing or waning moon), etc. From this account we know when the present Brahmā came into being. Even if we concede that he made his appearance millions and millions of years ago, he cannot be claimed to be anādi. How can then creation be said to have no beginning in time? When creation itself has an origin, how do we justify the claim that the Vedas are anādi?

The Paramātman, being eternal, was present even before creation when there was no Brahmā. The Paramātman, the Brahman or the Supreme Godhead, is eternal. The cosmos, all sentient beings and insentient objects, emerged from him. The Paramātman did not create them himself : he did so through the agency of Brahmā. Through Viṣṇu he sustains them and through Rudra he destroys them. Later Brahmā, Viṣṇu and Rudra are themselves destroyed by him. The present Brahmā, when he becomes a hundred years old, will unite with the Paramātman. Another Brahmā will appear and he will start the work of creation all over again. The question arises : Does the Paramātman create the Vedas before he brings into being another Brahmā?

We learn from the śāstras that the Vedas had existed even before creation. In fact, they say, Brahmā performed his function of creation with the aid of the Vedic mantras. I shall be speaking to you about this later, how he accomplished creation with the mantras manifested as sound. In the passage dealing with creation, the *Bhāgavata* also says that Brahmā created the world with the Vedas.

Is this the reason (that Brahmā created the world with the Vedic mantras) why it is said that the Vedas are anādi? Is it right to take such a view on the basis that both the Vedas and Īśvara are anādi? If we suggest that Īśvara had produced these scriptures even before he created the world, it would mean that there was a time when the Vedas did not exist and that would contradict the claim that they are anādi.

If we believe that both Īśvara and the Vedas are anādi it would mean that Īśvara could not have created them. But if you believe that Īśvara created them, they cannot be said to be without an origin. Everything has its origin in Īśvara. It would be wrong to maintain [according to this logic] that both Īśvara and the Vedas have no beginning in time. Well, it is all so confusing.

What is the basis of the belief that the Vedas are anādi and were not created by Īśvara? An answer is contained in the Vedas themselves. In the *Bṛhadāraṇyaka Upaniṣad* (2.4.10)[2] — the Upaniṣads are all part of the Vedas — it is said that the Ṛg, Yajus and Sāma Vedas are the very breath of Īśvara. The word "niḥśvasitam" is used here.

It goes without saying that we cannot live even a moment without breathing. The Vedas are the life-breath of the Paramātman who is an eternal living Reality. It follows that the Vedas exist together with him as his breath.

We must note here that it is not customary to say that the Vedas are the creation of Īśvara. Do we create our own breath? Our breath exists from the very moment we are born. It is the same case with Īśvara and the Vedas. We cannot say that he created them.

When Vidyāraṇyasvāmin[3] wrote his commentary on the Vedas he prayed to his guru regarding him as Īśvara. He used these words in his prayer : "Yasya niḥśvasitam Vedāḥ" (whose — that is Īśvara's — breath constitutes the Vedas). The word "niḥśvasitam" occurs in the Upaniṣads also. Here too it is not stated that Īśvara created the Vedas.

The Lord says in the Gītā[4]: "It is I who am known by all the Vedas "(Vedaiśca sarvair aham eva vedyaḥ)". Instead of describing himself as "Vedakṛd" (creator of the Vedas), he calls himself "Vedāntakṛd" (creator of the philosophical system that is the crown of the Vedas). He also refers to himself as "Vedavid" (he who knows the Vedas). Before Vedānta that enshrines great philosophical truths had been made known to mankind, the Vedas had existed in the form of sound, as the very breath of Īśvara — they were (and are) indeed Īśvara dwelling in Īśvara.

The *Bhāgavata* too, like the Gītā, does not state that the Lord created the Vedas. It declares that they occurred in a flash in his heart, that they came to him in a blaze of light. The word used in this context is "sphuraṇam", occurring in the mind in a flash. Now we cannot apply this word to anything that is created anew, anything that did not exist before. Brahmā is the primordial sage who saw all the mantras. But it was the Paramātman who revealed them to him. Did he transmit them orally? No, says the *Bhāgavata.* The Paramātman imparted the Vedas to Brahmā through his heart : "Tene Brahma hṛdā ya Ādikavaye"[5], says the very first verse of that Purāṇa. The Vedas were not created by the Paramātman. The truth is that they are always present in his heart. When he merely resolved to pass on the Vedas to Brahmā the latter instantly received them. And with their sound he began the work of creation.

The Tamiḷ *Tevāram*[T] describes Īśvara as *"Vediyā, Vedagitā".* It says that the Lord keeps singing the hymns of the various śākhās or recensions of the Vedas. How are we to understand the statement that the "Lord sings the Vedas"? Breathing itself is music. Our out-breath is called "haṁsa-gīta". Thus, the Vedas are the music of the Lord's breath. The *Tevāram* goes on : "Wearing the sacred thread and the holy ashes, and bathing all the time, Īśvara keeps singing the Vedas." The impression one has from this description is that the Lord is a great "ghanapāṭhin"[S]. Apparsvāmigal[T] refers to the ashes resembling milk applied to the body of Īśvara which is like coral. He says that the Lord "chants" the Vedas, "sings" them, not that he creates (or created) them. In the Vaiṣṇava *Divyaprabandham*[T] too there are many references to Vedic sacrifices. But somehow I do not remember any reference in it to the Lord chanting the Vedas.

In the story of Gajendramokṣa[6] told by Puhazhendi Pulavar[T] (a Tamiḷ Vaiṣṇava saint - poet), the elephant whose leg is caught in the jaws of the crocodile cries in anguish. *"Ādimūlame"* [vocative in Tamiḷ of Ādimūla, the Primordial Lord]. The Lord thereupon appears, asking "What?" The poet says that Mahāviṣṇu "stood before the Vedas" *("Vedattin mun ninrān").* According to the poet the Lord stood in front of the Vedas, not that he appeared at a time earlier than the scriptures. The Tamiḷ for "A man stood at the door" is *"vīṭṭin mun ninrān".* So *"Vedattin mun ninrān"* should be understood as "he stood at the commencement of all the Vedas". Another idea occurs to me. How is Perumāḷ[T] (Viṣṇu or any Vaiṣṇava deity) taken in procession? Preceding the utsava-mūrti (processional deity) are the devotees reciting the *Tiruvāymozhi*[T]. And behind the processional deity is the group reciting the Vedas. Here too we may say that the Lord stood before the Vedas (*"Vedattin mun ninrān").*

In the Vaiṣṇava Āgamas[S] and Purāṇas, Mahāviṣṇu is referred to specially as "Yajñasvarūpin" (one personifying the sacrifice) and as "Vedasvarūpin" (one who personifies the Vedas). Garuḍa is also called "Vedasvarūpa". But none of these texts is known to refer to Viṣṇu as the creator of the Vedas.

It is only in the "Puruṣasūkta", occurring in the Vedas themselves, that the Vedas are said to have been "born" "(ajāyata)". However, this hymn is of symbolical and allegorical significance and not to be understood in a literal sense. It states that the Parama-Puruṣa (the Supreme Being) was sacrificed as an animal and that it was in this sacrifice that creation itself was accomplished. It was at this time that the Vedas also made their appearance. How are we to understand the statement that the Parama-Puruṣa was offered as a sacrificial animal ? Not in a literal sense. In this sacrifice the season of spring was offered as an oblation (āhuti) instead of ghee : summer served the purpose of samidhs (firesticks); autumn was havis[S] (oblation). Only those who meditate on the mantras and become absorbed in them will know their meaning inwardly as a matter of experience. So we cannot construe the statement literally that the Vedas were "born".

To the modern mind the claim that the breath of Īśvara is manifested in the form of sound seems nonsensical, also that it was with this sound that Brahmā performed his function of creation. But on careful reflection you will realise that the belief is based on a great scientific truth.

I do not mean to say that we must accept the Vedas only if they conform to present-day science. Nor do I think that our scripture, which proclaims the truth of the Paramātman and is beyond the reach of science and scientists, ought to be brought within the ken of science. Many matters pertaining to the Vedas may not seem to be in conformity with science and for that reason they are not to be treated as wrong. But our present subject—how the breath of the Paramātman can become sound and how the function of creation can be carried out with it — is in keeping with science.

Notes & References

1 "Anādi" literally means "without a beginning". But this meaning is ambiguous with reference to the Vedas. As applied to our scripture it means "existing from eternity", that is without any origin. For the sake of convenience the term "anādi" is used in this book without its English equivalent given every time.

2 Sa yathā'rdraidhāgnerabhyāhitātpṛthagdhūmā viniścarantyevaṁ vā are'sya mahato bhūtasya nihśvasitametadyadṛgvedo Yajurvedo Sāmavedo' tharvāṅgirasa itihāsaḥ purāṇam vidyopaniṣadaḥ ślokāḥ sūtrāṇyanuvyākhyānāni vyākhyānānyasyaivaitāni niḥśvasitāni.

— Bṛhadāraṇyaka Upaniṣad, 2.4.10.

3 Vidyāraṇyasvāmin was a polymath and was the founder of the Vijayanagara Empire (1336). When he is spoken of as the commentator of the Vedas, Vidyāraṇyasvāmin is noted along with his younger brother Sāyaṇācārya, the actual producer of the commentary.

4 *Sarvasya cā'ham hṛdi saṁniviṣṭo*
Mattaḥ smṛtirjñānam apohanaṁ ca
Vedaiśca sarvair aham eva vedyo
Vedāntakṛd Vedavid eva cā'ham

— Bhagavadgītā, 15.15.

5 *Janmādyasya yato'nvayāditarataścārtheṣvabhijñaḥ svarāt*
Tene Brahma hṛdā ya Ādikavaye muhyanti yatsūrayaḥ
Tejovārimṛdām yathā vinimayo yatra trisargo' mṛṣā
Dhāmnā svena sadā nirastakuhakam satyam param dhīmahi

— Bhāgavata, 1.1.

6 The famous story of Viṣṇu saving an elephant-king from the jaws of a crocodile. It is told to illustrate how the Lord is ever anxious to come to the rescue of his devotees.

Chapter 7

Sound and Creation

[This chapter must be read in conjunction with Chapter 8, Part Three, and Chapter 13 of this part.]

What is sound? According to modern science, it is vibration. "If you examine the core of an atom you will realise that all matter is one." This Advaitic conclusion is arrived at according to nuclear science and the concepts of Einstein. All this world is one flood of energy (śakti); everything is an electro-magnetic flow. But how do we account for the manifestation of different objects? It is to be attributed to different types of vibrations.

Where there is a vibration there is a sound. Conversely, to produce a sound the vibration corresponding to it must also be created. The scientific concept that the different vibrations of the same energy are the cause of creation is the same as the belief that the world was created with the breath of the Paramātman manifesting itself as the sound of the Vedas.

Consider human beings and other creatures. What is it that determines their health and feelings? The breath that passes through our nāḍis[S], blood vessels[1], during respiration produces vibrations and on them depends the state of our health. Those who keep their breathing under control through the practice of yoga are healthy to an amazing degree. They do not bleed even if their veins are cut. They are able to remain buried in the earth in samādhi[S] stopping their pulse and heartbeat. They are not poisoned even if they are bitten by a snake or stung by a scorpion. The reason is that they keep the vibrations of the nāḍis under control during breathing.

Breath is vital not only to the body but also to the mind. The mind which is the source of thought and the vital (prāṇik) energy that is the source of breath are the same. Healthy or unhealthy thoughts are to be attributed to different vibrations of the nāḍis. You may test this for yourself. See for yourself how you breathe when you are at peace before the sanctum of a deity or in the presence of a great and wise person and how you breathe when your mind is quickened by desire or anger. The happiness you experience when you take part in something divine, like a *bhajan* or a temple festival, must be different from the pleasure that sensual gratification gives you: the vibrations of the nāḍis concerned will also be correspondingly different.

When you experience joy of an elevated kind the passage of breath will be through the right nostril, but when you are enjoying sensual pleasure it will be through the left. When you meditate, with increasing concentration, on the Reality Serene which is the source of all your urges and feelings, the breath will pass through both nostrils slowly, evenly and rhythmically. When you are absorbed in the object of your meditation breathing itself will cease, but there will still be life. The great awareness called jñāna will then be in bloom as it were.

The inert body of a man and the awareness that is the vital essence of his life are both dependent on the course of his breathing. They grow or decay according to it. The course of a man's breath keeps his inner vibrations in order.

Is it not from the Paramātman that so many countless inert objects and so many sentient beings have originated and grown? The movements appropriate to these should have also occurred in the Ultimate Object that is the Paramātman.

Even according to non-dualism, the Brahman that is utterly still and is unconditioned and has no attributes (nirguṇa) manifests itself in the countless disguises of this cosmos with the power of Māyā,[S] Māyā that cannot be described. Disguises or no disguises, we have to concede the existence, in a mundane sense, of the inert world and of the sentient beings. But we must remember that even Māyā has its source in Īśvara who is "Māyin". But the power of Māyā apart, all that we see have arisen from the vibrations in the Object called the Parabrahman. At the same time, with all these vibrations, this Object remains still and tranquil inwardly. This stillness notwithstanding, there are movements that are apparent to our perception. They are not disorderly movements but constitute a system embracing vast heavenly bodies like the sun at the one end and the tiniest of insects on the other or even something as humble as a blade of grass.

It is this orderliness that goes to make worldly life happy. The Paramātman has created this by bringing all powers of nature within an orderly system. But if you sometimes see flaws in it and the natural forces going against us, it is because he likes to be playful now and then.

The human mind can go astray to any length. Indeed it keeps wandering aimlessly like a goblin or an imp. Whatever the extent to which cosmic life is orderly, it (the human mind) breaks free from all control and runs about like a mad dog.

When the powers of nature are unfavourable to us, is there a way to change their behaviour and make them favourable to us? Is there also a means by which our mind could be brought under control when it goes haywire? If everything is caused by vibration, by sound, there must be a way of making the forces of nature favourable to us and of purifying our mind and bringing it under control through this very sound. The Vedas constitute such sound.

By controlling our breath through the practice of yoga, it is possible to gain access to the breath of the Paramātman and by this means perform such actions as can uplift our own Self as well as mankind. Here the vibrations of the nāḍis do not produce the sound that is audible to us. Science tells us that there are sounds outside the range of human hearing in the same way as there is light that does not pass through the lens of the human eye.

However, it is possible to bring within us (within our reach) that which is without. When a musician sings on the radio, the sound of his music is converted into electromagnetic waves which travel through space. But how do we hear the music? The receiving set captures the electromagnetic waves and reconverts them into sound waves.

(Science is not opposed to religion. It seems to me that it even helps in the growth of religion. A century ago[2], before the radio and the telephone were invented, it would not have been easy to counter the arguments of an atheist who dismisses claims made on behalf of the sound of the Vedas as absurd. Now the discoveries of science have come to our rescue.)

It is possible for humans to earn the power or energy possessed by such an inert object as the radio set. Indeed we can earn much more, do much more. It is tapas[S], ascetic endeavour, that will give us such energy. What is tapas? It is the determination to find the truth: it is keeping the mind one-pointed in this search, forsaking food, sleep, home, everything. But when you are a seeker like this, you must remain humble and erase the least trace of egoism in you. You must realise that the truth you seek will be revealed to you only with the grace of Īśvara. The sages performed austerities in this manner and attained to the highest plane of yoga. They could perceive the vibrations in creation, that is the course taken by the breath of the Supreme Godhead. Besides, they also knew them as sound capable of being heard by the human ear in the same manner as electric waves converted into sound waves. It is these sounds that they have passed on to us as the mantras of the Vedas.

The Vedas are called "Śruti." That which is heard is Śruti. "Śrotra" means the "ear". The Vedas have been handed down orally from generation to generation and have not been taught or learned from any written text. That is how they got the name of "Śruti". Why were these scriptures not permitted to be written down? Because the sound of the Vedas cannot be properly transcribed. There are sounds or phonemes that cannot be accurately represented in any script. For instance, the one between "zha" and "ḷa". Such sounds have to be learned by listening. Besides there are svaras for Vedic mantras (tonal variations, proper accentuation): "udātta" (raised syllable), "anudātta" (lowered syllable) and "svarita" (falling syllable)[S]. Mistakes in enunciation are likely even if diacritical or some other marks are used in the printed text. Wrong chanting will not bring the desired results. There is much difference in the vibrations caused by pronouncing a syllable laying stress on it and pronouncing it without any stress. Correspondingly, there will be changes in our feelings and urges and the divine forces that rule nature. There is a story in the *Taittirīya Saṁhitā* of the Vedas which illustrates how wrong chanting can produce results contrary to what is intended. Tvaṣṭā, the divine carpenter, chanted a mantra with the object of begetting a son who would be the slayer of Indra. But he went wrong in the intonation of some syllables. So, unwittingly, he prayed for a son who would be slain by Indra instead of one who would slay that celestial. And his prayer (that had gone wrong in the intonation) was answered. When the wavelength shifts even minutely on our radio we receive the broadcast of a different transmitting station. Fine-tuning has to be done to get the required station. So is the case with the intonation of Vedic mantras. There should not be the slightest mistake in the svaras[S]. Just as we receive a different station on our radio when the wavelength is changed, so the result is different when we go wrong in the intonation.

This is the reason why it is of the utmost importance to learn the Vedas by listening — hence the name "Śruti", in Tamiḷ "*Ezhutākkiḷavī*" (unwritten old text). Another explanation occurs to me for the name "Śruti". The sages heard, did they not, the sound of the divine vibrations that cannot be perceived by the common people? Did they read the Vedas in any book or did they compose them themselves? Śruti is an apt name for the Vedas since they were made known to the world after they had been first heard by the sages.

The Vedic seers have the name of "mantra-draṣṭās" -- a "draṣṭā" is one who sees. In Tamiḷ it is "*pārppavan*". "*Pārppān*" also means the same thing. If the sages "saw" the mantras it would mean that they did not "hear" them. Which of the two versions is correct? Did the sages see the mantras or did they hear them? If they saw them, in what script did they appear? There was no script at the time, neither Devanāgarī nor Grantha[S] nor Brāhmī, the basis of all. But, then, the sound of the Vedas, their svaras, cannot be truly written down in any script.

The answer to this problem is that when the sages were meditating the mantras of the Vedas appeared to them in a flash in their hearts. It may be that in this state of theirs they could neither see nor hear anything. The mantras must have appeared in a flash in the inner recesses of their minds.

"Seeing" or "looking" does not denote merly what is perceived by the eye. It is a term that covers a variety of perceptions and experiences. When we say that a man has "seen" all sorrows in his life, does the term "seen" imply only what he "saw" with his eyes? Does it not mean what he has "experienced"? The term "mantra-draṣṭā" also could be taken in a similar manner as referring to what is perceived through experience. It is further believed that the sages were able to hear the Vedas with their divine ears.

Arjuna wished to see the Lord's cosmic form (visvarūpa). The Gītā has it that Krṣṇa Paramātman said to him[3]: "You will not be able to see my cosmic form with this eye of yours. I will give you a celestial eye...."

Just as Arjuna was endowed by the Lord with a divine eye, the sages must have been invested with celestial ears to grasp the sound emanating from the Paramātman and pervading the vast space.

The vibrations of the Vedas serve the purpose not only of creation and the conduct of life. There are indeed Vedic mantras that help us to transcend this life and become one with the Ultimate Truth. When a man returns by the same way as he comes, does he not arrive at the starting point? In the same way when we go seeking how creation came about, we are led to the point where there are no vibrations, no movements, where there is utter stillness. Some mantras that create vibrations in our nāḍis accomplish the same noble task of taking us to such a goal. Such are the Upaniṣadic mahāvākyas[4] and Praṇava[5].

In sum, the Vedas are not anyone's compositions. The sages did not create them, nor were they inscribed by the Paramātman on palm-leaves.

Notes & References

[1] The term "nāḍi" also denotes a nerve.

[2] "Wireless telegraphy" or the "radio" was born in 1901 while the telephone was first patented in 1876. But we must remember that this discourse was given long before 1976.

[3] Na tu māṁ śakyase draṣṭum anen'aiva svacakṣuṣā
Divyaṁ dadāmi te cakṣuḥ paśya me yogam aiśvaram

— Bhagavadgīta, 11.8

[4] The "mahāvākyās" will be dealt with in the chapter on the Upaniṣads.

Chapter 8

Western Vedic Research

In the present sorry state in which the nation finds itself it has to learn about its own heritage like the Vedas from the findings of Western scholars called "orientalists" and from Indians conducting research on the same lines as they. I concede that European scholars have made a very valuable study of the Vedas. We must be thankful to them for their work. Some of them like Max Müller[1] conducted research out of their esteem for our scriptures. They took great pains to gather the old texts and published volume after volume incorporating their findings.

Two hundred years ago Sir William Jones[2], who was a judge of the Calcultta high court, started the Asiatic Society. The number of books this institution has published on Vedic subjects should arouse our wonder. With the help of the East India Company, Sir William published the Ṛgveda with the commentary of Sāyaṇa and also a number of other Hindu works. Apart from Englishmen, indologists from France, Germany and Russia have also done outstanding work here. "The discovery of the Vedas of the Hindus is more significant than Columbus's discovery of America," thus exclaimed some indologists exulting in their findings.

These foreigners discovered Vedic and Vedāntic texts from various parts of the country. They translated the dharma-, gṛhya- and śrauta-sūtras[3]. The Kuṇḍalinī Tantra gained importance only after Arthur Avalon[4] had written extensively on it. A number of Westerners have contributed studies of other aspects of our culture also. It was because of the Protection of Ancient Monuments Act that came into force during the viceroyalty of Lord Curzon[5] that our temples and other monuments were saved from vandals. Fergusson[6] took photographs of our artistic treasures (sculptures) and made them known to the world. Men like Cunningham[7], Sir John Marshall and Mortimer-Wheeler[8] did notable work in Indian archaeology. It was because of the labours of Mackenizie[9] who gathered manuscripts from various parts of India that we have come to know about many of our śāstras. The department of epigraphy was started during British rule.

We suffered in many ways at the hands of the British but it was during their time that some good was also done. But this good was not unmixed and had undesirable elements in it. The intention of many of those who called themselves orientalists or indologists was not above reproach. They wanted to reconstruct the history of India on the basis of their study of the Vedas and, in the course of this, they concocted the Āryan-Dravīḍian theory of races and sowed the seeds of hatred among the people. Purporting to be rationalists they wrongly interpreted, in an allegorical manner, what cannot be comprehended by our senses. In commenting on the Vedas they took the view that the sages were primitive men. Though some of them pretended to be impartial, their hidden intention in conducting research into our religious texts was to propagate Christianity and show Hinduism in a poor light.

A number of Westerners saw the similarity between Sanskrit and their own languages and devoted themselves to comparative philology[10].

We may applaud European indologists for their research work, for making our śāstras known to a wider world and for the hard work they put in. But they were hardly in sympathy with our view of the Vedas. What is the purpose of these scriptures? By chanting them, by filling the world with their sound and by the performance of rites like sacrifices, the good of mankind is ensured. This view the Western indologists rejected. They tried to understand on a purely intellectual plane what is beyond the comprehension of the human mind. And with this limited understanding of theirs they printed big tomes on the Vedas to be preserved in the libraries. Our scriptures are meant to be a living reality of our speech and action. Instead of putting them to such noble use, to consign them to the libraries, in the form of books, is like keeping living animals in the museum instead of in the zoo.

Notes & References

[1] Friedrich Max Müller (1823-1900) was born in Germany but spent most of his working years in England. He is perhaps the best-known Western indologist. Here is one of his oft-quoted pronouncements on India: "If we were to look over the whole world to find out the country most richly endowed with all the wealth, power and beauty that nature can bestow—in some parts a very paradise on earth — I should point to India. If I were asked under what sky the human mind has most fully developed some of its choicest gifts, has most deeply pondered over the greatest problems of life, and has found solutions to some of them which will deserve the attention even of those who have studied Plato and Kant — I should point to India. And if I were to ask myself from what literature, we here in Europe, we who have been nurtured almost exclusively on the thoughts of Greeks and Romans, and of one Semitic race, the Jewish, may draw the corrective which is most wanted in order to make our inner life more perfect, more comprehensive, more universal, in fact more truly human a life, not for this life only, but a transfigured and eternal life — again I should point to India."

Despite all his apparent admiration for Hindu thought Max Müller wanted the British to propagate Christianity in India.

[2] Sir William Jones (1746-94), a pioneer in indology, landed in Madras on September 1, 1783. The Asiatic Society was founded in the following year. Sir William was the first to translate *Śākuntalam* into a European language and it had a profound impact on European thinkers and poets.

[3] These sūtras will be dealt with separately in Part Fifteen.

[4] Arthur Avalon (Sir John Woodroffe) made an important contribution to Tāntric studies and to the literature of the Śākta system early in this century. His *The Serpent Power* is particularly famous.

[5] Lord Curzon was viceroy of India between 1899 and 1905.

[6] James Fergusson's *The History of Indian and Eastern Architecture* contains photographs of 3,000 Indian monuments and was published in the seventies of the last century.

[7] To Sir Alexander Cunningham we owe some of the most remarkable archaeological discoveries in India. He came to this country in 1833 and spent more than 50 years here.

[8] Sir John Marshall and Sir Mortimer-Wheeler contributed to our knowledge of the Indus (or Harappan) civilization. The excavations were carried out in the 1920s. There were also a couple of distinguished Indian archaeologists associated with this work.

[9] Colonel Colin Mackenizie was the first surveyor-general of India. In the late 18th and the early 19th centuries he made a prodigious collection of manuscripts and inscriptions (mainly South Indian). He was also interested in ancient Hindu mathematics.

[10] It was Sir William Jones who first discovered the affinities between Sanskrit and the classical languages of Europe. He was thus the father of comparative philology.

Chapter 9

Date of the Vedas : Inquiry not Proper

The idea that the Vedas are eternal does not fit into the mental outlook of Western indologists. Their claims to impartiality and to conducting research in a scientific manner notwithstanding, they are not prepared to accord an elevated status to the Hindu texts. Many Hindu research scholars have also found themselves unable to accept the view that the Vedas are eternal.

Modern historians have adopted chiefly two methods to determine the date of the Vedas: the first is based on the astronomical references in the scripture and the second on the morphology of the language of the same. But have they, using either method, come to any definite conclusion? Each investigator has arrived at a different age. Tilak[1] has assigned the date 6000 B.C. to the Vedas. According to some others it is 3000 B.C or 1500 B.C.

There is no difference of opinion among historians about the dates of the scriptures of other religions. They are agreed that the Buddhist Tripīṭaka was written during the time of Aśoka but that the teachings of the Buddha included in it belong to an earlier time. There is similar unanimity of view in that the New Testament is 2,000 years old. And all are agreed that the Qur'ān was composed 1,300 years ago. In the case of the Vedas alone have historians not arrived at a decisive date.

I mentioned that two methods were adopted in reckoning the age of the Vedas. There are references in these scriptures to the position of certain heavenly bodies. The date of the Vedas, fixed at 6000 B.C. or so, is based on an astronomical conjunction mentioned in them.

But is it right to say that such an astronomical conjunction would not have occurred earlier too? Conjunctions similar to the one on the basis of which the date of 6000 B.C. has been arrived at must have occurred not only before the present creation but even far far earlier. Which of these is to be taken as the one mentioned in the Vedas? The sages had a vision that could penetrate through the eons. So such calculations will not hold in the case of the Vedas which the great sages brought together with their trans-sensual powers of perception. We find thus that the internal astronomical "evidence" found in the Vedas and made much of by modern researchers does not help in fixing their date.

The second method is linguistic. Here we have to consider not only the language but also the script. Brāhmī is the source of all the scripts in use today in most parts of the country. Devanāgarī and the Tamiḷ scripts may seem totally unrelated, but the fact is otherwise. A study has been conducted on the changes the Brāhmī script has undergone during all these centuries on the basis of the edicts found throughout the land. A chart made from the results of this study shows that the scripts in use today in different parts of the country, though seemingly unrelated, were evolved from the original Brāhmī. An amusing thought occurs to me that the scripts prevalent today are Brāhmī letters with moustaches and horns. Something like a moustache affixes itself to the middle of Brāhmī letters. The Devanāgarī उ and ऊ (u and ū) appear similarly formed. Many letters of the Tamiḷ alphabet look like Brāhmī letters that have sprung horns. From the edicts and inscriptions we can find out with some precision the period taken for each alteration in the script. It is in this manner that the dates of some edicts have been determined.

The Vedas, however, have never been inscribed on stone anywhere. So there is no question of our fixing their date on the basis of any of the scripts. Other aspects of language have to be considered in this context. The morphology of words and the character of their sound keep changing with time. Many Tamiḷ words belonging to the Saṁgam period[2] have changed thus. It is a phenomenon common to all languages. An erosion takes place in the case of some sounds. Sometimes their meaning also does not remain the same. Take the Tamiḷ word "*veguḷī*" : it now means a "simpleton", but earlier it meant "anger" or "an angry man". In the old days the Tamiḷ "*māṇḍa*" did not mean "dead" : a Tamiḷ scholar told me that it meant "famous". Such instances are to be met with in Sanskrit also. We do not undersand the Vedas in the same way as later poetical works in Sanskrit. Compared to other languages such changes are not numerous in our own tongues. Even an Englishman cannot follow one line of Anglo-Saxon English (Old English) which is only 1,000 years old. In the course of about 300 years English has changed so much in America as to merit a name of its own, "American English".

The period over which a phoneme changes its character has been calculated. But the time taken for a change in the meaning of a word has not been determined with the same definiteness. Scholars have tried to fix the date of the Vedas by examining the character of the sound of their words. "Every two hundred years the sound of a word undergoes such and such a change," observes one authority on linguistics. "A Vedic sound, in the form we know it today, is the result of a number of mutations. If it has undergone ten mutations, it means that the Vedas are 2,000 years old. Or, if thirty, they are 30 x 200 = 6,000 years old, which would mean [according to this logic] that our scripture did not exist before 4000 B.C." We hear such views expressed frequently.

One example would be enough to prove how wrong such a basis of calculation is to fix the date of the Vedas.

We have so many utensils at home. We use some of them more often than others. The bell-metal vessel in which we cook rice morning and evening has to be washed twice a day. So it wears faster. Suppose we have another vessel, quite a big one, an *aṇḍā*[3] for instance. It is kept in the store-room and not used except perhaps during a wedding or some other festive occasion. Since it is washed only at infrequent intervals, it does not wear as fast as the bell-metal vessel which we perhaps bought as recently as last year. The *aṇḍā* must have come as part of grandmother's dowry and must be very old. Even so, it does not show any sign of wear. Are we to infer that the bell-metal pot was bought before the *aṇḍā*? The dinner-plate and the rosewater sprinkler came together as your daughter-in-law's dowry. In ten years, the plate has gone out of shape but the sprinkler still retains its glitter and polish.

The same is the case with the sounds of the words of everyday speech on the one hand and of Vedic words on the other, the difference between them being similar to that between the two types of vessels mentioned above. Words in common daily use undergo erosion in many ways. Though the Vedas are chanted every day special care is taken to preserve the original sound of their words. I shall tell you later about the Vedāngas, Śikṣā and Vyākaraṇa[4], and about how a system was devised by our forefathers to preserve the sound of each Vedic syllable from undergoing any mutation. The Vedic sounds are not subject to erosion like the utensils in daily use or the words in common speech. They are like the *aṇḍā* which, though old, is well preserved.

Modern indologists have also put forward the view that the Ṛgveda is the oldest of the Vedas, that the Yajurveda, the Sāmaveda and the Atharvaveda came later (in that order). They also believe that in each recension or śākhā of a particular Veda, the Saṁhitā is the oldest part, the Brāhmaṇa and Āraṇyaka being of later origin. They try to fix the dates of these different texts on the basis of the differences in their language. Also they have carried out research into how certain words used in the Vedas are seen in a different form in the Rāmāyaṇa, the Mahābhārata and in the works of poets like Kālidāsa.

The linguistic research conducted by these indologists will not yield true results because they ignore the basic differences that I have pointed out between the sound of the Vedas and that of other works. The slight changes perceived today in certain Vedic sounds, despite all the care taken to preserve them in the original form, could not have come about in 200 years but over some thousands of years. If you realise that the "wear and tear" we speak of cannot apply to the Vedas but may be to other works or to spoken languages, you will agree that to fix the date of the Vedas, as modern indologists have tried to do, is not right.

Hindī is only some centuries old. However, since it is spoken in a large area and contains Sanskrit, Arabic and Persian words, it has changed in a comparatively short period. Tamiḷ, though spoken in a smaller region, has not changed so much. Even so you will not understand Kamban's[T] Rāmāyaṇa to the same extent as you will the songs of Tāyumānavar[T]. As for Jñānasambandhar's *Tevāram*[T] itself you will not understand it as easily as Kamban's Rāmāyaṇa. And then there is the *Tirumurugaṟṟupaḍai*[T] which is more difficult than the *Tevāram*. So Tamiḷ has also not remained the same all these centuries. Though Sanskrit was known all over India it was not a spoken language like Hindī or Tamiḷ. It was a literary language and has not changed even to the extent Tamiḷ has. As for the Vedas, they have been preserved with greater care than the poetical works and it is rarely that you see changes in them. So, according to linguistic experts, if it takes 1,000 years for certain changes to occur in other languages, it should take 100,000 years for the same in the Vedas.

The Vedas have been preserved with the utmost care in the firm belief that the mantras will be efficacious only if each syllable is chanted with precision so far as its sound and textual correctness are concerned. It was for this purpose that a separate caste was assigned with the mission of caring for them. Research conducted without realising this truth will not serve any purpose. Modern investigations have not succeeded in establishing that the Vedas are not eternal. Faith in the belief that they are anādi will be strengthened if you appreciate the care with which they have been preserved during all these ages and also consider the different ways in which their sound has been kept alive.

Notes & References

1 Lokamānya Bāl Gangādhar Tilak discusses the date of the Vedas in his book, *The Orion*. In his Preface to this work, Tilak says: "... as I was reading the Bhagavadgītā it occurred to me that we might derive important conclusions from the statement of Kṛṣṇa that he 'was Mārgaśīrṣa of the months'." He further says that he has "endeavoured to show.... that the traditions recorded in the Ṛgveda unmistakably point to a period *not later* than 4000 B.C. when the vernal equinox was in Orion". (Orion is the Greek name of Mṛgaśīrṣa.)

2 Saṁgam poetry is believed to belong to the second or third centuries A.D., if not earlier.

3 Usually a copper boiler.

4 See Parts Six and Seven.

Chapter 10

Methods of Chanting

Our forefathers devised a number of methods to preserve the unwritten Vedas in their original form, to safeguard their tonal and verbal purity. They laid down rules to make sure that not a syllable was changed in chanting, not a svara[S] was altered. In this way they ensured that the full benefits were derived from intoning the mantras. They fixed the time taken to enunciate each syllable of a word and called this unit of time or time interval "mātrā[S]". How we must regulate our breathing to produce the desired vibration in a particular part of our body so that the sound of the syllable enunciated is produced in its pure form: even this is determined in the Vedānga called Śikṣā. The similarities and differences between the svaras of music and of the Vedas are dealt with. So too those between the sounds voiced by birds and animals on the one hand and the Vedic svaras on the other. With all this the right way is shown for the intonation of Vedic mantras.

A remarkable method was devised to make sure that words and syllables are not altered. According to this the words of a mantra are strung together in different patterns like "vākya", "pada", "krama", "jaṭā", "mālā", "śikhā", "rekhā", "dhvaja", "daṇḍa", "ratha ", "ghana".

We call some Vedic scholars "ghanapāṭhins", don't we ? It means they have learnt the chanting of the scripture up to the advanced stage called "ghana". "Pāṭhin" means one who has learnt the "pāṭha". When we listen to a ghanapāṭhin chant the ghana, we notice that he intones a few words of a mantra in different ways, back and forth. It is most delightful to the ear, like nectar poured into it. The sonority natural to Vedic chanting is enhanced in ghana. Similarly, in the other methods of chanting like krama, jatā, śikhā, mālā and so on the intonation is nothing less than stately, indeed divine. The chief purpose of such methods, as already mentioned, is to ensure that not even a syllable of a mantra is altered to the slightest extent. The words are braided together, so to speak, and recited back and forth.

In "vākyapāṭha" and "saṁhitāpāṭha" the mantras are chanted in the original (natural) order, with no special pattern adopted. In the vākyapāṭha some words of the mantras are joined together in what is called "sandhi"[1]. There is sandhi in Tamiḷ also; but in English the words are not joined together. You have many examples of sandhi in the *Tevāram*[T], *Tiruvācakam*[T], *Tirukkural*[T], *Divyaprabandham*[T] and other Tamiḷ works. Because of the sandhi the individual words are less recognisable in Sanskrit than even in Tamiḷ. In padapāṭha each word in a mantra is clearly separated from the next. It comes next to saṁhitāpāṭha and after it is kramapāṭha. In this the first word of a mantra is joined to the second, the second to the third, the third to the fourth, and so on, until we come to the final word.

In old inscriptions in the South we find the names of some important people of the place concerned mentioned with the appellation *"kramavittan"* added to the names. *"Kramavittan"* is the Tamiḷ form of "kramavid" in the same way as "*Vedavittan*" is of "Vedavid". We learn from the inscriptions that such Vedic scholars were to be met throughout the Tamiḷ country.

In jaṭāpāṭha, the first word of the mantra is chanted with the second, then the order is reversed — the second is chanted with the first. Then, again, the first word is chanted with the second, then the second with the third, the third with the second, and, again, the second with the third, and so on. In this way the entire mantra is chanted, going back and forth. In śikhāpāṭha the pattern consists of three words of a mantra, instead of the two of jaṭā.

Ghanapāṭha is more difficult than these. There are four types of this method. Here also the words of a mantra are chanted back and forth and there is a system of permutation and combination in the chanting. To explain all of it would be like conducting a class in arithmetic.

We take all kinds of precautions in the laboratory, don't we, to protect a life-saving drug? The sound of the Vedas guards the world against all ills. Our forefathers devised these methods of chanting to protect the sound of our scripture against change and distortion.

Saṁhitāpāṭha and padapāṭha are called "prakṛtipāṭha" (natural way of chanting) since the words are recited only once and in their natural order. The other methods belong to the "vikṛtipāṭha" (artificial way of chanting) category. (In krama, though the words do not go in the strict natural order of one-two-three, there is no reversal of the words — the first after the second, the second after the third, and so on. So we cannot describe it fully as vikṛtipāṭha). Leaving out krama, there are eight vikṛti patterns and they are recounted in verse to be easily remembered.

Jaṭā mālā śikhā rekhā dhvaja daṇḍo ratho ghanaḥ
Ityaṣṭau-vikṛtayaḥ proktāḥ kramapūrvā maharṣibhiḥ

All these different methods of chanting are meant to ensure the tonal and verbal purity of the Vedas for all time. In pada the words in their natural order, in krama two words together, in jaṭā the words going back and forth. The words tally in all these methods of chanting and there is the assurance that the original form will not be altered.

The benefits to be derived from the different ways of chanting are given in this verse[2].

Saṁhitāpāṭhamātreṇa yatphalam procyate budhaiḥ
Pade tu dviguṇam vidyāt krame tu ca caturguṇam
Varṇakrame śataguṇam jaṭāyāntu sahasrakam

Considering that our ancestors took so much care to make sure that the sound of the Vedas did not undergo the slightest change, it is futile for modern researchers to try to establish the date of our scripture by finding out how the sounds of its words have changed.

Notes

1 "Sandhi" means putting together, the coalescence of the final and initial letters. There are elaborate rules of sandhi in Sanskrit grammar.

2 Padapāṭha is twice as beneficial as saṁhitāṭha; kramapāṭha is four times more beneficial; the method called "varṇakrama" is a hundred times more beneficial; while jaṭāpāṭha is a thousand times more beneficial.

Chapter 11

Word of God

We must not distrust the belief that the Vedas are not the work of mere mortals. Followers of other religions too ascribe a divine origin to their scriptures. Jesus says that he merely repeats the words of God and, according to Muslims, the Prophet speaks the words of Allah. What we call "apauruṣeya" is revealed text in their case. The word of the Lord has come through the agency of great men to constitute religious texts.

Whatever our field of work, we must be dedicated to it with one-pointedness of mind for its truths to be revealed. They say that such truths come to us in a flash. A professor told me that the Theory of Relativity occurred to Einstein in a flash, that he knew it intuitively. If we accept such claims, how can we dismiss the belief that the Vedas are not the work of mortals, that they revealed themselves to the seers in their heart-space[1], seers who were inwardly pure[2]?

Notes

[1] "Heart-space", hṛdayākāśa, is a mystical concept.

[2] The Paramaguru describes the seers here as men possessing pure "antaḥ-karaṇas" or "inner organs".

Chapter 12

The Vedas are Infinite

If the cosmos of sound (śabda-prapañca) enfolds all creation and what is beyond it, it must naturally be immensely vast. However voluminous the Vedas are, one might wonder whether it would be right to claim that they embrace all activities of the universe. "Anantāḥ vai Vedāḥ", the Vedas themselves proclaim so (the Vedas are endless). We cannot claim that all the Vedas have been revealed to the seers. Only about a thousand śākhās or recensions belonging to the four Vedas have been revealed to them.

Brahmā, the Creator, alone knows the Vedas in their entirety. Before the present Brahmā there was a great deluge and, preceding it, there was another Brahmā. And, similarly, before him too there must have been another Brahmā. But through all these vast vistas of time, through successive deluges, the vibrations caused by the Paramātman's breath have existed in space, the vibrations that urged the first Brahmā to do the work of creation. These vibrations are indestructible. The Brahmā who appears after each great deluge performs his function of creation with them.

The sounds we produce are never destroyed. I remember reading that what Jesus Christ spoke 2,000 years ago could still be recaptured in his own voice and that efforts are being made for the same. I don't know how far these efforts have succeeded. But I do know that there does exist such a possibility (of receiving a voice or sound from the past). We know that a sound, once it is produced, remains in space without ever being destroyed.

Brahmā created this world with the sound of the Vedas and this sound is not destroyed even during a great deluge. We build a village or town with stone, earth, timber, iron, etc. All these materials are derived from the will of the Paramātman, from his thought, from the vibrations that are his will or thought. Brahmā saw the sounds corresponding to these vibrations as the Vedas and he chanted them and brought all the world into existence.

We often see reports in the newspapers of trees flowering or fruiting in abundance in response to the vibrations of certain sounds. Some vibrations have also the effect of stunting the growth of plants. Here is proof of the fact that sound can create, sustain and destroy.

Brahmā could create the universe with the sound of the Vedas because of his power of concentration. A siddha[S] can cure a sick man if he intones the

Pañcākṣara[S] mantra — the mantra that we mutter every day — and applies holy ashes to the patient's body. He is able to do it because he has greater power of concentration than we have. If the mantra is to be efficacious it has to be chanted without any tonal error whatsoever. Only then will it bring the desired result. Brahmā had the power of concentration to the full since he came into being as an "instrument" for creation.

Much could be accomplished from the void of space through electricity. From the spiritual reality called the Nirguṇa Brahman (the unconditioned Brahman without attributes) emanates everything. During the deluge, this spiritual reality goes to sleep. Take the case of a sandow. When he is asleep his strength is not evident. But when we see him wrestling with an opponent we realise how strong he is. Similarly, during the time of creation, the spiritual reality is revealed to perform manifold functions. From the Nirguṇa Brahman comes a flow of energy to perform such functions. Brahmā came into being as a part of this flow. Since he was all tapas[S], all concentration, he could grasp all the Vedas with his extraordinary power. He created the world with their sound. The Vedas are infinite and so too creation takes forms that are countless.

The great sage Bharadvāja kept chanting the Vedas over three lifetimes. Parameśvara appeared before him and said to him: "I will grant you a fourth life. What will you do during it?" The sage replied: "I will keep chanting the Vedas again." It is not possible to learn the Vedas in their entirety even over many, many lifetimes. Parameśvara took pity on Bharadvāja for all his efforts to accomplish a task that was impossible to accomplish. Wanting to change his mind, Parameśvara caused three great mountains to appear, took a handful of earth and said to the sage: "The Vedas you have learned all these years are like this handful of earth. What you have yet to learn is vast, like these mountains." It is believed that Vedagiri or Tirukkazhukkunram[1] is the place where the Vedas appeared in the form of these mountains. When I was circumambulating the hill there, people accompanying me intoned, "Deva, Deva, Mahādeva," in the course of their *bhajan*. I asked them to intone instead, "Veda, Veda, Mahāveda".

The story of Bharadvāja occurs in the *Kāṭhaka*[2] of the Vedas. We learn from it that the Vedas are infinite. The classification into the four Vedas and the one thousand or so recensions was a later development. As Brahmā came into being, his heart was filled with all Vedic sound. The Vedas showed him the way to perform his function of creation. He recognised that the sound of the Vedas pervaded everywhere. To him occur all Vedas. Only some mantras have revealed themselves to the sages and these constitute the Vedas that are our heritage.

At the time of chanting a mantra we usually mention the ṛṣi associated with it, its chandas or metre and the name of the deity invoked. In the Telugu country they mention the three for all mantras. The sages learned the mantras with the power of concentration acquired through austerities. They were bestowed with celestial ears, so they could hear the mantras in space. It is said in the science of yoga that if our heart-space becomes one with the transcendent outward space we will be able to listen to the sounds in it. Only those who have attained the state of undifferentiated oneness of all can perceive them. It is in this way that the seers became aware of the mantras and made them known to the world. It must be remembered that they did not create them. They brought us immeasurable blessings by making the mantras known to us.

If someone offers us water from the Gangā (Gangā-tīrtha, *Gangājal)* we receive it, prostrating ourselves before him. The man did not of course create the Gangā, but all the same we reverence him in recognition of the fact that he must have travelled a thousand miles to bring us the few drops of the holy water. We cannot adore the seers sufficiently for their having made us the gift of the mantras which are beyond the grasp of our ears. That is why before chanting a mantra we hold the sacred feet of the ṛṣi concerned with our head.

Notes

[1] This is in Cengalpaṭṭu district, Tamiḷ Nāḍu.

[2] Of the Yajurveda.

Chapter 13

Mantrayoga

The fourteen worlds[1] constitute an immensely vast kingdom. It has an emperor and all living beings are his subjects. This kingdom as well as its ruler is eternal and it has its own laws. If the kingdom and the king-emperor are eternal, the law also must be so. This law is constituted by the Vedas. Though the kingdom, the cosmos, is called "anādi", it is dissolved and created again and again. The only eternal entities are the Paramātman and his law, the Vedas.

The world comes into being, grows and is dissolved in the deluge. Thus it alternates between being and non-being. The emperor and the law remain eternal. At the time of every creation the emperor, the Paramātman, also creates authorities or "officials" and invests them with the yogic power necessary for them to function. In the yoga śāstra is taught the truth that one's ears are not to be differentiated from outward space. When we meditate on this truth we acquire a celestial ear. It is with this ear and with the grace of the Paramātman that the authorities appointed by him obtain the sound waves that are always present in outward space. They were the first to know the Vedas and they are the maharṣis (the great seers or sages) of the mantras.

Vedic chanting is a mantrayoga. The vibration in each nāḍi[S] creates certain feelings or urges in the consciousness. Sensual desire is aroused by some, sloth by some and sorrow by some others. To reverse this, when there is sensual desire there is a vibration in some nāḍis, and when there is anger there is vibration in some other nāḍis, and so on for each type of feeling or emotion or urge. We know this from actual experience. When we are at ease there is a special glow on our face and this glow is caused by some nāḍis being cool and unagitated. There is a saying: "One's inner beauty is reflected outwardly on one's face." Our emotions cause their own reactions in our nāḍis. If we succeed in bringing the nāḍis under control we shall be masters of our urges and feelings. There will then be no need to depend on any external agency for the purpose.

One way of acquiring control over the nāḍis is the practice of Rājayoga[2] of which prāṇāyāma is the most important feature. Mantrayoga is another. When we vocalise a syllable, the vital breath is discharged through the space intervening our throat, tongue, lips, the upper and lower parts of the mouth, etc. It is then that the syllable is voiced or the "akṣara-dhvani" produced. Vibrations are created in the nāḍis located in those parts of the body where the vital breath courses through as a consequence of the akṣara-dhvani.

What are the Vedic mantras like in this context? Chanting them means only voicing such syllables as would cause beneficent vibrations of the nāḍis, beneficent vibrations that would produce such mental states as would lead to well-being in this world and the hereafter and ultimately to liberation. No other type of vibration is caused by the chanting of the mantras.

What is a mantra? "Mananāt trāyate" : that which protects you by being turned over again and again in the mind. By birth the Brahmin is invested with the duty of chanting mantras again and again and producing such vibrations in the nāḍis as would bring Ātmic well-being. Through the power of the mantras he must create this well-being not only for himself but for all creatures.

How are the mantras to be chanted so that we may master them and derive the full benefit from them? But first let us consider the faulty ways of chanting.

Gītī śīghrī śirahkampī tathā likhitapāṭhakaḥ
Anarthajño'lpakaṇṭhaśca ṣaḍete pāṭhakādhamāḥ

"Gītī" means one who chants a mantra as he likes setting it to tune, as it were, like a rāga[S]. The Vedas must be recited only in accordance with the tones appropriate to them. "Śīghrī" is one who hurries through a hymn. To derive the full benefit from the mantras the right mātras[S] must be maintained in the chanting. "Śiraḥkampī" denotes one who keeps shaking his head as he chants. There must be a certain poise about the man who chants the Vedas. The nāḍi vibrations must be such as are naturally produced in the course of the intonation. There must be no other vibrations. If the head is shaken as in a music recital the nāḍi vibrations will be affected. The "likhitapāṭhaka" is one who chants, reading from the written text. As I have said so often the Vedas must be taught and learned without the help of any written text. The "anarthajña" is one who does not know the meaning (here one who does not know the meaning of what he chants). All those belonging to these six categories[3] are described as "pāṭhakādhamāḥ", belonging to the lowest types among those who chant the Vedas.

Notes & References

[1] The fourteen worlds: atala, vitala, nitala (or pātāla), sutala, talātala, mahātala, rasātala; and bhūloka, bhuvarloka, svarloka, maharloka, janaloka, tapoloka and satyaloka.

[2] Rājayoga is the superior yoga of meditation. Prāṇāyāma is control of the vital breath.

[3] The meaning of "alpakaṇṭha" is explained in the next chapter.

Chapter 14

Sound and Meaning

An interesting thought occurs to me here. In Sanskrit the suffix "taram" is used for the comparative degree. "Vīryavat" means "strong", "vīryavattaram" means "stronger". It is said in the *Chāndogya Upaniṣad* (1.1.10)[1] that he who meditates on the truth of Omkāra (Aumkāra) with a knowledge of its meaning, will gain benefits that are "vīryavattaram". The implication here is that those who practise such meditation without knowing the meaning will obtain benefits that are "vīryavat". In his commentary on this Upaniṣad, Śankarācārya remarks that those who meditate on Omkāra, even without grasping the principle behind it, will gain much benefit though it may not be the same measure as that gained by those who meditate on it knowing its meaning.

We may or may not know the meaning or significance of a religious rite, but we will be duly rewarded if we perform it in deference to the great men who have urged us to do it or because we follow the example of our forefathers who have done it. What matters is the faith inspiring our action. This applies particularly to mantra upāsanā (worship through chanting mantras) more than to anything else. The reason is that in such worship the proper voicing of the syllables of the mantra and the vibrations created are what matter in bringing beneficial results. The meaning of the mantras comes later.

In this context it seems to me that performing a rite without knowing its meaning yields results that are "vīryavattaram", that is more potent than performing it with a knowledge of its meaning (the benefits in the latter case are "vīryavat"). The chanting of a mantra, or the muttering of it, without knowing its meaning, is also more rewarding than chanting or muttering it knowing the meaning. How?

A man sends a petition to the collector through his lawyer. Another man, an unlettered peasant, has his petition written by somebody else but he personally hands it to the collector. He requests the official to treat his case sympathetically. The latter is moved by the man's simple faith and decides to help him. If we approach the collector through a lawyer and if he takes it amiss, he might turn against us. Also, if he finds that we have knowingly committed a wrong, he will have greater reason to be displeased with us. But if he realises that we have committed a mistake unknowingly, he may be inclined to forgive us.

We must not refuse to perform a rite because we do not know its meaning, nor must we ask why we should perform what is prescribed in the śāstras. Conducting a ritual without knowing its significance, it occurs to me, is "vīryavattaram".

You may take it that this observation of mine has not been made in any seriousness. But, when I see that intellectual arrogance and deceit are on the increase and that the ignorant are being deprived of their one asset, humility, it seems to me that doing things in mere faith is to be lauded.

You must, in fact, be intellectually convinced about the need to perform a religious duty and, at the same time, you must be humble. The mantras are the laws of the dharmaśāstras. If we knew their meaning we would be better able to live according to them.

The term "alpakaṇṭha" in the verse quoted above [in the previous chapter] means one who has a thin voice (one who chants the Vedas in a thin voice). The Vedic mantras must be intoned full-throatedly, sonorously and their sound must pervade space to the maximum extent possible.

The sound of the mantras does good to the man chanting them as well as to the listener by producing vibrations in the nāḍis of both. As it fills the air it will be beneficent both in this world and in the next. This is the reason why the Vedas must be chanted with vigour, so that their sound reaches the utmost limits possible.

Reference

[1] Tenobhau kuruto yaścaitadevaṁ veda yaśca na veda nānā tu vidyā cāvidyā ca; yadeva vidyayā karoti śraddhayopaniṣadā, tadeva viryavattaram bhavatiti khalvetasyaivākṣarasyopavyākhyānam bhavati.

— Chāndogyopaniṣad, 1.1.10.

Chapter 15

The Glory of the Vedas

The Vedas are eternal and are the source of all creation and their greatness is to be known in many different ways. As I have already stated, their sound produces in our nāḍis[S] as well as in the atmosphere vibrations that are salutary not only to our own Self but to the entire world. Here we must understand "lokakṣema" or welfare of the world to mean the good of mankind as well as of all other creatures. This concern for all creation that finds expression in the Vedas is not shared by any other religion. "Śanno astu dvipadeśañcatuṣpade" -- this occurs in a mantra: the Vedas pray for the good of all creatures including bipeds, quadrupeds, etc. Even grass, shrubs, trees, mountains and rivers are not excluded from their benign purview. The happy state of all these sentient creatures and inert objects is brought about through the special quality of the sound of the Vedas.

The noble character of their sound apart, the Vedas are also notable for the lofty truths that find expression in the mantras. The tenets of these scriptures have aroused the wonder of people of other lands, of other faiths. They are moved by the poetic beauty of the hymns, the subtle manner in which principles of social life are dealt with in them, the metaphysical truths embedded and expounded in them, and the moral instruction as well as scientific truths contained in them.

Not all mantras that create benign vibrations are necessarily meaningful. In this context we have the example of music. The ālāpana of a rāga (the elaboration of a musical mode) is "pure" sound, that is it has no words, but it is still capable of producing emotions like joy, sorrow, etc. During the researches conducted by a university team, it was discovered that the vibrations created by instrumental music quickened the growth of plants and resulted in a higher yield of fruits and vegetables. Here is proof that sound has the power of creation. Also to be noted is the fact that the instrumental music played to the plants does not obviously have any verbal content — this establishes that sound has its own power.

The remarkable thing about the Vedas is that they are of immeasurable value as much for their sound as for their verbal content. While the sound has its own creative power, the words are notable for the exalted character of the meaning they convey.

There are Tamiḷ hymns of a very high order. To read them is to be moved by them; they touch our hearts with their intense devotion. But we have recourse only to a few of them for repeated incantation to expel a poison or to cure a disease. The authors of these hymns like Nakkīrar[T], Aruṇagirināthar[T] and Sambandamūrti[T] have composed poems that are more moving and beautiful. But the sound of the hymns chosen for repeated incantation are potent like mantras. Among our Ācārya's devotional works are the *Saundaryalaharī* and the *Śivānandalaharī*. The recitation of each stanza of the *Saundaryalaharī* brings in a specific benefit. The same is not said about the *Śivānandalaharī*. The reason is the special māntrik power (of the sound) of the former.

There are mantras that are specially valuable for their sound but are otherwise meaningless. Similarly, there are works pregnant with meaning but with no special māntrik power. The glory of the Vedas is that they are a collection of mantras that are at once notable as much for the energising character of their sound as for the lofty truths they proclaim. A medicine, though bitter, does the body good, while some types of food, though delicious, do harm. Are we not delighted to have something like kūśmāṇḍa-lehya[1] which is sweet to taste and is at the same time nourishing to the body? Similarly, the Vedas serve a twofold purpose: while they have the māntrik power to do immense good to each one of us and to the world, they also contain teachings embodying great metaphysical truths.

It must here be emphasised that on the doctrinal level the Vedas deal both with worldly life and the inner life of the Self. They teach us how to conduct ourselves in such a manner as to create Ātmic well-being. And their concern is not with the liberation of the individual alone; they speak about the ideals of social life and about the duties of the public. How the Brahmin ought to lead his life and how the king must rule his subjects and what ideals women are to follow: an answer to these -- stated in the form of laws -- is to be found in these scriptures. The Vedas indeed constitute the apex of our law-books.

Note

[1] Kūśmāṇḍa-lehya is an Āyurvedic preparation consisting of ash-gourd, jaggery and other ingredients.

Chapter 16

Yajña or Sacrifice

I spoke about the glory of the Vedas, about the features that contribute to their greatness as a scripture. One such feature yet to be dealt with is yajña or sacrifice.

What is a yajña? It is the performance of a religious duty involving Agni, the sacrificial fire, with the chanting of mantras. The word itself is derived from the root "yaj" meaning "to worship", to evince devotion. The performance of a yajña is meant to please the Paramātman and various deities. Yajña is also called "yāga".

We have already seen the definition of the word "mantra": "mananāt trāyate iti mantraḥ" (that which protects us by being repeated and meditated upon). "Trāṇam" means to protect. All of you must be familiar with the words in the Gītā: "Paritrāṇāya sādhūnām" (to protect the virtuous)[1]. "Mananam" means repeating, turning over something in the mind. There is no need to vocalise the words of the mantra. Even if it is repeated mentally, healthy vibrations will be produced in the nāḍis[S]. If the same — the Vedic mantra — is chanted loudly ("Vedaghoṣa") it will give divine joy to the listeners even if they do not understand its meaning. Such a sound has the power to make mankind happy.

Mind, speech and body are dedicated to the Vedas when you mutter a Vedic mantra mentally and vocalise it outwardly during the performance of a rite involving the body. Of the Vedic rites of this kind yajña or yāga is the most important.

(See Chapter 5, Part Nineteen, for a detailed account of the various sacrifices.)

Reference

1. *Paritrāṇāya sādhūnām vināśaya ca duṣkṛtām*
   Dharmasaṁsthāpanārthāya saṁbhavāmi yuge yuge.

   — Bhagavadgītā, 4.8

Chapter 17

Not in Other Religions

The concept of yajña or sacrifice is not present in other systems of worship. There is a big difference between our religion, the "Vedic mata", and other faiths. Religions like Christianity and Islam speak of one God. The Vedas too proclaim that there is but one God and that even an ordinary mortal is to be identified with him. This Paramātman, this Godhead, is to be realised as an experience by constant inquiry conducted with our inner being. It needs much wisdom and maturity to attain this state. When we unite with this one and only Reality, all this world disappears for us.

How do we prepare ourselves for such a state? The answer is : now itself, when we are deeply involved in worldly affairs. In the very midst of our mundane existence we must live according to the dictates of dharma and the teachings of the śāstras. In this way our consciousness will be purified. We will become mature within and will be severed from the world. The duties and rites that will take us to this goal are enshrined in the Vedas. The most important of the rites is yajña. There is a very old Tamiḷ word for it — "*veḷvi*". In yajña offerings are made to different deities instead of to the one and only Paramātman. This sacrament is unique to our religion.

In a yajña we are enjoined to offer various materials in the sacred fire with the recitation of mantras. Making such offerings in the sacrificial fire is called "homa". Though the materials are placed in the fire it does not mean that they are necessarily offered to Agni. Only such materials as are placed in the fire with the chanting of mantras invoking Agni himself are meant for that deity. But the oblations meant for other deities like Rudra, Viṣṇu, Indra, Varuṇa, Mātariśvan (Vāyu), and so on are also made in the holy fire. Agni conveys them to the deities invoked. Just as letters addressed to various people are put in the same letter-box, the oblations meant for various deities are conveyed through one devatā, Agni.

An important difference between the Vedic religion and other faiths is this: while followers of other religions worship one God we worship many deities and make offerings to them in the sacrificial fire.

We often say, don't we, that the Lord is pleased if we keep helping one another? Reformists forsake pūjā and ritual, saying, "Serving people, serving the poor, is as good as serving God." We will receive the Paramātman's blessings if we serve the devas also through sacrifices, for they too are his creation.

The Vedas proclaim that the one Brahman, call it the Truth or Reality, is manifested as so many different devatās or deities. Since each devatā is extolled as the Paramātman we know for certain that monotheism is a Vedic tenet. It is wrong to believe that the Vedas subscribe to polytheism merely because they speak of many deities. In doing so they mean that the one and only Brahman is revealed as many deities. It is for the conduct of the affairs of the cosmos that the Paramātman has created the various divine powers. These divinities are also in charge of the forces of nature, the feelings and urges of man. The Supreme Godhead has created them in the same way as he has created us. He fashioned us out of himself -- which means that he it is that came to be so many human beings also.

This is the reason why non-dualism proclaims that the Paramātman and the jīvātman (the individual self) are one and the same. In the same way it is he who is manifested as the many deities. However, until we are mature enough to recognise the truth of non-dualism and realise it within, and until we reach the state in which we realise that we are not separate from the Paramātman, we have to perform rituals and help one another. In the same way the deities are also to be looked upon as separate entities and are to be worshipped through sacrifices. This is the law of the Vedas.

If we and all other creatures are to be happy in this world, we must have the blessings of the deities who govern the cosmic forces. It is for this purpose, to propitiate and please them for their grace, that the Vedas impose on us the duty of performing sacrifices.

If we attain jñāna, the wisdom to realise within the oneness of all, there will be no need for these deities. We may worship the Paramātman directly. However, so long as we make efforts to find release from this pluralistic cosmos, we have to worship the deities as separate entities.

Chapter 18

The Threefold Purpose of Yajña

The Vedic sacrifices have a threefold purpose. The first is to earn the blessings of the deities so that we as well as all other creatures may be happy in this world. The second is to ensure that, after our death, we will live happily in the world of the celestials. But our stay in devaloka, the celestial world, is not for all time. It will last only until such time as we exhaust the merit earned by us in this world. The joy known in the celestial world is also not full or entire unlike the bliss experienced by great devotees and jñānins. It is nowhere equal to the bliss of the Ātman: which is also described as "experiencing" Īśvara.

Śankara has stated in his *Māniṣa-Pañcaka* that the joy that Indra knows is no more than a drop in the ocean of Ātmānanda or the bliss of Self-realisation. However, life in svarga, the paradise of the celestials, is a thousand times happier than life on earth with its unceasing sorrows. The second purpose of performing sacrifices is to earn residence in this paradise.

The third purpose is the most important and it is achieved by performing sacrifices, as taught by the Gītā, without any expectation of reward[1]. Here we desire neither happiness in this world nor residence in paradise. We perform sacrifices only because it is our duty to invoke the blessings of the gods for the welfare of the world. In this way our consciousness will be cleansed, a pre-requisite for enlightenment and final liberation. In other words the selfless performance of sacrifices means that we will eventually be dissolved in the Paramātman.

Śankara, who has expounded the ideals of Self-realisation and jñāna, says: "Vedo nityam adhīyatām taduditam karma svanuṣṭhīyatām" (Chant the Vedas every day. Perform with care the sacrifices and other rites they enjoin upon you). The Ācārya wants us to conduct sacrifices not for happiness in this world, nor for the enjoyment of the pleasures of paradise. No, not for any petty rewards. Śankara exhorts us to carry out Vedic works without our hearts being vitiated by desire. This, according to his teaching, is the way to make our mind pure in order to realise the Self.

Reference

1. Karmaṇyevādhikāraste mā phaleṣu kadācana
Mā karma-phala-hetur bhūr ma te saṅgo'stvakarmaṇi

— Bhagavadgītā, 2.47

Chapter 19

The Celestials and Mortals Help Each Other

The sacrifices, you will have seen, are of the utmost importance to our Vedic religion. The Lord himself has spoken about them in the Gītā. When Brahmā created the human species he also brought the yajñas or sacrifices into existence, bidding mortals thus: "Keep performing sacrifices. You will obtain all good fortune. May these sacrifices of yours be the cow (Kāmadhenu[S]) that grants you all you desire"[1].

Saha-yajñāḥ prajāḥ sṛṣṭvā puro'vāca Prajāpatiḥ
Anena prasaviṣyadhvam eṣa vo'stviṣṭa-kāmadhuk

If we assume that Brahmā "created humans and with them sacrifices", it is likely to be construed that he first created human beings and then sacrifices. But actually it is stated in the Gītā that Prajāpati created yajña along with humankind (saha-yajñāḥ prajāḥ sṛṣṭvā). Yajña is mentioned first and then prajā (mankind).

Since the mantras of the Vedas are the source of creation, the vibrations produced by chanting them will bring the divine powers invested with the authority of performing certain functions. To recite such mantras at a sacrifice is like writing the address on an envelope. It is by performing homa[S] in this way that the oblation is conveyed to the deity invoked by Agni.

The dog is stronger than the cat, the horse stronger than the dog, the elephant stronger than the horse, and the lion stronger than the elephant. To extend this sequence, who are stronger than men? The devas, or celestials. While in this world they remain dissolved in the five elements, in the celestial world they exist in a visible form. Those who have obtained siddhi[S] or perfection by chanting the mantras can also see them in their gross form in their celestial abode besides receiving their blessings in their subtle form. The gods emanated from the Paramātman as a result of the vibrations produced by the mantras. We may therefore describe the mantras as the "sonic" form of the deities.

The deity appears during a sacrifice when he is invoked with mantras. Those who are wise and mature will perceive them with their eyes. Even if they do not, the power of the deities will be subtly revealed to them. However, offerings cannot be made directly to them. When you write a letter you have to stick a stamp on it or put the seal of the registrar. According to the "regulations" of the Vedas, any oblation intended for the celestials must be offered in the sacred fire in a form acceptable to them.

What remains after the sacrificial fire has consumed the offering ("yajñaśiṣṭa") is taken as prasāda[S] by the performers of the sacrifice. The question is asked: how does the same reach the deities invoked? We should not entertain such doubts. The deities are not like us created of the five elements. So they do not require food in the gross form. Even in our case the food we eat is burned (digested) by the gastric fire. Its essence alone is conveyed to all parts of the body in the form of blood. The subtle essence of the offerings are conveyed by the sacrificial fire to the deities invoked.

You know how a toast is proposed to the guest of honour at a dinner or banquet. The host and invitees drink to his health. This means that, when a group of people drink or eat ceremonially, the benefit goes to someone else. Do you ask how this is possible? Such things can be explained only on the basis of a certain mental attitude. Good intentions and good thoughts have their own creative power.

When the thought waves of the Paramātman have come to us in the form of mantras, they must truly be pregnant with the utmost power for good. The offerings made to the deities with the chanting of mantras will increase their strength. The celestials are of course strong but they are neither almighty nor full. They too have their wants and desires and these are met by the sacrifices performed by us. If they help us by making our mundane existence happier we have to help them by performing sacrifices. If we conduct yajñās so that they may flourish, they will in return bless us with well-being. Śrī Kṛṣṇa says in the Gitā[2]:

Devān bhāvayatā'nena te devā bhāvayantu vaḥ
Parasparaṁ bhāvayantaḥ śreyaḥ param avāpsyatha

Our religious texts are replete with accounts of how people have merited the grace of Īśvara and pleased the celestials by performing sacrifices.

If the celestials bring us rains, bless us with food, health, etc, why should we perform sacrifices so as to provide them with food, we are asked. "Why should we feed the deities when we ourselves are dependent on them for our food and clothing? Why cannot they manage to obtain food on their own? How would you explain the Lord's statement (in the verse quoted above), 'Parasparam bhāvayantaḥ'? To say that we must regard the celestials as great beings and make obeisance to them seems reasonable enough. So let us worship them. But, instead of this, why are we seemingly elevated and placed on an equal footing with them? What is the meaning of our being told: 'You sustain them and let them sustain you — you feed them by performing sacrifices and let them bless you with rains'?"

When I consider such questions, it seems to me that the world of the celestials is like England and that they themselves are like Englishmen. Is there much agricultural land in England? No. Yet Englishmen lorded it over the world. They boasted: "The sun never sets on our empire[3]." What was the secret of their world dominance?

England is poor in food resources. It has plenty of coal and chalk — coal that is black and chalk that is white. These are the main resources of Englishmen but they cannot eat them. If machines and factories are to be installed in countries where food crops are grown in plenty, they will need a lot of coal and chalk. That coal is essential to industry is well known. (Petrol and electricity came later. Now there is atomic power also.) For some industries like cement, chalk (limestone) is essential.

Englishmen thought up a shrewd plan. They induced other countries to start factories using machinery and fomented new, unnecessary desires among people there. And they sold lumps of coal and chalk to these countries and got in return foodgrains, cotton, etc, in abundance. In this way they brought country after country under their heel.

There are no agricultural lands in the celestial world. The devas have no means to feed themselves. "Durbhikṣam devalokeṣu manūnām udakam gṛhe," so it is said in the first praśna (first part) of the *Taittirīya Āraṇyaka.* Rain is produced when the clouds precipitate. It is only on earth that rain can be made use of — it fills the rivers, lakes and wells. The celestials have to come to our households for water. On earth alone is there plenty because of cultivation carried on by irrigating the fields. There is famine in the celestial world since it has no agricultural land: this is the meaning of the words quoted from the Āraṇyaka.

However, we need the grace of the gods if we are to be blessed with rains. To deserve such grace we must perform sacrifices. Otherwise there will be no rains on earth. The result will be famine or the rain will fall into the sea and not on land, or it will be either ativṛṣṭi (too much rain) or anāvṛṣṭi (no rain). We have to depend on the denizens of the celestial world to send us the right quantity of rain to create abundance on this planet.

Just as England has plenty of coal but does not have sufficient agricultural land, the celestials have an abundance of grace but no crops to grow -- they cannot also sustain themselves with their power of grace. Because they send us rain we are able to raise crops and sustain ourselves. For our part we can enhance their power of grace by chanting the Vedas. The oblations offered in the sacrificial fire with such chanting become their nourishment.

Our country grows cotton. When our spinning mills did not prosper, the English took our cotton to Lancashire, made "nice" cloth and sold it to us, making in the process four times profit. The celestials produce rain for us from the water vapour formed from our own seas. But, unlike the English, they do not make any profit out of it (in the transaction). In fact the blessings they give us are far more than the sustenance we give them. As I said earlier, the celestials are much stronger than we are. The Lord has assigned us the duty of performing various rites and the celestials have to find satisfaction in them. By doing so, it seems, he has raised us to the level of the celestials. "Parasparam bhāvayantaḥ," he says in the Gītā. The gods and mortals support each other.

References

[1] Bhagavadgītā, 3.10.

[2] With this shall you sustain the gods so that the gods may sustain you (in return). Sustaining one another you shall achieve the highest goal.

- Bhagavadgītā, 3.11

[3] Christopher North said in 1829: "His majesty's dominions, on which the sun never sets."

Chapter 20

The Capacity to Work and the Capacity to Protect

The Lord has endowed us with the capacity to work and the celestials with the capacity to protect. There is a similar division of functions in this world also.

The field and the factory are associated with labour. The police station, the lawcourt and other offices have the function of protection. The administrative offices are meant to ensure that what is produced in the field and in the factory is made available to the households in an equitable manner. The offices do not "produce" anything, nor do they have any crops to harvest. They are free from the noise of the machines and from cowdung and dust. Those who work in an office need not make their hands and nails dirty and can spend their time sitting comfortably on chairs with the fans whirling over them. There is hardly any bodily exertion—it is all pen-pushing. The celestial world is like this: it is the office that affords protection to all the worlds. We do not find fault with people who man offices for not ploughing the fields or operating the machines. If they start doing such work, they will not be able to do their duty of protecting us. The celestials resemble these officials.

The earth is the field as well as the factory. It is all slush and mud, all din and noise, and it is oily, sticky, dusty. We have to toil here all day long. Performing the rites according to the canons means suffering all this, like the smoke of the sacrificial fire, exhaustion due to fasting — indeed you have to sweat through the elaborate rites.

The Lord does not regard the celestials as belonging to a higher plane nor does he think that we mortals belong to a lower one. The peasant and the factory worker produce food and other articles. The official sitting stylishly in his cubicle will starve and will be denied essential goods but for the work done by the peasant and the factory hand. All the same, it is because of the protection afforded by the official that the corn harvested by the farmer and other essential articles produced by the factory worker are made available to all members of society.

The engineer gives the order to dig irrigation canals. The agricultural officer supplies pesticides. Another official issues the licence to start a factory. The government, which means also the police, assists in the just distribution of the goods manufactured by it. (It is for this purpose that the government is constituted, no matter how it functions in practice.) Thus it is a system in which one is dependent on another. A contributes to B's happiness and B to A's.

It is against such a background that we have to consider the words of the Gītā, "Parasparam bhāvayantaḥ". Though the devas look to us for our help, it must not be forgotten that they belong to a higher plane and that we must be respectful towards them.

In other religions the one God is worshipped directly by all. They do not have a system of sacrifices meant to please a number of deities. Among us, only sannyāsins worship the Paramātman directly. Others have to please and propitiate the various deities and obtain well-being through their blessings. It is to please the deities that we perform a variety of sacrifices.

A big king is not directly approached by all. The subjects have their favours granted by the officials appointed by him. These officials do not function on their own; they look after the welfare of the people under royal orders. Some customs of our religion are reminiscent of such a system. Parameśvara is the supreme king-emperor. We, human beings, are his subjects. Varuṇa, Agni, Vāyu and such celestials are his officials. We have to obtain a number of benefits through them and we perform sacrifices with a view to enhancing their power to do us good. The oblations we make in the sacrificial fire constitute their food: "Agnimukhāḥ devāḥ".

We say "na mama" (not mine) when we offer any material in the sacred fire. Such an oblation is consumed by Agni and conveyed to the celestials invoked. It is thus that they obtain their sustenance. In this way we also propitiate our fathers (pitṛs), those belonging to our vaṃśa or clan. The Vedas contain directions about how rites meant for the pitṛs are to be performed.

Chapter 21

Rites for Celestials, Rites for Fathers

The rites meant for the deities must be performed with devotion and those meant for the pitṛs or fathers must be performed with faith. What is done with devotion is yajña and what is done with faith is śrāddha. While performing the former, the śikhā[S] must be gathered into a knot and the sacred thread must rest on the left shoulder, and while performing the latter the śikhā must be worn loose and the sacred thread must rest on the right shoulder.

The śikhā and the sacred thread are meant for these two purposes. Sannyāsins do not have either. When they renounce the world they also renounce the rites for the fathers and cease to worship a number of deities. They adore the Paramātman directly without any worldly desire in their hearts. The followers of other religions too wear neither a śikhā nor a sacred thread and they worship the Supreme God directly [that is without going through the stages in which the various deities are worshipped].

Let me tell you about the two positions of the sacred thread while performing the rites for the celestials and the fathers. We must face the east as we conduct various rituals. The north is the direction in which we make the passage to the celestials. This path is called "uttarāyaṇa". Our departed fathers reside in the south. The saint-poet Tiruvaḷḷuvar[T] calls them *"tenpulattār"*, those dwelling in the south. "Dakṣiṇāyana" is the way to the world of the fathers. Bhagavān Kṛṣṇa speaks of the two paths in the Gitā[1].

When we sit facing the east to perform rites for the pitṛs, which shoulder is to the south? The right one. So the sacred thread must rest on it.

To do "pradakṣiṇa" means to go facing the south. (In the majority of temples the rāja-gopuram — the main entrance tower— is in the east. When you enter it and start circumambulating you will be facing the south.)

When we sit facing the east to perform rites for the gods our left shoulder is to the north. So the sacred thread must rest on it. When we are not engaged in either of these two rites— that is when we are doing our office work or something else— the sacred thread must not rest on either shoulder and must be worn like a garland. (No one seems to observe this rule in practice now. Except during the rites for the fathers, most people have their sacred thread resting on the left shoulder.)

Reference

[1] Agnir jyotir ahaḥ śuklaḥ ṣaṇmāsā uttarāyaṇam
Tatra prayātā gacchanti Brahma Brahṃavido janāḥ

Dhūmo rātristathā kṛṣṇaḥ ṣaṇmāsā dakṣiṇāyanam
Tatra cāndramasaṁ jyotir yogī prāpya nivartate

Śukla-kṛṣṇe gatīhyete jagataḥ śāśvate mate
Ekayāyātyanāvṛttim anyayā'vartate punaḥ

— Bhagavadgītā, 8. 24, 25 & 26.

Chapter 22

The Purpose of Sacrifices

Why is it that our religion alone has the rites called yajñas or sacrifices?

If a crop grows in surplus in our place we trade it with what is available in plenty in another and is not produced in our own. The carpenter, the blacksmith and other artisans make useful articles and serve us in many ways. In return we give them what they need for their upkeep. We feed the cow grass and it yields us milk. We pay the government taxes and it gives us protection. The affairs of the world are conducted on the basis of a system of exchange. Similarly, we conduct an exchange even with worlds other than our own. Engineers and other experts can canalise water obtained from the rains but they cannot produce the rains. If we want the rains to come, we have to despatch certain goods to the abode of the celestials. It is this kind of exchange that the Gītā speaks of:

Devān bhāvayatā'nena te devā bhāvayantu vaḥ
Parasparaṁ bhāvayantaḥ śreyaḥ param avāpsyatha

It means: "You keep the devas satisfied with the performance of sacrifices. And let them look after your welfare by producing rain on earth. Thus, helping each other, be more and more prosperous and happy."

Chapter 23

Is Sacrificial Killing Justified?

A yāga or sacrifice takes shape with the chanting of the mantras, the invoking of the deity and the offering of havis (oblation). The mantras are chanted (orally) and the deity is meditated upon (mentally). The most important material required for homa[S] is the havis offered in the sacrificial fire — in this "work" the body is involved. So, altogether, in a sacrificial offering[1] mind, speech and body (mano-vāk-kāya) are brought together.

Ghee (clarified butter) is an important ingredient of the oblation. While ghee by itself is offered as an oblation, it is also used to purify other sacrificial materials — in fact this is obligatory. In a number of sacrifices the vapā[S] (fat or marrow) of animals is offered.

Is the performance of a sacrifice sinful, or is it meritorious? Or is it both?

Madhvācārya[S] was against the killing of any paśu for a sacrifice. In his compassion he said that a substitute for the vapā must be made with flour and offered in the fire. ("Paśu" does not necessarily mean a cow. In Sanskrit any animal is called a "paśu".)

In his *Brahmasūtra,* Vyāsa has expounded the nature of the Ātman as found expressed in the Upaniṣads which constitute the jñānakāṇḍa[2] of the Vedas. The actual conduct of sacrifices is dealt with in the Pūrvamīmāṁsā which is the karmakāṇḍa[3] of the Vedas. The true purpose of sacrifices is explained in the Uttaramīmāṁsā, that is the jñānakāṇḍa. What is this purpose or goal? It is the cleansing of the consciousness and such cleansing is essential to lead a man to the path of jñāna.

The *Brahmasūtra* says : "Aśuddhamiti cen na śabdāt"[4]. The performance of sacrifices is based on scriptural authority and it is part of the quest for Self-realisation. So how can it be called an impure act? How do we determine whether or not an object or an act is impure or whether it is good or bad? We do so by judging it according to the authority of the śāstras. Vyāsa goes on to state in his *Brahmasūtra* that animal sacrifice is not sinful since the act is permeated by the sound of the Vedas. What is pure or impure is to be known by the authority provided by the Vedas or rather their sound called Śabda-pramāṇa. If sacrifices were impure acts according to the Vedas, they would not have accepted them as part of the Ātmic quest. Even if the sacrificial animal is made of flour (the substitute according to Madhvācārya) it is imbued with life by the chanting of the Vedic mantras. Would it not then be like a living animal and would not offering it in sacrifice be taken as an act of violence?

Tiruvaḷḷuvar[T] says in his *Tirukkural*[T] that not to kill an animal and eat it is better than performing a thousand sacrifices in which the oblation is consigned to the fire. You should not take this to mean that the poet speaks ill of sacrifices.

What is in accordance or in pursuance of dharma must be practised howsoever or whatsoever it be. Here questions of violence must be disregarded. The *Tirukkural* says that it is better not to kill an animal than perform a thousand sacrifices. From this statement it is made out that Tiruvaḷḷuvar condemns sacrifices. According to Manu himself conducting one aśvamedha (horse sacrifice) is superior to performing a thousand other sacrifices. At the same time, he declares that higher than a thousand horse sacrifices is the fact of one truth. If we say that one thing is better than another, the implication is that both are good. If the performance of a sacrifice were sinful, would it be claimed that one meritorious act is superior to a thousand sinful deeds? You may state that fasting on one Śivarātri is superior to fasting on a hundred Ekādaśīs[S]. But would you say that the same is better than running a hundred butcheries? When you remark that "this rite is better than that rite or another", it means that the comparison is among two or more meritorious observances.

In the concluding passage[5] of the *Chāndogya Upaniṣad* where ahiṁsā or non-violence is extolled you find these words. "Anyatra tīrthebhyaḥ". It means ahiṁsā must be practised except with regard to Vedic rites.

Considerations of violence have no place in sacrifices and the conduct of war.

If the ideal of non-violence were superior to the performance of sacrifices, it would mean that "sacrifices are good but that non-violence is better". The performance of a thousand sacrifices must be spoken of highly but the practice of non-violence is to be regarded as even higher: It is in this sense that the *Kural* stanza concerning sacrifices is to be interpreted. We must not also forget that it occurs in the section on renunciation. What the poet wants to convey is that a sannyāsin does better by abstaining from killing than a householder does by conducting a thousand sacrifices. According to the śāstras also a sannyāsin has no right to perform sacrifices.

There are several types of sacrifices. I shall speak about them later when I deal with "Kalpa" (an Anga or limb of the Vedas) and "Gṛhasthāśrama" (the stage of the householder)[6]. What I wish to state here is that animals are not killed in all sacrifices. There are a number of yajñas in which only ghee (ājya) is offered in the fire. In some, haviṣyanna (rice mixed with ghee) is offered and in some the cooked grains called "caru" or puroḍāśa", a kind of baked cake. In agnihotra[7] milk is poured into the fire; in aupāsana[8] unbroken rice grains (akṣata) are used; and in samidādhāna[S] the sticks of the palāśa (flame of the forest). In sacrifices in which the vapā of animals is offered, only a tiny bit of the remains of the burnt offering is partaken of — and of course in the form of prasāda[S].

One is enjoined to perform twenty-one sacrifices. These are of three types: pākayajña, haviryajña and somayajña[9]. In each category there are seven subdivisions. In all the seven pākayajñas as well as in the first five haviryajñas there is no animal sacrifice. It is only from the sixth haviryajña onwards (it is called "nirūḍhapaśubandha") that animals are sacrificed.

"Brahmins sacrificed herds and herds of animals and gorged themselves on their meat. The Buddha saved such herds when they were being taken to the sacrificial altar," we often read such accounts in books. To tell the truth, there is no sacrifice in which a large number of animals are killed. For vājapeya[10] which is the highest type of yajña performed by Brahmins, only twenty-three animals are mentioned. For aśvamedha (horse sacrifice), the biggest of the sacrifices conducted by imperial rulers, one hundred animals are mentioned.

It is totally false to state that Brahmins performed sacrifices only to satisfy their appetite for meat and that the talk of pleasing the deities was only a pretext. There are rules regarding the meat to be carved out from a sacrificial animal, the part of the body from which it is to be taken and the quantity each ṛtvik[11] can partake of as prasāda (iḍāvataraṇa). This is not more than the size of a pigeon-pea and it is to be swallowed without anything added to taste. There may be various reasons for you to attack the system of sacrifices but it would be preposterous to do so on the score that Brahmins practised deception by making them a pretext to eat meat.

Nowadays a large number of animals are slaughtered in the laboratories as guinea-pigs. Animal sacrifice must be regarded as a little hurt caused in the cause of a great ideal, the welfare of mankind. As a matter of fact there is no hurt caused since the animal sacrificed attains to an elevated state.

There is another falsehood spread these days, that Brahmins performed the somayajñas only as a pretext to drink somarasa (the essence of the soma plant). Those who propagate this lie add that drinking somarasa is akin to imbibing liquor or wine. As a matter of fact somarasa is not an intoxicating drink. There is a reference in the Vedas to Indra killing his foe when he was "intoxicated" with somarasa. People who spread the above falsehoods have recourse to "arthavāda"[12] and base their perverse views on this passage.

The principle on which the physiology of deities is based is superior to that of humans. That apart, to say that the priests drank bottle after bottle of somarasa or pot after pot is to betray gross ignorance of the Vedic dharma. The soma plant is pounded and crushed in a small mortar called "graha". There are rules with regard to the quantity of essence to be offered to the gods. The small portion that remains after the oblation has been made, "huta-śeṣa", which is drunk drop by drop, does not add up to more than an ounce. No one has been knocked out by such drinking. They say that somarasa is not very palatable[13].

The preposterous suggestion is made that somarasa was the coffee of those times. There are Vedic mantras which speak about the joy aroused by drinking it. This has been misinterpreted. While coffee is injurious to the mind, somarasa cleanses it. It is absurd to equate the two. The soma plant was available in plenty in ancient times. Now it is becoming more and more scarce: this indeed is in keeping with the decline of Vedic dharma. In recent years, the Rājā of Kollengode[14] made it a point to supply the soma plant for the soma sacrifice wherever it was held.

Notes & References

[1] See Chapter 16 of this part.

[2] & [3] These terms are explained in Chapter 32 of this part.

[4] Roughly the statement means: "Sacrifices cannot be said to be impure since they have scriptural authority (or is accompanied by the sound of the Vedas"). The Paramaguru has of course given his own clear explanation.

[5] *Taddhaitad Brahmā Prajāpataya uvāca, Prajāpatir Manave, Manuḥ prajābhyaḥ. Ācārya-kulād Vedam adhītya yathā-vidhānam, guroḥ karma atiśeṣeṇa abhisamāvṛtya, kuṭumbe, śucau deśe svādhyāyam adhīyānaḥ, dhārmikān vidadhat, Ātmani sarvendriyāṇi sampratiṣṭhāpya, ahiṁsan sarva-bhūtāni anyatra tīrthebhyah. sa khalvevaṁ vartayan yāvad āyuṣaṁ Brahmalokam abhisampadyate, na ca punarāvartate, na ca punarāvartate.*

— Chandogya Upaniṣad, 8.15.1

[6] These are dealt with in Part Eleven and Part Nineteen respectively.

[7], [8], [9], & [10] All these terms are explained in Part Nineteen.

[11] Ṛtviks are the priests conducting a sacrifice. See Chapter 26 of this part.

[12] "Arthavāda" is explained in Chapter 34 of this part.

[13] Some matters dealt with in this section are from the explanations of Vedic practices given by Śrī Agnihotram Tātācāriyār. —Ra.Ga.

[14] Kollengode was once a small principality south of Pālakkād in Keraḷa. The Rājā of Kollengode received a pension from the British.

Chapter 24

Animal Sacrifice in the Age of Kali?

An argument runs thus: In the eons gone by mankind possessed high ideals and noble character. Men could sacrifice animals for the well-being of the world because they had great affection in their hearts and were selfless. They offered even cows and horses in sacrifice and had meat for śrāddha[S]. As householders, in their middle years, they followed the karmamārga (the path of works) and performed rites to please the deities for the good of the world. But, in doing so, they desired no rewards. Later, they renounced all works, all pūjā, all observances, to become sannyāsins delighting themselves in their Ātman. They were men of such refinement and noble character that, if their brother, a king, died heirless they begot a son by his wife without any passion in their hearts and without a bit detracting from their brahmacarya[S]. Their only motive was that the kingdom should not be plunged in anarchy for want of an heir to the throne.

In our own Kali age we do not have such men who are desireless in their actions, who can subdue their minds and give up all works to become ascetics and who will remain chaste at heart even in the company of women. So it is contended that the following are to be eschewed in the Kali age: horse and cow sacrifices, meat in the śrāddha[S] ceremony, sannyāsa, begetting a son by the husband's brother. As authority we have the following verse:

Aśvālaṁbham gavālaṁbham sannyāsam palapaitṛkam
Devareṇa sutotpattim kalau pañca vivarjayet

According to one view "aśvālaṁbham" in this verse should be substituted with "agniyādhānam"[1]. If you accept this version it would mean that even those sacrifices in which animals are not killed should not be performed. In other words it would mean a total prohibition of all sacrifices. The very first in the haviryajña category is agniyādhāna. If that were to be prohibited it would mean that, apart from small sacrifices called "pākayajñas", no yajña can be performed.

According to great men such a view is wrong. Śankara Bhagavatpāda, whose mission in life was the re-establishment of the Vedic dharma, did not stop with the admonishment that the Vedas must be chanted every day ("Vedo nityam adhīyatām"). He insisted that the rites imposed on us by the Vedas must be performed: "Taduditam karma svanuṣṭhīyatām." Of Vedic rites, sacrifices occupy the foremost place. If they are to be eschewed what other Vedic rites are we to perform? It may be that certain types of sacrifices need not be gone through in the age of Kali.

If, according to the verse, agniyādhāna is interdicted, and no big sacrifice is to be performed in the age of Kali, why should gavālambha (cow sacrifice) have been mentioned in the prohibited category? If agniyādhāna is not permissible, it goes without saying that gavālaṁbha also is prohibited. So, apart from certain types, all sacrifices are to be performed at all times.

According to another verse quoted from the Dharmaśāstra, so long as the varṇāśrama system is followed in the age of Kali, in however small a measure, and so long as the sound of the Vedas pervades the air, works like agniyādhāna must be performed and the sannyāsāśrama followed, the stage of life in which there is no karma. The prohibition in Kali applies to certain types of animal sacrifices, meat in śrāddha[S] ceremonies and begetting a son by the husband's brother.

Reference

[1] See Chapter 8, Part Nineteen.

Chapter 25

The One Goal

Briefly told, a yajña is making an oblation to a deity in the fire with the chanting of mantras. In a sense the mantras themselves constitute the form of the deities invoked. In another sense, the mantras, like the materials placed in the fire, are the sustenance of the celestials invoked. They enhance their powers and serve more than one purpose. We pay taxes to the government. However, the various imposts — professional tax, land tax, motor vehicles tax, and so on — are collected by different offices. There are also different stamp papers for the same. Similarly, for each karma or religious work there is an individual deity, a separate mantra, a particular material, etc, but the ultimate goal of all these is dedication to the Supreme God. We know that the different taxes paid to different departments are meant for the same government. Similarly, we must realise that the sacrifices performed for the various deities have behind them one goal, the Paramātman.

The king or the president is not personally acquainted with us who pay the taxes. But Parameśvara, the Supreme Monarch, knows each one of us better than we know ourselves. He also knows whether we pay the taxes properly, the taxes called sacrifices. Parameśvara cannot be deceived.

As mentioned before, for each sacrifice there are three essential requirements: the mantra, the material for oblation, and the deity to be invoked, the three bringing together speech, hand [body] and mind.

Chapter 26

Those who conduct Sacrifices

One who performs a yajña or sacrifice spending on the material and dakṣiṇā[S] is called a "yajamāna." "Yaj" (as we have seen already) means to worship. The root meaning of "yajamāna" is one who performs a sacrifice. In Tamiḷ Nāḍu nowadays we refer to a "*mudalāḷi*"[1] as *yajamān*. It is the *mudalāḷi* who pays the wages. So it is that we have given him the same place as the yajamāna who pays dakṣiṇā in sacrifices. That even common folks refer to the *mudalāḷi* as *yajamān* shows how deep-rooted the Vedic culture is in the Tamiḷ land[2].

There is another word which also testifies to the fact that Tamiḷ Nāḍu is steeped in the Vedic tradition. A place where people are fed free is called a "*cattiram*" by Tamiḷs[3]. In the North the corresponding word for the same is "*dharamśālā*" (dharmaśālā).

How would you explain the use of the word *cattiram* in the South? It is derived from "sattram" which is the name of a type of Vedic sacrifice. In other sacrifices there is one yajamāna who spends on the material and dakṣiṇā. The priests receive the dakṣiṇā from him and conduct the sacrifice on his behalf. In a sattra all are yajamānas. As we have mentioned earlier any sacrifice brings benefits to all mankind and also serves to cleanse the minds of all those who participate in it — even those who witness the rites are benefited. But the merit accrues chiefly to the yajamāna.

The speciality of a sattra is that all the priests conducting it are yajamānas. It is a kind of socialist yajña in which the merit is equally shared. From this type of sacrifice has originated the term signifying a place or establishment where anyone can come and eat as a matter of right. In a *cattiram* the one who feeds does not consider himself superior to the one who eats. There is reason to believe that sattras had a special place in the tradition of Tamiḷ Nāḍu.

Among the ṛtvik Brahmins there are three classes. The "hotā" (hotṛ) chants the ṛks, the hymns from the Ṛgveda in praise of the deity, invoking the devatā to accept the oblation. Because of the high place accorded him in a sacrifice we hear even today the remark made with reference to anyone occupying a high position, "Ah, he is showing so much of his "*hotā*"[4].

The Ṛgveda is replete with hymns to various deities. The Yajurveda contains mostly the methods and directions for the conduct of sacrifices. The Brahmin who looks after the conduct of the sacrifice is the "adhvaryu". The "udgātā" (udgātṛ) intones the mantras of the Sāmaveda to please the deities. There is a Brahmin supervising the sacrifice and he is called the brahmā.

The Vedas themselves are called "Brahma". That is why one who learns them (the student) is called a "brahmacārin". The supervisor of the sacrifice, brahmā, performs his function in accordance with the Atharvaveda. Thus the hotā, the adhvaryu, the udgātā and the brahmā represent the four Vedas in a sacrifice. In later times, however, the opinion emerged that the brahmā is not connected with the Atharvaveda to the same extent as the hotā, adhvaryu and udgātā are connected respectively with the Ṛg, Yajur and Sāma Vedas. In actual practice also we see that those taking part in sacrifices are conversant with the first three Vedas only and not with the Atharvaveda. For this reason the view is put forward that all sacrifices, from the somayāga to the aśvamedha, are to be performed only on the basis of the Ṛg, Yajur and Sāma Vedas[5].

There are sacrifices which come independently under the Atharvaveda. According to Vālmīki's Rāmāyaṇa, Indrajit performed the Nikumbhilā sacrifice mentioned in this Veda. The other three Vedas have a far wider following. Though we customarily speak of the four Vedas (Caturveda), the Ṛg, Yajur and Sāman are bracketed together and specially spoken of as "Trayī".

(There are three types of sacrifices mentioned in the Atharvaveda: "śāntikam" for peace; "pauṣṭikam" for strength; and "ābhicārikam" to bring injury to enemies).

Notes & References

[1] *Mudalāḷi* is a term used in the South to denote an employer (as already mentioned by the Paramaguru here) or a capitalist.

[2] & [3] See Appendix 1, "Vedic Dharma and Tamiḷ Nāḍu".

[4] Here "hotā" is used as an abstract noun.

[5] The supervisory function of the brahmā in a sacrifice is very small indeed. In the course of the rites the adhvaryu seeks his permission, now and then, for the conduct of the sacrifice. The brahmā grants it with an "Om". In the soma sacrifices he has a slightly bigger role. The Atharvaveda lays down the rules in this connection. In the soma sacrifice the brahmā comes as the head of the three ṛtviks — brāhmaṇācchāmsi, agnīdhra and potā. His function is described in the *Atharvaveda Saṁhitā* (19.20.).

It is the responsibility of the brahmā to point out mistakes or lapses in the conduct of a sacrifice and lay down the prāyaścitta or expiation for the same.

The Atharvaveda itself declares that the position of the brahmā is determined by it. Its *Gopatha Brāhmaṇa* has it that no sacrifice can be conducted on the basis of the other three Vedas alone. It also states that none other than an Atharvavedin can be made a brahmā.

Notwithstanding this, for some reason or other, authors of dharmaśāstras like Āpastamba have excluded the Atharvaveda from sacrifices and permitted the participation in them of brahmās belonging to the other Vedas. However, they have not said that Atharvavedins are not required. (This information was provided by Śrī Agnihotram Rāmānuja Tātācāriyār.) — Ra.Ga.

Chapter 27
The Four Vedas

"Anantāḥ vai Vedāḥ", the Vedas are unending. The seers have, however, revealed to us only a small part of them but it is sufficient for our welfare in this world and the next. We are not going to create many universes like Brahmā that we should know all the Vedas. We need to know only as many as are necessary to ensure our good in this world.

In each of the four Vedas there are different "pāṭhas" and "pāṭhabhedas" or "pāṭhāntaras"[1]. The same musical composition or rāga is sung in different "*pāṇis*"[2]. For instance, the same composition or rāga is expounded in different styles by, say, Mahā-Vaidyanātha Ayyar, Konerirājapuram Vaidyanātha Ayyar and Śarabha Śāstrī[3]. Just as in some *pāṇis* there are more saṅgatis[4] to a composition than in some others, there are more sūktas in some pāṭhas than in others. There may also be differences in the order of the mantras.

Each pāṭhāntara or each version is called a śākhā or recension. The various śākhās are the branches of the Vedic tree, indeed a great tree like the Aḍyār banyan [in Maḍrās]. The branches big and small belong to one or another of the four Vedas, Ṛg, Yajur, Sāman and Atharvan.

Modern indologists are of the view that the Ṛgveda came first, that the Yajurveda came later and so on. But, according to our śāstras, all Vedas are eternal. To state that one Veda belongs to a period prior to, or later than, another is not correct since all the Vedas are associated with the sacrifice that came to mankind with creation itself. The same argument holds good in the matter of fixing the dates of the divisions of any of the śākhās — the Saṁhitā, the Brāhmaṇa and Āraṇyaka. The Vedas belong to a realm in which there is no scope for any research. If we believe that they were discovered by seers who knew past, present and future — themselves, though, remaining in a state beyond time — we will realise that it is meaningless to attempt to fix their date.

In the Ṛgveda itself the Yajurveda and the Sāmaveda are mentioned in a number of passages. In the Puruṣasūkta occurring in the Ṛgveda (tenth maṇḍala, 90th sūkta) there is a reference to the other Vedas. We learn from this, don't we, that one Veda does not belong to a period prior to, or later than, another?

I stated that each recension consisted of the Saṁhitā, the Brāhmaṇa and the Āraṇyaka. When we speak of "Veda-adhyayana" (the study or chanting of the Vedas) we normally have in mind the Saṁhitā part only. When we bring out a book consisting of the Saṁhitā alone of the Ṛgveda we still call it the "Ṛgveda". The Saṁhitā is indeed the very basis of a śākhā, its life-breath. The word means "systematised and collected together".

The Ṛgveda Saṁhitā is all in the form of poetry. What came to be called "śloka" in later times is the "ṛk" of the Vedas. "Ṛk" means a "stotra", a hymn. The Ṛgveda Saṁhitā is made up entirely of hymns in praise of various deities. Each ṛk is a mantra and a number of ṛks in praise of a deity constitute a sūkta.

The Ṛgveda, that is its Saṁhitā, has 10,170 ṛks and 1,028 sūktas. It is divided into ten maṇḍalas or eight aṣṭakas[5]. It begins with a sūkta to Agni and concludes with a sūkta to the same deity. For this reason some believe that the Vedas must be described as the scripture of fire worship, a view with which we would be in agreement if Agni were believed to be the light of the Ātman (the light of knowledge of the Reality). The concluding sūkta of the Ṛgveda contains a hymn that should be regarded as having a higher significance than the national anthem of any country: it is a prayer for amity among all nations, a true international anthem[6]. "May mankind be of one mind," it goes. "May it have a common goal. May all hearts be united in love. And with the mind and the goal being one may all of us live in happiness."

"Yajus" is derived from the word" "yaj" meaning "to worship". "Yajña" (as we have already noted) is also from the same root. Just as "ṛk" means a hymn, "yajus" means the worship associated with sacrifices. The chief purpose of the Yajurveda is the practical application of the Ṛgvedic hymns in the religious work called yajña or sacrifice. The Yajurveda describes in prose the actual conduct of the rites. If the Ṛgveda serves the purpose of adoring the deities verbally the Yajurveda serves the same purpose through rites.

The Yajurveda is different from the other Vedas in that it may be said to be divided into two Vedas which are considerably different from one another: the Śukla-Yajurveda and the Kṛṣṇa-Yajurveda. "Śukla" means white, while "kṛṣṇa" means "black". The Saṁhitā of the Śukla-Yajurveda is also called "Vājasaneyī Saṁhitā". "Vājasani" is one of the names of the sun god. It was the sun god who taught this Saṁhitā to the sage Yājñavalkya.

There is a long story about this, but let me tell it briefly. Before the time of Yājñavalkya, the Yajurveda was an undivided scripture. Yājñavalkya learned it from Vaiśampāyana. Later some misunderstanding arose between the two and the guru bade his student to throw up what he had taught him. Yājñavalkya did so and went to the sun god for refuge. The latter taught him a new Veda, an addition to the scripture that is endless. That is how we came to have Vājasaneyī or Śukla-Yajurveda. The other Yajurveda already taught by Vaiśampāyana acquired the appellation of "Kṛṣṇa", so "Kṛṣṇa-Yajurveda".

In the Kṛṣṇa-Yajurveda, the Saṁhitā and the Brāhmaṇas do not form entirely different parts. The Brāhmaṇas are appended here and there to the mantras of the Saṁhitā.

The glory of the Ṛgveda is that it is replete with hymns to all deities. Scholars are of the opinion that, besides, it contains teachings for our life. The wedding rites are based on that part of this Veda which pertains to the marriage of the daughter of the sun god. There are also passages of a dramatic character like the dialogue between Purūravas and Urvaśī. In later times Kālidāsa based one of his dramatic works on this [the *Vikramorvaśīyam*]. The hymn to Uṣas, the goddess of dawn, and similar mantras are considered to be of high poetic beauty by men of aesthetic discernment.

Since the Ṛgveda is placed first among the four Vedas it must naturally have an exalted position. It is the matrix of the works (karma) of the Yajurveda and the songs of the Sāmaveda.

The importance of the Yajurveda is that it systematises the karmayoga, the path of works. The *Taittirīya Saṁhitā* of the Kṛṣṇa-Yajurveda deals with sacrifices like darśa-pūrṇamāsa, somayāga, vājapeya, rājasūya, aśvamedha[7]. Besides it has a number of hymnic mantras of a high order not found in the Ṛgveda. For example, the popular Śrī Rudra mantras are from the Yajurveda. The Ṛgveda does contain five sūktas known as "Pañcarudra", but when we mention Śrī Rudra we at once think of the mantras to this deity in the Yajurveda. That is why a supreme Śaiva like Appayya Diksita[S] laments that he was not born a Yajurvedin — he was a Sāmavedin.

Among the followers of the four Vedas, Yajurvedins predominate. The majority in the North (Brahmins) belong to the Śukla-Yajurveda while most people in the South belong to the Kṛṣṇa-Yajurveda. The day on which Yajurvedins perform their upākarma[S] is declared a holiday[8]. There is no such holiday for the upākarma of Ṛgvedins and Sāmavedins. This is because Yajurvedins are in a majority. The Puruṣasūkta of the Ṛgveda occurs with some changes in the Yajurveda. Today it is generally understood to be a Yajurvedic hymn.

For non-dualists, the Yajurveda has a special importance. A doctrine and its exposition consist of three parts: the sūtra, the bhāṣya and the vārtika. The sūtra states the doctrine in an apophthegmatic form; the bhāṣya is a commentary on it; and the vārtika is an elucidation of the commentary. To non-dualists the term "vārtikakāra" at once brings to mind Sureśvarācārya[S]. What is the commentary or bhāṣya for which he wrote his vārtika? Śankara's bhāṣya on the Upaniṣads are to be regarded as sūtras. He wrote, in addition, a bhāṣya for the *Brahmasūtra* also. His disciple Sureśvara wrote a vārtika on his master's commentaries. In this work he chose only two of the ten Upaniṣads for which Śankara had written his commentary — the *Taittirīya Upaniṣad* and the *Bṛhadāraṇyaka Upaniṣad*. These two are from the Kṛṣṇa and Śukla - Yajurvedas respectively, which means both are from the Yajurveda. Another distinction of the Yajurveda is that of the ten Upaniṣads ("Daśopaniṣad") the first and the last are from it — the *Īśāvāsyopaniṣad* and the *Bṛhadāraṇyaka Upaniṣad*.

"Sāma" denotes that which brings equipoise or tranquillity to the mind. There are four well-known ways of dealing with an opponent or rival: sāma, dāna, bheda and daṇḍa. The first method is that of conciliation, making an enemy a friend through affection. The Sāmaveda enables us to befriend the divine forces, even the Paramātman. How do we make a person happy? By praising him. If the panegyric is set to music and sung he would be doubly pleased. Many of the mantras of the Ṛgveda are intoned with a cadence in the Sāmaveda; thus we have Sāmagāna. While the ṛks are chanted with the tonal differences of udātta, anudātta and svarita[S], the sāmans are intoned musically according to certain rules. Our music, based on the seven notes (saptasvara), has its origin in Sāmaveda. All deities are pleased with Sāmagāna. We become recipients of their grace not only through the offerings made in the sacrificial fire but through the intoning of the sāmans by the udgātā[9]. Sāmagāna is particularly important to soma sacrifices in which the essence of the soma plant is offered as oblation.

Though the sāmans are indeed Ṛgvedic mantras, they are specially capable of pleasing the deities and creating Ātmic uplift because they are intoned musically. This is what gives distinction to the Sāmaveda. Śrī Kṛṣṇa Paramātman says in the Gītā : "Vedānām Sāmavedosmi" (Of Vedas I am the Sāmaveda)[10]. The Lord is everything, including good as well as bad. Even so, as he speaks to Arjuna about the things in which his divine quality specially shines forth, he mentions the Sāmaveda among them. In the *Lalitā-Sahasranāma* (The One Thousand Names of the Goddess Lalitā), Ambā has the name of "Sāmagāna-priyā (one who delights in Sāmagāna); she is not called "Ṛgveda-priyā" or "Yajurveda-priyā". Śyāmāśāstrī[11] refers to the goddess Mīnākṣī as "Sāmagāna-vinodinī" in one of his compositions. In the *Śiva-aṣṭottaram* ["Siva aṣṭottara-śatam", the 108 names of Śiva], Śiva is worshipped thus: "Sāma-prīyāya namaḥ." The *Tevāram*[T] extols Śiva as one who keeps chanting the Chandoga-Sāman (*Chandoga-Sāman odum vāyān).* Appayya Dīkṣita has sought to establish that Īśvara or Śiva, Ambā and Viṣṇu are "Ratna-trayī" (the Three Gems) occupying the highest plane. And all three have a special relationship with the Sāmaveda.

"Atharvan" means a purohita, a priest. There was a sage with this name. That which was revealed by the seer Atharvan is the Atharvaveda. It contains mantras with which one wards off misfortunes and disasters and brings about the destruction of one's enemies. The Atharvaveda is a mixture of prose and poetry. The mantras of other Vedas also serve the same purpose as those of the Atharvaveda. But what is special about the latter is that it has references to deities not mentioned in the others and has mantras addressed to fierce spirits. What has come to be known as "māntrikam" (magical rites) has its source in this Veda.

But it is to be noted that the Atharvaveda also contains mantras that speak of lofty truths. It has the Pṛthivī-sūkta, the hymn to earth, which glorifies this planet with all its creatures.

The Atharvaveda is noteworthy for the fact that the brahmā, the supervisor of sacrifices, is its representative. The Atharvaveda, that is its Saṁhitā, is rarely chanted in the North and is not heard at all in the South. But we must remember that of the ten important Upaniṣads three belong to this Veda — *Praśna, Muṇḍaka and Māṇḍūkya*. It is believed that those who seek liberation need nothing to realise their goal other than the *Māṇḍūkya Upaniṣad*.

We learn from stone inscriptions that the Atharvaveda had a following until some centuries ago. Information about Vedic schools is provided by such inscriptions found near Peraṇi, not far from Tiṇḍivanam, at Eṇṇāyiram and a place near Wālājabād[12], in the neighbourhood of Kāñcīpuram. Even during the reign of the later Coḷas the Atharvaveda was learned in the Tamiḷ country.

There are eighteen divisions among the Brahmins of Orissa. One of them is made up of "Atharvaṇikas", that is Atharvavedins. Even today Atharvavedins are to be met, though their number is small, in parts of Gujarāt like Saurāṣṭra and in Kosala (in U.P.)[13].

Gāyatrī is the mantra of mantras and it is believed to be the essence of the three Vedas — which means that the Atharvaveda is excluded here. According to one view, before he starts learning the Atharvaveda, a brahmacārin must go through a second upanayana[S] ceremony. Generally, the Gāyatrī imparted to a child at the Brahmopadeśa[S] ceremony is called "Tripadā-Gāyatrī" — it is so called because it has three padas or three feet. Each foot encompasses the essential spirit of one Veda. The Atharvaveda has a separate Gāyatrī and if people belonging to other Vedas want to learn this Veda they have to go through a second upanayana to receive instruction in it. For the followers of the first three Vedas, however, there is only one Gāyatrī and those belonging to any one of them can learn the other two Vedas without another upanayana.

(See Chapters 36 and 38 of this part for more on śākhās or recensions of the Vedas).

Notes & References

[1] Different pāthas, versions, variants.

[2] *Pāṇi* is a school or style of music.

[3] Mahā-Vaidyanātha Ayyar (1844-1893) and Konerirājapuram Vaidyanātha Ayyar (1878-1920) were great Carṇāṭic vocalists. Śarabha Śāstrī (1872-1904) was a distinguished Carṇāṭic flautist.

[4] Saṅgati means variation of a melodic line.

[5] The Saṁhitās of all the four Vedas together have 20,500 mantras. — Ra. Ga.

[6] *Saṅgacchadhvam samvadadhvam*
Samvo manāṁsi jānatām
Devābhāgam yathā pūrve
Sañjānānā upāsate

Samāno mantraḥsamitissamānī
Samānam manahsahacittameṣām
Samānam mantramabhimantrayevaḥ
Samānena vo haviṣā juhomi

Samānī va ākūtiḥ
Samānā hṛdayāni vaḥ
Samānamastu vomano
Yathāvahsusahāsati

—Ṛgveda, 10.191. 2, 3 & 4

[7] These terms are explained in Chapter 5, Part Nineteen.

[8] This is no longer the case today.

[9] The Sāmaveda Saṁhitā contains the part called "Arcikā" of the Ṛgveda, and the part called "Gāna". Gāna is subdivided into "krama gāna", "āraṇya gāna" and "ūhya gāna". — Ra. Ga.

[10] Vedānām Sāmavedo'smi devānam asmi Vāsavaḥ
Indriyāṇāṁ manaścāsmi bhūtanām asmi cetanā

— Bhagavadgitā, 10.22

[11] Śyāmāśāstrī (1762-1827) is one of the foremost vāggeyakāras of Carṇāṭic music. A vāggeyakāra (literally word-song-maker) is one who not only creates the text of a song but also determines its musical form and content.

[12] Places in Tamiḷ Nāḍu.

[13] Owing to the efforts made by the Paramaguru and Śrī Jayendra Sarasvatī Svāmī, the study of the Atharvaveda has been revived in the South. Students from Tamiḷ Nāḍu have been sent for this purpose to Sinor in Gujarāt. — Ra. Ga.

Chapter 28

To Discover the One Truth

All Vedas have one common goal though there are differences among their adherents. What is this goal? It is the well-being of the entire world and all creatures living in it, and the uplift of the Self of each one of us and its everlasting union with the Ultimate Reality.

We may take pride in the Vedas for another reason also. They do not point to a single way and proclaim, "This alone is the path" nor do they affirm, "This is the only God" with reference to their own view of the Supreme Being. Instead, they declare that, if one adheres to any path with faith or worships any deity with devotion, one will be led towards the Truth. The scripture of no other religion speaks thus of the many paths to liberation. On the contrary, each of them insists that the way shown by it alone will lead to liberation[1]. The Vedas alone give expression to the high-minded view that different people may take different paths to discover the one and only Truth.

Note

[1] "Salvation" perhaps is the word more commonly used in Christianity in this context.

Chapter 29

Brāhmaṇa, Āraṇyaka

So far, in speaking of the Vedas, I have dealt mainly with the Saṁhitā part of each śākhā or recension. We have already seen that the Saṁhitas are the main text of the Vedas. Apart from them, each śākhā has a Brāhmaṇa and an Āraṇyaka.

The Brāhmaṇa lays down the various rites — karma — to be performed and explains the procedure for the same. It interprets the words of the mantras occurring in the Samhitā, how they are to be understood in the conduct of sacrifices. The Brāhmaṇas constitute a guide for the conduct of yajñas.

The word "Āraṇyaka" is derived from "araṇya". You must have heard of places like "Daṇḍakāraṇya" and "Vedāraṇya". "Araṇya" means a "forest". Neither in the Saṁhitā nor in the Brāhmaṇa is one urged to go and live in a forest. Vedic rites like sacrifices are to be performed by the householder (gṛhastha) living in a village. But after his mind is rendered pure through such rites, he goes to a forest as a recluse to engage himself in meditation. It is to qualify for this stage of vānaprastha, to become inwardly pure and mellow, that Vedic practices like sacrifices are to be followed.

The Āraṇyakas prepare one for one's stage in life as an anchorite. They expound the concepts inherent in the mantras of the Saṁhitās and the rites detailed in the Brāhmaṇas. In other words, they explain the hidden meaning of the Vedas, their metaphorical passages. Indeed, they throw light on the esoteric message of our scripture. For the Āraṇyakas, more important than the performance of sacrifices is awareness of their inner meaning and significance. According to present-day scholars, the Āraṇyakas incorporate the metaphorical passages representing the metaphysical inquires conducted by the inmates of forest hermitages.

The *Bṛhadāraṇyaka Upaniṣad,* as its very name suggests, is both an Āraṇyaka and an Upaniṣad and it begins with a philosophical explanation of the horse sacrifice.

Chapter 30

The Upaniṣads

The Upaniṣads come at the close of the Āraṇyakas. If the Saṁhitā is the tree, the Brāhmaṇa the flower and the Āraṇyaka the fruit (i.e. in its unripe stage), the Upaniṣads are the mellow fruit — the final fruit or "phala"[1]. The Upaniṣads are to the seeker the direct means of realising the non-difference between the jīvātman (individual self) and the Paramātman. The purpose of the Saṁhitā and the Āraṇyaka is to take us to this path of knowledge. Though a number of deities are mentioned here and there in the Upaniṣads, the chief objective of these texts is inquiry into the Ultimate Reality and the attainment of the stage in which one becomes wise enough and mature enough to sever oneself from all karma. It is on this basis that the Vedas are divided into the karmakāṇḍa and the jñānakāṇḍa, the part dealing with works and the part dealing with knowledge [enlightenment]. The two are also spoken of as the Pūrvamīmāṁsā and the Uttaramīmāṁsā respectively.

The great sage Jaimini's śāstra based on his inquiry into the karmakāṇḍa is called Pūrvamīmāṁsā. His teaching is that the karmakāṇḍa, constituting the Vedic rites and duties, is itself the final fruit of the scripture. Similarly, Vyāsa has in his work, the *Brahmasūtra,* inquired into the jñānakāṇḍa and come to the conclusion that it represents the ultimate purpose of the Vedas. The Upaniṣadic jñānakāṇḍa is small compared to the karmakāṇḍa. The *Jaiminisūtra* has a thousand sections ("sahasrādhikaraṇī"), whileVyāsa's *Brahmasūtra* has only 192 sections. Just as the leaves of a tree far outnumber its flowers and fruits, in the case of the Vedic tree the karmakāṇḍa is far bigger than the jñānakāṇḍa.

In other countries philosophers try to apprehend the Truth on an intellectual plane. The Upaniṣadic inquiry is different, its purpose being to realise inwardly the Truth perceived by the mind or the intellect. Is it enough to know that *halva* is sweet? You must experience its sweetness by eating it. How are the Upaniṣads different from other philosophical systems? They (the Upaniṣads) consist of mantras, sacred syllables, and their sound is instinct with power. This power transforms the truths propounded by them into an inward reality. The philosophical systems of other countries do not go beyond making an intellectual inquiry. Here, in the Vedas — in the karmakāṇḍa — a way of life is prescribed for the seeker with actions and duties calculated to discipline and purify him. After leading such a life and eventually forsaking all action, all Vedic karma, he meditates on the truths of the Upaniṣads. Instead of being mere ideas of intellectual perception, these truths will then become a living reality.

The highest of these truths is that there is no difference between the individual self and the Brahman.

It is to attain this highest of states in which the individual self dissolves inseparably in the Brahman that a man becomes a sannyāsin after forsaking the very karma that gives him inward maturity. When he is initiated into sannyāsa he is taught four mantras, the four [principal] mahāvākyas[2]. The four proclaim the identity of the individual self (jivātman) with the Brahman. When these mahāvākyas are reflected upon through the method known as "nididhyāsana"[S], the seeker will arrive at the stage of realising the oneness of the individual self and the Brahman. The four mahāvākyas occur in four different Upaniṣads. Many are the rites that you have to perform, many are the prayers you have to recite and many are the ways of life you are enjoined to follow — all these according to the Saṁhitās and the Brāhmaṇas. But, when it comes to achieving the highest ideal, the supreme goal of man, you have no alternative to the Upaniṣads and their mahāvākyas.

"The Brahman means realising the jñāna that is the highest" (Prajñānam Brahma): this mahāvākya occurs in the *Aitareya Upaniṣad* of the Ṛgveda. "I am the Brahman" (Aham Brahmāsmi) is the mahāvākya belonging to the *Bṛhadāraṇyaka Upaniṣad* of the Yajurveda. "That thou art" or "the Paramātman and you are one and the same" (Tat tvam asi) is from the *Chāndogya Upaniṣad* of the Sāmaveda. The fourth mahāvākya, "This Self is the Brahman" (Ayam Ātma Brahma), is from the *Māṇḍūkya Upaniṣad* of the Atharvaveda.

In his *Sopana Pañcaka,* which contains the sum and substance of his teachings, the Ācārya urges us to chant the Saṁhitās (of the Vedas), perform the duties laid down in the Brāhmaṇas and, finally, to meditate on the mahāvākyas after receiving initiation into them, the purpose being our oneing with the Brahman.

The Vedas find their final expression in the Upaniṣads. Indeed, the Upaniṣads are called "Vedānta". They form the final part of the Vedas in two ways. In each recension we have first the Saṁhitā, then the Brāhmaṇa which is followed by the Āraṇyaka, the Upaniṣad coming at the close of the last-mentioned. The Upaniṣads throw light on the meaning and purpose of the Vedas and represent the end of the scripture in more than one sense: while their text forms the concluding part of the Vedas, their meaning represents the Ultimate Truth of the same. A village or town has a temple; the temple has its gopuram; and the gopuram has a śikhara[S] over it. The Upaniṣads are the śikhara, the summit, of our philosophical [and metaphysical] system.

"Upa-ni-sad" means to "sit near by". The Upaniṣads are the teachings imparted by a guru to his student sitting by his side [sitting at his feet]. You could also take the term to mean "that which takes one to the Brahman". "Upanayana" may be interpreted in two ways: leading a child to his guru; or leading him to the Brahman. Similarly, the term Upaniṣad could also be understood in the above two senses.

If a student sits close to the teacher when he is receiving instruction it means that a "rahasya" (a secret or a mystery) is being conveyed to him. Such teachings are not meant to be imparted to those who are not sufficiently mature and who are not capable of cherishing their value. That is why in the Upaniṣads themselves these words occur where subtle and esoteric truths are expounded: "This is Upaniṣat. This is Upaniṣat". What is held to be a secret in the Vedas is called a "rahasya". In the Upaniṣads the term "Upaniṣat" itself is used to mean the same.

(See Chapter 33 of this part, entitled "The Ten Upaniṣads".)

Notes

[1] "Phala" means a fruit as well as the benefit gained from any action or the result or reward of any work or endeavour.

[2] The "mahāvākyas" are "great pronouncements", "great formulas", "great dicta", found in the Upaniṣads.

Chapter 31

The Brahmasūtra

I said that every doctrine or system has a sūtra (text consisting of aphoristic statements), a bhāṣya (commentary) and a vārtika (elucidation of the commentary). The systems founded by Śankara, Rāmānuja, Madhva, Śrikaṇṭha (ācārya of Śaiva-Siddhānta) belong to Vedānta. All these ācāryas cite the authority of the Vedas in support of their respective doctrines and they have chosen the same ten Upaniṣads to comment upon according to their different philosophical perceptions. The Upaniṣads are not in the form of sūtras; yet for the Vedāntic system they must be regarded as having the same "place" (or force) as the sūtras.

How is a sūtra to be understood? It must state truths in an extremely terse form. What is expressed in the least possible number of words to convey an idea or truth is a sūtra, an aphorism. According to this definition the Upaniṣads cannot be said to be sūtras. However, there does exist a basic text for all Vedāntic schools in the form of sūtras. This is the *Brahmasūtra.*

In the *Brahmasūtra,* on which there are commentaries according to the various philosophical schools, Vyāsa presents in an extremely terse form the substance of the ten (principal) Upaniṣads. Since he dwelt under the badarī tree (jujube) he came to be called "Bādarāyaṇa" and his work became well known as "Bādarāyaṇa-sūtra". Who or what is man (the individual self)? What is the nature of the world (jagat) in which he lives? And what is the truth underlying all this? The *Brahmasūtra,* which is a basic text of all Vedāntic schools, seeks to answer these fundamental questions. Vyāsa does not project his personal views in his work. All he does is to make a penetrating study of the science of Vedānta that is already constituted by the Upaniṣads. Since it is an inquiry into the Upaniṣads which form the latter part of the Vedas, the *Brahmasūtra* is called "Uttaramīmāṁsā".

There are 555 sūtras in the *Brahmasūtra* which is divided into four chapters, each consisting of four padas (or "feet"). Altogether there are 192 sections or "adhikaraṇas" in it. The *Brahmasūtra* is also called "Bhikṣu-sūtra" since it deals with sannyāsa, the final goal of the seeker. And, because it is all about the Self in the body, it has another name, "Śārīraka".

"Sūtra" literally means a rope or a string. The word occurs in the term "maṅgaḷa-sūtra", the thread worn by the bride at her wedding. Keeping the meaning of thread or string in mind, our Ācārya has made a pun on the word in his commentary: "Vedānta-vākya-kusuma-grathanārthatvāt sūtrāṇām". If the flowers that are the Upaniṣads in the tree called the Vedas are strewn all over the earth, how can we gather them to make a garland? Our Ācārya remarks that in the *Brahmasūtra* the flowers that are the Upaniṣads are strung together to form a garland.

All Hindu philosophical systems are based on the *Brahmasūtra,* but the *Brahmasūtra* itself is based on the Upaniṣads. That is why it has become customary to describe all Vedic schools of thought as "Upaniṣadic systems". When Westerners keep extolling our philosophy, chanting, "Vedānta! Vedānta!", they have in mind the Upaniṣads. If a person turns against the petty pleasures of this world and makes some remark suggestive of jñāna, people tell him, "*Arre,* are you mouthing Vedānta?"

If the Vedas were personified as Puruṣa, the Upaniṣads would be his head or crown. That is why these texts are called "Śruti-śiras".

Chapter 32

Veda and Vedānta : Are They Opposed to One Another?

The rituals mentioned in the karmakāṇḍa of the Vedas are sought to be negated in the jñānakāṇḍa which is also part of the same scripture. While the karmakāṇḍa enjoins upon you the worship of various deities and lays down rules for the same, the jñānakāṇḍa constituted by the Upaniṣads ridicules the worshipper of deities as a dim-witted person no better than a beast.

This seems strange, the latter part of the Vedas contradicting the former part. The first part deals throughout with karma, while the second or concluding part is all about jñāna. Owing to this difference, people have gone so far as to divide our scripture into two sections: the Vedas (that is the first part) to mean the karmakāṇḍa and the Upaniṣads (Vedānta) to mean the jñānakāṇḍa.

Vedānta it is that the Lord teaches us in the Gītā and in it he lashes out against the karmakāṇḍa. It is generally believed that the Buddha and Mahāvīra were the first to attack the Vedas. It is not so. Śrī Kṛṣṇa Paramātman himself spoke against them long before these two religious leaders. At one place in the Gītā he says to Arjuna[1]: "The Vedas are associated with the three qualities of sattva, rajas and tamas[S]. You must transcend these qualities. Full of desire, they (the practitioners of Vedic rituals) long for paradise and keep thinking of pleasures and material prosperity. They are born again and again and their minds are never fixed in samādhi[S], these men clinging to Vedic rituals." In another passage Kṛṣṇa declares[2]: "Not by the Vedas am I to be realised, nor by sacrifices nor by much study. ..."

Does not such talk contradict all that I have spoken so far about the Vedas, that they are the source of all our dharma ?

With some thinking we will realise that there is in fact no contradiction. Would it be possible for us, in our present condition, to go beyond the three guṇas even to the slightest extent and realise the true state of the Self spoken of in the Upaniṣads? The purpose of the Vedic rituals is to take us, by degrees, to this state. So long as we believe that the world is real we worship the deities so as to be vouchsafed happiness. And this world, which we think is real, is also benefited by such worship. Thinking the deities to be real, we help them and in return we are helped by them. Living happily on this earth we long to go to the world of the celestials and enjoy the pleasures of paradise. So far so good. But if we stopped at this stage would it not mean losing sight of our supreme objective? Is not this objective, this goal, our becoming one with the Paramātman? Would it not be foolish to ignore this great ideal of ours and still cling to mundane happiness?

In our present state of immaturity it is not possible to think of the world being unreal. Recognising this, the Vedas provide us the rituals to be performed for happiness in this world. Because of our inadequacies we are unable to devote ourselves to a formless Paramātman from whom we are not different. So the Vedas have devised a system in which a number of deities are worshipped. But, in course of time, as we perform the rituals and worship the deities, we must make efforts to advance to the state of wisdom and enlightenment in which the world will be seen to be unreal and the rites will become unnecessary. Instead of worshipping many deities, we must reach the state in which we will recognise that we have no existence other than that of our being dissolved in the Paramātman. We must perform Vedic sacraments with the knowledge that they prepare us to go to this high state by making our mind pure and one-pointed.

If we perform rituals with the sole idea of worldly happiness and carry on trade with the celestials by conducting sacrifices (offering them oblations and receiving benefits from them in return), we will never come face to face with the Truth. Even if we go to the world of the celestials, we will not be blessed with Self-realisation. Our residence in paradise is commensurate with the merit we earn here and is not permanent. Sooner or later we will have to return to this world and be in the womb of a mother. The ritual worship and other sacraments of the Vedas are to some extent the result of making an adjustment to our present immature state of mind. But their real purpose is to take us forward gradually from this very immature state and illumine us within. It would be wrong to refuse to go beyond the stage of ritual worship.

If, to begin with, it is not right to refuse all at once to perform Vedic rites, it would be equally not right, subsequently, to refuse to give them up. Nowadays, people are averse to ritual to start with itself. "What?" they exclaim. "Who wants to perform sacrifices? Why should we chant the Vedas? Let us go directly to the Upaniṣads." Some of them can speak eloquently about the Upaniṣads from a mere intellectual understanding of them. But none has the inward experience of the truths propounded in them and we do not see them emerging as men of detachment with a true awareness of the Self. The reason for this is that they have not prepared themselves for this higher state of perception through the performance of rituals. If this is wrong in one sense, refusal to take the path of jñāna from that of karma is equally not justifiable.

If one has to qualify for the B.A. degree one has to begin at the beginning — one has to progress from the first standard all the way to the degree course. One cannot naturally join the B.A. class without qualifying for it. At the same time, is it not absurd to remain all the time as a failure in the first standard itself?

In the old days there were many people belonging to the latter category (that is people who refused to take the path of knowledge and wished to remain wedded to the path of karma). Now people belonging to the former category predominate (that is those who want to take the path of jñāna, without being prepared for it through karma). During the time of Śrī Kṛṣṇa also the majority clung to rituals. His criticism is directed against them, against those who perform Vedic sacraments without understanding their purpose and who fail to go beyond them. Unfortunately, this is mistaken for criticism of the Vedas themselves. The Lord could never have attacked the Vedas *per se.* After all, it was to save them that he descended to earth again and again.

In keeping with his times, Kṛṣṇa Paramātman spoke against people who confined themselves to the narrow path of karma. If he were to descend to earth again to teach us, he would turn against those who plunge into a study of the Upaniṣads, spurning Vedic rites. It seems to me that he would be more severe in his criticism of these people than he was against those who were obsessed with karma.

Graduating to the Upaniṣads without being prepared for them through the performance of Vedic rites is a greater offence than failure to go along the path of jñāna from that of karma. After all, to repeat what I said before, one has to go through the primary and secondary stages of education before qualifying for admission to college. The man who insists on being admitted to the B.A. class without qualifying for it is not amenable to any suggestion. The one who wants to remain in the first standard learns at least something; the other type is incapable of learning anything.

The Vedas and Vedānta are not at variance with one another. The karmakāṇḍa prepares us for Vedānta or the jñānakāṇḍa. The former has to do with this world and with many deities and its adherents are subject to the three guṇas[S]. But it is the first step to go beyond the three guṇas and to sever oneself from worldly existence. If we perform the rites laid down in the karmakāṇḍa, keeping in mind their true purpose, we shall naturally be qualifying for the jñānakāṇḍa.

Some questions arise here. The sound of the Vedas and the sacrifices benefit not only the person who chants the Vedas and performs the sacrifices but all creatures. If such a man (that is like the one who learns the Vedas and conducts sacrifices) renounces the world thinking it to be unreal and becomes a jñānin, what will happen to the world, to its welfare? Even if you think that the world is unreal, it is real in the sense that it is the cause of so much suffering. The jñānin does not perform any rites like sacrifices so as to rid the world of its troubles. Who will then work for the welfare of the world?

The answer: the jñānin is in an exalted state of awareness and while being in it he does not have to perform any sacrifices or other rites to ensure the good of the world. His life itself is a sacrifice, a yajña, and through him the world will receive the Lord's blessings even if he looks upon it as unreal or as a "sport" of the Supreme Being. Why do people flock to a jñānin? Why do they fall at his feet even if he keeps himself aloof from them? It is because they receive his grace. Whether or not he wants to give any blessings, the Lord's grace flows into this world through him. In his very presence people feel tranquil and, sometimes, even their worldly desires are satisfied. A jñānin who realises within that there is no deity apart from himself can give his blessings in greater measure than the deities themselves. So it is wrong to think that, since he does not perform sacrifices, he does not do anything for the good of the world.

Followers of other faiths are mistaken in their view of Hinduism. They separate the Vedāntic system from the Vedic system of sacraments and observe: "To the Hindus what matters is individual salvation. They ignore the well-being of the world. Meditation, yoga, samādhi[S] are a means of individual liberation. Hindus are unlike the followers of Jesus Christ and the Prophet Mohammed because they do not preach love and brotherhood nor do they promote the growth of social consciousness among themselves."

One who has a proper understanding of our religion will recognise that it is wrong to divide Hinduism into two compartments, the Vedic religion and the Vedāntic. As a sannyāsin in the final stage of his life a man becomes a Vedāntin and jñānin and merits liberation for himself. But we must remember that he leaves behind him another stage of life in which he has worked for the welfare of the world by chanting the Vedas and by performing rituals. Indeed it was because of this work that he became mentally pure and qualified for the Vedāntic path and for his own release from worldly existence.

Also to be noted is that even after achieving perfection in Vedānta and becoming a jñānin he keeps blessing the world without performing any rites and, indeed, by virtue of his mere presence. I am not examining here the big question of which of the two goals of a religion is greater, individual liberation or collective welfare. That is a separate subject. Let us leave aside for the present the question of social welfare. The question to be answered now is this: If an individual owing allegiance to a religion does not become a jñānin with inward experience of the Truth of the Supreme Being, what does it matter whether or not that religion exists ?

All rituals, all worship, are meant to make a man aware of the Reality. Varṇāśrama with its one hundred thousand differences and with its countless stipulations as to who can do what is a preliminary arrangement to arrive at the stage in which there is a oneing of all, with all the differences banished. If we fail to go beyond the stage of karma, observing all the differences of varṇāśrama, we shall be committing a wrong. Kṛṣṇa Paramātman directs his criticism against those who claim that the karmakāṇḍa of the Vedas alone matters, that the jñānakāṇḍa does not serve any purpose. In doing so he seems to attack the Vedas themselves. In reality he faults those who are, in his words, "Veda-vāda-ratāḥ", those who are deceived by flowery accounts of the Vedas without realising their true meaning and those who do not exert themselves to rise to the level of experiential jñāna.

To start with, we must perform the rites prescribed by the Vedas. But in this there must be the realisation that they are but steps leading us to the higher state in which we will ultimately find bliss in our Self, a state in which there will be neither rites nor duties to perform. Similarly, to start with, the deities must be worshipped but again with the conviction that such worship serves the ultimate purpose of arriving at the point where we will recognise that the worshipper and the worshipped are one. Thus, to begin with, all differences in functions must be recognised and life lived according to them. Different divisions of people have different duties, and the customs and rites assigned to each are such as to help them in the proper discharge of those duties. But in the very process of maintaining such differences there must be the conviction within that ultimately there are no differences, that all are one.

If the Vedas are to be learned and chanted and if the Vedic rituals are to be practised — and the Vedas must be learned and chanted even as the Vedic rituals must be practised — it is because in this way we shall be led to that supreme experience of the Reality in which there will be no need for these very Vedas. First the flowers and from them the fruit. Though the flower looks beautiful, the fruit emerges only when it wilts or falls to earth. A tree does not fruit before it flowers. In the same way, to plunge into Vedānta without first going through a life of Vedic discipline is neither wise nor in keeping with reality. It is equally wrong to remain confined to the karmakāṇḍa and refuse to make an effort to acquire Vedāntic knowledge: it is like wishing that we must have only flowers and no fruits. There must be a sense of balance, a sense of proportion, in everything we do.

There is a passage in the *Bṛhadāraṇyaka Upaniṣad* similar to that in the Gītā: "He who becomes aware of the nature of the Ātman — for him the Vedas will no longer be Vedas, the gods will cease to be gods, Brahmins will no longer be Brahmins...[3]"

As we have already seen, "Śruti" by which we mean the Vedas contains not only the Saṁhitās but also the Brāhmaṇas, Āraṇyakas and the Upaniṣads. The Gītā is not a Śruti and it is customary to regard it as belonging to the category of Smṛti. I shall speak to you later about Smṛti when I deal with Dharmaśāstra, one of the fourteen branches of learning (caturdaśa-vidyā). The Smṛti that is the Gītā observes: "Vedic rites and worship are futile if they do not take you to the path of jñāna." The Purāṇas too are among the three categories of authoritative texts of our religion — the other two being Śruti and Smṛti — and they have the same view about a life confined to rituals. The sages in the Dāruka forest were proud about their sacrificial worship, but Parameśvara curbed their pride — how he did so is narrated in the Śaiva Purāṇas. The *Bhāgavata* tells us how the yajñapatnis, the simple and unpretentious wives of the sages, were able to see Mahāviṣṇu as he appeared in the form of the Yajñapuruṣa. But their husbands who were wedded to ritual could not see the Lord and very much regretted it.

Śruti is higher as an authority than Smṛti or the Purāṇas. I referred to a passage from the *Bṛhadāraṇyaka Upaniṣad* to show that we have the testimony of the Śruti itself to prove that rituals are not enough for Ātmic advancement. However, it might be argued that Śruti itself is divided into the karmakāṇḍa and the jñānakāṇḍa and that, after all, it is natural that in the jñānakāṇḍa the quest for jñāna should be spoken of highly. So there is nothing remarkable about its declaring that rituals cannot be the final goal of the seeker.

However, in the karmakāṇḍa itself there is criticism of the view that rituals are all and that they are the ultimate goal. Śrī Kṛṣṇa declares in the Gītā[4] that it is laudable to perform the many sacrifices mentioned in the Vedas realising their true purpose ("Evaṁ bahuvidhā yajñā vitatā Brahmaṇo mukhe"). However, all these sacraments have their culmination in jñāna ("Sarvaṁ karm'akhilaṁ Partha jñāne parisamāpyate").

The same idea is expressed forcefully through an illustration in the Vedic karmakāṇḍa itself: "He who performs only rituals, without wakening to Īśvara feeds the fire to raise smoke and nothing else" (*Taittirīya Kāṭhakam,* first praśna, last anuvāka, fourth vākya). If you feed the fire with firewood you must keep the pot over it to cook rice. One who does not exert oneself to be "cooked" in jñāna is like the man who lights the kitchen fire without keeping the cooking pot on it. This is what the Vedas say. What purpose is served by building a big sacrificial fire if you do not offer the oblation in it? The result will be only smoke and more smoke. A sacrifice must be performed with the consciousness that you are offering the fruit of your karma itself as an oblation. Otherwise there will be nothing but smoke.

"The Self must be offered as an oblation in the fire of the Brahman. All sensual pleasures must be offered in the fire of self-control. The five vital breaths must be given over in sacrifice in one another"[5], says the Gītā. Vedic sacrifices involving materials and works have this goal. A man may perform any number of sacrifices but he would be a fool to perform them without realising this truth. The Vedas too say that such a man is unintelligent. What do you expect his buddhi (intuitive intelligence) to become? It would also be like the smoke of the sacrificial fire that darkens everything in its course and ends up in nothing.

When Vedic rites are performed in a spirit of dedication to Īśvara they will loosen your ties little by little, instead of keeping you bound to this world. If you perform rites to please the Lord, without expecting any reward, your mind will be cleansed and you will transcend the three guṇas[S]. This is the meaning and purpose of "yajña". Is not the word understood in English as "sacrifice"? "Yāga" also means sacrifice, "tyāga". When an offering is placed in the fire we say "na mama" ("not mine"): it is this attitude of self-denial that is the life and soul of a sacrificial rite. Is it possible to retrieve what has been offered in the fire? Even if it were, it would soon disintegrate. In this way you must reduce your ego-sense to ashes, also your possessiveness ("ahaṁkāra-mamakāra"). One who performs a sacrifice without being conscious of such high ideals but with the purpose of petty gains like ascending to paradise — is he not a fool?

There is no contradiction between the karmakāṇḍa and the jñānakāṇḍa. *In the karmakāṇḍa itself jñāna is given an elevated place and the limitations of karma mentioned.* There are hymns incorporating high philosophical truths in the Saṁhitā part itself of the Vedas like, for instance, the "Nāsādīyasūkta", the "Puruṣasūkta" and the "Tryaṁbaka mantra". *Also to be noted is the fact that the Upaniṣads themselves mention rites (karma) like the "Naciketāgni".* How would you explain this if the karmakāṇḍa and the jñānakāṇḍa were opposed to one another? The underlying idea is that we must graduate from the one to the other [from karma to jñāna].

As we have already seen, the Gītā (which is a Smṛti) says that sacraments performed in a spirit of dedication to Īśvara are a means of obtaining jñāna. The same idea is found expressed in a Śruti text, the *Īśāvāsya Upaniṣad.* The first of the ten major Upaniṣads, it commences with the statement[6]: "Live a hundred years performing Vedic rites. But do so in a spirit of dedication to Īśvara. Then it will not keep you bound". So it would be wrong to believe that the Upaniṣads teach inaction.

Karma, however, is not the goal of the Vedas. You must go beyond the stage of performing Vedic rituals even if they be for such a noble purpose as that of creating welfare in the world, cleansing your consciousness and propitiating the deities. You must rise higher to the plane where you will realise that nothing other than the Paramātman exists, that the phenomenal world is unreal, that there are no entities called deities (devatās) with an independent existence of their own and that there is no "I". When you come to this state there will be no need for the Vedas too for you: this is stated in the Vedas themselves.

The Vedas are the laws laid down by Parameśvara. All people, all his subjects, must obey them. But there is no need for the man who is always steeped inwardly as well as outwardly in the Reality that is the Paramātman to refer to this law with respect to all his actions. That is why it is said that for such men the Vedas cease to be Vedas. (We too do not respect the Vedas as the law. For us also the Vedas are not Vedas. But we do not have even a whiff of jñāna!)

If you do not realise that the karmakāṇḍa is a means to take you to the "parāvidyā"[7] that is constituted by the Upaniṣads, then the Vedas (that is their karmakāṇḍa) is an aparā vidyā[8] like any other subject such as history or geography that is learned at school. It is for this reason that the *Muṇḍaka Upaniṣad* includes the Vedas in the category of aparā-vidyā[9]. This Upaniṣad describes a person who performs Vedic rites for ephemeral enjoyments, mundane benefits, as a mere beast (paśu).

To the jñānin who is united with the Paramātman the deities are not entities outside of himself for they too have emanated from the same Paramātman. Indeed, these deities inhere in him since he is dissolved in the Paramātman to become the Paramātman. If he does not have such inward experience of being dissolved in the Supreme Godhead, when he worships a deity as an entity separate from him, he must do so regarding it as integral to the Ātman. Even if it be necessary to carry out all our outward functions according to a system based on differences, we must always be conscious of the truth that in the end we will be united with that fundamental Reality in which all these differences will cease to exist. The *Bṛhadāraṇyaka Upaniṣad* declares: "He who worships the deities as entities entirely separate from him does not know the truth. For the gods he is like a paśu (beast)" (1.4.10)[10].

The word "paśu" is very meaningful here. In a superficial sense it means one who does not possess the sixth sense of a human and lives on an animal level. Let me tell you the inner meaning. Why do we keep a cow? Because it gives us milk. That is why we feed it grass, oil cake, cottonseed and so on. We offer oblations in the fire to please the gods. In return they grant us blessings in the form of rain, crops, etc. These celestials, as we have seen, are superior to us but they do not know the bliss that is boundless. Indeed they are unaware of even a fraction of the bliss that a jñānin who is but a mortal experiences.

The *Taittirīya Upaniṣad* (2.8.1)[11] and the *Bṛhadāraṇyaka Upaniṣad* (4.3.33)[12] deal with the ānanda, bliss, experienced by various orders like humans, the fathers, the celestials. We have here something of an arithmetical table on bliss. The bliss experienced by each order is a hundred times greater than that experienced by the preceding one — it is all in the ascending order. Among the celestials the degrees of bliss known to Indra, Bṛhaspati and Prajāpati are given separately. The highest bliss is experienced by the jñānin, the bliss of knowing the Brahman (Brahmānanda). Thus the devas (celestials) are deficient in the matter of bliss. Also, they do not make any effort to attain to the highest state of blessedness. They look forward to the gains to be made from us, from the sacrifices we perform, from our worship. For this reason they do not like us humans to become jñānins. This is clearly stated in the *Bṛhadāraṇyaka Upaniṣad:* "The celestials do not like humans who realise the Self" (1.4.10)[13]. Why? When a man realises himself he will not perform any sacrifices and other rites to please the deities.

Take the case of our domestic servant. We pay him a small wage and we know that we will have to pay more if we appoint a new man in his place. He wants to go to school, pass some examination or other so that, eventually, he will be able to take up some better job and do well in life. If he really appeared for an examination, would we honestly like him to pass? No. We would like him to fail. If he passes he will find a better job for himself and have a better "status" than now. We may not find it easy to hire a new servant on the same small wages. We are similarly situated in our relationship to the celestials. They will not like us to become jñānins because we will then cease to worship them.

If a jñānin is not dear to the devas, it follows that one who is not a jñānin is dear to them. In other words he who is dear to the gods is an ajñānin. That is why in grammar an idiot ("mūrkha") has the name of "devānāṁpriya" ("dear to the gods or celestials"). This term has its source in the Upaniṣads. In his commentary on the *Brahmasūtra,* Śankara Bhagavatpāda says to one who maintains that the Paramātman and the jivātman (individual self) are different: "Idam tāvad devānāmpriyaḥ praṣṭavyaḥ" (This is what you idiot should be asked). You had probably thought that "devānāṁpriya" to be a big title of honour.

(In the Aśokan edicts the emperor is referred to as "devānāṁpriya". Even before the time of Aśoka, Pāṇini had said that the term meant an idiot. For this reason it would be wrong to believe that the followers of the Vedic religion in later times took the word to mean an idiot with the deliberate intent of denigrating the Buddhist Aśoka. Our Ācārya, as I have said earlier, refers in his commentary on the *Brahmasūtra* to one who does not know the true purpose of the Vedas as a "devānāṁpriya", meaning by the term an "idiot". But now in the Aśokan edicts the same appellation is given to one opposed to the Vedas, one who belongs to the non-Vedic Buddhist religion.

(One who follows the Vedic tradition and becomes a jñānin by learning the truths propounded in the Upaniṣads no longer performs sacrifices to please the gods. No more will he be dear to them now. Since sacrifices are prohibited in Buddhism obviously the celestials do not like followers of that religion. Then why is Aśoka, who was a great supporter of Buddhism, called "devānāṁpriya"? As a Buddhist he would not have performed Vedic rituals, but at the same time he would not have come under the influence of Vedānta to become a jñānin. Aśoka must have earned the appellation of "devānāṁpriya" in the sense that anyone who did not follow the teachings of Vedānta does not become a jñānin.

(It is also likely that someone not acquainted with such matters, a sculptor or a government official, must have inscribed the title "devānāṁpriya" thinking it to be highly complimentary to the emperor.)

When a man, dear to the celestials, ceases to perform sacrifices on turning to the path of jñāna, they place obstacles before him. We read in the Purāṇas stories of the apsarases[S] who disturb the sages in their meditation and austerities.

Until a man becomes a jñānin he keeps performing the rites intended for the celestials. In return they bring him various benefits. They have to be given their share of the oblations. If a man helps us we have to help him in return. Is that not so? We have to help the celestials who bring us rain and other benefits. That is why we perform sacrifices. Some Brahmin or other gives the "havirbhāga" (a share in the oblations) to the devas, doing so as a representative of us all. It is like one man paying taxes on behalf of all.

To the celestials a person who performs Vedic rituals is like a milch cow. When the cow goes dry what use is it to a man (its owner)? The celestials will be pleased with a person so long as he remains a milch cow (performing sacrifices and other rites). If he ceases to be a milch cow they will dislike him, cause him suffering. That means man is like a cow to the devas in more than one sense: in the sense that he is ignorant (not a jñānin);' and in the sense that they do not protect him when he stops performing rites (do we take care of a cow that has gone dry?).

It is part of wisdom and enlightenment to realise that the gods are not separate from us. Vedānta points a way to realise this truth, and shows us how we may free ourselves from works and even worship of the gods and reach the stage where there is no difference between us and all the rest. Let me tell you about the great esteem in which Vedānta has been held in this country.

Though the Vedas are infinite, the seers have brought us only a few of them. But since, in this age of Kali, even these are difficult to master, they divided them into 1,180 śākhās or recensions, each with a Saṁhitā, Brāhmaṇa, Āraṇyaka and Upaniṣad. Later, out of these many passed into oblivion. Now the remaining too are threatened with extinction because people belonging to this generation have brought Vedic studies to such a sad state and earned merit thereby!

We have some Upaniṣads belonging to recensions of which neither the Samhitās nor the Brāhmaṇas are studied. Even their texts are not available. The Saṁhitā of the *Śāṅkhāyana Śākhā* of the Ṛgveda is no longer chanted now; the fact is we have lost it. But the *Kauṣītaki Upaniṣad* which is a part of this recension is still extant. The *Bāṣkala Mantropaniṣad,* also from the Ṛgveda, is still available: I am told a palm-leaf manuscript of the same is in the Aḍyār Library, Maḍrās. But neither the Saṁhitā nor the Brāhmaṇa of the *Bāṣkala Śākhā* is known to us. The *Kaṭha Upaniṣad* belongs to the *Kaṭha Śākhā* of the Kṛṣṇa- Yajurveda. Did I not tell you that the Upaniṣad comes at the end of the Āraṇyaka? The *Kaṭhopaniṣad* is very famous and is one of the major Upaniṣads; but its Āraṇyaka is not available. The Atharvaveda is totally forgotten in the South and is studied but in one or two parts of the country. But still extant are *Praśna, Muṇḍaka* and *Māṇḍūkya* which belong to this Veda and which form part of the Daśopaniṣad.

All this points to the fact that, while parts of many Vedic recensions that pertain to karma or works have become extinct or have been forgotten, many of the Upaniṣads which are the means of jñāna have been preserved. Great care has been taken to protect that part of our heritage which shows us the way to wisdom and light.

The Upaniṣads are believed to have been large in number. Two hundred years ago, an ascetic belonging to Kāñcīpuram wrote a commentary on 108 Upaniṣads. He earned the name of "Upaniṣad Brahmendra". His monastic institution is still to be seen in Kāñcī.

Notes & References

[1] Yām imāṁ puṣpitāṁ vācaṁ pravadanti avipaścitaḥ
Vedavādaratāḥ Partha nānyad astī'ti vādinaḥ

Kām'ātmānaḥ svarga-parā janma-karma-phala-pradām
Kriyā-viśeṣa-bahulāṁ bhog'aiśvarya-gatiṁ prati

Bhog'aiśvarya-prasaktānāṁ tayā'pahṛta-cetasām
Vyavasāy'ātmikā buddhiḥ samādhau na vidhīyate

Traiguṇya-viṣayā Vedā nistraiguṇyo bhavā'rjuna
Nirdvandvo nitya-sattvastho niryogakṣema Ātmavān

— Bhagavadgītā, 2. 42-45

[2] Na Veda-yajñ'ādhyayanair na dānair
Na ca kriyābhir na tapobhir ugraiḥ
Evaṁ-rūpaḥ śakya ahaṁ nṛloke
Draṣṭum tvad-anyena Kurupravīra

— Ibid, 11.48

[3] Brahma taṁ parādāt yo'nyatrātmano Brahma veda: Kṣatram tam parādāt, yo'nyatrātmanaḥ Kṣatram veda: lokāstam parāduḥ, yo'nyatrātmano lokān veda; devāstam parāduḥ, yo'nyatrātmano devan veda; Vedāstam parāduḥ, yo'nyatrātmano Vedān veda; bhūtāni tam parāduḥ, yo'nyatrātmano bhūtāni veda; sarvam tam parādāt, yo'nyatrātmanaḥ sarvam veda; idam Brahma, idam Kṣatram, ime lokāḥ, ime devāḥ, ime Vedāḥ, imani bhūtāni, idam sarvam, yad ayam, Ātmā.

— Bṛhadāraṇyaka Upaniṣad, 4.5.7.

[4] Evaṁ bahuvidhā yajñā vitatā Brahmaṇo mukhe
Karmajān viddhi tān sarvān evam jñātvā vimokṣyase

Śreyān dravyamayād yajñajjñāna-yajñaḥ paraṁtapa
Sarvaṁ karm'ākhilam Pārtha jñāne parisamāpyate

— Bhagadvadgītā, 4.32-33

[5] Brahm'ārpaṇaṁ Brahmahavir Brahm'āgnau Brahmaṇā hutam
Brahmai'va tena gantavyaṁ Brahma-karma-samādhinā

Daivam ev'āpare yajñaṁ yoginaḥ paryupāsate
Brahm'āgnāvapare yajñaṁ yajñen'ai'vo'pajuhvati

Śrotrādīni'ndrīyāṇyanye saṁyam'āgniṣu juhvati
Śabdādīnviṣayān anya indriy'āgniṣu juhvati

Sarvāṇī'ndriya-karmāṇi prāṇa-karmāṇi cā'pare
Ātma-saṁyama-yog'āgnau juhvati jñāna-dīpite

— Ibid, 4. 24-27

[6] Iśāvāsyamidaṁ sarvam yatkiñca jagatyām jagat
Tena tyaktena bhuñjithā ma gṛdhaḥ kasyasviddhanam

Kurvanneveha karmāṇi jijīviṣecchataṁ samāḥ
Evam tvayi nānyatheto'sti na karma lipyate nare

— Īśāvāsya Upaniṣad, 1 & 2

[7] Higher knowledge.

[8] Lower knowledge.

[9] Tatrāparā Ṛgvedo Yajurvedaḥ Sāmavedo'tharvavedaḥ Śīkṣā Kalpo Vyākaraṇam Niruktam Chando Jyotiṣam iti. Atha parā yayā tadakṣaram-adhigamyate

— Muṇḍaka Upaniṣad 1.1.5

[10] Brahma vā idam agra āsīt, tadātmānam evāvedaham Brahmāsmīti: tasmāt tat sarvam abhavat, tad yo yo devānām pratyabudhyata, sa eva tad abhavat, tatharṣīṇām, tathā manuṣyāṇām, taddhaitat paśyan ṛṣir Vāmadevaḥ pratipede, aham Manur abhavam Sūryaśceti, tad idam api etārhi ya evam veda, aham Brahmāsmīti sa idam sarvam bhavati; tasya ha na devāśca nābhūtyā īśate, Ātmāhyeṣām sa bhavati. Atha yo anyām devatām upāste, anyo'sāvanyo'ham asmīti, na sa veda; yathā paśur, evam sa devānām; yathā ha vai bahavaḥ paśavo manuṣyam bhuñjyuḥ, evam ekaikaḥ puruṣo devān bhunakti; ekasminneva paśāvādīyamāne'priyam bhavati, kimu bahuṣu? Tasmād eṣām tan na priyam yad etan manuṣyā vidyuḥ.

— Bṛhadāraṇyaka Upaniṣad, 1.4.10

[11] Bhīṣāsmād vātaḥ pavate, bhīṣodeti sūryaḥ, bhīṣāsmād agniścendraśca, mṛtyur dhāvati pañcama iti.

Saiṣānandasya mīmāṁsā bhavati;

Yuvā syāt sādhu yuvādhyāyakaḥ āśiṣṭho dṛḍhiṣṭho baliṣṭhaḥ, tasyeyam pṛthivī sarvā vittasya pūrṇā syāt, sa eko mānuṣa ānandaḥ te ye śataṁ mānuṣā ānandāḥ, sa eko manuṣya-gandharvāṇām ānandaḥ, śrotriyasya cākāmahatasya;

Te ye śataṁ manuṣya-gandharvāṇām ānandāḥ sa eko deva-gandharvāṇām ānandaḥ, śrotriyasya cākāmahatasya;

Te ye śataṁ deva-gandharvāṇām ānandāḥ sa ekaḥ pitṛṇāṁ cira-loka-lokānām ānandaḥ, śrotriyasya cākāmahatasya;

Te ye śataṁ pitṛṇāṁ cira-loka-lokānām ānandāḥ, sa eka ajānajānāṁ devānām ānandaḥ, śrotriyasya cākāmahatasya;

Te ye śataṁ ajānajānāṁ devānām ānandāḥ, sa ekaḥ karmadevānām devānām ānandaḥ ye karmaṇa devān apiyanti, śrotriyasya cākāmahatasya;

Te ye śataṁ karma-devānām devānām ānandāḥ, sa eko devānām ānandaḥ, śrotriyasya cākāmahatasya:

Te ye śataṁ devānām ānandāḥ, sa eka Indrasyānandaḥ, śrotriyasya cākāmahatasya;

Te ye śataṁ Indrasyānandāḥ, sa eko Bṛhaspater ānandaḥ, śrotriyasya cākāmahatasya;

Te ye śataṁ Bṛhaspater ānandāḥ, sa ekaḥ Prajāpater ānandaḥ, śrotriyasya cākāmahatasya;

Te ye śataṁ Prajāpater ānandāḥ, sa eko Brahmaṇa ānandaḥ, śrotriyasya cākāmahatasya;

Sa yaścāyam puruṣe, yaś cāsāvāditye sa ekah, sa ya evaṁ-vit asmāllokāt pretya, etam annamayam Ātmānam upasaṁkrāmati, etaṁ prāṇamayam Ātmānam upasaṁkrāmati, etam manomayam Ātmānam upasaṁkrāmati, etam vijñānamayam Ātmānam upasaṁkrāmati, etam ānandamayam Ātmānam upasamkrāmati

Tadapi eṣa śloko bhavati.

— Taittiriya Upaniṣad, 2.8.1.

[12] Sa yo manuṣyāṇām rāddhaḥ samṛddho bhavati, anyeṣām adhipatiḥ, sarvair mānuṣyakair bhogaiḥ sampannatamaḥ, sa manuṣyāṇām paramānandaḥ; atha ye śatam manuṣyaṇām ānandāḥ, sa ekaḥ pitṛṇām jitalokānām ānandaḥ; atha ye śataṁ pitṝṇāṁ jitalokānām ānandāḥ. sa eko gandharvaloka ānandaḥ: atha ye śataṁ gandharvaloka ānandāḥ, sa eka karma-devānām ānandaḥ, ye karmaṇā devatvam abhisampadyante; atha ye śataṁ karma-devānām ānandāḥ, sa eka ājāna-devānām ānandaḥ, yaśca śrotriyo'vṛjino 'kāma-hataḥ; atha ye śatam ājāna-devānām ānandāḥ, sa ekaḥ Prajāpatiloka ānandaḥ, yaśca śrotriyo'vṛjino' kāma-hataḥ: atha ye śatam Prajāpatiloka ānandāḥ, sa eko Brahmaloka ānandaḥ, yaśca srotriyo'vṛjino' kāma-hataḥ: athaiṣa eva paramanandah; yaśca śrotriyo'vṛjino kāma-hataḥ; athaiṣa eva paramānandaḥ. Eṣa Brahmalokaḥ, samrād, iti hovāca Yājñavalkyaḥ. So'ham Bhagavate sahasram dadāmi; ata ūrdhvam vimokṣāyaiva brūhīti. Atra ha Yājñavalkyo bibhayām cakāra; medhāvī rājā, sarvebhyo māntebhya udarautsīd iti.

— Bṛhadāraṇyaka Upaniṣad, 4.3. 33

[13] See note 10 above.

Chapter 33

The Ten Upaniṣads

Śankara Bhagavatpāda selected ten out of the numerous Upaniṣads to comment upon from the non-dualistic point of view. Rāmānuja, Madhva and others who came after him wrote commentaries on the same based on their own philosophical points of view. These ten Upaniṣads are listed in the following stanza for the names to be easily remembered.

Īśa-Kena-Kaṭha-Praśna-Muṇḍa-Māṇḍūkya-Tittari
Aitareyam ca Chāndogyam Bṛhadāraṇyakam daśa

Śankara has followed the same order in his Bhāṣya (commentary).

"Īśa" is *Īśāvāsya Upaniṣad (Īśāvāsyopaniṣad)*[1]. It occurs towards the end of the Saṁhitā of the Śukla-Yajurveda. The name of this Upaniṣad is derived from its very first word, "Īśāvāsya". The next, *"Kena"*, is *Kenopaniṣad*. The *Īśāvāsyopaṇisad* proclaims that the entire world is pervaded by Īśvara and that we must dedicate all our works to him and attain the Paramātman.

An elephant made of wood looks real to a child. Grown-ups realise that, though it resembles an elephant in shape, it is really wood. To the child the wood is concealed, revealing the elephant; to the grown-up the animal is hidden revealing the wood. Similarly, all this world and the five elements are made of the timber called the Paramātman. We must learn to look upon all this as the Supreme Godhead.

Marattai maraittadu māmada yānai
Marattil maraindadu māmada yānai
Parattai maraittadu pārmudal bhūtam
Parattil maraindadu pārmudal bhūtam

Tirumūlar[T] says in this stanza that, because of our being accustomed to seeing the five elements all the time, we must not forget that the Paramātman is hidden in them. We must recognise that it is indeed he who pervades them and learn to see that everything is instinct with Īśvara. Śankara expresses exactly the same idea in his Bhāṣya when he speaks of "dantini dāru vikāre". I don't wish to enter into a debate as to who came first, Tirumūlar or Śankara. Great men think alike.

The *Kenopaniṣad* is also called the *Talavakāra Upaniṣad* since it occurs in the *Talavakāra Brāhmaṇa* of the *Jaiminī Śākhā* of the Sāmaveda. This Upaniṣad contains a story about the devas. The celestials in their arrogance failed to recognise the Supreme Being whose crown and feet are unknown. Ambikā then appeared to give instruction in jñāna to Indra, the king of the devas. She explained to him that all our power emanated from the one Great Power, from the one Mahāśakti.

The Ācārya has written two types of commentaries for this Upaniṣad, the first word by word as in the case of the other Upaniṣads and the second sentence by sentence. In his *Saundaryalaharī* he has the *Kenopaniṣad* in mind when he prays to Ambā: "Place your feet on my head, the feet that are held by Mother Veda." The Upaniṣads (Vedānta) are also called "Veda-śiras", "Śruti-śiras", the "head" or "crown" of the Vedas — the Upaniṣads which are the "end" of the Vedas (Vedānta) are also their crown. To say that Ambā's feet are placed on the head of Mother Veda means that they are held by the Upaniṣads. It is in the *Kenopaniṣad* that we see Ambā appearing as Jñānāmbikā (the goddess of jñāna). "Sāmagānapriyā" is one of her names in the *Lalitāsahasranāma* (The One Thousand Names of Lalitā): this is in keeping with the fact that Ambā's glory is specially revealed in an Upaniṣad belonging to the Sāmaveda.

What we see is the object and we who see it are the subject: the seen is the object, the seer is the subject. We can see our body as an object, we can know about it, know whether it is well or ill. It follows that there is an entity other than it that sees it, the subject called "we". That which sees is the Ātman. The subject called the Ātman cannot be known by anything else. If it can be known, it also becomes an object and it would further mean that there is another entity that sees: and that will be the true "we". The Ātman that is the true "we" can only be the subject and never the object. We may keep aside objects like the body and *experience* ourselves, the subject called "we", but we cannot *know* the "we". "To know" means that there is something other than ourselves to be known. It would be absurd to regard the Ātman as something other than ourselves. The true "we" is the Ātman, the Self. "Knowing" it implies that that which knows it ("we") is different from that which is known (the Self). What can be there that is different in us from our true Self? What is it that is other than the Self that can know the Self? Nothing. We say "Ātmajñāna" which literally means "knowing the Ātman". But is the phrase, "knowing the Ātman", used in the sense of a subject knowing an object? No. "Ātmajñāna" means the Self experiencing itself, and that is how "jñāna" or "knowing" is to be understood. This is the reason why the *Kenopaniṣad* says that "he who says that he knows the Ātman does not know it". It goes on: "He who says that he does not know knows. He who thinks that he knows does not know and he who thinks he does not know knows[2]."

The *Kaṭhopaniṣad* comes next. It occurs in the *Kaṭha Śākhā* of the Kṛṣṇa-Yajurveda. This Upaniṣad contains the teachings imparted by Yama to the brahmacārin[S] Naciketas. It begins as a story and leads up to the exposition of profound philosophical truths. The Gītā contains quotations from this Upaniṣad.

What I said just now about the subject-object relationship is explained in depth in the concluding part of the *Kaṭhopaniṣad*. How do we remove the ear of grain from the stalk? And how do we draw the pith from the reed? Similarly, we must draw the subject that is the Self from the object that is the body, says the *Kaṭhopaniṣad*[3]. "Desire, anger, hatred, fear, all these appertain to the mind, not to the Self. Hunger, thirst and so on appertain to the body — they are not 'mine'." By constant practice we must learn to reject all such things as do not belong to the Self by "objectifying them". If we do so with concentration, in due course we will be able to overcome the idea that has taken root in us that the body and the mind constitute the "we". We can then exist as the immaculate Self without the impurities tainting the body and the mind.

The *Kaṭhopaniṣad* compares the spiritual exercise of separating the Self from the body and the mind to that of drawing off the pith, bright, pure and soft, from the reed. Before you is the spadix of a plantain. When it wilts do you also droop? Think of the body as a lump of flesh closer to you than this spadix of the plantain. This spadix is not the subject that is "we", but the object. On the same lines you must become accustomed to think of the body as an object in relation to the subject that is the Self. During our life in this world itself — during the time we seem to exist in our body — we must learn to treat the body as not "me", not "mine". Mokṣa or liberation does not necessarily mean ascending to another world like Kailāsa or Vaikuṇṭha. It can be attained here and now. What is mokṣa? It is everlasting bliss that comes of being freed from all burden. He who lives delighting in his Self in this world itself without any awareness of his body is called a "jīvanmukta". The supreme goal of the Vedas and Vedānta is making a man a jīvanmukta.

Kṛṣṇa Paramātman speaks of the same idea in the Gītā[4]. He who, while yet in this world ("ihaiva"), controls his desire and anger before he is released from his body ("prak śarīravimokṣaṇāt") — he will remain integrated (in yoga) and achieve everlasting bliss. "Ihaiva" = "iha eva", while yet in this world. If you realise the Self, as an inner experience, while yet in this world, at the time of your death you will not be aware that your body is severed from you. The reason is that even before your death, when you are yet in this world, the body does not exist for you. So is there any need for what is called death to destroy it? There is no death for the man who has absolute realisation of his body being not "he" (when you mention the body the mind is also included in it). Where is the question of his dying if he knows that the body is not "me" (that is "he")? The death is only for his body.

The man who has no death thus becomes "amṛta" ("immortal"). Hymns like the Puruṣasūkta which appear in the karmakāṇḍa of the Vedas also speak of such deathlessness. This idea recurs throughout the Upaniṣads.

The body, and the mind that functions through it, are the cause of sorrow. All religions are agreed that liberation is a state in which sorrow gives place to everlasting happiness. However, according to religious traditions other than Advaita (non-dualism), a man has to go to some other world for such bliss after his death. Śankara Bhagavatpāda establishes that true liberation can be won in this world itself if one ceases to identify oneself totally with the body and remains rooted in the Self.

"Tadetat aśarīratvam mokṣākhyam," so he proclaims in his *Sūtrabhāṣya* (1.1.4). The word "aśarīrī" is popularly understood as a voice we hear without knowing its origin (disembodied voice). It means to be without a body. "Aśarīratvam", bodylessness (being incorporeal), is a state in which one is not conscious of the existence of one's body. This is liberation, says the Ācārya. To remain bodyless, disincarnate, does not mean committing suicide. When we reduce our desires little by little a stage will be reached when they will be totally rooted out. When they are thus eradicated, consciousness of the body will naturally cease too. The Self alone will remain then, shining. To arrive at such a state it is not necessary to voyage to another world. It is this idea that the Vedas and Vedānta refer to when they say, "Ihaiva, ihaiva" (Here itself, here itself) — the ideal of liberation here and now.

We have two enemies who prevent us from reaching the state of amṛta (deathlessness): according to the Gītā they are desire and anger. The basis for this is the *Chāndogya Upaniṣad* (8.12.1)[5] which is part of the Śruti — the passage in which "priya apriya" occurs: the words mean "what one likes and what one hates". The first is denoted by desire, or Kāma, the second by anger. The *Chāndogya Upaniṣad* says that one who has no body (that is one who is not conscious of his body) is not affected either by desire or by anger. That is (it says): "If you wish to be free from the evils of desire and anger you ought to make yourself without your body (free yourself of your body) right now when you are yet in this world."

A jīvātman (individual self) is divided into three parts in association with the ego: "gauṇātman", "mithyātman" and "mukhyātman". These are mentioned in Śankara's commentary on the *Brahmasūtra*.

Gauṇa-mithyātmano'sattve putradehādi bādhanāt
Sadbrahmātmāhamityevam bodhe kāryam katham bhavet

— Sūtrabhāṣya, 1.1.4

It is part of human nature to believe that one's children and friends are the same as oneself and that their joys and sorrows are one's own. That is what is meant by "gauṇātman". "Gauṇa" denotes what is ceremonial or what is regarded as a formality. We know that our children and friends are different from us and yet we want to believe that they are our own.

The "I-feeling" in relation to the body which is closer to us than our children and friends is "mithyātman".

There is a state in which the pure Self is seen separate from the body and identified inwardly with the Brahman: it is called "mukhyātman".

When the first two — gauṇātman and mithyātman — are separated from us we will be freed from attachments to our children, friends and the body as well as its senses. The realisation will dawn then that "I am the Brahman". Now there will be nothing for us to "do". This is the meaning of the *Sūtrabhāṣya* passage.

Svāmī Vivekānanda who wanted to rouse the people of India chose a mantra[6] from the *Kaṭhopaniṣad* ("Arise, awake", etc) for the Rāmakṛṣṇa Mission. This Upaniṣad is the source of many a popular quote. For instance, there is the mantra[7] which states that the Self cannot be known either by learning or by the strength of one's intellect. "Know that the Self is the Lord of the chariot, that the body is the chariot and that the intellect is the charioteer," is another[8].

"In the cavern of the heart the Supreme Being is radiant like a thumb of light..."[9]

Then there is the mantra[10] we recite at the time of the "dīpārādhana rite" ("Na tatra suryo bhāti..."): "The sun does not shine there, nor the moon, nor the stars. There is no flash of lightning. Agni too does not shine there. When he (the Paramātman) shines everything shines; all this shines by his light." All our knowledge is derived from that Great Light. With our limited knowledge we cannot shed light on that Reality.

Later, the *Kaṭhopaniṣad* mentions what Śrī Kṛṣṇa Paramātman says in the Gītā about the cosmic *pīpal* tree, the symbol of saṁsāra or worldly existence[11]. If all the desires of the heart are banished a man can become immortal and realise the Brahman here itself.

After the *Kaṭhopaniṣad* comes the *Praśnopaniṣad*, the *Muṇḍakopaniṣad* and the *Māṇḍukyopaniṣad,* all three being from the Atharvaveda. "Praśna" means "question". What is the origin of the various creatures? Who are the deities that sustain them? How does life imbue the body? What is the truth about wakefulness, sleep and the state of dream? What purpose is served by being devoted to Om? What is the relationship between the Supreme Godhead and the individual self? These questions are answered in the *Praśnopaniṣad*.

"Muṇḍana" means "tonsure". Only sannyāsins, ascetics with a high degree of maturity, are qualified to study the *Muṇḍakopaniṣad* — that is how it came to be so called. This Upaniṣad speaks of the Akṣarabrahman, akṣara meaning "imperishable"[12] and also "sound". We speak of "Pañcākṣara", "Aṣṭākṣara"[13] and so on. The source of all sound is "Praṇava", or "Omkāra". Praṇava is a particularly efficacious means to attain the Akṣarabrahman.

One mantra[14] in the *Muṇḍakopaniṣad* asks us to string the bow of Oṁkāra with the arrow of the Ātman and hit unperturbed the target called the Brahman. Like the arrow you must be one with the Brahman. It is also in this Upaniṣad that the individual self and the Paramātman are compared to two birds perched on the body that is the pippala tree[15]. The jīvātman (individual self) alone eats the fruit (of karma) and the Paramātman bird is merely a witness. This is the basis of the biblical story of Adam (Ātman) and Eve (jīva). Adam does not eat the apple (pippala) but Eve does.

The motto of the Union of India — "Satyameva Jayate" — is taken from this Upaniṣad[16].

There is also a mantra[17] which speaks of sannyāsins who, after being jīvanmuktas in this world, become "videhamuktas" (liberated without their body). It is chanted when ascetics are received with honour with a "pūrṇakuṁbha"[18].

The *Muṇḍakopaniṣad* speaks of the jñānin thus[19]: "Different rivers with different names lose their names and forms in the ocean. Similarly the knower (jñānin) freed from name and form unites inseparably with the Brahman."

Next is the *Māṇḍūkyopaniṣad*. "Maṇḍūka" means a "frog". Why the name "Frog Upaniṣad"? One reason occurs to me: the frog does not have to go step by step. It can leap from the first to the fourth step. In the *Māṇḍūkyopaniṣad* the way is shown to reach the turīya or fourth state from the state of wakefulness through the states of sleep and dream. By devoting oneself to (by intense meditation of) Om (that is by akṣara upāsanā) one can in one bound go up to the fourth state. That perhaps is the reason why this Upaniṣad is called *"Māṇḍūkya"*. According to modern research scholars, the *Māṇḍūkya Upaniṣad* belonged to a group of people who had the frog as their totem! (It is also said that the sage associated with the Upaniṣad is Varuṇa who took the form of a frog.)

The text of the *Māṇḍūkyopaniṣad* is very brief and contains only twelve mantras. But it has acquired a special place among seekers because it is packed with meaning. It demonstrates the oneness of the individual self and the Brahman through the four feet (padas) of Praṇava. There is a famous passage occurring towards the end of this Upaniṣad which describes the experience of the turiya or fourth state in which all the cosmos is dissolved in "Śiva-Advaita" (Sivo'dvaita)[20]. Śankara Bhagavatpāda's guru's guru, Gauḍapādācārya, has commented on this Upaniṣad *(Māṇḍūkyopaniṣad- Kārikā)* and Śankara has written a further commentary on this work.

Now the *Taittirīya Upaniṣad.* I had referred earlier to the misunderstanding that developed between Vaiśaṁpāyana and his disciple Yājñavalkya. In his anger the teacher asked his student to eject the Veda he had taught him. Yājñavalkya did as bidden. Later the sun god taught him the Śukla-Yajurveda which had until then not been revealed to the world.

It was with the power acquired through mantras that Yājñavalkya became a gander to throw up the Veda he had first learned from Vaiśampāyana. Now that master's other disciples, bidden by him, assumed the form of tittiri birds (partridges) and consumed what had been ejected by Yājñavalkya. Thus this recension of the Yajurveda came to be called "*Taittirīya Śākhā*". The name "Taittirīya" is also applied to the Saṁhitā, Brāhmaṇa and Āraṇyaka of this śākhā. The *Taittirīya Upaniṣad* is part of the *Taittirīya Āraṇyaka* and it is perhaps studied more widely than any other Upaniṣad. Many mantras employed in rituals are taken from it. There are three parts to it — "Śīkṣāvallī", "Ānandavallī" and "Bhṛguvallī".

Śīkṣāvallī contains matters relating to education, rules of the brahmacaryāśrama (the celibate student's stage of life), its importance, order of Vedic chanting, meditation of Praṇava[S]. The "Āvahantī homa"[21] is in Śīkṣāvalli. It is performed by the ācārya to ensure that disciples come to learn from him without any let or hindrance. We know from our own experience that, even today, as a result of performing this sacrifice, Vedic schools which were in decay have received a new lease of life with the admission of many new students.

Śīkṣavāllī mentions "Ātma-svarājya"[22] that is eternal, a state which transcends in meaning the "svarājya" we are familiar with in politics.

"Satyam vada, dharmam cara" (Speak the truth, do your duty according to dharma): such exhortations to students are contained in this Upaniṣad[23]. Students are urged not to neglect the study of the Vedas at any time. They are asked to marry and beget children so that Vedic learning will be kept up from generation to generation. "Mātṛ-devo bhava, pitṛ-devo bhava, ācārya-devo bhava, atithi-devo bhava" (Be one to whom your mother is a god; be one to whom your father is a god; be one to whom your teacher is a god; be one to whom your guest is a god) — all such mantras are in this Upaniṣad. The importance of charity and dharma is specially stressed here.

Earlier I spoke to you about a "multiplication table" of bliss in which each successive type of bliss is a hundredfold greater than the previous one[24]. Ānandavallī is the part of the *Taittirīya Upaniṣad* in which you see this. The highest form of bliss or ānanda in this "table" is Brahmānanda (the bliss of realising the Brahman).

Different sheaths (kośas) of man are mentioned in this Upaniṣad. The first is the "annamaya-kośa" (the sheath of food), the flesh that grows with the intake of food. Inside it is the "prāṇamaya-kośa (the sheath of vital breath). Then comes the "manomaya-kośa" (the sheath of mind) that gives rise to thoughts and feelings. The fourth is "vijñānamaya-kośa" (the sheath of understanding). And, finally, the fifth, the "ānandamaya-kośa" (the sheath of bliss). It is here that the Self dwells in blessedness. Each sheath is personified as a bird with head, wings, body, belly — there is a philosophical significance in this. This Upaniṣad contains the oft-quoted mantra ("Yato vāco..")[25]. It says: "He who knows the bliss of the Brahman, from which speech and mind turn away unable to grasp it, such a man does not have to fear anything from anywhere."

"Bhṛguvallī" is the teaching (upadeśa[5]) imparted by Varuṇa to his son Bhṛgu. "Upadesa" here is not to be understood as something dictated by the guru to his student. Varuṇa encourages his son to ascend step by step through his own experiments and experience. Bhṛgu performs austerities and thinks that the sheath of food is the truth. From this stage he advances gradually through the sheaths of breath, mind and understanding and arrives at the truth that is the sheath of bliss. He realises as an experience that the Ātman (the nature of bliss) is the ultimate truth.

This does not mean that the *Taittirīya Upaniṣad* rejects the factual world represented by the sheath of food. While being yet in this world, taking part in its activities, we must become aware of the supreme truth. For this we must strive to make life more dhārmic, as a means of Ātmic advancement. That is why even those who have attained the sheath of bliss are admonished[26]: "Do not speak ill of food. Do not throw it away. Grow plenty of food." Even the government has used this mantra for its grow more food campaign. The *Taittirīya Upaniṣad* concludes with the mantra which says : "I am food, I am food, the one who eats it...."[27]

The *Aitareya Upaniṣad* forms part of the *Aitareya Āraṇyaka* of the Ṛgveda. The name is derived from the fact that it was the sage Aitareya who made it widely known. A jīva (individual self) originating in the father, says the Upaniṣad, enters the womb of the mother. He is born in this world and goes through his life of meritorious and sinful actions. Then he is born again and again in different worlds. Only by knowing the Ātman does he find release from the bondage of phenomenal existence.

The sage called Vāmadeva knew about all his previous births when he was in his mother's womb. He passed through all fortresses and, like an eagle soaring high in the skies, voyaged seeking liberation. In this context prajñāna, direct perception of the Ātman, is spoken of in high terms. It is not merely that one attains the Brahman through such jñāna (prajñāna) — the fact is such prajñāna itself is the Brahman. And this is the mahāvākya[S] of the Ṛgveda[28]: "Prajñānam Brahma".

The *Chāndogya* and *Bṛhadāraṇyaka Upaniṣads* are the last two of the ten major Upaniṣads and also the biggest. They are bigger than all the other eight of the ten put together. The first is part of the *Chāndogya Brāhmaṇa* of the Sāmaveda. "Chāndogya" means relating to "chandoga", one who sings the Ṣāman. The Tamiḷ *Tevāram*[T] refers to Parameśvara as "*Candogan kān*". The Zoroastrian scripture called the Zend-Avesta could be traced back to "Chandoga-Avesta."

Just as there are passages in the Gītā from the *Kaṭhopaniṣad,* so has the *Brahmasūtra* passages from the *Chāndogya Upaniṣad.* In these two Upaniṣads the teachings of a number of sages are put together.

The introductory mantras of the *Chāndogya Upaniṣad* refer to Omkāra as "udgītā" and explains how one is to meditate on it. A number of vidyās are mentioned like "Akṣi", "Ākāśa", "Madhu", "Śāṇḍilya", "Prāṇa", and "Pañcāgni". These help in different ways in knowing the Ultimate Reality. "Dahara vidyā" is the culmination of all these : it means perceiving the Supreme Being manifested as the transcandent outward sky in the tiny space in our heart. A number of truths are expounded in this Upaniṣad in the form of stories.

From the story of Raikva we learn about the strange outward behaviour of one who has realised the Brahman. There is then the famous story of Satyakāma who does not know his gotra[S], but is accepted as a pupil by Gautama. The guru thinks that Satyakāma must be a true Brahmin since he does not hide the truth about him. Before the pupil is taught he is made to undergo many tests. The guru's wife, out of concern for the pupil, speaks to her husband for him. When we read such stories we have before us a true picture of gurukulavāsa[S] in ancient times.

In character Śvetaketu was the opposite of Satyakāma and was proud of his learning. His father Uddālaka Āruṇi teaches him to be humble and in the end imparts to him the mantra, "Tat tvam asi" (That thou art), the mantra which proclaims the non-difference between the individual self and the Brahman. "Tat tvam asi" is the mahāvākya of the Sāmaveda[29].

Unlike Śvetaketu, the sage Nārada, who had mastered all branches of learning, was humble and full of regret that he had remained ignorant of the Ātman. He finds enlightenment in the teachings of Sanatkumāra which are included in the *Chāndogya Upaniṣad*. In the *Taittirīya Upaniṣad* Bhṛgu is taught to go step by step to obtain higher knowledge [from the sheath of food to the sheath of bliss]. Here Sanatkumāra teaches Nārada to go from purity of form to purity of the inner organs ("antaḥ-karaṇas). That is the time when all ties will snap and bliss realised.

Another story illustrates how different students benefit differently from the same teaching according to the degree of maturity of each. Prajāpati gives the same instruction to Indra, the king of the celestials, and to Virocana, the king of the asuras. This is what Prajāpati teaches them: "He who sees with his eyes, he is the Self." He subtly hints at the object that is behind the eye, knowledge, etc, and that is the basis of all these. Without understanding this, the two see themselves in a mirror and take the reflection to be the Self. You see only the body in the mirror and Virocana comes to the conclusion that that is the Self. It is from this idea that atheism, materialism and the Lokāyata system developed. Although Indra also took this kind of wrong view from his reflection, eventually [similar to the story in the *Taittirīya Upaniṣad* of Bhṛgu advancing from the sheath of food to the sheath of bliss] he goes in gradual stages from the gross body to the subtle body of sleep and later to the turīya or fourth state mentioned in the *Māṇḍūkyopaniṣad* — the turiya is the Self.

The *Bṛhadāraṇyaka Upaniṣad* comes last. "Bṛhad" means "great". It is indeed a great Upaniṣad, *Bṛhadāraṇyaka*. Generally, an Upaniṣad comes towards the close of the Āraṇyaka of the śākhā concerned. While the *Īśāvāsyopaniṣad* occurs in the Saṁhitā of the Śukla-Yajurveda, the *Bṛhadāraṇyaka Upaniṣad* is in the Āraṇyaka of the same Veda: as a matter of fact the entire Āraṇyaka constitutes this Upaniṣad. There are two recensions of it: the *Mādhyandina Śākhā* and the *Kāṇva Śākhā*. Śankara has chosen the latter for his commentary.

This Upaniṣad consists of six chapters. The first two are the "Madhu-kāṇḍa", the next two are the "Muni-kāṇḍa" in the name of Yājñavalkya, and the last two are the "Khila-kāṇḍa". Madhu may be understood as that which is full of the flavour of bliss. If we have the realisation that all this world is a personification of the Parabrahman it would be sweet like nectar to all creatures — and the creatures would be like honey to the world[30]. The Ātman then would be nectar for all. This idea is expressed in the Madhu-kāṇḍa.

It is in this Upaniṣad that the celebrated statement occurs that the Ātman is "neither this, nor this" ("Neti, neti")[31]. The Self cannot be described in any way. "Na-iti" — that is "Neti". It is through this process of "Neti, neti" that you give up everything — the cosmos, the body, the mind, everything — to realise the Self. After knowing the Ātman in this manner you will develop the attitude that the phenomenal world and all its creatures are made up of the same essence of bliss.

The first kāṇḍa contains the teachings received by the Brahmin Gārgya from the Kṣatriya Ajātaśatru. This shows that kings like Ajātaśatru and Janaka were knowers of the Brahman. We also learn that women too took part on an equal footing with the sages in the debates in royal assemblies on the nature of the Brahman. There was, for instance, Gārgī in Janaka's assembly of the learned. The *Bṛhadāraṇyaka Upaniṣad* also tells us about Yājñavalkya's two wives: of the two Kātyāyanī was like any housewife and the second, Maitreyī, was a Brahmavādini (one who inquires into the Brahman and speaks about it). The instruction given by Yājñavalkya to Maitreyī occurs both in the Madhu-kāṇḍa and the Muni-kāṇḍa. Here we have a beautiful combination of story-telling and philosophical disquisition.

When Yājñavalkya is on the point of renouncing the world, he divides his wealth between his two wives. Kātyāyanī is contented and does not ask for anything more. Maitreyī, on the other hand, is not worried about her share. She tells her husband: "You are leaving your home, aren't you, because you will find greater happiness in sannyāsa than from all this wealth? What is that happiness? Won't you speak about it?"

Yājñavalkya replies: "You have always been dear to me, Maitreyī. Now, by asking this question, you have endeared yourself to me more." He then proceeds to find out what is meant by the idea of someone being dear to someone else. His is indeed an inquiry into the concept of love and affection. He says: "A wife is dear to her husband not for the sake of his wife but for the sake of his Self. So is a husband dear to his wife for the sake of her Self. The children too are dear to us not for their sake but for the sake of the Self. So is the case with our love of wealth. We have affection for a person or an entity because it pleases our Self. It means that this Self itself is of the nature of affection, of love, of joy. It is to know this Self independently of everything else that we forsake all those who are dear to us and take to sannyāsa. When we know It, the Self or the Ātman, we will realise that there is nothing other than It. Everything will become dear to us. To begin with, when we had affection for certain people or certain things, we had dislike for certain other people and certain other things. If we cease to be attached to those people or to those things that we loved and realise the Ātman, then we will become aware that there is nothing other than the Ātman. Then, again, we will dislike none and will love all without any distinction."

Before renouncing the world, Yājñavalkya held disputations on the Ultimate Reality with Kahola, Uddālaka Āruṇi and Gārgī in Janaka's royal assembly. These debates, together with the teachings he imparted to Janaka, are included in the Muni-kāṇḍa. The concept of Antaryāmin (Inner Controller) belongs to Viśiṣṭādvaita (qualified non- dualism). The basis for this is to be found in Yājñavalkya's answer to a question put to him by Uddālaka Āruṇi.

According to non-dualism all this phenomenal world is Māyā. The idea behind the concept of Antaryāmin is that if the world is the body, the Paramātman dwells in it as its very life. Though Yājñavalkya accepts this concept on a certain level, at all other times his views are entirely in consonance with non-dualism. In his concluding words to Maitreyī, the supreme Advaitin that he is, Yājñavalkya remarks : "Even if you be a little dualistic in your outlook, it means that you look at something other than yourself, smell, taste, touch and hear something other than yourself. But when you have realised the Self experientially, all these 'other things' cease to exist. That which is the source of seeing, hearing, tasting, smelling, and so on — how can you see, hear, taste, smell That?" Expounding non-dualism Yājñavalkya tells Janaka (4.3.32)[32], "Like water mingled with water all become one in the Paramātman." "He who is freed from all desire exists as the Brahman even when he is in this world (with his body) and when he dies he is united with the Brahman"[33] .

The two concluding chapters that form the Khila-kāṇḍa of the Upaniṣad bring together scattered ideas. (If a thing is broken or divided it is called "khila". That which is whole and unbroken is "akhila".)

A story in the Khila-kāṇḍa illustrates how the same teaching is interpreted differently according to the degree of maturity of the aspirants. The devas (the celestial race), humans and the demons (asuras) seek instruction from Prajāpati (the Creator). Prajāpati utters just one syllable, "Da", as his teaching. The devas who do not possess enough control over their senses take it to mean "dāmyata" ("control your senses"). Humans who are possessive understand the syllable as "datta" ("give", "be charitable"). The asuras who are cruel by nature take the same as "dayadhvam" (be compassionate).

A mantra occurring in the concluding part of the *Bṛhadāraṇyaka Upaniṣad* seems to me not only extremely interesting but also comforting. What does it say? "If a man suffers from fever it must be taken that he is practising austerities (tapas). If he recognises illnesses and afflictions to be tapas, he passes on to a very high world" (5.11.1). [Etadvai paramam tapo yadvyāhitastapyate paramaṁ haiva lokam jayati ya evam veda...]

What is the meaning of this statement and what is interesting about it? And how is it comforting?

By observing vows, by fasting, by living an austere life and by suffering physically, we will become less attached to the body, and the sins accumulated in our past lives will diminish. Tapas is a way of expiating the sins of past lives. The offences committed with our body are wiped away by the very body when it undergoes suffering (that is by bodily tapas).

That is why the Purāṇas speak of great men having performed austerities. Ambikā herself — she is the mother of the universe — performs tapas. Not heeding the word of her husband Parameśvara, she [as Satī] attends the sacrifice conducted by her father Dakṣa. Because of the humiliation she suffers there she immolates herself in the sacrificial fire and is reborn as the daughter of Himavān. As atonement for disobeying her husband's command during her past life and for the purpose of being united with him again, she performs severe austerities. Kālidāsa gives a beautiful and moving account of this. How bitterly cold it will be during the winter in the Himālaya. But in that season Pārvatī (that is Ambikā) performs austerities seated on icy rocks or standing on frozen lakes. In the summer, when the sun is beating down harshly, she does tapas with fires burning all round her[34]. Performing austerities with the fires on four sides and with the sun burning above is called "pañcāgni-tapas".

Many great men have performed such severe austerities.

How about ourselves? If they, the great men, were guilty of one or two lapses, we cannot even keep count of our sins. But we have neither the will nor the strength to perform a fraction of the austerities that they went through. How then are we going to wipe away our sins?

It is when we are troubled by such thoughts that we find the foregoing Upaniṣadic mantra comforting. Since ours is not a disciplined life we keep suffering from one ailment or another. The Upaniṣadic mantra seems to be directed to us: "You must learn to think that the affliction you are suffering from is tapas. If you do so you will be freed from your sins and liberated." Though the message is not given in such plain terms, such is the meaning of the mantra.

We often speak of "jvara-tāpa" or "tāpa-jvara" (literally "hot fever"). "Tāpa" means "boiling" or "cooking". The root is "tap" to burn. "Tapana" is one of the names of the sun. Even if we do not perform the austerities mentioned in the śāstras, we must take it that the fever contracted by us is the tapas Īśvara has awarded us to become free from our sins.

When we are down with malaria we keep shivering in spite of covering ourselves with blankets. Our attitude now must be to suffer the affliction in lieu of the tapas we ought to perform in the winter months remaining on snow. Do you feel that your body is being roasted when you are suffering from typhoid or pneumonia and running a temperature of 105^0 or 106^0 F? You must comfort yourself, believing that God has given you the fever as a substitute for the pañcāgni-tapas you are unable to perform.

You will in due course learn to take such an attitude and develop the strength to suffer any illness. Instead of sending for the doctor or rushing to the medicine chest you may take it easy, telling yourself, "Let the illness take its course." When we happen to fall ill as a means of reducing our burden of sin, is it right to seek a cure for it? Also we save on doctor's fees, medicine, etc. The gain bigger than all the rest is that of learning to take the high attitude of treating suffering as not suffering. This is called "titikṣā".

All this is briefly indicated in the Upaniṣadic mantra. When we keep lamenting that we are unable to expiate our sins — when we are unable to perform tapas — we may take comfort from the fact that when we suffer from a disease it is God's way of making us perform austerities.

In the last chapter of the *Bṛhadāraṇyaka Upaniṣad* we have strong proof of the fact that Vedānta is not opposed to the karmakāṇḍa. Here are mentioned the pañcāgni-vidyā and the rites to be performed to beget virtuous children (suprajā).

Notes & References

1 Or, simply, *Īśa Upaniṣad.*

2 *Yadi manyase suvedeti dabhramevāpi nūnaṁ tvaṁ vettha Brahmaṇo rūpam yadasya tvaṁ yadasya ca deveṣvatha nu mīmāṁsyameva te manye viditam*

Nāha manye suvedeti no na vedeti veda ca
Yo nastadveda tadveda no na vedeti veda ca

Yasyāmatam tasya matam matam yasya na veda saḥ
avijñātaṁ vijānatām vijñātamavijānatām

— Kenopaniṣad, 2.1, 2 & 3

3 *Anguṣṭhamātraḥ puruṣo'ntarātmā sadā janānām hṛdaye sanniviṣṭaḥ. Tam svāccharīrātpravṛhenmuñjādiveṣīkāṁ dhairyeṇa taṁ vidyācchukramamṛtaṁ taṁ vidyācchukramamṛtam iti*

— Kaṭhopaniṣad, 6.18.

4 *Śaknoti'hai'va yaḥ soḍhum prak śarīra-vimokṣanāt*
Kāma-krodh'odbhavaṁ vegam sa yuktaḥ sa sukhī naraḥ

— Bhagavadgītā, 5.23

5 *Maghavanmartyaṁ vā idaṁ śarīramāttam mṛtyunātad-asyāmṛtasyāśarīrasyātmano'dhiṣṭhānamātto vai saśarīraḥ priyāpriyābhyām, na vai saśarīrasya sataḥ priyāpriyayorapahatirastyaśarīram vāva santaṁ na priyāpriye spṛśataḥ.*

— Chāndogya Upaniṣad, 8.12.1

6 *Uttiṣṭhata jāgrata prāpya varān nibodhata. Kṣurasya dhārā niśitā duratyayā durgam pathastatkavayo vadanti*

— Kaṭhopaniṣad, 3.14

7 *Nāyamātmā pravacanena labhyo na medhayā na bahunā śrutena .*
Yamevaiṣa vṛṇute tena labhyastasyaiṣa Ātmā vivṛṇute tanūm svām .

— Ibid, 2.23

8 *Ātmānaṁ rathinam viddhi śariram ratham eva tu*
Buddhiṁ tu sārathim viddhi manah pragraham eva ca

— Ibid, 3.3

9 *Anguṣthamatrah puruṣo madhya Ātmani tiṣṭhati.. Īśāno bhūtabhavyasya natato vijugupsate. Etadvai tat.*

Aṅguṣṭhamātrah puruṣojyotirivādhūmakaḥ. Īśāno bhūtabhavyasya sa evādya sa u śva etadvai tat.

— Ibid, 4.12 & 13

10 *Na tatra sūryo bhāti na candra-tārakam nema vidyuto bhāti kuto'yam agniḥ. Tameva bhāntamanubhāti sarvam tasya bhāsa sarvamidam vibhāti*

— Ibid, 5.16

11 *Urdhvamūlo'rvākśākhaḥ eṣo'svatthaḥ sanātanaḥ. Tadeva śukraṁ tadbrahma tadevāmṛtam ucyate*

— Ibid, 6.1

12 "Aksara" also means a letter or syllable.

13 "Pañcākṣara" and "Aṣṭākṣara" are mantras with five and eight syllables respectively ("Namaḥ Śivāya"; "Om Namo Nārāyaṇāya").

14 Praṇavo dhanuḥ śaro hyātmā Brahma tallakṣyamucyate. Apramattena veddhavyam śaravattanmayo bhavet

— Muṇḍakopaniṣad, 2.2.4

15 *Dvā suparṇā sayujā sakhāyā samānaṁ vṛkṣam pariṣasvajāte. Tayoranyaḥ pippalaṁ*

svādvattyanaśnannanyo abhicākaśīti.

— Ibid, 3.1.1.

16 *Satyameva jayate nānṛtam satyena panthā vitato devayānaḥ. Yenākramantyṛṣayo hyāptakāmā yatra tatsatyasya paramam nidhānam*

— Ibid, 3.1.6

17 *Vedānta-vijñāna-suniścitārthāḥ sannyāsa-yogādyatayaḥ śuddhasattavāḥ. Te Brahmalokeṣu parāntakāle parāmṛtāḥ parimucyanti sarve.*

— Ibid, 3.2.6.

18 It is customary to receive acāryas and other distinguished men with a pūrṇa-kuṁbha, a pot or jar filled with water and decorated with mango leaves, darbha grass, etc.

19 *Yathā nadyaḥ syandamānāḥ samudre'stam gacchanti nāma-rūpe vihāya. Tathā vidvānnāmarūpādvimuktaḥ parātparam puruṣamupaiti divyam*

—— Muṇḍakopaniṣad, 3.2.8.

20 *Amātraścaturtho'vyavahāryaḥ prapañcopaśamaḥ Śivo'dvaita evamonkara Ātmaiva saṁviśatyātmanā'tmānaṁ ya evam veda ya evam veda.*

— Māṇḍūkyopaniṣad, 12

21 *Āvahantī vitanvānā kurvāṇā cīramātmanaḥ. Vāsāmsi mama gāvaśca. Annapāne ca sarvadā. Tato me śriyamāvaha. Lomaśām paśubhih saha svāhā. Ā māyantu brahmacāriṇah svāhā. Vi māyantu brahmacāriṇaḥ svāhā. Pra māyantu brahmacāriṇaḥ svāhā. Da māyantu brahmacāriṇaḥ svāhā. Śa māyantu brahmacāriṇaḥ svāhā.*

— Taittirīya Upaniṣad, 1.4.2

22 *Suvarityāditye, maha iti Brahmaṇi, āpnoti svārājyam āpnoti manasaspatim, vākpatiścakṣuṣpatiḥ, śrotrapatiḥ vijñānapatiḥ, etat tato bhavati, ākāśaśarīram Brahma, satyātmaprāṇārāmaṁ mana ānandaṁ. Śānti samṛddhamamṛtam iti prācīnayogyopāsva.*

—- Ibid, 1.6.2.

23 *Vedam anūcyācaryo'ntevāsinam anuśāsti. Satyam vada, dharmam cara, svādhyāyān ma pramadaḥ, acāryāya priyam dhanam āhṛtya prajātantum mā vyvacchetsīḥ. Satyānna pramaditavyam, dharmānna pramaditavyam, kuśalānna pramaditavyam, bhūtyai na pramaditavyam, svādhyāya- pravacanābhyam na pramaditavyam, deva-pitṛ-karyābhyām na pramaditavyam.*

Mātṛdevo bhava, pitṛdevo bhava, ācārya-devo bhava, atithi-devo bhava, yānyanavadyāni karmāni tāni sevitavyāni, no itarāṇi, yañyasmākam sucaritāni tāni tvayopāsyāni, no itarāṇi.

Ye ke cāsmaccchreyāṁso Brāhmaṇāh. Teṣām tvayā'sanena praśvasitavyam. Śraddhayā deyam, aśraddhayā'deyam, śriyā deyam, hṛiyā deyam, bhiyā deyam, saṁvidā deyam.

— Ibid, 1.11. 1, 2 & 3

24 See notes appended to Chapter 32 of this part.

25 *Yato vāco nivarttante, āprāpya manasā saha, ānandam Brahmaṇo vidvān, na bibheti kutaścaneti. Etam ha vāva na tapati, kim ahaṁ sādhu nākaravam, kimahaṁ pāpam-akaravamiti, sa ya evam vidvānete Ātmānam spṛnute. Ubhe hyevaiṣa ete Ātmānam spṛṇute, ya evam veda, ityupaniṣat.*

—— Taittiriya Upaniṣad, 2.9.1

26 *Annam na nindyāt. Tad vratam. Prāno va annam, śarīram annādam. Prāṇe śarīram pratiṣṭhitam, śarīre prāṇaḥ pratiṣṭhitaḥ, tadetadannamanne pratiṣṭhitam. Sa ya etadannamanne pratiṣṭhitaṁ veda pratitiṣṭhati, annavānannādo bhavati, mahān bhavati, prajayā paśubhir Brahma-varcasena mahān kīrtyā.*

— Ibid, 3.7.1.

27 *Aham annam aham annam aham annam; ahamannādo' hamannādo'ham annādaḥ; aham ślokakṛdaham ślokakṛdaham ślokakṛt; aham asmi prathamajā ṛtāsya, pūrvam devebhyo amṛtasya nabhāyi, yo mā dadāti, sa id eva mā, vāh, aham annam annamadantam ādmi, aham viśvaṁ bhuvanam abhyabhavām, suvarṇa jyotiḥ. Ya evam veda ityupaniṣat.*

— Ibid, concluding mantra.

28 *Eṣa Brahmaiṣa Indraḥ. Esa Prajāpatirete sarve devā imāni ca pañcamahābhūtāni pṛthivīvāyurākāśa āpojyotīṁṣītyetānīmāni ca kṣudramiśrāṇīva bījānītarāṇi cetarāṇi cāṇḍajāni ca jārujāni ca svedajāni codbhijjāni cāśvā gāvaḥ puruṣā hastino yatkimcedam prāṇi jaṁgamam ca patatri ca yacca sthāvaram sarvam tatprajñānetram prajñāne pratiṣṭhitam prajñānetro lokaḥ prajñā pratiṣṭha.*

Prajñānam Brahma.

— Aitareya Upaniṣad, 3.1.3

29 *Sa ya eṣo'ṇimaitadātmyamidam sarvam tatsatyam sa Ātmā Tattvamasi Śvetaketo iti bhūya eva mā Bhagavān vijñāpayitviti tathā somyeti hovāca.*

— Chāndogyopaniṣad, 6.8.7

30 *Iyam pṛthivī sarveṣām bhūtānam madhu, asyai pṛthivyai sarvāṇi bhūtani madhu; yaścāyam asyām pṛthivyām tejomayo'mrtamayaḥ puruṣaḥ, yaścāyam adhyātmaṁ śārīrastejomayo'mṛtamayaḥ purusah, ayam eva sa yo'yam Ātmā, idam amṛtam, idam amṛtam, idam Brahma, idam sarvam.*

— Bṛhadāraṇyaka Upaniṣad, 2.5.1.

31 *Sa vā eṣa mahānaja Ātmā yo'yam vijñānamayaḥ prāṇeṣu ya eṣo'ntarhṛdaya ākāśastasmiñchete sarvasya vāśī sarvasyeśānaḥ sarvasyādhipatiḥ sa na sādhunā karmaṇā bhūyānno evāsādhunā kanīyāneṣa sarveśvara eṣa bhūtādhipatireṣa bhūtapala eṣa seturvidharaṇa eṣām lokānāmasaṁbhedāya tametam Vedānuvacanena Brāhmaṇā vividiṣanti yajñena dānena tapasā'nāśakenaitameva viditvā munirbhavatyetameva pravrājino lokamicchantah pravrajantyetaddha sma vai tatpūrve vidvāṁsaḥ prajām na kāmayante kim prajaya kariṣyāmo yeṣām no'yamātmā'yam loka iti te ha sma putraiṣaṇāyaśca vittaiṣaṇāyaśca lokaiṣaṇāyaśca vyutthāyātha bhikṣācaryam caranti yā hyeva putraiṣaṇā sā vittaiṣaṇā ya vittaiṣaṇā sā lokaiṣaṇobhe hyete eṣane eva bhavataḥ. Sa eṣa neti netyātmā'gṛhyo na hi gṛhyate'śīryo na hi śīryate'saṅgo na hi sajyate' sito na vyathate na riṣyatyetamu haivaite na tarata ityataḥ pāpamakaravamityataḥ kalyāṇamakaravamityubhe u haivaiṣa ete tarati nainam kṛtākṛte tapataḥ.*

— Ibid, 4.4.22

32 *Salila eko draṣṭādvaito bhavati, eṣa Brahmalokaḥ, samrāḍ iti, hainam anuśaśāsa Yājñavalkyah; eṣasya paramā gatiḥ, eṣasya paramā sampadeṣo'sya paramo lokaḥ, eṣo'sya paramā ānandaḥ; etasyaivānandasyānyani bhūtāni mātrām upajivanti.*

— Ibid, 4.3.32.

33 *Tad eṣa śloko bhavati: — Tad eva saktaḥ saha karmaṇaiti liṅgam mano yatra niṣaktam asya. Prāpyāntaṁ karmaṇastasya yat kim ceha karotyayam. Tasmāllokāt punaraiti asmai lokāya karmaṇa iti nu kāmayāmānaḥ; athākāmayamānaḥ, yo'kāmo niṣkāma āpta-kāma Ātmakāmo na tasya prāṇā utkrāmanti, Brahmaiva sanbrahmāpyeti*

Tad eṣa śloko bhavati— Yadā sarve pramucyante kāmā ye'sya hṛdi śritāḥ, Atha martyo'mṛto bhavati, atra Brahma samaśnute iti; tad yathāhinirvlayanī valmike mṛtā pratyastā śayīta, evam evedam śarīram śete. Athāyam aśariro'mṛtah prāno Brahmaiva, teja eva; so'ham Bhagavate sahasram dadāmi, iti hovāca Janako vaidehaḥ

—— Ibid, 4.4. 6 & 7.

[34] *Śucau caturṇām jvalatām havirbhujām*
Śucismitā madhyagatā sumadhyamā
Vijitya netrapratighātinīm prabhā-
Mananyadṛṣṭiḥ savitāramaikṣata

Tathātitaptam saviturgabhastibhir-
Mukham tadīyam kamalaśriyam dadhau
Apāngayoḥ kevalamasya dīrghayoḥ
Śanaiḥ śanaiḥ śyāmikayā kṛtam padam

— Kumārasaṁbhavam, 5. 20 & 21.

Chapter 34

What do the Vedas Teach Us?

The Vedas speak of a variety of matters. So how are we to accept the view that their most important teaching is the concept of Self-realisation expounded in the Upaniṣads constituting Vedānta? They mention a number of sacrifices like agnihotra, somayāga, sattra and iṣṭi and other rituals in addition. Why should it not be maintained that it is these that form their chief purpose?

What are the rites to be performed at a marriage? Or at a funeral? How best is a kingdom (or any country) governed? How must we conduct ourselves in an assembly? You will find answers to many such questions in the Vedas. Which of these then is the main objective of our scripture?

The Vedas tell you about the conduct of sacrifices, ways of worship, methods of meditation. How is the body inspired by the Self? What happens to it (the body) in the end? And how does the Self imbue the body again? We find an answer to such questions in these sacred texts. Also we learn from them methods to keep the body healthy, the rites to protect ourselves against enemy attacks. What then is the goal of the Vedas?

The Upaniṣads proclaim that all the Vedas together point to a single Truth *(Kaṭhopaniṣad, 2.15)*[1]. What is that Truth ? "The Vedas speak in one voice of a Supreme Entity revealing itself as the meaning of Omkāra."

There was a judge called Sadāśiva Ayyar. He had a brother, Paramaśiva Ayyar, who lived in Mysore. "The Vedas deal with geology," so wrote Paramaśiva Ayyar. "In those early times, people in India looked upon the sun and the moon with wonder," some Westerners remark. "It was an age when science had not made much advance. People then regarded natural phenomena according to their different mental attitudes. Not all are capable of turning their thoughts into song. But some have the talent for the same. The songs sung by people in the form of mantras constitute the Vedas."

Though the Upaniṣads declare that the Vedas speak of the One Reality, there is an impression that they speak of a variety of entities. There is a well-known stanza on the Rāmāyaṇa :

Vedavedye pare pumśi jate Daśarathātmaje
Vedaḥ Prācetasādāsītsākṣādrāmāyaṇātmanā

"Vedavedye" = one who is to be known by the Vedas. Who is he ? "Pare puṁsi" = the Supreme Being. The Supreme Being to be known by the Vedas descended to earth as Rāma. When he was born the son of Daśaratha, the Vedas took the form of Vālmīki's child Rāmāyaṇa. According to this stanza, the goal of the Vedas is the Supreme Being or Omkāra, the One Truth. Just as the *Kaṭhopaniṣad* speaks of "sarve Vedāḥ", the Lord says in the Gītā: "Vedaiśca sarvair ahameva vedyaḥ" (I am indeed to be known by all the Vedas)[2].

Considering all this, we realise that, although the Vedas deal with many matters, all of them together speak of one goal, the One Reality. But the question arises why they concern themselves with different entities also when their purpose is only the One Entity ?

It is through the various entities, through knowledge of a multiplicity of subjects, that we may know this One Object. Yoga, meditation, austerities, sacrifices and other rites, ceremonies like marriage, state affairs, social life, poetry: what is the goal of all these? It is the One Reality. And that is the goal of the Vedas also. All objects and all entities other than this true Object are subject to change. They are like stories remembered and later forgotten. [In our ignorance] we do not perceive the One Object behind the manifoldness of the world. The Vedas take us to the One Reality through the multifarious objects that we do know.

To attain this One Reality we need to discipline our mind in various ways. Performing sacrifices, practising austerities, doing the duties of one's dharma, building gopurams, digging ponds for the public, involving ourselves in social work, saṁskāras like marriage, all these go to purify our consciousness and, finally, to still the mind that is always agitated (cittavṛtti-nirodha). The purpose of different works is to help us in our efforts to attain the Brahman.

"Ved" [from "vid"] means to know. The Upaniṣads proclaim: "The Ātman is that by knowing which all can be known." The goal of the Vedas is to shed light on this Ātman. The rituals enjoined on us in their first part and the jñāna expounded in the second have the same goal — knowing Īśvara, the Brahman or the Ātman. The beginning of the beginning and the end of the end of our scripture have the same ultimate aim. During the "mantrapuṣpa"[S] ceremony at the time of welcoming a great man this mantra is chanted: "Yo Vedā'dau svaraḥ prokto Vedānte ca pratiṣṭhitaḥ." These words are proof of the truth mentioned above. The mantra means: "What is established in the beginning of the Vedas as well as in their end is the One Truth, the Reality of Īśvara." The works associated with the beginning and the jñana associated with the end — there is no difference between the goals of the two.

For the rituals that are divided in a thousand different ways and for the knowledge (jñāna) that is but one, the subject is common. That is the Vedas have a common subject. The senses are incapable of perceiving the Self. They are aware only of outward objects and they keep chasing them. This is mentioned in the *Kaṭhopaniṣad* (4.1)[3]. When one's attention is diverted from the object in hand we say *"parākku pārppadu"* [in Tamiḷ]. Our object is the Self. To be diverted from it and to look round — or look away — is to be "parāmukha" — it is the same as *"parākku pārppadu"*. It is this idea that is expressed by the *Kaṭhopaniṣad.* But the mind does not easily remain fixed on our goal. So it is only by performing outward functions that we will gain the wisdom and maturity to turn our look inward. We will develop such inner vision only by refusing to be dragged down by the mind and the senses, and for this we must perform Vedic works.

After learning about, or knowing all other matters, by inquiring into them and by making an assessment of them, we are enabled to grasp that by knowing which we will know everything. That is the reason why the Vedas deal with so many branches of learning, so many types of worship, so many different works and so many arts and so many social duties. By applying the body in various rites we lose consciousness of that very body. By directing our thoughts to various branches of learning, by examining various philosophical systems and by worshipping various deities the mind and the intellect will in due course be dissolved.

We are more conscious of our body when we are engaged in evil actions than otherwise. By thinking about evil matters the mind becomes coarser. Instead, if we perform Vedic sacraments and worship and chant Vedic mantras for the well-being of the world, the desires of the body and the mind will wilt. Eventually, we will develop the maturity and wisdom to gain inner vision. In this way we will obtain release here itself ("ihaiva"). Release from what? From saṁsāra, from the cycle of birth and death. When we realise that the body and the mind are not "we" and when we become free from them — as mentioned in the Upaniṣads — we are liberated from worldly existence.

The purpose of the Vedas is achieving liberation in this world itself. And that is their glory. Other religions promise a man salvation after his departure for another world. But we cannot have any idea of that type of deliverance. Those who have attained it will not return to this world to tell us about it. So we may have doubts about it or may not believe in it at all. But the Vedas hold out the ideal of liberation here itself if we renounce all desire and keep meditating on the Self. Mokṣa then will be within our grasp at once. There is no room for doubt in this[4].

Other paths give temporary relief like quinine administered to a person suffering from malaria. If malarial fever is never to be contracted by the patient again the root cause of the disease must be found and eradicated. The Vedic religion goes deep into the roots of life and cuts away that which separates it from the Supreme Being. The freedom realised in this manner is eternal and not "temporary relief" [from the pains and sorrows of wordly existence].

The karmakāṇḍa of the Vedas deals with matters that give only such temporary relief. However, it must be realised that a man racked by difficulties cannot at once be placed in a position where he would remain all the time delighting in his Self. Through the "temporary relief" gained from performing Vedic rites, his consciousness is freed from impurities and he becomes "qualified" for everlasting peace. Sacrifices, vows, philanthropic work, and so on, do not take us to the final goal but they are necessary to reduce ourselves physically, to cleanse our consciousness and make our mind one-pointed in our effort to reach the final goal.

A variety of subjects are spoken about in detail in the Vedas but all of them have the one purpose of leading us to the Vedāntic inquiry into Truth and jñāna. The concluding portion of a work, speech, article, etc, is usually the most significant. If we want to find out what so-and-so has said in a speech or in an article, we do not have to read all of it. We glance through the first para and, skipping through, come to the last. Here we get the message of the speech or article. We are able to decide on the content of either by going through the first and concluding passages. The first and last parts alike of the Vedas speak of the Paramātman; so that can be said to be the "subject" of the Vedas.

The government enacts many laws. But later, in the course of their enforcement, doubts arise with regard to their intention. Then another law is enacted to settle its meaning: it is called the law of interpretation. In this way, Mīmāṁsā has come into being as the law of interpretation for the Vedas which constitute the eternal law of the Lord. I will speak to you later[5] in detail about Mīmāṁsā which is one of the fourteen branches of Vedic lore. But one aspect of it I should like to mention here itself.

According to the Mīmāṁsā śāstra, there are six ways in which to determine the meaning of a Vedic pronouncement or "vākya". They are listed in this verse :

Upakrama-upasaṁhārau abhyāsao'pūrvatā phalam
Arthavādo'papattī ca liṅgam tātparya-nirṇaye

"Upakrama" and "upasaṁhāra" together form the first method. The other five are "abhyāsa", "apūrvatā", "phala", "arthavāda" and "upapattī". These six are employed to determine the meaning or intent not only of Vedic passages but of, say, an article or discourse.

"Upakrama" means the initial part of a work, treatise, and "upasaṁhāra" the conclusion. If the first and concluding parts of a work speak of the same idea, it is to be taken as its subject. "Abhyāsa" is repeating the same thing, the same idea, again and again. If the same view or idea is repeated in a work, it must be understood as its theme. "Apūrvatā" denotes an idea not mentioned before or mentioned for the first time. So a view or idea expressed afresh in the course of a work or discourse is to be taken as the purpose or message intended. "Phala" is fruit, benefit, reward or result. If, in the course of a work or speech, it is said, "If you act in this manner you will gain such and such a fruit or benefit", it means that the purpose of the work or speech is to persuade you to act in the manner suggested so that you may reap the fruit or "phala" held out.

Suppose a number of points are dealt with in a work or discourse. Now, based on them, a story is told and, in the course of it, a particular matter receives special praise. This particular point must be regarded as the purpose of the work or speech in question. The method employed here is "arthavāda". If a viewpoint is sought to be established with reasoning it must be treated as the subject of the work concerned. Here you have "upapatti".

A gentleman told me his view of the Vedas based on his reading of the first and last hymns: "The chief point about the Vedas is fire worship (Agni upāsanā). In the upakrama there is 'Agnimīḷe' and in the upasaṁhāra also there is a hymn to Agni. Both the beginning and the end being so, the purpose of the Vedas (their 'gist') is fire worship." There is an element of truth in this view. Agni is the light of the Ātman, the light of jñāna. The light of jñana is nothing but the spirit of the Self which is the knower, the known and the knowledge: this is the ultimate message of the Vedas.

However, to understand the hymns in question in a literal sense and claim that the Vedas mean fire worship is not correct. The greatness of our scripture consists in the fact that it does not glorify one deity alone. The Vedas proclaim that the Ātman, the Self, must be worshipped, the Ātman that denotes all deities (*Bṛahadāraṇyaka Upaniṣad),* 4.5.6.[6]: "Verily. O Maitreyī, it is the Self that should be perceived, that should be seen, heard and reflected upon. It is the Self that must be known. When the Self is known everything is known." This truth that Yājñavalkya teaches his wife Maitreyī is the goal of the Vedas.

What is the implication of the word "goal"? Now we are here at a particular point. From this point, where we start, we have to go to another point which is final. Such a meaning is suggested by the word "goal". "Ataḥ" is what is pointed to at a distance ("that") as the goal. "Itaḥ" is where we are now (here), the starting point. From "here" we have to go "there" to reach the goal.

But, as a matter of fact, is not "that", the goal, here itself (this)? Yes, when we recognise that everything is the Brahman, we will realise that "that" and "this" (or "here" and "there") are the Brahman — in other words, "that" and "this" are the same. What we now think to be "this" becomes the true state denoted by "that".

Like "ataḥ", the Vedas refer to the Paramātman as "Tat" which means "That". At the conclusion of any rite or work it is customary to say "Om Tat sat". It means, "That is the truth."

We add the suffix "tvam" to some words: "puruṣatvam", "mahatvam", and so on. Here *"tvam"* means the quality or nature of a thing. The quality of "mahat" (or being "mahat") is "mahatvam". The nature of a "puruṣa", being a "purusa", is "puruṣatvam". All right. What do we mean when we refer to a truth, the Ultimate Truth, as "tattvam"? "Tattvam" means "being Tat". When we speak of inquiry into tattva or instruction in tattva it means inquiring into the nature of the Brahman (or rather Brahmanhood or what is meant by the Brahman).

If the Vedas proclaim the Paramātman as "Tat", that is a distant entity, how does it help us? Actually it is not so. What is far away is also close by. The Vedas proclaim: "Dūrāt dūre antike ca."

Once the parents of a girl arranged her marriage to a boy who happened to be a relative[7]. But the girl said: "I'll marry the greatest man in the world." She was stubborn in her decision and the parents in their helplessness said to her, "Do what you like."

The girl thought that the king was the greatest of men and that she would get married to him. One day, as the king was being taken in a palanquin, an ascetic passed by. The king got down and prostrated himself before the sannyāsin and got into his palanquin again. Witnessing the scene, the girl thought to herself: "I was wrong all these days in thinking that the king was the greatest among men. The ascetic seems to be greater. I must marry him." She then followed the holy man.

The ascetic stopped on his way to worship an idol of Gaṇapati installed under a *pīpal* tree. The girl saw it and came to the conclusion: "This Gaṇapati is superior to the sannyāsin. I must marry him." She gave up her chase of the ascetic and sat by the idol of Gaṇapati.

It was a lonely place and no devotee came up to worship the god. After some days a dog came and relieved itself on the idol. The girl now decided that the dog must be greater than Gaṇapati. She went chasing the dog and as it trotted along, with the girl keeping pace with it, a boy threw a stone at it and it wailed loudly in pain. A young man saw this and reprimanded the boy for his cruelty. The girl now told herself. "I had thought that the boy was superior to the dog. But here comes a young man to take him to task. So he must be the greatest of them all." Eventually, it turned out that the young man was none other than the groom her parents had choosen for her.

The girl in the story went in pursuit of one she thought was far away but in the end it turned out that what she had sought was indeed close by.

"You look for God thinking him to be far from you. So long as you are ignorant (that is without jñāna) he is indeed far from you. Even if you look for him all over the world you will not find him. He is in truth with you." "Dūrāt dūre antike ca," says the Śruti (Farther than the farthest, nearer than the nearest).

When we look afar at the horizon it seems to us to be the meeting point of the earth and the sky. Suppose there is a palm-tree there. We imagine that if we go up to the tree we will arrive at the point where the earth and the sky meet. But when we actually arrive at the spot where the tree stands we see that the horizon has receded further. The further we keep going the further the horizon too will recede from us. "We are here under the palm-tree but the horizon is still far away. We must also go further to overtake it." Is it ever possible to overtake the horizon? When we were at a distance from the palm, the horizon seemed to be near it. But when we came to it the horizon seemed to have moved away further. So where is the horizon? Where you are there it is, the horizon. You and the horizon are on the very same spot. What we call "That", the Lord, who we think is far away, is by your side. No, he is *in you.* "That thou art," declare the Vedas — He is you (or you are He).

"That you are" or "That thou art" (Tat tvam asi) is a Vedic mahāvākya. The "tvam" here does not mean the quality or essential nature of any entity or object. The word has two meanings: "essential nature" ("beingness") is one meaning; and "you" or "thou" is another. The Ācārya has used "tvam" as a pun in a stanza in his *Saundaryalaharī.*

It is as a combination of the two words "tat" and "tvam" that the term "tattvam" has come into use. Any truth arrived at at the conclusion of an inquiry is "tattva"[8] — thus it denotes the One Truth that is the Paramātman.

What we call "I", what we think to be "I", that indeed is Īśvara: or such awareness is Īśvara. If you do not possess the light within you to discern this truth you will not be able even to conceive of an entity called Īśvara. The consciousness of "I" is what we believe to be the distant "That". "That and you are the same, child," is the ultimate message of the Vedas.

What we call "this" ("idam") is not without a root or a source. Indeed there is no object called "this" without a source. Without the seed there is no tree. The cosmos with its mountains, oceans, with its sky and earth, with its man and beast, and so on, has its root. Anger, fear and love, the senses, power and energy have their root. Whatever we call "this" has a root. What we see, hear and smell, what we remember, what we feel to be hot or cold, what we experience — all these are covered by the term "idam". Intellectual power, scientific discoveries, the discoveries yet to come — all come under "idam" and all of them have a root cause. There is nothing called "this" or "idam" without a root. Everything has a root or a seed. So the cosmos also must have a root cause; so too all power, all energy, contained in it.

To realise this truth, examine a tamarind seed germinating. When you split the seed open, you will see a miniature tree in it. It has in it the potential to grow, to grow big. Such is the case with all seeds.

The mantras have "bījākṣaras" [seed letters or rather seed syllables]. Like a big tree (potentially) present in a tiny seed, these syllables contain immeasurable power. If the bījākṣara is muttered a hundred thousand times, with your mind one-pointed, you will have its power within your grasp.

Whatever power there is in the world, whatever intellectual brilliance, whatever skills and talents, all must be present in God in a rudimentary form. The Vedas proclaim, as if with the beat of drums : "All this has not sprung without a root cause. The power that is in the root or the seed is the same as the power that pervades the entire universe. Where is that seed or root ? The Self that keeps seeing all from within, what we call 'idam,' is the root."

When you stand before a mirror you see your image in it. If you keep four mirrors in a row you[9] will see a thousand images of yourself. There is one source (or root cause) for all these images. The one who sees these one thousand images is the same as the one who is their source. The one who is within the millions of creatures and sees all "this" is Īśvara. That which sees is the root of all that is seen. That root is knowledge and it is the source of all the cosmos. Where do you find this knowledge? It is in you. The infinite, transcendent knowledge is present partly in you — the whole is present in you as part.

Here is a small bulb. There you have a bigger bulb. That light is blue, this is green. There are lamps of many sizes and shapes. But their power is the same — electricity, electricity which is everywhere. It keeps the fan whirling, keeps the lamps burning. The power is the same and it is infinite. When it passes through a wire it becomes finite. When lightning strikes in flashes, when water cascades, the power is manifested. In the same way you must try to make the supreme truth within you manifest itself in a flash. All Vedic rites, all worship, all works, meditation of the mahāvākyas, Vedānta — the purpose of all these is to make the truth unfold itself to you - in you - in a flash.

Even the family and social life that are dealt with in the Vedas, the royal duties mentioned in them, or poetry, therapeutics or geology or any other śāstra are steps leading towards the realisation of the Self. At first the union of "Tat" and "tvam" (That and you) would be experienced for a few moments like a flash of lightning. The *Kenopaniṣad* (4.4)[10] refers to the state of knowing the Brahman experientially as a flash of lightning happening in the twinkling of an eye. But with repeated practice, with intense concentration, you will be able to immerse yourself in such experience. It is like the electricity produced when a stream remains cascading. This is mokṣa, liberation, when you are yet in this world, when you are still in possession of your body. And, when you give up the body, you will become the etenal Truth yourself. This is called "videhamukti" (literally bodiless liberation). The difference between jīvanmukti and videhamukti is only with reference to an outside observer; for the jñānin the two are identical.

The goal of the Vedas is inward realisation of the Brahman here and now. We learn about happenings in the world from the newspapers. The news is gathered by reporters stationed in different countries, at different centres, also through news agencies. It is received through letters, telegrams or teleprinter messages. There are things that cannot be known by such means, things that are not comprehended by the ordinary human mind. Should we not have a special newspaper to keep us informed about them? The Vedas constitute such a paper. They tell us about things that cannot be known to ordinary news-gatherers and also about things occurring in a place where there is neither telegraphy nor any teleprinter. It is through the medium of this newspaper that the sages who possess trans-sensual powers keep us informed about matters that are beyond this world and beyond the comprehension of the average man.

There are, however, certain portions in the Vedas that are to be discarded. "To be discarded" is not to be taken to mean to be rejected outright as wrong. There cannot be anything wrong about any part of the Vedas. Even to think so is sacrilegious. There are matters in these texts that are preliminary to an important subject or that lend support to it. According to the arrangement made by our forefathers the important part is to be retained and the other preliminary or supporting portion is to be excluded. Certain things are necessary at a certain stage of our development. But these are to be excluded as we go step by step to a higher stage.

There are then passages that are of the utmost importance and have the force of law. These are to be accepted in full. Things that are to be discarded belong to the category of "arthavāda" or of "anuvāda".

The Vedas contain stories told to impress on us the importance of a concept, stories that raise ideas to a high level. The injunctions with which these stories are associated must be accepted in full but the stories themselves may be discarded as "arthavāda", that is they need not be brought into observance.

What is "anuvāda"? Before speaking about a new rule or a new concept, the Vedas tell us about things that we already know. They go on repeating this without coming to the new rule or concept, that is things known to us in practical life and not having the authority of Vedic pronouncements. This is "anuvāda."

Anuvāda and arthavāda are not of importance and are not meant to convey the ultimate purpose or message of the Vedas. What we do not know otherwise through any other authority and what the Vedas speak of is "vidhi". And that is the chief "vāda", the true tattva, the true intent of the Vedas.

To explain further. What is mentioned in the Vedas but can be known by other (mundane) means is not incontrovertible Vedic authority. The purpose of the Vedas is to make known what is not known. They speak about things we know and do not know, but their chief purpose is the latter — what they state about what we do not know. It is out of compassion that they speak about what is known to us as a prelude to telling us what we do not know. But if telling us what we already know is the purpose of the Vedas — their truth — why should they deal with things that we do not know? If the Vedas deal at length with the things that we are ignorant about, would it not be ridiculous to discard them and retain only what we know already? Indeed such an act would be sacrilegious. The question, however, arises : why should things known to us have been dealt with at length?

The Vedas could have been silent about them. Well, what is it that we know, what is it that we do not know?

There are two views about all mundane objects, worldly phenomena. Do all the objects that we perceive constitute one entity or are they all disparate?

Opinion is divided on this. Based on our physical perceptions we regard all objects to be separate from one another. It is only on such a basis that our functions are carried out properly in the workaday world. Water is one thing and oil is another. To light a lamp we need oil [to feed the wick]. We cannot use water for the same. But if the lamp flares up and objects near by catch fire we will have to put it out with water. With oil the fire will only spread. We have thus to note how one object is different from another and to learn how best each is to be used.

To view each object as being distinct from another is part of "Dvaita", dualism. Many of the rituals in the Vedas, many of the ways of worship found in them, are based on the dualistic view. As Advaitins (followers of the non-dualistic doctrine) we need not raise any objections on this score. We must, however, find out whether or not the Vedas go beyond dualism. If they do not, we have to conclude that their message is Dvaita. But what is the truth actually found expressed in them?

The non-dualist truth is proclaimed in a number of hymns and in most of the Upaniṣads, but this is not in keeping with our outward experience. The ultimate Vedic view is that all objects are indeed not separate from one another but are the outward manifestation of the same Self.

Our religious and philosophical works have two parts — pūrvapakṣa and siddhānta. In the pūrvapakṣa or initial section of a work, the point of view to be refuted [the view opposed to that of the author of the work] is dealt with. If we read only this part we are likely to form an impression opposite to what the work intends to convey. To refute an opinion other than one's own, one has naturally to state it. This is the purpose of the pūrvapakṣa. In the sīddhānta section there is a refutation of the systems opposed to one's own before the latter is sought to be established. Scholars abroad are full of praise for the fact that in our darśanas or philosophical works the views of systems opposed to those expressed in the darśanas are not concealed or ignored but that their criticisms and objections are sought to be answered.

From what is said before, does it mean that non-dualism is incorporated in the pūrvapakṣa of the Vedas so as to be refuted in the latter part? No, it is not so. The jñānakāṇḍa in which the Upaniṣads lay emphasis on non-dualism is the concluding part of the Vedas. The karmakāṇḍa which speaks of dualism precedes it. So if the Vedas first speak about the dualism that we know[11] and later about the non-dualism that we do not know, it means that the non-dualistic teaching is the supreme purpose of the Vedas.

I will tell you why the dualism in the pūrvapakṣa in the Vedas is not rebutted. The works and worship performed with a dualistic outlook are not a hindrance for us to advance on the path of non-dualistic experience. On the contrary, they are a means to make precisely such progress. So the works and worship are not to be taken as constituting a point of view opposed to the main message of the Vedas and to be refuted in the second part. First the flower, then the fruit. Similarly, we have to advance to non-dualism from dualism. The flower is not opposed to the fruit, is it ? Do we despise the flower because the fruit represents its highest [natural development]?

From the non-dualistic standpoint there is no need to counter other systems, viewed on their own proper levels. It is only when these levels are exceeded that the need arises to counter them. That is how our Ācārya and other exponents of non-dualism countenanced other systems.

By the grace of Īśvara scientific advancement so far has done no injury to things Ātmic and indeed modern science takes us increasingly close to Advaita whose truth hitherto could not be known by anything other than the Vedas. In the early centuries of science it was thought that all objects in the world were different entities, separate from one another. Then scientists came to the conclusion that the basis of all matter was constituted by the different elements, that all the countless objects in the world resulted from these elements combining together in various ways. Subsequently when atomic science developed it was realised that all the elements had the same source, the same energy[12].

Those who meditate on the Self and know the truth realise that this power, this Ātman, is made up of knowledge, awareness. And it is knowledge (jñana) that enfolds not only inert objects but also the individual self to form the non-dualistic whole.

Whether it is one energy or one caitanya[S], the One Object that both vijñānins (scientists) and jñānins (knowers) speak of is not visible to us. We see only its countless disguises as different objects, that is we see the One Object dualistically [or pluralistically]. You need not seek the support of the Vedas for this, for what is obvious. Why do you need the testimony of the Vedas for what our eyes and intellect recognize ? If they speak of a truth that we are not aware of but which we can realise from what we know, and if this truth is proclaimed to be their final conclusion, we must accept it as their ultimate message. This message is the doctrine, the truth, that the individual self is inseparably (non-dualistically) dissolved in the Paramātman to become the Paramātman.

Notes & References

1 *Sarve Vedā yatpadamāmananti, tapāṁsi sarvāṇi ca yad-vadanti; yadicchanto brahmacaryaṁ caranti, tatte padaṁ saṁgraheṇa bravimi Omityetad.*

— Kaṭhopaniṣad, 2.15

2 See Note 4 appended to Chapter 6 of this part.

3 *Parāñci khāni vyatṛṇatsvayambhūstasmātparāṅ paśyati nāntarātman. Kaścid dhīraḥ pratyagātmānamaikṣadāvṛttacakṣuramṛtatvamicchan.*

— Kaṭhopaniṣad, 4.1.

4 The reference is to liberation in this world itself, not in an unknown next world.

5 See Part Twelve.

6 *...Ātma va are draṣṭavyaḥ śrotavyo mantavyo nididhyāsitavyo, Maitreyyātmani khalvare dṛṣte, śrute, mate, vijñate, idam sarvaṁ viditam.*

— Bṛhadāraṇyaka Upaniṣad, 4.5.6.

7 There is a custom in the South of a girl being married to her maternal uncle's or paternal aunt's son.

8 The word is also used in the sense of a "principle". Literally, "tattva" may be understood as "thatness".

9 Parallel mirrors.

10 *Tasyaiṣa ādeśo yadetadvidyuto vyadyutadā iti tinyamīmiṣadā, ityadhidaivatam.*

—Kenopaniṣad, 4.4

11 "...first speak about the dualism that we know": what is meant here is the fact that to our direct perception the phenomenal world appears divided and manifold. "The non-dualism we do not know": it means that the oneness of all objects is not directly perceived or is not apparent.

12 The Paramaguru said many years before nuclear science had developed that countless objects were formed by different combinations of two or more of the elements. He also observed that with further research scientists would discover that the source of all the elements would be the same. Is there any wonder that what he foresaw has come true? — Rā. Ga.

Chapter 35

Essence of the Upaniṣadic Teaching

What is the essence of the Upaniṣadic teaching? How do we realise the ideal state mentioned in the Upaniṣads [the oneing of the individual self and the Overself]?

The phenomenal universe, in the view of modern science, is embraced by the concepts of time and space [it exists in the time-space frame]. The Upaniṣads declare that only by being freed from the time and space factors can we grasp the ultimate truth that is at the source of the cosmos. I told you about the horizon — where we are right there the horizon is. A recognition of this truth takes us beyond space. In this way we must also try to transcend time.

Is it possible?

To give us the confidence that it is, an example could be cited from everyday life. To spend the time we lap up newspaper reports of the fight going on in a distant country like, say, the Congo [now called Zaire]. If a dispute or trouble erupts nearer home, in a country like Pākistān (or at home in Kāśmīr), we forget the Congo and turn to Pākistān or Kāśmīr. The newspapers themselves push reports of the Congo trouble to some corner and highlight developments in Pākistān or Kāśmīr. But when a quarrel breaks out even nearer, say, a quarrel over Tiruttaṇi[1] between the Tamiḻs and the Telugus, Pākistān and Kāśmīr are forgotten and the boundary quarrel claims all our interest. Now, when we come to know about a street brawl in our neighbourhood, we throw aside the newspaper to go out and see for ourselves what the trouble is all about. Again, when we are watching the street fight, a friend or relative comes and tells us that a war is going on in our own home, a fight between the wife and the mother. What do we do then? We forget the street brawl and rush home at once.

On an international level the Congo dispute is perhaps of great importance. But we pass from that to quarrels of decreasing importance. Our interest in each, however, is in inverse proportion to its real importance. Why ? The Congo is far away *in space*. We are more concerned about what happens nearer us than about distant occurrences. It is all like coming to the horizon, the spot where we are.

Now let us turn our gaze inward. If we become aware of the battle going on within us, the battle fought by the senses, all other quarrels will become distant affairs like the Congo dispute. Let us try to resolve this inner conflict and try to remain tranquil. In this tranquillity all will be banished including place, space, and so on. When we are asleep are we conscious of being in any particular place? In sleep we are not aware of either knowledge or space, but in jñāna (in the state of enlightenment of the inner truth) we will experience knowledge without any consciousness of space.

The time factor is similar. How inconsolably we wept when our father died ten years ago. How is it that we do not feel the same intensity of grief when we think of his death today? On the day a dear one passes we weep so much, but not so much on the following day. Why is it so? Last year we earned a promotion, or won a prize in a lottery. We jumped for joy then, didn't we? Why is it that we don't feel the same thrill of joy when we think about it today?

Just as nearness in space is a factor in determining how we are affected by an event, so too is nearness in time. Even when we are turned outward and remain conscious of time and space, they lose their impact without any special effort on our part. So the confidence arises that we can be totally freed from these two factors of time and space if we turn inward. When we are asleep we are oblivious of time and space without any effort on our part. But we do not then have the awareness of being free from them. We must go to the state spoken of by Tāyumānavar[T], the state in which we sleep without sleeping and are full of jñāna and are immersed in the bliss of freedom from time and space. Then nothing will affect us, not even a quarrel right in our presence, in our home. Even when we receive a stab wound we will not be affected by it — it would be like a happening in a remote land like the Congo. When someone very dear to us dies in our presence — husband, wife or child — it would be an occurrence remote in time, like our father's passing ten years ago.

Let us, for the time being, forget arguments about non-dualism and dualism. Let us think about our real need. What is it ?

Peace. Tranquillity.

We are affected by good and bad things alike. We cry, we laugh. Both sorrow and joy have their impact on us. Even excessive laughter causes pain in the stomach, enervates us. When we are tickled we react angrily. "Stop it!" we cry. Even when we dance for joy we are fatigued. We like to remain calm without being affected by anything, without giving way to any type of emotion. Such is our need. Not dualism or non-dualism.

Let us consider what we must do for this goal. One point will become clear if we think about how the impact produced by a happening or an emotion is wiped away. "When news about the Congo war broke how we became engrossed in newspaper reports of the dispute. How did we lose interest in it later? Why does it not have any impact on us now?" If we think on these lines we will realise that the impact of any event — or whatever — is progressively reduced as it is pushed further in space. If we also consider why we are not as much affected now by our father's death as we were ten years ago when he died, we will realise that with receding time we are less and less affected by past events. So if we are to remain detached we must learn to think that what happens close by is happening in a remote place like the Congo.

Similarly, we must also learn to think that all the happy and unhappy incidents of the moment occurred ten years ago. We must assiduously train ourselves to take such an attitude. No joy or sorrow is everlasting. They are all relative [that is they do not have their own integral or independent force but rely on other factors]. So, without being part of anything or else dependent on anything, we must remain in the absolute state of being ourselves. Then alone will we be free from all influences and experience eternal peace. This is how Einstein's Theory of Relativity is applied to the science of the Self (Ātmavidyā).

The essence of the Upaniṣadic message is the burning desire to be free from time and space. It would be in proportion to the extent to which we burn within in our endeavour to be free from the spatio-temporal factor that we will be rewarded with the grace of Īśvara and be led towards the fulfilment of the great ideal.

There is no need to go to the mountains or to the forest for instruction. Space and time teach us how to remain unaffected by events. All that we need do is to pray to the Lord and make an effort to develop the will and capacity to put happenings of the moment back in time and distant in space.

The first of the ten [major] Upaniṣads. *Īśāvāsya,* says[2]: "It is in motion and yet it is still. It is afar and yet near. It is indeed within....". This statement refers to space and time and creates the urge in us to be freed from both. The next mantra[3] asks us to see time and space and all creatures in our Self itself. Then there will be no cause for hatred, delusion or sorrow, that is nothing will affect us. Another mantra[4] of the same Upaniṣad declares that the Self is all-pervading, going beyond space, and distributing things through the endless years according to their natures.

On the whole, the Upaniṣads speak of the same basic truth of space and time that modern science teaches. But there is this difference. For science this truth is a mere postulate. For the Upaniṣads it is a truth to be realised within as an experience.

This is the conclusion of the Upaniṣads which are themselves the concluding part of the Vedas.

Notes & References

[1] Tiruttaṇi in Tamiḷ Nāḍu is on the border of that state with Āndhra Prades. Years ago when the states were reorganised there was a dispute over this town (it has a famous temple to Subrahmaṇya), the Āndhras demanding its inclusion in their state and the Tamiḷs refusing to yield to the demand. (We must remember that the Paramaguru is speaking here to a Tamiḷ audience.)

[2], [3] & [4] Tadejati tannaijati taddūre tadvadantike
Tadantarasya sarvasya tadu sarvasyāsya bāhyataḥ

Yastu sarvāṇi bhūtānyātmanyevānūpaśyati
Sarvabhūteṣu cātmānam tato na vijugupsate

Yasmin sarvāṇi bhūtānyātmaivābhūdvijānataḥ
Tatra ko mohaḥ kaḥ śoka ekatvamanupaśyataḥ

Sa paryagācchukramakāyamavraṇamasnāviram śuddhamapāpaviddham. Kavirmanīṣī parībhūḥ, svayambhūryāthātathyato'rthān vyadadhācchāśvatībhyaḥ samābhyaḥ

—Īśāvāsya Upaniṣad, 5, 6, 7 & 8.

Chapter 36

Vedic Śākhās

When the Vedas are said to have no end, how can one talk of there being an "end to the Vedas (Vedānta)"? The message of the Vedas, the truths proclaimed by them, the teachings with respect to Self-realisation occur in the concluding part (Upaniṣad) of each of the Vedas, that is Vedānta.

Why should the Vedas, which are infinite, have been divided into so many śākhās or recensions? A man must be imparted all that is necessary to purify his mind and prepare him for Self-realisation. For this purpose he needs hymns, mantras, employed in the performance of sacrifices and other works; he has to examine the principles behind the sacrifices; and, finally, he has to inquire into the Paramātman adopting the meditative practice called nididhyāsana[S] so as to make the Ultimate Truth an inner experience. It is not necessary for him to learn all the countless Vedas; in any case it would be an impossible task. You remember the story I told you of the great sage Bharadvāja who could go only three steps up the Vedic mountain.[1] What a man needs to learn to refine himself, become free from all impurities and finally mingle in the Supreme Being — the text conforming to such needs is separated from the unending Vedas to make a śākhā.

A Vedic recension includes all the works relating to a Brahmin's life from birth to death. A Brahmin must memorise the mantras of the Saṁhitā, perform sacrifices according to the Brāhmaṇas to the chanting of the mantras, and later cross the bridge constituted by the Āraṇyaka, the bridge that connects the outward with the inward, that is study intensely the Upaniṣads that are concerned exclusively with the inward. In this way he finally becomes liberated, with the inward and the outward becoming one.

For the wise and the mature a single mantra is enough to free them from worldly existence. But to become pure an ordinary man needs to perform many works and conduct worship in many ways. He has to do japa[S] and meditation. Each śākhā contains mantras, rituals and instruction in the science of the Self to enable him to find release.

(See Chapter 38 of this part entitled "Śākhās now Studied".)

Reference

1 See Chapter 12 of this part.

Chapter 37

Brahmins and Non-Brahmins

What about non-Brahmins? Is it not necessary for them too to become pure within? Even if they do not have to perform Vedic rituals or chant mantras, they too have to become cleansed inwardly by doing their allotted work. Whatever his caste or jāti, if a man performs his hereditary work in a spirit of dedication to Īśvara he will become liberated. This is stated clearly in the Gītā[1]: "Svakaramaṇā tam abhyarcya siddhiṁ vindati mānavaḥ."

One man has the job of waging wars, another that of trading and rearing cattle, a third has manual work to do. What work does the Brahmin do for society ?

Is not the grace of the Supreme Being important even in wordly life? The Brahmin's vocation is doing such works as would enable all jātis earn this grace. The devas or celestials are like the officials of the Paramātman. It is the duty of the Brahmin to make all creatures of the world dear to them. The work he performs, the mantras he chants are intended to do good to all jātis. Since he has to do with forces that are extra-mundane, he has to follow a religious discipline of rites and vows more strictly than what others have to follow so as to impart potency to the mantras. If it were realised that he has to perform rituals and observe vows for the sake of other communities also, people would not harbour the wrong notion that he has been assigned some special [privileged] job.

Apart from this, the Brahmin has to learn the arts and śāstras that pertain to worldly life, the trades and vocations of all other castes and instruct them in such work as is theirs by heredity. His calling is that of the teacher and he must not do other jobs. His is a vocation entailing great responsibility and is more important than the job of affording bodily protection to people, or of trade or labour. For the Brahmin's duty is to preserve the arts and crafts and other skills by which other communities maintain themselves, to nurture their minds and impart them knowledge.

If the man discharging such a responsibility is not mentally mature, his work will not yield the desired results. If he himself is not noble of mind he will not be able to raise others to a high level. At the same time, he has a handicap which he does not share with others. If he believes that he is superior to others because he does intellectual work he will only be a hindrance to himself. That is why the Brahmin has to be rendered pure. Since there are reasons for him to feel superior to others, there must be the assurance that he does not suffer from the least trace of egoism or arrogance. That is why he is tempered by means of the forty saṁskāras[2] and his impurities wrung out.

If the mantras are to be efficacious, the one who chants them must be disciplined and must observe a variety of vows. There is, for instance, the mantra to cure a person stung by a scorpion. The man who chants it must observe certain strict rules. If he is lax in the matter, the mantra will have no effect— this is what the māntrikas themselves say. There are rules for the recitation of each mantra, a time when it is to be chanted and when it is not to be. If the rules are violated it will have no effect. It is said that the mantras are more efficacious when recited during eclipses.

A Vedic śākhā contains all the rites needed to be performed by a Brahmin to become pure within.

References

[1] Yataḥ pravṛttir bhūtānāṁ yena sarvam idam tatam
Svakarmaṇā tam abhyarcya siddhiṁ vindati mānavaḥ

—Bhagavadgītā, 18.46

[2] Described in detail in Part Sixteen.

Chapter 38

Śākhās now Studied

People in the distant past had remarkable abilities and possessed great yogic and intellectual power. So they could gain mastery of many Vedic recensions. As for the great sages it was a matter of the Vedas revealing themselves to them in a flash. Others with their unusual abilities were able to master not only the Vedas but other branches of learning. The Vedas in their infinitude being like the expanse of an endless ocean, no one has been able to master all of them. Even so in the remote past there were individuals conversant with a large number of śākhās.

In later times men began to lose their divine yogic power. At the beginning of the age of Kali it became very weak indeed. The life-span of man began to get shorter and his health and intelligence declined. It is all the sport of the Paramātman. Why should there have been a diminution in human power and human intelligence? It is difficult to answer the question. Would it not be natural to expect an increase, generation after generation, in the number of people learning the Vedas, performing sacrifices and conducting Ātmic inquiry? Why is it not so? Again it is a question that is hard to answer.

The Paramātman conducts the cosmic drama playing in strange and ever new ways. Although scientists like Darwin speak of evolution, in the matter of Ātmic strength, intellectual enlightenment, character and yogic power, we seem to have been going further and further down on the scale.

Since the Kṛta-Yuga there has been a decline in the powers of man. In that age a man lived so long as his skeleton lasted. Even if his blood dried up and his flesh was destroyed he survived until his bones collapsed. People in the Kṛta age had much power of knowledge. They were called "asti-gata-prāṇas".

In the Tretā age people were "māṁsa-gata-prāṇas", that is they lived so long as their flesh lasted and did not perish even when their blood dried up. They had a special capacity for performing sacrifices. In the Dvāpara age people were "rudhira-gata-prāṇas" and lived until such time as their blood dried up. They were known especially for the pūjā they performed. We of the Kali age are "anna-gata-prāṇas" and life will remain in our body so long as the food [nourishment] lasts. We have little capacity to meditate, perform rituals and pūjā. But we are capable of chanting the names of the Lord — Kṛṣṇa, Rāma, and so on. It is true that by muttering the names of the Lord we will be liberated.

Even so we must not allow the Vedas to become extinct. They were bequeathed to us from the time of creation. Must we allow them to be lost?

When Śrī Kṛṣṇa departed from this world, grim darkness enveloped the world. There is "darkness" in his name itself ("Kṛṣṇa" means dark). He was also born in darkness, in the dungeon of a prison at midnight. But he was the radiance of knowledge for all the world, the light of compassion. When he departed much injury was done to jñāna, and darkness descended into the world. Kali, who is evil incarnate, acceded to authority. All this is the sport of the Paramātman, the sport that is inscrutable. Śrī Kṛṣṇa came as a burst of light but later he created a state in which the fear of darkness arose everywhere. Then, urged by his compassion, he decided that the world must not go to waste. He thought that it could be saved by administering an antidote against the venom of Kali. This antidote was the Vedas. It would be enough if precautions were taken to make sure that the "Kali Man" did not devour them — the world would be saved. In the darkness surrounding everything they would serve the purpose of a lamp lighting the path of mankind. In the age of Kali they would not shine with the same effulgence as in the previous ages. But the Lord resolved that they must burn with at least the minimum of lustre to be of benefit to mankind and this he ensured through Vedavyāsa who was partially his incarnation.

The sage who was to carry out Bhagavān Kṛṣṇa's resolve was not then called Vedavyāsa. His name too was Kṛṣṇa and, since he was born on an island, he had the appellation "Dvaipāyana" (Islander). Bādarāyaṇa is another name of his. Kṛṣṇa Dvaipāyana knew all the 1,180 śākhās (recensions) of the Vedas revealed to the world by various sages. They were mingled together in one great stream. Being remarkably gifted, our ancestors could memorise all of them. For the benefit of weaker people like us, Vyāsa divided them into four Vedas and subdivided each into śākhās. It was like damming a river and taking the water through various canals. Vyāsa accomplished the task of dividing the Vedas easily because he was a great yogin with vision and because he had the power gained from austerities.

The Ṛgvedic śākhās contain hymns to invoke the various deities; the Yajurvedic śākhās deal with the conduct of sacrifices; the Sāmaveda śākhās contain songs to please the deities; and the Atharvaveda śākhās, besides dealing with sacrifices, contain mantras recited to avert calamities and to destroy enemies. The Sāmaveda had the largest number of recensions, 1,000. In the Ṛgveda there were 21; in the Yajus 109 (Śukla-Yajurveda 15, and Kṛṣṇa Yajurveda 94); and in the Atharvaveda 50.

Śākhās now Studied

While, according to one scholar, the *Viṣṇu Purāna* mentions the number of śākhās to be 1,180, another version has it that there were 1,133 recensions—the Ṛgveda 21, the Yajurveda 101, the Sāmaveda 1,000 and the Atharvaveda 11.

Considering that people in the age of Kali would be inferior to their forefathers, Kṛṣṇa Dvaipāyana thought that it should be sufficient for them to learn one śākhā of any one of the four Vedas. It was the Lord that put this idea into his head. Vyāsa assigned the Ṛgveda śākhās to Paila, the Yajurveda śākhās to Vaiśampāyana, the Sāmaveda śākhās to Jaimini and the Atharvaveda śākhās to Sumantu.

Kṛṣṇa Dvaipāyana came to be called "Vedavyāsa" for having divided the Vedas into four and then having subdivided them into 1,180 recensions. "Vyāsa" literally means an "essay" or a "composition". Classifying objects is also known as "vyāsa".

According to Kṛṣṇa Dvaipāyana's arrangement, though it is obligatory for a person [that is a Brahmin] to learn only one recension, it does not mean that there is a bar on learning more. The intention is that at least one śākhā must be studied. Even after Vyāsa's time, there have been examples of paṇḍitas mastering more than one śākhā from the four Vedas. (Vyāsa divided the Vedas some 5,000 years ago. This has been established to some extent historically. Instead of accepting this date arrived at according to our śāstras, modern historians maintain that the date of the Mahābhārata must be 1500 B.C. But of late opinion is veering round to the view that the epic dates back to 5,000 years ago.[1])

I said that there was no bar on anyone learning more than one śākhā. Even today we find North Indians with appellations like "Caturvedī", "Trivedī" and "Dvivedī".

We had a "Trivedī"[2], who was governor of one of our states. "Duve" and "Dave" are derived from "Dvivedī". One descended from a family well versed in the four Vedas is called a "Caturvedin". In Beṅgāḷ he is called "Catterjī". Those who have mastered three Vedas are "Trivedins". Today it is rare to see a man who has learned even one Veda, but the fact that members of some families still call themselves "Trivedins" or "Caturvedins" show that in the past there must have been individuals who knew more than one Veda. Jñānasaṁbandhar[T] calls himself *"Nānmarai Jñānasaṁbandhar"*[3]. Since he was suckled by Ambā herself it must have been easy for him to master the four Vedas.

During these 5,000 years and more since Vedavyāsa divided the Vedas, many śākhās have been lost. Out of the 1,180 we are in the unfortunate position of having only six or seven. Of the 21 śākhās of the Ṛgveda there is only one extant — it is called the *Śākala Śākhā*, or the *Aitareya Śākhā*, since the *Aitareya Upaniṣad* occurs in it. Of the 15 recensions of the Śukla-Yajurveda only two are extant, the *Kāṇva Śākhā* having a large following in Mahārāṣṭra and the *Mādhyandina Śākhā* in North India. Of the 94 śākhās of the Kṛṣṇa-Yajurveda, the *Taittirīya* has a large following, particularly in the South. We have lost 997 of the 1,000 śākhās of the Sāmaveda. In Tamiḷ Nāḍu those who follow the *Kauthūma Śākhā* are more in number than those who follow the *Talavakāra Śākhā*, while in Mahārāṣṭra there is a small following for *Rāṇāyanīya*. Once it was feared that out of the 50 recensions of the Atharvaveda none was extant. But on inquiry it was discovered that there was a Brahmin in Sinor, Gujarat, who was conversant with the *Śaunaka Śākhā* of this Veda. We sent students from here (Tamiḷ Nāḍu) to learn the same from him.

The *Aitareya Brāhmaṇa* and the *Kauṣītaki Brāhmaṇa* (also called *Śānkhāyana Brāhmaṇa*) of the Ṛgveda are still available to us. The *Aitareya Upaniṣad* and the *Kauṣītaki Upaniṣad*, which are part of the Āraṇyakas belonging to these, are still extant.

Of the Śukla-Yajurveda we have the *Śatapatha Brāhmana*. This is common — with minor differences — to both the *Mādhyandina* and *Kāṇva Śākhās*. It is a voluminous work which serves as an explanation for all the Vedas. Only one Āraṇyaka is extant from this Veda and it constitutes the *Bṛhadāraṇyaka Upaniṣad*. I have already mentioned that the *Īśāvāsya Upaniṣad* belongs to the Saṁhitā part of this Veda.

Of the Kṛṣṇa-Yajurveda the *Taittirīya Brāhmaṇa* alone is extant. Among the Āraṇyakas of this Veda we have the *Taittirīya;* the *Taittirīya Upaniṣad* and the *Mahānārāyaṇa Upaniṣad* are part of it. The latter contains a number of mantras commonly used. The *Maitrāyaṇi Āraṇyaka* and the Upaniṣad of the same name also belong to the Kṛṣṇa-Yajurveda. As mentioned before, of the *Kāṭha Śākhā* only the Upaniṣad *(Kaṭhopaniṣad)* is available, not the Saṁhitā, Brāhmaṇa and Āraṇyaka.

(Similarly, the *Śvetāśvataropaniṣad* of the Kṛṣṇa-Yajurveda is still extant, but no other part of the relevant śākhā.)

Nine hundred ninety-seven śākhās of the Sāmaveda are lost and of its Brāhmaṇas only some seven or eight have survived — *Tāṇḍya, Ārṣeya, Devatādhyāya, Saṁhitopaniṣad, Vaṁsa, (Ṣadvimśa, Chāndogya, Jaiminīya)*. The *Talavakāra Āraṇyaka* of this Veda is also called the *Talavakāra Brāhmaṇa*. The *Kenopaniṣad* comes at the end of it: so it is also known as the *Talavakāra Upaniṣad*. The *Chāndogya Brāhmaṇa* has the *Chāndogya Upaniṣad*.

Śākhās now Studied

To repeat what I mentioned earlier, we still have three important Upaniṣads from the Atharvaveda — *Praśna, Muṇḍaka and Māṇḍūkya.* (The *Nṛsimha-Tāpinī Upaniṣad* also belongs to this Veda.) The only Brāhmaṇa of this Veda to have survived is *Gopatha.*

We should be guilty of a grave offence if the seven or eight śākhās of the 1,180 that still survive become extinct because of our neglect: there will be no expiation for the same.

In the South, which is called "Drāviḍadeśa", Vedic learning is still kept alive by the Nampūtiris in Keraḷa. And it was well maintained in Āndhra Pradeś until recently. A great encouragement to this was the annual Navarātri festival at Vijayavāda every year when examinations for Vedic students and an assembly of Vedic scholars were held. Those who took part in the assembly were given cash awards as well as certificates. Brahmacārins[S] and *paṇḍits* came from all over the country to take part in the examination and the assembly respectively. The certificate was highly valued. A scholar returning home with the certificate was honoured by householders all along the way. There was a custom in Āndhra Pradeś to set aside a tidy sum to be presented to Vedic scholars at weddings. Vedic learning flourished in that state because of such incentives.

A Brahmin ought not to run after money; if he does he ceases to be a Brahmin. However, we have to consider the fact that today any occupation or profession other than that of the Vedic scholar is lucrative. One learned in the Vedas cannot make ends meet. Such being the case it becomes incumbent on us to devise a system by which the Vedic scholar too can live without any care. It is because the minimum needs of Vedic students and scholars were met in the Telugu country that scriptural learning flourished there.

We are making efforts to promote Vedic learning[4] all over India and in particular in Tamiḷ Nāḍu — and a scheme has been drawn up to raise funds for pāṭhaśālās (Vedic schools). In Tamiḷ Nāḍu there was patronage for Vedic learning until the reign of Hindu rulers like the Nayakas[5]. Later it received encouragement from the princely states. A Brahmin who has mastered an entire Vedic śākhā is called a "śrotriya", from "Śruti" meaning the Vedas. It was customary for Tamiḷ rājās to donate land to such Brahmins and sometimes an entire village was given away, it being exempt from taxes. This is described as "*iraiyili*" in the old inscriptions. "Brahmadeśam" is the name given to lands made over to Brahmins as gifts. In the royal edicts the word used is "*Brahmadeyam*". "Caturvedimaṅgalam" was the name given to a village donated by royalty to Brahmins proficient in all the four Vedas. Those who spent all their time in learning and teaching the scriptures had no other source of income. So they were exempt from *kisti*[6]. This exemption was in force even during the rule of the Nawabs, the East India Company and its successor British government. Even though the British did nothing to promote Vedic studies, they exempted śrotriya villages from taxes. However, the Brahmins during the time sold their lands, converting them into certificates, and abandoned the villages of their forefathers to settle in towns. This also meant something most unfortunate, severing their connection with the long Vedic tradition.

Our country has an ages-old tradition— and it is a glorious tradition— that has no parallel in any other part of the world. It is that a section of its people have, generation after generation, worked not only for their own Ātmic uplift but for the well-being of the entire society. And this they have done to the exclusion of being involved in worldly affairs. Later, however, they (Brahmins) failed to recognise the unique importance of such a tradition and broke away from it to take to the Western way of life. A situation soon arose in which others also forgot the importance of having a class of people devoting themselves solely to the Ātmic quest.

Notes & References

[1] The implication is that Vedavyāsa lived during the same time.

[2] C.M. Trivedī.

[3] "Jñānasaṁbandhar who knows the four Vedas."

[4] The Kāñcī Maṭha under the inspiration of the Paramaguru himself started the scheme. For details see Appendix 2.

[5] The Nayakships of Tañjāvūr and Madurai were established about the same time, in the 16th century.

[6] *"Kisti"* is a tax on landed property.

Chapter 39

Duty of Brahmins

If any purpose has been served by listening to me all the while, it is up to you [Brahmins] to take whatever steps you think fit to promote Vedic learning. Every day you must perform "Brahmayajña" which is one of the five great sacrifices (mahāyajñas). The term "Brahma" in "Brahmayajña" means the Vedas. The power of the mantras must be preserved in us as an eternal reality. It must burn bright like a lamp that is never extinguished. For this reason it is that we perform Brahmayajña. We must offer oblations to the presiding ṛṣi or seer of our Vedic recension. Failing that, the least we can do is perform the Gāyatrī-japa[S] every day. Gāyatrī is the essence of the Vedas, their substance. To qualify to chant it, you must be initiated into it by a guru. The Gāyatrī you thus learn must be mentally repeated at least a thousand times every day. Again, the least you can do — and you must do it — is to chant the mantra ten times morning, noon and dusk. The sun god is the presiding deity of Gāyatrī. Sunday, the day of the sun, is a universal holiday. On this day you must get up at 4 in the morning and, after your ablutions, recite the Gāyatrī a thousand times. This will ensure your well-being as well as of all mankind.[1]

All Brahmins must learn to chant the Puruṣasūkta, the Śrīsūkta, Śrī Rudram[2], etc. I am speaking particularly to officegoing Brahmins here. Since they will find it difficult to devote themselves fully to Vedic learning they must try to acquire at least a minimum of scriptural knowledge. But it should be creditable if they accomplish something — in the present case learning the Vedas -- in the face of difficulties. If you start learning the scripture now you will be able to complete your study in a few years. But you need faith and devotion. The Vedas are a vidyā[S] that has come down to us through the millennia. If you study them with determination you are bound to succeed. Haven't you seen 50- or 60-year-old people engaged in research in the hope of gaining a Ph.D. or some such degree? If you have the will you will have the way to accomplish anything however difficult. There are examples of individuals who at 40 had been totally in the dark about the Vedas but who later learned to chant them with ardour. As a matter of fact there are such men among the office-bearers of our Veda Rakṣaṇa Nidhi Trust. So what is needed is faith as well as resoluteness.

Leave aside the question of Brahmins who are in jobs and are middle-aged or older. Whether or not they themselves can chant the Vedas or want to learn to chant them, they must see to it that their sons at least receive instruction in the scriptures. Perhaps the children cannot be sent for a full-time course in the Vedas, but the parents could at least ensure that, after they perform the upanayana[S] of their sons at the age of eight years, the boys are taught the Vedas for one hour every evening for a period of eight years. A Vedic tutor may be engaged on a cooperative basis for all children of a locality or village. This should be of help to the children of poor Brahmins.

Above all, efforts must be made to ensure that the existing Vedic schools that are in bad shape are not forced to close down. These institutions must be reinvigorated and more and more students encouraged to join them. To accomplish this task both teachers and taught must be adequately helped with money.

Let me repeat that Brahmins ought not to be afforded more than the minimum cash or creature comforts. But we see today that there are many lucrative jobs to tempt them. So there is the danger of their not being fully involved in their svadharma (own duty) of learning and teaching the Vedas if they are not kept above want. We must provide them with certain facilities so that we are not faced with the unfortunate situation in which such Brahmins become more and more scarce. There are new comforts, new avenues of pleasure, not known in the past. It is unrealistic to expect a few Brahmins alone to deny themselves all these and adhere to their svadharma. If we adopt such an attitude the Vedic dharma will suffer. So when some Brahmins are engaged exclusively in their dharma it is obligatory on our part to help them with money and material. Though they must not be afforded any luxuries, we must provide them with enough comforts so that they are not enticed into other jobs. We have drawn up a number of schemes bearing this mind.

References

[1] See Part Seventeen

[2] Vedic hymns.

Chapter 40

Veda-bhāṣya

The sound of the Vedas must be kept alive. For this purpose, it would be enough if Brahmins memorised the mantras and chanted them every day. The power of the sound, the power of the mantras vocalised, is sufficient to bring good to mankind. I said, you will remember, that chanting the Vedas with faith, even though without knowing their meaning, is "vīryavattaram"[1]. The statement, however, does not fully reflect my view. .

A student will have to spend many years to memorise the Vedas and study their meaning. It is not easy to keep him confined to the Vedic school for such a long time. I must explain here why I said that "it is not necessary to know the meaning of the Vedas and that their sound is all we need". To insist that a student should chant the Vedas only if he knows the meaning of the mantras is expecting too much of him. It might also mean that nobody would come forward even to memorise the hymns. In that case how will their sound be kept alive? That is why I said, half seriously and half sportively, that "the meaning is not necessary, the sound would be sufficient ...".

There must indeed be a large number of people who can chant the Vedas and keep their sound alive. In addition, there must be a system by which some of them at least will be taught their meaning. That is how we have come to be seriously involved in teaching the Veda-bhāṣya (commentary on the Vedas). It is because the Vedas are profound in their import that a number of great men have commented upon them. Their efforts must not go in vain.

We perform a number of rites in our home: marriage, śrāddha[S], upākarma[S], and so on, and during these functions we chant Vedic mantras as instructed by the priest. By the grace of Īśvara we have not reached the unfortunate state of totally discarding such rites. However, there is a declining trend, a weakening of Vedic practices. One important reason for this is that we do not know the meaning of the mantras chanted. Educated people nowadays have no true involvement in rites in which they have to repeat the mantras after the priest without knowing the meaning.

We cannot expect to convince people that the chanting of the mantras (even without knowing their meaning) is beneficial. The hymns for each function are different and also different in significance. If we appreciate this fact, we will realise that there is a scientific basis for them. Besides, they have an emotional appeal which will be evident only when we know their meaning. So to know the meaning of the mantras is to have greater involvement in the functions in which they are chanted. That is the reason why the mouthing of syllables purposelessly has come to be [irreverently] likened to the chanting of "śrāddha mantras". The meaning of the mantras (including those chanted at śrāddhas) must be understood by the priest as well as by the performer of the rites; we must evolve a scheme for this purpose.

First the priest himself must know the meaning of the mantras and the significance of the rituals at which he officiates. Today the majority of priests are ignorant of the meaning of what they chant. If a kartā or a yajamāna (the man on whose behalf a rite is conducted) asks his priest, "What does this mean?", the latter is unable to give an answer. How would you then expect the kartā to have faith in the rites?

I believe that many middle-aged people today are keen to know the meaning of the mantras. I also think that if they tend to lose faith in the rituals it is because they have to repeat parrot-like the hymns chanted by the priest. So we are making efforts to ensure that those who officiate at rituals (the upādhyāyas) acquire proficiency in Veda-bhāṣya to enable them to explain the meaning of the mantras.

According to the Nirukta[2] (one of the six Angas of the Vedas) a Brahmin comes under a curse by chanting the Vedas without knowing their meaning.

A number of great men have written commentaries on the Vedas so as to inspire faith in the sacraments. Śrī Madhvācārya has written a commentary for the first 40 sūktas of the first kāṇḍa of the Ṛgveda. Skandasvāmin has also written a bhāsya on the Ṛgveda. To Bhaṭṭa Bhāskara we owe a commentary on the Kṛṣṇa-Yajurveda, and to Mahīdhara on that of the Śukla-Yajurveda. In recent times, Dayānanda Sarasvatī[3] and Aravinda Ghose[4] as well as his disciple Kapālī Śāstrī have written expository treatises on the Vedas. Though there are so many commentaries, the one by Śrī Sāyaṇācārya is particularly famous: many scholars, including Western indologists, treat it as authoritative.

There are five Vedas if you reckon the Yajurveda to be two with its Śukla and Kṛṣṇa divisions. Sāyaṇa has written commentaries on all the five. Expository treatises on the Vedas had been written before him, but he was the first to write a bhāṣya for all the Vedas.

Though Sāyaṇācārya's commentary had been studied for centuries, a stage came recently when we feared that it would cease to hold any interest for students. Those who learned to chant the Vedas, without knowing their meaning, became priests while those who studied poetry and other subjects did not learn even to chant the mantras. So much so interest in the study of the Veda-bhāṣya declined. It was at this time that the Ṣaṣṭyabdapūrti Trust[5] was formed with a view to maintaining the study of the Veda-bhāṣya.

When the Trust started to conduct examinations, the Veda-bhāṣya meant no more than the printed text of the Vedic commentary kept in bookshops. The publishers were then worried that not many copies would be sold. After the creation of the Trust we gave students not only scholarships but also copies of the Veda-bhāṣya. Our worry now was whether there would be enough copies in stock for fresh students. It is with the grace of Parāśakti, the Supreme Goddess, that we have succeeded in reviving the study of the Veda-bhāṣya. And so long as we have her grace there will be students ready to learn the subject and there will also be enough copies of the text.

On the eve of a wedding, upanayana or sīmanta ceremony[6], we must consult a Vedic scholar who knows the Veda-bhāṣya to explain the meaning of the mantras employed in these rituals. On the day of the function itself the time at our disposal would be short. If we grasp the meaning and significance of the mantras beforehand we will have a more rewarding involvement in the function.

Nowadays, we do not have a month's time in which to prepare for a wedding. The problem facing the bride's people is which group is to play the band, who is to give the dance recital, how the marriage procession is to be conducted... We attach the least importance to that which is the very soul of a marriage sacrament, I mean the Vedic mantras chanted at the time. Those who recite these mantras, the Vedic paṇḍitas, are also treated as the least important to a marriage celebration. There are perhaps a few who have faith in the mantras and for their benefit and enlightenment at least some Brahmins must be instructed in the Veda-bhāṣya.

We print invitation cards for wedding and upanayana ceremonies and distribute them among a large number of friends and relatives — in fact we invite an entire town or village to the function. And we spend thousands. But we do not pay any attention to the ritual itself, to its significance. This is not right.

If we know the meaning of the mantras chanted at a function, we stand to gain more benefits from it. We go through rites because we do not have the courage to give them up. Similarly, we must come to realise that it is wrong to perform a rite without knowing the meaning of the mantras chanted; we must therefore take the help of a paṇḍita in this matter. As mentioned before, going through works with a knowledge of the significance and meaning of the mantras is more beneficial[7]. We must have faith in the Upaniṣadic saying, "Yadeva vidyayā karoti tadeva vīryavattaram bhavati."

At an upanayana, it is the brahmacārin (as the kartā) who chants the mantras; similarly it is the groom alone who intones them at a marriage. What do you expect of all the invitees to do at such functions? Do they come only for the luncheon or dinner, or to keep chatting, to see the dance recital or to listen to the *nāgasvaram*[S] music? Is their part only to make themselves happy in this manner? No. The Vedic mantras deserve our highest respect. When they are being intoned we must honour them by listening to them intently. The mantras create well-being for all. If the invitees and others at a function listen to them and are able to follow their meaning they will earn merit even though they do not have the role of the kartā in it.

Take the case of the aśvamedha (horse sacrifice). Only a king who has subdued all other rulers, that is a mahārāja or a sārvabhauma[S], is qualified to perform it. So only a monarch during a particular period in history, a monarch whose sway extends all over the world[8], is entitled to conduct this sacrifice. The aśvamedha brings more benefits than any other rite. Now the question arises: In any generation only one individual is perhaps capable of earning so much merit (by performing the horse sacrifice). Why are the Vedas so partial that they have made it impossible for the vast majority of people (who cannot perform the sacrifice themselves) to earn such merit? Is it true that only a ruler, who has immense strength and enormous resources at his command, is capable of benefiting from such a sacrifice? If people of good conduct and character are denied the same merit as a powerful emperor can earn, does it not amount to deceiving them? How can the Vedas be so partial to one man?

In truth no partiality can be ascribed to the Vedas. A Vedic rite is admittedly beneficial to the man who performs it. But, at the same time, it does good to all the world. If I light a lamp in the darkness here does it not bring light to all the people present and not to me alone?

It may be that the performer of a Vedic work receives more special benefits than others. But the śāstras show the way by which these others may also reap the same fruits as the kartā[S] — in fact the Vedas themselves mention it. If ordinary people cannot conduct a horse sacrifice they may get to know how it is performed. They may pay attention to the hymns chanted during the sacrifice and also try to follow their meaning. In this way they derive the full benefits of the sacrifice performed by an imperial ruler. This fact is referred to in the section dealing with horse sacrifices in the Vedas.

In the same way, whether it is a marriage or a funeral, the merit will be earned in full if we closely follow the rite and listen to the mantras with due knowledge of their meaning.

Notes & References

1 See Chapter 14 of this part.

2 Part Nine deals with this Aṅga.

3 Svāmī Dayānanda Sarasvatī (1824-83), reformer and founder of the Ārya Samāj. To him only the Vedas and the six darśanas (or systems of philosophy) mattered.

4 Śrī Aurobindo (1872-1950) was a patriot and revolutionary who turned to philosophy and mysticism. The āśrama founded by him in Poṇḍicerri (Pondicherry) is called Auroville.

5 The Trust formed on the 60th birthday of the Paramaguru in 1954.

6 Dealt with in Chapter Sixteen.

7 —— than performing them without knowing their meaning.

8 Perhaps what is meant is no more than a monarch who holds undisputed sway over a large kingdom.

Chapter 41

My Duty

My duty is to impress upon you again and again that it is your responsibility to keep the Vedic tradition alive. Whether or not you listen to me, whether or not I am capable of making you do what I want you to do, so long as there is strength in me, I will keep telling you tirelessly: "This is your work. This is your dharma." It is for the sake of the Vedas that the Ācārya established this Maṭha. So, no matter how I keep deceiving you in other ways, as one bearing his name I should be guilty of a serious offence if I failed to carry out with all sincerity at least the responsibility placed on my shoulders of protecting the Vedic dharma. That is why I keep speaking again and again, not minding the tedium, about the need to sustain this dharma.

It has not been all talk. A number of concrete schemes have been and are being implemented in pursuance of our ideal. I have come here to beg of you for your help. If you think I am not begging for your help, take it that I am issuing you a command to serve the cause of the Vedas. However it be, the work I have undertaken must be done.

Vedam odiya Vediyarkkor mazhai
Nīti mannar neriyinarkkor mazhai
Mādar karpuḍai maṅgaiyarkkor mazhai
Mādam mūnru mazhai enappeyyume

According to this well-known Tamiḷ poem, the earth will become cool and the crops will grow in plenty only if it rains thrice a month. It rains once for the Brahmin who chants the Vedas in the right manner; it rains once for the king who rules justly; and again it rains once for the woman who remains true and constant to her husband.

It is not in my hands to make sure that the rulers rule justly, strictly adhering to dharma. Sannyāsins like me have nothing to do with the government. But I believe that, as the head of a Maṭha with the duty of protecting dharma, I have a responsibility with regard to the other two matters. How does a religious head see to it that a woman adheres to her dharma, remains true to her husband? The trends seen today are contrary to strīdharma (code of conduct for women). I have the title of "guru" and so it is my duty to warn womanhood against things that are likely to undermine their dharma. When child marriages were prevalent there was little opportunity for women to go astray. If a girl is already married before she attains puberty she will develop strong attachment for her husband. If she is not married at this age she is likely to feel mentally disturbed. But our hands are tied because of the Sārda Act[1].

But, if I have not entirely washed my hands of the subject, it is because of the hope that public opinion could be created against the Sārda Act and the government compelled to respect it. After all, so many other laws have been changed in response to public opinion or otherwise. Unfortunately, the attitude of parents and of women in general has become perverse. Instead of trying to conduct the marriage of their daughters in time, parents send them to co-educational colleges and later to work along with men. When I see all this I inwardly shed tears of blood: I am losing my confidence in my ability to arrest this trend.

If Brahmins keep chanting the Vedas, the rulers will rule justly and women will remain steady in their wifely dharma. It is in this hope that all my efforts are turned to maintaining the Vedic dharma.

You must make a gift of your sons for this purpose, also of your money. Well-to-do people must help children of the poor with cash so that they may be encouraged to learn the Vedas. We need money to pay the teachers, to buy books, to administer the Vedic schools. We have drawn up a modest scheme to raise funds. You pay one rupee a month and in return you will receive (by post), apart from the blessings of the Veda Mātā (Mother Veda), the prasāda[S] of Śrī Candramaulīśvara after the pūjā performed to him at the Kāñcī Maṭha. If you send your donation mentioning your nakṣatra [the asterism under which you are born] the prasāda will be sent to you every month on the day on which the asterism falls.

Nowadays, we receive "chain letters" invoking the name of Śrī Venkaṭācalapati (of Tirupati) and with the threat added, "If you don't send copies of this letter to such and such number of people, you shall turn blind or shall be crippled." Out of fear many people make copies of the letter to be sent to various addressees. I too sometimes wonder whether we could do something similar to promote the Vedic dharma!

I do not ask you much — just one rupee a month. Don't you pay the government taxes, whether or not you like to do so? Take this — the one rupee — as a levy imposed by me. It is a tax you pay to run my government, my *sarkār* which is no bigger than a mustard seed[2]. You deny yourself a bit of your pleasure for this, your outing to the beach or your visit to the cinema. You will thus carry out a fraction of your duty and my duty will have been fulfilled.

Notes

1 The Child Marriage Restraint Act came into force in 1929 mainly through the efforts of Harbilās Sārda. The Paramaguru speaks more on the subject when he comes to the marriage samskāra, Part Eighteen. This discourse must have been given before the comprehensive new Hindu Code came into force.

2 In comparison with the vast government establishment.

Chapter 42

Greatness of the Vedas

The glory of the Vedas knows no bounds and it is manifested in the affairs of the world in a manner that defies comparison.

Of all the sacred places on earth Kāśī comes foremost. When we speak in praise of other hallowed centres, we say that they are equal to Kāśī in holiness. From this we know the importance of that city. In the South there is a pilgrim centre which has come to be called "Daksiṇa Kāśī" (Southern Kāśī). There is an Uttara Kāśī (Northern Kāśī) in the Himālaya. Vṛddhācalam in Tamiḷ Nāḍu is also known as "Vṛddha-Kāśī". In Tirunelveli district (of Tamiḷ Nāḍu) there is a town called "Tenkāśī" (this also means "Southern Kāśī"). When we speak in praise of a sacred place it is customary to describe it as being "equal to Kāśī". But Kuṁbhakoṇam is considered greater than Kāśī ("in greatness it weighs one grain more than Kāśī"). Here is a stanza that speaks of the high place accorded to Kuṁbhakoṇam :

Anyakṣetre kṛtam pāpam puṇyakṣetre vinaśyati
Puṇyakṣetre kṛtam pāpam Vārāṇasyām vinaśyati
Vārāṇasyām kṛtam pāpam Kuṁbhakoṇe vinaśyati
Kuṁbhakoṇe kṛtam pāpam Kuṁbhakoṇe vinaśyati

"The sin committed in any (ordinary) place is washed away in a sacred place. That committed in any sacred place is washed away in Vārāṇasī (that is Kāśī). The sin committed in Vārāṇasī is wiped away in Kuṁbhakoṇam. And the sin earned in Kuṁbhakoṇam, well, it is destroyed only in Kuṁbhakoṇam."

The glory of Kāśī is that all other sacred places are likened to it. Even when a place is said to be superior to Kāśī the implication is that Kāśī is uniquely great. It has acquired a distinction by being made an object of comparison. A great man has composed a poem on Kāśī. "Ksetrāṇaṁ uttamānām api yad upamayā kā'pi loke praśastiḥ," so it begins. It means: "By being likened to it even highly esteemed places become famous — that is Kāśī."

Similarly, when you speak highly of sacred tīrthas[S] you liken them to the Gangā or say that they are more holy than that river. We must conclude from the foregoing that Kāśī comes first among the sacred places and that the Gangā is the holiest of the tīrthas.

It is in this way that, when any work is to be extolled, it is said to be "equal to the Vedas". The Rāmāyaṇa is a very famous poetic work. There are many versions of it. Take any language in India: the story of Rāma will be seen to be a theme in drama, poetry, music, etc, in its literature. The greatness of the Rāmāyaṇa is such that it is exalted to the position of a Veda. "Vedaḥ Prācetasādāsītsākṣādrāmāyaṇātmanā." The Veda itself was born as Rāmāyaṇa to Vālmīki, the son of Pracetas.

The Mahābhārata too is celebrated as a Veda: in fact it is called the fifth Veda ("pañcamo Vedaḥ").

Vaiṣṇavas glorify the *Tiruvāymozhi*[T] as a Veda. It is the work of Nammāzhvār[T], who is also called Śaṭhakopan and Māran. They say : "Māran Śaṭhakopan composed the Tamiḷ Veda." The famous Tamiḷ work on ethics, the *Tirukkural*[T], is also called the "Tamiḷ Veda".

During the time of the author of the *Kural*, Tiruvaḷḷuvar, there was the "Kaḍai Saṁgam"[1] in Madurai. In that city there was a seat received as a gift from Sundareśvara[2]. Only the worthy could sit on it. The unworthy would be pushed aside. Was such a thing possible? We cannot believe it; but we do believe that when a coin is inserted in a machine we get a ticket.

[Here the Paramaguru tells the story of Tiruvaḷḷuvar and his Kural *and how the poets of his time came to regard Tamiḷ as great as Sanskrit since it had now come into possession of a work like* Kural *which, they said, was equal to the Vedas. This story occurs in Chapter 5, Part Two, "The Vedas in their Original Form."]*

Śaivas [in Tamiḷ Nāḍu] regard the *Tiruvācakam* as the Tamiḷ Veda. To the Christians in India the Bible is the "Satya-Veda". Thus we see that the Vedas have a special place of honour. The Vedic river is ageless and it traverses the length and breadth of our land as the very life- blood of our culture. This river should not be allowed to dry up. There is no greater responsibility for a Hindu than that of keeping the Vedas a live and vibrant tradition.

The sound of the Vedas must pervade everywhere, must fill all space. The truths enshrined in them must be spread far and wide and the rituals enjoined on us by them must be made to flourish. Sufficient it would be if the Vedic dharma remains vigorous and is maintained at least in our land. If a man's heart is stout he will survive even if all other parts of his body are afflicted. In the same way, if the Vedas flourish in this land all nations will prosper and live in peace and happiness. This is the prayer of the Vedic dharma.

"Lokāḥ samastāḥ sukhino bhavantu."

Notes

[1] The third and last Madurai academy which had 49 men of letters.

[2] Sundareśvara is Śiva, the consort of Mīnākṣī of the famous Madurai temple.

Ṣaḍanga

The discourses dealing with Ṣaḍanga, the six "limbs" of the Vedas, are divided into six parts — Part Six to Part Eleven. On the pages immediately following appears the introductory lecture.

Chapter 43

The Six "Limbs" of the Vedas

Among the basic texts of Hinduism, the six Angas or limbs of the Vedas are next in importance to the Vedas themselves. The Vedapuruṣa has six limbs or parts — mouth, nose, eye, ear, hand, foot. These are called "Ṣaḍanga". The Tamiḷ term "*caḍangu*" denoting any ceremonial is derived from this word[1]. The Tamiḷ *Tevāram*[T] refers to Ṣaḍanga in this line, "*Vedamo(ḍu) āru angam āyinān.*"

In the past all moral and religious edicts were inscribed on the stone walls of temples. In a sense the temple in ancient and medieval times was the "sub-registrar's office" that "registered" all [acts of, contribution to] dharma. In the princely state of Travancore[2] there used to be an official called "*Tirumantira olai*". In the old days all kings in Tamiḷ Nāḍu had such an official. He was like the present-day private secretary. His duty was to write down the ruler's orders or communication and the royal message would be sent to the people concerned.

In those days the rājā had to be informed about all private charities. In fact they required the royal assent and were instituted on royal orders. These were written down by the *olai* with these concluding words, "to be inscribed on stone and copper". The royal command was passed on to the place which received the charity. The authorities there had all this inscribed on the walls of the local temple. Most of the stone inscriptions to be found in temples are of this nature.

Inscriptions were also made on copper-plates. If more than one plate was needed, the plates were pierced and held together with a ring. The local council or assembly had to accept these inscriptions. The copper-plates were kept underground in the temple premises in a place called "kṣema". The life of a land, its destiny, was entrusted in the hands of the Lord and it was natural that the temple was considered the standing monument to its life. It had something of the function of the registrar's office, the epigraphy department, and so on.

Let me now come to the subject of the local assembly.

Every village had a Brahmin sabhā or assembly. Its membership was open to those who knew the Vedas and the Mantra-Brāhmaṇa. People guilty of certain offences and their relatives were debarred from membership. The names of candidates wanting to be members were written on pieces of palm-leaf and a child would be asked to pick one from the lot. The one whose name was inscribed on it was adopted as a member. Details of such elections to the local assembly are mentioned in the Uttaramerūr Inscriptions[3]. There were a number of divisions of the sabhā to look after different subjects like irrigation, taxation, etc. All charities, whether in the form of land or money, had to be made through the sabhā. So too cattle offered to the temple or the lamps to be lighted there. The members of the sabhā had to give their written consent for all this. This is how we have come to know the names of some of them. We also learn the titles conferred on some Brahmins like "Ṣaḍanganiratan" and "Ṣaḍangavi", the latter being an eroded form of "Ṣaḍangavid" — "Ṣad + anga + vid" = one who knows the six Angas or limbs of Vedic learning. From these old inscriptions we come to know that there were many such Brahmins even in small villages, Brahmins proficient in the "Ṣaḍanga". That is why Vedic rites themselves came to be called *"caḍangu"* in Tamiḻ Nāḍu. The Brahmin who gave away his daughter in marriage to Sundaramūrtiśvāmī[T] was called *"Caḍangavi Śivācāriyār"*.

The six Angas are: Śikṣā (phonetics); Vyākaraṇa (grammar); Nirukta (lexicon, etymology); Kalpa (manual of rituals); Chandas (prosody); Jyotiṣa (astronomy-astrology). A Brahmin must be acquainted with all. That he must be well-versed in the Vedas goes without saying. He must first learn to chant them and proficiency in the six Angas will later help him to gain insights into their meaning.

Śikṣā is the nose of the Vedapuruṣa, Vyākaraṇa his mouth, Kalpa his hand, Nirukta his ear, Chandas his foot and Jyotiṣa his eye. The reason for each śāstra being identified with a part of the body will become clear as we deal with the Angas individually.

Notes & References

1 See Appendix 1.

2 Now part of the state of Keraḷa.

3 The Uttaramerūr Inscriptions (10th century A.D.) show that the Colas had an advanced system of local self-government. The Paramaguru has dealt with the subject in detail in one of his discourses and we hope to include it in a subsequent volume.

Part Six

ŚIKṢĀ

Chapter 1

Nose of the Vedapuruṣa

Śikṣā comes first among the six limbs of the Vedas, the nose of the Vedapuruṣa. The function of the nose here is not to be taken only as that of perceiving smells. It has also the function of breathing; in fact it is one of the organs of breathing. Śikṣā serves as the life-breath of the Vedic mantras.

Where is the life of a Vedic mantra centred? Each syllable of a hymn is to be enunciated strictly according to its measure. Clarity of pronunciation is what is intended. Apart from this, each syllable is raised, lowered or pronounced evenly[1] — udātta, anudātta, svarita[S]. If attention is paid to these points, there will be tonal purity. A mantra yields the desired fruit if each syllable is vocalised with clarity and tonal accuracy. The phonetic and tonal exactitude of a mantra is even more important than its meaning. In other words, even though the meaning is not understood, if the tonal form takes shape correctly, the mantra will bring the intended benefit. So the life-breath of the Vedas, which are a collection of mantras, is their sound [the "sound form"].

There is a mantra to cure scorpion sting. Its meaning is not to be revealed. Its potency is in its sound. Certain sounds have certain powers associated with them. It is sometimes asked: Why should the śrāddha[S] mantras be in Sanskrit? May they not be in English or Tamiḷ? Those who raise these questions do not realise that it is the sound that matters here, not the language as such. If the teeth of a sorcerer were knocked off, his witchcraft [magic] would have no effect. Why? Because the man would not be able to recite his spell properly.

Enunciation of the mantras is most important to the Vedas. What do we do about it? Śikṣā is the science that deals with the character of Vedic syllables — it determines their true nature. The science of the sounds of human speech is called phonetics and it is more important to the Vedic language than to any other tongue. The reason is that even if there is a slight change in how you vocalise a syllable the efficacy of the mantra will be affected. [The result sometimes will be contrary to what is intended.]

It is because of the importance of Vedic phonetics that Śikṣā has been placed first among the six Angas. It is dealt with in the *Taittirīya Upaniṣad.* Its "Śīkṣāvallī" begins like this: "Let us now explain the Śīkṣā śāstra"[2]. The name of the śāstra occurs here as well as in many other Vedic texts with a long "i" ("Śīkṣā"). Śankara observes in his commentary : "Dairghyam Chāndasam": it means that the usually short "i" occurs as long [in the Vedas]. (Such examples are to be found in Tamil poetry also.) I told you that the Vedic language is not called Sanskrit but "Chandas"[3]. "Chāndasam", from "Chandas", denotes here a Vedic usage.

Notes & References

[1] "Pronounced evenly" is svarita, the falling tone. See Sanskrit Glossary.

[2] "Śikṣāṁ vyākhāsyāmaḥ. Varṇaḥ, svaraḥ, mātrā, balam, sāma, santānah, ityuktaḥ Śīkṣādhyāyaḥ."

[3] The discourse in which the Paramaguru speaks of "Chandas" being the language of the Vedas appears as part of Appendix 1 in this book.

Chapter 2

Yoga and Speech

When you play the harmonium, the *nāgasvaram*[S] or the flute, the sound is produced by the air discharged in various measures through different outlets. Our throat has a similar system to produce sound. It is not that the throat alone is involved in this process. How do we speak and sing? Speaking or singing is an exercise that has its source below the navel in the "mūlādhāra" or "root-base"[1] of the spinal column. From this point the breath is brought up in various measures as we speak or sing. The human instrument made by the Lord is far superior to the harmonium, the *nāgasvaram* or the flute. These latter can produce only mere sounds and cannot articulate the syllables *a, ka, ca,* etc. Man alone possesses this faculty. Animals can produce one or two types of sound but do not have the ability to articulate.

We may gauge the importance of articulate speech from the fact that the Lord has bestowed this faculty only on man. Such a wonderful gift of Īśvara must not be squandered or abused in idle gossip or useless talk. We must use it to grasp the divine powers and endeavour to create the well-being of mankind thereby. And we must also try to raise our own Self with it. All these lofty purposes can be served with the Vedic mantras that the sages have gathered from space for our benefit.

If you recognise this fact you will realise why there should be a śāstra called Śikṣā specially for the purpose of guiding us in the enunciation of Vedic mantras. This science as developed by our forefathers arouses the wonder of linguistic scientists even today. It teaches us how the syllables are to be produced accurately and describes in the minutest detail how the passage of the breath coming from the pit of the stomach is to be controlled. Further, it tells us on which parts of the body the breath must impinge and how it must be discharged from the mouth.

In a sense, air going into our body in different ways is a manifestation of the yogic science : it is because of the vibrations caused in our nāḍis[S] as a result of the passage of our breath that our emotions and powers take shape. There is a saying, "What is in the macrocosm is present in the microcosm." As mentioned before, the vibrations within us produce vibrations outside also and these are the cause of worldly activities. That is why those who have mastered the mantras have the same powers as those who have achieved yogic perfection by controlling their breath. The one is mantrayoga, the other is Rājayoga.

Śikṣā explains how each syllable of a mantra is to be produced by the human voice, what its tone should be like. It lays down the duration or mātra for each syllable. In determining the mātra the short and long syllables (the "hṛsva" and "dīrgha") are taken into account. Śikṣā also describes how words that are joined together (according to the rules of "sandhi"[2]) are to be enunciated without splitting them. All such matters as help in the correct chanting of the mantras are included in this śāstra.

Śikṣā explains in very fine detail how the sounds of the various syllables are to be produced. A sound like "ka"[3] is to be created from between the neck and the throat; another like "ña" is nasal. To produce the sound of "ta"[4] the tongue should come into contact with particular teeth -- this is mentioned in this śāstra; so too how the tongue should touch the upper palate for a sound like "na". Phonemes like "ma" arise from completely closing the lips together and those like "va" (labio-dental) are produced using both the lips and the teeth. It is all scientific and at the same time part of mantrayoga and śabdayoga.

(See Chapter 13 on Mantrayoga in Part Five)

Notes & References

1 One of the six cakras in the body according to yoga. "Cakra" is literally wheel, but means here centre or lotus. Mūlādhāra is the seat of the Kuṇḍalinī,the "coiled one", thought to be a sleeping serpent of the yogic body and situated between the anus and the genitals. Some understand the term cakra as plexus. The other cakras in the "yogic body" are svādhiṣṭhāna, maṇipūra, anāhata, viśuddha, and ājña. The sahasrāra-padma (the one-thousand-petalled lotus) is situated close to the Brahmarandhra (see Sanskrit Glossary).

2 For the meaning of "sandhi" see notes appended to Chapter 10, Part Five.

3 Guttural — some classify it as velar.

4 Dental.

Chapter 3

Root Language—Sanskrit

In speaking about the Vedas I stated that the sound of a word was more important than its meaning. That reminds me. In the Vedic language called "Chandas" and in Sanskrit which is based on it, there are words the very sound of which denotes their meaning. Take the word "danta". You know that it means a tooth. We have to use our teeth to produce the sound of the word "danta" -- the tongue has to make an impact on the teeth. You will note this phenomenon when you ask a toothless person to say "danta". He will not be able to vocalise the word clearly.

From such small observations comparative philology can discover an important fact: which word has come first in what language. Sanskrit, Greek, Latin, German, French, etc, have been jointly referred to as belonging to the Indo-European group and derived from one mother language. Western philologists do not accept Sanskrit as the original language, the mother of all Indo-European tongues. But words like "danta" point to the fact that Sanskrit *is* the root language.

Consider the English word "dental". There is so much similarity between "dant" and "dent". In languages like French and Latin also the word for tooth is akin to "dent", though it is "ḍa-kāra" and not the "da-kāra" of Sanskrit. "Why should'nt you derive the Sanskrit word 'danta' from 'dental'?" it might be asked. But you must consider the fact that to say "danta" you have to make use of your teeth. Not so to say "dental". You get the sound "dental" as a result of the tip of your tongue touching your upper palate. It is only in Sanskrit that the sound of the word itself signifies its meaning. So that must be the root form of the word. Hence languages like English, French, Latin, etc, must have been derived from Sanskrit.

By interchanging the letters of some words you get other words which are related in meaning to the original. What is the nature of the animal called lion, the quality you associate with it most? It is violence. "Himsā" is violence and the word turns into "simha" to denote the lion. Kaśyapa was the first among the sages. Celestials, non-celestials, human beings, all may be traced back to him. He knew the truth or, rather, saw the Truth. Jñāna is also called "dṛśya". Kaśyapa is thus a seer, "Paśyaka": "Paśyaka became "Kaśyapa".

In Tamiḷ one who sees, the seer, is *"pārppān"*. It is in this sense, as men who know the Truth or Reality, that Brahmins in the Tamiḷ land came to be called *"Pārppāns"*. But now the word is used in a pejorative sense.

Chapter 4

Pronunciation

Śikṣā deals with "uccāraṇa", "svara", "mātra", "bala", "sāma" and "santāna"[1]. The sound of each mantra is determined with the utmost accuracy. How different sounds have their source in different parts of the body and how they are vocalised, all such details which are of scientific and practical importance are dealt with in this Anga. If it says, "Join your lips in this way and such and such a sound will be produced as you speak", you may verify it for yourself in practice and find it to be true.

Here I am reminded of an interesting fact. The lips come into use in "pa", "ma" "va". They are not used in "ka", "ṅga", "ca", "ña", "ṭa", "ṇa", "ta" and "na". A poet has composed a Rāmāyaṇa which can be read without using your lips. It is called *"Niroṣṭhya-Rāmāyaṇa[2]."* "Oṣṭha" means "lip". "Auṣṭraka", the word for camel, is derived from it and the Tamiḷ word *"oṭṭagai"* has the same origin. "Nir-oṣṭhya" means without lips. *Niroṣṭhya-Rāmāyaṇa* was perhaps composed by its author to demonstrate his linguistic ingenuity. But another reason occurs to me. The poet must have been very much concerned about ritual purity and felt that the story of Śrī Rāmacandra must be read without bringing the lips together.

There is a beautiful verse in *Pāninīya Śikṣā* (its author, as the name itself suggests, is Pāṇini) which tells us how careful we must be in pronouncing Vedic syllables:

Vyāghrī yathā haret putrān
Daṁṣṭrābhyām na ca pīḍayet
Bhītāpatanabhedābhyām
Tadvad varṇān prayojayet

"The Vedic syllables must be pronounced with clarity. The character of their sound should not be distorted a bit. But no force must be used in vocalising the syllables. There should be no damage done — no erosion of the sound — and no violence should be suggested in the pronunciation. How does a tigress carry its cubs? Tigresses and cats carry their young ones by holding them firmly with their teeth, yet in doing so they do not cause any hurt to the little ones. The Vedic hymns must be chanted in the same way, the syllables enunciated gently and yet distinctly. Pāṇini, the author of the above stanza, has written the most important work on grammar, a subject which comes next (after Śikṣā) among the Vedāngas. Apart from him many others have written on Śikṣā. There are thirty works in this category[3]. Pāṇini's and Yājñavalkya's are particularly important.

Each Veda has attached to it a "Prātiśākhya"[S] which examines Vedic sounds. There are also ancient commentaries on them and these too are included in Śikṣā.

Notes

[1] These terms may be roughly translated as pronunciation or enuniciation, tone or accent, duration in pronouncing vowels, force or stress, continunity or combination.

[2] The author of this work is Mallikārjunabhaṭṭa who belonged to the court of the Kākatīya king Pratāparudradeva (13th - 14th centuries).

[3] Abhicalī, Candrakomi, Yājñavalkya, Vasiṣṭha, Kātyāyana, Parāśara, Māṇḍavya, Nārada and Lomaśa are some authors of Śikṣā śāstra whose works are extant. — Ra.Ga

Chapter 5

Scripts

The evolution of the script of any language must be based on symbols or signs denoting various "units" of its speech (phonemes). Most of the European languages including English are written in the Roman script. There is a script called Brāhmī and the Aśokan edicts are in it. In fact it is from Brāhmī that the scripts of most Indian languages have evolved and these include not only the Devanāgarī script in which Sanskrit is written but also the Tamiḷ and Grantha[S] scripts.

The Brāhmī lipi or script has two branches. Of the two, the Pallava Grantha script was prevalent in the South and it is from it that scripts of most of the Draviḍian languages evolved[1].

The Telugu script has a unique feature. While in all other scripts the letters are written in a clockwise fashion, in Telugu there are letters written in an anticlockwise fashion, that is the loops are shaped leftward. Parāśakti, the Supreme Goddess, is to the left of Īśvara and there is leftist worship associated with her ("vāma- mārga"). For this reason it is believed that some letters of the Śrīcakra[2] should be written in Telugu. The Āndhra language itself is said to have a Śaiva character. In most other parts of India, the child is first taught to write the "Aṣṭākṣarī"[S], [prayer to Viṣṇu] but in Āndhra Pradeś it is the "Siva-Pañcākṣara"[S]. There are places sacred to Śiva in three corners of this state: Kāḷahasti in the south, Śrīśailam in the west and Koṭiliṅgakṣetram in the north. It is because this land is within the area marked by these liṅgas that it is called "Teluṅgu-deśa" (from "Triliṅga"). Appayya Dīkṣita[S] has composed a stanza in which he expresses his regret that he was not born an Āndhra:

Āndhratvam Āndhrabhāṣacāpyāndhradeśa svajanmabhūḥ
Tatrāpi Yajūṣī Śākhā na'lpasya tapasaḥ phalam

Appayya Dīkṣita was a Sāmavedin by birth. "Of the Vedas I am the Śāmaveda," so says Bhagavān in the Gītā. But Dīkṣita, a great devotee of Śiva, regrets that he was not born in Āndhra, and that too as a Yajurvedin, and states that the reason for this was his failure to perform austerities in sufficient measure. The Yajurveda, it will be remembered, contains the Śiva-Pañcākṣara mantra.

Let me revert to the question of script. As I said before, almost all the scripts in India today have evolved from Brāhmī. But it is hard to make out elements of the original Brāhmī in them. So anything that we find difficult to understand or make out is referred to as "Brāhmī-lipi". Later this came into usage as "Brahma-lipi", the Creator's "writing" on our forehead [our destiny]. Now anything we find difficult to understand or cannot make out is called "Brahma-lipi". Another old script is "Kharoṣṭhī". "Khara-oṣṭham" means the lips of a donkey — these resemble bellows. The loops protrude in this script. Persian is written in Kharoṣṭhī.

Brāhmī was our common script just as Roman is today for most European languages. Now Devanāgarī [with variations] is the common script for most Northern languages. We do not realise that each letter or syllable represents a particular sound or phoneme. There are two different letters in Tamiḷ to represent "na". Why should there be two to represent the same sound, we wonder, thinking it to be unique to that language. But there is a subtle difference between the two "na"s.

In Telugu there is only one "na". So is the case with other languages. There are two types of "r" common to Tamiḷ and Telugu. But the two types differ in the two languages. In Tamiḷ, two 'r's together of one of these two types form a consonant with a special sound value (*kuṟṟam, maṟṟum, soṟṟunai,* etc).[3] In Telugu it is different. The Tamiḷ word for horse is *"kudirai"*; in Telugu it is *"kurram"* — the two r's are pronounced fully. In Tamiḷ there is no such phoneme. There are some other unique phonemes in Telugu. In some words "ja" is pronounced as "za". Āndhras pronounce *"śāla"* as *"tsāla"*. The Devanāgarī and Grantha alphabets have 50 letters. In Telugu there are 52 (including the additional letters in the "ja" and "ca" groups. The Telugu-speaking people sometimes interchange "tha" and "dha". I am told you find this in some of the compositions of Tyāgarāja himself[4].

When we transliterate passages from one language into another we must keep these peculiarities in mind. In English also for the same labial there are two letters, "v" and "w". A professor told me that there is a difference between the two. The English "v" should be pronounced with the lower lip folded and the upper row of teeth coming into contact with it. When "w" is pronounced the lips do not come into contact with the teeth but are turned round. Words like "Sarasvatī" and "Īśvara" must be written with a "v" (not as "Saraswatī" and "Īśwara").

Sanskrit, more than any other language, exemplifies the principle of phonetic spelling. In English the spelling is erratic and confusing. I remember reading a newspaper heading recently: "Legislature wound up." Absent-mindedly I read the word "wound" in the sense of a hurt or injury. Of course it was actually used as the past participle of "wind". Now the word "wind" can also mean a breeze but then it is pronounced differently. So it is all confusing. Is the word "put" pronounced in the same way as "cut" or "but"? In "walk" and "chalk", the "l" is silent.

Seemingly, such is not the case with Tamiḷ which contains many words from other languages like Sanskrit. In other Indian languages for each series of consonants there are four different letters in place of the one in Tamiḷ. For instance, the same "ka" is used for *"kaṇ"* (Tamiḷ for eye) and the Sanskrit "mukha" (in Tamiḷ it is written as *"mukam"*), while "Gangā" is written as "*Kangā*", and "ghaṭam" (pot in Sanskrit) is written as "*kaṭam*". In Tamiḷ the word for mace (the weapon wielded by Bhīma) and for story are written alike as "*katai*", instead of as "*gadai*" and *"kathai"*.

In Tamiḷ, unlike in other Indian languages, "ka" serves the purpose of "kha", "ga" and "gha"[5]; "ta" serves for "da" also; and "ṭa" for "ḍa" also. Words that have almost opposite meanings are spelt identically: "*Doṣam*" and "*toṣam*" meaning blemish and happiness respectively are written identically. Letters from the Grantha script are added in Tamiḷ for proper pronunciation — "sa", "ha", "ja", "ṣa", "kṣa", etc. In the past these letters were not used in Tamiḷ poetry following the tradition of poetic usage. But now some authors do not use these Grantha characters even in prose. Since they find it difficult to get rid of Sanskritic words from the Tamiḷ vocabulary, the next best thing they can do perhaps is to rid the language of the letters representing the phonemes of Sanskrit which have no equivalents in the Tamiḷ alphabet. This causes confusion. If an author writes "*cātakam*" in the strict Tamiḷ manner it can be read also as "sād(h)akam" or "jātakam". From the very beginning Tamiḷ has not had all the consonants. But why should characters added to meet this deficiency be dropped? Does it mean "victory" for Tamiḷ and "defeat" for Sanskrit? Why should there be a fight over languages? There is no need to nurse any bitterness against languages that we think are not our own.

The Tamiḷ script is adequate to write words that are strictly Tamiḷ. The difficulty is when it comes to its adopting words from other languages with sounds representing "kha", "ga", "gha", etc. In Sanskrit, Telugu, Kannaḍa and so on, there are letters for the entire "ka-varga", "ca-varga", "ta-varga", "ṭa-varga", and "pa-varga". In English, as we have already seen, we cannot pronounce the words according to their spelling. It is not so in Tamiḷ. But in that language too the script is not entirely self-sufficient. You may not agree. But I will tell you what I learned from my own experience.

A Northerner learned the Tamiḷ alphabet sufficiently well, that is he learned to read the individual letters of the alphabet. But he had no one to help him in pronouncing the words properly. He wanted to learn Tamiḷ because he was keen to read the *Tevāram*[T] and the *Tiruvācakam*[T] in the original. After learning the alphabet he tried to read the *Tevāram* from a book. Though he had no knowledge of the language he thought he could earn merit by reading the hymns of the great saints even without understanding their meaning. Then, one day, he came to me and announced: "I am going to recite the *Tevāram*." I felt happy and asked him to go ahead.

His recitation caused me amusement. The passage he read was a famous one — what Appar[T] had sung at Tiruvaiyāru of his experience of seeing everything in the form of Umāmaheśvara [that is the entire cosmos revealed as Śiva] and the song was "*Mādar piraikkaṇṇiyānai...*" He got the very first word wrong. Instead of "*mādar*" he said "*mātar*". It sounded strange to me. Then he said "*malaiyān makaḷotu*" for "*malaiyān mahaloḍu*" laying stress on the "k" and the "ṭ". For "*pādi*" he said "*pāṭi*". I was on the verge of laughter. His recitation went on in this fashion. He said "*pukuvar*" instead of "*puhuvar*".

I heard him silently because I thought a Northerner learning a Tamiḷ song deserved to be encouraged. But soon I found that I could no longer suffer his erratic reading. So I told him in a friendly manner that his pronunciation was faulty. To this he said: "What can I do? It is all in the book." What he said was right and it showed that in Tamiḷ too the words are not always written according to how they are pronounced. Letters that come in the middle of a word are not pronounced as they are written. We write "*makalotu*" but say "*mahaloḍu*"; we write "*atarkāka*" but say "*adarkāha*". "Ka" becomes "ha" in the middle and end of a word. "Ta" in the beginning of a word remains "ta" but in the middle becomes "da". For instance, "*tantai*" (father) is pronounced as "*tandai*" and "*Kaṭavūḷ*" (God) and "*iṭam*" (place) pronounced as "*Kaḍavūl* and "*iḍam*". Such matters are dealt with in detail in Tamiḷ grammar books.

Like Sanskrit, Tamiḷ too has excellent works on grammar -- for example, the *Tolkāppiyam* and *Nannūl*. They deal with the morphology of words and their vocalisation. For instance there are such rules: After such and such a syllable "sa" becomes "ca", "ka" becomes "ha".

Generally speaking, if "ka" is the initial letter of a word in Tamiḷ it retains its sound of "ka". In the same way if the initial letter of a word is "ta" it retains its true sound, but in the middle or end of a word it sounds "da". "Pa" is "pa" if it is the initial letter of a word but sounds "ba" in the middle of a word. (In Tamiḷ we do not see "pa" occurring as an independent letter in the middle or end of a word. "*Anpu*" (love), "*ampu*" (arrow), "*inpam*"[6] (pleasure) — "pa" in these words is joined with other letters. Words like "japa" (muttering the names of the Lord or any mantra); "śāpam" (curse), "*kapam*" ("kapham", phlegm), "*śupam*"[7] ("śubham", auspicious) have letters belonging to the "pa-varga" independently in the middle of the words but they are from the Sanskrit.

There is something interesting about "ca". While in Tamiḷ "*ka*", "*ta*", "*pa*", etc, retain their true sound when they are the initial letters of words, "*ca*" as the initial letter is voiced as "*śa*". "*Caṭṭi*" (cooking vessel) and "*civappu*" (red) are pronounced as "*śaṭṭi*" and "*śivappu*". But when the letters come together as "*cca*", they are not pronounced as "*śśa*"— for example, "*accam*" (fear), "*paccai*" (green). "*Col*" (to speak) is pronounced as "*śol*", but "*peyarccol*" and "*vinaiccol*" are not pronounced "*peyerśśol*" and "*vinaiśśol*". But in Malayāḷam which is derived from Tamiḷ "ca" in the beginning of a word is pronounced as "ca": "*civappu*" is "*civappu*". But at other times when the "*cca*" comes in the middle of a word the word is pronounced as "*śśa*", not "*cca*", e.g, place names like "Kāviśśeri", "Nelliśśeri", while Tamils pronounce the same as "Kavicceri" and "Nellicceri". In words like "*accan*" (father) and "*Ezhuttaccan*", however, there is no change.

The genius of the Tamiḷ language is to be known from its works on grammar — how a word is changed and where. However, the pronunciation is not in strict consonance with the spelling.

It is only in Sanskrit that the pronunciation is fully phonetic but for two exceptions. One is when there is a visarga[S] before "pa". Visarga more or less has the same sound as "ha" — not a full "ha", though. In Tamiḷ Nāḍu it is pronounced fully as "ha" and Northerners who slur over it are made fun of. But their pronunciation is correct according to the rules of Śikṣā. With the visarga occurring before it, "pa" becomes "fa".

The second exception : "Subrahmaṇya", "Brahma", "vahni" (fire) are pronounced as "Subramhanya", "Bramha" and "vanhi". But all words with "ha" coming as a conjunct consonant are not like this as, for example, "jahvara" (deep, inaccessible), "jihva" (tongue), "guhya" (secret), and "Prahlada" [son of the demon Hiraṇyakaśipu and a great devotee of Viṣṇu].

Notes & References

[1] Probably the scripts of some of the languages of countries like Burma, Cambodia, Thailand and so on are based on Brāhmī. Indeed they resemble the scripts of the Dravidian languages.

[2] Śrīcakra is a yantra or diagram for the worship of the Supreme Goddess.

3 The words in brackets are pronounced in the same way as the term familiar to people in many parts of India, *araṅgetram,* meaning in Tamiḷ debut or exhibition of a new art. Strictly, the word is spelt "*arangeṟṟam*". The words in brackets are pronounced: "*kutram*" (fault, defect, crime); "*matrum*" (and so on). The "t" in these words has more or less the same sound as the t's in "matter".

4 For instance the composition in the rāga Nādanāmakriya, "Karuṇājaladhe". Here "jaladhe" is voiced as "jalathe". -- Ra. Ga. (Tyāgarāja, 1769-1847, is the most celebrated composer of Carṇātic music.)

5 As indicated by the Paramaguru, in most Indian languages including even Dravīḍian tongues other than Tamiḷ, each of the five "vargas" (ka-varga, ca-varga, ṭa-varga, ta-varga, pa-varga) have all the letters. In Tamiḷ the consonants have been reduced to 18 in number, omitting the voiced and aspirated plosives and the sibilants. But certain retroflex and alveolar letters are added.

6 Pronounced "*anbu*", "*ambu*", "*inbam*".

7 Pronounced "*śubam*" in Tamiḷ.

Chapter 6
A Language that has all Phonemes

From the foregoing it is clear that Sanskrit has the "f" sound. In fact there is no sound vocalised by humans that is not present in that language. "Zha"[1] is not, as is usually imagined, unique to Tamiḷ. It exists in the Vedic language which is the source of Sanskrit. The "ḍa" in the Yajurveda has to be pronounced as "zha" in the corresponding passages in the Sāmaveda. In the Ṛgveda also in some places the "ḍa" has to be similarly pronounced. The very first word in the first sūkta of the Ṛgveda, "Agnimiḷe", has to be pronounced almost as "Agnimīzhe" — not a full "zhe" for "ḷe", but almost.

There is a sound very close to "zha" in French. But neither in that language nor in Sanskrit is there a separate letter to represent that sound. "Ja" and "ga" serve the purpose of "zha" in French. In Sanskrit "ḷa" serves the same purpose.

(I am told there is "zha" in Chinese.)

The three-dot symbol in Tamiḷ. (∴), called "*āytam*"[2], is present in Sanskrit also. There is a Pāṇini sūtra, "ḥ kap pauc". According to it, if a visarga comes before a word beginning with "ka" (Rāmaḥ + Karuṇākaraḥ), it will not have the sound of "ḥ", as mentioned before, but of "ḥ" in the "*āytam*". Here it is the visarga that is the *āytam* that becomes the "f" before "pa-kāra".

Rāmaḥ + Karuṇākaraḥ = Rama ∴ Karuṇākaraḥ. Rāmaḥ + paṇḍitaḥ = *Rāma f paṇḍitaḥ*. This "f" sound is called "upatmānīya"[3]. "Tma" suggests the sound created by blowing the pipe to build the kitchen fire. When you blow thus you get the "f" sound. The initial letter of the English word "flute" is "f", is it not?

One more point about "fa". We generally pronounce "fa" as "pa". But it would be wrong to think that we [in the South] pronounce coffee as "*kāpī*" in the same way. In Sanskrit "kapiśa" means dark brown — that is the colour of coffee powder. Our kapiśa is the white man's coffee.

What Tamiḷs call *kuṟṟiyalukaram* is present in Sanskrit also — ṛ and ḻ. People write both "Rigveda" and "Rugveda" — the first letter of the word is neither "Ri" nor "Ru". It represents in fact the *kuṟṟiyalukara* sound. It is between "u" and "i". We write "Krishṇa" in Roman. In the North some people write the same as "Krushṇa". It is amusing to listen to Āndhras pronouncing "hṛdayam" as "*hrudayam*". Both the "ra-kāra" and "la-kāra" of Sanskrit have vocalic forms. But in "la-kāra" the vocalic form comes only in conjunction with another consonant. In the ra-kāra vocalic form we have examples like "Ṛg", "ṛsi"; in the "la-kara" vocalic form we have "kḻpta".

In Sanskrit the vocalic "*ṛ*" and "*ḻ*" are not included among the consonants but regarded as vowels : a, ā, i, ī, u, ū, ṛ, ḻ, e, ai, o, au, aṁ, aḥ.

There is no short "e" or "o" in Sanskrit. I felt this to be a minus point for that language. Parāśakti, the Supreme Goddess, is the personification of all sounds. So should there not be all sounds in a language (like Sanskrit)? Why should it lack these two (short "e" and short "o")? On going through Patañjali's commentary on the sūtras of Pāṇini, I discovered that Sanskrit too had these short vowels and it was a comforting discovery. Patañjali says that, in chanting the *Sātyamugrī* and *Rāṇāyanīyā Śākhās* of the Sāmaveda the short "e" and "o" are used[4].

Thus Sanskrit embraces all sounds. It has also a script in which the sound of every letter is determined with the utmost accuracy.

Notes & References

1 A retroflex affricate sound.

2 Winslow's *A Comprehensive Tamil and English Dictionary* defines *"āytam"* thus: "The letter so called from the indistinctness of its sound, or the peculiarity or minuteness of its form. It is chiefly a consonant, but sometimes occurs as a vowel; yet it cannot be confounded with another letter."

3 It is defined as the aspirate visarga before p and ph.

4 *Chandogānām Sātyamugrī*
Rāṇāyanīyā ardham-ekāram
Ardham okāram ca adhīyate. — Rā.Ga.

Chapter 7

Languages and Scripts : Indian and Foreign

A special feature of our languages is that each syllable of every word is pronounced distinctly. Take the English word "world". The sound of the first syllable has no clear form; it is neither "we" nor "wo". Then the letter "r" is slurred over. There are many such indistinct words in foreign tongues. They come under the category of "avyakta-śabda" (indistinct sounds). In our country all languages are "spaṣṭa" (clear and distinct).

In the languages of many other countries there is no accord between spelling and pronunciation. For the sound of "ka" there are three letters in English "k", "c" and "q". Such is not the case with our languages. The "f" sound in English is represented in three different ways as illustrated in the words "fairy", "philosophy", "rough". When you say "c" as a letter of the English alphabet, it sounds like a "sa-kāra" letter, but many words with the initial letter "c" have the "ka-kāra" sound. The "sa-kāra" sound occurs only in a few words like "cell", "celluloid", "cinema". The spelling is totally unrelated to the pronunciation as in "station" and "nation".

The Roman alphabet has only 26 letters and is easy to learn. The alphabets of our languages have more letters and are comparatively difficult to learn. But, once you have learned them, our languages are easier to read and write than their European counterparts. Take English, for instance. Even a person who has passed his M.A. has often to consult the dictionary for spelling and pronunciation.

But among Indian languages themselves Sanskrit is the best in the matter of spelling and pronunciation. By saying this I do not mean that the languages of other countries are inferior to ours. At the same time, so far as our own country is concerned, I do not wish to downgrade other tongues in comparison with Sanskrit. I merely mentioned some facts to underline the point that Sanskrit fully represents the Supreme Being manifested as the Śabda-brahman.

If we develop the attitude that all languages are our common heritage, we will not run down other people's tongues. We often forget the fact that the purpose of language, any language, is communication, exchange of ideas. It is our failure to recognise this basic fact that is the cause of fanatical attachment to our mother tongue and hatred of other languages. We are often asked to be broad-minded and to develop an international outlook, but in the matter of language we remain narrow-minded. I feel sad when I think of it.

Chapter 8
Akṣamālā

"Rudrākṣa"[S] means the eye of Rudra or Śiva. "Rudrākṣa-mālā" is a "garland" (or rosary) made up of such "eyes". "Akṣa" means eye. In Tamiḻ the rudrākṣa is called "*tirukkaṇmaṇi*" [the sacred pupil of the eye].

What is the meaning of "akṣamālā" or "sphaṭika-akṣamālā"? Here the word "akṣa" is not taken to mean the eye but the letters of the alphabet from "a" to "kṣa". In the Sanskrit alphabet "a" comes first and "kṣa" comes last. To learn the "A" to "Z" of a subject means to have a thorough grasp of it. To convey the same idea in Sanskrit we say "*a*-kārādi *kṣa*-kārāntam". There are 50 letters from "a" to "kṣa". So an akṣamālā consists of 50 beads. There is of course a 51st bead which is bigger than the rest and it is called "Meru". The sun, the legend goes, does not go beyond the Meru mountain during his daily journey. When we make one round thus, muttering the name of the Lord or a mantra, first clockwise up to the Meru and then anticlockwise up to the Meru again, we will have told the beads a hundred times.

Chapter 9

Importance of Enunciation, Intonation

You must not go wrong either in the enunciation or intonation of a mantra. If you do, not only will you not gain the expected benefits from it, the result might well be contrary to what is intended. So the mantras must be chanted with the utmost care. There is a story told in the *Taittirīya Saṁhitā* (2.4.12) to underline this.

Tvastā[1] wanted to take revenge on Indra for some reason and conducted a sacrifice to beget a son who would slay Indra. When he chanted his mantra, "Indraśatrur varddhasva...", he went wrong in the intonation. He should have voiced "Indra" without raising or lowering the syllables in it and he should have raised the syllables "tru" and "rddha" (that is the two syllables are udātta). Had he done so the mantra would have meant, "May Tvastā's son grow to be the slayer of Indra". He raised the "dra" in Indra, intoned "śatru" as a falling svara and lowered the "rddha" in "varddhasva". So the mantra meant now: "May Indra grow to be the killer of this son (of mine)". The words of the mantra were not changed but, because of the erratic intonation, the result produced was the opposite of what was desired. The father himself thus became the cause of his son's death at the hands of Indra.

The gist of this story is contained in this verse which cautions us against erroneous intonation:

Mantrohīnaḥ svarato varṇato vā
Mithyā prayukto na tamarthamāha
Sa vagvajro yajamānam hinasti
Yathendraśatruḥ svarato'parādhāt

What was the weapon with which Tvastā's son[3] was killed? Not Indra's thunderbolt but the father's wrongly chanted mantra.

Notes

1 Tvastā (Tvastṛ) is the divine carpenter.

2 Indra is the lord of the celestials

3 The son was Vṛtra

Chapter 10

Versions with Slight Differences

I have spoken about the importance of maintaining the purity of Vedic syllables. All over India, from the Himālaya to Rāmeśvaram and all through the ages, the Vedas have been taught entirely in the oral tradition, without the aid of any printed books and without one part of the country being in touch with another. And yet 99 per cent of the texts followed everywhere is the same to the letter.

So it means that there is a difference of one per cent, is there not? Yes, there is, among the recensions in the different regions. Is it proper to have such slight differences? After claiming that the consequences would be unfortunate even if one syllable of a mantra goes wrong, how are we to accept that the same mantra in the different recensions or in the different regions differ by one per cent? If the original Vedas in their true form are one, will not the departure by even one per cent mean undesirable consequences?

There is an answer to this question. You will come to harm if the medicine you take is different from what your physician has ordered. Similarly, if you chant a mantra with its syllables changed, you will suffer an adverse consequence. The rule that the medicine prescribed must not be changed applies to the patient, not to the doctor. The patient cannot, on his own, change the medicine that his doctor has prescribed. But the doctor can, cannot he? There is more than one medicine available to treat a particular ailment. So there is nothing wrong if the doctor substitutes one medicine for another. While treating two patients suffering from the same illness the doctor may, while prescribing essentially the same medicine for both, make small changes in the ingredients according to their different natures.

It is in the same manner that the sages have introduced slight changes in the different Vedic recensions, but these are not such as to produce any adverse effect: indeed, even with the changes, the mantras yield the expected benefits. As a matter of fact, the sages have introduced the changes for the benefit of people who are entitled to learn the particular recensions. The rules with regard to these are clearly stated in the Prātiśākhyas[S].

The syllables of the mantras in the different recensions do not vary to any considerable degree. Nor are they unrelated to one another. On the whole they sound similar. Even when the letters vary there is a kinship to be seen between them.

Chapter 11

Vedic Vocalisation and the Regional Languages

If we relate certain unique characteristics of the different languages of India to how Vedic chanting differs syllabically from region to region, we will discover the important fact that the genius of each of these tongues and the differences between them are based on how the Vedas are chanted in these regions. I make here certain observations based on my own philological researches.

The letters ḍa, ra, la, ḷa and zha are phonetically close to one another. Ask a child to say "rail" or "Rāma", in all likelihood it will say "ḍail", "Dāma". The reason is "ḍa" is phonetically close to "ra". Quite a few people say "Śivalātri" for "Śivarātri". And some say "*tuḷippora*" for "*tuḷippola*" (Tamiḷ for "just a little"). Here "la" and "ra" sound similar. I spoke about how "ra" and "ḍa" change. So "la" can also change to "ḍa". "La" is very close to "ḷa". Usually what we pronounce as "laḷitā", "naḷina", and "śītaḷa" will be found in Sanskrit books as "lalita", "nalina" and "śitala". There is no need to say how "ḷa" and "zha" are close friends. Madurai is indeed *the* city of Tamiḷ but here people say "*vāḷa-paḷam*" (plaintain) for "*vāzha-pazham*". That is they use "ḷa" for "zha", a letter we believe to be unique to the Tamiḷ (or Tamizh) language.

Here I should like to mention an idea likely to sound new to you. What is considered unique to Tamiḷ, "zha" [retroflex affrative], is present in the Vedas also. *Jaimini* is one of the Sāmaveda śākhās: it is also called the *Talavakāra Śākhā*. The "ḍa" or "ḷa" of other Vedas or śākhās sounds like "zha" in the *Talavakāra Śākhā*. Those who have properly learned this recension say "zha" for "ḍa" or "ḷa". Perhaps it is not a full "zha" sound but something approximating to it, or something in which the "zha" sound is latent.

The "zha-kāra" occurs even in the Ṛgveda in some places. Usually "ḍa" and "ḷa" are interchanged and where there is "ḍa-kāra" in the Yajurveda it is "ḷa-kāra" in the Ṛgveda. The very first mantra in the Vedas is "Agnimīḍe". "Agnimīḍe" is according to the Yajurveda which has the largest following. In the Ṛgveda the same word occurs as "Agnimīḷe". The "ḷe" here is to be pronounced almost as "zhe". In the famous Śrī Rudra hymn of the Yajurveda occurs the word "Mīḍuṣṭamāya". The same word is found in the Ṛgveda also and the "ḍu" in the "mīḍu" sounds like "zhu" instead of sounding like "ḷu" — that is the "zha-kāra" is latent in how the syllable is vocalised.

Generally speaking, the "ḷa" in the Ṛgveda is "ḍa" in the Yajurveda and "zha" in the Talavakāra Sāmaveda. Now let us take up the regions where each of the Vedas has a large following and consider the special features of the language spoken in each such region.

The view is propagated that the Vedas belong to the Āryans, that the Dravīḍians have nothing to do with them. Let us take three of the four Dravīḍian states for consideration, that is the regions where Tamiḷ, Telugu and Kannaḍa are spoken.

The "zha-kāra" is special to Tamiḷ, "ḍa" to Telugu and "ḷa" to Kannaḍa. Where "zha" occurs in Tamiḷ, it is "ḍa" in Telugu and "ḷa" in Kannaḍa. Take the Sanskrit word "pravāḷa" (coral). It is "*pavazham*" in Tamiḷ, "*pakaḍalu*" in Telugu and "*havāḷa*" in Kannaḍa.

"*Pavazham*" is derived from "pravāḷa", so too "*pakaḍalu*" in Telugu, in which language the original Sanskrit word has changed more than in Tamiḷ: the "vā" of "pravāḷa" has become "ka" but it is according to the genius of that language. How has the word changed in Kannaḍa? In Tamiḷ and Telugu the change from the Sanskrit "pra" to "pa" is but small. But in Kannaḍa the "pra" becomes "ha" and that of course is according to the genius of that language. The "pa" in the other languages becomes "ha" in Kannaḍa. Thus "Pampā" becomes "Hampā" and then "Hampi" (you must have heard of the ruins of Hampi)[1]. The Tamiḷ "*pāl*" for milk is "*hālu*" in Kannaḍa and the Tamiḷ "*puhazh*" (fame) is "*hogaḷu*" in Kannaḍa. In the same manner "pravāḷa" becomes "*havāḷa*" in Kannaḍa.

It was not my purpose to speak about the "pa-ha" relationship. All I wanted to point out was how the "ḷa" of Sanskrit is the "zha" of Tamiḷ and the "ḍa" of Telugu. In Kannaḍa, however, there is no change. The "ḷa" remains "ḷa".

You see this difference not only with respect to words of Sanskritic origin but also with respect to those belonging to the Dravīḍian group. The word "*puhazh*" *(or pugazh)* cited earlier is an example in this connection — it is not a Sanskrit word.

(From our present state of investigations we know this: our people belong to one family. They are not racially divided into Āryans and Dravīḍians but are divided into those speaking languages related to Sanskrit on the one hand and those speaking Dravīḍian tongues on the other. Further research is likely to reveal that even this linguistic difference is not real and that both Sanskritic and Dravīḍian languages are from the same parent stock. Some linguists are known to be examining the possible bonds that unite Sanskrit and Tamiḷ. If we go back to very early times, we may discover that the two languages are of the same stock. But, during the thousands of years subsequent to that period, the Dravīḍian languages must have evolved separately. It is in this sense that I speak of the "Dravīḍian" languages as being distinct from Sanskrit.)

I wondered whether there was any special reason why the "zha" of Tamiḷ should be the "ḍa" of Telugu and the "ḷa" of Kannaḍa. I came to the conclusion that the differences were related to how the Vedas are chanted in the regions where these three languages are spoken.

The predominant Veda in the western region [of Peninsular India], including Mahārāṣṭra and Karṇāṭaka, is the Ṛgveda. In the region from Nāsik to Kanyākumārī, the Ṛgveda has the widest following. Kannaḍa is one of the languages spoken here and "ḷa" has a unique place in it. And this "ḷa", special to Kannaḍa, which is considered a Dravīḍian regional language, is Vedic in origin.

If we go to that part of the eastern seashore and the hinterland that form Āndhra Pradeś, we find that 98 out of 100 people (Brahmins) here are Yajurvedins. The remaining two per cent are Ṛgvedins. There are practically no Sāmavedins in Āndhra Pradeś. Since Yajurvedins are the predominant group the Ṛgvedic "ḷa" is "ḍa" here, so also the "ḷa" of other languages.

In Tamiḷ Nāḍu also Yajurvedins are in a majority though not to the same extent as in Āndhra Pradeś. Here 80 per cent are Yajurvedins, 15 per cent Sāmavedins and 5 per cent Ṛgvedins. In ancient times, however, the Sāmavedins formed quite a large group — there is evidence for such a belief. It is likely that there were Brahmins belonging to all the 1,000 recensions of the Śāmaveda in the Tamiḷ land. Īśvara is extolled in the *Tevāram*[T] as "*Āyiram-śākhai- uḍaiyān*" (one with a thousand Vedic recensions).

Among the Sāmavedins those belonging to the *Kauthūma Śākhā* form the majority. But in the old days the followers of the *Jaiminīya* or *Talavakāra Śākhā* were quite large in number. Cozhiyar are people of the Cola land. Even today they are all Sāmavedins and they follow the *Talavakāra Śākhā* — the Cozhiyar residing in Tirunelveli (which is identified as a Pāṇḍya territory) still belong to this recension. Originally the Sāmaveda had a great following not only in the land of the Coḷas but also in that of the Pāṇḍyas.

"Cozhiyar" may be understood as Brahmins belonging to the Tamiḷ land from very ancient times. They are indeed the Brahmin "Ādivāsīs" of that region. I will tell you how. Among Tamiḷ Smārta Brahmins there is a sect called "Vaḍamas" ("Vaḍamar")[3]. They must have come to the Tamiḷ land from the North, specifically from the Narmadā valley. Their very name suggests that they are from the North. Cozhiyar must have been inhabitants of Tamiḷ Nāḍu from the earliest times.

From what I have said about "Vaḍamar" I should not be taken to mean that I believe that all Brahmins in the South came from the North as is suggested by some people today. As a matter of fact, in the very word "Vaḍamar" there is proof that all Brahmins *did not* come from the North. If all Brahmins in Tamiḷ Nāḍu or in the rest of the South had their original home in the North, why should one sect have been singled out for the name of "Vaḍamar"? The rest of the Brahmins must have belonged to the Tamiḷ land from the very beginning. Cozhiyar are among these first Brahmins.

There is one proof to show that "Vaḍamar" originally belonged to the Narmadā valley. Only they, among the Brahmins [in the South], recite the following verse in their sandhyāvandana[S]; it is a prayer for protection from snakes.

Narmadāyai namaḥ prātaḥ Narmadāyai namo niśi
Namostu Narmade tubhyam pāhi mām viṣa-sarpataḥ

Among the Cozhiyar there was a great man called Somāśimāra Nāyanār who was one of the 63 Nāyanmārs[5]. "*Somāśī*" is not an eatable, but means a "somayājin", one who has performed the soma sacrifice. Śrī Rāmānujācārya's father had also performed the same sacrifice and he was called "Keśava Somayājin". The Sāmaveda has an important place in the soma sacrifice.

If there were a large number of Cozhiyar Brahmins in the very early times in Tamiḷ Nāḍu, it means that the *Talavakāra Śākhā* of the Sāmaveda must have had a large following then. I have spoken about the Coḷa and Pāṇḍya kingdoms but not of the Pallava and Cera lands. In the dim past there was no Pallava kingdom. The *"Mūvendar"* are the Ceras, Colas and Pāṇḍyas. The region where the Pallava kingdom arose later was then part of the Cola territory. So the early Brahmins who had come from the North, the Vaḍamar, settled in the northern part of Tamiḷ Nāḍu, that is the Pallava territory. Subsequently they came to be called "Auttara Vaḍamar". There are Sāmavedins among the "Vaḍamar" also, but they do not belong to the *Talavakāra Śākhā* but to the *Kauthūma Śākhā*. The "Vaḍamar" came to the Tamiḷ land long after the Tamiḷ language had developed into its classical stage. So their Vedic chanting is not germane to our subject. The same could be said about the Pallavas after the Samgam[T] literature came to flourish.

Let us now turn to the Cera land. Malayāḷam is spoken in Keraḷa. If I did not touch upon this language when I dealt with Tamiḷ, Telugu and Kannaḍa, it was because of the fact that it appeared much later than the other three. Until about a thousand years ago, Keraḷa was part of the Tamiḷ land and its language too was Tamiḷ. Malayāḷam evolved from Tamiḷ. If the Tamiḷ "zha" is "ḍa" in Telugu and "ḷa" in Kannaḍa, it remains "zha" in Malayāḷam. Tamiḷs say *"puzhai"* for a river, Malayāḷis say *"puzha"*. If the former say "Ālappuzhai" and "Ambalappuzhai" [both names of places in Keraḷa], the latter say "Ālappuzha" and "Amblappuzha".

Leaving aside the question of the Malayāḷam language, let us turn to the subject of the Vedic tradition of Keraḷa. The Malayāḷa Brahmins called Nampūtiris have a long tradition of learning the Vedas in the śāstric manner. There are among them Trivedins (those well- versed in the Ṛgveda, Yajurveda and Sāmaveda, and among the last-mentioned a number of people following the *Talavakāra Śākhā*). The Pāñcānmana family is one such and it has behind it a fine Vedic tradition. They belong to the *Talavakāra Śākhā*. Today those who follow the *Kauthūma Śākhā* are in a majority among the Sāmavedins in Tamil Nāḍu but in Keraḷa the Sāmavedins belong to the *Talavakāra Śākhā*.

From generation to generation, the Nampūtiris have been chanting the *Talavakāra Śākhā*. They pronounce the "ḍa" or "ḷa" of other śākhas as "zha" — which means they follow the same practice as in Tamiḷ Nāḍu. Both the palm-leaf and printed versions of the *Talavakāra Śākhā*, in Tamiḷ Nāḍu as well as in Keraḷa, have "zha" in the relevant places.

Thus we see that from very early times the *Talavakāra Śākhā* of the Sāmaveda has had a following in the Tamiḷ land larger than in any other part of the country. And with this recension has come the "zha" which is a phoneme not found elsewhere. Naccinārkkiṇiyar[T] is among the commentators of the Tamiḷ Samgam works. In his commentary on the *Tolkāppiyam* (famous Tamiḷ grammatical treatise), he mentions "four Vedas": *"Taittirīyam, Pauḍikam, Talavakāram* and *Sāmam."* He mistakes recensions for full-fledged Vedas. However, we note from his list that the *Talavakāra Śākhā* had the place of a full-fledged Veda in Tamiḷ Nāḍu. *"Taittirīyam"* is a recension of the Kṛṣṇa-Yajurveda. The *Kauṣītaki Brāhmaṇa* of the *Śānkhāyana Śākhā* of the Ṛgveda is called *"Pauṣya"*. What Naccinārkkiṇiyar calls *"Pauḍiyam"* is referred to by the Āzhvārs as *"Pauzhiyam"* — here again you see the relationship between "zha" and "ḍa".

All told the phonemes unique to the languages spoken in the different regions have evolved on the basis of the differences in pronunciation in the various Vedic recensions.

So far I have confined myself to the languages of the Dravīḍian region. Now I will speak on the same theme with reference to other parts of India and to other countries of the world.

It is customary in the North to use "ja" for "ya" and "ba" for "va" — both in literary and colloquial usage. The use of "ba" for "va" is noticeable particularly in Beṅgāḷ and "ja" for "ya" in Uttar Pradeś, Punjāb, etc.

In Beṅgāḷ they follow the dictum, "vabayorabhedam" — there is no difference between "va" and "ba". In Tamiḷ too "Bhīṣma" is sometimes referred to as "Vīṭṭumar" and Bhīma as "Vīma". In Beṅgāḷ, all "va's" are vocalised as "ba's". Indeed "Beṅgāḷ" itself is from "Vaṅga".

Beṅgāḷis say "Baṅgabāsī" for "Vaṅgavāsī" (a resident of Bengāḷ). Once they realised that changing all "va's" universally into "ba's" was not right and called a pariṣad [a meeting of scholars] to consider the question — it was called the "Vaṅga Pariṣad". According to one of its decisions all "ba-kāra" in Beṅgāḷi books to be printed thenceforth was to be changed to "va-kāra". They strictly carried out the decision. But in doing so they also changed what should naturally be "ba" into "va" — for instnace, "bandhu"[6] into "vandhu", "Baṅgabandhu" into "Vaṅgavandhu".

As observed earlier, in other regions of the North too "ba" is used for "va". For example, the name "Bihār" itself is from "Vihār". (Once there were many Buddhist vihāras, temples or monasteries, in this region.) The name "Rāsbihārī" is from "Rāsavihārī". How would you explain this practice? Such usage is laid down in the Prātiśākhya of the Vedic recensions followed in these parts. People there applied the rule of the Prātiśākhya to their ordinary writing and speech also. It also follows that the rules laid down by the Vedic śāstras have been faithfully followed in this region.

Yajurvedins, it will be remembered, form the majority in the country taken as a whole: The Kṛṣṇa-Yajurveda is followed in the South and the Śukla-Yajurveda in the North. There is a śākha of the latter called" *"Mādhyandina"* and it has a large following in the North. In its Prātiśākhya it is said that "ja" may be used in place of "ya", and "ka" in place of "ṣa". We say in the South "yat Puruṣena haviṣā" (from the Puruṣasūkta); the Northern version of the same is "jat Puruṣena havikā". We are amused by such chanting and we even feel angry that the Vedas are being distorted. At the same time we feel proud that we in the South maintain the purity of the Vedic sound. However, the "ja" and "ka" in the Northern intonation have the sanction of the Śikṣā śāstra.

It is only phonemes that are close to one another that are interchanged. There are examples in Tamiḷ also to show that "ja" and "ya" are closely related. Jāvā (the "Jāvaka" island) is referred to in Tamiḷ works as "Yāvaka". Generally, if "ja" comes as the initial letter of a word it is spelt as "śa" in Tamiḷ, but if it comes in the middle it becomes "ya" — *"Aja(n)" and "Pankaja(m)"* become

"Ayan and *"Pangayam".* "Ṣa" is a form of śa. If "ṣa" and "ka" are interchangeable so too, it seems, "śa" and "ka". In keeping with this what is *"kai"* (hand) in Tamiḷ is *"śey"* in Telugu. "Doing" (performing some work) is the function of the hand (in Tamil *"śeyvadu"*). So better than the Tamiḷ *"kai"* is the Telugu *"śey"* which denotes the function of the hand. In Sanskrit the word "kara" has the meaning of "to do" as well as the hand -- "Śamkara" ("Śankara") one who does good; "karomi" is "I do." One wonders whether in Tamiḷ too *"śey"* was originally used to denote the hand and then *"kai"* came to be used. Now *"śey"* is a verb in that language. The "śa" (or "ṣa"), it is likely, changed to "ka" and then "kai". One more point: "ṣa" and "kṣa" are related sounds. So for "kṣa" to become "ka" is natural. "Akṣam"- *"akkam"*; "dakṣinam"- *"dakkāṇam"*; "kṣaṇam" - *"kaṇam"*. Such examples could be multiplied.

We have seen that "ba" becomes "va" in Tamiḷ while in the Northern languages it is the other way round. Similarly, "ja" becomes "ya" and "sa" becomes "ka" in Tamiḷ while in the Northern languages "ya" and "ṣa" become "ja" and "ka" respectively. That is according to the Vedic recension followed there and the rules of the Śikṣā relating to it. That is the reason why Northerners chant "jat Puruṣena havikā" for "yat Puruṣena haviṣā".

This change is to be seen in so many other words in the North: "Jamunā" for "Yamunā"; "jogi" for yogi(n); "jug-jug" for yuga-yuga; "jātra" for "yātra." "Ṣa" is changed to "ka" and so "ṛṣi" becomes *"riki".* As we have seen, "kṣa" and "ṣa" are related. Even in the South we hear people saying "Laṣimī" for "Lakṣmī" — they even write like that. In the North "ka" is used for "kṣa" -- for instance *"khīr"* for "kṣīra". The same applies to Tamiḷ usage also — "Ilakkumi" for "Lakṣmī".

Let us now turn to other countries, first to the land which saw the birth of Christianity, to the Semitic countries like Palestine and Israel. The Old Testament is basic to the Qur'ān also. Some characters are common to Christianity and Islam, but in Arabic they are pronounced differently. Joseph becomes "Yusuf" and Jehovah becomes "Yehovah." There are differences among the Christian nations too. In some languages you see "ja-kāra" to be prominent. "Jesu" and "Yesu", the name of the very founder of Christianity, is spelt differently. "Ja-kāra" is a characteristic of Greek also. We could trace the root of all this to the Vedas. Jehovah or Yehovah is the same as the Vedic deity Yahvan. "Dyau-Pitār" (Dyāva- Pṛthivī) becomes Jupiter. Sanskrit words lose their initial letter when borrowed by other languages. So Dyau-Pitār becomes "Yau-Pitaṛ"and then Jupiter.

What were originally Yahvan and Dyau-Pitaṛ changed to Jehovah and Jupiter with the addition of the "ja-kāra". In the beginning the Vedic religion was practised everywhere. It is likely that the *Mādhyandina Śākhā* was followed in Greece and its neighbourhood.

Notes & References

1 The ruins of Hampi, on the Tungabhadrā, are such as to proclaim the splendour of the Vijayanagara Empire.

2 Folks in Tamiḷ Nāḍu pun on the word "Vaḍama". "*Vada*" is a snack popular all over the South and in Tamiḷ "*mā*" means flour or the batter for *dośa* and *iḍḍali.* So goes the joke: "What, *vaḍamā or dośa mā?*" The Paramaguru himself tells this joke in this discourse.

3 "Vaḍamar" — from *Vaḍakku* or North. Here "North" should be understood simply in the sense of being north of Tamiḷ Nāḍu. Otherwise the word usually refers to Northern India.

4 See *The Guru Tradition*, pages 222 to 230.

5 A relative or friend.

Chapter 12

Impact of Śikṣā Śāstra

In the foregoing we noticed that certain Vedic syllables had a special association with certain regions and that these were absorbed in the languages spoken there. We also learned from this that the Vedas flourished in all countries. There was never a period in Tamiḷ Nāḍu, the land we know intimately[1], when Vedic dharma was not practised there.

The name "Tamizh"[2] itself has the "zha" characteristic of the *Talavakāra Śākhā* of the Sāmaveda. Am I right in making such a claim? Or is it all the other way round? Suppose the argument goes like this: it is the "zha" characteristic of Tamiḷ and the "ja" characteristic of Northern tongues that are seen as the distinguishing phonemes in the Vedic texts prevalent in Tamiḷ Nāḍu and the North respectively. In other words what was already present in the regional languages came to be absorbed in the Vedic śākhās prevalent in the areas concerned. Did I put the whole thing topsyturvy when I made the statement that the Vedic "zha", "ja" and "ba" became characteristic for the Tamiḷs, Northerners and Beṅgāḷis respectively, that these were reflected in the speech of each of these linguistic groups?

That the rules of the Śikṣā śāstra had their impact on the regional languages is the correct view. The rules of the Prātiśākhya[S] do not apply to one area alone but to all those parts where the Vedic recension concerned is followed. If there is a Brahmin chanting the *Talavakāra* in Kāmarūpa (Assam) or Kāśmīr, he will use "zha" where others use "ḍa" or "ḷa" in the mantras. A Brahmin who chants hymns from the Kṛṣṇa-Yajurveda has to use "ḍa" instead of "zha" or "ḷa" whether he belongs to Gujarāt or Mahārāṣṭra or any other place in India. In the same way, it is not only the Kannaḍiga, any Ṛgvedin anywhere will use "ḷa" where others use "ḍa" or "zha" in chanting the mantras. The Prātiśākhya determines the sound of Vedic mantras not for a particular area alone but for the whole country. In course of time the local language takes on the characteristics of the śākhā where it is practised.

The name of the month "Mārgaśīrṣī" is derived from the fact that generally the full moon falls on the day to which is conjoined the asterism of Mṛgaśīrṣa during that month. Mārgaśīrṣī is *Mārgazhi* in Tamiḷ. "Ṣī" changed to "ḍi" and "ḍi to "zhi". It is according to the genius of that language that "ṣa" becomes "ḍa". "Puruṣa" is called *"puruḍan"* in Tamiḷ and "Nahuṣa" is *"Nag(h)uḍan"* in Tamiḷ poetry. Kambar[T] calls Vibhīṣana "Vīḍaṇan". But, if Mārgaśīrṣī changed to "Mārgaśīrḍi" and then the "śīr" in the middle dropped, should not the word have the final form of "Mārgaḍi"? How do you explain the presence of the "zha-kāra"? In other words, how does the name of the month finally take the name *"Mārgazhi"*? The "zha-kāra" must be attributed to the *Talavakāra Śākhā* that was predominant in Tamiḷ Nāḍu.

People belonging to this recension use "zha" and Kṛṣṇa- Yajurvedins use "ḍa", don't they? This habit they still retain unconsciously. The Telugu Vaiṣṇavas sing the Tamiḷ *Divyaprabandham*[1] during worship in the temples. In Tirupati the Tamiḷ *Tiruppāvai* is sung before the Lord. It starts with the words *"Mārgazhi-t-tiṅgaḷ"*. "Zhi" is difficult for Telugus to vocalise. How is it that they do not say *"Mārgaḷi"* or *"Mārgali"* then? They say *"Margaḍi-t-tiṅgaḷ"*, that is with the "ḍa-kāra" instead of the "zha-kāra". When they chant hymns from the Sāmaveda that is prevalent in Tamiḷ Nāḍu they unconsciously use the "ḍa-kāra" for the "zha- kāra". "Da is in the blood of Yajurvedins, so they say *"Mārgaḍi"* instead of *"Mārgazhi"*.

Notes & References

[1] The Paramaguru is here speaking to a Tamiḷ audience.

[2] "Tamiḷ" is strictly "Tamizh".

Chapter 13

Names of Months

From our inquiry into the derivation of the Tamiḷ *Mārgazhi* from Mārgaśīrṣī, you must have formed an idea of how the genius of one language differs from that of another. You may note this from how the original Sanskrit names of other months have changed in Tamiḷ. Usually, as observed before, the name of a month is derived from the asterism under which the full moon falls in that month. Citrā-Pūrṇimā is a sacred day. The Tamiḷ *Cittirai* does not represent much of a change from the Sanskrit "Citrā".

Vaiśākhā is connected with the asterism Viśākhā; it is *"Vaikāsi"* in Tamiḷ. Just as Madurai becomes Marudai, so the Sanskrit Vaiśākhī has changed to *"Vaikāsi"* in Tamiḷ. (In Beṅgāḷ the month is called "Baisākhī".) Viśākhā is the asterism under which Nammāzhvār[T] was born. Now Vaiśākhā Pūrṇimā is celebrated as Buddha Purṇimā.

The month Ānuṣī is associated with the asterism of "Anuṣa" [Anurādhā]. The full moon usually falls under this asterism during this month. In Tamiḷ the month is called "Āni" — the "ṣa-kāra" of the original has dropped.

There are two "Āṣaḍhās" — Pūrvaṣāḍhā and Uttarāṣaḍhā (Earlier Āṣāḍhā and Later Āṣāḍhā). Pūrvāṣāḍhā is called *"Pūrāḍam"* in Tamiḷ: in the Tamiḷ name the "rva" of the original is eroded and the "ṣa" has dropped. Similarly, Uttarāṣāḍhā is *"Utrāḍam"* in Tamiḷ. The Sanskrit "Aṣāḍhī" is the Tamil month of *"Āḍi"*.

Śrāvaṇa means that which is associated with the asterism Śravaṇa. In the Tamiḷ *"Oṇam"* the "śra" of the original has dropped and "vaṇa" has become "oṇam". Since it is the asterism sacred to Mahāviṣṇu the honorific *"Tiru"* [equivalent of Śrī] is prefixed to its name — thus we have *"Tiruvoṇam"*. (Ārdrā is the asterism sacred to Śiva. It is called *"Ādirai"* in Tamiḷ and with the prefixing of *"Tiru"* it becomes *"Tiruvādirai"*. It is not customary to add *"Tiru"* to the Tamiḷ names of other asterisms. In the South, there is a festival of lights in the month of *"Kārttigai"*— the original Sanskrit name is Kṛttikā. During this time alone is *"Tiru"* added to *"Kārttigai"*. But to the asterisms sacred to Hari and Hara -- Viṣṇu and Śiva -- *"Tiru"* is added. Here is proof of the fact that it is part of the religious culture of Tamiḷs not to maintain any distinction between these two gods.) To come back to Śrāvaṇa. The full moon in this month generally falls under the asterism of Śravaṇa. In the Tamiḷ name of *"Āvani"*, the "śra" of the original has dropped.

For this linguistic phenomenon of letters dropping off in Tamiḷ there is the example of "Īzham" for Siṁhaḷa [the island nation known today as Śrī Lanka]. "Sa" and "śa" become "a" in Tamiḷ. If "sahasra" is *"sāsiram"* in Kannaḍa, it is *"āyiram"* in Tamiḷ.

"Āyiram" reminds me of other numbers. The Tamiḷ numbers *onru, iraṇḍu, mūnru* (one, two, three) seem to have no connection with the Sanskrit eka, dvi, tri. But *añcu* and *eṭṭu* (five and eight) seem to be related to the Sanskrit pañca and aṣṭa. The English "two" and "three" are related to the Sanskrit dvi and tri. Sexta, hepta, octo, nona, deca — these are obviously connected with the Sanskrit ṣaṣta, sapta, aṣṭa, nava and daśa. But the very first number "one" seems totally unrelated to the Sanskrit "eka". But, strangely enough, it appears to have some connection with the Tamiḷ *"onru"*. The Telugu equivalent is made up of the "o" of the Tamiḷ *"onru"* and the "ka" of the Sanskrit "eka" — *"okaṭī"*. If we consider all this, just as we are one racially, in the matter of language also we are one. There must have been a common root language for Sanskrit and the Dravīḍian tongues.

In Siṁhaḷa the "sa" and "ha" of "Simha" have dropped off and the word has become "Īḷam" and the "ḷa" has changed to "zha" to become "Īzham".

Like Āṣaḍhā, Prosṭhapadā has also a Pūrva and an Uttara. Pūrva-Proṣṭhapadā is *"Pūraṭṭādi"* in Tamiḷ: "aṣṭa" changing to *"aṭṭa"* is already known to us. Uttara-Proṣṭhapadā is *"Utraṭṭādi"* in Tamiḷ. The full moon falls under this asterism or the one near it in the Tamiḷ month *Puraṭṭāśi* which name is derived somehow from Proṣṭhapadī.

We call Āśvayuja Aśvinī or *"Asvati"*. The full moon conjoined with the asterism Āśvayuja makes the month Āsvayujī which in Tamiḷ is *"Aippaśi"*.

The "Kārttika" of Sanskrit (adjective of Kṛttikā) has not changed much in its Tamiḷ equivalent of *Kārttigai*. The *"Tirukkārttigai"* festival of lights usually falls on a full moon. I started with how Mārgaśirṣī changes to *"Mārgazhi"*. The full moon of that month is celebrated as *Tiruvādirai,* the day sacred to Śiva.

"Puṣyā" is the Tamiḷ *"Pūśam"*. (We in Tamiḷ Nāḍu have got so used to *"Pūśam"* that we have made the asterism "Punarvasu" into *"Punarpūśam"*. Of course there is no Sanskrit equivalent like "Punarpuṣyā".) "Pauṣyā" means what is associated with Puṣyā. Puṣyā is also known as Taiṣyā. The Tamiḷ name of the month *"Tai"* is the result of the second syllable of "Taiṣyā" dropping off.

The month "Māgha" is named after the asterism Maghā — in Tamiḷ it is *"Māśi"*. The "śi" ending is reminiscent of *"Vaikāśi"*, *"Puraṭṭāśi"* and *"Aippaśi"*.

There are two asterisms called Pūrva-Phālguna and Uttara- Phālguna. In the corresponding Tamiḷ names the important part of the Sanskrit original, "Phalguna", has dropped off. So "Purva-Phālguna" is mere *"Puram"* in Tamiḷ and "Uttara-Phalguna" is mere *"Utram"*. But the month in which the full moon falls under the asterism of Uttara-Phālguna is *"Panguni"* for Tamiḷs. It is a festive day in many parts of the South. We celeberate it as *Panguni-Utram Tiru-k-kalyāṇam*[T].

From an examination of the Tamiḷ names of the months we form an idea of how the phonemes of Sanskrit change in Tamiḷ.

Chapter 14
Other Notable Aspects of Śikṣā

The general rule is that the sound of the Vedas ought not to be changed, that there should be no tonal alterations. But there are rules permitting slight modifications based on the differences between the recensions. — and these rules are according to the Śikṣā śāstra. Slight tonal changes are also allowed. In some hymns of the Ṛgveda the "a-kāra" and "e-kāra" are drawn out further than in the other Vedas. In some recensions we have "ṁ" and in some others "gṁ" — these are called "anusvāra"[1]. The differences are not so much related to letters or syllables as they are to tone and accent.

Sound means so much to the Vedic tradition, so due importance must be given to it. Thus Śikṣā śāstra is the Vedapuruṣa's organ of breathing.

The 50 letters of the Sanskrit alphabet are derived from the Vedic sounds. If you add "jña" to them you will have 51. These letters are called "mātṛkā". The word has more than one meaning. Importantly, "mātṛ" or "mātā" means Ambā, the World Mother. The 51 letters make up her form — Ambā, Parāśakti, personifies them. If the cosmos is the creation of this Supreme Goddess and, if it is also remembered that creation was accomplished with sound, Ambā must be the incarnation of the 51 letters. The Śākta Tantras declare that the 51 letters are the limbs of Ambā and correlate the letters with different parts of her sacred body. The 51 Śakti pīthas [seats of the Supreme Goddess] are associated with one or another of these letters.

If Śikṣā is particularly esteemed as the breathing organ of the Vedapuruṣa, we must also remember that it is made more glorious by the fact that it sheds light on the 51 letters which personify Ambā.

Notes

[1] "Anusvāra" literally is "after-sound". One authority describes it as the unmodified nasal following a vowel.

Part Seven

VYĀKARAṆA

Chapter 1

Mouth of the Vedapuruṣa

Vyākaraṇa or grammar is the "mukha" of the Vedapuruṣa, his mouth. The Tamiḻ word for grammar is "*ilakkaṇam*". Grammar deals with the "lakṣaṇas" of a language. "Lakṣmaṇa(n)" is "Ilukkumaṇan" in Tamiḻ. In the same way, "laksaṇa(m)" becomes "*ilakkaṇam*" in that language.

There are a number of works on Sanskrit grammar. The most widely used and important is the one by the great sage Pāṇini. There is a gloss — a vārtika— on his "Vyākaraṇa-sūtra"[1] by Vararuci. Patañjali has written a bhāṣya or commentary on Pāṇini's sūtras. These three are the chief works on Sanskrit grammar.

There is a difference between grammar and other śāstras. In the case of other subjects the original sūtras constituting them are esteemed more than their bhāṣyas. But, in the case of grammar or vyākaraṇa, the vārtika is more valued than the sūtras and still more valued is the bhāṣya.

According to one reckoning, there are six śāstras. Vyākaraṇa is one of them. Four of the śāstras are particularly important : apart from Vyākaraṇa, Tarka (logic), Mīmāṁsā and Vedānta. Vyākaraṇa is also one of the Vedic Ṣaḍanga (six limbs of the Vedas).

"Sūcanāt sūtram," so it is said. (The sūtra is just an indication of something, a truth or a principle.) Every śāstra has a bhāṣya and each such bhāṣya is known by a particular name. The vyākaraṇa bhāṣya (of Patañjali) alone is called "Mahābhāṣya", "the great commentary".

Note

[1] Also known as the *Aṣṭādhyāyī*.

Chapter 2

Grammar and Śiva

Śiva temples have a maṇḍapa (pavilion or hall) called "vyākaraṇa-dāna-maṇḍapa". In Tamiḷ it has come to be called "*vakkānikkum maṇḍapam*". There are such halls in many temples in the Cola territory of Tamiḷ Nāḍu. One such is in Tiruvoṟṟiyūr near Madras. Why should there be a maṇḍapa for grammar in Śiva temples? What is Śiva's connection with language? Is not Śiva in his form of Dakṣiṇāmūrti all silence?

Nṛttāvasāne Naṭarāja-rājo nanāda ḍhakkām navapañcavāram
Uddhartukāmaḥ Sanakādisiddhānetadvimarśe Śivasūtrajālam

I will speak briefly about this stanza. The silent Śiva remains still [as Dakṣiṇāmūrti]. But the same Śiva [in another form of his] keeps dancing all the time and it was from his dance that the science of language was born.

Naṭarāja is the name of the dancing Parameśvara. "Naṭa" is a member of a troupe which also consists of the "viṭa" and "gāyaka"[1]. The naṭa dances. Naṭarāja is the king of all dancers — he who cannot be excelled as a dancer— and he is also called Mahānaṭa [the great dancer]. The *Amarakośa,* the Sanskrit lexicon[2], has these two words: "Mahākālo mahānaṭaḥ." In Tamiḷ they say "*Aṁbala-k-kūttāḍuvān*". We find from royal inscriptions that in the old days Brahmins too had such Tamiḷ names — "*Aṁbala-k-kūttāḍuvān Bhaṭṭan*", for instance.

There used to be a publishing establishment in Bombay called the Nirṇaya-Sāgara Press. It once brought out old poetical works in Sanskrit under the general name, "Kāvyamālā Series". There were some books in this series with the name "Prācīnalekhāmālā". Reproduced in one of them is the text of a copper-plate inscription belonging to the Veṅgi kingdom. Veṅgi is situated between the Godāvarī and the Kṛṣṇā.

The Coḷa rulers of the Telugu country and the Coḷas of Tañjāvūr were related by marriage. Rājarāja Coḷa (Narendra) reigned in Tañjāvūr; it was he who built the Bṛhadīśvara temple[3]. Kulottuṅga Coḷa who belonged to the family of the grandson of a king of Veṅgi ruled as a member of the Coḷa dynasty of Tañjāvūr. Once he visited the Cola kingdom and on his return took some 500 Brahmins with him to promote Vedic learning in Vengi. The "Drāviḍalu" of Āndhra Pradeś are the descendants of these Brahmins.

The names of all these Brahmins and their gotras[S] are mentioned in the copper-plate inscription together with the subjects in which they were proficient and the duties they had to perform. The landed property allotted to each is referred to, so also the names of the donors and of the donees. The Brahmins brought from Tamiḷ Nāḍu had to teach the Vedas and the śāstras. That is why gifts of lands were made to them.

"Rūpāvatāra-vaktuḥ eko bhāgaḥ": these words are from the inscription. It means "one share to the Brahmin who is proficient in the *Rūpāvatāra.*" *Rūpāvatāra* is a work on grammar.

In Eṇṇāyiram, near Tiṇḍivanam (Tamiḷ Nāḍu), there was a school with 340 students. Of them 40 studied *Rūpāvatāra,* says an inscription of Rājendra Coḷa I. In Tribhuvanam, Poṇḍicerri (Pondicherry), also there was a Vedic school supported by Rājādhirāja (A.D. 1018-1050) where the *Rūpāvatāra* was taught. We also learn from an inscription of Vīra-Rājendra Deva, dated A.D. 1067, that this grammatical work was taught at a school in Tirumukkūḍal, near Kāñcī.

Siddhānta-Kaumudī is a very popular treatise on grammar. It is a commentary on Pāṇini's sūtras by Bhaṭṭoji Dīkṣita who was a disciple of Appayya Dīkṣita. The latter was born in Aḍayappalam and was the author of 104 works, many of them on Śaiva themes. His *Kuvalayānanda,* a work on poetics, is also famous.

Ardha-mātrā-lāghavena putrotsavam
mānyante vaiyākaraṇāḥ

This speaks of the great joy experienced by grammarians: if they gain as much as half a mātra[S] it is a cause for jubilation like the birth of a son to a man who has been long childless.

The sūtras are very brief and very precise. The *Siddhānta-Kaumudī* is also famous for its brevity and exactitude; there is no circumlocution in it, no beating about the bush. May be the sūtras themselves are wordy but not Bhaṭṭoji Dīkṣita's commentary on the same. Written some 400 years ago, it is very popular even today and is the first book of grammar prescribed for students. (Bhaṭṭoji Dīkṣita also wrote the *Tattvakaustubha* and dedicated it to his guru, Appayya Dīkṣita. In this he seeks to establish that there is no Truth other than the Brahman and that, to claim that there is, is not in keeping with the teachings of the Upaniṣads. Bidden by his guru, he also wrote an attack on Madhvācārya's philosophy of dualism. The work, *Madhvamata-viddhvaṁsanam,* is a cause of dispute among philosophers but Bhaṭṭoji Dīkṣita's commentary on grammar is acceptable to all systems.)

Before *Siddhānta-Kaumudī, Rupāvatāram* was the grammar work famous among students. "Rūpam" here means the "complete form of sound"; "avatāram" is descent, but in the present context "history". *Rūpāvatāram* was published by Raṅgācāri, of Presidency College, Madras.

That gifts of land were made to scholars who taught *Rūpāvatāram* [the reference here is to the Veṅgi inscription], shows the importance attached to Sanskrit grammar in those times.

The Veṅgi inscription dates back to 850 years ago. As mentioned earlier, the names of Brahmins who received gifts are given in it. Many of them had the title "Ṣaḍangavid" (learned in the six Vedic Angas). Some had Tamil names — "*Aṁbala-k-kūttāḍuvān Bhaṭṭan*", "*Tiruvarangamuḍayān Bhaṭṭan*", etc. Of the foregoing two names the first is associated with the Cidaṁbaram temple which is Śaiva and the second with the Śrīrangam temple which is Vaiṣṇava. Both Brahmins were Smārtas, even the one with the Vaiṣṇava name. There has been as much devotion to Śiva as there has been to Viṣṇu at all times. In the North and in Keraḷa, even today, Smārtas perform pūjā in all temples. The man called "*Tiruvarangamuḍayān Bhaṭṭan*" is not to be taken as a Vaiṣṇava from his name. The Sanskrit equivalent of the name is Rangasvāmin. "*Uḍayān*" means "svāmin", "svam" denoting possession.

The Tamiḷ name of Naṭarāja is "*Tiruvaṁbala Kūttāḍuvān*". I wanted to speak about Naṭarāja and his connection with grammar. Let us go back to the stanza with the first word, "Nṛttāvasāne..." Naṭarāja performs an awe-inspiring dance. It seems to bring together all the dance that all of us have to perform, the rhythms of all our lives. The head of the Naṭarāja idol has something that seems spread over it, something falling down on both sides. What is it? It is the god's mass of matted locks. I am reminded of the snapshot photographs taken nowadays. A snapshot is a rapid photograph that captures an object in one of its fleeting moments. It is not a study that is static but one suggestive of motion. Naṭarāja dances fast, but momentarily seems to stop dancing. His matted locks give the impression of fanning out over the two sides of his face. The sculptor of those times seems to have taken a mental snapshot of that moment to create the image of Naṭarāja.

Naṭarāja has a drum in one hand, called the ḍhakka or ḍamaruka. The tāḷa of this drum (the time kept by it) is in keeping with the "footwork" of the dancing god, the movement of his feet. The beat of his drum is referred to in the words, "nanāda ḍhakkām".

There are chiefly three types of musical instruments. Those made of skin like the ḍhakka, the *tavil* (drum accompaniment to *nāgasvaram* music), the *kañjira* (a kind of hand drum), the mṛdanga; stringed instruments like the vīṇa, the violin; wind instruments like the *nāgasvaram*, the flute. The final beat of the drum is called *cāppu*[4]. Similarly at the end of Naṭarāja's dance ("nṛttāvasāne") the ḍamaruka produced the *cāppu* sound

When Naṭarāja dances, Sanaka and his brother sages, Patañjali, Vyāghrapāda and so on stand round him. They are great ascetics, so they are able to see the dance. Naṭarāja's dance can be seen only by those who have the inner vision of jñāna. The Lord himself bestowed on Arjuna the divine eye with which the Pāṇḍava could see his cosmic form[5]. Vyāsa imparted the same power to Sañjaya so that he could describe this wondrous form to Dhṛtarāṣṭra. Only they (Arjuna and Sañjaya) could see Kṛṣṇa's universal form. Others on the battlefield of Kurukṣetra could not. Because of the great efforts made by them, the celestials, the sages and yogins obtained the divine eye to see the dance of Naṭarāja. In the Gītā such sight is called "divya-cakṣus" (divine eye).

Sanaka and others[6] saw the dance with their real eyes. Viṣṇu played the drum called the maddaḷa, while Brahmā kept time. At the close of the dance, the concluding beats (*cāppu*) produced fourteen sounds. It is these fourteen that are referred to in the stanza *("Nṛttāvasāne",* etc) as "navapañcavāram"; "nava" is nine and "pañca" is five, so fourteen in all. "Nanāda ḍhakkām navapañcavāram." If the number of sounds produced by Naṭarāja's ḍhakka is fourteen, the branches of Vedic learning are also the same number (caturdaśa-vidyā). If the foundation of Hindu dharma is made up of these fourteen vidyās, Naṭarāja's *cāppu* produced fourteen sounds which, according to the verse, were meant for the [Ātmic] uplift of Sanaka and others. You must have seen in the sculptural representations of Dakṣināmūrti in temples four aged figures by his side. They are the Sanaka sages. It is not Śaiva works like the *Tevāram*[T] and the *Tiruvācakam*[T] alone that mention how instruction was given to the four but also the Vaiṣṇava songs of the Āzhvārs[T].

The fourteen sounds produced by Naṭarāja's drum are the means by which the reality of Śiva is to be known and experienced within us in all its plenitude. Nandikeśvara has commented upon the fourteen sounds in his *Śivabhaktisūtra.*

Among those present at Naṭarāja's dance was Pāṇini. His story is told in the *Bṛhatkathā* which was written by Guṇāḍhya in the Prākṛt called Paiśācī. Kṣemendra produced a summary of it in Sanskrit and, based on it, Somadeva Bhaṭṭa wrote the *Kathā-sarit-sāgara.* It is the source of some of the stories of *The Arabian Nights, Pañcatantra,* and *Aesop's Fables. Peruṅkathai* is a Tamiḷ version, the title being Tamiḷ for *Bṛhatkathā.*

The story of Pāṇini is told in the *Kathā-sarit-sāgara*. In Pāṭaliputra (modern Patna), in Magadha, there were two men called Varṣopādhyāya and Upavarṣopādhyāya — the second was the younger of the two. Upākosalā was Upavarṣopādhyāyā's daughter. Pāṇini and Vararuci were Varṣopādhyāya's students. Pāṇini made little progress in his lessons. So his teacher asked him to go to the Himālaya and practise austerities. The student did so and through the grace of Īśvara received the power to witness the tāṇḍava[S] dance of Naṭarāja. With this divine gift of the Lord, Pāṇini indeed saw the tāṇḍava and heard the fourteen sounds at its conclusion. For him these sounds meant the fourteen cardinal sūtras of grammar and on them he based his *Aṣṭādhyāyi*. As its very name suggests, this work, which is the source book of Sanskrit grammar, has eight chapters.

The fourteen sounds are recited at the upākarma[S] ceremony. Since they emanated from the drum of Maheśvara (Naṭarāja), they are called "Māheśvara-sūtras". Human beings can produce only inarticulate sounds on the musical instruments played by them. The hand of Parameśvara is verily the Nādabrahman and Śabdabrahman incarnate, so his *cāppu* on the ḍamaruka at the conclusion of his tāṇḍava sounded as a series (garland) of fourteen letters:

1. a i uṇ; 2. ṛḷk; 3. e oṅ; 4. ai auc; 5. hayavaraṭ; 6. laṇ; 7. ñama ṅaṇa nam; 8. jha bha ñ; 9. gha ḍa dha ṣ; 10. ja ba ga ḍa da ś; 11. kha pha cha ṭha tha caṭatav; 12. kapay; 13. śa ṣa sar; 14. hal— iti Māheśvarāṇi sūtraṇi[7].

When you listen to these sūtras at the upākarma ceremony, you are amused. You repeat them after the priest without knowing what they are all about. They are the concluding strokes Śiva made on his drum as he stopped dancing, stopped whirling round and round.

We say, don't we, that the anklets sound "*jal-jal*", that the ḍamaru sounds "*timu-timu*", that the *tavil* sounds "*dhum-dhum*"? These are not of course the sounds actually produced by the respective drums. Even so the words give us some idea of the beats. We don't say "*pi-pi*" to describe the sound of a drum or "*dhum-dhum*" to describe the sound of a pipe. The sound produced by plucking the strings of instruments like the viṇa is usually described as "*toyn-toyng*". From this it follows that, though the musical instruments do not produce articulate sounds, they create the impression of producing the phonemes of human speech. If this be so in the case of instruments played by humans, why should not the drum beaten by Naṭarāja during his pañcakṛtya dance[8] produce articulate sounds?

How did Pāṇini make use of the fourteen sounds? He created an index[9] from the sūtras to vocalise the letters or syllables together. According to the arrangement made by him, the first letter or syllable of a sūtra voiced with the last letter or syllable of another sūtra will indicate the letters or syllables in between. For example, the first syllable of "hayavaraṭ", "ha", and the last letter of "hal", "l", together make "hal". This embraces all the consonants in between. Similarly, the first letter of the first sūtra, "a", and the last letter of the fourth sūtra together form "ac" — this includes all the vowels. The first letter of the first sūtra and the last letter of the fourteenth sūtra together form "al" — it includes all letters.

"Halāntasya" is one of the sūtras of *Aṣṭādhyāyī.* "Al" itself has come to mean writing.

"A-kāra" is the first letter in all languages. In Urdu it is *alif;* in Greek it is alpha. Both are to be derived from "al". So too "alphabet" in English. Here is another fact to support the view that, once upon a time, the Vedic religion was prevalent all over the world.

We know thus that the prime source of grammar is constituted by the Māheśvara-sūtras emanating from the drum of Naṭarāja. Since Parameśvara was the cause of the śabda-śāstras (all sciences relating to sound, speech), "grammar pavilions" have been built in Śiva temples, but not in Viṣṇu shrines.

By the side of Naṭarāja are Patañjali and Vyāghrapāda. I had been to a temple near Śirkāzhi (in Tamiḷ Nāḍu). There, beside Naṭarāja, were Patañjali and Vyāghrapāda. Beneath their images were inscribed their names. Patañjali's name was seen here as "*Padaṁcollī*" — the error must be attributed to the ignorance of the man who had inscribed the names. I was however happy that ironically enough, this name befitted the sage and that even ignorance was the cause of something appropriate. "Padam" has the meaning of grammar [as in] "padavākya pramāṇa." Here "pada" means grammar. So "*Padaṁcollī*" [the second half of the name is Tamiḷ] means one who "says" grammar.

When I saw this inscription I was reminded of another thing. We speak of "guṇākṣara-nyāya". "Guṇa" here means an insect like the white ant which eats into wood and palm-leaves. Sometimes in this process letters are formed accidentally. If something meaningful results from an act committed unconsciously or unwittingly it is said to be according to the "guṇāksara-nyāya". This term is thus applicable to Patañjali being written as "*Padaṁcollī*".

Some years ago I happened to see the *Sāhitya-Ratnākara.* The author of this poetical work is Yajñanārāyaṇa Dīkṣita who composed it 400 years ago during the reign of Raghunātha Nāyaka of Tañjāvūr. Dīkṣita was a great devotee of Śiva and in one of his hymns there is a reference to grammar.

Ādau pāṇi-ninādato'kṣara-samāmnāyopadeśena yaḥ
Śabdānāmanuśāsanānyakalayat śāstreṇa sūtrātmanā
Bhāṣyam tasya ca pādahamsakaravaiḥ prauḍhāśayam tam gurum
Śabdārthapratipatti-hetumaniśam Candrāvataṁsam bhaje

— Sāhitya-Ratnākara, 11.124

"Akṣara-samāmnayam" in this stanza means grammar, a grouping together of letters. Īśvara's breath constitutes the Vedas. The wind produced by his hand [as he beats the drum] is "Akṣara-Veda", the Māheśvara-sūtras. It is called "śabdānuśāsanam". "Pāṇi-ninādataḥ" means "produced sounds with your hands" or "the sounds came by to Pāṇini". Thus the words have two meanings. The idea is that Pāṇini created his grammar with the sounds produced by Īśvara with his hand.

The stanza goes on to say: "With the movement of your hand the sūtras of grammar were created and with the movement of your feet[10] its commentary has been produced." Patañjali, author of the *Mahābhāṣya,* was an incarnation of the primordial serpent Ādiśeṣa. Ādiśeṣa is now the anklet of Parameśvara. It is in keeping with this that the poet says that Śiva created the bhāṣya with the movement of his feet. He concludes by remarking that sound and meaning originate in Śiva.

In this way, Śiva is the prime source of grammar. That is why there are maṇḍapas in his temples where vyākaraṇa is to be taught.

Notes & References

1 "Naṭa" is a dancer or actor; "viṭa" is one who is conversant with music and literature and who also serves as the royal jester; "gāyaka" is a musician.

2 Not to be understood as a dictionary arranged in alphabetical order.

3 Work on the temple was completed in A.D. 1009.

4 *Cāppu* in Carṇāṭic music means beating with the open palm the upper part of the right-hand side of the mṛdanga. It represents the final beats.

5 Na tu mām śakyase draṣṭum anenai'va svacakṣuṣā
Divyam dadāmi te cakṣuḥ paśya me yogam aiśvaram

— Bhagavadgītā, 11.8.

6 "Sanaka and others" : the four "mind-born sons" of Brahmā, apart from Sanaka, are Sananda, Sanātana and Sanatkumāra.

7 अइउण् । ऋलृक् एओङ् । ऐओच् । हयवरट् । लण् । ञमङणनम् । झभञ् । घढधष् । जबगडदश् । खफछठथ-चटतव् । कपय् । शषसर् । हल् । इति माहेश्वराणि सूत्राणि ॥

8 The dance of Naṭarāja is called "pañca-kṛtya paramānanda tāṇḍava". Through this dance

he performs the function of creation with the sound of his drum; protects the world with his abhaya-hasta (the "fear not" mudra); carries out the function of destruction with the fire held in one of his hands; with the foot placed on Mūsalaka he accomplishes the function of tirodhāna or tirobhāva, that is concealment or Māyā; and the fifth function of anugraha or conferring blessings on devotees he performs by pointing a finger at his sacred left foot.

[9] The word the Paramaguru himself uses here is "saṁjña".

[10] What is called "footwork" in a dance.

Chapter 3

Works on Grammar

In the stanza [in the previous chapter] we saw that the poet calls Śiva "Candrāvataṁsa". It means the god who has the moon for a head ornament. "Candraśekhara" and "Induśekhara" mean the same. Remarkably enough, "Induśekhara" occurs in the titles of two grammatical works. One is *Śabdenduśekharam,* and the other *Paripoṣenduśekharam.* A student who has read grammar up to *Śabdenduśekharam* is considered a master of the subject.

If there are about thirty books on Śikṣā, there are any number on grammar. Foremost among them are Pāṇini's sūtras, Patañjali's bhāṣya for it and Vararuci's vārtika (mentioned earlier). I make this statement in the belief that Vararuci and Kātyāyana are the same person. Some think that they are not. Vararuci was one of the "Nine Gems" of Vikramāditya's court.

Bhartṛhari's *Vākyapādīyam* is also an important grammatical treatise. There are said to be nine [notable] Sanskrit grammar works, "nava-vyākaraṇa". Hanumān is believed to have learned them from the sun god. Śri Rāma praises him as "nava-vyākaraṇa-vettā". One of these nine works is *Aindram* authored by Indra. It is said that the basic Tamiḷ grammar book, the *Tolkāppiyam,* follows *Aindram.*

Chapter 4

Sanskrit and Tamiḷ Grammar

Just as "*ilakkaṇam*", the Tamiḷ word for grammar, is derived from the Sanskrit "lakṣana", so too a number of other words that have to do with grammar in that language are of Sanskritic origin. For instance, there are two terms used in Tamiḷ grammar, *pakuti (pahuti)* and *vikuti (vihuti).* To illustrate: in the word "*Rāmanukku*" (for Rāman), "*Rāman*" is *pakuti* and "*ku*" is "*vikuti*". Both terms *pakuti* and *vikuti* are derived from Sanskrit grammar. "How do you say so?" it might be asked. "Is not *pakuti* an original Tamiḷ word derived from "*pakuttal*?"

Pakuti in the sense of that which has been divided is indeed a Tamil word. But I say that there is another *pakuti* that is a corrupt form of the Sanskrit "prakṛti". It is in the sense of "prakṛti" that the word "*Rāman*" in "*Rāmanukku*" is described as *pakuti.* As for "*vikuti*" it is from the Sanskrit "vikrti": there is no such word as "*vikuttal*" in Tamiḷ corresponding to *pakuttal.* From the undisputed fact that *vikuti* is from vikṛti, we may conclude for certain that *pakuti* is from prakṛti.

(Vikṛti is also called "pratyaya", that which gives many meanings to the same prakṛti. When it is said "*Rāmanai aḍitten*" — (I) beat *Rāman* — the pratyaya "*ai*" added makes *Rāman* the person who is beaten. If it is said *Rāmanāl aḍipaṭṭen*— (I) was beaten by *Rāman*— the prakṛti *Rāman* with the *āl* makes him the one who beat.)

It is not my purpose to claim that Sanskrit is superior toTamiḷ. When do feelings of superiority arise to make us happy? When we are conscious of differences between what we believe is "ours" and what we believe is "theirs". Were we to have a racial bias, we would be tempted to speak in appreciative terms of what is "ours" and to deprecate what is "theirs." If we realise that to harbour feelings based on racial differences is itself wrong, that our languages have sprung from the same family, from the same cultural tradition, there will be no cause for speaking highly of one language at the expense of another.

On the subject of grammar I have mentioned certain facts and it is not my intention to elevate one language above another.

Chapter 5

Sanskrit: The Universal Language

Sanskrit is the language of all mankind; it is an international language and also the language of the gods. The gods are called "gīrvāṇas"; so Sanskrit is called "Gairvāṇī". While the emperor of Tamiḷ poetry, Kambar[T], describes it as the "devabhāṣā", the Sanskrit poet Daṇḍin[S] calls it "daivī vāk" (divine speech) in his *Kāvyādarśa*: "Samskṛtam nāma daivī vāk."

Sanskrit has no syllable that is indistinct or unclear. Take the English "word". It has neither a distinct "e-kāra" nor "o- kāra". There are no such words in Sanskrit. Neither is the "r" in "word" pronounced distinctly nor is it silent.

Sanskrit, besides, has no word that cannot be traced to its root. Whatever the word it can be broken into its syllables to elucidate its meaning. Sanskrit is sonorous and auspicious to listen to. You must not be ill disposed towards such a language, taking the narrow view that it belongs to a few people.

To speak Sanskrit is not to make some noises and somehow convey your message. The sounds, the phonemes, in it are, as it were, purified and the words and sentences refined by being subjected to analysis. That is why the language is called "Sanskrit" [Saṁskṛtam]. The purpose of Śikṣā, and in greater measure of Vyākaraṇa, is to accomplish such refinement.

To speak the language of Sanskrit itself means to be refined, to be cultured. As the language of the gods it brings divine grace. The sounds of Sanskrit create beneficial vibrations of the nāḍis[S] and strengthen the nervous system, thereby contributing to our health.

Chapter 6

Linguistic Studies and Religion

Śikṣā, Vyākaraṇa and the subjects I have yet to deal with — Chandas and Nirukta — are Vedāngas (limbs of the Vedas) connected with language. After I said that I would deal with matters basic to our religion, I have been speaking about linguistic studies and grammar. Next I am going to deal with prosody. By works on religion we ordinarily mean those [directly] relating to God, worship, devotion, jñāna, dharma and so on. Would not the right thing for me then be to speak about such works?

When we dealt with the Vedas a number of matters cropped up, matters regarded as germane to religion. Religion will find a prominent place in the subjects that I have yet to speak about, Kalpa, Mīmāṁsā, the Purāṇas and Dharmaśāstra. But in between has arisen the science of language that has *apparently* no connection with religion.

In the Vedic view everything is connected with the Lord. There is no question of dividing subjects into "religious" and "non-religious". Even the science of medicine, Āyurveda, which pertains to physical well-being, is ultimately meant for Ātmic uplift — or for that matter, military science (Dhanurveda). That is why they were made part of traditional lore. So too political economy which is also an Ātma-śāstra.

Why are works belonging to these fields held in great esteem? All subjects, all works, that teach a man to bring order, refinement and purity in every aspect of his life and help him thus to take the path to liberation are regarded as religious in character.

Sound is the highest of the perceived forms of the Paramātman and language is obviously connected with it. It is the concern of Śikṣā and Vyākaraṇa to refine and clarify it and make it a means for the well-being of our Self.

Grammar is associated with the Śabdabrahman. Worship of the Nādabrahman, which is the goal of music, is a branch of this. If sounds are well discerned and employed in speech they will serve not only the purpose of communication but also of cleansing us inwardly. The science of language is helpful here.

I have already mentioned that Patañjali's commentary on Pāṇini's sūtras is called the *Mahābhāṣya.* The prefix "Mahā" in the name of the work is an indication of the high degree of importance given to grammar in our tradition. Illustrious teachers have written commentaries on the Vedas, on the *Brahmasūtra,* on the Upaniṣads, on the Bhagavadgītā, and so on. But none of these has "mahā" prefixed to it. There is a saying that a scholar derives as much happiness from learning the *Mahābhāṣya* as from ruling an empire.

Mahābhāṣyam vā paṭhanīyam
Mahārājyam vā śāsanīyam

I recently came across another piece of evidence like the Veṅgi inscription to prove how in the old days our rulers nurtured and propagated the science of grammar.

Dhār was a state in the former Central Provinces (now a part of Madhya Pradeś). It is the same as Dhāra which was the capital of Bhojarāja who was a great patron of arts and who made lavish gifts to poets and artists. There is a mosque in the town of Dhār now. Once a cave was discovered in the mosque which, on examination, revealed some writings in Sanskrit. But the department of epigraphy could not carry out any investigations until some years after freedom. Then, with the permission of the authorities of the mosque, they studied their finding.

To their amazement they saw a wheel inside with verses dealing with grammar inscribed on it in the form of a chart. The mosque stands today where a temple to Sarasvatī stood during Bhojarāja's time. The idea behind the wheel is that the science of language (grammar) must form part of the temple to Sarasvatī, the goddess of speech — and grammar is the Vedapuruṣa's mouth. They say that grammar could be learned at a glance from this wheel. It is because the science of language is worthy of worship that the wheel inscribed with grammar was installed in the temple. With the blessings of Vāgdevī (Sarasvatī) we have obtained the wheel, though long after the mosque was built at the site. The department of epigraphy has published the text of the inscription with an English translation.

We learn thus that śāstras like grammar were not regarded merely as of worldly imterest but in fact considered worthy of worship. That is why rulers promoted them.

Part Eight

CHANDAS

Chapter 1

Foot of the Vedapuruṣa

We so often hear people [Tamils] speak of "*Chanda-t-Tamizh*". Men of devotion[1] say that the praises of the Lord must be sung in "*Chanda-t- Tamizh*". "*Chanda(m)*" is derived from "Chandas".

"Chandas", as I have already said, means the Vedas. Bhagavān says in the Gītā that the Vedas are leaves of the *pīpal* tree called Creation — "Chandāṁsi yasya parṇāni"[2]. Instead of "Veda", the Lord uses the word "Chandas". However, the "Chandas" I am going to speak about does not mean the Vedas but prosody and represents the foot of the Vedapuruṣa.

The Ṛgveda and the Sāmaveda are entirely poetical in form. The Yajurveda consists of both prose and poetry. It is because poetry forms their major part that the Vedas are called Chandas.

The tailor takes your measurement to make your suit. He will not otherwise be able to cut the cloth properly. Similarly, poetry gives form to our thoughts and feelings. Your shirt has to be so many inches wide, so many inches long, isn't that so? Similarly, poetry also has its measurement expressed in "feet" and number of syllables. The śāstra that deals with such measurement is "Chandas" and the text on which it is chiefly based is the *Chandas Sūtra* by Piṅgaḷa. People who have received initiation into a mantra touch their head with their hand, mentioning the name of the sage associated with the mantra, touch their nose mentioning the chandas and touch their heart mentioning the deity invoked.

All Vedic mantras in verse are Chandas. Non-Vedic poetry is in the form of "ślokas". Prose is called "gadya" and poetry "padya". In Tamiḷ, poetry is called *"śeyyuḷ"*, in Telugu "*padyam*". The term chandas also refers to poetic metre (prosody). There are many types of "vṛtta" (metre) in poetry. Ślokas are of course vṛttas. There is a metre called "Anusṭubh" in which are composed the Rāmāyaṇa and the Purāṇas.

There are rules governing the number of feet in each stanza, and the number of syllables in each foot. The metre "Āryā" is based on mātras[S], syllables short and long. Take the word "Rāma": the long syllable "Rā" is two mātras while the short one "ma" is one mātra. There are stanzas in which each foot is determined by the number of syllables, no matter whether they are short or long. Other metres are based on mātras.

Notes & References

[1] The word the Paramaguru actually uses for "men of devotion" is the Tamiḷ *aḍiyārs,* meaning those who support the feet of the Lord with their head or those who are at the feet of the Lord.

[2] *Ūrdhvamūlam adhaḥśākham aśvattham prāhuṛ avyayam*
Chandāṁsi yasya parṇāni yastaṁ Veda sa Vedavit.

— Bhagavadgītā, 15.1

[3] Vedic metres are described here and there in the Vedic catalogues called *Ṛg-sarva-Anukramaṇī, Atharvavedīya Bṛhat-sarva anukramaṇikā, Bṛhat Devatā* and the *Ṛg-Prātiśākhya.* The prosody of other types of poetry is dealt with in *Chandomanjarī* and *Vṛttaratnākara.* — Ra. Ga.

Chapter 2

Pāda or Foot

I said Chandas is the foot of the Vedapuruṣa. Poetry also has its foot. In Tamiḻ poetry there are *"īraḍikkural"* (stanzas with two feet), *nālaḍiyār* (stanzas with four feet), etc: *"aḍi"* here has the same meaning as "pāda", that is foot. *Nālaḍiyār* does not mean four *aḍiyars*. Great devotees are called *aḍiyars* because they lie at the lotus feet of the Lord. (In Sanskrit too we have similar terms like "Ācāryapāda", "Govindapāda" and "Bhagavatpāda". *Nālaḍiyār* means stanzas with four feet.

If "foot" is called "pāda" or "pada" in Sanskrit, it is known as *"aḍi"* in Tamiḻ. (It goes without saying that "foot" is the English equivalent.) A stanza must have a certain number of feet and its metre must have a certain number of letters or syllables. "Pāda" ("pada"), *"aḍi"*, "foot" — thus all languages have words with the same meaning to denote a line of a stanza. The realisation that there is something common to all mankind, something that shows the unity of the human race, is inwardly satisfying.

One-fourth of a mantra or a stanza is called a "pāda". In Tamiḻ one out of four parts is known as *"kāl"* (that is "foot"). The foot (leg) forms one-fourth of the human body. From the head to the waist is one-half of the body, and from the waist to the feet is another half. And half of the latter half, i.e. one-fourth is *kāl* in Tamiḻ or foot (leg). The waist is called *"arai"* in that language, meaning half.

In Tamiḻ *"kāl"* usually means the entire leg and *"padam"* or *"pādam* is used to denote the foot. But in some contexts *kāl* is also used in the sense of the foot. For instance, in the terms *"ullaṅgāl"* and *"puraṅgāl* (sole and upper part of the foot respectively) only the foot is referred to. In Sanskrit too "pāda" means both leg and foot.

Chapter 3

Feet and Syllables

A Vedic mantra or the stanza of an ordinary poem is divided into four parts. In most metres there are four feet and each foot is divided into the same number of syllables or mātras. When the feet are not equal we have what is called a metre that is "viṣama": "vi+sama" = "viṣama". "Sama[1]" indicates a state of non- difference, of evenness. When we do something improper, departing from our impartial "middle position", our action is characterised as "viṣama". The word is also used in the sense of "craftiness" or "cunning". But the literal meaning of "viṣama" is "unequal".

To repeat, if all pādas of a stanza are not uniform they are said to be "viṣama". If alternate lines or pādas are equal they are called "ardha-sama-vṛtta". The first and second are unequal here, so too the third and the fourth. But the first and the third and the second and the fourth are equal.

In most poems the pādas are equal. Let me illustrate with a śloka[S] with which, I suppose, all of you are familiar:

The four feet of this stanza :

1. Śuklāmbaradharam Viṣṇum
2. Śaśivarṇam caturbhujam
3. Prasannavadanam dhyāyet
4. Sarvavighnopaśāntaye

Each pāda in this has eight syllables.

Only vowels and consonants in conjunction with vowels are to be counted as syllables; other consonants are not to be counted. Then alone will you get the figure eight. The eight syllables in the first pāda are : 1. śu; 2. klām; 3. ba; 4. ra; 5. dha; 6. ram; 7. Vi; 8. ṣṇum. The other pādas will have similarly eight syllables each.

The stanza with four feet, each foot of eight syllables, is "Anuṣṭubh", which metre is used in the Vedas and in poetical works of a later period.

Note

[1] Literally, "same", "identical".

Chapter 4

How Poetry was Born

There is no tonal variation in poetry as there is in Vedic mantras. The unaccented poetic stanza corresponding to the accented Vedic mantra owes its origin to Vālmīki, but its discovery was not the result of any conscious effort on his part.

One day Vālmīki happened to see a pair of krauncа[1] birds sporting perched on the branch of a tree. Soon one of the birds fell to the arrow of a hunter. The sage felt pity and compassion but these soon gave way to anger. He cursed the hunter, the words coming from him spontaneously: "O hunter, you killed a krauncа bird sporting happily with its mate. May you not have everlasting happiness."

Mā niṣāda pratiṣṭhām tvam
Agamaḥ śāśvatīḥ samāḥ
Yat krauncamithunādekam
Avadhīḥ kāmamohitam

Unpremeditatedly, out of his compassion for the birds, Vālmīki cursed the hunter. But, at once, he regretted it. "Why did I curse the hunter so?" When he was brooding thus, a remarkable truth dawned on him. Was he not a sage with divine vision? He realised that the very words of his curse had the garb of a poetic stanza in the Anustubh metre. That the words had come from his lips, without his being aware of them himself (in the same way as he had, without his knowing, felt compassion and anger in succession), caused him amazement.

It occurred to him that the stanza he had unconsciously composed had another meaning. The words aimed at the hunter were also words addressed to Mahāviṣṇu. How? "O consort of Lakṣmī, you will win eternal fame by having slain one of a couple who was deluded by desire." Rāvaṇa and his wife Maṇḍodarī are the couple referred to here and Rāvaṇa was deluded by his evil desire for Sītā. Śrī Rāma won everlasting fame by slaying him. Without his being aware of it, the words came to Vālmīki as poetry. Realising it all to be the will of Īśvara, the sage composed the Rāmāyaṇa in the same metre.

The "śloka" (without the Vedic tonal variation) was born in this manner. Vālmīki was filled with joy that he had come upon the śloka as a medium that facilitated the expression of the highest of thoughts in a form that made it easy to remember like the Vedas themselves.

Prose is not easily retained in memory, not so poetry composed in metrical form. That is why in ancient times everything was put down in verse. Prose developed [in any significant sense] only after the advent of the printing press after which books began to be produced in large numbers for ready reference, obviating the need to memorise everything.

However it be, in conveying an idea or a message (or in imparting information) poetry has greater beauty and greater power. The Rāmāyaṇa was the first poetical work[2], hence its name "Ādikāvya". We received the gift of chandas as the prasāda[S] of Bhagavān (as the Lord's grace). Chandas helped in the birth of various metrical forms used in the hymns to various deities, in the Purāṇas and in other poetical works.

Notes

[1] Egrets(?)

[2] Vedic hymns like sūktas are not regarded as constituting a "poetical work". Besides, the Vedic mantras were not "composed" but "seen" by the ṛsis.

Chapter 5

Some Metrical Forms

"Indravajrā", "Upendravajrā", "Bhujangavijṛmbhita", "Sragdharā" are some of the metres used in devotional and other poetical works. Some of them are intricate and only highly gifted people are capable of composing in them.

As mentioned earlier, the foot of a stanza with eight syllables is Anustubh. With nine syllables it is "Bṛhatī" and with ten "Paṅkti". "Triṣṭubh" has eleven syllables and "Jagatī" twelve. We have a 26-syllable metre ("Bhujangavijṛmbhita") which belongs to the category of "Utkṛti". Beyond this is "Daṇḍaka" of which there are several types. The metre in which Apparsvāmigal's *Tiru-t-taṇḍagam* is composed is related to this metre.

Some metres have beautiful names. In poems composed in a certain metre the flow of words reminds us of a playful tiger lunging forward; the metre is appropriately called "Śārdūlavikrīḍita". "Śardūla" means a tiger; "vikrīdita" is playfulness. (This metre, belonging to the category of "Atidhṛti", has 19 syllables.) Each pāda in it is divided into 12 and 7 syllables. Ādi Śankara's *Śivānandalaharī* is partly in this metre (a number of verses from the 28th stanza onwards). The initial verses of the part called "Stuti- śatakam" of the *Mūka-Pañcaśatī* (which is a hymn to Kāmākṣī) are in this metre. The concluding one hundred verses, "*Mandasmita-śatakam*", are entirely in this metre. "Bhujangaprayāta" is the name of another metre which suggests a snake (bhujanga) gliding along. Our Ācārya's *Subrahmaṇya-bhujangam* is in this metre. It belongs to the Jagatī type with 12 syllables a foot, divided into six and six as in

Ma-yū-rā-dhi-rū-ḍham
Ma-hā-vā-kya-gū-ḍham

Our Ācārya's *Saundaryalaharī* is in the Śikhariṇī metre. It has 17 syllables in each pāda. (It belongs to the category of Atyaṣṭi.) The 17 syllables are divided into two parts of six and 11. The "Pādāravinda-śatakam" of the *Mūka-Pañcaśatī* is in this metre. The metre called "Sragdharā" suggests a flow of words breaking through the floodgates of poetry. It has 21 syllables (belonging to the "Prakṛti" class) and each pāda has three sets of seven syllables. Our Ācārya's hymns to Śiva and Viṣṇu (describing them from foot to head and head to foot -- pādādi-keśānta and keśādi-pādānta) are in this metre.

I mentioned "Indravajrā" first. It belongs to the Triṣṭubh category with 11 syllables in each pāda. Another 11-syllable metre is "Upendravajrā". A mixture of both is "Upajāti": Kālidāsa's *Kumārasaṁbhavam* is in this metre.

All these metres belong to the post-Vedic period and are employed in poetical works as well as in hymns to various deities. "Gāyatrī", "Uṣṇik", "Anustubh", "Paṅkti", "Triṣṭubh" and "Jagatī" are Vedic metres.

"Gāyatrī" is a mahā-mantra, the king of mantras. A mantra is usually named after the deity it invokes. "Śiva-Pañcākṣarī", "Nārāyaṇa-Aṣṭākṣarī", "Rāma-Trayodaśī": in each of these the name of the deity as well as the number of syllables in the mantra are combined. The deity for Gāyatrī is Savitā. Gāyatrī is the name of the metre also. The metre too, one should infer from this, has divine power expressed through the sound and tone of a mantra.

Gāyatrī, unlike most other mantras and ślokas, has only three feet. Each foot has eight syllables and altogether there are 24 syllables. Because it has only three pādas or feet it is called "Tripadā-Gāyatrī". There are other Gāyatrīs also. The first Vedic mantra, "Agnimīḷe", is in the Gāyatrī metre.

(The 24-syllable Gāyatrī metre used in poetry and non-Vedic hymns has four pādas, each of six syllables. Uṣṇik has also four padas, each of seven syllables.)

So far I have spoken about metres based on the number of syllables, that is without worrying about whether a syllable is long or short. In prosody the long and short syllables are called "guru" and "laghu" respectively. Poems that make no distinction between "short" and "long" are called "vṛttas": those based on mātras are called "jāti". In the latter type, a short syllable is one mātra and a long syllable is two mātras. Instead of the number of syllables what matters here is the number of mātras.

The "Āryā-śatakam" of *Mūka-Pañcaśatī* is in the Āryā metre. Ambā, as Āryā, belongs to the most exalted plane; so it is proper that the verses used in singing her praises should also belong to an equally high order. That is why they are in the Āryā metre, which is based on mātras and not on the number of syllables. If you go by the number of syllables you are likely to be misled into thinking that the metre differs from verse to verse.

Chapter 6

Uses of Chandas Śāstra

Śikṣā śāstra may be said to be a "guard" to ensure the right enunciation of a (Vedic) mantra. But it is Chandas that determines whether the form of the mantra is right. Of course the form of a mantra can never be wrong. The mantras, as mentioned so often, were not created by the sages and are not the product of their thinking. It was Bhagavān who caused them to be revealed to them. Man, beast, tree and other sentient creatures and insentient objects of creation exist as they should be according to the law of nature. In the same way, the metre of a Vedic mantra must be naturally correct. However, Chandas helps us to find out whether a mantra or sūkta that is being taught or chanted has come down to us in its true form. We may check the hymn according to its metre and if we find it faulty we may correct it in consultation with people who are well-versed in such matters.

Apart from the mantras, which appeared on their own, are the compositions of poets. Chandas is of help in giving shape to poetic thought and imagination. Like tāla to music is chandas to poetry.

It is because poetry is composed according to a certain measure and its rhythm determined in a certain order of syllables that it acquires a definite form. It is also easy to memorise. Modern society is discarding all those rules of discipline meant to give it a definite character and purpose. In keeping with this new trend, poetry too is being written without any metre and "poets" compose as they please. People do not realise that to be free means to be firmly attached to a system, that discipline is the road to a higher freedom.

Chandas is the means by which we ensure that the Vedic mantra is preserved in its original form, it being impossible to add one letter to it or take away another. The very purpose of the Vedas is the raising up of the Self. Must we then permit a single sound to be added to it or to be taken away?

Chapter 7

Foot for the Vedas, Nose for the Mantras

Each mantra has a deity (the deity it invokes), its own metre and its own seer (the seer who revealed it to the world). Mentioning the name of the ṛṣi and touching our head with our hand have their own significance, that of holding his feet with our head. We first pay obeisance to the sages because it is from them that we received the mantras. We then mention the chandas or metre of the hymn and touch our nose with our hand. Chandas protects the sound of a mantra and is like its vital breath. So we place our hand on that part of our body with which we breathe. Without breath there is no life. While for all the Vedas taken as a whole Śikṣā is the nose and Chandas the foot, for the mantras proper Chandas is the nose.

When we commence to chant a mantra we must meditate on its adhidevatā, or presiding deity, and feel his presence in our hearts. This is the reason why we touch our hearts as we mention the name of the deity.

The Vedapuruṣa stands on Chandas. "Chandaḥ pādo Vedasya" : the Vedic mantras are supported by Chandas.

Part Nine

NIRUKTA

Ear of the Vedapuruṣa

Nirukṭa serves the purpose of a Vedic dictionary, or "kośa". A dictionary is also called a "nighanṭu", which term is used in Tamiḷ also. Nirukta, which deals with the origin of words, their roots, that is with etymology, is the ear of the Vedapuruṣa. It explains the meaning of rare words in the Vedas and how or why they are used in a particular context. Many have contributed to Nirukta, the work of Yāska being the most important.

Take the word "hṛdaya" (heart). The Vedas themselves trace its origin. "Hṛdayam" is "hṛdi ayam": it means that the Lord dwells in the heart. "Hṛd" itself denotes the physical heart. But with the suffixing of "ayam" — with the Lord residing in it — its Ātmic importance is suggested. The purpose of any śāstra is to take you to the Supreme Being. "Hṛdaya" is so called because Parameśvara resides in "hṛd". Thus each and every word has a reason behind it. Nirukta makes an inquiry into words and reveals their significance.

"Dhātu" means "root" in English. In that language one speaks of the root only of verbs, not of nouns. In Sanskrit all words have dhātus. Such words, transformed or modified, must have been adopted in other languages. That is why we do not know the roots of many words in these tongues. After all, such an exercise would be possible only if the words in question belonged naturally to them. Take the English word "hour". Phonetically it should be pronounced "h o u r" ("h" being not silent) or "h o a r". At one time the word indeed must have been pronounced "hoar". "Hora-śāstra" is the name of a science in Sanskrit, "hora" being from "ahorātram" (day and night). "Hora" is 2 1/2 nāḍikas[S] or one hour. The English "hour" is clearly from this word. In the same way "heart" is from "hṛd". There are so many words like this which could be traced to Sanskrit. It must have taken a long time for words in other languages to evolve into their present form. That is why those who speak them find it difficult to discover their origin [or root].

How does it help to listen to someone speaking a language without understanding what he says? It is as good as not listening to him. In other words it is like being deaf. Nirukta finds the meaning of words by going to the root of each. That is why it is called the ear of the Vedapuruṣa: it is the ear of Śruti which itself is heard by the ear.

Western scholars learned Vyākaraṇa and Nirukta from *paṇḍits* in Kāśī and acquainted themselves with the origin of words as described in the latter śāstra. From this they developed the new science of philology. It is primarily from our Vyākaraṇa and Nirukta that the linguistic science has developed.

From their researches, Western scholars have arrived at the conclusion that all languages have one source. People all over the world are the descendants of the original inhabitants of the area where this primal language was spoken. There are differences of opinion with regard to this area, the home of this tongue. We need have no worry about it. After all, we believe that all places on earth are our home. "*Yādum mūre!*"[1] is a famous Tamiḷ declaration. "Svadeśo bhuvanatrayam" — the three worlds are our motherland.

Note

[1] "*Yādum mūre, yāvarum keḷir!*" ("All places are our places and all people are our kin". Or, to paraphrase the statement: "The whole world is my motherland and all mankind my family." This celebrated declaration is attributed to Kaṇiyan Pūṅkunran and occurs in the *Puranānūru* -- see Tamiḷ Glossary. It is an expression of the universal spirit that inspires the Tamiḷ heritage.

Part Ten

JYOTIṢA

Chapter 1

Eye of the Vedapuruṣa

Of the fourteen branches of learning basic to our Vedic religion, I have so far dealt with Śikṣā, Vyākaraṇa, Chandas and Nirukta[1]. These four form part of Ṣaḍaṅga (the six limbs of the Vedas). I will now speak about Jyotiṣa, it being the first of the remaining two of the Ṣadaṅga. Jyotiṣa, which is the science of celestial bodies, and the eye of the Vedapuruṣa, consists of three "skandhas" or sections. So it is called "Skandha-trayātmakam". Sages like Garga, Nārada and Parāśara have written saṁhitās (treatises) on this subject. The sun god, in disguise, taught the science to Maya, the carpenter of the asuras. The work incorporating his teachings is called the *Sūryasiddhānta*. There are treatises on astronomy written by celestials and sages and ordinary mortals. Of them some are by Varāhamihira, Āryabhaṭa and Bhāskarācārya. In recent times we had Sundareśvara Śrautin who wrote a work called *Siddhānta-Kaustubham*.

Why is Jyotiṣa regarded as the eye of the Vedapuruṣa?

What purpose is served by the eye? Near objects may be perceived by the sense of touch. With our eyes we learn about distant objects. Just as our eyes help us to know objects that are distant in space (that is just as we see distant objects with our eyes), Jyotiṣa śāstra helps us to find out the position of the heavenly bodies that are distant in time (their configuration many years ago in the past or many years hence in the future).

We can find out directly the positions of the sun and the moon and other heavenly bodies. Just as we can know near objects, even if we are blind, by feeling them with our hands, we can learn about the position of heavenly bodies near in time even without the help of astronomy. What is 50 feet away is to be perceived by the eye. Similarly, if you want to know the position of planets 50 years ago or 50 years hence, you have to have recourse to Jyotiṣa.

We cannot, however, form a full picture of near objects only by feeling them. For instance we cannot know whether they are green or red. For this we must see them with our eyes. Again, even if we are able to see a planet with our naked eye, we will need the help of astrology to find out its effects on our life, how its position in the heavens will influence our destiny.

This is the reason why Jyotiṣa is called the eye of the Vedapuruṣa. Vedic rituals are performed according to the position of the various planets [and the sun and the moon]. There are rules to determine this. The right day and hour [muhūrta] for a function is fixed according to the position of the celestial bodies. Here again Jyotiṣa performs the function of the eye.

This Anga of the Vedas is indeed called "nayana" which word means "to lead". A blind man needs to be led by another. So it is the eye that leads. Astronomy/astrology is the eye that enables us to fix the hours for Vedic rituals.

Note

1 We must add to this list the four Vedas which were dealt with in Part Five.

Chapter 2

Astronomy and Astrology

Astronomy examines the position of the planets and other heavenly bodies. It does not concern itself with how they affect the life of the world or the individual. It is not its function to find out how far the celestial bodies are beneficial to us or how they may be made favourable to us. Such functions belong to astrology. Jyotiṣa includes both astronomy and astrology.

Telling us about the results of performing a ritual at a given time, keeping in mind the position of the planets, the sun and the moon and the nakṣatras (asterisms[1]), comes under the purview of astrology. The hours favourable to the performance of Vedic rites are determined according to calculations based on the movement of planets. All this entails mathematical work.

The measurements of the place where a sacrifice is to be conducted (yajñabhūmi) are based on certain stipulations. These must be strictly adhered to if the sacrifice is to yield the desired benefits. Mathematics developed in this way as a handmaid to the Vedic dharma.

Note

[1] Also called "lunar mansions". They are 27 in number, though there were originally 28 including Abhijit.

Chapter 3

Ancient Mathematical Treatises

Jyotiṣa, as we have seen, consists of three sections. There was a scholarly man in the Maṭha who was particularly learned in this science. We wished to honour him with a title and decided upon "Triskandha-Bhāskara"[1]. "Skandha" literally means a big branch springing from the trunk of a tree. The three skandhas of Jyotiṣa are : siddhānta, hora and saṁhitā.

The siddhānta-skandha deals with arithmetic, trigonometry, geometry and algebra. The higher mathematics developed by the West in later centuries is found in our ancient Jyotiṣa.

Arithmetic, called "vyakta-gaṇita" in Sanskrit, includes addition, subtraction, multiplication and division. "Avyakta-gaṇita" is algebra. "Jya" means the earth and "miti" is method of measurement. "Jyāmiti" evolved with the need to measure the sacrificial place: "geometry" is derived from this word. The "geo" in geography is from "jya". There is a mathematical exercise called "samīkaraṇa" which is the same as "equation".

The sixth Anga of the Vedas, Kalpa (I will speak about it later), has a great deal to do with the fifth, that is Jyotiṣa. Kalpa has a section on "śulba-sūtras". These sūtras mention the precise measurements of the "yajñavedi" (sacrificial altar). The character of the yajñabhūmi is called "cayana"[S]. The śulba-sūtras deal with a number of cayanas like, for instance, the one shaped like Garuḍa. They tell us how to construct a brick-kiln — the number of bricks required for the cayana of such and such shapes. The siddhānta-skandha is used in all this.

There is an equation in the Āpastamba śulba-sūtras which could not be proved until recently. Westerners had thought it to be faulty merely because they could not solve it. Now they have accepted it as right. That Indians had taken such great strides in mathematics, thousands of years ago, has caused amazement in the West. There are a number of old equations still to be solved.

Our śāstras mention branches of mathematics like "rekhāgaṇita", "kuṭṭaka", "angapāka", etc. "Avyakta-gaṇita" is also called "bījagaṇita".

Eight hundred years ago there lived a great mathematician called Bhāskarācārya. An incident in his life illustrates how relentless destiny is. Bhāskarācārya had a daughter called Līlāvatī. The great astrologer that he was, he found that she had "māṅgalya-doṣa"[2] in her horoscope, but he felt confident that he could change his daughter's destiny, as foreshadowed by the stars, with his ingenuity and resourcefulness as an astrologer. He decided to celebrate Līlāvatī's marriage during a lagna[S] in which all planets would be in positions favourable to the bride. This should, he thought, ensure that Līlāvatī would remain a "dīrgha- sumaṅgalī"[S].

In those days there were no clocks as we have today. A water-pot was used to measure time. It consisted of an upper as well as a lower part. The water in the upper receptacle would trickle down through a hole into the lower container. This lower part was graduated according to the unit of time then followed — *nāzhikai* (nāḍikā), one sixtieth of a day or 24 minutes. So the time of day was calculated by observing the level of the water in the lower container. ("Water-clock" and "hour-glass" are English names for such an apparatus. Since water evaporates quickly sand was sometimes used instead.)

According to the custom then prevailing, Līlāvatī's marriage was to be celebrated when she was still a child. On the appointed day, she sat beside the water-clock and bent over it fascinated by the apparatus. As she fumbled around, a pearl from her nose-stud got loosened and fell into the apparatus lodging itself in its hole. The flow of the water into the lower receptacle was reduced. So what the clock indicated as the hour fixed for the marriage was not the right one — the auspicious hour had passed. Nobody, including Līlāvatī, had noticed the pearl dropping into the water-clock. When her father and others came to know about it, it was too late. They realised that destiny could not be overcome.

Later, Bhāskarācārya wrote a mathematical treatise and named it "Līlāvatī" after his daughter. The father taught his widowed daughter mathematics and she became highly proficient in the subject. *Līlāvatī* deals with arithmetic, algebra, etc. It is a delightful book in which the problems are stated in verse as stories. Bhāskarācārya also wrote the *Siddhānta- Śiromaṇī* which deals with how the position and movement of heavenly bodies are determined.

We learn from the text of an edict in the *Prācīnalekhāmālā* that a Gūrjara (Gujarāt) king had made an endowment to popularise the works of Bhāskarācārya.

Parts 7, 8, 9 and 10 of Euclid's Geometry are believed to be lost. All the twelve books on mathematics in Sanskrit are still available. "Making additions several times is multiplication; carrying out subtraction several times is division." We remain ignorant of such easy methods of calculation dealt with in our ancient mathematical texts.

Varāhamihira lived much before Bhāskarācārya, that is about 1,500 years ago. He wrote a number of treatises including the *Bṛhat-Saṁhitā* and the *Bṛhajjātaka*. The first is a digest of many sciences, its contents being a wonderful testimony to the variety of subjects in which our forefathers had taken strides. *Bṛhajjātaka* is all about astrology.

Āryabhaṭa, famous for his *Āryabhaṭīya-Siddhānta,* also lived 1,500 years ago. The *vākya-gaṇita* now in use is said to be based on his *Siddhānta.* Varāhamihira and Āryabhaṭa are much acclaimed by mathematicians today.

All these books on mathematics also deal with the movements of celestial bodies. There are seven "grahas" according to the ancient reckoning — the five planets and the sun and the moon. Rāhu and Ketu are called "chāyā-grahas" (shadow planets) and their orbits are the opposite of the sun's and the moon's.

Notes

[1] "The Sun of the Three Sections of Jyotiṣa."

[2] "Fault" in a girl's horoscope that suggests early widowhood: this is dependent on the position of Mars.

Chapter 4

Planets, Stars

How do the planets differ from the stars? The planets revolve round the sun; the stars do not belong to the sun's "maṇḍala" [they are not part of the solar system]. If you hold a diamond in your hand and keep shaking it about, it will glitter. The stars glitter in the same way and twinkle, but the planets do not twinkle.

The sun and the stars are self-luminous. The stars dazzle like polished diamonds. The planets Jupiter and Venus shine like the bigger stars but they do not twinkle. The sun too has the brilliance of the stars [it is in fact a star]. If you gaze intently at the sun for a moment the watery haziness surrounding it will vanish. Then it will look like a luminous disc of glass floating in water and it will not be still. The moon is not like it. I will tell you how to prove that the sun twinkles. Observe the sun's light pouring down from an opening in the roof. Observe similarly the moon's light also coming into your room. You see the sun's rays showing some movement but not the moon's. The planets are also like the moon.

If the star is a big one, we may be able to see its light refracted into the seven colours (vibgyor), like the colours emanating from a brilliant diamond.

The sun is called "Saptāśva" (one with seven horses — the sun god's chariot is drawn by seven horses). It is also said that there is only one horse drawing the chariot but that it has seven different names. "Aśva" also means "kiraṇa" or ray. So "Saptāśva" could mean that the sun emits seven types of rays or colours. It is of course the same light that is split into seven colours. In the *Taittirīya Āraṇyaka* it is clearly stated that the same "aśva" or ray has seven names: "Eko aśvo vahati saptanāma."

The stars are self-luminous, while the planets shine by reflected light. The light of the stars is not still. That is how we say, "Twinkle, twinkle, little star"[1]. The stars rise in the east and set in the west. The planets too travel westward but they keep moving a bit towards the east every day. It is like a passenger walking westward on a train speeding eastward. The seven planets thus keep moving eastward.

Reference

[1] *Twinkle, twinkle, little star,*
How I wonder what you are!

— from "The Star" by Jane Taylor

Chapter 5

The Grahas and Human Life

The condition of man corresponds to the changes in the position of the nine grahas[1]. A human being does not enjoy happiness all the time nor does he always suffer hardships — that is he experiences a mixture of happiness and sorrow. While he may be pushed up to a high position today, he may be thrust down to the depths tomorrow. It is not man alone that is subject to changes of fortune. Establishments too have their ups and down, so also nations.

The ṣages saw a relationship between the position and movements of the planets and the destiny of man, the sorrow and happiness experienced by him. There is a branch of astrology called "hora-skandha". If we knew the planetary position at the time of commencing a job or enterprise, with its help we should be able to find out how it would take shape, how we would fare in it. If our horoscope is cast on the basis of the configuration of the planets at the time of our birth, our fortunes over the entire period of our life can be predicted.

Different reasons are given for the ups and downs in a man's life, for his joys and sorrows. It is similar to finding out the different causes of the ailment he suffers from. The physician will explain that the disease is due to an imbalance in the "dhātus"[2]. The mantravādin[S] will say that it is due to the gods being displeased with the patient, while the astrologer will observe that it is all in his (the patient's) stars. The *paṇḍit* versed in Dharmaśāstra will explain that the illness is the fruit of the man's past actions, his karma. And the psychologist will express the view that the bodily affliction is related to an emotional disturbance. What is the true cause?

All these different causes may be valid. All of them together go to create an experience. When it rains it becomes wet and the place is swarmed with winged white ants. Frogs croak. All these are indicators of the rain. Many outward signs manifest themselves as the fruits of our past karma. They are all related to one another. The course of the planets governing our life is in accordance with our karma. We come to know the consequences of our actions in previous births in various ways. Astrological calculations help us to find out such consequences as indicated by the heavenly bodies

Notes

1 The nine grahas: the sun, the moon, Mars, Mercury, Jupiter, Venus and Saturn, and the shadow planets Rāhu and Ketu.

2 The dhātus: vāyu (wind), pitta (bile) and kapha (phlegm)

Chapter 6

Omens, Signs

Where can you discover water? Where does ground water occur? Or where do streams flow inside the earth? By what signs on the surface do you make out the presence of water underground? How are perfumes manufactured? What are the right measurements for a house? These questions are discussed in the saṁhitā-skandha of Jyotiṣa. Also omens and signs.

"Śakuna" is one thing, "nimitta" quite another. "Śakuna" literally means a bird: only signs connected with birds come under the category of "śakuna". All things in this world are interrelated: all happenings are linked to one another. If we knew the precise scale and manner in which events are woven together, we would be able to know everything. Everything in this world occurs according to the will of the One Being and according to a precise system. So with reference to one we can know all others. Palmistry, "ā*ruḍam*" (a method of divination), astrology, all are interrelated.

What does a bird flying from right to left indicate? What is foretold by the chirping of such and such a bird? Questions like these belong to śakuna-śāstra. "Nimitta" means omen. "Nimittāni ca paśyāmi viparītāni Keśava"[1] says Arjuna to Kṛṣṇa before the start of the battle of Kurukṣetra. He uses the right word "nimitta" while we use the word "śakuna" carelessly. When a cat crosses our path it is an omen; when an eagle flies above us it is a śakuna.

To go back to Arjuna. The Lord tells Arjuna: "Nimittamātram bhava Savyasācin"[2]. This is in answer to Arjuna telling Kṛṣṇa, lamenting, that it is sinful to kill one's enemies [or one's kin]. Says Kṛṣṇa: "I have already resolved to slay them in this battle. So they are already as good as dead. It is I who will kill them. You are a mere tool" (Nimittamātram bhava).

A nimitta does not produce any result on its own. It points to the result that has already been ordained by some other factor -- or, in other words, it merely indicates the fruits of our past karma.

References

1 *Nimittāni ca pasyāmi viparītani Keśava*
Na ca śreyo'nupaśyāmi hatvā svajanam āhave

— Bhagavadgītā, 1.31

[2] *Tasmāt tvam uttiṣṭha yaśo labhasva*
Jitvā śatrūn bhuṅkṣva rājyam samṛddham
Mayai'vai'te nihatāḥ pūrvam eva
Nimittamātram bhava Savyasācin

— Ibid, 11.33

Chapter 7

Modern Discoveries in Ancient Works

There are few scientific discoveries that are not found mentioned in Varāhamihira's *Bṛhat-Saṁhitā*.

How do heavenly bodies remain in the skies? How is it that they do not fall? Everybody thinks that it was Newton who found the answer to such questions. The very first stanza in the *Sūryasiddhānta,* which is a very ancient treatise, states that it is the force of attraction that keeps the earth from falling.

In Śankara's commentary on the Upaniṣads there is a reference to the earth's force of attraction. If we throw up an object it falls to the ground. This is not due to the nature of the object but due to the earth's force of attraction. "Ākarṣaṇa-śakti" is force of attraction, the power of drawing or pulling something. The breath called "prāṇa" goes up, "apāna" pulls it down. So the force that pulls something downward is apāna. The Ācārya says that the earth has apāna-śakti. The *Praśnopaniṣad* (3.8)[1] states : "The deity of the earth inspires the human body with apāna." In his commentary on this Śankara observes that, just as an object thrown up is attracted by the earth, so prāṇa that goes up is pulled down by apāna. This means that our Upaniṣads contain a reference to the law of gravitation. There are many such precious truths embedded in our ancient śāstras. Because of our ignorance of them we show inordinate respect for ideas propounded by foreigners, ideas known to us many centuries before their discovery by them. Our Jyotiṣa is also some thousands of years old. Even so it foresaw the mathematical systems prevalent in the world today.

At the beginning of the kalpa[S], all grahas were in alignment. But over the ages they have changed their courses. When another kalpa commences, they will again remain in alignment.

The "saṁkalpa"[S] we make before the performance of any ritual contains a description of the cosmos, a reference to the time cycle, and so on. All this is part of Jyotiṣa.

Centuries ago, we knew not only about the earth's force of attraction but also about its revolution round the sun. Āryabhaṭa, Varāhamihira and others spoke of the heliocentric system long before Western astronomers or scientists. Until the 16th century people in Europe believed that the earth remained still at the centre of the universe and that the sun revolved round it[2]. They further believed that this was how day and night were created. If anybody expressed a different view he was burned at the stake by the religious leaders.

"It is the earth that revolves round the sun, not the sun round the earth," declared Āryabhaṭa[3]. He used a beautiful term to describe the logic behind his view: "lāghava-gaurava nyāya". "Laghu" means light, small, etc, and "lāghava" is derived from it. The opposite of "laghu" is "guru", weighty, big, etc. "Guru" also denotes a weighty personality, a great man, like an ācārya or teacher, one who has mastered a śāstra. If the ācārya is guru, the disciple must be laghu. The student is small and "light" compared to his guru. So he goes round the latter. This is based on the "lāghava-gaurava nyāya". By adducing this reason for the earth going round the sun, Āryabhaṭa combined science with a traditional śāstric belief.

In the old days religious leaders in Europe were opposed to science and even burned scientists as heretics. But today we join the descendants of the very same people to make the preposterous charge that the Hindu religion stood in the way of scientific advancement, that it ignored matters of this world because of its concern for the other world. As a matter of fact our traditional śāstras are a storehouse of science.

"The sun remains still and it is the earth that goes round it. It is only because the earth revolves round the sun that it seems to us that the sun rises every day in the east and sets in the west". This is mentioned in the *Aitareya Brāhmaṇa* of the Ṛgveda. The text says clearly:" "The sun neither rises nor sets."

That all learned people in India knew about the earth's revolution is shown by a passage in the *Śivotkarṣa-Mañjarī* by Nīlakaṇṭha Dīkṣita[S] who was minister to Tirumala Nāyaka. One stanza in this work begins like this: "Bhūmir bhrāmayati" and from it we must also gather that the author's great- uncle, Appayya Dīkṣita[S], also knew about this truth. What is the content of this verse?

Śiva is called "Aṣṭamūrti". Earth, water, air, fire, space, the sun and the moon, the yajamāna or sacrificer — they are all the personification (mūrti[S]) of Īśvara. Among them only the yajamāna has no bhramaṇa or motion. All the rest have bhramaṇa, says Appayya Dīkṣita. That he has said so is mentioned in the verse in question by his younger brother's grandson, Nīlakaṇṭha Dīkṣita.

We see that air has movement, that fire does not remain still, that water keeps flowing. When we look up into the sky, we notice that the sun and the moon do not remain fixed to their spots. As for space, it is filled with sound and it cannot be still. But the earth apparently stands still. Even so, says Appayya Dīkṣita,it has motion. "It revolves."

Let us now consider the shape of the earth. Europeans claim that they were the first to discover that the earth is like a ball, that in the past it had been thought to be flat like a plate. All right. What word do we use for "geography"? "Bhūgola śāstra", not just "bhū- śāstra". We have known from early times that the earth is a "gola", a sphere.

We call the universe, with all its galaxies, "Brahmāṇḍa". It means the egg created by Brahmā (the cosmic egg). An egg is not exactly spherical in shape, but oval. According to modern science the universe too is oval in shape. The cosmos is always in motion, so observe modern astronomers. "Jagat" is the word by which we have known it from Vedic times. What does the word mean? That which does not stand still but is always in motion, that which "is going".

In our country too there were people who refused to believe that the earth rotates on its axis. I will tell you the view of one such school of thought. The earth's circumference is about 25,000 miles. So if it rotates once in 24 hours then it means it rotates more than 1,000 miles an hour or 16 or 17 miles in one minute. Those who did not accept the fact of the earth's rotation tried to prove their point thus: "There is a tree in Mylapore [in Madras]. Imagine there is a crow perched on one of its branches. It leaves its perch this moment and soars high and, by the next minute, it perches itself again on the branch of the same tree in Mylapore. If the rotation of the earth were a fact how would this be possible? The crow should have descended to a place 16 or 17 miles away from where it had started[4]".

I have not checked on how this argument was answered. But when I asked people who know modern science they said: "Surrounding the earth for some 200 miles is its atmosphere. Beyond that there are other spheres. When the earth rotates these too rotate with it." I may have gone slightly wrong in stating the view of modern science. However it be, there is no doubt that when the earth rotates, its atmosphere also rotates with it.

What are called Arabic numerals actually belong to India. This fact was discovered by Westerners themselves. The zero is also our contribution and without it mathematics would not have made any advance. Bhāskarācārya establishes the subtle truth that any quantity divided by zero is infinity ("ananta"). He concludes one of his mathematical treatises with a benedictory verse in which he relates zero to the Ultimate Reality.

When the divisor goes on decreasing the quotient keeps increasing, does it not? If you divide 16 by 8 the quotient is 2; if the same quantity is divided by 4 the result is 4. Divided by 2, the quotient is 8. Divided by zero? The quotient will be infinity. Whatever the number divided the result will be infinity if the divisor is 0. Bhāskarācārya gives it the name of "khāhara". "Kham" means zero, "haram" means division. Bhāskarācārya says: "I pay obeisance to the Paramātman that is Infinity."

Notes & References

1 *"Adityo ha vai bāhyaḥ prāṇa udayatyeṣa hyenam cākṣuṣaṁ prāṇamanugṛhṇānaḥ, Pṛthivyām yā devatā saiṣā puruṣasyāpānamavaṣṭabhyāntarā yadākāśaḥ sa samāno, vāyur-vyānaḥ*

— Praśnopaniṣad, 3.8

2 It was in 1543 that the Polish astronomer Nicolaus Copernicus published his book in which he said that the sun, not the earth, be considered the centre of the universe.

3 "For purposes of calculation the planetary system was taken as geocentric, though Āryabhaṭa in the 5th century suggested that the earth revolved round the sun and rotated on its axis; this theory was also known to later astronomers... The precession of the equinoxes was known and calculated with some accuracy by medieval astronomers, as were the lengths of the year, the lunar month and other astronomical constants. These calculations were reliable for most practical purposes, and in many cases more exact than those of the Graeco-Roman world. Eclipses were forecast with accuracy and their true cause understood." — A. L. Basham in *The Wonder that was India.*

4 There is a remarkable similarity between this argument and the imaginary experience of a famous French writer recounted by Ya. Perelman in his *Physics for Entertainment:* "In his statirical History of Lunar States and Empires (1657) the witty 17th-century French writer Cyrano de Bergerac describes an amazing thing which had supposedly happened to him. Experimenting one day, he was lifted up into the air with all his retorts. On landing several hours later, he was astonished to find himself not in his own land of France nor even in Europe, but in Canada. Strangely enough Cyrano de Bergerac believed his transatlantic flight quite possible, claiming that while he was up in the air, the earth had continued to rotate eastwards which was why he had landed in North America and not France.

"A very cheap and simple mode of travel, I must say! Just ascend and stay suspended a few minutes and you'll return to a totally different place much further westwards..."

Chapter 8

Not Blind Belief...

"Hindu śāstras are all nonsensical," exclaim critics of our religion. "They say that north of the earth is the Meru mountain, that our one year is one day for the celestials residing there, and that the sun revolves round it. They believe that, besides the ocean of salt, there are oceans of sugarcane juice and milk, in fact seven kinds of oceans. They describe the earth with its five continents as consisting of seven islands. It is all prattle."

Why should the ocean be salty? Who put the salt in it? Why should not there have been an ocean tasting sweet or one of milk? Is the talk about the seven islands and the seven oceans absurd? What do the śāstras say about the position of the earth, the same śāstras that speak about the seven oceans, and so on? "Meru is situated on the northern tip of the earth," they state. "Directly opposite to it is the Pole star (Dhruva)."

The northern tip of the earth is the North Pole. Is the Pole star directly opposite to it? No. "Eons ago," scientists explain, "it was so. But later big changes took place and the earth tilted a bit." The śāstras refer to a time when the Pole star was directly opposite the North Pole and at that time the seven islands and the seven oceans must have existed. When the rotating earth tilted a bit the oceans must have got mixed and become salty and in the process the seven islands must have become the five continents.

If there is a place above the North Pole it must be Meru where we have our svarga or paradise. Let us imagine that this earth is a lemon. A spot on its top is the Meru peak. In relation to that spot any other part of the fruit is south. Where can you go from there, east or west? You can go only south. You will learn this if you mark a point on the top of the lemon. For all countries of the earth, for all "varṣas", north is Meru. "Sarveṣāmapi varṣāṇām Meruruttarataḥ sthitaḥ."

On the North Pole it is six months day and six months night. We must have been taught this in our primary classes. It means our one year is one day on the North Pole. This is what is meant by saying that our one year is one day for the celestials.

When the earth rotates, the northernmost and southernmost points are not affected. In some places there will be sun for 18 hours and in other places only for six hours. There are many differences in the durations of day and night with regard to different places on earth. Only on some days does the sun rise directly in the east and is overhead without departing even by one degree. On other days it rises from other angles (from north-east to south-east). Such is not the case on the North Pole. There the sun shines six months and the other six months it is darkness. And, again, during the sunny months it would seem as if the sun were revolving round this place (the North Pole).

The six-month period when there is sun in the North Pole is called uttarāyaṇa and the similar sunny period on the South Pole is dakṣiṇāyana.

The North Pole is called "Sumeru" and the South Pole "Kumeru". ("Sumeria" is from Sumeru. In that land, it is said, the Vedic gods were worshipped.) Just as the North Pole is the abode of the gods, the South Pole is the abode of the fathers (pitṛs) and hell. To see the gods and the pitṛs who are in the form of spirits and the denizens of hell one must obtain divine sight through yoga. Merely because we do not possess such sight we cannot deny their existence. There was Blavatsky[1] who was born in Russia, lived in America and later came to India. She speaks about the worlds of the gods and of the spirits. A great scientist of our times, Sir Oliver Lodge, affirmed the existence of spirits and deities and stated that mankind could benefit from them. If you ask why Jyotiṣa, after dealing with the science of astronomy, should turn to spiritualism, the answer is that there is no contradiction between the two as supported by the example of a scientist like Sir Oliver who too turned to spiritualism.

Our śāstras came into existence at a time when mortals mixed with the gods. We would be able to appreciate this fact if we tried to understand the saṁkalpa[S] we make at the time of performing any religious function. The saṁkalpa traces the present from the time of creation itself. From Jyotiṣa we learn the position of the grahas[S] at the commencement of the yuga: then they were all in a line.

Some calculations with regard to heavenly bodies today are different from those of the past. And, if the findings at present are not the same as seen in the śāstras, it does not mean that the latter are all false. The śāstras have existed from the time the grahas were in a line and the North Pole was directly opposite the Pole star. Since then vast changes have taken place in nature. Valleys have become mountains, mountains have become oceans, oceans have become deserts and so on. Geologists speak about such cataclysmic changes, and astronomers tell us about the change in the courses of the heavenly bodies. So what we see today of the earth and the heavenly bodies is different from what is mentioned in the śāstras.

The date of creation according to Jyotiṣa agrees more or less with the view of modern science.

Kali yuga — the age of Kali — has a span of 432,000 years. Dvāpara yuga is twice as long, 864,000 years, Tretā yuga is 1,296,000 years and Kṛta yuga 1,728,000 years. The four yugas together, called a mahāyuga, are 4,320,000 years long. A thousand mahāyugas add up to the period of 14 Manus. The regnal period of a Manu is a manvantara. There are royal and republican rulers on earth, but God has appointed Manu as ruler of all the worlds. There are fourteen Manus ruling the world successively from the creation of man. The word "manuṣya" and "manuja" are derived from Manu. So too the English word "man". In the saṁkalpa for any ritual we perform we mention the year of the seventh Manu, Vaivasvata. If we go back to the first Manu, Svāyambhuva, we arrive at a date for the origin of the human species which agrees with the view of modern science.

The Sanskrit word, "man", means to think. Manu was the first of the human race with its power of thinking. There is a saying in English: "Man is a thinking animal." Since man's distinctive characteristic is his capacity to think the descendants of Manu came to be called "manuṣyas."

The life-spans of the fourteen Manus put together make one day (daytime) of Brahmā, that is 4,320,000,000 years. His night has the same length. While one day of Brahmā is thus 8,640,000,000 years his one year is 365 such days and his life-span is 100 such years. The life of this cosmos is the same. When Brahmā's life comes to an end the Brahman alone will remain and there will be no cosmos. Then another Brahmā will start creation all over again. It is believed that Hanumān will be the next Brahmā.

Bhūloka, Bhuvarloka, Suvarloka, Maharloka, Janaloka, Tapoloka and Satyaloka comprise the seven worlds. The gods, mortals and so on live in these worlds. Bhūloka, Bhuvarloka and Suvarloka form one group. "Bhūrbhuvassuvaḥ," we pronounce this so often while performing rituals. The remaining four belong to higher planes. When Brahmā goes to sleep at night the first three worlds will be dissolved in the praḷaya (deluge). This is called "avāntara-praḷaya" ("intermediate deluge"). All other worlds will perish when his life-span ends.

Scientists say that the heat of the sun is decreasing imperceptibly. Without the warmth of the sun there will be no life on earth. Scientists have calculated the time when the sun's heat will be reduced so much that life on earth cannot be sustained. Then this world itself will perish. The date on which this will occur agrees with that given by our śāstras for the next "avāntara-praḷaya".

Half of Brahmā's allotted life-span is over. This life-span is divided into seven "kalpas"[S]. Now we have come more than half way of the fourth kalpa, "Śvetavarāha". We mention in the saṁkalpa how old Brahmā is at the time we perform a rite, which year we are in of the Śāka era, also the year according to the 60-year cycle[2] beginning with Prabhava — all details of the almanac including the day, the asterism and the lagna[S]. The date of Brahmā's appearance, according to this calculation is said to agree with the view of modern science of when this cosmos came into being.

Brahmā is called "Parārdha-dvaya-jīvin". It means that he lives for two "parārdhas". A "parārdha" is half the number meant by "para". When Brahmā is called "Parārdha-dvaya-jīvin" it means he lives as many years as is meant by 2 x 1/2 paras. Two half paras are the same as one para. Then why say "parārdha-dvaya" instead of just one "para". The reason for this is that Brahmā has already completed half of one para and is going on 51. So it is meaningful to use the term "half of para" [two half-paras].

Fourteen Manus reign successively during one daytime of Brahmā which lasts a thousand caturyugas. So one manvantara is 71 caturyugas. Now running is the 28th caturyuga, the Vaivasvata manvantara. And of it, it is Kali yuga now. In our saṁkalpa we mention all this and, in addition, the day according to the moon, the lagna, etc. We also mention how we are situated in space, from the Brahmāṇḍa down to the locality where we are performing the function (for which the saṁkalpa is made). It is all similar to writing the date and address on a letter.

Notes

1 Madame Blavatsky founded the Theosophical Society in 1875

2 This is the Bārhaspatīya or Jovian circle

Chapter 9

Empirical Proof

A ray of light pouring through an opening in the roof of a building falls on a particular spot. Normally, we shall not be able to tell where the same ray of light will fall next year. But a prediction can be made with the help of Jyotiṣa. This is how it was done in the old days. A pearl attached to a thread was hung from the roof. If a man was able to indicate correctly in advance where its shadow would fall on a particular day, he received a reward from the king. One's competence in other śāstras is established though argument, but in Jyotiṣa it has to be proved by actual demonstration. You cannot deceive anyone by employing the methods taught by this science. The sun and the moon are witness to what you do. "Pratyakṣam Jyotiṣam śāstram."

Part Eleven

KALPA

Chapter 1

Hand of the Vedapuruṣa

The sixth limb or Anga of the Vedapuruṣa is Kalpa, his hand. The hand is called "kara" since it does work (or since we work with it). In Telugu it is called *"sey"*[1]. Kalpa is the śāstra that involves you in "work". A man learns to chant the Vedas, studies Śikṣā, Vyākaraṇa, Chandas, Nirukta and Jyotiṣa. What does he do next? He has to apply these śāstras to the rites he is enjoined to perform. He has to wash away his sins, the sins earned by acting according to his whims. This he does by the performance of good works. For this he must know the appropriate mantras and how to enunciate them correctly, understanding their meaning. Also certain materials are needed and a house that is architecturally suited to the conduct of the rituals. The fruits yielded by these must be offered to Īśvara. Kalpa concerns itself with these matters.

Why does a man learn the Vedas? Why does he make efforts to gain perfection with regard to the purity and tone of their sound by learning Śikṣā, grammar and prosody? And why does he learn Jyotiṣa to find out the right time to perform rituals? The answer is to carry out the injunctions of Kalpa.

How is a rite to be performed, what are the rituals imposed upon the four castes and on people belonging to the four āśramas (celibate students, householders, forest recluses and ascetics)? What are the mantras to be chanted during these various rites and what are the materials to be gathered? What kind of vessels are to be used, and how many ṛtviks (priests) are needed for the different rituals? All these come under the province of Kalpa.

A number of sages have contributed to the Kalpa śāstra. Six sages have composed Kalpasūtras for the Kṛṣṇa-Yajurveda which is predominantly followed in the South — Āpastamba, Baudhāyana, Vaikhānasa, Satyāṣādḥa, Bhāradvāja, Agniveśa. Āśvalāyana and Śāṅkhāyana have written Kalpasūtras for the Ṛgveda but the former's is the most widely followed. For Śukla-Yajurveda there is the Kalpasūtra by Kātyāyana. For the *Kauthūma, Rānāyanīya* and *Talavakāra Śākhās* of the Sāmaveda, Lāṭyāyana, Drāhyāyana and Jaimini respectively have composed Kalpasūtras.

Kalpa contains Gṛhyasūtras and Śrautasūtras[2] for each recension. Both deal with the 40 saṁskāras to be performed from conception to death. The cremation of the body is also a sacrifice, the final offering: it is called "antyeṣṭi" and it is also to be performed with the chanting of mantras. "Iṣṭi" means a sacrifice and in antyeṣṭi the body is offered in the sacred fire as a "dravya" or material.

A Brahmin has to perform 21 sacrifices: seven "haviryajñas" based on agnihotra; seven pākayajñas and seven somayajñas. Of them the seven haviryajñas and the seven somayajñas are not included in the Gṛhyasūtras. They belong to the Śrautasūtras. Together with these there are forty rites for a Brahmin — they are called saṁskāras. A saṁskāra is that which refines and purifies the performer.

Agnihotra is performed at home and yajñas [of a bigger type] in specially constructed halls. While the Śrautasūtras contain instructions for the conduct of big sacrifices, the Gṛhyasūtras are concerned with domestic rites. The names given before are of the authors of Śrautasūtras.

The Kalpasūtras deal with the forty saṁskāras and with the eight "Ātmaguṇas" [qualities to be cultivated by individuals][3]. Apart from the seven haviryajñas and seven somayajñas (together 14), the remaining 26 belong to the category of Gṛhyasūtras. Among them are garbhādhāna, puṁsavana, sīmanta, jātakarma, nāmakarana, annaprāśana, caula, upanayana and vivāha. I shall be dealing with them later.

The eight Ātmaguṇas are compassion, patience, freedom from jealousy, purity or cleanliness, not being obstinate, keeping a cool mind, non-covetousness and desirelessness. These are among the "sāmānya-dharmas", universal virtues, to be cultivated by all jātis.

When we do "abhivādana"[S] [as we prostrate ourselves before the fire or before a preceptor or any elder], we mention, among other things, the sūtra that we follow. To illustrate: Sāmavedins mention *Drāhyāyaṇa-sūtra.* Drāhyāyaṇa has authored only a Śrautasūtra. Another, Gobhila, has written a Gṛhyasūtra. In the old days when it was a common practice to conduct big sacrifices the Śrautasūtras which deal with them were mentioned in the abhivādana. This practice continues though we no longer perform śrauta sacrifices and go through only such functions as marriage which are dealt with by the Gṛhyasūtras.

In the past even poor people performed śrauta rituals. They got all the materials required by begging. Brahmins who were called "prati-vasanta-somayājins" conducted soma sacrifices every year during the spring [that is what the term means]. If a man had enough income to meet three years' expenses (of his family) he conducted the soma sacrifice during every season of spring.

Now there is decay in all fields. Things have turned topsyturvy. People spend three times their annual income but, ironically enough, owing to changes in trade and commercial practices all, including the rich, suffer from poverty and hardship. There must be moderation in everything. All the ingenuity and resourcefulness of our times have led only to indigence even in the midst of plenty. The rich man has brought himself to a position of not being able to afford all his expenses. With moderation alone will there be the means to do good works.

The śikhā[S], the puṇdra[S] and the religious rites vary from sūtra to sūtra. Some wear "ūrdhva-śikhā" [lock of hair on the crown of the head], some "pūrva-śikhā" [lock of hair on the forepart of the head]. Similarly there are differences in wearing the marks on the forehead: some wear vertical marks (ūrdhva-puṇḍra) and some horizontal (tripuṇḍra)[S]. These are according to the tradition one follows.

Cayana[S] is an important feature of sacrifices. There are two types of śulba-sūtras in Kalpa: "sāmānya" (ordinary or common) and "viśeṣa" (special). There are śulba-sūtras by Kātyāyana, Baudhāyana, Hiraṇyakeśin and so on. In the South there is what is called "*Āṇḍapiḷḷai-prayoga.*" "Āṇḍapiḷḷai" belonged to Tiruppanantāḷ and was named after the deity Gaṇeśa ("*Piḷḷayar*") of Tiruviḍaimarudūr (Tañjāvūr district). It is according to his method that śrauta works are performed. The śrauta sacrifices are large-scale sacraments not conducted in the home but in a "yāgaśālā". Rites that are not so big are "gṛhya" and performed at home. Since big sacrifices have become rare, the Gṛhyasūtras have gained greater importance. Besides, alien śāstras, alien practices, are becoming more and more popular.

All our śāstras have one goal, that of holding the lotus-feet of Īśvara. Whatever we read must be in the form of an offering to the Lord and it must be capable of bringing us Ātmic merit. Our śāstras belong to such a category. It is a matter for regret that the conduct of śrauta works (havir and soma sacrifices), which are of the utmost importance to the Vedic religion, has become very rare.

Among those who have authored Kalpasūtras, but for Drāhyāyana and Kātyāyana, all the rest, like Āpastamba, Baudhāyana and Āśvalāyana, have written both Śrauta and Gṛhya sūtras.

Apart from the above two types of sūtras, we have the "Dharmasūtras". These deal with a man's individual, domestic and social life. The Dharmaśāstra is based on them. What we understand by the English term "law" is derived from them. They are also the basis of the moral and legal śāstras of Manu, Mitākṣara and so on. (The following Dharmasūtras have been handed down to us: those of Vasiṣṭha and Viṣṇu for the Ṛgveda; those of Manu, Baudhāyana, Āpastamba and Hiraṇyakeśin for the Kṛṣṇa-Yajurveda; and those of Gautama for the Sāmaveda.) Since the Atharvaveda has hardly any following its Kalpasūtras are not in observance.

Kalpa deals with rites in their minutest detail. All the actions of a Brahmin have a Vedic connection. Through each and every breath he takes in, with each step he takes, he will be able to grasp the divine powers for the well-being of the world because of this Vedic connection and only because of it. The Kalpasūtras contain rules with regard to how a Brahmin must sit, eat, wear his clothes and so on.

This "limb" of the Vedas also deals with the construction of houses. Why? The design — or architecture — of a Brahmin's dwelling must be such as to help him in the performance of his duties according to the scriptures. If, say, there is a rule about the doorway where he should offer the "vaiśvadeva-bali"[4], should not the doorway be constructed in the required śāstric manner? Is the modern "flat" suitable for such rites? The character of the place where the "aupāsana"[5] is to be performed is described in Kalpa. A class-room where children are taught has to meet certain requirements: it must have a desk, benches, etc. The laboratory has to be different from it. Similarly, the architecture of a house and the design of a class-room differ functionally.

I perform pūjā. The place where I do it must have a certain special character. All rooms are similar in a bungalow. If a pūjā is performed in such a place, rules regarding ritual purity and differences based on varṇa and āśrama cannot be properly maintained since people will come crowding together. The bungalow is built according to the white man's way of life. *There must be separateness and at the same time togetherness;* there must be a place for everybody. Even if we wish to have a place according to our customs and traditions, the new type of house does not help in this way. Our architecture has developed according to our traditions and needs. A cement floor cannot be maintained clean after eating. When washed or scrubbed with water, the "*eccil*"[6] will spread. Westerners living in bungalows (or flats) eat at table[7].

We must build our houses according to our architectural science. The term "gṛhastha" itself is from "gṛha" (house). Those who observe ritual purity in matters like eating, living and clothing, must build their houses according to our architectural concepts. But we are now accustomed to living in houses built in an alien style. At first we may feel some qualms about the difficulty in practising our customs and traditions. Eventually, however, we are likely to get used to the new style of living and become careless about our religious observances. Instead of abandoning such houses, we abandon the religious and other practices which are part of our dharma.

I shall be speaking to you in some detail about the 40 saṁskāras included in Kalpa when I deal with Dharmaśāstra.

We have discussed ten of the caturdaśa-vidyā, the fourteen branches of Vedic lore — the four Vedas, Śikṣā, Vyākaraṇa, Chandas, Nirukta, Jyotiṣa, and Kalpa. Four remain.

Notes & References

[1] See Chapter 11, Part Six.

[2] Gṛhyasūtras, Śrautasūtras, the 21 sacrifices, etc, are discussed in Part Sixteen.

[3] The eight Ātmaguṇas are dealt with in Part Sixteen.

[4] & [5] To be explained in the chapter on Saṁskāras.

[6] Tamiḷ word meaning what has come into contact with the mouth, spittle, etc, remains of food. It is impure and defiled.

[7] Eating at table is now a common practice among all castes, especially in towns and cities.

Part Twelve

MĪMĀṀSĀ–KARMAMĀRGA

While examining the beliefs of Pūrvamīmāṁsā, which is the main theme of this part, the Paramaguru also deals with Sānkhya and briefly touches upon yoga.

Chapter 1

Explication of Vedic Laws

Of the fourteen branches of learning (caturdaśa-vidyā), after the four Vedas and the Ṣaḍaṅga, we have the four Upāṅgas of the Vedas remaining. "Upa + anga " = "Upāṅga." The prefix "upa" is added to suggest what is auxiliary to a subject. "Sabhānāyaka" means speaker; "upa-sabhānāyaka" means deputy speaker. In the same way we have, after the six Angas (Ṣaḍaṅga), the four Upāṅgas. These are Mīmāṁsā, Nyāya, the Purāṇas and Dharmaśāstra.

"Mām" is the root of the word "Mīmāṁsā"; "san" is the pratyaya[1]. "Mīmāṁsā" means "esteemed or sacred inquiry", an exposition. What is esteemed or worthy of worship? The Vedas. Mīmāṁsā is an exegesis of the Vedas. Nirukta explains the meaning of the words of the Vedas, also their etymology in the fashion of a dictionary. Mīmāṁsā goes further, to find out the significance of the mantras, their intent. It also gives its decisions on these points.

We have already discussed the karmakāṇḍa and jñānakāṇḍa of the Vedas. Karmakāṇḍa is called the pūrva-bhāga, the first or early part of each Vedic recension, and the second or concluding part is the uttara-bhāga. Mīmāṁsā too is divided in this way into Pūrvamīmāṁsā and Uttaramīmāṁsā. The first holds that sacrifices and other rites of the karmakāṇḍa form the most important part of the Vedas, while the second maintains that the realisation of the Self taught in the jñānakāṇḍa is their true goal. I spoke about the Uttaramīmāṁsā when I dealt with the Upaniṣads and the *Brahmasūtra*.

Uttaramīmāṁsā, that is the *Brahmasūtra* as well as the Upaniṣads, constitutes "Brahmavidyā" or Vedānta here. It is the foundation of the three important philosophic systems — Advaita (non-dualism or monism), Viśiṣṭadvaita (qualified non-dualism or qualified monism) and Dvaita (dualism).

Our present subject is Pūrvamīmāṁsā. As a matter of fact the term "Mīmāṁsā" itself usually denotes "Pūrvamīmāṁsā". But mention of it brings to mind Uttaramīmāṁsā also.

Every system has, as we have seen, its sūtras, bhāṣya[s] and vārtika[s]. The *Pūrvamīmāṁsā-sūtra* is by Jaimini Maharṣi, its bhāṣya by Śabarasvāmin and its vārtika by Kumārilabhaṭṭa. Kumārilabhaṭṭa's *Bhaṭṭadīpikā* remains the most important Pūrvamīmāṁsā work. Kumarila was an incarnation of

Kumārasvāmin or Subrahmaṇya. Prabhākara has written a commentary on Pūrvamīmāṁsā in which he expresses views which, on some points, are divergent from Kumārilabhaṭṭa's. So two different schools are identified in Mīmāṁsā -- "Bhaṭṭa-mata" and "Prabhākara- mata". Let us consider Mīmāṁsā in general terms, ignoring the differences between the two schools. "Bhaṭṭa-mata", it is obvious, gets its name from the fact that it represents the views of Kumārilabhaṭṭa[2].

Jaimini's *Pūrvamīmāṁsā-sūtra* is a voluminous work and has twelve chapters, each having a number of "pādas" and each pāda having a number of "adhikaraṇas". In all, there are 1,000 adhikaraṇas.

The Vedas constitute the law of Īśvara. Since they are eternal and endless the law is also eternal. All of us are the subjects of the monarch called Īśvara. He has engaged many officials, authorities, like Indra, Vāyu, Varuṇa, Agni, Yama, Īśana, Kubera, Nirṛti and so on to take care of this world. They need a law to protect the creatures of all the fourteen worlds. How should we, the subjects of Īśvara, conduct ourselves according to this law, how are the officials appointed by Īśvara to rule over his domain? We may find out the answer to these by examining the Vedas. There are judges who deliberate on the laws of this world and resolve doubts concerning them with the help of lawyers. If the Vedas are the law that determines how dharma is to be practised, it is Jaimini who interprets the meaning of this law. His interpretation is Mīmāṁsā.

When there is a legal dispute, a verdict is given, say, according to the decision of the Allahabad or Bombay high court based on similar cases. The decision given by one court with regard to one case may be applied to a similar case that comes up before another court. In Jaimini's Mīmāṁsā a thousand issues (or points) are examined, taking into account the views opposed to those of the author of the sūtras, and the meaning of the Vedic passages determined with cogent reasoning. To explain: first, a Vedic statement is taken up; second, questions are raised about its meaning ("samasya"); third, the opposing school's point of view is presented ("pūrvapakṣa"); fourth, that point of view is refuted ("uttarapakṣa"); and, fifth, a conclusion is arrived at ("nirṇaya"). The process of arriving at the meaning of each issue or point constitutes an adhikaraṇa.

The sūtras of Jaimini are very terse. Śabara's commentary on them is called *Śābaram*[3]. The word "śabara" usually means a hunter. "Śabarī" of the Rāmāyaṇa, they say, was originally a huntress. Śabara, the Mīmāṁsā commentator, had an aspect of Īśvara in him. It is believed that Īśvara composed the commentary (*Śābaram*) when he appeared as a hunter to grant the Pāśupata weapon to Arjuna.

Since it has one thousand adhikaraṇas, Pūrvamīmāṁsā is called "Sahasrādhikaraṇī". One must add here that in this work the meaning of the Vedic texts are determined by countering many a captious argument ("kuyukti").

While Pūrvamīmāṁsā concerns itself with the meaning of the karmakāṇḍa of the Vedas, Uttaramīmāṁsā deals with the meaning of the jñānakāṇḍa, that is the Upaniṣads. The Upaniṣads speak primarily of the Paramātman and our inseparable union with him. Vyāsa, in his *Brahmasūtra,* determines the meaning of the divine law constituted by the Upaniṣads. Ironically enough, the sage who composed the sūtras for Uttaramīmāṁsā, Vyasa, was the guru of Jaimini who composed the sūtras of Pūrvamīmāṁsā.

Sureśvarācārya[S] wrote a commentary on the *Taittirīya* and *Bṛhadāraṇyaka Upaniṣads* from the non-dualistic point of view. It is noteworthy that he had earlier been an adherent of Pūrvamīmāṁsā. He made the transition from the path of works to the path of jñana, on becoming a disciple of Śankara and wrote a commentary on his guru's bhāṣya. Before becoming a disciple of our Ācārya and a sannyāsin he was called Maṇḍanamiśra. The story goes that Śankara approached Maṇḍanamiśra for a philosophical disputation during a śrāddha[S] performed by the latter. Vyāsa and Jaimini were the two Brahmins[4] to take part in the ceremony.

Notes & References

[1] Qualifying suffix.

[2] Tirupputkuzhi Kṛṣṇatātacāriyār's *Bhāṭṭasāram,* as its name suggests, is a summary of the ideas of Kumārilabhaṭṭa. It was first published early in the century. — Ra. Ga.

[3] Laksmīpuram Śrī Śrīnivasācāriyār's *Śabara-bhāṣya-bhūṣaṇam* is an elucidation of the Śabara-bhāṣya. — Ra. Ga.

[4] One of the two Brahmins represents the Viśvedeva and the second represents the fathers.

Chapter 2
No Concept of God in Mīmāṁsā

Why should the Ācārya have sought a debate with Maṇḍanamiśra, the mīmāṁsaka? (A mīmāṁsaka is an adherent of Pūrvamīmāṁsā. We Uttaramīmāṁsakas are called "Vedantins".) The Ācārya it was who revivified the Vedic religion and re-established it on a firm footing. Why, then, should such a preceptor have been critical of Mīmāṁsā which is an Upāṅga of the very Vedas he promoted?

Before answering this question, we must consider the goal of any śāstra or system, whether it be Mīmāṁsā or anything else. Any discipline, to repeat what I said before, must have the ultimate purpose of leading us towards Īśvara. I further observed that even subjects like grammar, lexicography, prosody had such an end in view and that was the reason why they were included among the fourteen branches of Vedic learning. Now what is the concept of God like in Pūrvamīmāṁsā?

We must here consider how Vedānta or Uttaramīmāṁsā views God, for it is the system to which the Ācārya gave his whole-hearted support and which he also commented upon. After all, it is the Ācārya who chiefly matters to us. And to him it is that Vyasa's *Brahmasūtra* matters most. What does this text have to say about Īśvara?

The *Brahmasūtra* declares: "Kartā śāstrārthavattvāt." It means Īśvara is the creator of the cosmos. Even adherents of other religions call God "Kartā"[1]. But Īśvara is more than a Kartā and has one more function. We do good and bad — good actions and bad actions. It is Īśvara who vouchsafes us the fruits of such actions: "Phalam ata upapatteḥ". Īśvara is the "phaladātā" (giver of the fruits of our actions) of our karma. We do good and evil with our mind, speech and body. The Lord is witness to all this and he dispenses the fruits of our actions. These are the two characteristics (lakṣaṇas) of Īśvara according to Uttaramīmāṁsā.

What does Pūrvamīmāṁsā say about Īśvara?

Both Sāṅkhyas[2] and mīmāṁsakas belong to the Vedic system. But the Sāṅkhyas believe that Īśvara is not the Kartā or author of the jagat (universe). "Īśvara is pure knowledge, jñāna," they say. "This cosmos is insentient, made of earth and stone. What constitutes jñāna cannot be the cause of insentient matter. To believe that Īśvara is the author of the universe is not right." Such is the Sānkhya view. Supporters of Sānkhya describe Īśvara, who is unattached to the universe and is pure jñāna, as "Puruṣa". It is this Puruṣa that our Ācārya calls the ultimate "Nirguṇa-Brahman" (the Brahman without attributes). However, he criticises the Sānkhya concept maintaining that the Nirguṇa-Brahman itself becomes the Saguṇa-Brahman of Īśvara to create the world and to engage itself in other activities.

To mīmāṁsakas only such rites matter as are enjoined on us by the Vedas. They are silent on the question of Īśvara and of who created the world. However, they are emphatic on one point — that Īśvara is not the one who dispenses the fruits of our actions. They do not quarrel on the point of whether or not Īśvara is the Kartā of the universe. They declare: "It is wrong to claim that Īśvara gives us the fruits of our actions according to whether they are good or evil. He is not the one who metes out the fruits of our actions. It is the Vedic works performed by us that decide the fruits to be earned by us."

So adherents of both Sānkhya and Mīmāṁsā, in their different ways, reject the view of the Vedas and the *Brahmasūtra* that Īśvara possesses the two lakṣaṇas (mentioned earlier). The mīmāṁsakas believe that Īśvara does not dispense the fruits of our actions because, according to them, the Vedic works we perform give rewards on their own. We earn merit or demerit according to how the Vedas and śāstras view our actions. So it is our karma that brings its rewards or retribution, as the case may be, not Īśvara.

Among the religious systems that accept the Vedas, Sānkhya and Mīmāṁsā alone hold the view that Īśvara is not the creator of the world, that he does not award the fruits of our actions.

Notes

1 Or they use equivalents of this word.

2 Those who support the Sānkhya system of philosophy, Sānkhya being one of the six darśanas.

Chapter 3

Nyāya and Mīmāṁsā: They brought about the Decline of Buddhism

Many believe that Buddhism ceased to have a large following in India because it came under the attack of Śankara. This is not true. There are very few passages in the Ācārya's commentaries critical of that religion, a religion that was opposed to the Vedas. Far more forcefully has he criticised the doctrines of Sānkhya and Mīmāṁsā that respect the Vedic tradition. He demolishes their view that Īśvara is not the creator of the world and that it is not he who dispenses the fruits of our actions. He also maintains that Īśvara possesses the lakṣaṇas or characteristics attributed to him by the Vedas and the *Brahmasūtra* and argues that there can be no world without Īśvara and that it is wrong to maintain that our works yield fruits on their own. It is Īśvara, his resolve, that has created this world, and it is he who awards us the fruits of our actions. We cannot find support in his commentaries for the view that he was responsible for the decline of Buddhism in India.

Then how did Buddhism cease to have a considerable following in our country? Somebody must have subjected it to such rigorous attack as to have brought about its decline in this land. Who performed this task? The answer is the mīmāṁsakas and the tārkikas. Those who are adept in the Tarka-śāstra (logic) are called tārkikas. Tarka is part of Nyāya which is one of the fourteen branches of Vedic learning and which comes next to Mīmāṁsā. People proficient in Nyāya are naiyāyikas; those well versed in grammar are "vaiyākaraṇis"; and those proficient in the Purāṇas are "paurāṇikas".

Udayanācārya, the tārkika, and Kumārilabhaṭṭa, the mīmāṁsaka, opposed Buddhism for different reasons. The former severely criticised that religion for its denial of Īśvara. To the mīmāṁsakas, as I have said earlier, Vedic rituals are of the utmost importance. Even though they do not believe that it is Īśvara who awards us the fruits of our actions, they believe that the rituals we perform yield their own fruits and that the injunctions of the dharmaśāstras must be carried out faithfully. They attacked Buddhism for its refusal to accept Vedic rituals. Kumārilabhaṭṭa has written profusely in criticism of that religion. He and Udayanācārya were chiefly responsible for the failure of Buddhism to acquire a large following in this country. Our Ācārya came later and there was no need for him to make a special assault on that religion on his own. On the contrary, his chief task was to expose the flaws in the systems upheld by the very opponents of Buddhism, Kumārilabhaṭṭa and Udayanācārya. He established that Īśvara is the creator of the universe and that it is he who awards the fruits of our actions.

I am mentioning this fact so as to disabuse you of the wrong notions you must have formed with regard to Śānkara's role in the decline of Buddhism. There is a special chapter in one of Kumārilabhaṭṭa's works called "Tarkapādam" in which he has made an extensive refutation of Buddhism. So too has Udayanācārya in his *Bauddhādhikāram*. These two ācāryas were mainly responsible for the decline of Buddhism in our land and not Śankara Bhagavatpāda. What we are taught on the subject in our textbooks of history is not true.

Chapter 4

Buddhism and Indian Society

In my opinion at no time in our history did Buddhism in the fullest sense of that religion have a large following in India. Today a number of Hindus, who are members of the Theosophical Society, celebrate our festivals like other Hindus and conduct marriages in the Hindu way. There are many devotees of Śrī Rāmakṛṣṇa Paramahaṁsa practising our traditional customs. Śrī C. Rāmānujācāriyār[T], "Aṇṇā" (Śrī N. Subrahmaṇya Ayyar[T]) and some others are intimately associated with the Rāmakṛṣṇa Mission but they still adhere to our traditional beliefs.

When great men make their appearance people are drawn to them for their qualitics of compassion and wisdom. In the organisations established after them our sanātana dharma[S] is followed with some changes. But a large number of the devotees of these men still follow the old customs and traditions in their homes.

Many regard Gāndhījī as the founder almost of a new religion (Gāndhīsm), and look upon him as one greater than avatāras like Rāma and Kṛṣṇa. But in their private lives few of them practise what he preached — for instance, widow marriage, mixing with members of other castes, and so on. People developed esteem for Gāndhījī for his personal life of self-sacrifice, truthfulness, devotion and service to mankind. But applying his ideas in actual life was another matter.

It was in the same way that the Buddha had earned wide respect for his lofty character and exemplary personal life. "A prince renounces his wife and child in the prime of his youth to free the world from sorrow": the story of Siddhārtha, including such accounts, made an impact on people. They were moved by his compassion, sense of detachment and self-sacrifice. But it did not mean that they were ready to follow his teachings. They admired the Buddha for his personal qualities but they continued to subscribe to the varṇāśrama system and the ancient way of religious life with its sacrifices and other rites. Contrary to what he wished, people did not come forward in large numbers to become monks but continued to remain householders adhering to Vedic practices.

Emperor Aśoka did much to propagate Buddhism; but in society in general the Vedic dharma did not undergo any change. Besides, the emperor himself supported the varṇāśrama dharma as is evident from his famous edicts. But for the Buddhist bhikṣus (monks), all householders followed the Vedic path. Though they were silent on the question of Īśvara and other deities, some books written by great Buddhist monks open with hymns to Sarasvatī. They also worshipped a number of gods. It is from Tibet that we have obtained many Tāntrik works relating to the worship of various deities. If you read the works of Śrīharṣa[S], Bilhaṇa[S] and so on in Sanskrit, and Tamiḷ poetical works like that of Ilango Aḍigaḷ[T], you will realise that even during times when Buddhism wielded influence in society, Vedic customs and varṇāśrama were followed by the generality of people.

Reformists today speak in glowing terms about Vyāsa, Śankarācārya, Rāmānujācārya and others. But they do not accept the customs and traditions I ask people to follow. Some of them, however, come to see me. Is it not because they feel that there is something good about me, because they have personal regard for me, even though they do not accept my ideas? Similarly, great men have been respected in this country for their personal qualities and blameless life notwithstanding the fact that they advocated views that differed slightly from the Vedic tradition or were radically opposed to it. Our people anyway had long been steeped in the ancient Vedic religion and its firmly established practices and, until the turn of the century, were reluctant to discard the religion of their forefathers and the vocations followed by them. Such was our people's attitude during the time of the Buddha also. When his doctrines came under attack from Udayanācārya and Kumārilabhaṭṭa even the few who had first accepted them returned to the Vedic religion.

Chapter 5

Śankara and Non-Vedāntic Systems

The Ācārya views the last stage or āśrama in a man's life as the years during which he renounces Vedic works and devotes himself to meditation and metaphysical inquiry. But, unlike the Buddha, he does not want Vedic karma to be given up in the earlier stages. According to him, only after a man cleanses his consciousness through years of Vedic rituals is he to become exclusively devoted to Ātmic inquiry. First accept the karma that Mīmāṁsā asks us to perform and finally give up that very karma as suggested by Buddhism.

The Ācārya goes along with systems like Buddhism, Mīmāṁsā, Sānkhya and Nyāya up to a point. He accepts them on a certain level, but on another level he disapproves of them. Each of these systems regards one aspect of truth to be final. Our Ācārya harmonises them all into a single whole Truth.

Chapter 6

Sānkhya

According to Sānkhya, the Ātman is "Puruṣa" and is the basis of all, though, at the same time, detached from everything. In its view Māyā which keeps everything going is "Prakṛti". The cosmos is contained in 24 "tattvaṣ" ["thatnesses" or principles or categories] of which Prakṛti is one — Prakṛti indeed is the first of these and it has the name of "pradhāna". From it arises the second tattva of "mahat" which is the intellect of Prakṛti (like the intellect of man). From mahat (the great) is derived the third tattva of "ahaṁkāra", the ego, self-consciousness, the feeling that there is a separate entity called "I".

Ahaṁkāra divides itself into two: first as the sentient and knowing life of a man, his mind, his five jñānendriyas[S] and five karmendriyas[S]. The second is constituted by the five "tanmātras" and the five "mahābhūtas"[1] of the insentient cosmos. The jñānendriyas are faculties with which a man gets to know outside objects: the eyes that see objects, the nose that smells, the mouth that tastes, the ear that hears and the skin that feels by touch. With his karmendriyas he performs various actions. The mouth serves as a karmendriya also since it performs the function of speech. The hand, the leg, the anus and the genitals are all karmendriyas. The "āśrayas" for jñānendriyas are sound (ear), feeling, sparśa (skin), form (eye), flavour or taste (mouth), smell (nose). These five are tanmātras. The tattvas in their expanded insentient forms are space (sound), air (feeling or touch), water (flavour), earth (smell), fire (form) — these are mahābhūtas. Thus Prakṛti, mahat, ahaṁkāra, mind, the five jñānendriyas, the five karmendriyas, the five tanmātras, the five mahābhūtas — all these make the 24 tattvas.

These tattvas are accepted by non-dualistic Vedānta also. According to it, it is Īśvara (the Brahman with attributes) who unites Puruṣa (or the Ātman without attributes) with Prakṛti or Māyā. Sānkhya, however, is silent on Īśvara.

The three "qualities" of sattva, rajas and tamas, according to the Sānkhya philosophy, are accepted by all Vedāntic systems including non-dualism. Sattva denotes a high state of goodness, clarity and serenity; rajas is all speed and action and passion; and tamas denotes sleep, inertia, sloth. The Gītā has much to say on the subject in its "Gunatraya-vibhāga yoga". The Lord says: "Nistraiguṇyo bhava" (Go beyond all three guṇas and dwell in the Ātman)[2]. Sānkhya also believes that all undesirable developments are due to an imbalance of the guṇas and that they must be maintained evenly. But, unlike the Gītā,

Sānkhya does not tell us the means to achieve this — like worship of Īśvara, surrender to him, Ātmic inquiry and so on.

Puruṣa alone has life, Prakṛti is inert. By itself Prakṛti is incapable of performing any function. It manifests itself as the 24 tattvas only in the presence of Puruṣa. But Sānkhya also speaks contradictorily that Puruṣa is "kevala-jñāna-svarūpin" unrelated to Prakṛti. "Kevala" means what is by itself, isolated, without the admixture of anything else. "Kaivalya" is the name Sānkhya gives to liberation. The state in which an individual, after discarding the 24 tattvas and being released from inertia, remains in the vital Puruṣa by himself is "kaivalya". (In Tamiḷ "*kevalam*" has somehow come to mean "inferior" or "unworthy".)

Advaita also has the goal of one being absorbed in Puruṣa, that is the Ātman, and discarding all else as Māyā. To attain this state, the Ācārya has cut out a path for us, the path that takes us to final release through works, devotion and philosophic inquiry. Sānkhya does no such thing. Most of its teaching relates to forsaking the 24 tattvas.

Another unsatisfactory aspect of Sānkhya is this. Puruṣa (the Ātman) is jñāna by itself and has no function. Prakṛti has a function but is insentient and without jñāna. How does this insentient Prakṛti unfold itself as the 24 tattvas? According to Sānkhya, this phenomenon occurs in the presence of Puruṣa. This is not a convincing explanation. How does Prakṛti perform its function under Puruṣa that has no function? Supporters of Sānkhya answer: "Are not iron filings brought into motion by the presence of a magnet. Does the magnet consciously want to keep them in motion? The magnet is by itself and the iron filings are in motion. Similarly, though Puruṣa is by himself, Prakṛti is activated as a consequence of its vitality."

Puruṣa and Prakṛti work together like a cripple carried by a blind man. The cripple cannot walk and the blind man cannot see. So the cripple perched on the shoulders of the blind man shows the way and the latter follows his directions. Similarly, Prakṛti which has no jñāna carries Puruṣa who is full of jñāna, but Prakṛti without jñāna is behind all the affairs of the world. This may sound good as a story or as a metaphor but it does not make sense unlike the explanation provided by the Advaita concept — that the Nirguṇa-Brahman becomes the Saguṇa-Brahman (Īśvara) to conduct the world.

Another important difference between Advaita and Sānkhya is this. Although Sānkhya believes in a Puruṣa made up of jñāna it does not state unequivocally like Advaita that all individual souls are the same as Puruṣa. All individual souls, according to Sānkhya, exist by themselves. Though the ideas of Sānkhya are confusing sometimes, it is regarded as one of our basic systems of philosophy. ("Sankhya" means enumerating, numbers: from it comes "Sānkhya".)

The author of the *Sānkhya-sūtra* is Kapila Maharṣi. Notable works of this system are Īśvarakṛṣna's *Sānkhya-kārikā* and Vijñānabhikṣu's commentary on the *Sānkhya-sutra*[2].

The Gītā too deals with Sānkhya. When Bhagavān Kṛṣṇa speaks of the two paths, Sānkhya and yoga, he means jñāna by the former and karmayoga by the latter (not Rājayoga).

Sānkhya does not go beyond asking us to have an awareness of Puruṣa as separate from Prakṛti. Rājayoga, however, goes further from this point and tells us the practical means, the "sādhana", to be followed to become aware of Puruṣa dissociated from Prakṛti. The concept of Īśvara and devotion to him is part of yoga and it has lessons to bring the mind under control. What generally goes under the name of yoga is Patañjali's Rājayoga, according to which yoga is stopping the mental process (or the oscillating vitality of consciousness). It is this yoga that has become popular in Western countries.

Sānkhya and yoga are not included in caturdaśa-vidyā but, all the same, they are important among our śāstras.

Though devotion to Īśvara is not part of Mīmāṁsā, it accepts the authority of the Vedas. Likewise, Sānkhya too respects the authority of the Vedas and does not support belief in Īśvara.

Buddhism on the one hand, Nyāya and Mīmāṁsā on the other which were opposed to it, and Sānkhya, which does not accept Īśvara but respects the pramāṇas of the Vedas: of these our Ācārya accepts elements that are to be accepted and rejects elements that are to be rejected. He establishes the Vedāntic system which harbours all these and which is their source. Śankara's view is not at variance with the ultimate message of Buddhism, that is the exalted state of jñāna. He accepts some of the basic concepts of Sānkhya like Puruṣa that is jñāna by itself and equivlalent to the Nirguṇa-Brahman and Prakṛti which is the same as Māyā. At the same time, he accepts the Vedic rituals of Mīmāṁsā and the Īśvara of Nyāya. But he sees each of them as an aspect of the One Truth, not as the final goal which it is to the various individual systems mentioned. He integrates these different aspects into a harmonious whole in his own system of thought.

Notes & References

[1] "Tanmātras" and "mahābhūtas" may be understood as the "subtle elements" and the "material elements" respectively.

[2] See notes appended to Chapter 32, Part Five.

[3] The commentaries on *Sānkhya-kārikā* written by Gauḍapāda and Vācaspati are important contributions to Sānkhya literature. There is a difference of opinion as to whether this Gauḍapāda is the same as the paramaguru of Ādi Śankara [that is Śankara's guru's guru]. — — Ra. Ga.

Chapter 7

Mīmāṁsā and Ādi Śankara

As we have already seen, Udayana and other supporters of the Nyāya system criticised Buddhism on the score that it was silent on the question of God, while the mīmāṁsakas like Kumārilabhaṭṭa attacked the same because it did not favour Vedic rituals. The Ācarya was in sympathy with these views and believed that Vedic sacraments, considered all-important by the mīmāṁsakas, were essential to the cleansing of the mind and to the proper conduct of the affairs of the community. However, he was opposed to the mimāṁsakas not only because they did not accept an entity like Īśvara as the dispenser of the fruits of our actions but also because they did not believe that, after being rendered pure by works, there is any need for one to go further and take the path of jñāna. He did not also agree with their view that to become a sannyāsin giving up all karma is not right.

Kumārilabhaṭṭa and Maṇḍanamiśra are particularly important among mīmāṁsakas. The Ācarya had a debate with Kumārilabhaṭṭa during the last days of that mīmāṁsaka and won him over to his viewpoint. Similarly, Maṇḍanamiśra also became a convert to Advaita Vedānta and came to be one of the Ācarya's chief disciples assuming the name of Sureśvarācarya.

If the Ācarya opposed Mīmāṁsā, which is one of the fourteen branches of Vedic lore, it was not because he thought it to be wholly unacceptable. He was in agreement with the sacraments dealt with in that system, but he differed from it on the question of devotion to the Lord. He further believed that the fruits yielded by the rites, rewards like paradise, must be dedicated to Īśvara and that in this very act of renunciation the mind is purified. Śankara's teaching is this: it is only if we realise that Īśvara is the phala-dātā, the one who awards the fruits of our actions, that we will not be tempted by petty rewards like paradise. Only then will we be inspired to go beyond to attain the higher reward of inner purity. The Vedic works were wholly acceptable to our Ācarya. But for the mīmāṁsakas they were an end in themselves; they did not transcend them to become devoted to the Supreme Godhead and to acquire jñāna, the final realisation that Īśvara and we are one and the same. Śankara criticised mīmāṁsakas for their failure to understand this truth. That he did not oppose Vedic karma is proved again by the fact that in his upadeśa[1] (teaching) — it is called *Sopāna-Pañcaka* — before giving up his body he made the admonishment that the Vedas must be chanted every day and that the rites mentioned in them must be performed :

Vedo nityam adhīyatām
Taduditam karma svanuṣṭhīyatām

The Ācārya, however, taught us not to stop with karma (performed for the sake of karma), but to go beyond it. The rites that we conduct must be made an offering to Īśvara. This is a means of obtaining inner purity and also that of receiving instruction in jñāna. That is the time when we must give up all karma to meditate upon the teaching we have received, indeed meditate on it with intensity and make it our own inner experiential reality. Śankara takes us, step by step, in this way to final release. He opposed the mīmāṁsakas because they failed to understand the purpose of Vedic karma and refused to go beyond it.

We must accept the Mīmāṁsā system's interpretation of the Vedas, especially because it surrenders wholly to the "Śabda-pramāṇa", the sound of the Vedas, its authority, and it is in this spirit that it has understood the meaning of the scripture. An interesting thought occurs to me. Mīmāṁsā does not surrender to a perceptible God nor seek to understand his form. Does that matter? The Vedas themselves constitute a great deity. The sound of the Vedas does not take the form of a deity that can be seen with our eyes but one that can be perceived with our ears. Let us perform the works that that sound bids us to do without asking questions. Such an act implies an attitude of surrender and it is in this spirit that the mīmāṁsakas have determined the meaning of the Vedas. So whether or not they believed in a tangible God, they knew the God that could be grasped by the ears (that is they had a good understanding of the meaning of the Vedas).

Note

[1] See Sanskrit Glossary for the correct meainng of "upadeśa."

Chapter 8

Determining the Meaning of Vedic Texts

The Vedas, as we know, contain "vākyas"[S] and "adhyāyas"[S]. How are we to know their content, their meaning? What must we do to find out their purpose, their message?

The rules according to which the Vedas are to be interpreted are contained in the Mīmāṁsā śāstra. If the Vedas are the law, Mīmāṁsā is the law of interpretation. As I said before, when the government enacts a great number of laws doubts arise as to their intention and application. So to interpret these the government enacts another law, the law of interpretation. Mīmāṁsā is such a law with reference to the Vedas. It formulates certain methods to discover the meaning of the Vedic texts.

Six methods are mentioned: upakrama-upasaṁhāra, abhyāsa, apūrvatā, phala, arthavāda, upapatti. According to Mīmāṁsā the meaning, the intent, of Vedic mantras may be understood by applying these methods.

The reader is requested to refer to Chapter 34, Part Five, in which these six methods of Mīmāṁsā śāstra are dealt with.

Chapter 9

Mīmāṁsā Beliefs

Let me now speak a little more on the doctrines of Mīmāṁsā.

Let us not worry about whether or not there is a God. Let there be a God or let there be none. Our duty is to perform the rites prescribed by the Vedas and they will yield fruits on their own. Any work we do produces its own results, doesn't it? Why do we need God in between? The work generates results on its own. Do we pay the greengrocer if he fetches plantain leaves from our own garden? It is the same to give credit to Īśvara for the fruits we reap by performing karma. We till the land and rice grows in it. It is the same with Vedic works. If we do what we do not know, as told by the Vedas, we will derive certain benefits. Why should we think that the cosmos was created by God? It has always existed as it exists today: why should we believe that it came into being all of a sudden? "Na kadācit anīdṛśam jagat." This universe has always existed as it exists today. Do works; they will yield fruits on their own. When the engine is wound the car starts. It is all like that.

The Vedas speak about things not comprehended by the human mind. If we perform the rites imposed on us by them, the fruits thereof will naturally follow. Sound has always existed: it has indeed no beginning and the Vedas are this sound. Like time and space they are ever-present.

If you do evil, the consequence shall be evil; if you do good the result shall be correspondingly good. The rites keep yielding fruits, and we keep enjoying them — and thus we go on and on. No God is required for all this. We should never cease to do work becaue not to work is sinful. It will take us to hell.

There are three types of karma: "nitya", "naimittika" and "kāmya". "Nitya-karma" as the name suggests includes sacraments that must be performed every day. "Naimittika" rites are conducted for a specific purpose or reason or on a specific occasion. For instance, when there is an eclipse we must bathe and offer libations to our fathers. When a great man visits our home he has to be honoured ceremonially — this is also naimittika. Nitya and naimittika rites are to be performed by all. A kāmya-karma is a ritual that has a special purpose. When there is a drought we conduct Varuṇa-japa to invoke the god and seek his blessings in the form of rain. When we are desirous of a son we perform the "putrakāmeṣṭi" (sacrifice to beget a son). These belong to the kāmya category.

The sacraments to be performed every day are defined in Mīmāṁsā. "Akaraṇe pratyavāya janakam, karaṇe'bhyudayam" — this statement refers to two types. The non-performance of some rites brings us ills, troubles — these form one type. On the other hand some rites bring us happiness — these form the second type. A good house, wealth, sons, fame, knowledge are part of "abhyudaya". Vedānta speaks of "nihśreyas", the supreme bliss of liberation. "Abhyudaya" is different; it is happiness on a lower plane. Mīmāṁsā is concerned with the latter, and does not speak of the ultimate blessedness of release from worldly existence.

If rites belonging to the category of "nitya" are not performed, we will have to face trouble. Suppose you ask a man to perform sandhyāvandana[S] and he replies: "I won't do it. I don't care whether or not it does me good." Mīmāṁsā has an answer to it: Sandhyāvandana is not a kāmya or optional rite and its non-performance will bring you unhappiness.

It stands to reason to say that the performance of certain rites will bring you happiness. But how do you justify the statement that the non-performance of certain other rites will have ill effects? Not performing sandhyāvandana is sinful, but its performance is not claimed to bring any good. It is because this rite belongs to the category referred to in the statement, "akaraṇe pratyavāya janakam.."

Worshipping the deity in a temple, feeding the poor, such acts are said to be beneficial and belong to the second category referred to in the statement, "....karaṇe abhyudayam". This makes sense. But how is it sensible to say "akaraṇe pratyavāya janakam"? Are there examples to illustrate this dictum? Yes, there are.

We give alms to beggars, or make a donation to some organisation or other in the belief that there is merit to be earned thereby. Sometimes we do not practise such charity because we may not feel the urge to earn any special merit. We have, of course, to do our duty, but not helping people with money or material cannot be said to be sinful.

Suppose we have borrowed Rs 500 from a friend or an acquaintance. How far are we justified in refusing repayment of the loan, saying: "I don't wish to earn any merit by returning your money?" Is it possible to escape the obligation to the lender in this manner? He will naturally tell us: "I came to ask you for my money. I don't care about whether you or I earn any merit." If we refuse to repay a loan we will be taken to court and eventually we will have to repay it along with a penalty. This illustrates the statement: "Akaraṇe pratyavāyajanakam..."

Not performing sandhyāvandana is like not repaying a debt. In Tamiḷ the sandhyāvandana performed at dawn and dusk are aptly called "*kālai-k-kaḍan*" and "*mālai-k-kaḍan*" ["morning debt" and "evening debt"]. These are beautiful terms.

You may wonder how sandhyāvandana can be described as something "borrowed". The *Taittirīya Saṁhitā* (6.3) of the Vedas says: "A Brahmin is born with three debts. These are 'ṛṣi-ṛṇa', 'deva-ṛṇa' and 'pitṛ-ṛṇa' (that is a Brahmin is indebted to the sages, the devas and to his fathers)." The first debt is repaid by chanting the Vedas; by conducting sacrifices and other rites the second is repaid; and by offering libations and performing the śrāddha[S] ceremony the third is repaid. The Vedas enlighten us on matters of which we are ignorant. From the pronouncements made in them, those who have faith will find reasons to perform the rites. Others who are perverse in their reasoning will find an excuse for not performing the same.

There are two brothers. One is a magistrate and the other a Vedic scholar. The first cannot refuse to attend the court saying, "My brother does not go to any lawcourt. Why should I?" The authorities will tell him: "You applied for the job of magistrate. We issued orders appointing you to the office and you accepted the job. So there is no choice for you but to attend the court." Similarly, we have applied for liberation, for mokṣa, and have received orders that we have to perform certain rites. The one who issued the orders is not seen by us but he sees all and is witness to all. Such is the view of Vedānta.

Mīmāṁsā believes that the karma that we "applied for" gives its own reward. According to it, the fruits of Vedic works come to us "automatically".

Our birth in this world is according to our past karma and we have to perform the rites that are proper to it. If we do not, we will suffer. The customs and rites must be adhered to properly. The duty of a Brahmin is to know the truths contained in the Vedas, to bring solace to those who are sorrowing and to give instruction to people in their respective vocations. Similarly, each man must perform the duties allotted to him by virtue of his birth. The oil-monger must produce oil; the cobbler must make footwear; and so on. The Brahmin must keep his body, mind and Self pure and he must be careful about what he eats. The reason for this is that not only has he to remain meditating on the Paramātman, he has also the duty of bringing others to the path of dhyāna[S]. It was for the proper discharge of such duties that in the old days he was given gifts of rent-free lands. Then every worker was allotted land. If he stopped doing the work assigned to him society would suffer. So he forfeited his land and it was allotted to another worker.

According to the śāstras, not to do the work assigned to us is not only sinful but also disadvantageous in a worldly sense. In the past one earned respect only because one did one's karma, the duties expected of one. Our nation is in a lamentable state today only because of the failure on the part of people to follow their respective callings, callings inherited from their forefathers. If everybody does his allotted job, performs the duties expected of him by birth, there should be happiness for all even in a mundane sense. If there is so much poverty in the country today it is because of our failure to maintain the social order in which everybody is expected to do his allotted work, contributing to social prosperity and harmony.

Sandhyāvandana and the like are every-day rites. The non-performance of nitya-karma is a sin; performance means we will not incur any demerit. That apart, there will be general well-being. If we repay a loan in instalments it means that we shall no longer remain indebted to the lender (here we see a gain); additionally we earn a name for being honest and trustworthy. By performing nitya-karma no sin will attach to us and, besides, it should mean some good to us. Thus there are two types of gain.

Vedānta too accepts the idea implicit in the statement "Akaraṇe pratyavāya janakam, karane' bhyudayam." We must never fail to perform nitya-karma; for instance, Śrauta rites like agnihotra and Smārta rites like aupāsana.

It is the view of mīmāṁsakas that agnihotra must be performed so long as one is alive. So they do not favour the sannyāsāśrama (the last stage of life, that of the ascetic). In this āśrama there are no rites like agnihotra. Giving up works, according to the mīmāṁsakas, is extremely sinful. To do so consciously and become an ascetic is like embracing another religion. The *Īśāvasyopaniṣad* (second mantra) says that a man must live a hundred years performing works[1]. The *Taittirīya Brāhmaṇa* has it that to extinguish the agnihotra fire is to earn the demerit of killing a hero.

According to Mīmāṁsā, to give up nitya-karma is tantamount to doing evil karma. "The sannyāsin deprives himself of karma ('karma- bhraṣta'). To look at him is sinful and you must atone for it. To look at the sinner, to talk to him, to touch him, to dine with him," say Maṇḍanamiśra and mīmāṁsakas like him, "is to earn sin. To look at a sannyāsin is equally sinful."

The jñānakāṇḍa of the Vedas speaks of sannyāsa, the Parabrahman, liberation, jñāna and so on. Why should such concepts be attacked? What is the answer of mīmāṁsakas to this?

It is true, they say, that the Upaniṣads speak of jñāna and the Parabrahman. But what are the Vedas? The Vedas are sound, they are made up of words. Why did they come into existence? To tell us about the things that we do not know. The Vedas constitute the Śabda-pramāṇa which speaks about things that cannot be perceived by the eyes and are beyond conjecture. Their purpose is not to tell us about matters that are of no use. All words serve a twofold purpose. They bid you: "Do this" or "Do not do this."

Pravṛttirvā nivṛttirvā nityena kṛtakena vā
Puṁsām yenopadiśyeṭe tacchāstram abhidhīyate

Words that speak of things that serve no purpose belong to the category of useless, idle talk. Suppose a man says, "The crow flies." How does the statement help you? "The crow is black." Do these words also help you in any way? Take this sentence for example: "Tomorrow night a discourse will be held here." This has some purpose. It gives a bit of information and implicit in it is an invitation to people to come and listen to the discourse. Such usefulness is "pravṛtti". If someone says that there will be a discourse at Kuṁbhakoṇam tomorrow, it is as good as gossip. You are in Maḍrās and how will you go to Kumbhakoṇam in such a short time to listen to the discourse? Any word, any śabda, must have some objective or other. It must either involve you in work, "pravṛtti", or keep you out of it, "nivṛtti". If the Vedas mention all the five terrible sins (pañca-mahā- pātakas) and bid us not to commit them, it is nivṛtti, because they warn us against committing those dreadful crimes.

Words that do not serve the purpose of either pravṛtti or nivṛtti are useless. One part of the Vedas asks you to do this or that and another part asks you not to do this or that [ordinances regarding what you must do and what you must not]. But there is another part which is like story-telling. The stories are meaningful only if they are connected with the injunctions and interdictions of pravṛtti and nivṛtti.

Suppose there is an advertisement of a tonic that claims to give you vigour and strength. It carries an illustration showing a man wrestling with a lion. What is the purpose of this drawing? It is a kind of deception, the idea behind it being to induce you to buy the tonic and make money. Such "stories" in the Vedas become purposeful only because of the injunctions associated with them and they belong to the category of "arthavāda"[2]. Why does a doctor print his certificate in advertising his medicine? To persuade people to buy it (the medicine). In this way in arthavāda untruth is mixed with truth. The untrue part is called "guṇavāda". There is another term called "anuvāda". It means stating what is already known. For instance, the statement that "fire burns".

Mentioning the ingredients of a medicine is an example of "bhūtārthavāda." "Guṇārthavāda" is to tell a story, even though untrue, to make it useful for the observance of a rule. "Do not drink liquor" is an injunction (or interdiction). To tell the "story" that a man who got drunk was ruined is arthavāda. The purpose — or moral — is that one must not drink. To say that if a man drinks he will be intoxicated is anuvāda. All told, the stories or statements belonging to arthavāda must make us conform to the commandments of the Vedas.

In dealing with a sacrifice, the Vedas ask us to pay the dakṣiṇā in gold, not in silver. According to the *Taittirīya Saṁhitā* silver should not be given as dakṣiṇā in sacrifices. In this connection a long story is told to illustrate the "niṣedha" or the prohibitory rule regarding silver. ("Do this" is a "vidhi"; "do not do this" is a "niṣedha".) But the words by themselves in such arthavāda do not serve any purpose.

It is in this manner that the mīmāṁsakas try to counter the objections raised against their system by adherents of the jñānakāṇḍa of the Vedas.

When the Upaniṣads speak about the Brahman there is no mention of any work to be performed. The Upaniṣads themselves show that the realisation of the Brahman is a state in which there is no action. When do the Vedas become an authority? When they speak about the performance of a karma. So the Upaniṣads belong to the arthavāda category because they deal with existing things. What is it that we must know? Existing things or the karma we ought to perform?

"The Brahman exists. The Ātman is the Brahman." In such pronouncements there is no mention of any rites to be performed. It is obligatory for us to conduct sacrifices and we need the Vedas only for that purpose, to tell us about such works, not to speak about things that exist. What exists will be known at one time or another, even if we do not know it now. That part of the Vedas which speaks of existing things belongs to arthavāda. So the Upaniṣads are not to be regarded as an authority. Then what is their purpose? They are meant to elevate the sacrificer. By extolling him he would be made to perform more and more works. It is not right to forksake karma to become a sannyāsin. The Upaniṣadic declaration that the individual self is the same as the Brahman is meant only to glorify one who leads a life of works. The man who takes the tonic (in the story mentioned earlier) will never be able to wrestle with the lion. Similarly, the individual self will never attain the Brahman. The Upaniṣads are in the nature of a story and we do not need any talk of the Brahman, jñāna, mokṣa, Īśvara, and so on. Karma is all for us. So goes the argument of the mīmāṁsakas.

References

[1] *Kurvanneveha karmāṇi jijviṣecchatam samāḥ*
Evaṁ tvayi nānyatheto'sti na karma lipyate nare

— Īśāvāsyopaniṣad, 2

[2] See Chapter 34, Part Five.

Chapter 10

Śankara's Reply

What is Śankara's reply to this argument?

What the Vedas state need not necessarily serve the purpose of involving us in any work. The mīmāṁsakas accept the Vedas because, according to them, the karma mentioned in them serves a purpose. So the purpose served by karma is the message of the Vedas, not the karma itself. If to be without any karma, without any work, is itself a great purpose, must not the jñānakāṇḍa of the Vedas then be acceptable since it deals with a condition in which there is no karma to be performed, or nothing is to be done? That is if being without karma is "useful" by itself — if it serves a "purpose" — that can also then be the message of the Vedas. So the underlying goal of the Vedas is not karma itself but the purpose behind it.

The Vedas admonish us: "Do not drink wine." How do we react to this interdiction? We react by doing nothing; there is indeed nothing for us to do. The message of this Vedic commandment is that we ought not to ruin ourselves by drinking. To remain without doing anything is called "abhāva". All niṣedha (prohibition) belongs to the abhāva category. The mīmāṁsakas themselves admit that the Vedas forbid certain actions. If it is beneficial not to perform certain actions, how can you object to the possibility that not doing any karma at all can also constitute a great purpose? Vedānta has great "use" thus since it serves the supreme purpose of the actionless or quiescent state in which we realise the Self. This cannot be rejected as arthavāda.

Kṛṣṇa says in the Gītā: "Sarvam karmā'khilam Partha jñāne parisamāpyate" (All works, Partha, find their goal in jñāna)[1]. All karma must be consecrated to Parameśvara, must be laid at the feet of the Supreme Lord. To be without work, and experience the bliss of the Brahman is the greatest of "uses". In this state there is no birth again and it means freedom from worldly existence. That is the ultimate message of the Vedas. The karmakāṇḍa must be woven together with the jñānakāṇḍa if it is to be meaningful and if it is to serve a purpose.

Śankara succeeded in convincing Maṇḍanamiśra, Kumārilabhaṭṭa and others about the rightness of this view. To recapitulate his argument: "The karmakāṇḍa of the Vedas mentions works because their performance is of some use in cleansing the mind. If the purpose achieved by not performing them is a million million times greater than that gained by performing them, then that must be understood to be the message of the Vedas, the ultimate teaching of the jñānakāṇḍa. The karmakāṇḍa helps a seeker in his early stages. The performance of rites creates inner purity and takes him to Īśvara. Karma performed for the sake of karma leads a man nowhere. The Vedas speak of the sannyāsin's stage of life in which the ascetic, as he attains the Paramātman, becomes the Paramātman." The Ācārya spoke in this vein to Maṇḍanamiśra [converted him to his point of view] and gave him initiation into sannyāsa.

In the karmakāṇḍa certain acts are declared sinful. If a person keeps doing them it is because he feels he finds some pleasure in them. But such pleasure is momentary and becomes an obstacle in his efforts to know the joy that is greater. The mīmāṁsakas, respecting the injunctions of the Vedas, abjure sinful acts. By the performance of Vedic karma they derive certain fruits, a certain degree of happiness, find well-being in their mundane existence and go to the pitṛ-loka or devaloka[2]. But these do not mean everlasting bliss. When the fruits of their virtuous acts are exhausted, the joys also come to an end. Even if they go to the world of the celestials they will have to plunge into this world again on exhausting their merit. "Kṣiṇe puṇye martyalokam viśanti."

What is that well-being which is eternal? The answer is that which is experienced by the jñānin when he dissolves in the Supreme Godhead. Then there is no "doing" for him. One must abjure sinful acts that afford petty momentary pleasure and instead perform noble works such as those mentioned in the Vedas. But what use are even these if they do not lead to the experience of plenary bliss? Are we, however, capable of directly attaining such blessedness abandoning Vedic karma? No. Jñāna is not easy to obtain. For it the consciousness, the mind, must be made pure and unoscillating. So Vedic rituals are essential.

But they must be performed not for impermanent rewards like paradise but for the removal of inner impurities. We must not be deflected from the higher path by the fruits yielded by karma — these must be placed devotedly at the feet of the Lord. He will bless us with the higher fruit of inner purity and then the mind will become mellow enough for Ātmic inquiry, for the inward journey. That is the way to the supreme blessedness, the quiescent state in which one is oneself.

Note & Reference

[1] See notes appended to Chapter 32, Part Five.

[2] "Pitṛ-loka", world of the fathers (the manes); devaloka, world of the celestials, svarga or paradise.

Chapter 11

Vedānta and Mīmāṁsā

Advaita or non-dualism is in agreement with Mīmāṁsā up to a point. It accepts Vedic karma as well as the six pramāṇas (perceptions or sources of knowledge) defined by Kumārilabhaṭṭa. Śankara's non-dualism, Rāmānuja's qualified non-dualism and Madhva's dualism are all Vedāntic doctrines and all three are not against Vedic rituals. While non-dualism accepts all the six pramāṇas of Mīmāṁsā, qualified non-dualism accepts only three — pratyakṣa, anumāna and the Vedas. I will explain these terms when I deal with Nyāya.

The three leading Vedāntic teachers (Śankara, Rāmānuja and Madhva), do not completely reject Mīmāṁsā, but the paths they have cut out go beyond the mīmāṁsic view: devotion in the case of Viśiṣṭadvaita and Dvaita and jñāna in the case of Advaita.

Mīmāṁsā is called karmamārga since it teaches that karma is all. But karma here does not have the same meaning as in Vedānta which speaks of the three paths — karma, bhakti and jñāna. In Vedānta karma is not performed for the sake of karma and is not an end in itself, but consecrated to Īśvara without any expectation of reward. This is also karmamārga or karmayoga. It is this view of karma that the Lord expounds in the Gītā. In the karmamārga of mīmāṁsakas there is no bhakti. But, all the same, the Vedic rituals create well-being in the world, lead to a disciplined and harmonious social life and bring inner purity to the performer. Mīmāṁsā holds karma to be a goal in itself; Vedānta regards it as a means to a higher end.

Chapter 12

How Mīmāṁsā is Esteemed

Mīmāmsā is of great help in understanding the meaning of the Vedic texts. For this reason many scholars, including those opposed to its karmamārga, have made a thorough study of it and also written books on it. Rāju Śāstrī of Mannārguḍi (Tañjāvūr district), who was an outstanding Vedāntin, Venkaṭasubba Śāstrī of Tiruviśanallūr, Nīlamegha Śāstrī of the same place, Kṛṣṇamācāriyār of Rāyampeṭṭah, Kṛṣṇatātācāriyār, Cinnasvāmi Śāstrī of Nandakulattūr, and so on, were "scholar-lions"[1] who made a deep study of Mīmāmsā. Ironically enough, Tiruviśanallūr Rāmasubba Śāstri,[2] who was the guru of Venkaṭasubba Śāstri and Nīlamegha Śāstri, was opposed to sacrificial rites. However, though he was against the śrauta karma that is such an important part of Mīmāṁsā, he was impressed by the theoretical excellence of the system and was himself recognised as an authority on the subject.

The Sanskrit College, Mylapore, Maḍrās, has produced outstanding mīmāṁsakas.

Notes

1 "Paṇḍita-siṁhas" is the term used by the Paramaguru.

2 Rāmasubba Śāstrī has attacked sacrifices in his book "Paśu-māraka-mardanam". —— Ra. Ga.

Part Thirteen

NYĀYA

The Paramaguru briefly deals with the Vaiśeṣika darśana also in this part.

Chapter 1

Science of Reasoning

Nyāya is also called Tarka-śāstra and its author is Gautama. Its main purpose is to establish by reasoning that the Kartā or Creator of all this world is Parameśvara. Indeed, it seeks to prove the existence of Īśvara through inference. Reasoning thus has a major place in Nyāya.

Logic or reasoning is of course indispensable to any study. The Vedas make a statement and Mīmāṁsā determines its meaning. Though we have faith in the Vedas, doubts arise in our minds regarding the meaning of scriptural passages. If these doubts are cleared through reasoning the message of the Vedas will be affirmed. When we construct the marriage *paṇḍāl* we test the strength of the bamboo or timber posts by trying to shake them. In the same way we must subject truths to proper tests so as to confirm them. All logical reasoning must be accepted but it must be firmly rooted in authority. Also, arguments must not be of a carping character, stemming from the urge to be merely contrary.

When Śankara was about to depart from this world his disciples requested him for a brief upadeśa[S]. It was then that he imparted his succinct teaching in the form of five stanzas which go by the name of *Upadeśa-Pañcaka* or *Sopāna-Pañcaka*. "Dustarkāt suviramyatām — Śrutimatastarko'nusandhīyatām", is a line from it. It means that you must give up the habit of captious arguments and that in dealing with a question you must employ proper reasoning, duly respecting the views of the Vedas.

Without reason to guide us it is like roaming aimlessly in the forest. But reason must be founded on authority. Nyāya finds the meaning of Vedic passages in this manner.

Kaṇāda too created a Nyāya śāstra: it is called Vaiśeṣika. One object is distinguished from another on the basis of the special characteristics or "particularities" of the two. The name "Vaiśeṣika" is derived from the fact that it inquires into such particularities. There is a good deal of science in this Nyāya śāstra. Ātmic matters like the individual self, the cosmos, Īśvara, mokṣa or liberation are examined (in Vaiśeṣika "mokṣa" is known by the name of "apavarga").

The Nyāya inquiry into truth is through the four pramāṇas or instruments of knowledge of "pratyakṣa", "anumāna" "upamāna" and "śabda"[1]. Pratyakṣa is direct perception, what is perceived by the eyes and the ears and so on. It is anumāna or inference that is central to Nyāya. What is anumāna? We see smoke rising from the summit of a distant mountain: we notice only the smoke, not the fire, which is concealed by the rocks perhaps. But even if we do not see the fire we may infer that the forest has caught fire. This is anumāna. Here the fire is called "sādhya" and the means by which we infer its presence is "sādhana", "liṅga" or "hetu".

In our Vedāntic system we must reflect upon the teaching imparted by our guru. This is manana and it means going over an idea (in this case the instruction received from the teacher) again and again in the mind, making use of our own ability to reason. Here anumāna is of help. Is it not through inference that we are able to know things that cannot otherwise be perceived? The individual self and the Paramātman are not directly perceived by our senses. Nor do we know the nature of liberation or how to attain it. We have to know such things by inference. Knowing an object on the basis of another known object is anumāna. When we hear the roar of thunder we know, by inference, that there are clouds [that the sky is overcast].

By performing Vedic works [let us take it] we have become pure within. We have also found a good teacher and we have faith in his instruction. But, if we happen to hear something different from what he tells us, doubts naturally arise in our minds. These doubts have to be cleared; they must be discussed and a decision arrived at. Here we must have recourse to a pramāṇa (source or instrument of knowledge) like anumāna or inference. Both Nyāya and Vaiśeṣika conduct inquiries based on anumāna.

Note

[1] "Pratyakṣa" is direct perception; "anumāna" is inference; "upamāna" is inference by analogy or comparison; and "śabda" is the pronouncement of a reliable authority like the Vedas.

Chapter 2

Padārthas

Our religious system is such that if we go to the root of all padārthas (categories[1]) and understand their source, the Truth will become illumined. We must make use of all pramāṇas (sources or instruments of knowledge) for this purpose. (That by which we perceive objects is a pramāṇa).

Objects that are apprehended by the senses, that is by the eyes, ears, etc, are not many. Others have to be known by inference. And inference helps us in understanding the truths of the Vedas. That is why Nyāya is called an Upānga (an auxiliary "limb") of the Vedas.

In Nyāya the padārthas are divided into seven categories. Of them there are two divisions: "existent" and "non-existent" — "bhāvo abhāvaśca", the latter being the seventh padārtha. "Bhāva" or the existent is further divided into six sub-categories.

How does that which does not exist become a padārtha? What does "padārtha" mean? In a literal sense, it is the meaning of a pada or word. Is there not a word which means No? There is non-existence of certain objects in some places, and not in some others. Here there are no flowers. There, in the pavilion where the pūjā is performed, there are flowers, which means that the non-existence of flowers does not apply to the pavilion. So there is non-existence [of objects] in some places and on certain occasions. Thus the fact of non-existence [of a thing] in certain places and at certain times is also to be known as padārtha.

The seven padārthas are : dravya (substance), guṇa (quality), karma (action), sāmānya (association), viśeṣa (difference), samavāya (inherence) and abhāva (non-existence). Dravya, guṇa and karma are padārthas that belong to the category of "sat" or being. We can demonstrate their existence but not of the other four padārthas. Dravya can also be shown in its gross form. But qualities like jñāna, desire, happiness, sorrow, etc, cannot be shown as independent entities. Redness is the quality of, say, the lotus and it cannot be separated from that flower. That on which it is dependent is dravya. And, though qualities like happiness and sorrow cannot be "shown", we can know whether a person is happy or sad: we "see" in him happiness or sorrow. When we see a red lotus we know what is red. Karma is work, activity. Such "work" as movement, running, is karma and it is also dependent on dravya. When a man runs, his "running" cannot be separated from him. But we do see him running and know that he is not sitting or lying down. That means we "see" the running. Sāmānya is the fourth padārtha and it means "jāti" ("species"[2]). We see a number of cows. They have the common quality of being cows. This common quality is of jāti. Among objects or individuals that have a common quality there may still be differences. This is what is called "viśeṣa". Suppose there is a herd of cows (they belong to the same jāti): among them we will be able to tell apart individual cows because of their distinctive characteristics.

What is "samavāya"? The quality of a substance cannot be separated from it (the substance), nor the work associated with it. The parts of a whole object cannot be separated if it is still to remain the object that we know it to be. Here we have samavāya, the quality inhering in something. Fire has a radiant form. But this radiance cannot be separated from it. Here again is an example of samavāya. When one dravya or substance combines with another substance we have "saṁyoga". The two can remain independently without combining. There is samavāya when a substance combines with guṇa or quality and there is samavāya again when dravya and karma combine. The quality and the karma cannot be separated from the substance.

I have already spoken about "abhāva".

Each of the seven padārthas is now further subdivided. Dravya or substance is subdivided into nine: pṛthivī (earth), ap (water), tejas (fire), vāyu (air), ākāśa (space), kāla (time), dik (direction), the Ātman (Self), manas (mind). The first five are called "pañcabhūtas". Corresponding to them in the body are the five sense organs, the eyes that see, the ears that hear, the tongue that tastes, the organ of touch that feels warmth and cold, the nose that smells. The organ of touch is not the skin alone; the entire body possesses the sense of touch. It is because it exists within the body too that we feel stomach ache, chest pain, etc.

These faculties are associated with individual parts of the body. Sight is in the eyes; the ears cannot see. Music is heard by the ears; the eyes and the nose cannot hear it. If an object comes into contact with your tongue, you know its taste but not its smell — the nose does not know that sugarcane is sweet. So these five qualities can be recognised individually by the five sense organs. The eye recognises the quality called tangible form, "rūpa", which means colour, size, shape, etc. White, yellow, green, red, brown are some of the colours. The nose percieves pleasant and unpleasant smells. Heat and cold are known by the skin. The tongue apprehends the six different flavours (rasas). Thus there are five different sense organs for the five different qualities and they are called the jñānendriyas.

Without the sense organs or indriyas the quality of an object will not be recognised. If we had six sense organs we could perhaps know six guṇas or qualities and if we had a thousand sense organs we could perhaps appreciate a thousand qualities. We have no knowledge of all objects of the universe. If we did not possess the sense organ of touch we would not be able to feel heat and cold. We cannot claim that we have knowledge of cold or heat (that is we can feel heat and cold) because they exist. We recognise qualities only by means of our sense organs. The blind and the deaf do not perceive form or sound though form and sound do exist in the world. All the five qualities, form, flavour, smell, touch and sound, are known respectively with the eye, tongue, nose, skin and ear. The Lord has invested the pañcabhūtas, the five elements, with these five qualities. The earth has all the five guṇas or qualities. It has form and flavour. Our body, aubergines, *jaggery* — all are earth. Earth has smell. The fragrant flower is indeed earth. Earth has qualities like cold and heat known by the sense of touch and it has also sound. If you drop one end of a string to earth and keep the other end of it to your ear you will hear sound. Water has four of the five qualities but not smell. It smells only when we mix perfume in it. If we beat its surface it sounds. Though earth has all the five qualities its special quality is smell which is absent in the other four elements. The special quality of water is flavour. Without water there is no rasa. That is why the sense organ of taste, the tongue, is always wet. If the tongue becomes dry you will not be able to appreciate any taste. As a matter of fact, the word "rasa" itself also means water. Fire has neither smell nor flavour but it has form, sound and touch, form being its special quality. Vāyu or air has no form, but it has sound and touch — the last-mentioned is its special quality. That is how we know when the wind blows on us. Ākāśa or space has only one quality, sound.

To sum up, ākāśa or space has only one quality, sound ; vāyu or air has, in addition to sound, the quality of touch; agni or fire has the three qualities of sound, touch and form; water has the qualities of sound, touch, form and rasa; but earth has all the five qualities. Such are the pañcabhūtas or five elements.

The remaining four subdivisions of dravya (substance) are time, dik, the Ātman and manas. Terms like "hour", "yesterday", "today", "year", "yuga" indicate time. "Dik" means direction or area, the points of the compass, what we mean by "here" or "there". In short it denotes "space", ākāśa. The Ātman is the entity that knows all this. He or It is of two types, the intelligent and the unintelligent, the Paramātman and the jīvātman. The Paramātman is a mere witness to all that passes in the world while the jīvātman or the individual self is trapped in it (the world) and given to sorrow. The individual souls are many while the Paramātman is one and only one. Both the jivātman and the Paramātman are spiritual entities of jñāna.

According to Vedānta, knowledge itself is the Ātman; the Ātman is jñāna in a plenary sense. Apart from it, and outside it, there is nothing to be known. Indeed we cannot speak of different jīvātmans[3]. According to Nyāya, the Ātman is a dravya or substance, knowledge (jñāna) being its quality.

Nyāya describes the Paramātman alone as jñāna that is full since there is nothing that is not known to him. The individual self possesses only a little knowledge. So we are called "kiñjijñas", "kiñjit" meaning little. The Paramātman is "Sarvajña", the One who knows all. We are in a mixed state of being dependent both on jñāna and ajñāna. The Paramātman is dependent on (or is) jñāna alone. The Ātman is "vibhu", all-pervading. Nyāya also says that the Paramātman is all - pervading, but it does not speak of the two being the same, the Ātman and the Paramātman. The reason for this is that, according to Nyāya, knowledge exists independently in each individual as a separate factor. The place where it dwells is the mind — and it is the mind that causes sorrow and happiness.

In Nyāya guṇa is divided into 24 categories and karma into five. The Truth will be known, says Nyāya, if we have knowledge of the padārthas and develop detachment that will lead to release. Liberation is a state in which we know neither sorrow nor happiness. Even if we adhere to the Vedāntic concept of liberation, Nyāya affords a method to reflect upon the instruction received from our guru. We are able to know the pañcabhūtas or the five elements, the individual self and the mind. But how are we to know the Paramātman? He alone is not known. It is to know him that we must employ anumāna, the method of inference. To know the rest "pratyakṣa pramāṇas" or direct sources of knowledge are sufficient. The Vedas proclaim the existence of Īśvara; Nyāya establishes it with anumāna or inference.

Let us now see a small example of inference. We know that the throne on which I am seated must have been made by someone. Because we do not know him, can we describe the fact of its having been made itself to be false? We have seen other thrones being made and from that we deduce that there must be somebody who must have made this one also. Similarly, there must be someone who must have created this universe. He is omniscient, omnipotent and compassionate — and he is the protector of all. Such matters are dealt with in Nyāya: a proposition is stated, objections raised and answered.

Notes

1 Literally, the meaning of a word or an object.

2 It is also understood as "generality" as opposed to the "particularity" of "viśeṣa".

3 The idea is that the jīvātman is not separate from the Paramātman.

Chapter 3

Pramāṇas

The pramāṇas other than "pratyakṣa" and "anumāna" are "upamāna" and "śabda". What is "upamāna"? It is knowing what is not known by means of comparison with the known. There is an animal called "gavaya". We do not know what it looks like. It is like a wild buffalo: to look at it is like a cow, so it is said. We go to the neighbourhood of the forest and there we spy an animal resembling a cow, so we conclude that it must be a gavaya. Here we have recourse to upamāna.

"Śabda-pramāṇa" is verbal testimony, the pronouncements of the Vedas and the words of great men. When the scriptures speak of things that we do not know, their words must be accepted as authority. The naiyāyikas, or exponents of Nyāya, believe that the Vedas are the words of Īśvara. The words of great men who are wedded to truth are also verbal testimony.

These four pramāṇas are accepted in Kumārilabhaṭṭa's school of Mīmāṁsā. To them he has added two more: "arthāpatti" and "anupalabdhi"[1]. Thus there are six pramāṇas in all and they are part of the non-dualistic doctrine also.

Our śāstras give a clear idea of arthāpatti through an illustration. "Pīno Devadatto divā na bhuṅkte." What does the statement mean? "The fat Devadatta doesn't eat during daytime." Though Devadatta does not eat during daytime, he still remains a fat fellow. How? We guess that he must be eating at night. There is something contradictory about an individual not eating and still not being thin. Here arthāpatti helps us to discover the cause of Devadatta being fat. Our guess that he eats at night does not belong to the category of anumāna. To make an inference there must be a hint or clue in the original statement itself. There must be a "liṅga" like smoke from fire, thunder from clouds. Here there is no such liṅga.

It is the same with upamāna. When we come to the conclusion that the animal we have seen is the beast called "gavaya", it does not mean that we made an inference or anumāna. We did not recognise the animal by means of any sign but from the fact that its appearance tallied with the description we had been given.

The last pramāṇa is anupalabdhi. It is the means by which we come to know a non-existent object. I spoke about "abhāva", the last of the seven padārthas according to Nyāya. Anupalabdhi is the means by which we know abhāva. Suppose someone tells us, "Go and see if the elephant is in the stable." We go to the stable to see for ourselves whether or not the elephant is there. We find that there is no elephant in the stable: to recognise such absence (non-existence) is anupalabdhi.

Arthāpatti and anupalabdhi are part of Mīmāmsā and Vedānta, not of Nyāya. (However, anupalabdhi is mentioned only in the Kumārilabhaṭṭa school of Mīmāmsā, not in the Prabhākara school.)

Note

[1] "Arthāpatti" is (intuitive) presumption, "anupalabdhi" is non-perception.

Chapter 4

Rational Way to Know God

Vaiśeṣika takes up the thread of inquiry from where Nyāya leaves it with its pramāṇas. According to the great sage Kaṇāda, the founder of Vaiśeṣika, everything ultimately is made up of atoms. Īśvara created the world by different combinations of atoms. In both Nyāya and Vaiśeṣika, the cosmos and the individual self are entities separate from Īśvara.

As we inquire into the origin of conscious life and the insentient atom and go step by step ahead in our inquiry, we realise in the end the monistic truth that everything is the manifestation or disguise of the same Paramātman. Nyāya is an intermediate stage to arrive at this truth.

Nyāya or Tarka (logic) gives rationalism its due place, but this does not lead to materialism, atheism or the Lokāyata system. Through intellectual inquiry, Nyāya comes to the conclusion that, if the world is so orderly with so many creatures in it, all of them interlinked, there must be an Īśvara to have created it. Nyāya recognises that there are areas that cannot be comprehended by human reason and that the truths that cannot be established rationally must be accepted according to how the Vedas see them. This means that Nyāya takes every care to see that reasoning does not take a course that is captious (remember what I told you about the Ācārya's view that tarka should not become kutarka) and that it leads to the discovery of truth.

To examine something with the instrument of knowledge is to purify that very knowledge. It is also a means of obtaining intellectual clarity. When there is lucidity the truth that is beyond the reach of this very intellect will appear to us in a flash. [In other words there will be an intuitive perception of the truth.]

It is indeed commendable to have faith in the Lord and in the śāstras even without carrying out any intellectual inquiry. But are we able to have such complete faith that will take us across worldly existence? Instead of idling away one's time, without making any intellectual effort to discover the truth, would it not be better to keep thinking about things even if it be to arrive at the conclusion that there is no God? A person who does so is superior to the idler who has no intellectual concern whatsoever. Perhaps the atheist, were he to continue his inquiry, would develop sufficient intellectual clarity to give up his atheism. But the idler has no means of advancing inwardly.

This is one reason why even "Cārvākam" was accepted as a system in India. "Cāru-vākam" = "Cārvākam": that which is pleasing to the ear. Cārvākam believes that there is no need to worry about God or any Spirit or to observe vows and fasts or to control one's senses. Live as you please according to your whims and according to the dictates of your senses.

Sorrow, however, is inevitable even in a life in which we consciously seek pleasure. Indeed sorrow will predominate. The purpose of religion is overcoming sorrow.

Chapter 5

We Need All Types of Knowledge

We must make good use of our brain and mind. Indeed, we must make them sharp as if by frequent honing so that they will help us in finding the truth. Why did Śankara master all the śāstras, all the arts, all the sciences, Śankara who thought the world was Māyā? Why did he ascend the "sarvajña-pīṭha" (seat of omniscience)?

I said Nyāya was also known as Tarka, "Ānvīkṣikī". We learn from the *Śankara-Vijaya* that the Ācārya mastered Nyāya or Ānvīkṣikī, Kapila Maharsi's "Kāpilam" (Sānkhya), Patañjali's Yoga-śāstra ("Pātañjalam"), Kumārilabhaṭṭa's Mīmāmsā ("Bhāṭṭa-śāstra").

Ānvīkṣikyaikṣi tantre paracitiratulā
Kāpile kāpi lebhe
Pītam Pātañjalāmbhaḥ paramapi viditam
Bhāṭṭa ghattārtha-tattvam

Advaita embraces even those śāstras that apparently do not speak about it. That is why I am speaking about all such śāstras though I am called "Śankarācārya". Non-dualism inheres dualism, qualified non-dualism, Śaivism, Vaiṣṇavism and so on. It enfolds even those systems that are critical of it. Advaita does not state that other systems are totally false. If it opposes them it is only to the extent needed to counter their agrument against itself. It concedes them the place they deserve.

Chapter 6

Tarka Treatises

Gautama Maharṣi who composed the *Nyāya-sūtra* is called "Akṣapāda". He was always so wrapped up in thought that he was often oblivious of the outside world. We call scientists, professors and such people "absent-minded" and retail jokes about them. Gautama too was absent-minded. One day as he was walking along, brooding over some philosophical problem, he fell into a well. Īśvara then rescued him and fixed eyes to his feet. Thus, as he walked, he would be guided by the pair of new eyes. That is how he came to be called "Akṣapāda", one with eyes on his feet. So goes the story.

Vātsyāyana wrote a bhāṣya[S] for the *Nyāya-sūtra* and Uddyotakara a vārtika[S]. Vācaṣpatimiśra, who was a great non-dualist, wrote a gloss called *Nyāya-vārtika-tātparya-ṭīkā*. Udayanācārya wrote a gloss on this gloss: it is known as *Tātparya-ṭīkā-parisuddhi*. He also wrote the *Nyāya-kusumañjalī*. To recall what I said before, he was foremost among those responsible for the decline of Buddhism in India. Jayanta wrote a commentary on the *Nyāya-sūtra* called *Nyāya-mañjarī*. Annaṁbhaṭṭa wrote the *Tarka-saṁgraha* and himself wrote a commentary on it called *Dīpikā*. Usually, students of Nyāya start with the last-mentioned two works.

It is believed that the *Rāvaṇa-bhāṣya,* a commentary on Kaṇāda's *Vaiśeṣika-sūtra,* is no longer available. However, a bhāṣya-like work called *Padārtha-dharma-saṁgraha* by Praśastapāda is still extant. Udayana has commented on it. Recently, Uttamūr Śrī Vīrarāghavācariyār wrote a book called *Vaiśeṣika-rasāyana.*

Vaiśeṣika came to be called "Aulukya-darśana". "Ulūka" means an owl — the English word "owl" is from "ulū". What belongs to, or what is connected with, the owl is "aulūkya". Kaṇāda himself was called "Ulūka". If Gautama, always lost in thought, fell one day into the well, Kaṇāda was so absorbed in his philosophical investigations by day that he had to go begging for his food at night. He got the nickname of "Ulūka" from this fact, that is he was not seen during daytime and went about at night. (Bhagavān says in the Gītā[1] that the night of the ignorant man is the day of the wise and enlightened man, jñānin. So all jñānins are owls in this sense).

Vaiśeṣika is also called "Kāṇāda-śāstra" after the name of its founder, Kaṇāda. Not the Tamiḷ *"kāṇāda"*[2]. A scholar has said jocularly that Kaṇāda founded his system after having *seen (kaṇḍu)*[3]. Grammar and Vaiśeṣika are believed to be of great help in the study of all subjects. So the saying:

Kāṇādam Pāṇinīyam ca sarvaśāstropakārakam.

Like grammar (which originated in Naṭarāja's ḍamaru), Nyāya and Vaiśeṣika are also connected with Śiva. In the Vaiśeṣika treatises obeisance is paid to Maheśvara who is regarded as the Paramātman. The Śaiva schools hold the view that Īśvara is the "nimitta" or cause of the universe.

Notes & References

1 *Yā niśā sarva-bhūtānāṁ tasyāṁ jāgarti saṁyamī*
Yasyāṁ jāgrati bhūtāni sā niśa paśyato muneḥ

—— Bhagavadgītā, 2.69

2 "*Kāṇāda*" means "not seen" in Tamiḷ.

3 In Tamiḷ, "*kaṇḍu*" means after having seen.

Chapter 7

Cause of Creation

"Causes" or "kāraṇas" are divided into two categories: "nimitta" and "upadāna". You need earth or clay as a material to make a pot. So earth is the upadāna for the pot. But how does it become a pot? Does it become a pot by itself? It has to be shaped by a potter. So the potter is the cause — he is the nimitta. (The "nimitta" we spoke about in Jyotiṣa is different.)

Nyāya and Vaiśeṣika believe that Īśvara created the universe with the ultimate particles called "aṇu-s". Here Īśvara is the nimitta-kāraṇa and the "aṇu-s" are the upadāna-kāraṇa. To shape the clay into a pot a potter is needed. Without him there is no earthen pot, or in other words, the pot without the potter is non-existent. So when he shapes it out of clay he is the cause and the pot the effect. This is called "ārambha-vāda" or "asat-kārya-vāda". "Sat" means that which exists (the real) and "asat" that which does not. There is no pot in mere clay. The non-existent pot is produced from the clay. It is in similar fashion that Īśvara created the universe with the "aṇu-s" — what he created did not exist in the particles. This is the doctrine of Nyāya.

Adherents of Sānkhya, as we know, do not believe in an Īśvara. According to them Prakṛti itself exfoliated into the universe. Such a belief is not to be mistaken for the contemporary atheistic view. I say so because Sānkhya also postulates a Puruṣa who is jñāna, similar to the Nirguṇa-Brahman. According to it the inert Prakṛti can function in such an orderly fashion only in the presence of Puruṣa. The presence of Puruṣa is the cause but he is not directly involved in creation. Crops grow on their own in sunshine. Water dries up, clothes become dry and it is all because of the sun. Does the sun worry about which crop is to be grown or which pond is to be dried up? Your hand becomes numb when you hold a lump of ice in it. Is it right to reason that it is the intention of ice to benumb your hand? Similar is the case with Puruṣa for he is not attached to creation. But with the power received from him, Prakṛti creates the world out of itself. There is no Īśvara as a nimitta-kāraṇa. According to Sānkhya, Prakṛti has transformed itself as the created world. This is called "pariṇāma-vāda".

While asat-kārya-vāda is the principle on which the naiyāyikas base their view of creation, supporters of Sānkhya base their theory on sat-kārya-vāda. Adherents of the former believe that the clay is the upadāna (material cause) for the making of the non-existent pot while the potter is the nimitta or efficient cause. The sat-kārya-vādins belonging to Sānkhya argue thus: "The pot was there in the clay in the beginning itself. The oil-monger presses the sesame seeds to extract the oil that is already present in them. Similarly, the pot concealed in the clay emerged as a result of the work of the potter. It is only by using the clay that you can make the pot. You cannot make a pot with sesame seeds nor do you get oil by pressing the clay. The pots are all aṇu-s of the clay; they came into existence by the aṇu-s being shaped."

Our Ācārya says: "There is neither ārambha-vāda nor pariṇāma-vāda here. It is the Brahman, with its power of Māyā, that appears in the disguise of creation. For the potter who is the Paramātman there is no other entity other than himself called clay. So the ārambha-vāda is not right. To say that the Paramātman transformed himself into the cosmos is like saying that the milk turns into curd. The curd is not the same as the milk. Would it not be wrong to state that the Paramātman became non-existent after becoming the cosmos? So the pariṇāma-vāda also is not valid. On the one hand, the Paramātman remains pure jñāna, as nothing but awareness, and, on the other, he shows himself through the power of his Māyā as all this universe with its living beings and inert objects. It is all the appearance of the same Reality, the Reality in various disguises. If a man dons a disguise he does not become another man. Similar is the case with all these disguises, all this jugglery of the universe. With all the apparent diversity, the one Reality remains unchanged." This argument is known as "vivarta-vāda".

There is vivarta in the phenomenon of a rope appearing to be a snake. The upadāna-kāraṇa (material cause) that is the rope does not change into a snake by nimitta-kāraṇa (efficient cause). So the ārambha-vāda does not apply here. The rope does not transform itself into a snake; but on account of our nescience (avidyā) it seems to us to be a snake. Similarly, on account of our ajñāna or avidyā the Brahman too seems to us as this world and such a vast plurality of entities.

Nyāya lays the steps by which we may go further to realise the truth on which our Ācārya has shed light.

Nyāya and Vaiśeṣika teach us how we may become aware of padārthas (categories) through reasoning and become detached from them to realise "apavarga" in which there is neither sorrow nor joy. But they do not take us to a higher realm. Dualism also has its limitations thus. To grasp the One Reality that is non-dual and realise inwardly that we too are that Reality is to experience absolute liberation.

It must be said as one of the distinctive features of Nyāya that it inspires us to go in quest of apavarga by creating discontent in our worldly existence.

Another of its distinguishing features is that it employs all its resources of reasoning to contend against the doctrines of the Buddhists, the Sānkhyas and Cārvākas to establish the principle of Īśvara as Kartā (Creator).

Chapter 8

Some Stories, Some Arguments

Gangeśa Miśropādhyāya deals with 64 methods of logic in his *Tattvacintāmaṇi*. Since we were taxing our brains with philosophical questions, let me tell you a story, the story of Gangeśa.

Gangeśa was dull-witted in his youth. He belonged to a "kulīna" Brahmin community of Beṅgāḷ. "Kulīna" means one from a good "kula" or clan. It was a custom in Beṅgāḷ to give away a number of "inferior" Brahmin girls in marriage to young men born in "kulīna" families. A kulīna would sometimes take more than fifty wives. Gangeśa had only one wife and he lived with his in-laws. Who would give away more than one girl in marriage to a dull fellow?

Beṅgāḷis eat fish. Six months in a year the whole land is inundated. There is no place then to grow vegetables. So during these months Beṅgāḷis eat fish. In the eastern parts of Beṅgāḷ[1] fish is called "jala-puṣpa" and regarded as a vegetable.

Fish was regularly cooked in the house of Gangeśamiśra's in-laws. People would call him "Gangā". Since he was slow-witted he was thought to deserve only the bones of fish at mealtime. Others were served the flesh and everybody would make fun of him. Gangeśa, unintelligent though he was, could not stand it any more. One day he ran away from home, went to Kāśī without telling anyone. Nobody bothered about it at home. "Let the stupid fellow go wherever he likes," they told themselves.

Many years passed. One day, Gangeśa returned home. People thought that he must still be an idiot. When he sat down to eat he was as usual served the bones of fish. Thereupon Gangeśa exclaimed: "Nā'ham Gangā kintu Gangeśamiśraḥ" (I am not Gangā but Gangeśamiśra). Were he still the dim-witted Gangā of the past it would have been all right to serve him the bones. Now there was a "Miśra" tagged on to his name. It meant that he had returned home with a qualification or title, that he was now a learned man. The message was brief but clear.

The in-laws realised that Gangā was now a great man. It was the same Gangeśamiśra who later wrote the *Tattvacintāmaṇi*. Many have written commentaries on it. The one by Raghunāthaśiromaṇi is called *Dhītiti*. It was after his time that the title "Śiromaṇi" came into use. Gadādhara has written a big tome to comment on ten sentences of *Tattvacintāmaṇi,* and not one sentence of it is superfluous. If a student reads five arguments presented in *Gadādharī* (Gadādhara's work) he would become a wise man; if he studies ten he would be wiser still. Prāmāṇya-vāda is dealt with in it and it is believed that he who studies it would be brighter than all others. *Gadādharī* is still read by students of logic.

To explain prāmāṇya-vāda is to tax one's brain. But during the time of our Ācārya even parakeets, it is believed, were capable of discussing it. (Arguments about pramāṇas is prāmāṇya-vāda.)

Śankara Bhagavatpāda went to Māhiṣmati, the home town of Maṇḍanamiśra, where he happened to see women carrying water to their homes from the river. He asked one of them about Maṇḍanamiśra's house. In that city even ordinary women were learned. So their reply to the Ācārya's question came in verse. Here is one of the stanzas from it:

Svataḥ pramāṇam parataḥ pramāṇam
Kīrāṅganā yatra ca sangīranti
Dvārastha nīḍāntara sanniruddhāḥ
Jānīhi tan-Maṇḍanapaṇḍitaukaḥ

From such incidents we know how wrong it is to say that in olden days only men in India were educated and that the women were condemned to remain unlettered. Not only females of the human species, even birds — in the present case "young parakeet women" (kīrāṅganās) — discussed philosophy. "When you come to the doorstep of that house where the female parakeets discuss svataḥ-pramāṇa and parataḥ-pramāṇa, know that house to be that of Maṇḍanamiśra," is what the women said to Śankara.

Svataḥ-pramāṇa and parataḥ-pramāṇa are part of the prāmāṇya-vāda I spoke to you about earlier. Let us now try to have some idea of this vāda. An interesting story comes to mind.

A Southerner went to Navadvīpa in Beṅgāḷ to learn logic. Most of the logicians in the country were then in Beṅgāḷ. This Southerner who went there was a poet. Through his poetry he had earned a small fortune. Tarka was too tough for him and he could not make head or tail of it. All his efforts to study it were in vain. In the bargain he lost his poetic muse and now he had also spent all his money. If he had retained his poetic talent he could have still earned some money. With the little poetic talent left in him he lamented thus: "Namaḥ prāmaṇya-vādāya mat-kavitvā'pahāriṇe" (I bow to prāmāṇya-vāda that has robbed me of my poetic talent).

Let us briefly examine the prāmāṇya-vāda which the parakeets were discussing.

When we see an object we form a certain idea of it. Some kinds of knowledge are right and some wrong. When we see a piece of glass we may think it to be sugar-candy. This is wrong knowledge. Right knowledge is "pramā", wrong knowledge is "bhramā". Then there is "samśaya-jñāna" as well as "niścaya-jñāna". "Samśaya-jñāna" is knowledge about which we have doubts and "niścaya- jñāna" is knowledge of which we feel certain. Sometimes, though our knowledge of an object (as we see it) is wrong, we think it to be right. An example is that of glass being mistaken for sugar-candy. Then there is the case of our perception of an object being recognised to be wrong at the very time we see it. For example a tree seen reflected upside down in a pond: this is "apramāṅa". At the very moment of our recognition of an object we have two kinds of knowledge about it — pramāṇa and apramāṅa. What seems true to us at the very moment of our seeing an object is "prāmāṇya-graha-jñāna"; and what seems untrue at such a moment is "apramāṇya-graha-askandhikajñāna". In bhramā too as in pramā there is pramāna-jñāna. That is why when we mistake glass for sugar-candy our knowledge seems pramāṇa.

When an object appears to be true (pramāṇa) or false (apramāṇa), is the perception subjective (arising out of ourselves) or objective (arising from the object itself)? If it is subjective it is "svataḥ-pramāṇa"; if objective "parataḥ-pramāṇa". The parakeets in Maṇḍanamiśra's house were discussing these two pramāṇas.

Whether our perception is pramāṇa or apramāṇa is not a subjective matter. It is dependent on the quality of the object perceived. It is only when we know its usefulness in practice that we can confirm whether our perception is right or wrong. This is the view of Nyāya — whether our perception is right or wrong is objective. The view of Maṇḍanamiśra and other mīmāmsakas is the opposite. Maṇḍanamiśra's view is this: certainty about jñāna is dependent on the jñāna itself. But that our jñāna is apramāṇa is dependent on the outside object. "Prāmāṇyam svataḥ; apramāṇyam parataḥ".

The word "vāda" itself is nowadays wrongly taken to mean stubbornly maintaining that one's view is right. As a matter of fact it truly means finding out the truth by weighing one's view against one's opponent's. It was in this manner that Śankara held debates with scholars like Maṇḍanamiśra and it was only after listening to the other man's point of view that he arrived at non-dualism as the ultimate Truth. Vāda means an exchange of thoughts, not a refusal to see the other man's point of view. To maintain that one's view of a subject is the right one without taking into account the opinions of others is "jalpa", not vāda. There is a third attitude. It is to have no point of view of one's own and being just contrary: it is called "vitaṇḍa".

Nyāya received a new impetus, particularly in Beṅgāḷ, after the dull-witted Gangeśa, having blossomed into a great intellect, returned from Kāsī, that is from the 12th century onwards; and it came to be called "Navya-Nyāya", "navya" meaning new. There is also another reason for the name. Gangeśa and those who came after him belonged to Navadvīpa in Beṅgāḷ. The area is now called "Nadiad". Śrī Kṛṣṇa Caitanya[2] belonged to Navadvīpa. He was a great scholar, a master of many śāstras and had the name of Kṛṣṇa always on his lips. He propagated bhakti, especially through bhajana (singing the praises of the Lord) as the path to liberation.

Nyāya holds that the world is real (not Māyā), that the Paramātman is different from the individual self. Even so it was opposed to atheism and established the existence of Īśvara. Besides it laid the foundations for the path leading us to Advaita.

Nyāya is an Upāṅga of the Vedas and is highly intellectual in character. Purāṇas come next in the fourteen branches of learning (caturdaśa-vidyā) but they are dismissed by educated people as a product of superstition.

Notes

[1] Now Bāṅgḷādeś.

[2] Caitanya Mahāprabhu (Viśvambhara Miśra), a great figure of Beṅgāḷi Vaiṣnavism, lived between 1485 and 1533.

Part Fourteen

PURĀṆAS

Chapter 1

Magnifying Glass of the Vedas

The Purāṇas are the magnifying glass of the Vedas. The principles and rules of dharma that are briefly dealt with in the Vedas are enlarged or elaborated upon in them in the form of stories. A subject briefly touched upon may not make a deep impression on the mind. If the same were told as an absorbing story it would at once make an impact on the mind of the listener or reader.

The Vedas urge us to speak the truth ("Satyam vada"). How one becomes exalted by remaining truthful at all costs is illustrated by the story of Hariścandra. "Dharmam cara" (Follow dharma, live a life of dharma) is a Vedic injunction consisting of just two words. The importance of the pursuit of dharma is explained through the long story of Dharmaputra [Yudhiṣṭhira] in the Mahābhārata. "Mātṛ-devo bhava" and "Ptiṛ-devo bhava" ("Be one to whom the mother is a god" — "Be one to whom the father is a god"): these two admonishments are enlarged on, as it were, through the magnifying glass in the story of Śrī Rāma. Such dhārmic virtues as humility, patience, compassion, chastity, which are the subject of Vedic ordinances, are illustrated through the noble examples of men belonging to ancient times, women of hallowed reputation. By reading their stories or listening to them we form a deep attachment to the virtues and qualities exemplified by them.

All these men and women whose accounts are contained in the Purāṇas had to undergo trials and tribulations. We keep committing so many wrongs. But consider these Purāṇic characters who had to suffer more than we suffer. Indeed some of them had to go through terrible ordeals. However, by reading their stories we do not form the impression that adherence to dharma means suffering. On the contrary, etched in our minds is the example of men and women of great inner purity who in their practice of dharma stood like a rock against all difficulties and challenges. At the same time, we are moved by their tales of woe and thereby our own inner impurities are washed away. Finally, the glorious victory they achieve in the end and the fame they achieve help to create a sturdy bond in us with dharma.

Chapter 2

Purāṇas and History

Our nation, it is often alleged, does not have a sense of history. In my opinion the Purāṇas *are* history. But to our educated people today history means the history of the past two thousand years since the birth of Christ. They do not believe that the events of earlier eras, including those mentioned in the Purāṇas, are history. Some of them admit, though, that there is an element of truth in the Purānic stories as shown by recent researches. But these relate to theories like the division of the Indian people into races like Āryans and Dravīḍians, theories they fancy are supported by the Purāṇas. The rest, like the miracles or accounts of supernatural occurrences, they dismiss as fables or as a tissue of lies. Since they are unable to comprehend matters that are beyond our senses they treat the Purāṇas as mystery.

Now children have no choice but to read the textbooks of history written by such people. But I believe that it is not good to keep children ignorant of the Purāṇas. It is not my purpose to say that you should not read history, but I should like to mention that the Purāṇas are also history and that our youngsters have a great deal to learn from them, a great deal that will help in moulding their conduct and character. No such purpose is served by the history taught in schools.

One reason why they say history must be read is their belief that "history repeats itself". The idea is that the lessons of the past would be helpful to us in the future. We learn from history about the circumstances that usually lead to war and about how great civilizations rise and fall. We can be on guard against a repetition of these circumstances and this, we are told, is one of the "uses" of history.

The same events are repeated kalpa[S] after kalpa. According to our śāstras, the Rāmāyaṇa, the Mahābhārata, the *Bhāgavata,* the Daśāvatāra (the story of the ten incarnations of Viṣṇu) and the Purāṇas are re-enacted kalpa after kalpa. Here too we see history repeating itself.

Have we in reality learned any lesson from history, I mean from the history taught in schools? No. We learn how such men as Cenghiz Khān, Timūr, Ghazni and Mālik Kāfur[1] appeared from time to time and caused devastation in various countries and how they massacred innocent people. But by reading accounts of their infamous deeds have we been able to prevent the appearance of such scourges again? Hitler and Mussolini rose to perpetrate the same kind of outrages on people.

We are witness in our own times to governments losing their support because of charges of bribery and corruption made against them and other malpractices ascribed to them including partisanship and nepotism. When one such government falls, another group forms a new government and they too lose the support of the people in the subsequent elections for the same reasons. Here is an example of our failure to learn any lesson from history.

History must be taught along with lessons in dharma; then alone will it serve the purpose of bringing people to the right path. The Purāṇas do precisely this.

History contains no more than accounts of monarchs and other rulers in a chronological order. It does not give importance to their moral character : whether wicked rulers suffered an ill fate or whether just and righteous rulers earned a high place. According to the law of Karma, Īśvara determines the fate of people on the basis of their actions, meritorious and sinful. Such justice is not necessarily meted out during the lifetime of a person. The fruits of a man's actions are reaped in subsequent births. It is not the task of history to deal with such questions, nor do historians have the capacity to inquire into such matters. Whether a wicked ruler like Hitler was consigned to hell on his death and whether he had a lowly rebirth is a subject for the Purāṇas. Those who composed these texts had the requisite insight to deal with such questions; indeed the very purpose of these stories is this, to impart moral lessons. From history we do not derive any edification.

The Purāṇas are also, as I said before, history. Besides, they contain lessons in pāpa and puṇya (demerit and merit). In fact, their choice of stories and narration are such as to bring people closer to the path of dharma. Again, the Purāṇas contain accounts of individuals who by virtue of their steadfast adherence to dharma attained to an elevated state in this birth itself. At the same time, they also tell us about persons who, by their acts of adharma, came to harm in this very birth itself. There are in fact no Purānic stories that do not contain some moral lesson or other.

"The experiences of the past narrated in history are a pointer to future events. The stories of good men who performed virtuous deeds and benefited from them should be a source of inspiration for us. In the same way, the stories of wicked men who brought evil to the world and themselves suffered on account of their acts contain a warning for us." Is the study of history really useful in this way? It is not. To improve ourselves morally and spiritually we must turn to the Purāṇas.

The purpose of the Purāṇas is not to give [as history does] a chronological account of kings or their quarrels without imparting lessons on good and evil. We do not need such history since it does not contain any guide for the conduct of our life. History must be capable of bringing us Ātmic rewards.

The Purāṇas too deal with the lineages of various ruling houses. They give accounts of dynasties descended from the moon and the sun (candravaṃśa and sūryavaṁśa) and contain lists of successive rulers of various kingdoms. But in most cases only the names of rulers are mentioned or only brief references made to them. Detailed accounts are given only of rulers whose lives have a lesson for us. For instance, the *Bhāgavata* tells the story of Uttānapāda, the father of Dhruva, and of Dhruva's son, but only very briefly. However, the story of Dhruva himself is told in detail, Dhruva who is an example for all of us in devotion, determination and courage.

English historians dismiss the Purāṇas as false. But on the pretext of carrying out impartial research they twist history to suit their ends like, for instance, their "divide and rule" policy. It is in this way that they have propagated the Āryan-Dravīḍian theory. If the Purāṇas are a lie, what about the history written by these Englishmen? Efforts are going on to reconstruct our history. But prejudicial accounts cannot be ruled out in these new attempts also. Whatever claim the historians make to impartiality, it is hard to say how far the new history (or histories) are likely to be truthful.

Vyāsa, who composed the eighteen Purāṇas, the great men who wrote the various Sthala Purāṇas[2], and the Tamiḷ author Śekkizhār[T] were unbiased in their accounts.

It is not right to view history merely as an account of the rise and fall of empires or of wars, invasions, dynasties and so on. Each and every subject has a history of its own. But we find that political history is given a dominant place. The emphasis in the Purāṇas is on dharma and, incidentally, they also deal, in a subsidiary manner, with the ruling dynasties, with holy men as well as with ordinary folk. They contain details also of cultural life, the arts and the sciences. The thrust of the Purāṇas, however, is dhārmic and Ātmic.

Notes & References

[1] Cenghiz Khān (*c.* 1155-1227), regarded as one of the greatest military leaders produced by the world, conquered much of China and Central Asia. India escaped his fury although he came up to the Indus. This Mongolian conqueror was a Shamaist by faith. Timur (1336-1405), a Turko-Mongol and one of the most flagitious characters known to history, was descended on his mother's side from Cenghiz Khān. His invasion of India during the declining days of the Tughlaq dynasy is a story of butchery, loot and destruction. During the sack of Delhi he

massacred 100,000 Hindu prisoners. Mahmud of Ghazni, called the "Sword of Islam", led seventeen infamous expeditions to India (1000 - 1027). A perfervid iconoclast, he destroyed numerous temples, including the shrine of Somanātha, and enriched his Afghān capital with the loot brought from India. Mālik Kāfur, during the reign of Alauddin Khilji, started his Southern adventure in 1307. He went up to Rāmeśvaram and created havoc wherever his expedition took him. He returned to Delhi in 1311 with immense booty.

2 Sthala Purāṇas are dealt with later in this part. They are essentially histories of places, especially those noted for temples. (They may be called "local Purāṇas".)

Chapter 3

Are the Purāṇas a Lie or Are they Metaphorical?

Those who distrust the Purāṇas maintain that they contain accounts that are not in keeping with day-to-day realities. The stories in these texts refer to the arrival and departure of celestials and of their awarding boons to devotees. To the critics such accounts seem false. A woman is turned into a stone because of a curse, then the curse is broken with the grant of a boon; or the sun is stopped from rising — such stories seem untrue to us because they are beyond the realms of possibility and refer to acts beyond our own capacity.

Since such things do not happen these days, is it right to argue that they could not have occurred at any time? In the past the mantras of the Vedas had their own vibrant power because of the exemplary life led by those who chanted them. Then people practised severe austerities and cultivated yogic power of a high order. These facts are borne out by ancient books. Through their mantras, austerities and yoga, people then could easily draw to themselves powers of a divine nature. Where there is light there is shadow. So with divine powers there also existed demonic forces that could be seen in their gross form during those times. Today the war between the celestials and the demons is still being waged (the combat between good and evil). Eons ago people could perceive these forces of good and evil because of the special vision gained from their austerities. Scientists say that all light waves and sound waves cannot be grasped by the human sense organs. Some of them go a step further to observe, on the basis of their researches, that there are indeed "good and evil deities".

Even today there are present in this world any number of yogins and siddha-puruṣas[S]. They are unscathed by fire or snow, they can produce rain or stop it, and have powers that cannot be comprehended by our senses. But we do not have faith in such phenomena and we keep doubting everything. In the past there must have been more people than we find today with such abilities or "siddhis"[S]. The Purāṇas contain accounts of many a miracle.

Historians dismiss miracles as not part of history. Jñānasambandhar[T] cured Kūn Pāṇḍyan[T] of his fever with the sacred ashes that had the potency imparted by his muttering the Pañcākṣara[S]. The Pāṇḍyan was made upright with his hunch removed ("*kūn*" in Tamiḷ means "hunch" or "hump"). Historians disbelieve such stories. Mahendra Pallava[T] bound Apparsvāmigal[T] with ropes to a stone and threw him into the Kaḍila river. The saint remained floating down the stream. It was this phenomenon that persuaded the Pallava king to return to the Vedic religion from Jainism.

Again, historians refuse to accept such accounts as true. There is, however, circumstantial evidence to show that a Pallava and a Pāṇḍyan king were restored to Śaivism from Jainism. Historians agree that in the sixth and seventh centuries Jainism declined in Tamiḷ Nāḍu and that the Vedic religion (particularly Śaivism) came to be on the ascendant. If such a big change was to happen, that is if two important monarchs of the time felt it necessary to change their religion, the sort of miracles mentioned in the stories of Jñānasaṁbandhar and Appar must have occurred. The fact that these rulers did not record the incidents in stone or copper-plate does not mean that they (the incidents) did not take place at all.

There is a story told in the tradition relating to gurus about Rāmānujācārya. He exorcised a ghost from the daughter of the Jaina king Piṭṭideva who ruled Hoysala [in Karṇātaka]. Thereupon the monarch embraced Vaiṣṇavism. Historians do not lend credence to such stories of exorcism. Rāmānuja lived in the 11th century. Jainism languished in the Hoysala kingdom and Vaiṣṇava worship and temples prospered. Piṭṭideva himself came to be called Viṣṇuvardhanadeva. This is now confirmed as a historical fact. How can you deny that these changes occurred as a result of the incidents narrated in the story told above? English-educated people dismiss such accounts in the Purāṇas as lies since they cannot be proved scientifically. This attitude is not right.

Even today human skeletons that are ten or twelve feet long are found here and there. Also are discovered the skeletons of huge animals which are extinct today but which agree with the descriptions contained in the Purāṇas. From such discoveries it seems likely that in the hoary past demons as tall as palm-trees must have existed, also animals like yāḷis with the body of a lion and the trunk of an elephant. A human skeleton of which the legs alone measure 16 feet and the remains of an animal ten times bigger than an elephant have been discovered in the Arctic region.

It has been determined that the animals belonged to many hundred thousand years ago. If we take the help of mythology also it would be seen that our Purāṇic stories are not untrue.

Man, who was as tall as a palm, is now only six feet; at another time he was only the size of our thumb. The physical characteristics of creatures change from age to age. This is stated in the Purāṇas.

The Purāṇas are ridiculed because they contain references to vānaras, monkeys akin to humans, to creatures with the face of a man and the body of an animal; and then to a character with ten heads. It is all lies, critics say. Some, however, believe that the Purāṇic stories are all "symbols", that they are allegorical representations.

It is true that in the Purāṇas certain principles, certain truths, are conveyed in the form of stories. But, for that reason, the stories themselves cannot be called false. Even in modern times we read in the papers about the birth of a child with two heads and four hands or one that is neither human nor animal. They call such children freaks. A freak is the product of an error in nature, nature in which we do not usually meet with an error. What are called freaks today could have been created in the past in larger numbers for a special purpose. People in those days had supernatural powers and, in keeping with the same, the birth of such unusual children would not have been impossible. We cannot claim that what we know now is all that is to be known and that there could not have existed anything different from the existing orders of creatures.

It does not stand to reason to treat what we do not know and what we cannot know as untrue. In our own times we see that what we normally regard as unbelievable happens now and then. We read reports of children and older people recalling their past births. In recent years such reports seem to have become more common than before.

We distrust the Purāṇic story, according to which, Kāśyapa had a wife called Kadru who gave birth to snakes. But many of you must have read a newspaper report last year (1958) of a snake born to a Mārwāri woman. When I read it I was reminded of another story.

It refers to a family I had heard about before I became *Svāmigaḷ*[T]. In that family neither the daughters nor the daughters-in-law wore screwpine flowers[1] in their hair. When asked the reason for it they told a "story" — but by story is not meant anything made up.

"Ten or fifteen generations ago," one of the family members, a woman, said, "a snake was born in our family. The family was ashamed of its birth and concealed the fact from others, but, all the same, it was brought up in the home, fed milk, etc. This wonder child could not be taken out. The mother went out only when she had some work of the utmost importance. There is a saying: if you are married to a stone, well, the stone is your husband. Likewise, if a snake is born to you, the snake is your child. One day the mother had to go to the wedding of a very close relative.

"There was an old woman in the house. We do not know who she was, whether she was the grandmother of the snake child. In those days the family cared for even distant relatives who were otherwise helpless. Nowadays children are over-anxious to leave their parents to set up their own households. The joint family was then still a strong institution. A great-aunt or a distant cousin of the grandfather's was looked after by the family. The old woman in our story was blind. The mother of the snake child left it in the care of this woman when she went to the wedding.

"What have you to do to a snake child? You don't have to bathe it or do up its hair. Do you have to dress it? Or carry it in your arms? But it had to be fed at fixed hours. Before leaving, the mother had told the woman: 'Feed it boiled milk. Feel around for the stone mortar and pour the milk in the cavity. The snake will feed on it.' She had probably trained the snake to feed in this manner.

"The old woman did as she had been told. But one day she probably overslept and it was past the time to feed the snake. When the snake crept up to the mortar it didn't find any milk in it. It waited for some time but soon fell asleep crouching in the mortar itself. It was now that the old woman brought the milk. It had not been cooled and was piping hot. She could not naturally see the snake lying coiled in the mortar as she poured the hot milk into it.

"Alas, the milk was too hot for the snake and it died.

"The mother who had gone to attend the wedding had a dream in which the snake child appeared and said to her: 'Mother, I am dead. You come and cremate me amid the clump of screwpine. Hereafter no daughter or daughter-in-law in your family shall wear screwpine flowers in the hair.

"From that day, no one in our family has worn screwpine flowers," the woman said concluding her story.

When I heard this account first I was astounded and wondered whether such things really happened.

Many years later, after I had become *Svāmigal,* people belonging to that family [in which the snake child was born] came to see me. It was not to speak about the snake child of the past. There was an old copper-plate inscription in their family. They had come to know about my interest in old inscriptions and they brought the copper-plate for me to see.

The inscription on it belonged to the time of Acyutarāya[2] who reigned after Kṛṣṇadevarāya[3]. According to it a Brahmin had donated lands to 108 fellow Brahmins. He had done so on behalf of his king. I will tell you why. The Brahmin's time is taken up by chanting the Vedas and performing rituals. He is not expected to earn a salary or do any work other than practising Vedic dharma (today of course Brahmins work in offices and other establishments). But he had to maintain his family. That is why the śāstras permit him to receive gifts, and that is how in the past kings and wealthy citizens honoured Brahmins with donations. But, contrary to present-day allegations, Brahmins did not extort such offerings, but maintained their self-respect, receiving only the minimum needed for their upkeep. They would accept gifts of land only from Kṣatriyas belonging to a high lineage.

Some kings were unhappy that Brahmins did not accept gifts from them and so were denied the opportunity of earning merit. A way out presented itself to them (and to affluent citizens who were in a similar predicament). They prevailed upon an indigent Brahmin to accept a large gift, say, an entire village. But the gift was not wholly intended for him. He was expected to keep only a small plot of land to himself and divide the rest among other Brahmins. These latter did not incur "pratigraha-doṣa" (the taint of receiving gifts) by accepting charity from a fellow Brahmin. This was how the affluent donor managed to earn puṇya.

But would not such a practice bring demerit to the Brahmin who first receives the gift of land? It is not wrong on the part of a wealthy man to honour a Vedic scholar with a donation. But what about the Brahmin who receives it? Legally the property becomes his, and when he keeps only a small part of the land to himself and gives away the rest to others not a trace of pāpa sticks to him.

It is, however, bad to receive charity from a king. Great men like Tyāgarāja[4] spurned the gifts offered them by rulers like Śarabhoji[T]. Tyāgarāja sang in anger: *"Nidhi cāla sukhamā..?"* (Is it money that brings happiness?)

The Nāṭṭukkoṭṭai Ceṭṭis (Nagarattār) built many *cattirams*[T] (dharmaśālās) but Brahmins were reluctant to eat in them. So the Ceṭṭis made over the *cattirams* to a Brahmin and thereby it was made to appear that he was feeding the other Brahmins.

According to the copper-plate inscription I mentioned earlier, a Brahmin had distributed the land received from Acyutarāya among 108 fellow Brahmins. All their names and gotras[S] are mentioned in it, together with the subjects in which they were proficient. Among them figures the name of the ancestor of the people who came to see me, people descended from the family in which the snake child was born. The copper-plate had come as a family heirloom through so many generations. An interesting fact emerging from the inscription was that the name of the ancestor mentioned on the copper-plate was Nāgeśvara[5]. I was told by my visitors that the family had a Nāgeśvara every successive generation.

I could guess at once that the name was associated with the snake child. It seemed to answer my doubts about its story. When I heard the news last year of the birth of a snake to a woman, I had more reason to believe the earlier story of the snake child.

It is wrong on my part to blame you for not having sufficient faith in the Purāṇas. I myself had doubts about the story of the snake child — it had all the character of a legend. It was only when I read the newspaper report of the birth of a similar snake child that I believed it to be fully authentic.

Today we are prepared to believe any story however bizarre it be if it is printed in the papers. But we treat the Purāṇas as no more than fables. "Those who composed the Purāṇas had nothing worthwhile to do. They had the stylus and palm-leaves and they went on inscribing story after story. Some of the stories seem ingenious enough but most are absurd," such is our way of thinking.

Notes & References

1 *"Tāzhambu"* in Tamil, Ketakī in Sanskrit.

2 Acyutarāya ruled the Vijayanagara empire between 1530 and 1542

3 Kṛṣṇadevarāya (1509-30) was the greatest of the Vijayanagara rulers.

4 For Tyāgarāja see notes appended to Chapter 1, Part Six.

5 "Lord of snakes."

Chapter 4
Meaningful even if Imaginary

There is perhaps an element of the imaginary in the Purāṇas. It is also possible that they contain interpolations. But who is to determine what parts are imaginary and what passages constitute the interpolations? And who is to separate the authentic from the spurious ? If each one of us removes what seems interpolatory, nothing will be left of the stories in the end. So it would be better to preserve the Purāṇas in the form in which they have bean handed down to us notwithstanding the apparent errors and distortions.

If there are stories in the Purāṇas that read like fables, let them be so. Do they not bring us mental peace and take us nearer to the Lord? We go shopping and make good purchases. Are we to be happy on this score or are we to be unhappy that there was something wrong with the shop or the shopkeeper? There may be mistakes in the Purāṇic accounts of the earth and the heavens. After all, we can have accurate knowledge of such matters from our books on geography and astronomy. The point to remember is that the Purāṇas contain what geography, astronomy and history do not: the truth of the Ultimate Reality. Besides, they speak about devotion and dharma.

It is argued that Rāma could not have lived hundreds of thousands of years ago, i.e., in the Tretā yuga, that it is not likely that the sort of civilization described in the Rāmāyaṇa would have obtained in that distant period. Similar criticisms are made about stories in the Purāṇas and the epics. I do not accept them. But, for the sake of argument, let it be that Rāma did not live in the Tretā age. And let us also presume that all those stories that happened, according to the Purāṇas, in the earlier Kṛta yuga, did not really belong to that age. Let us suppose that they date back to a comparatively recent period to 7,000 or 8,000 years ago. But for that reason would the story of Rāma or others be less valuable ? And would the lessons we learn from such accounts be less meaningful?

The Purāṇas mention the ages in which the stories recounted in them really happened. According to critics it is not these ages alone that are wrong but also the date(s) traditionally ascribed to the Purāṇas themselves.

According to the śāstras, Vyāsa composed the Purāṇas 5,000 years ago, at the beginning of the age of Kali. But they must have existed before him also. In the *Chāndogya Upaniṣad* Nārada speaks about the subjects learned by him and they include the Purāṅas. From this we infer that they must have existed during the time of the Vedas and the Upaniṣads. Just as Vyāsa divided the Vedas into a number of branches for the benefit of people of later times with their diminished capacity to learn, he also composed the Purāṇas, which are detailed in their treatment, with the same purpose in view.

Western-educated people think that the Purāṇas are not very ancient. So let them be. Devotees throng the Kandasvāmī[1] temple in Madras. They feel the presence of the deity there. If they think that there is an end to their sorrows by worshipping at this shrine, what else is required of a temple? Is there any purpose in conducting an investigation into the origin of the temple, whether it had existed during the time of Aruṇagirināthar[T] and whether he had sung his *Tiruppugazh*[T] in it? Carrying out research into the Purāṇas is similarly futile. If we bear in mind that their purpose is the cleansing of our mind there should be no need to harbour any doubts concerning them.

There is no bigger superstition than the belief that the results of [historical] investigations represent the absolute truth. Much of today's research is hollow, much of it faulty. However, even the view of modern research scholars that the Purāṇas are imaginary serves to show up the purpose for which they are intended: to demonstrate that one who does good prospers, that another who does evil suffers — or is raised up by the compassionate Lord.

Somehow the Purāṇas are regarded as of secondary importance not only by people who claim to have a "modern" outlook, but also by those proficient in the śāstras. Also paurāṇikas (those who have made a thorough study of the Purāṇas and give discourses) are regarded as inferior to those who give talks on other branches of learning. However, scholars who have earned the title of "Mahāmahopādhyāya" like Yajñasvāmī Śāstrī and Kābe Rāmacandrācār have given purāṇic discourses. Today Śrīvatsa Somadevaśarmā[2] is devoting himself fully to the printing of all the Purāṇas in Tamiḷ (even though in an abridged form).

Notes

[1] Kandasvāmī (Skandasvāmī) is Subrahmaṇya.

[2] Śrī Somadevaśarmā passed away in 1973.

Chapter 5

Vyāsa's Priceless Gift to Us

Vyāsa divided the Vedas to make them easier for people to learn. It was to help mankind similarly that he composed the "aṣṭādaśa Purāṇas" (the eighteen Purāṇas).

I regard Vyāsa as the first journalist, the ideal for all newspapermen of today. He composed the Purāṇas and made a gift of that great treasure to humanity. How have they (the Purāṇas) benefited us? They encompass stories, history, geography, philosophy, dharma, the arts. Vyāsa's narration holds the interest not only of intellectuals but of ordinary people, even the unlettered. Is this not the aim of journalists, holding the interest of the general reader? However, most of them stop with this, exciting the interest of people or pandering to their taste. But Vyāsa had a loftier purpose: he made the Purāṇas engrossing with the purpose of taking the reader (or listener) to the goal of dharma and the Supreme Being. If holding the interest of people somehow is their sole objective, the papers are likely to propagate subjects or views that are contrary to the ideals of dharma. If journalists keep Vyāsa as their forerunner and ideal, their writing will assume a noble character and contribute to the good of the world.

Vyāsa composed the Purāṇas in 400,000 "granthas". A grantha is a stanza consisting of 32 syllables. Of these the *Skānda Purāṇa* alone accounts for 100,000. It is perhaps the world's biggest literary work. The remaining 17 Purāṅas add up to 300,000 granthas. Apart from them Vyāsa composed the Mahābhārata, also nearly 100,000 granthas.

Each Purāṇa is devoted to a particular deity. There are Śaiva, Vaiṣṇava and Śākta Purāṅas. The 18 Purāṅas: *Brahmā Purāṇa (Brāhma), Padma Purāṇa (Pādma), Nārada Purāṅa (Nāradīya), Mārkaṇḍeya Purāṇa, Viṣṇu Purāṇa (Vaiṣṇava), Śiva Purāṇa (Śaiva), Bhāgavata Purāṇa, Agni Purāṇa (Āgneya), Bhaviṣya Purāṇa, Brahma-Vaivarta Purāṇa, Liṅga Purāṇa, Varāha Purāṇa (Vārāha), Skānda Mahāpurāṇa, Vāmana Purāṇa, Kūrma Purāṇa (Kaurma), Matsya Purāṇa (Mātsya), Garuḍa Purāṇa (Gāruḍa) and Brahmāṇḍa Purāṇa.*

Our Ācārya in his commentary on the "Viṣṇu-Sahasranāma" cites many passages from the *Viṣṇu Purāṇa*. This Purāṇa, composed by Vyāsa's father Parāśara[1], is an important source of Rāmānuja's Viśiṣṭadvaita (qualified non-dualism).

One of the precursors of qualified non-dualism was Āḷavandār. Rāmānuja wanted to meet him but as he arrived at his place he saw him lying dead. Āḷavandār had wanted to entrust Rāmānuja with three important tasks. When he passed away three fingers of his right hand were seen bent in. Rāmānuja understood the meaning of this phenomenon, that he had three tasks to perform. When he spoke out what they were, the three fingers unbent. One of the three tasks was to write a commentary on the *Brahmasūtra* from the standpoint of qualified non-dualism. The second was to do a commentary on the *Tiruvāymozhi*[T] and the third to perpetuate the memory of Parāśara and Vyāsa. As the author of the *Viṣṇu Purāṇa,* Parāśara occupied a high position. It was with this in mind that Rāmānuja named the two sons of his chief disciple, Kūrattāzhvār, Parāśarabhaṭṭa and Vedavyāsabhaṭṭa. The first grew up to be an important teacher of Vaiṣṇavism.

Though Parāśara was the original author of the *Viṣṇu Purāṇa* it was Vyāsa who wrote it in the present form. The sage who had divided the Vedas now composed the Purāṇas so that the truths embedded in the Vedas would make a deep impression on the minds of the common people. There was also another reason. Not all people have the right to learn the Vedas. It is believed that Vyāsa composed the Purāṇas to enlighten such people (as have no access to the Vedas) on the scriptural truths.

If Vyāsa's father was the author of the original *Viṣṇu Purāṇa,* his son Śukācārya it was who instructed King Parīkṣit in the *Bhāgavata.* There is a difference of opinion about the *Bhāgavata,* whether the term should refer to *Viṣṇu-Bhāgavata* or *Devī-Bhāgavata.* The former is devoted to the incarnations of Viṣṇu, particularly Kṛṣṇa, while the latter deals with the divine sport of Ambā. We need both and both are great works. In the systems propagated by Caitanya, Nimbārka and Vallabhācārya[2], the *Viṣṇu - Bhāgavata* has a place no less important than that of the Vedas. At the same time, non-dualists who are opposed to their ideas also treat this *Bhāgavata* with the utmost respect.

Though there is a separate *Śiva Purāṇa,* three-fourths of the *Skānda Purāṇa* is devoted to Śiva. It also includes the story of Skanda or Muruga[3]. Kacciyappa Śivācariyār of Kāñcīpuram has written a *Kanda Purāṇam* in Tamiḷ: it is devoted [as the name itself suggests] mainly to Subrahmaṇya or Skanda. "Durgā-Saptaśatī" is part of the *Mārkaṇḍeya Purāṇa.* "Caṇḍī-homa", in which oblations are made to the goddess Caṇḍī, is performed with the recitation of the 700 stanzas of this hymnal work: each stanza is regarded as a mantra.

"Bhaviṣya" means the future. The *Bhaviṣya Purāṇa* contains many matters including the evil doings of the age of Kali. In the Purāṇas, apart from the story of the Mauryas and other rulers, there is also a reference to the advent of the white man. Critics discount such accounts believing that they could not have been written by Vyāsa at the beginning of the Kali yuga. "Somebody must have written them recently." they argue, "and put the name of Vyāsa to them." Admittedly, there must be interpolations here and there in the Pūraṇas but it is not correct to say that the Purāṇas were all recently written. Men with yogic power can see past, present and future. Sitting in one spot they can see happenings all over the world. It is not easy for people to write works like the Purāṇas and ascribe their authorship to the great men of an earlier era.

The *Garuḍa Purāṇa* deals with the world of the fathers and related matters. It is customary to read it during the śrāddha[S] ceremony.

"Lalitopākhyāna", the story of Lalitāmbikā, occurs in the *Brahmāṇḍa Purāṇa,* so also the "Lalitā-Sahasranāma" (The One Thousand Names of Lalitā). The reading of the 18 Purāṇas is to be concluded with this Purāṇa which contains a description of the coronation of Rājarājeśvarī. Devotees of the goddess take special pride in this fact.

The Purāṇas contain many hymns, hymns that include the one hundred and eight or the one thousand names of various deities. But the "Viṣṇu Sahasranāma" (The One Thousand Names of Viṣṇu) and the "Śiva-Sahasranāma" (The One Thousand Names of Śiva) are part of the Mahābhārata. The "Pradoṣa-stotra" is in the *Skānda Purāṇa.*

Notes & References

1 See a later paragraph to resolve any apparent contradiction.

2 For Caitanya, see Notes, Chapter 8, Part Thirteen. Both Nimbārka (13th century) and Vallabhācārya (1479-1531) were Telugu Brahmins. The former was settled in Mathura; the latter was born in Vārāṇasī.

3 Tamiḷs know Skanda or Subrahmaṇya as Muruga or Kanda.

Chapter 6

Upa-purāṇas and Others

Apart from the 18 major Purāṇas there are an equal number of Upa-purāṇas. Among them are the *Vināyaka Purāṇa* and the *Kalki Purāṇa*. There are also, in addition, a number of minor Purāṇas. The Purāṇas that speak of the glory of various months such as the *Tulā Purāṇa*, the *Māgha Purāṇa* and the *Vaiśakha Purāṇa* are parts included in the 18 major Purāṇas or Upa-purāṇas. There are also what are called Sthala Purāṇas[1], some of them part of the Purāṇas mentioned above and some existing independently. The Purāṇas that sing the glory of the Kāverī and the Gangā exist both separately and as part of the major Purāṇas or of the Upa-purāṇas. In the *Tulā Purāṇa*, for instance, the importance of the Kāverī is the theme. It mentions how auspicious it is to bathe in that river in the month of Tulā (October-November).

If there are Purāṇas devoted to deities there are those dealing *with* devotees. The Tamiḷ *Periyapurāṇam* tells the story of the 63 Śaiva saints called Nāyanmārs[T]. The same is available in Sanskrit as *Upamanyu Bhaktavilāsa*. *Bhakta-Vijaya* deals with poet-saints like Tukarāma and Nāmadeva who were specially devoted to the deity Pāṇḍuranga of Panḍharpūr.

Reference

[1] See Chapter 15 of this part.

Chapter 7

Itihāsas and Purāṇas

For the learned and the unlettered alike in our country the Rāmāyaṇa and the Mahābhārata have for centuries been like their two eyes, pointing to them the path of dharma. The two poetic works are not included among the Purāṇas and are accorded a special place as "itihāsas"[1].

"Purā" means "in the past". That which gives an account of what happened in the past is a "Purāṇa", even though it may contain predictions about the future also. The term can also mean what was composed in the past. The genre called "novel" written in prose came after a long period in literature dominated by poetry and drama. When the novel was introduced into India it came to be called "*navīnam*"[2]. If "*navīnam*" means new, purāṇa means old.

A Purāṇa must have five characteristic features — (lakṣaṇas). The first is "sarga" (creation of the cosmos); the second is "prati-sarga" (how eon after eon it expanded); the third is "vaṁśa" (the lineage of living creatures beginning with the children of Brahmā); the fourth is Manvantara (dealing with the ages of the 14 Manus, forefathers of mankind during the 1,000 caturyugas); and the fifth is "vaṁśānucarita" (genealogy of the rulers of the nation including the solar and lunar dynasties). Besides there are descriptions of the earth, the heavens, the different worlds.

"Itihāsam" = "iti-hā-asam" (it happened thus). The "hā" in the middle means "without doubt", "truly". So an "itihāsa" means a true story, also a contemporary account. Vālmiki composed the Rāmāyaṇa during the lifetime of Rāma. Vyāsa, author of the Mahābhārata, lived during the time of the five Pāṇḍavas and was witness to the events narrated by him in his epic.

In the Purāṇas Vyāsa has dealt with the stories or events of the past which of course is in keeping with their name (that is "Purāṇas"). But how? Vyāsa could see into the past as he could into the future. So what he has written of the past must be an eyewitness account. However, his contemporaries would not have known about them. The Mahābhārata and the Rāmāyaṇa are different. When these works were first made known to the world most people must have been familiar with the characters and events described in them. There is thus no reason to doubt their authenticity. The "hā" in "itihāsa" confirms this.

The word "itihāsa" can also mean "thus speak they" (that is "great men say that it must be so").

"Aitihya" is not an account of what is directly witnessed: it is to be accepted as a matter of faith. It is also derived from "iti" ("thus great men have spoken"). What we actually observe is "this"; what is told by others is "thus".

Notes

[1] Explained later in this discourse.

[2] In Hindi the novel is called *"upanyās"*

Chapter 8

The Epics and their Greatness

If the Purāṇas are described as constituting an Upāṅga of the Vedas, the itihāsas (the epics) are so highly thought of as to be placed on an equal footing with the Vedas. The Mahābhārata is indeed called the fifth Veda ("pañcamo Vedaḥ"). Of the Rāmāyaṇa it is said: "As the Supreme Being, who is so exalted as to be known by the Vedas, was born the son of Daśaratha, the Vedas themselves took birth as the child of Vālmīki [in the form of the Rāmāyaṇa]."

Vedavedye pare puṁsi
Jāte Daśarathātmaje
Vedaḥ Prācetasādāsīt
Sākṣādrāmāyanātmanā

(As the son of Pracetas Vālmīki is called Prācetas.)

The stories of the Rāmāyaṇa and the Mahābhārata are in the blood of our people, so to speak. Today not many read these epics, but forty or fifty years ago[1] it was not so. If our people were then known in the rest of the world for their truthfulness and moral character, the most important reason for it was that they were steeped in the Rāmāyaṇa and the Mahābhārata. In the old days Tamiḷ rājās made gifts of land to learned men to give year-round discourses on the Mahābhārata in the temples. Until thirty or forty years ago people gathered in their hundreds to listen to the *pūśāri*[T] tell stories from the Mahābhārata through song to the accompaniment of his drum *uḍukku*. For common folks then the *pūśari's* performance was both "cinema" and "drama". Cinema and drama have their own ill effects but not the art of the *pūśāri*. By listening constantly to stories from the Mahābhārata people remained guileless, respecting such virtues as truthfulness and morality. The esteem in which the Mahābhārata was held in the Tamiḷ country may be known from the fact that the temple of the village deity was called "*Draupadai Amman koyil*"[2].

The bigger Purāṇas contain a number of independent stories, each highlighting a particular dharma. In the itihāsa or epic it is one story from beginning to end. In between there are episodes but these revolve round the main story or theme. In the Purāṇas, as mentioned above, each story speaks of a particular dharma, while in the itihāsa the main or central story seeks to illustrate all dharmas. For instance, "Hariścandra Upākhyāna" illustrates the dharma of truthfulness alone; the story of Śravaṇa speaks of filial affection; that of

Naḷāyanī of a wife's chastity and uncompromising loyalty to her husband; the story of Rantideva speaks of self-sacrifice and utter compassion. But in the Rāmāyaṇa and the Mahābhārata, based on the life of Rāma and the Pāṇḍavas respectively, all dharmas are illustrated through the example of the different characters portrayed in them.

Notes

1 It must be some 40 years since the Paramaguru made this observation.

2 Temple of the goddess Draupadī.

Chapter 9

Why Differences among the Gods?

Each Purāṇa is in the main devoted to a particular devatā. In the *Śiva Purāṇa* it is stated: "Śiva is the Supreme Being. He is the highest authority for creation, sustenance and dissolution. It is at his behest, and under him, that Viṣṇu functions as protector. Viṣṇu is a mere bhogin[1], trapped in Māyā. Śiva is a yogin and jñāna incarnate. Viṣṇu is subject to Śiva and worships him. Once when he opposed Śiva he suffered humiliation at his hands." Stories are told to illustrate such assertions.

In the Vaiṣṇava Purāṇas you see the reverse. They contain stories to support the view that Viṣṇu is superior to Śiva. "Is Śiva a god, he who dwells in the burning grounds with spirits and goblins for company?" these Purāṇas ask.

In each Purāṇa thus a particular deity is exalted over others. It may be Subrahmaṇya, Gaṇapati or Sūrya. Each such deity is declared to be the Supreme God and all others are said to worship him. When, out of pride, they refuse to worship him they are humbled.

Doubts arise in our minds about such contradictory accounts. "Which of these stories is true?" we are inclined to ask. "And which is false? They cannot all of them be true. If Śiva worships Viṣṇu, how does it stand to reason that Viṣṇu should adore Śiva? If Ambā is superior to the Trimūrti (Brahmā, Viṣṇu and Maheśvara), how is it right to say that she remains submissive to Parameśvara as his devoted consort? The Purāṇas cannot all of them be true. Or are they all lies?"

Logical thinking seems to point to the conclusion that all Purāṇic stories cannot be true. But, as a matter of fact, they are. A deity that suffers defeat at one time at the hands of another emerges triumphant on another occasion. And a god who worships another deity is himself the object of worship at other times. How is this so and why?

The Paramātman is one and only one. He it is that creates, sustains and destroys. And it is he who exfoliates as the many different deities. Why does he do so? He has not cast people in the same mould. He has created them all differently, with different attitudes, the purpose being to make the affairs of the world interesting by imparting variety to them. The Paramātman himself assumes different forms to suit the temperament of different people so that each may worship him in the form he likes and obtain happiness. This is the reason why the one and only Paramātman manifests himself as so many different deities.

Everybody must have firm faith in, and devotion for, his chosen deity. He must learn to believe that this deity of his is the Paramātman, that there is no power higher. That is the reason why each manifestation or form of the Supreme Godhead reveals itself to be higher than other forms or manifestations. It is thus that these other forms are shown to have worshipped it or suffered defeat at its hands. Altogether it means that each deity worships other deities and is in turn worshipped by these others. Also each god suffers defeat at the hands of other gods and, at the same time, inflicts defeat on them.

In the Śaiva Purāṇas all those aspects that proclaim the glory of Śiva are brought together. Similarly, in the case of the Vaiṣṇava Purāṇas that deal with Viṣṇu. Ambā, Subrahmaṇya and other deities are each of them dealt with in such a way as to show him or her to be the highest among the devatās.

The purpose of exalting a particular deity over another is not to depreciate the latter. The underlying idea is that a person who worships his chosen god has unflinching faith in him and becomes totally devoted to him. Such exclusive devotion is called "ananyabhakti". The idea here, however, is not to regard other devatās as inferior to one's own chosen deity -- an example of "nahi nindā nyāya".

Those who are capable of looking upon all deities as the manifestations of the one and only Paramātman have no cause for exclusive devotion to any one of them. It is only when we think that one deity is separate from — or alien to — another that the question arises of giving up one for another. If we realise that all are the different disguises of the One Reality, the various gods and goddesses portrayed in the Purāṇas, with all the differences among them, will be understood to be nothing but the līlā or sport of the Supreme Being. It is the One alone that seems divided into manifold entities. This is to help men of various attitudes and temperaments. If this truth is recognised we shall be able to see the stories in the Purāṇas — stories that seem contradictory — in the true light.

In the story of Bāṇāsura we see that Śiva is vanquished by Kṛṣṇa. But in the story of Tiruvaṇṇāmalai, Viṣṇu meets with failure in finding the feet of Śiva. Both stories must be treated as truthful. The first is to make devotees of Kṛṣṇa worship him as the Paramātman and the second to make devotees of Śiva adore him similarly. Although we think that the one is the winner and the other the loser or that the one is superior to the other or inferior to him, the two know themselves to be one. Does one triumph over oneself — or does one inflict defeat upon oneself? So all this is play. The Paramātman indulges in sport assuming multifarious forms.

The purpose of the Purāṇas is to show people the right path. Pātivratya[S] is a virtue that is of the utmost importance. Ambā herself exemplifies it. The Parāśakti, the Supreme Power that she is, remains subject to her husband. Faith and devotion must grow in the world and for it the Lord himself must show the way. This is why in some temples Viṣṇu is represented as a worshipper of Śiva and in some other shrines Śiva is seen as a devotee of Viṣṇu. The same with other deities. I have spoken more about Śiva and Viṣṇu since Śaivism and Vaiṣṇavism are the two major divisions.

To sum up, if a deity is glorified in the Purāṇas, and stories told in support of it, it is to create exclusive devotion to him as the Paramātman. And, if any god is portrayed as inferior to another, the true purpose of it is not to denigrate him but to develop unflinching faith in the latter.

Chapter 10

The One as Many

As already emphasised, the one and only Paramātman is revealed as so many different deities. If one person develops a great liking for a certain deity, another chooses to have a liking for some other. To make a man a confirmed devotee of the form in which he likes to adore the Lord, the Paramātman on occasion diminishes himself in his other forms.

Tirukaṇḍiyūr is in Tañjāvūr district, Tamiḷ Nāḍu. In the temple here Śiva is seen to be a lesser god than Viṣṇu. He once plucked off one of Brahmā's heads, became thus the victim of a curse and was freed from it through the grace of Viṣṇu. In the same district is Tiruvīzhimalai where it is Viṣṇu who is seen to be a lesser god than Śiva. Reciting the "Śiva-Sahasranāma" (The One Thousand Names of Śiva), Viṣṇu offers lotuses at the feet of Śiva. When he is nearing the end of his worship he finds that he is short of one lotus. What does he do now? Viṣṇu, the lotus-eyed, digs out one of his own eyes and offers it at the feet of Śiva. The latter is pleased and gives him the cakra or discus. Śiva is called here "Netrārpaṇeśvara" (Śiva to whom an eye has been offered); at Tirukaṇḍiyūr Viṣṇu is "Hara-śāpa-vimocana" (one who freed Śiva from a curse). When we listen to the story of Tirukaṇḍiyūr we learn that Viṣṇu is a god of great compassion who frees his devotees from the most terrible of curses. Similarly, from the Tiruvīzhimalai story we realise that no sacrifice is too great for a devotee — Viṣṇu offers one of his own eyes to the god he worships, that is Śiva. The question here is not who is the greater of the two, Śiva or Viṣṇu.

In the old days we used to have lanterns in our homes. There were lanterns with glass on all the four sides — or three sides. Let us take the latter type. The wick inside the glass case is lighted. The three sides made of glass are painted in three different colours [or only two sides are painted]. The light burning inside will be seen to be a different colour from each side. We may take these three sides to represent creation, protection and dissolution, the three functions performed by the Paramātman. It is the one Light that is responsible for all the three, like the wick burning inside the lamp with the three sides.

One side of the lantern, let us assume, is painted red. It symbolises creation. If we remove red from the pure light of the spectrum, the other six colours also will be separated. This is what is meant by the one becoming the many of creation. Brahmā, the Creator, is said to be red in colour. Another side of the lantern is painted blue. The first and last colours of the spectrum are violet and red. The beginning is red (or infrared) and the end violet (or ultraviolet). Mahāviṣṇu, during the very act of sustaining all creation, demonstrates through jñāna that this world is not the whole self-fulfilling truth but the disguise of the Paramātman, his sport. In the fire of jñāna the cosmos is charred. This is the state in which an object, without being entirely disintegrated, retains its form but loses its colour: it is like a lump of charcoal. Such an entity as the world still exists, but its own quality, Māyā, is burned out and is suffused with Viṣṇu — "Sarvam Viṣṇumayam jagat". In Tamiḷ Viṣṇu is called "*Kariyān, Nīlameniyān*" (one who is like charcoal, one whose body is blue). Blue, black and violet are more or less similar colours. The light coming from the blue side of the lantern is Viṣṇu.

The third side of the lamp is not painted. We saw that when all is burnt in jñāna the residue is a lump of charcoal. But if this charcoal is burned further the ultimate product is ash. It has no form and is just powder or dust. Now the colour also changes from black to white. White is the colour close to pure light. All the colours are inherent in that light, which means all the cosmic functions and activities emanating from the Paramātman are made extinct, are burnt out. Now the Paramātman alone remains. That is the ashes remain when everything is burnt out — that is what lasts in the end. It is indeed Parameśvara otherwise called Mahābhasma. Saṁhāra, destruction, may seem a cruel function. But what Śiva does, though seemingly cruel, is truly an act of compassion because he goes beyond destruction to unite us with the Truth. When Viṣṇu sportingly bestows jñāna on us the cosmos seems like a lump of charcoal. "Sarvam Viṣṇumayam jagat," we say. But now all the sport has ended and we have come to the state of supreme jñāna: there is neither "sarvam" nor "jagat". Now it is all "Śivamayam". It is the one lamp that is the light of the Brahman. When it is seen through the red side of the lantern it becomes Brahmā; through the blue side it is Viṣṇu; and through the unpainted side it is Śiva.

Our great men have in the past sung of the One manifesting as three ("*Oruvare mūvuruvāy*"). There were great poets in our country who were not interested in propagating any philosophy or any system of thought — they were men possessing a broad outlook and an open mind who expressed their views freely. These poets have said that it is the same entity that is manifested as the Trimūrti (Brahmā, Viṣṇu and Maheśvara) and indeed as the 33 crore devatās. Bāṇa[S] says that the same Object becomes three to perform three functions, "sarga-sthiti-nāśa-hetave". Kālidāsa clearly states, "Ekaiva mūrtirbibhide tridhā sā" (The Paramātman is One; it is this One that divides itself into three for the three different functions)[1].

If we were divided into two schools, the one insisting that the Śaiva Purāṇas alone are authoritative among the Purāṇas and the other claiming that only the Vaiṣṇava Purāṇas are to be relied upon, we would keep quarrelling without ever being able to take a clear and dispassionate view of things. "The Truth is One. The wise speak of it by different names." There is no greater authority for us than this Vedic pronouncement. So all of us, without making any distinction between the Śaiva and Vaiṣṇava systems, must listen to the stories of all deities and be rewarded with freedom from worldly existence.

Tiruviśanallūr Ayyāyāl[S] was a great man. His real name was Śrīdhara Venkaṭeśvara. But out of respect people referred to him as "Tiruviśanallūr Ayyāvāḷ". He lived some three hundred years ago and was the senior contemporary of Bhagavannāma Bodhendra[S]. Bodhendra propagated devotion to Rāma and Govinda, that is he taught people to sing these names of the Lord. At the same time Ayyāvāḷ spread the glory of Śiva by singing his names. Neither of the two respected any distinction between Śiva and Viṣṇu. So the two of them jointly propagated the "nāma siddhānta" in Tiruviśanallūr. They had respect and affection for one another and established the doctrine that in the age of Kali repeating the names of the Lord [nāma japa] is the sovereign remedy for all ills. Whenever a bhajana is held obeisance is paid to these two (first Bodhendra and then Ayyāvāl) before singing the praises of the deities.

During a śrāddhā[S] ceremony Ayyāvāḷ fed an untouchable. The village headman gave the ruling that he had to bathe in the Gaṇgā in expiation. Ayyāvāḷ made the sacred river rise in the well in the backyard of his house. This story is well known. The incident took place on the new moon of the month of *Kārttigai* (November-December). Even today devotees in large numbers bathe in the water of this well in the belief that it is as good as taking a dip in the holy Gangā.

Ayyāvāl gives his own accc unt of how Śrī Rāmā broke the bow of Śiva. "Svakara pratipādita svacāpaḥ," this is how he puts it. That is Rāma broke *his* bow with his own own hands. The story usually told is that the bow of Śiva was cracked by Nārāyaṇa and that later Nārāyaṇa who descended to earth as Rāma broke it completely. Ayyāvāḷ does not like the idea of Śiva being represented as inferior to Rāma. He does not make any distinction between Śiva and Viṣṇu and believes that Śiva is Viṣṇu and Viṣṇu is Rāma (so Śiva and Rāma are the same). Logically, in his view, the bow of Śiva is the bow of Rāma. That is why he says that Rāma broke his own bow with his hands. All such acts are needed for his sport, he declares.

Reference

[1] Ekaiva mūrtirbibhide tridhā sā
Sāmānyameṣām prathamāvaratvam
Viṣṇorharastasya Hariḥ kadācid-
Vedhāstayostāvapi Dhāturādyau

-- Kumārasaṁbhavam, 7.44

Chapter 11

Many Paths to the One Goal

The Āzhvārs[T] sing the glory of Viṣṇu and the Nāyanmārs[T] of Śiva. In the Vedas all deities are hymned in the same way. The Upaniṣads do not speak much about deities; they are concerned with truths of the Self. Tiruvaḷḷuvar[T] speaks about God and philosophical matters and his views are in keeping with the Vedic tradition. But the emphasis in his work is on morals and ethics. As for Tirumūlar[T], he does not deal so much with God, devotion, etc, as he does with aspects of yoga like prāṇāyāma, dhyāna, dhāraṇa and samādhi[S]. "Each great man, like each great work, speaks about a particular system, a particular path. Which of these is to be followed?" such a question arises in the minds of people. Whatever system or path you follow, follow it with faith. Do not give it up midway. In the end it will lead you to the Paramātman. In the beginning the paths may seem different but all of them take you to the same goal.

Devar kuraḷum Tirunānmarai muḍivum
Mūvar Tamizhum munimozhiyum — Kovai
Tiruvācakamum Tirumūlar śollum
Oruvāçakam en(ru)uṇar[1]

The same idea is expressed in the "Śivamahimna-stotra". This hymn glorifying Śiva is by Puṣpadanta. He was a gandharva who, under a curse of Īśvara, was condemned to live on earth. One stanza in his hymn says : "Trayī (the three Vedas), Sānkhya (philosophical inquiry), yoga, the Pāśupata system, Vaiṣṇavism — people follow any of them according to their different dispositions. Like the rivers merging in the ocean all these paths have one meeting point, the Paramātman."

It is in this spirit of catholicism that Englishmen exclaim: "Jehovah, Jove or Lord!"[2] Jehovah is the Semitic God of the region of Israel, the home of the Bible. Jove is another name of Jupiter. The word "Lord" applies to the God of any faith; it is common to all religions. Realised people in the West also speak that the one Being is the same, call him by any name you like.

If the Purāṇas are read in an attitude of respect and humility and with the honest intention that we should benefit by reading them, there will be no cause for any confusion. We will gain the wisdom to treat them as works meant for our ultimate well-being.

Note & Reference

[1] "Know that the *Tirukkural,* the four Vedas, the *Tevāram,* the words of Agastya and *Tirukovaiyār,* the *Tiruvācakam* and the *Tirumantiram*: teach the One Truth."

[2] This line occurs in Alexander Pope's "The Universal Prayer" :

Father of all! in ev'ry age,
In ev'ry clime adored,
By saint, by savage, and by sage,
Jehovah, Jove, or Lord!

Chapter 12

Who Taught the Purāṇas?

In the Purāṇas themselves it is mentioned that they were narrated by Śiva to Pārvatī or to Viṣṇu. It is also said that Viṣṇu taught them to Nārada or some other sage. Thus the stories told by the gods were later passed on from one sage to another sage or to a king. In the end the Purāṇas were narrated by Vyāsa to Sūta[1], and by Sūta to the sages in Naimiśāraṇya[2].

It was from a high seat offered by the sages of Naimiśāraṇya that Sūta taught the Purāṇas. We may gather from this the esteem in which the Purāṇas were held. Also that knowledge was respected more than birth. We also realise that caste was no consideration when it came to learning noble subjects. The learned man, whatever his caste, was listened to with respect.

Notes

[1] Sūta was a disciple of Vyāsa. (Sūtas were a half caste and were generally charioteers or actors.)

[2] Naimiśāraṇya, on the banks of the Gomatī river, was the hermitage of Śaunaka and other sages.

Chapter 13

They Speak like a Friend

There are three ways in which a good task may be accomplished. The first is by issuing an order or command backed by the authority of the government. This is called "prabhusammita". A rich or powerful man orders his servant to do some work: it is also "prabhusammita". Whether or not the servant likes the work, he is compelled to obey the order for fear of punishment. Without occupying any seat of authority a friend asks us to do something and we do it — not out of fear but out of affection. A friend who is well disposed towards us is a "suhṛd". His order given as a companion, as a sakhā, is "suhṛd-sammita". If there is any means by which you will do a work more willingly than in this manner, it is the loving words of your wife. The job your employer asks you to do is felt to be a burden, but the same is made lighter if it is a friend who asks you to do it. But if it is the wife who asks you to do the same it will be still lighter. This is "kāntāsammita".

The injunctions of the Vedas are "prabhusammita", the teachings of the Purāṇas are "suhṛd-sammita" and the works of poets are "kāntāsammita".

Yadvedāt prabhusammitādadhigatam
Śabdapramāṇācchiram

Yacchārthapravaṇāt-Purāṇavacanādiṣṭam
suhṛdsammitād

Kāntāsammitayā yayā sarasatāmāpādya-
kāvyāśriyā

Kartavye kutukī budho viracitas-tasyai
spṛhām kurmahe

— Pratāparudrīyam, stanza 8.

The Vedas ask you to "do like this" or "do like that". They do not say why. To question them, it is believed, is to dishonour them. The Purāṇas, however, tell you in a friendly manner: "If you do like this you will benefit in such and such a manner. If you do the same in some other way you will suffer..." Such lessons are driven home to people through stories. Yes, the special feature of the Purāṇas is that they not only tell you why you should do a work, they also state the reason for the same through absorbing stories. "Hariścandra acted like this. Nala did like that. That is why they were happy in the end though they had in between to suffer much. Besides, they earned such fame for their virtuous life and noble character that they will be remembered for all time." The moral derived from the stories of Hiraṇyakaśipu, Rāvaṇa, Duryodhana and so on are the opposite. They occupied high positions and wallowed in pleasure but in the end they were ruined and are remembered today for their wickedness and the evil they did. Such stories are a source of inspiration as well as a warning for us: they encourage us to do good and pull us back from evil. The Purāṇas tell us true stories. A suhṛd, a sincere friend, will not tell us false tales. He will speak to us only the truth and what is good for us in a persuasive manner.

What about poetry? What does the poet do? He mixes fact with fancy and invents stories with his power of imagination, exaggerating one thing, playing down another and repeating a third. He has the licence to do all this. The function of the poet is to invest reality with the imaginary or the fanciful so as to make his narrative compelling. The friend is unlike the wife. In trying to impress upon you your duty, he is persuasive but does not go beyond stating the facts. The wife is different. She is anxious to correct her husband and take him to the right path. She exaggerates a fact or plays down another, she adds and subtracts. By being "nice" to her husband she will somehow make him do the right thing. So goes at least the legend. Poetry, in the place of the wife; the Vedas, in the place of superior authority; and the Purāṇas, in between, in the place of a friend: the three teach us dharma in different ways.

Chapter 14

Purāṇic Discourses and Films

In the days gone by Mother would rise with birdsong and go about her household chores. As she sprinkled the house and surroundings with cowdung water[1], as she decorated the courtyard with *kolam*[2] and as she churned the curds, she recited tales from the Purāṇas. Children got to know such stories by listening to their mother or grandmother. A deep impression is made on their youthful minds by listening to narratives that contain lessons in dharma, stories told with such art that the characters come to life. When the boys and girls grow up they add to their knowledge of the Purāṇas by reading or by listening to the paurāṇikas.

Today all such good practices are forgotten. From childhood itself people become addicted to film songs, politics, fiction, newspapers. It is true that purāṇic themes are enacted on the stage or portrayed on the screen and may be some people benefit a little. But it is doubtful whether they will have the right kind of knowledge of the Purāṇas from them. More often than not the impact made by purāṇic films is unhealthy since the producers usually attempt to make them as spicy or as exciting as possible with the addition of undesirable features for, after all, the purpose of making movies is popular entertainment, not providing moral or spiritual instruction. Cinema does not come under the category of kāntā-sammita because the producers or directors abuse their licence, so much so the original story is changed in an objectionable manner.

Those who frequently go to see a film or a dramatic performance become more interested in the qualities of the actors and actresses than in those of the characters of the story itself.

You must listen to purāṇic discourses given by great men of virtuous conduct who are also steeped in the qualities of the high-souled characters whose stories they tell. Only then would you be drawn to the virtues exemplified by these characters and to the dharma practised by them. To listen to discourses given by paurāṇikas who are after money and fame and who do not practise the dharma that they ostensibly uphold is no better than seeing a drama or a movie. Dramatic (and cinematic) performances are likely to do good if they are based on the principles of drama enunciated in our canonical texts. For instance, only a couple married in real life can perform the roles of a hero and a heroine [husband and wife] in a play. The śāstras have also restrictions with regard to the enactment of erotic scenes [portrayal of śṛṇgāra].

Nowadays purāṇic and other religious discourses are held almost every day in towns and cities. I myself am amazed to see so many listed in the engagement columns of newspapers. Talks are given on religious themes, on stories, on the Purāṇas, in fact subjects I myself am not familiar with. People flock to them, educated people who may be said to be "modern" or "sophisticated". It seems as if there is a religious awakening.

But a point to consider is how far discourses given by paurāṇikas are in good taste. Adding a few stories on their own to the main theme is all right so as to enhance audience interest. Similarly, a little bit of humour and brief references to politics also seem to be not altogether improper. But these should not be far removed from the main story, the main theme, and must be without prejudice to the truths to be driven home to the listeners. Otherwise the whole exercise will be in bad taste ("rasābhāsa")[3]. That which calls the Lord to mind is "rasa", true flavour. The purāṇic stories must be told without straying too far from the text and a healthy impression must be made on the minds of the audience. The narrator must have faith in Īśvara, must adhere to traditional customs and must firmly believe in dharma and in the principles he himself expounds in the course of his discourse. If he has profound knowledge of the subject of his talk he will not be tempted to depart from the main theme to tell irrelevant stories or make tangential references to current political happenings. Purāṇic discourses will serve no purpose if they are treated as a pastime like films and fiction.

In the villages and the smaller towns not so many discourses and *bhajans* are held as in the cities and bigger towns. It is in places where more and more people have taken to the modern style of living (and perhaps as a reaction to it according to the Newtonian law) that you see a growth of interest in subjects related to our religious and cultural traditions. Religious or purāṇic discourses must be held in every village, also *bhajans*, at least on every Ekādaśī[S].

Notes & References

[1] Not perhaps a correct expression for "macerated cowdung".

[2] Designs drawn on the floor with dry or wet rice powder. Kolam is considered auspicious and is a ritual requirement. The word means "form" or "shape", "beauty", "ornament", "dress".

[3] See notes appended to Chapter 1, Part Three.

Chapter 15

Sthala Purāṇas

Even those who respect the Purāṇas are not prepared to accept that the Śthala Purāṇas, that is the short Purāṇas pertaining to particular places, are authentic. If educated people think the [major] Purāṇas to be nothing but lies, they go so far as to treat the Sthala Purāṇas as nothing better than rubbish. "It was here that Indra was freed from his curse..." "It was here that Agastya witnessed the marriage of Śiva and Pārvatī." Such statements give rise to scepticism about the Sthala Purāṇas. "How are such things possible?" they ask. "These Purāṇas must have been made up. They must have originated in the desire of some individuals to give a certain importance to places to which they belong."

People with faith who are acquainted with our traditions will tell you: "Kalpa[S] after kalpa, the same stories are repeated, but sometimes with slight differences. A story associated with one place in one kalpa may recur in another place in a different kalpa."

It is natural for people to take pride in claiming that their birthplace is associated with the great men mentioned in the Purāṇas. This is a fact that all of us must recognise. Ordinary unlettered folk like to believe that Rāma or Kṛṣṇa had once visited their village, also great sages, and that they were freed from terrible sins. Encouraged by such a belief they conduct the festivals of the local temples with great enthusiasm and are rewarded with faith and devotion. We should view this attitude with sympathy and understanding. Why should we who claim to be "intelligent" disturb the faith of these people of innocence and deprive them of their sense of fulfilment? The Lord himself says in the Gītā[1] that in such matters you must not produce some information as "fact" and create agitation in the minds of ordinary people. "Na buddhibhedam janayed ajñānām karmasaṅginām."

By this you should not take it that I am one with the critics who hold that the Sthala Purāṇas are not true, nor should you think that I accept them [these Purāṇas] only for the reason that, notwithstanding the fact that they are not true, they do some good to the people. I believe that the Sthala Purāṇas are by and large authentic. Some of the stories told in them may not be so, but for that reason I would not maintain that all Sthala Purāṇas are false.

Reference

[1] *Na buddhibhedam janayed ajñānāṁ karmasaṅginām*
Joṣayet sarva-karmāṇi vidvān yuktaḥ samācaran

—— Bhagavadgītā, 3.26

Chapter 16

The Authenticity of Sthala Purāṇas

We ought to have implicit faith in the Vedas, so too in the statements made in the Tamiḷ Vedas of Śaivas and Vaiṣṇavas — the *Tevāram*[T] and the *Divyaprabandham*[T]. There are places whose glory has been sung in the *Tevāram* of the Nāyanmārs and in the *pāsurams* of the Āzhvārs[T]. These songs allude to what is said about such places in the Sthala Purāṇas. That there are such references in these Tamiḷ devotional works, which are 1,500 years old, is proof of the antiquity of these Purāṇas.

For instance, take the Perumāl[T] of the Śrīraṅgam temple (Tamiḷ Nāḍu). The idol is unique in the sense that it faces south. There is an explanation for this in the Sthala Purāṇa pertaining to the temple. When Vibhīṣaṇa was returning to Lanka after attending the coronation of Śrī Rāmacandra, Rāma gave him the idol of Ranganātha that he himself had been worshipping. On his way the idol somehow got installed on the island skirted by the two arms of the Kāverī. Vibhīṣaṇa was sad that he could not take it with him to his capital Lankāpurī. So, out of compassion for him, Śrī Ranganātha lay facing south. This incident is described in detail in the Sthala Purāṇa of Śrīrangam. It is also mentioned in the songs of the Āzhvārs.

If the reason for Viṣṇu facing south in Śrīrangam was known during the time of the Āzhvārs, the Sthala Purāṇa of that place must surely predate the work of these Vaiṣṇava saint-poets.

The liṅga in the Ekāmranātha temple in Kāñcīpuram was shaped by Ambā herself. At the time she was worshipping it the Lord created a flood, but she kept embracing the liṅga and it was thus saved from being carried away in the flood. The Lord then appeared from the liṅga. This Sthala Purāṇa episode is told in the *Tevāram* also. Sundaramūrtisvāmin's[T] poems sing the glory of Ambā performing pūjā here.

In Jambukeśvaram (Tiruvānaikkā), near Śrīrangam, a great sage called Jambu was transformed into a jambu[S] tree. Śiva enshrined himself under it in his liṅga form. There a spider wove a canopy of web over the liṅga and worshipped the Lord. An elephant destroyed this canopy and performed abhiṣeka[S] to the liṅga. The spider, naturally enraged, crept into the elephant's trunk, ascended up and bore into its head. The animal then dashed against the jambu tree and it was killed along with the spider. The spider was reborn as Koccenkot Cola[T] who built the Jambukeśvaram temple. This story occurs in the

Sthala Purāṇa — and it is referred to in the *Tevāram* also. In the sanctum sanctorum of the temple, the Kāverī wells up all the time. This wonderful phenomenon is mentioned in the *Tevāram* of Appar[T] and in the *Pattupaṭṭu*[T].

At midday, in Tirukkazhukunram[1], two eagles descend on the hill and receive sweet rice offered by the temple priest. After consuming the rice the birds fly away. Some people have doubts about the antiquity of this phenomenon. From the time of the *Tevāram* itself the place is known as (Tiru)kazhukkunram. What better evidence is needed?

In Tiruviḍaimarudūr (in Tañjāvūr district) bathing on the occasion of Taippūśam[2] is specially auspicious according to the *Kṣetra-māhātmyam*[3]. Appar and Sambandhar have spoken about the festival in their songs dating back to 1,500 years ago.

Śrīrangam, Jambukeśvaram, Kāñcīpuram, Tirukkazhukunram and Tiruviḍaimarudūr[4] are great holy places. So, it may be argued, there is nothing remarkable about their being mentioned in the old Tamiḻ texts. But it is noteworthy that purāṇic stories associated even with smaller places are referred to in old Tamil religious works.

The Sthala Purāṇas have it that in certain places that are not so famous sages and celestials appeared as bees to worship the deities there. Even today we see huge honeycombs before the sanctum itself. One such place is Nannilam. It is also called "Madhuvanam". Śittāmbūr, near Tirutturaippūṇḍi, is called Tiruccirremam in the *Tevāram.* Here too there is a honeycomb before the sanctum. The story goes that siddhas[S] come here as honeybees to worship the Lord. Pūjā is performed to the honeycomb also every day. Similarly, there is a honeycomb in the Vaiṣṇava temple of Tirukkaṇṇamangai. There are references to such places in both the *Tevāram* and the *Divyaprabandham.*

The antiquity and authenticity of the Sthala Purāṇas are supported by such stories (stories relating even to minor incidents associated with not so big places) occurring in the *Tevāram, Tiruvācakam*[T] and the *Nālāyira-Divyaprabandham.*

Notes & References

[1] This "sacred hill of the eagles" is in Cengalpaṭṭu district, Tamiḻ Nāḍu.

[2] Taippūsam is a festival in honour of Subrahmaṇya and also Śiva in certain places. It is celebrated in January-February. See Chapter 13, Part Six, for how "*Tai*" and "*Pusam*" are derived.

[3] "Ksetra-māhātmyam" means glory or greatness or exalted position of a sacred place.

[4] The places mentioned in this para (as also in the previous one) are in Tamiḻ Nāḍu.

Chapter 17

Interconnected Stories

The events described in one Sthala Purāṇa are linked to those mentioned in another. Thus the strand of the same story is taken through a number of Purāṇas. We have to read them together to learn the entire story. That one Sthala Purāṇa begins where another ends is one proof of their authenticity. Another proof that could be adduced is that it is these Sthala Purāṇas that fill the gaps in the 18 main Purāṇas and Upa-purāṇas.

Once Śiva and Ambā (Pārvatī) played dice in Kailāsa. "I have won the game," said Ambā. "No, I am the winner," said Śiva. The two played thus to impart lessons in dharma to mankind. If now their game of dice ended in a quarrel it was because the divine couple wanted the world to learn that playing for stakes was an evil, that it leads to disputes and misconduct.

To resume the story. In his anger Śiva cursed Ambā thus: "You shall be born a cow and shall keep roaming the earth." Śiva is Paśupati, lord of animals. Yes, he is the Lord that controls the animal senses (the indriyas) that are in a frenzy. It is to demonstrate that he does not bless people with a big ego that he cursed even Parāśakti (the Supreme Power). Though she is Mahāśakti herself she realised her error and, the great pativratā[S] that she is, she became submissive to her husband. She roamed the earth as an ordinary cow.

In her One Thousand Names ("Sahasranāma") Ambā is extolled as "Gomātā, Guhajanmabhū." She came to the earth as Gomātā (Mother Cow).

Viṣṇu is Ambā's brother, is he not? He is very much attached to her and, as soon as he knew that his brother-in-law (Śiva) had "driven her out", he thought to himself: "Let him not protect her, lord of animals though he be. I will have my sister under my protection." So taking the guise of a cowherd he accompanied the divine cow. He was not the victim of any curse that he should roam the earth thus. It was to demonstrate to the world the dharma of filial affection that he came down to the world of mortals with her. (He developed a liking for the job of the cowherd now. That is how he took delight in grazing cows in his incarnation as Kṛṣṇa. He then came to be called Gopāla which name also means "Paśupati". If you reflect on these two names of Śiva and Viṣṇu you will cease to make any distinction between the two gods.)

Tiru-Azhundūr is the place to which sister and brother came as cow and cowherd. It is the same as "Terazhundūr". It also happens to be the birthplace of Kambar[T] and in fact there is a locality here called "Kambarmeḍu". Tirumaṅgai Āzhvār performed the "maṅgaḷā śāsanam"[T] in a temple here. Viṣṇu is in the sanctum sanctorum as Gopāla with the cow. Since he came as a companion of the cow he is called "Gosakhā". "Gosakhākṣetra" is another name for Terazhundūr. "Gosakhā" in Tamiḷ is "Ā*maruviyappan*", the initial "*ā*" in the name meaning cow. There is a temple to Śiva also here. According to our ancient system of town-planning there must be a temple to Śiva at one end of a village or town and one to Viṣṇu at the other. If the Viṣṇu temple at Terazhundūr is associated with the songs of the Āzhvārs the Śiva temple is associated with the *Tevāram*[T] hymns of Jñānasaṁbandhar[T]. The places sung by the Āzhvārs are said to have had "maṅgalā śāsanam", while any place associated with the *Tevāram* is called "*pāṭal peṟṟa sthalam*" [place that has been sung]. Many places in the South have had both types of distinction. Terazhundūr is one of them. Near it is a village called Pillūr where Viṣṇu, as the cowherd, grazed the cow that was Ambā. ("Pillūr" means a place where grass grows, *pil* meaning grass. In the Tañjāvūr region *pul* is known as *pil*.) Mekkirimaṅgalam also is one of the places where Viṣṇu grazed the cow and Ān-āngūr another (*ān* = cow).

For brother and sister to worship Śiva, Viṣṇu installed Vedapurīśvara (Śiva) in Gosakhākṣetra. (Both the Vedapurīśvara and Āmaruviyappan temples are today under the same management.)

The cow as well as the Brahmin is essential to the practice of Vedic dharma. Milk and ghee are indispensable to sacrifices, while without the Brahmin the sacrifices cannot be performed. This fact is underlined in the prayer, "Gobrāhmaṇebhyo śubhamastu nityam" [May cow and Brahmin ever prosper].

The one (that is Śiva) who had cast a curse on Ambā came as Vedapurīśvara to the same place where Ambā had also come. Until recently there were many Brahmins in this place learned in the Vedas and śāstras. Sambandhar[T] often refers to them as "*Azhundai Maraiyor*" (Vedic scholars of Azhundūr). The Āzhvārs call Viṣṇu by these names: "*Chandogā*", "*Pauzhiyā*", "*Taittirīyā*", "*Sāmavediyane*".

One day, when the cow (that is Ambā) was grazing, her hoof dug into the earth and a stone was revealed. It proved to be a Śiva liṅga. The cow, thinking that she had committed an offence against Śiva, ran about in bewilderment. Viṣṇu pacified her and brought her back. The place where this incident occurred is "Tirukkulaṁbiyam"[1]. Viṣṇu was pained by all these developments and regretted that his sister had shown herself to be egoisic, albeit playfully, and that this fact had led to such unfortunate consequences.

It was Viṣṇu who had married Mīnākṣī to Sundareśvara[2]. Wishing to unite them again he now performed pūjā to propitiate Śiva. The latter was pleased and he said to Viṣṇu: "Keep grazing the cow until you come to the river Kāverī. Bathe her in the river and she will be restored to her original form. I shall tell you later when I will marry her."

Viṣṇu, as bidden by Śiva, bathed the cow in the Kāverī. The place where the cow was seen after she had bathed in the river is "Tiruvāḍuturai". (It is also important for the reason that it was here that Tirumūlar[T] composed his *Tirumantiram*.)

Ambā was restored to her original form and Śiva himself appeared on the scene. But he wanted to play a game again. There is a place called Kuṟṟāḷam. (It is not the same as the Kuṟṟāḷam in Tirunelveli district that is famous for its waterfall. This Kuṟṟāḷam is near Māyūram[3] in Tañjāvūr district. It was once called Tirutturutti. This is one of the 44 places which Appar, Saṁbandhar and Sundaramūrti[T] have sung). A sage was performing austerities here for Ambā herself to be born as his daughter. Śiva thought that this was the opportune moment to grant his wish. He said to Ambā: "Go and be born the daughter of the sage at Tirutturutti. I will come and marry you at the appropriate time."

Śiva made his appearance as promised. There is proof for the fact that the one who gave his word at Gosakhākṣetra appeared here also in that in this place too the deity is called Vedeśvara. The sage and Viṣṇu — the latter had been waiting for the day his sister would be married again to Śiva — received Śiva and took him to the place of marriage. The spot where Śiva was received came to be called "Etirkoḷpāḍi". The "vrata" before the marriage was performed by Śiva in a nearby place which later came to be called "Veḷvikkuḍi". The spot where he saw Ambā as the bride and performed the pālikā[S] ceremony is called "Kurumuḷaippāli". The marriage *paṇḍal* was spread over two or three villages. The one in the middle came to be called "Tirumaṇañjeri"[4]. It was here that Viṣṇu married Pārvatī to Parameśvara and it was an occasion of great joy for him.

From this account you will realise how wrong it is to dismiss Sthala Purāṇas as of no significance. The present story contains a warning against the evil consequences of ahaṁkāra[S] and gambling and tells us how a wife should be dutiful towards her husband and how a brother should be affectionate towards, and concerned about, his sister. Actually I did not tell the story with this idea in mind. I wished to demonstrate how a number of Sthala Purāṇas fit into one another, how the incidents narrated in different Sthala Purāṇas are woven together — I mean those of Terazhundūr, Pillūr, Ānangūr, Tirukkulaṁbiyam, Tiruvāḍuturai, Kuṟṟāḷam, Etirkolpāḍi, Veḷvikkuḍi, Kurumuḷaippāli and Tirumaṇañjeri. The interconnected narrative also shows that the story must be authentic.

A story with which people of Tañjāvūr should be more familiar links Kuṁbhakoṇam with places in its neighbourhood.

During the great deluge Brahmā prepared himself for the next creation. He put all the seeds in amṛta (the elixir of immortality) and kept them together in a mudpot to the chanting of Vedic mantras. With due ceremony, he placed a coconut with mango leaves on it and invested the same with the sacred thread. Now he placed the pot on the summit of Meru. When it came floating in the waters of the deluge, Parameśvara wished to recommence creation. Then the coconut on the pot was dislodged in the storm and fell into the water. At once the water receded revealing the land there. This spot is four miles north-west of Kuṁbhakoṇam. The deity here is even today called "Nārikeḷeśvara", ("nārikeḷa" means coconut). Then the mango leaves fell off. The water receded there too revealing land. This is Tiruppuraṁbayam, four miles north-west of Kuṁbhakoṇam. "*Payam*" [or *bayam*] is "payas", that is water, but in this context deluge. "*Puram*" means outside or beyond something: the name of the place [Tiruppuraṁbayam] thus means "outside the waters of the deluge". Now the sacred thread (sūtra) also got loosened from the pot and fell off. The deity in the place where the sūtra fell is "Sūtranātha", "sūtra" meaning the "sacred thread".

The kuṁbha (pot) had a "nose" in addition to a "mouth" — it was like a *giṇḍi* or kamaṇḍalu. My pot too has a nose in addition to its mouth. Water is filled in the pot through the mouth and poured out through the nose. The pot with the amṛta was also similar. Parameśvara watched the scene. Since the pot with the elixir and the seeds in it were not overturned on their own, he decided to break it with his arrow so as to bring out its contents. The place where he discharged the arrow is called "Bāṇapuri" — now it is known as "Vāṇatturai". The deity here is "Bāṇapurīśvara" and the spot where the mouth of the pot fell in pieces is "Kuḍavāyil" ("Kuḍavaśal"). Parameśvara wanted the amṛta to be discharged in the śāstric manner, from the nose of the pot. The place where the nose broke and the elixir or ambrosia fell is holier than other places. It is called "Kuṁbhakoṇam", "kon" ("koṇam") meaning nose. In the *Tevāram* [T] the place is referred to as "Kuḍamūkku". Here the mudpot itself came to be the liṅga and even today it is so. The liṅga is ceremonially bathed along with a protective wear outside. "Kuṁbheśvara" is the name of the deity. The Mahāmagham pond is the spot where the amṛta first fell.

Since the place is hallowed by the fact that it was here that the amṛta fell, the Vaiṣṇava deity here, Śārṅgapāṇī, is called "Āra- amudan" by the Āzhvārs. To Vaiṣṇavas Kuṁbhakoṇam itself is "Kuḍandai".

Thus there are many sacred places that are interconnected, which fact also confirms that the Sthala Purāṇas are authentic. Tiruvazhundūr, Kuṁbhakoṇam, etc, are situated within a radius of four miles. There will be further confirmation of the authenticity of these Purāṇas if we note how the places mentioned in them and which are far apart are connected together. Rāmeśvaram, Vedāraṇyam and Paṭṭīśvaram are not near one another. Rāmeśvaram, in Rāmanāthapuram district, is on the seacoast. Vedāraṇyam is in a corner of Tañjāvūr district and is also on the seashore, in the *tālūqa* of Tirutturaipūṇḍi. In the same district, but by no means close by, is Paṭṭiśvaram which is near Kuṁbhakoṇam. These places which are far apart are connected by the same thread of a story. Would you call such a story baseless?

In all these three places there are great Śiva temples and the name of the deity in each is "Rāmaliṅga", suggesting that they are connected with Rāma. That he installed liṅgas in these places strengthens the concept of Śaiva-Vaiṣṇava unity. These places have some other special features too. Of the four great religious centres, known as *"cār-dhām"*, Rāmeśvaram alone is in the South. In the North is Badarināth(a), in the west Somanāth(a), in the east (Puri) Jagannāth(a) and, of course, Rāmeśvaram in the south.

Vedāraṇyam is associated with the salt satyagraha during the freedom movement. The place is mentioned in the *Tevāram*[T] as "Tirumaraikkā" (Tamiḷ for Vedāraṇyam). Here the temple door was closed after the Vedas had worshipped the deity Śiva. Appar[T] sang his *patigam*[T] here and the door flung open. Tirujñānasaṁbandhar[T] made the door shut again when he sang before the deity.

Paṭṭīśvaram is the place where Śiva was worshipped by Paṭṭi, one of the four daughters of Kāmadhenu[S]. Like Tiruvāḍuturai mentioned before there are many places where the cow has performed worship. Tiru-Āmattūr is near Panruṭṭi. It is connected with Appar. Here too the cow has performed pūjā. Paṭṭiśvaram is a similar place. When Jñānasaṁbandhar was a child he sang the praises of Śiva and went dancing before the deity in the hot sun. The Lord was moved by the sight and ordered his attendants to build a *paṇḍāl* to protect his devotee from the sun. Jñānasaṁbandhar was an incarnation of Subrahmaṇya. Govinda Dīkṣita was a minister to the Nayaka kings of Tañjāvūr. He was very much drawn to Paṭṭiśvaram and made additions to the temple there. Images of Dīkṣita and his wife may be seen before the sanctum of Ambā.

Where did Agastya witness the marriage of Śiva and Pārvatī? Three places are mentioned, that is three places are associated with the same event. As mentioned before, the Rāmaliṅga was installed in three places, but in each place for a different reason.

Rāma committed a threefold sin by slaying Rāvaṇa. Rāvaṇa, the son of the sage Viśravas, was a Brahmin. By killing him Rāma incurred the sin of "Brahmahatyā". To wipe away the same he installed the liṅga at Rāmeśvaram.

Some people today describe the war between Rāma and Rāvaṇa as a quarrel between Āryans and Dravịdians. Such a view is totally baseless and there is no better proof of this than the fact that Rāvaṇa was a Brahmin[5]. If the Rāmāyaṇa is a lie so must be the battle between Rāma and Rāvaṇa. It cannot be claimed that there is a historical basis for this battle alone. If the Rāmāyaṇa is accepted as true the account of Rāvaṇa contained in it must also be taken to be so. It is said again and again in the epic that Rāvaṇa was the son of a sage, that he was conversant with the Vedas, that he pleased Śiva by chanting the Sāmaveda and that it was for this reason that he was saved from being crushed under Kailāsa. It does not stand to reason to accept only that part of the Rāmāyaṇa which suits you and reject the rest.

Leave aside the Rāmāyaṇa and what it says about Ṛavaṇa: the temple of Rāmeśvaram is there for all of us to see. It has the biggest corridor in the world ("prākāra", ambulatory). All India worships Rāmanāthasvāmin in the form of the liṅga Rāma installed for the removal of the sin he had incurred by killing the Brahmin Rāvaṇa. For centuries our forefathers in Tamiḷ Nāḍu never thought of Rāvaṇa as belonging to a caste other than that of Brahmins.

Apart from being a Brahmin, Rāvaṇa was also a great warrior. All the worlds trembled before him. He fought successfully all the powerful rulers of the time except two — Kārtavīryārjuna and Vāli. By killing such a warrior Rāma committed the sin of "vīrahatyā". It was in expiation of it that he installed the liṅga (Rāmalinga) at Vedāraṇyam.

In addition to the qualifications already mentioned, Rāvaṇa had another; he was an ardent devotee of Śiva and proficient in playing the vīṇa, besides being a singer. Excellence such as this comes under the term "chāyā": it means both light and shadow. The goddess Mīnākṣī is addressed as "Marakata-chāyā" (emeraldine in radiance). By killing Rāvaṇa who possessed chāyā, Rāma also earned the sin of "chāyāhatyā." To expiate it he installed the liṅga at Paṭṭīśvaram.

From the śāstric point of view, by slaying Rāvaṇa Rāma brought on himself the threefold sin of Brahmahatyā, vīrahatyā and chāyāhatyā. Actually Rāma is patita-pāvana[6] and he cannot be tainted by any sin. By uttering his name a man is freed from the most terrible of sins. So Rāma has no need to perform any prāyaścitta (he does not have to do any expiatory rite) — he is "Tāraka Rāma"[7]. But he had descended to this world to serve as an ideal for all mankind and so he acted strictly according to the canons even with reference to matters that might be considered trivial. In the observance of dharma according to the śāstras no one excelled him. Throughout the Rāmāyaṇa we see this remarkable trait in his character. He regarded himself as an ordinary individual, observed all the rules of the śāstras; in this way he also performed the prāyaścitta according to them. This is not mentioned in the Rāmāyaṇa of Vālmīki; but the Sthala Purāṇas of Rāmeśvaram, Vedāraṇyam and Paṭṭiśvaram fill the gap.

"The Rāmāyaṇa does not contain these incidents. They must be some old wives' tales." To think so is not correct. The incidents described in the Sthala Purāṇas are in keeping with Rāma's character. He must have performed the three types of penitence. What is left out in the Rāmāyaṇa of Vālmīki is mentioned in the Sthala Purāṇas.

Rāváṇa had caused suffering to all mankind and it was with an evil intent that he had stolen Sītā, the mother of the world. Rāma killed such a wicked character and made all the world happy. At a time when there was universal rejoicing over his victory, Rāma thought himself to be a sinner because he had killed an enemy eminent in three different ways. The loftiness of his character is further enhanced by these acts. That he installed the liṅga in three different centres goes to demonstrate the unity of Hari and Hara (Viṣṇu and Śiva).

These Sthala Purāṇas do not contradict one another nor is there any overlapping in them. Those pertaining to Rāmeśvaram, Vedāraṇyam and Paṭṭīśvaram deal respectively with how Rāma, by installing the liṅga in each place, was freed from the sins of Brahmahatyā, vīrahatyā and chāyāhatyā. Rāma must have proceeded north from Rāmeśvaram along the coast. From Vedāraṇyam he must have gone to Paṭṭīśvaram in the interior. It is the strand of the same story that takes us through three Sthala Purāṇas. The three places are 150 or 100 miles apart from one another. When there were no fast modes of transport these distances correspond to 1,500 or 1,000 miles today. The fact that the stories belonging to the three places fit into one another shows that the Sthala Purāṇas relating to them must be true.

I should like to express a view that might seem strange to modern researchers and traditional scholars alike. It is generally believed that the

Sthala Purāṇas cannot be considered authoritative to the same extent as the Rāmāyaṇa. But I think that such of them as are authentic are more authoritative than the Rāmāyaṇa, the Mahābhārata, the *Viṣṇu Purāṇa* and the *Bhāgavata Purāṇa,* and so on. I have come to this conclusion from examples like the one I have cited above.

Now I am going to speak about Sthala Purāṇas that connect places in different parts of the country.

There are two versions of the *Kāverī Purāṇa.* One gives importance to the Ammā maṇḍapa on the Kāverī in Śrīrangam. It states that bathing in the Kāverī in the month of Tulā (October-November) is specially meritorious. The chief character in this Purāṇa is the Cola king Dharmavarman. He reigned from Niculāpurī. The Sanskrit words "nicula", "nicola", "coli" mean a garment covering the body [or a part thereof] like a case ("*uraī*" in Tamiḷ). The place called "Uraiyūr" is known in Sanskrit as "Niculāpurī". The kingdom with its capital as Niculāpurī came to be called Coḷadeśa (Cozhadeśa). What is remarkable about a corn-cob ? The grains growing on the top of the stalk are encased in the "cob". It means the grains of the cereal called *coḷam* or maize wear a *coli* so to speak.

In the second version of the *Kāverī Purāṇa* the bathing *ghāṭ* called *Tulāghaṭṭam* in Māyavaram [Māyūram] is given importance. It is popularly called "*Lagaḍam*": the word must be a distortion of "*Tūla-ghaṭṭam*". This *ghāṭ* has been specially built for the convenience of pilgrims who bathe in the Kāverī in the month of Tulā. There are such *ghāṭs* in six or seven other places on the Kaverī, all built to the same plan. While in the first version of the *Kāverī Purāṇa* Śrīrangam and Dharmavarman figure as important, in the second, apart from Māyavaram, a Brahmin couple find a prominent place. The couple were liberated by bathing at this *ghāṭ.*

The Brahmin was called Nāthaśarman and his wife Anavadyā. They were freed from worldly existence by bathing day after day in the Kāverī in the month of Tulā in the manner prescribed by the śāstras.

The Brahmin couple had during their pilgrimage visited Kedāra and Kāśī. (This story is known only in Māyavaram.) Kāśī is a thousand miles from here. One of the *ghāṭs* there is called "*Kedārghāṭ*". The Sthala Purāṇa of *Kedārghāṭ* mentions that the Brahmin couple, Nāthaśarman and his wife Anavadyā, bathed there.

People in our parts are not very much familiar with the story of Nāthaśarman. He is not like Rāma, Kṛṣṇa, Hariścandra, Nala and so on to be known all over the land. It is amazing that the story of such a man as told in the

Sthala Purāṇas of Māyavaram and of Kāśī, a thousand miles away, tally. This story shows how wrong it is to be sceptical about the authenticity of Sthala Purāṇas.

Kāśī, which is a thousand miles from Kāñcīpuram, is famous for the goddess Annapūrṇī. In Kāñcī too, when the World Mother observed the 32 dharmas, she distributed food among people. Opposite the doorway of the sanctum of the Kāmākṣī temple in Kāñcī is the sanctum of Annapūrṇeśvarī. It has a vimāna or tower that is unlike that of any other temple in the South. It has six spires ("śikharas"). The explanation for this is the fact that the tower of the Annapūrṇeśvarī temple in Kāśī too is similar. Even in such small matters there is agreement about places as far apart as Kāñcī and Kāśī. Are Sthala Purāṇas then to be dismissed as of no consequence?

Notes & References

1 The place associated with the sacred hoof.

2 Mīnākṣi is Pārvatī and Sundareśvara is Śiva. The two are deities of the famous Madurai temple.

3 Also known as Mayilaḍuturai.

4 The Tamiḷ place names in this story are significant. For instance, "Tirumaṇañjeri" suggests the place where the wedding (of Śiva and Pārvatī) was held, "Kurumulaippāli" the place where the pālika grains germinated.

5 Supporters of the Āryan-Dravīḍian theory — particularly politicians among them — claim that all Brahmins, including those in the South, are Āryans.

6 One who liberates the sinner; one who raises up the fallen.

7 Rāma, the liberator; Rāma who takes the devotee across from worldly existence or saṁsāra.

Chapter 18

Importance of Sthala Purāṇas

In my opinion, the Sthala Purāṇas not only enable us to have an insight into history but also enrich our knowledge of local culture and local customs. It seems to me that if they are read together in a connected manner they will throw more light on our history than even the 18 major Purāṇas and Upapurāṇas. In fact, they fill the gaps in the major Purāṇas.

Local legends do help in a proper understanding of history. For instance, educated people today do not believe that Śankara Bhagavatpāda visited any of the temples or that he brought the pūjā performed there under a certain system. "The great non-dualist that he was and exponent of the path of jñāna," they argue, "he would not have concerned himself with devotion, temple worship, the Āgamas[S], and the like." But let us examine the stories that tell us that he gave new life to certain temples, temples that are a thousand miles or more apart. Their connection with the Ācārya is confirmed from such stories and local legends. The priest who conducts the pūjā in Badarināth(a) in the Himālaya is a Nampūtiri Brahmin from Keraḷa — he is called "Rāwal". Here, in Maḍrās, the pūjā at the Tripurasundarī temple at Tiruvoṟṟiyūr is also by a Nampūtiri. This is proof of the oral tradition according to which the Ācārya was a Nampūtiri who engaged fellow Nampūtiris to conduct pūjā in the temples he revived.

In teaching us lessons in dharma also the Sthala Purāṇas are in no way inferior to the major Purāṇas. It is in fact these local Purāṇas which are a few hundred in number that throw light on the finer points of dharma. Unfortunately, even the religious-minded among the educated class today think poorly of them. But, until recently, these Purāṇas were treated with respect by learned men in Tamiḷ Nāḍu. Distinguished Tamiḷ scholars have written Purāṇas after those existing in the name of great sages and also a number of Sthala Purāṇas. There are works in Tamiḷ describing the importance and significance of places and temples — they are known variously as Sthala Purāṇas, *mānmiyam, kalaṁbagam, ula,* etc. ("Mahimā" means greatness or glory; *mānmiyam* is its Tamiḷ form.)

Tamiḷ literature is divided into the Saṁgam, *Tevāram-Divyaprabandham* and *Kambar-Oṭṭakūttar*[T] periods. Scholars describe the 16th century as the period of the Sthala Purāṇas. The chief authors of such works are Kamalai Jñānaprakāśar and Saiva Ellappa Nāvalar. We know the worthiness of Sthala

Purāṇas from the fact that among their authors are Kacciyappa Śivācāriyar (he composed the *Kanda Purāṇam)*, Parañjyoti Muni (he is the author of the *Tiruviḷayāḍal Purāṇam*), Umāpati Śivācāriyar (a distinguished teacher of Śaivism), Śivaprakāśa Svāmī, the Iraṭṭai Pulavars, Antakkavi Vīrarāghava Mudaliār, Koṭṭaiyūr Śivakkozhundu Deśigar, Trikūṭa Rāśappakkavirāyar. In recent times there was Mahāvidvān Mīnākṣisundaram Piḷḷai[T] who was the guru of U. V. Svāminātha Ayyar[T]. He has written a number of Sthala Purāṇas. We learn from this that Sthala Purāṇas have a place of honour in the Tamiḷ religious tradition and literature.

A distinguished Sanskrit scholar and authority on the śāstras, Karuṅguḷam Kṛṣṇa Śāstrī, has written a Tamiḷ work called *Vedāraṇya Māhātmyam.*

Tamiḷ rulers gave their support to Sthala Purāṇas and their propagation. More than four and a half centuries ago, the Purāṇa relating to Pañcanada-kṣetra (Tiruvaiyāru, Tañjāvūr) was translated into Tamiḷ. The translator mentions that he undertook the work as desired by Govinda Dīkṣita who was responsible for the founding of the Nāyaka kingdom of Tañjāvūr.

Chapter 19

Preserving the Purāṇas

For a thousand or ten thousand years our temples and the festivals associated with them have nurtured our religious traditions against various opposing forces. Every temple has a story to tell; every temple festival has a legend behind it. These have been preserved in the Purāṇas. To ignore or neglect this great heritage, this great treasure, is to cause serious hurt to the religious feelings of our people.

In the past, when there was no printing press, the palm-leaf manuscripts were jealously guarded generation after generation. Is it right to keep them in neglect when so many books are churned out by the printing presses today, the majority of them injurious to our inner advancement? It is our duty to preserve the Purāṇas for future generations. Not to do so is to deprive them of a great source of inspiration.

Chapter 20

Palm-leaf Manuscripts, Libraries

In the old days palm-leaf manuscripts were preserved in almost every house. They contained the texts of the epics, the Purāṇas, Sthala Purāṇas, and so on. When the palm-leaves were in danger of being damaged, their contents would be copied with a stylus on new leaves. The damaged leaves would be consigned to the Kāverī or some other sacred river, or to some pond on the occasion of *Patineṭṭām Per* [see next para].

The 18th day of the Tamiḷ month of Āḍi (July-August) has a special significance for the Kāverī. The river would be in spate. The swelling waters on this day are called *Patineṭṭām Perukku* or *Patineṭṭām Per.*

Our forefathers went on inscribing on palm-leaves with their stylus until their hands ached. They copied old texts to be preserved for posterity. This tradition lasted until perhaps the time of our fathers. People of our generation have thrown these precious manuscripts into the river without making copies of them. So much so it is doubtful whether the texts of many Purāṅas will ever be available to us. Not only Purāṇas, but also a number of śāstras. However, some scholars have taken great pains to go from place to place to collect manuscripts and preserve them in libraries. The Sarasvatī Mahaḷ Library in Tañjavūr, the Oriental Manuscripts Library and the Aḍyār Library, Maḍrās, have good collections of manuscripts. The Theosophical Society Library, Aḍyār, has done commendable work in this respect. Śarabhoji and other rulers of Tañjāvūr took great trouble to collect manuscripts for the Sarasvatī Mahaḷ.

The palm-leaf is called *eḍu* in Tamiḷ. It has two sides with a rib in between — either of the two sides after the removal of the rib is called an *eḍu.* The plantain leaf also has a rib. When it is split across the rib, each part is an *eḍu.* For long the palm-leaf was our paper, nature's paper which was not easily damaged. The letters had to be inscribed on it with a stylus.

The palm-leaves containing the text of Jñānasaṁbandhar's[T] *Tevāram* compositions went upstream against the current of the river Vaigai and were laid ashore. The spot where the manuscript lodged itself is called "Tiruveḍakam" ("Tiru + eḍu + akam"). Here the deity Śiva is called "Patrikā Parameśvara". Nowadays the word "paper" is understood as a newspaper, magazine, periodical, etc. "Patrika" means a magazine today. The Lord associated with the spot where the palm-leaves, nature's paper, were laid ashore is "Patrikā Parameśvara", which could be taken to mean "the Lord the journalist". "Patra" and "patrikā" mean the same, a leaf. In the past letters were written on palm-leaves. That is why a letter also came to be called "patra".

There is an interesting story about the Sarasvatī Mahaḷ. In the old days the worst injury an invader thought he could inflict on a country was to burn down its libraries. What the treasury is to the economy of a nation the library is to its culture; indeed the library represents its cultural treasury. Since there was no printing press then, there would not be many [palm-leaf] copies available of works, and of some works there would be only a single copy. To destroy the library of a nation, containing rare works, would be a greater outrage than looting its treasury or dishonouring its women. We must be proud of the fact that our śāstras on polity strictly forbid the destruction of an enemy country's treasures of knowledge and its places of worship, nor do they permit the dishonouring of its women.

When Jainas like Amarasiṁha lost to Hindu religious teachers in argument, they themselves wanted to burn their books. But great men like our Ācārya stopped them from doing so. Holding the hands of their opponents they requested them not to destroy their books. Their attitude was that no work must be destroyed whatever the philosophy or religious system it upholds.

Conquerors belonging to other countries took special delight in setting fire to the libraries of the conquered land if it was known to be culturally advanced. They perpetrated such outrages without reflecting for a moment on the fact that knowledge is common to all, even such knowledge as possessed by an enemy. They could cause anguish to people intellectually superior to them by destroying their books. It was thus that during the 15th-16th centuries Muslim invaders set fire to the library in Alexandria in Egypt (it had books collected from the time of Alexander) and the library in Constantinople (Istanbul) which had been built up over the centuries by the Greeks and the Romans. Once old Saṁgam works were swept off when the sea rose — it was an act of nature. But it is due to their cultural backwardness that foreign forces destroyed the libraries of the country they invaded.

The Sarasvatī Mahaḷ of Tañjāvūr was once under threat when Muslim forces had spread all over the South and the Nawab of Carnatic had the upper hand. For the Muslim invaders burning down the Sarasvatī Mahaḷ library was equivalent to destroying the great temple of Tañjāvūr[1]. At that time there was a Mahārāṣṭrian Brahmin called Dabīr Pant who was a minister to the Marāṭhā Rājā (the Marāṭhā rulers here belonged to Śivājī's family). An idea occurred to him just in time to save the library. He said to the vandals: "This library has of course Hindu books. But it also has many copies of the Qur'ān." "What? The Qur'ān also?" the invaders cried. "We won't set fire to the library in that case," so saying they departed.

Then came to India Englishmen, Frenchmen and others. They had a thirst for knowledge and research and were anxious to learn even from foreign sources. The Germans too came to our country and searched for palm-leaf manuscripts to take home with them. We must be grateful to some of these foreigners through whose efforts a number of our śāstras were rediscovered. There was, for example, Mackenzie who was surveyor-general of India[2]. He went from place to place to collect palm-leaf manuscripts. There was at the time no special department to deal with them but Mackenzie had them read by experts and took steps to have them preserved. Mackenzie's men came even to our Maṭha at Kuṁbhakoṇam to gather information.

It is believed that Westerners took with them some of our science manuscripts from the Sarasvatī Mahaḷ, especially those pertaining to the art of warfare. It is further claimed that Hitler made some types of weapons and aircraft on the basis of knowledge contained in these texts.

There are palm-leaf manuscripts still with us like Bhojarāja's *Samārangaṇa Sūtra*. From these we learn that we had long ago not only "astras" to be employed with mantras but also "śastras" that were the product of science. Digests like Varāhamihira's *Bṛhatsaṁhitā* bring together the various disciplines of our land.

Some of our ancient palm-leaf manuscripts contain texts not only of our religious systems but also of various arts and sciences. Also the Purāṇas. But we have lost many of our Sthala Purāṇas. We must do our best to preserve what remains and, at the same time, continue the search for more manuscripts.

The Purāṇas give us instruction, in the form of engrossing stories, on the truth of the Paramātman proclaimed by the Vedas, the dharmas, and the moral and ethical codes of conduct that they lay down. The teaching they impart touches our very hearts. The lessons of the Purāṇas, the stories of noble men and women contained in them, have shaped our lives. The Purāṇas have indeed served as a source of inspiration for our people from time immemorial. We must no longer be apathetic to them and must make a determined effort to preserve them as a treasure. Let us make a comparative study of purāṇic literature and take an integrated view. This will be to our own benefit as well as to that of all mankind.

Note & Reference

1 The great temple of Bṛhadīśvara, called *Periya Koyil* in Tamiḷ.

2 See Notes, Chapter 8, Part Five.

Part Fifteen

DHARMAŚĀSTRA

Chapter 1

Realising the Ideals of the Purāṇas

The noble characters who figure in the Purāṇas serve as an ideal for all of us to follow. When we read their stories we are inspired by their example and we ask ourselves why we cannot be like them ourselves, why we should not share their qualities. But, even if we wanted to emulate their lives, would we be able to live like them without deviating at any time from the high principles that they upheld?

Man by nature is always unstill: he cannot keep his mind quiescent even for a moment. Bhagavān says in the Gītā[1]: "Not for a moment can a man remain still, without doing work". So one must know the right path for work. One must make one's mind pure, acquire the highest of qualities and, finally, transcending these very qualities, realise the Brahman.

How can we live according to the tenets of our religion? How can we wash away our sins and cleanse our Self? And what must we do to attain everlasting happiness? Is not our present birth a consequence of the sins we committed in our past lives? We have to free ourselves from them and be careful not to sin afresh. We must elevate ourselves, our mind and character, so that we are not embroiled in sin again. The purpose of religion is this, to ennoble us and turn us away from sin. But how? How do we live according to the teachings of our religion? We do not know how.

In our present condition, what do we claim to know? Perhaps a little bit of the Rāmāyaṇa, the *Bhāgavata* and other Purāṇas. We learn about the religious life lived by the characters portrayed in these works. But neither the Purāṇas nor the epics deal with the rites in a codified form, nor do they contain directions for their proper performance.

The Purāṇas and the epics give a dominant place to devotion. Is it possible to be engaged in devotion all the time, or to keep singing the glory of the Lord day and night? Or, for that matter, to be similarly engaged in pūjā and meditation throughout? No. We have a family to look after. We have to bathe and eat and we have so much other work to do — all this takes time. The remaining hours cannot be set apart for pūjā. It would all be tiresome and we have, besides, to do other good works. How do we get such information?

From the Dharmaśāstra.

Of the fourteen branches of learning (caturdaśa-vidyā) Dharmaśāstra comes last. Purāṇic characters, who represent our ideal, show us the goal. The path to attain that goal starts with the performance of karma, works. The Dharmaśāstra contains practical instruction in our duties, in the rites to be performed by us. In the Vedas these duties are mentioned here and there. The Dharmaśāstra is an Upānga that deals with them in detail and in a codified form.

There is an orderly way of doing things, a proper way, with regard to household and personal matters including even bathing and eating. The ordinances of the Vedas cover all aspects of life and to conduct ourselves according to them is to ennoble our Self. Whatever we do must be done in the right manner — how we lie down, how we dress, how we build our house. The idea is that all this helps our inner being. Life is not compartmentalised into the secular, worldly and the religious. The Vedic dharma is such that in it even mundane affairs are inspired by the religious spirit. Whatever work is done is done with the chanting of mantras and thus becomes a means of Ātmic progress. Just as worldly life and religious life are integrated, harmonised, so are the goals of individual liberation and common welfare kept together.

The devotion we imbibe from the Purāṇas is part of the Vedas also. But with it is associated a good deal of karma. When devotion takes the form of the rite called pūjā there are certain rules to be observed. Apart from pūjā there are sacrifices and rites like śrāddha[S] and tarpaṇa[S] as important elements of the Vedic dharma. But these are not codified in the Vedas nor is any procedure laid down for each of them.

"Vedo'khilo dharmamūlam," says Manu. (The Vedas are the root of all dharma.) The works that the Vedas bid us perform for our inner well-being also serve the purpose of bringing good to the world. What is called dharma is that which fosters both individual and social welfare. The Vedas are the root of this dharma, its fountainhead.

But the rites and duties are not given in an orderly form in the Vedas, nor is the procedure for works laid down in detail. Of the Vedas that are infinite we have obtained only a very small part. And we do not comprehend fully the meaning of many of the passages even of this small part.

As we have seen, the sixth Vedānga, Kalpa, contains the Dharmasūtras, Gṛhyasūtras and Śrautasūtras, relating to rites based on the Vedas. But the sūtras are brief and do not constitute a detailed guide. The dharmaśāstras elaborate upon them without leaving any room for doubt.

The Dharmasūtras (by Āpastamba, Gautama and others) are terse statements and are so according to the very definition of the term "sūtras". The dharmaśāstras (by Manu, Yājñavalkya, Parāśara and others) are called Smṛtis and are in verse and detailed in treatment. Their basis, however, is constituted by the Vedas. The function of Dharmaśāstra is to analyse and explicate the sūtras of Kalpa which has to some extent systematised the Vedic rules and injunctions. If Kalpa gives instructions about the construction of the Vedic altar, of houses, etc, Dharmaśāstra provides a code of conduct embracing all human activity.

We want to perform a ritual, but how do we go about it? We do not know where the propriety or otherwise of performing it is mentioned in the Vedas. Nor do we know where instructions are given about it. What are we to do then? We do not know anyone who has mastered all the Vedas. Extracting information from them about the rite we want to perform is impossible because they are like the expanse of a vast ocean. If the Vedas bid us, "Do like this," we do so. But since we do not know their ordinances well enough, what are we to do? The answers to these questions are given by Manu: "The sages who had mastered the Vedas composed the Smṛtis. Find out what they have to say." What we call Smṛtis make up Dharmaśāstra.

"Vedo'khilo dharmamūlam / Smṛtiśile ca tadvidām".

"Smṛti" is what is remembered. "Vismṛti" is insanity. Manu observes: "There is Smṛti for the Vedas in the form of notes. The sages who had a profound understanding of the Vedas have brought together the duties and rites (dharma and karma) mentioned in them in the form of notes and they constitute the Smṛtis. They are written in a language that we can easily understand. Read them. They tell you about your duties in detail, the dos and don'ts, and how the rites are to be performed."

We have seen that the sixth Vedānga, Kalpa, contains instructions about the Vedic works. The Gṛhyasūtras, Dharmasūtras and Śrautasūtras of Kalpa deal with sacrifices and other rites. The Smṛtis elaborate on them and contain detailed instructions with regard to the rites one has to perform through one's entire life. Actually, there are rituals to be conducted from the time of conception until death. The Smṛtis also lay down the daily routine to be followed by all of us.

Reference

1 *Na hi kaścit kṣaṇam api jātu tiṣṭhati akarma-kṛt*
Kāryate hyavaśaḥ karma sarvaḥ prakṛtijair guṇaiḥ

— Bhagavadgītā, 3.5

Chapter 2

Smṛtis and Allied Works

Manu, Parāśara, Yājñavalkya, Gautama, Hārīta, Yama, Viṣṇu, Śaṅkha, Likhita, Bṛhaspati, Dakṣa, Angiras, Pracetas, Saṁvarta, Acanas, Atri, Āpastamba and Śātātapa are the eighteen sages who mastered the Vedas with their superhuman power and derived the Smṛtis from them. Their works are known after them like *Manusmṛti, Yājñavalkya-smṛti, Parāśara-smṛti* and so on, and they contain all that we need to know about all the dharmas to be adhered to and all the rituals to be performed during our entire life.

Apart from these eighteen, there are eighteen subsidiary Smṛtis called Upasmṛtis[1]. It is customary to include the Bhagavadgītā among the Smṛtis.

What we find in one Smṛti may not be found in another. There may also be differences between one Smṛti and another. These give rise to doubts which are sought to be cleared by works called "Dharmaśāstra Nibandhanas".

There are some Smṛtis that do not contain instructions with regard to all observances. For instance, some do not mention sandhyāvandana[S]. The reason must be it is such a common rite that everybody is expected to know it. Then some omit the śrāddha[S] ceremony and some others are silent on various types of "pollution" (for instance, that due to the birth of a child in the family or the death of a relative). Certain matters are taken for granted. After all, we do not have to be told about how to breathe or eat.

The nibandhanas do not leave out any rite or dharma. Differences between various Smṛtis are sought to be reconciled in them.

Each region follows its own nibandhana. In the North, it is the one authored by Kāśinātha Upādhyāya. In Mahārāṣṭra, it is the *Mitākṣara*: it has the force of law and is accepted as such by the lawcourts. *Nirṇayasindhu* by Kamalākara Bhaṭṭa is also accepted as an authority there. In the South, the *Vaidyanātha-Dīkṣitīyam* by Vaidyanātha Dīkṣita is followed. These are the important authorities for householders. Sannyāsins follow *Viśvesvara-saṁhitā*. In Tamiḷ Nāḍu the Dharmaśāstra means the *Vaidyanātha-Dīksitīyam*. This nibandhana has been translated into Tamiḷ.

The dharmaśāstras are not as difficult to follow as the Vedas and can be understood with a little knowledge of Sanskrit.

Notes

[1] The authors of these are : Jābāli, Nāciketas, Skanda, Laugākṣi, Kāśyapa, Vyāsa, Sanatkumāra, Śantanu, Janaka, Vyāghra, Kātyāyana, Jātukarṇya, Kapiñjala, Baudhāyana, Kāṇāda, Viśvāmiktra, Paiṭhīnasa, Gobhila.

— Rā. Ga.

Chapter 3

Vaidyanātha-Dīkṣitīyam

Vaidyanātha Dīkṣita's own name for his work is *Smṛti-Muktāphala-Nibandhana-Grantha.* We know very little about the author of this extremely useful book. Dīkṣita must have lived some two hundred years ago; he belonged to Kaṇḍiramāṇikkam, near Nācciyārkoyil (in Tañjāvūr district). It must be noted that he himself practised the dharmas he has dealt with in his nibandhana and he is also believed to have performed big sacrifices.

Vaidyanātha-Dīkṣitīyam is considered superior even to similar works by Medhātithi, Vijñeśvara, Hemādri and so on. Exhaustive in nature, it deals with the duties and rites pertaining to the different castes and aśramas (the four stages of life), ritual purity, śrāddha[S], prāyaścitta[S], strīdharma[S], dāyabhāga, dravya-śuddhi[S]. It even gives directions about the division of paternal property. When the Hindu Code Bill was introduced in free India some put forward the view that the division of property must be based on the śāstras. Such division is called "dāyabhāga". The division of property in Keraḷa, in the uncle-nephew line, is called *marumakkatāyam*[1]. The word "dāyādi" is derived from "dāya".

Dīkṣitīyam is the last among the nibandhanas. In the preparation of this work Vaidyanātha Dīkṣita had the advantage of making a comparative study of all the previous works on Dharmaśāstra. Before it the authority followed to some extent in the South was the nibandhana of Tozhappar. Vaiṣṇavas and Smārtas[S] alike today accept the *Dīkṣitīyam* as an authority.

The nibandhanas are not like the Vedas (Śruti), the Kalpa-sūtras and the Smṛtis. Since they came later it is not easy to make them acceptable to all. Dīkṣita, it must be noted, does not show the least trace of bias in his work and has followed the Mīmāṁsā in determining the meaning of Vedic texts. He has brought together previous śāstras and arrived at conclusions only after resolving the contradictions in them. This is the reason why his work is considered an authority in the South. When the Smṛtis differ in some matters, he takes a broad view and suggests: "Let each individual follow the practices of his region and the tradition of his forefathers."

Note

[1] This system (usually called matrilineal) is no longer in force in Keraḷa. According to *marumakkatāyam* when a man died, his property was inherited by his sister's sons.

Chapter 4

Freedom and Discipline

There are a hundred thousand aspects to be considered in a man's life. Rules cannot be laid down to determine each and every one of them. That would be tantamount to making a legal enactment. Laws are indeed necessary to keep a man bound to a system. Our śāstras do contain many dos and don'ts, many rules of conduct.

There is much talk today of freedom and democracy. In practice what do we see? Freedom has come to mean the licence to do what one likes, to indulge one's every whim. The strong and the rough are free to harass the weak and the virtuous. Thus we recognise the need to keep people bound to certain laws and rules. However, the restrictions must not be too many. There must be a restriction on restrictions, a limit set on how far individuals and society can be kept under control. To choke a man with too many rules and regulations is to kill his spirit. He will break loose and run away from it all.

That is the reason why our śāstras have not committed everything to writing and enacted laws to embrace all activities. In many matters they let people follow in the footsteps of their elders or great men. Treating me as a great man and respecting me for that reason, don't you, on your own, do what I do — wear ashes, perform pūjā and observe fasts? In some matters people are given the freedom to follow the tradition or go by the personal example of others or by local or family custom. Only thus will they have the faith and willingness to respect the rules prescribed with regard to other matters.

Setting an example through one's life is the best way of making others do their duty or practise their dharma. The next best is to make them do the same on their own by persuasion. The third course is compulsion in the form of written rules. Nowadays there are written laws for anything and everything. Anyone who has pen and paper writes whatever comes to his mind and has it printed.

Hindu Dharmaśāstra has come under attack for ordering a man's life with countless rules and regulations and not allowing him freedom to act on his own. But, actually, the śāstras respect his freedom and allow him to act on his own in many spheres. Were he given unbridled freedom he would ruin himself and bring ruin upon the world also. The purpose of the code of conduct formulated by our śāstras is to keep him within certain bounds. But this code does not cover all activities since the makers of our śāstras thought that people should not be too tightly shackled by the dhārmic regulations.

You may feel that with regard to some aspects of life there is an element of compulsion in the śāstras, but you may not feel the same when you follow the tradition, the local or family custom or the example of great men. Indeed you will take pride in doing so. This fact is accepted, in the large-heartedness of its author, by the *Vaidyanātha- Dīkṣitīyam.* Previous works on Dharmaśāstra shared the same view. The *Āpastamba-sūtra* is an authority widely followed. In its concluding part the great sage Āpastamba observes: "I have not dealt with all duties. There are so many dharmas still to be learned. Know them from women and from the fourth varṇa." From this it is clear that the usual criticism that men kept women suppressed or that Brahmins kept non-Brahmins suppressed is not true. In a renowned and widely accepted dharmaśāstra such as that of Āpastamba women and Śūdras are authoritatively recognised to be knowledgeable in some aspects of dharma.

Āśvalāyana and some other "original" authors of sūtras say that the word of women is to be respected in the matter of the ārati[S] in weddings and the application of *paccai*[T]. The posts supporting the marriage *paṇḍāl* are installed to the chanting of mantras. Even so, if the servant or worker erecting the *paṇḍāl* has a story to tell about it or some tradition connected with it, you must not ignore it. In this way everyone is respected in the śāstras and given what is called "democratic" freedom[1].

The dharmaśāstras include the saṁskāras and other rituals to be performed by the fourth varṇa. That caste has not been ignored and its duties and rituals are dealt with in the chapters on varṇāśrama, ānhika and śrāddha[S] in the *Dīkṣitīyam.*

The dharmaśāstras have usually chapters on "ācāra" and "vyavahāra". The first denotes matters of custom and tradition that serve as a general discipline. The second means translating them in terms of outward rites or works.

Note

[1] The Paramaguru uses the phrase "jananāyaka svātantryam".

Chapter 5

Signs, Marks

If we call ourselves Hindus we must bear certain external marks, outward symbols.

The boy scouts have a uniform of their own. Army and navy men are distinguished by certain external insignia. There are a number of divisions in the police force. Even though their functions will not change if they wear one another's uniforms or badges, there is a strict rule with regard to their dress and insignia. The policeman's cap must not be worn by the sailor. There is a certain discipline and orderliness among all these forces.

This discipline as well as orderliness is essential in religion also. That is why different jātis and different āśramas have different functions and signs. According to the dharmaśāstras we must wear the *dhoti* or the *sārī* in such and such a way or apply the mark to the forehead in a particular manner. All this is not meant for social discipline alone. There is a higher purpose, that of purifying our inner life.

The court attendant has a *ṭavāli*[1]. The official does not have it. Is it sensible to ask why? But we do not take the same attitude with regard to the different signs and marks assigned to people according to their vocations and family customs. We make a noise in the name of equality. Even though we remain divided in the matter of our vocations — which indeed is for the welfare of the entire community — we are of one heart. This is the ideal behind the social arrangement in which different jātis are assigned different rites and external symbols, these in keeping with their natural qualities and callings. There is no high or low in all this. But we keep fighting among ourselves imagining that there is.

Now we have come to such a pass that nobody wears any of the external marks of our religion. At the same time, we are not ashamed of wearing other types of signs or badges. To wear those marks that bring uplift of the Self we are ashamed. We dismiss all religious marks and symbols as part of superstition. But those who want to proclaim themselves to be reformers don a particular type of cap or upper cloth and these external trappings are given greater importance than symbols of a divine nature.

Note

[1] Hindi word meaning stripe on which the badge of a peon is placed.

Chapter 6

Smṛtis -- not Independent Works

There is a wrong impression about the dharmaśāstras even among those who treat them with respect. They think that the rules and duties of the Smṛtis were formulated by their authors on their own. They call these authors "lawgivers" who, in their opinion, laid down "laws" that reflect their own views. Further they think that the dharmaśāstras were composed in the same way as our Constitution. Such a view gives rise to another idea. We keep amending the Constitution whenever we find that it stands in the way of certain measures being introduced. It is asked, on the same logic, why the dharmaśāstras too should not be changed according to the beliefs and ideas of the present times.

People ask me[1]: "Why should not the śāstras be changed to suit the times? The government changes its laws, does it not?" They sing my praises and tell me: "You are like the sages, the authors of the Smṛtis. If only you make up your mind you can change the Smṛtis to suit our times." In effect what they respectfully suggest is this: "Please change the śāstras as we would like them to be changed."

If the Smṛtis really represent the views of their authors there is nothing wrong in what these people think about them and about what they want me to do about them. But those who want the dharmaśāstras changed do not seem to know that they (the Smṛtis) do not reflect the views of the sages who composed them. What the authors of the Smṛtis have done is to present us in an orderly fashion what is already contained in the Vedas. The Vedic word cannot and must not be changed at any time and on any account. The same applies to the rules and laws laid down in the Smṛtis.

I may not be capable enough, or worthy enough, to persuade you to live according to the śāstras. But changing them is certainly not my function. I have been installed here (in the Maṭha) to make people perform their duties and rites. That is according to the command of the Ācārya. I do not possess the authority to revise the śāstras according to what is felt to be convenient to the present times or what is in keeping with the new beliefs.

If the sages had created the Smṛtis on their own, to represent their own views, there would be no compulsion to accept them. If the Smṛtis were not needed we could reject them outright. If their contents are not based on the Vedas and include rules and directions that reflect the views of the authors, then we can do without them. In this way so many people have written down so much about so many things. We too may write down whatever comes to our mind. The Smṛtis must be looked upon as an authority for today and tomorrow and for all time because they are founded on the Vedas. But what is the proof for this claim?

Note

[1] See Chapter 1, Part Four. Here also there is a reference to people asking the Paramaguru why the śāstras should not be changed to suit the times. But the two contexts are different.

Chapter 7
The Source of Smṛtis is the Vedas

The best testimony to the claim that the Smṛtis are founded on the Vedas is provided by the words of a mahākavi (great poet). Śankara, Rāmānuja and Madhva, the founders of our religio-philosophical systems, proclaim that our dharmaśāstras are in accord with the Vedas. But they had, each of them, a doctrine to establish. Besides they had also the goal before them of preserving the tradition and they would not naturally go against it. With a poet it is different. He has no doctrine to establish, no belief to promote. He speaks what he feels to be the truth since he does not have to lend his support to any particular concept or system.

The greatest of the mahākavis, Kālidāsa, makes a reference to the Smṛtis in his *Raghuvaṁśam*.

As all of you know, Daśaratha was the father of Rāma. Daśaratha's father was Aja and Aja's father was Raghu. Rāma was named Raghurāma after his great-grandfather. We do not often come across "Dāśarathi" among the names of Rāma. Usually one is named after one's grandfather. But Rāma did not take the name of Aja and is better known after his great- grandfather. Raghu had such fame and glory. The name Rāghava also means one belonging to the family of Raghu.

Raghu's father was Dilīpa. For long he did not have a son. The guru of Dilīpa's family was Vasiṣṭha. Dilīpa approached him and said to him: "Svāmin, I don't have a child. Bless me that my family will continue and prosper." Vasiṣṭha had a cow called Nandinī, the daughter of Kāmadhenu. The sage asked the king to look after the cow and worship her with faith. He blessed Dilīpa thus: "A son will be born to you." Think of it, a king was asked to look after a cow — how humble he must have been.

Dilīpa took charge of the cow right away. Like a cowherd he took Nandinī to the forest, grazed her, bathed her and looked after her with devotion. He carried a bow with just one arrow to protect her from wild beasts. He scratched the cow, stopped on the way if she stopped, lay down if she lay down, walked if she walked. If we sit down our shadow too will seem to sit down, if we stand up so too our shadow will seem to stand up, if we run then too our shadow will seem to run. "Chāyeva tām bhūpatiranvagacchat,"[1] says Kālidāsa. Dilipa followed the cow like a shadow.

Every day, as Dilīpa took the cow to graze, his wife Sudakṣiṇā would follow him to some distance and then return home. Very religiously she would send her husband out with Nandinī and wait in the evening for them to return from the forest. Sudakṣiṇā kept caring for Dilīpa and, if the king followed Nandinī like a shadow, she too followed him in turn like a shadow.

The duties of a pativratā[S] are described by Janaka during the marriage of his daughter Sītā to Rāma. He says to Rāma: "My child Sītā will follow you like a shadow (chāyevānugatā)"[2]. This is in Vālmīki's Rāmāyana. Kālidāsa retells the story of Rāma that Vālmīki has told. He speaks about Lava and Kuśa who came after Rāma and also about Rāma's predecessors. And he gives to his great poetical work the title of *Raghuvaṁśam* after Rāma's great-grandfather Raghu of unsurpassed fame. Verily, to speak of this family is to sanctify one's speech.

In the passage describing how Sudakṣiṇā follows Dilīpa as he goes grazing the cow, the poet makes a reference to the sages creating the Smṛtis. He does so not in pursuance of any doctrine, not also after any deliberation. He speaks spontaneously about the Smṛtis, unpremeditatedly. The poet describes how Sudakṣiṇā follows the cow to some distance. Nandinī is in the front and Sudakṣiṇā walks behind. The cow raises a little dust with her hoofs and the queen goes some distance looking at the hallowed dust. Kālidāsa excels all other poets in similes. Each poet has some distinction or other. There is a saying: "Upamā Kālidāsasya" (For similes Kālidāsa — Kālidāsa excels in similes). It is in the context of Sudakṣiṇā following Nandinī that the poet brings in the simile of the queen following the cow like the Smṛtis following the Vedas.

Tasyāḥ khuranyāsapavitrapāṁsum
Apāmsulānām dhuri kīrtanīyā
Mārgam manuṣyeśvaradharmapatnī
Śruterivārtham Smṛtiranvagacchat

— Raghuvaṁśam, 2.2

"Pāmsu" means dust. As Nandinī goes grazing, dust is raised. "Khura" is hoof. "Khuranyāsa" means placing of the hoof and "pavitra pāṁsum" the sacred dust.

The dust raised by a cow is particularly sacred. It sanctifies any place. Such is the case even with the dust raised by an ordinary cow, not to speak of so sacred a cow as Nandinī, Kāmadhenu's daughter. Sudakṣiṇā is a woman of spotless character — there is not a speck of dust on it — and such a woman has now cowdust on her. "Apāṁsu" means free of dust and refers to Sudakṣiṇā of unblemished character. She goes step by step along the hallowed path following the dust raised by the hoofs of the cow. How? Like the Smṛtis composed by the sages that follow the Vedas — "Śruterivārtham Smṛtiranvagacchat."

"Anvagacchat" = (she) followed. Here the upamāna (that with which a comparison is made) for the cow is Śruti or the Vedas. The "hoofsteps" of the cow are to be taken as the meaning of the Vedas.

So Sudakṣiṇā followed in the "hoofsteps" of Nandinī like the Smṛtis following the meaning of the Vedas. Also, like the Smṛtis not going the entire way with the Vedas, she did not go all the distance with the cow. The idea is that the Smṛtis do not repeat all that is said in the Vedas. They are "notes from memory", but they truthfully follow the Vedas in their meaning. They do not, of course, represent all the thousands of mantras of the scriptures but, all the same, they tell us how to make use of the Vedas.

"Sudakṣiṇā with her pure antaḥ-karaṇa[S] followed her husband and, without deviating even a little, walked along the path of the dust raised by Nandinī's hoofs". Having said so much, Kālidāsa thought he must bring in a good simile for Sudakṣiṇā following the cowdust and it occurred to him in a flash: "Like the Smṛtis following faithfully the meaning of the Vedas."

The upamāna is always superior to the upameya[3]. If a face is compared to the lotus or the moon, the lotus or the moon must be more beautiful than the face. Here Sudakṣiṇā, of matchless purity of character, following her husband Dilīpa is likened to the Smṛtis *closely* following the Vedas. No better authority is needed to support the view that the Smṛtis are in accord with the Vedas.

Notes & References

1 Sthitaḥ sthitāmuccalitaḥ prayātām

Niśeduṣīmāsanabandhadhīraḥ

Jalābhilāṣī jalamādadānām

Chāyeva tam bhupatiranvagacchat

— Raghuvaṁśam, 2.6

2 Pativratā mahābhāga chāyevānugatā sadā

Ityuktvā prākṣipadrājā mantrapūrvam jalam tadā

— Vālmīki-Rāmāyaṇa

3 It means what is compared is inferior to what it is compared with.

Chapter 8

Śruti-Smṛti — Śrauta-Smārta

To discriminate between Śruti and Smṛti is not correct. Śruti, Smṛti and the Purāṇas, all three belong to the same tradition. Śankara is said to be the abode of the three ("Śruti-Smṛti-Purāṇanām ālayam"). If the three were at variance with one another how can they exist together in harmony in the same person?

Those who follow the tradition of the Ācārya are called "Smārtas". The word "Smārta" literally means one who adheres to the Smṛtis. To say that the Ācārya descended to earth to uphold the Vedas and that those who follow his path are Smārtas implies that the Vedas and the Smṛtis are one.

The rites that are not explicitly mentioned in the Vedas but are dealt with in the Smṛtis are called Smārta karmas and those that are explicitly mentioned are Śrauta karmas. This does not mean that Smārta rites are in any way inferior to Śrauta. The householder's Smārta works include such an important rite as aupāsana[1]; equally important are the domestic rites like śrāddha[S] and the seven pākayajñas[2]. Vedic mantras are chanted in all these. Those who composed the Smṛtis and laid down the performance of such rites must have been fully aware of the spirit of the Vedas. It is not proper to think that the Smṛtis are inferior to the Vedas or that the Purāṇas are inferior to the Smṛtis. We must learn to take an integrated view of all of them.

In the Purāṇas the Vedic truths are illustrated in the form of stories. The Smṛtis bring the Vedic dharmas and karmas in the form of instruction and injunctions and tell us how the rites are to be performed.

The sages had intuitive knowledge of the Vedas. As mentioned so often they did not compose them — they *saw* them. There was no intellectual effort on their part in this. "Śrutim paśyanti munayaḥ" (The sages see the Vedas). They used their intelligence to examine what they saw and, remembering it all, derived from the Vedas the duties and rites for various castes. This they gave us in a codified form called Smṛti. As I said before "Smṛti" means memory. For the sages the Vedas constituted an experience that just happened to them. The Smṛtis or dharmaśāstras are derived from their memory of it. "Saṁskāra-janyam jñānam Smṛtiḥ," the Nyāya-śāstra defines Smṛtis thus. It means that Smṛti is knowledge derived from saṁskāra. Here "saṁskāra" means "atīndriya". But what exactly is it?

We go to Kāśī and worship at the temple of Viśvanātha there. Many days after our return home, we go to the local temple which has a sanctum of "Kāśī Viśvanātha". At once we remember the experience we had of seeing the deity Viśvanātha at Kāśī. In between for many days, that is between our visit to Kāśī and to the local temple, we had no memory of this deity. We come across so many people every day but we hardly think of them later. But, when we happen to see them subsequently, we tell ourselves: "Ah, we must have seen them before somewhere." In between there was no memory of the people. This "in between state" is called "saṁskāra" or "atīndriya". In that state there is an impression of our experience within us. When this impression manifests itself as an "expression" we have "Smṛti" or memory. All told, Smṛti is the result of an experience and saṁskāra an impression of that experience within us.

The experience constituted by the Vedas and manifested as the memory is Smṛti or Dharmaśāstra. Smṛti does not become Smṛti without its Vedic root. Are not the Vedas the "experience" that is the source of the Smṛtis? Without such a source the name suggesting "notes of memory" would be meaningless. How can we describe as "notes of remembrance" anything that is new and is not founded on something prior to it?

There is no second opinion regarding the fact that what is called "Śrauta" (directly mentioned in the Vedas) is wholly authoritative. But what is not directly mentioned in Śruti but included in Smṛti — that is Smārta — is not to be taken to be less authoritative. Smārta never contradicts Śrauta. In some matters the Smṛtis may go beyond Śruti, but that too is fully authoritative being based on the inner spirit of Śruti. Just as the Sthala Purāṇas fill in the gaps in the major Purāṇas and the epics, so the Smṛtis speak of what is left out in the Vedas. We use the terms "Śruti pramāṇa" and "Smṛti pramāṇa" (the authority of the Vedas and the authority of the Smṛtis), but making such a distinction does not mean that we should treat Śruti and Smṛti as different or that we should think that the one is inferior to the other.

Reference

[1 & 2] See Chapters 2 and 5, Part Nineteen.

Part Sixteen

THE FORTY SAṀSKĀRAS

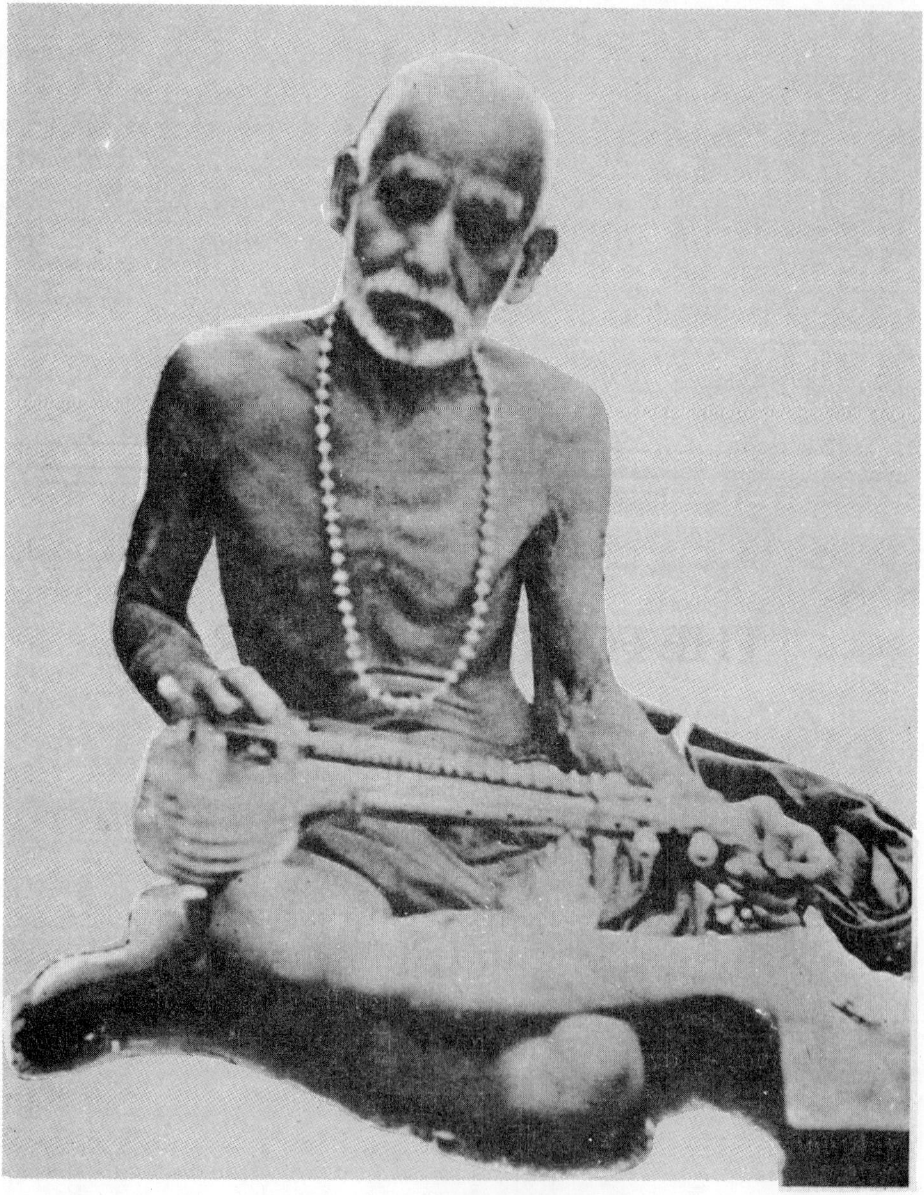

Chapter 1

Saṁskāra

I used the word "saṁskāra" above [in the previous chapter — of Part Fifteen]. I also explained its meaning according to the Tarka-śāstra (science of logic) as "impression on memory". But this is not how the word is generally understood. "Sam(s)" = well; "kara" = making. "Saṁskāra" means making something good, refining or purifying it.

The dharmaśāstras deal with such saṁskāras as purify a man so as to make him fit to be united with the Paramātman. From the dharmaśāstras we know in detail the forty saṁskāras that are based on the Kalpa-sūtras and that are to be performed by a man during his life's journey.

Chapter 2

Paradise or the Path of Ātmajñāna?

Our worldly existence is a mixture of joys and sorrows. Some experience more joy than sorrow and some more sorrow. Then there may be a rare individual here or there who can control his mind and keep smiling even in the midst of sorrow. On the other hand, we do see quite a number of people who have much to be happy about but who keep a long face. If a man lacks for something it means he is unhappy.

All creatures long for everlasting happiness. There are two abodes of eternal happiness. One is devaloka, the world of the celestials or paradise, the other is Ātmajñāna, the state of awareness of the Self[1]. The Ātman, the Self, is bliss; it is the Brahman. To realise this truth is to attain everlasting blessedness. But this state, this joy supreme, is not experienced by the mind or the senses. It is the highest, the most exalted state and it transcends the senses and the mind; it is a state in which a man becomes aware that "the body is not I, the intelligence is not I, the consciousness is not I".

Paradise is the place where happiness is always experienced by the mind and the senses. Music and dance — music of the gandharvas, dance by Rambhā and Menakā[S] — Kalpaka, the tree that grants all wishes, Kāmadhenu, the cow that grants all wishes, the garden known as Nandana: devaloka means all these. It is indeed a playground and there it is always joy. But a difference exists between the joy known in paradise and the bliss experienced by the knower of the Self. It is true that there is eternal happiness in paradise but not so for the man who goes there because he will not be a permanent resident of it. If he has earned a good deal of merit he will be able to reside there until he is reborn. When he has enjoyed the fruits of his meritorious actions, the Lord will send him back to earth. It is true that there are accounts in the Purāṇas of mortals who earn a great deal of merit and become gods themselves to reside in the celestial world. But the same Purāṇas also tell us that the gods themselves are not permanent denizens of paradise. There are stories in these texts of the celestials being hounded out of paradise by demons like Śūrapadma and Mahiṣāsura and of Indra, their king, himself being pushed down to earth to undergo suffering there.

On a hypothetical basis, eternal happiness may be ours in svarga or paradise. But there is no instance of anyone having actually lived there permanently nor does it seem possible for anyone to do so.

Happiness gained through the senses is derived from external objects. These cannot be ours for all time. There were occasions when Indra had to suffer all by himself when he lost everything, including Kāmadhenu, the Kalpaka tree, Airāvata[2] and even Indrāṇī[3]. So the happiness associated with paradise, which is dependent on external objects, can never be enduring. "Sadānanda" or eternal bliss is for him who has neither anything external nor internal and who dwells in his Self as a sthita-prajña (a man of steady wisdom) as explained by the Lord in the Gītā[4], one who remains nailed to his Self. The joy experienced by Indra is but a droplet of the vast ocean of Ātmic bliss, so says the Ācārya in his *Māniṣa-Pañcakam:* "Yad saukhyāmbudileśaleśata ime Śakrādayo nirvṛtāḥ".

According to the Upaniṣads you will have eternal bliss if the senses and the mind are removed in the same way as you draw off the rib from a stalk of corn and remain just the Ātman[5]. It needs great courage to pluck out the body and the senses realising that "I am not the body. Its joys and sorrows are not mine." Such courage is not earned without inner purity. Conduct of religious rituals is meant for this, for cittaśuddhi (purity of the consciousness). There are forty saṁskāras to "refine" a man with Vedic mantras and to involve him in the rites associated with those mantras. These are the first steps towards the indissoluble union of the individual self with the Absolute — it is Advaitic mukti, non-dualistic release.

We must strive to become inwardly pure by the performance of works. Then, with the inner organs (antaḥ-karaṇa) also cleansed, we must meditate on the Self and become one with It. This is the concept of Śankara. If a man has such a goal before him and keeps performing rituals throughout (that is even without becoming a sannyāsin) he goes to the Brahmaloka on death. During the great deluge when Brahmā is absorbed in the Brahman he too attains non-dualistic liberation, so says Śankara. But if a man performs rituals for the sake of rituals without keeping before him the goal of oneness with the Brahman he will be rewarded with paradise, but not the paradise that is eternal. Though the stay be brief he will enjoy greater happiness there than on earth. It is saṁskāras that earn a man heaven.

Notes & References

1 The state of Self-realisation.

2 The celestial elephant.

3 Consort of Indra.

4 *Prajahāti yadā kāmān sarvān Pārtha manogatān*

Ātmanyevā'tmanā tuṣṭaḥ sthita-prajñastad'ocyate

— Bhagavadgītā, 2.55

5 See Chapter 33, Part Five.

Chapter 3
Three Types of Worlds

We speak of three worlds: devaloka (world of the celestials), manuṣyaloka (this world of ours), and naraka (hell). The first has nothing but pleasure; in the second it is a mixture of happiness and sorrow; and in the third there is nothing but pain and sorrow. According to our śāstras a man who has committed terrible sins goes through the torments of hell before taking lowly birth again in this world.

Our śāstras also have it that this world of ours is better than the others. How? From here we may make the journey to any other world. If a man is condemned to hell he cannot escape from it and will be forced to stay there until he has paid for his sins. If we go to paradise we cannot extend our stay there however much we may wish to do so. When the fruits of our meritorious acts are exhausted we will have to tumble down to earth. It is only here that we have some freedom and we may earn merit or demerit by our actions. We may use our hands to perform pūjā — or we may use them to hurt others. We may sing the praises of Īśvara — or we may speak ill of people. We have the power to do good and evil in this world. For each of our faculties of action (karmendriya) God has given us this twin capacity.

There is not this kind of freedom in the other worlds. Is a cow capable of earning merit? The devas are like cows. So far as the cow is concerned there is neither merit nor sin in its life. On this earth (bhūloka) only those like us human beings can win liberation — we can do so through good actions. Other worlds are like hotels where the denizens eat what we harvest here. There you may enjoy the fruits you have merited here by your actions in proportion to the puṇya[S] you have earned or the pāpa[S] you have piled up. Our world alone is karmabhūmi (world of works). And even in this world only human beings are capable of thinking and acting on their own. All other creatures live by instinct. Those who live in the other worlds have no right for karma.

A man's actions, his works, together with his character, determine his passage to other worlds. Only in this karmabhūmi can we perfect our character by performing virtuous acts and thus qualify to go to another world.

There is a proper time and a proper place for the conduct of a religious rite. Do you think a śrāddha[S] can be performed at midnight? There is a right time for it as well as a proper place. It is in India particularly, that is Bhāratavarṣa, that Vedic karma must be performed, but even in this land it is not permitted during certain periods. It has to be carried out in hallowed places and during sanctified hours.

Chapter 4

Meaning of Saṁskāra

What is karma? It means work. Suppose you have to make a *veṣṭi (dhoti)*. There are a number of processes, a number of works for it. The cotton has to be gathered from the field; it has to be cleaned and spun into yarn; then the yarn has to be woven into cloth and dyed. In the same way a man has to be made a knower of the Ātman through a series of rituals. Karma has to be performed in such a way as to purify him both outwardly and inwardly. Such karma is called saṁskāra.

That which removes the impurities from an object, takes away all the bad or evil elements, and imparts good qualities to it is saṁskāra. For instance, we talk of "keśa-saṁskāra". It means shaving or delousing and applying oil to the hair. Saṁskāra is like combing the hair and applying oil to it. Certain types of saṁskāra are conducted on land. First the land is allowed to dry in the sun, then it is ploughed and irrigated. Seeds, say, of paddy, are sown and after they sprout the seedlings are transplanted. The weeds are removed, the field irrigated again and the excess water drained off. When the corn is ripe, the crop is harvested, threshed and the chaff winnowed. The paddy has to be "seasoned" and pounded before the rice is used.

How many different steps are there in making cotton into a *veṣṭi*. The weaver has to take great care that the yarn does not get tangled. Our Self is in a tangle caused by the senses. It has to be untangled and made eternally happy. There are many obstacles to accomplishing this. Now and then we experience some happiness in the midst of all our trouble and suffering. This happiness must be made to endure for ever. For that we must go to Brahmaloka. In the presence of Īśvara there will be no sorrow. After the great deluge we will become one with him. We have to prepare ourselves now itself towards that end.

The sages have laid down the forty saṁskāras and the eight "Ātmaguṇas" for this purpose.

When we use the term "Ātmaguṇa" or speak about the Ātman being rendered pure, there is a suggestion that we are dualists (Dvaitins) who hold that the individual self is different from the Paramātman. In truth there is only one Ātman, one Self, and there is no difference between the jīvātman or individual self and the Parabrahman. The Self is ever pure. So it is wrong to believe that it has to be purified by saṁskāras. It is nirguṇa, unconditioned and without attributes. So it is also wrong to speak of what are called Ātmaguṇas, since the Ātman has truly no guṇas or qualities or attributes.

However, in practice, owing to Māyā we do not realise that we are the Ātman without qualities. It is the Self perceived in our dualistic life that is referred to when we speak of saṁskāras and it is full of impurities that have to be removed through the saṁskāras. It has also durguṇas or bad qualities which have to be removed by cultivating the eight good qualities. Once we succeed in this, there will be neither any saṁskāra nor any guṇa. We will transcend all guṇas, all qualities, including the highest of them, sattvaguṇa. Finally there will be only the Self without any karma, without any guṇas, and without any distinction between the jīvātman and the Paramātman. But to come to this state we have to go through the process of saṁskāras and cultivate the eight Ātmaguṇas.

If we wish to emulate the example of the noble characters of the Purāṇas, we will have to contend against various obstacles like our attachments and desires, our feelings of hatred and fear. We will have to be disciplined through works and we will have to observe the rules about our daily routine, about how we should sit and stand and eat and dress. In this way we will rein in our mind, subdue our passions and ego, and our feelings of anger, hatred, fear and sorrow will gradually wither away. The saṁskāras and Ātmaguṇas are interconnected. They will help us to acquire the qualities of the noble Purāṇic characters whose stories we listen to or read.

Chapter 5

The Eight Qualities

The eight guṇas or qualities are: dayā, ksānti, anasūyā, śauca, anāyāsa, maṅgala, akārpaṇya, aspṛha.

"Dayā" implies love for all creatures, such love being the very fulfilment of life. There is indeed no greater happiness than that derived by loving others. Dayā is the backbone of all qualities.

"Ksāṇti" is patience. One kind of ksāṇti is patiently suffering disease, poverty, misfortune and so on. The second is forgiveness and it implies loving a person even if he causes us pain and trouble.

"Anasūyā" you know is the name of the sage Atri's wife. She was utterly free from jealousy: that is how she got the name which means non- jealousy. Heart-burning caused by another man's prosperity or status is jealousy. We ought to have love and compassion for all and ought to be patient and forgiving even towards those who do us wrong. We must not envy people their higher status even if they be less deserving of it than we are and, at the same time, must be mature enough to regard their better position as the reward they earned by doing good in their previous life.

"Śauca" is derived from "śuci", meaning cleanliness. Purity is to be maintained in all matters such as bathing, dress, food. There is a saying often quoted even by the unlettered: "Cleanliness makes you happy and it even appeases your hunger." To see a clean person is to feel ourselves clean.

In Manu's listing of dharmas that are applicable to all, ahiṁsā or non-violence comes first, followed by satya (truthfulness), asteya (non-covetousness; non-stealing is the direct meaning), śauca (cleanliness) and indriya-nigraha (subduing the senses or even obliterating them).

The fifth Ātmaguṇa is "anāyāsa". It is the opposite of "āyāsa" which denotes effort, exertion, etc. Anāyāsa means to have a feeling of lightness, to take things easy. One must not keep a long face, wear a scowl or keep lamenting one's hardships. If you lose your cool you will be a burden to yourself as well as to others. Anāyāsa is a great virtue. In many of our rituals there is much bodily exertion. When we perform a śraddha[S] we have to remain without food until 2 or 3 in the afternoon. There is no end to the physical effort we have to put in to conduct a sacrifice. Here anāyāsa means not to feel any mental strain. Obstacles, inevitable to any work or enterprise, must not cause you any mental strain. You must not feel any duty to be a burden and must develop the attitude that everything happens according to the will of the Lord. What do we mean when we remark that the musician we listened to yesterday touched the "tāra-sthāyī"[1] so effortlessly? Does it not mean that he performed a difficult musical exercise with ease? Similarly, we must learn to make light of all the hardships that we encounter in life.

What is "maṅgala", the sixth guṇa? Well, "maṅgala" is maṅgala[2]. There is maṅgala or an auspicious air about happiness that is characterised by dignity and purity. One must be cheerful all the time and not keep growling at people on the slightest pretext. This itself is extremely helpful, to radiate happiness wherever we go and exude auspiciousness. It is better than making lavish gifts and throwing money about.

To do a job with a feeling of lightness is anāyāsa. To be light ourselves, creating joy wherever we go, is maṅgala. We must be like a lamp spreading light and should never give cause for people to say, "Oh! he has come to find fault with everything." Wherever we go we must create a sense of happiness. We must live auspiciously and make sure that there is happiness brimming over everywhere.

"Akārpaṇya" is the next guṇa. Miserliness is the quality of a kṛpaṇa or miser. "Akārpaṇya" is the opposite of miserliness. We must give generously and whole-heartedly. At Kurukṣetra Arjuna felt dejected and refused to wage war with his own kin. In doing so, according to the Gītā, he was guilty of "kārpaṇya doṣa". It means, contextually, that he abased himself to a woeful state, he became "miserly" about himself. Akārpaṇya is the quality of a courageous and zestful person who can face problems determinedly.

"Aspṛha" is the last of the eight qualities. "Spṛha" means desire; a grasping nature. "Aspṛha" is the opposite, being without desire. Desire is at the root of all trouble, all evil and, all through the ages, it has been the cause of misfortunes. But to eradicate it from the mind of men seems an almost impossible task. By performing rites again and again and by constantly endeavouring to acquire the Ātmic qualities one will eventually become desireless. Says Vaḷḷuvar[3]:

Par̲r̲uga par̲r̲ar̲r̲ān par̲r̲iṇai appar̲r̲ai
par̲r̲uga par̲r̲u viḍarku

Tirumūlar goes a step further. "It is not enough," he says, "to be attached to Īśvara who is without attachment and be free from other attachments. You must be able to sever yourself from the attachment to Īśvara himself."

Āśai arumingal, āśai arumingal
Īśanodāyinum āśai arumingal

The Buddha calls desire thirst. Intense desire for an object is "tṛṣṇā". (The Buddha calls it "*tanha*" in Prākṛt.) His chief teaching is the conquest of desire.

Desirelessness is the last of the eight qualities. The first one, dayā, is the life-breath of Christianity. Each religion lays emphasis on a particular quality, though all qualities are included in the teachings of the Buddha, Jesus Christ, the Prophet Mohammed, Guru Nanak, Zoroaster, Confucius and the founders of all other religions. Even if these qualities may not have been pointedly mentioned in their teachings, it is certain that none of them would regard people lacking them with approval.

Notes

1 The upper octave or register.

2 This is similar to the statement: "A rose is a rose is a rose."

3 In order to abandon (earthly) desires, hold the feet of the Lord who is himself without any desire.

Chapter 6

Guṇas in Practical Life

All religions teach people to be loving, to be truthful and to be free from jealousy, desire and greed. But our religion goes further by imposing on us the performance of various saṁskāras to acquire these qualities in practical life. There is no use in merely preaching, in asking people to be like this or that. A man must be kept bound to a system consisting of such works as would help him in practice to acquire the noble qualities expected of them. Our religion alone does this.

Other religions, it is claimed, teach love and desirelessness. But Hinduism, it is alleged, does not give any importance to such qualities and is, besides, ritual-ridden. This view is totally erroneous. In fact, our religion does more than others: while laying emphasis on the eight qualities, it imparts lessons to take people beyond them, to a state that transcends these very qualities. It also believes that merely talking about the qualities will serve no purpose. After all, we know, don't we, that we have to be virtuous, truthful, loving and so on ? Still we find it difficult to live according to these ideals. What purpose is served if our canonical texts merely keep urging us again and again to acquire noble qualities? That is why, unlike other faiths which contain a great deal of ethical and moral instruction, our religion teaches ethics and morality only to the extent needed. But is that all? Without stopping with mere precept it tells us how we may — in actual practice — cultivate and acquire them. This it does first by telling us stories through the Purāṇas of virtuous people who obtained fame and of evil-doers who got ill fame. But it recognises that such examples are not enough to provide the necessary inspiration, so it lays down a number of saṁskāras for the purpose of obtaining inner purity. Ours is the only religion that gives practical training in making people virtuous and in acquiring moral excellence. Instead of being proud of this fact is it right to feel that there is something lacking in our religion?

The first of the eight qualities is love which is the chief teaching of Jesus and the last of them is desirelessness which is the cardinal teaching of the Buddha.

Is it enough to give oral instruction about the qualities? In other words, is it enough merely to preach them? It is man's nature to be engaged in some work or other. And, after all, if you want to accomplish something you will have to work for it. Gāndhījī taught truth and non-violence, spoke about them all his life. In his āśrama he was all the time not only doing some work or other himself, he was also urging others to do the same. His followers called him a hard taskmaster. He asked them to keep turning the *charkha* and expected them to clean their toilets themselves.

The dharmaśāstras have prescribed rites to make us inwardly pure and impart us the eight qualities. In this context the sūtras of Āpastamba and Gautama have a dominant place. Among the Smṛtis Manu's is the most important.

Āpastamba and Gautama deal with the dharmas common to all people. The former lays down the duties and saṁskāras separately for the different castes also. Gautama deals with the forty saṁskāras and the eight Ātmaguṇas. These forty-eight are the means to take a man to Brahmaloka on his death. He goes before the presence of Īśvara, which is like going to a great jñānin. He can remain quiescent in bliss. When Īśvara, who conducts the world himself becomes formless, he too [the man who attains Brahmaloka] will be dissolved in him. Until then he resides in the world of Īśvara (sāloka) and later attains sāyūjya, that is becomes one with him. "Yasyaite catvāriṁśat saṁskārāḥ aṣṭāvātmaguṇāḥ sa Brahmaṇaḥ sāyūjyam sālokatām jayati," so it is said.

The body is involved in various ways in performing the forty saṁskāras. When you work in an office you use your hands and feet and mouth, don't you? So is the case with the saṁskāras. He who performs them and cultivates the eight Ātmaguṇas goes directly to the Brahmaloka in which world there is neither sorrow nor happiness. When are you without sorrow and happiness? When you are with the One who creates them.

The Ātmic qualities are described as "Ātmaśakti"[1]. This term has recently come into use in newspaper language. In the old Sanskrit and Tamil texts we do not see the term "Ātmaśakti" used, only "Ātmaguṇas".

Note

[1] Gāndhījī often spoke about "soul force".

Chapter 7

Importance of Agni

The saṁskāras cover an individual's entire life-span — "Niṣekādi smaśānāntakam" — from the moment before he is conceived in his mother's womb to the time when his body is offered to Agni. "Niṣeka"[1] (impregnation) is a rite performed with the sacrificial fire as the witness; and the funeral rites which come last are performed in the fire.

Agni, the sacred fire, must be kept burning throughout a Brahmin's life. The brahmacārin or bachelor-student must perform the samidādhāna[S] every day. After he is married, with Agni as witness, he becomes a gṛhastha (householder). He must now perform the aupāsana in the fire. For the vānaprastha (forest recluse), there is a sacred fire called "kakṣāgni". The sannyāsin has no sacrament involving the sacred fire: he has the fire of knowledge (jñānāgni) in him. His body is not cremated — that is there is no Agni-saṁskāra for it — but interred as a matter of respect. Strictly speaking, it must be cut into four parts and consigned to the four quarters of a forest. There it will be food for the birds and beasts. In an inhabited place the severed parts of the body would cause inconvenience to people. That is why they were thrown into the forest. There it would be food for its denizens; if buried it would be manure for the plants. Now over the site of the interment of a sannyāsin's body a Bṛndāvana[S] is grown [or built]: this again is done out of respect. At such sites all that is to be done is to plant a bilva[S] or aśvattha[S] tree.

All castes have rites to be performed with the sacred fire. During marriage people belonging to all varṇas must do aupāsana and the fire in which the rite is performed must be preserved throughout. Today, only Pārsis[2] seem to keep up such a practice of preserving the fire. Their scripture is called the Zend-Avesta which name must have been derived from the Vedic "Chando-vasta". Their teacher was Zoroaster [Zarathuṣṭra]: this name must have been derived from "Saurāṣṭra". Their homeland is Iran (from "Ārya"). If the fire kept by them is extinguished at any time they spend a good deal of money in expiatory rites. With us rituals performed in the sacred fire have been on the decline from the turn of the century. The life style of our people has changed. If there is faith, this great treasure (rites performed in the fire) could be preserved. The most important reason for the loss of faith is the present system of education.

This body of ours has to be finally offered in the fire as an āhuti (oblation) to the deities. It is treated as a dravya (material for sacrifice) with ghee applied to it before it is offered in the fire. The ceremony is called "dahana-saṁskāra".

Notes

[1] The literal meaning of the word is "sprinkling".

[2] Zoroastrians.

Chapter 8

Names of Saṁskāras

The forty saṁskāras which are meant to purify the individual self are: garbhādhāna, puṁsavana, sīmanta, jātakarma, nāmakaraṇa, annaprāśana, cauḷa, upanayana, the four rites like prājāpatya (Vedavratas) performed during gurukulavāsa (the years the celibate student spends in the home of his guru), the ritual bath on completion of gurukulavāsa, marriage, the five mahāyajñas performed every day by the householder. We have listed nineteen so far. Then there are seven pākayajñas, seven haviryajñas and seven somayajñas to be conducted by the householder. Thus 19+21 = 40[1].

The seven pākayajñas are: aṣṭaka (anvaṣṭaka), sthālīpāka, pārvaṇa, śrāvaṇī, āgrahāyanī, caitrī, āśvayujī. The seven haviryajñas: agniyādhāna, agnihotra, darśa-pūrṇamāsa, āgrayaṇa, cāturmāsya, nirūḍhapaśubandha, sautrāmaṇī. The seven somayajñas: agniṣṭoma, atyagniṣṭoma, uktya, ṣoḍaśī, vājapeya, atirātra, aptoryāma.

Out of the forty saṁskāras some are to be performed every day, some at certain times and some at least once in a lifetime. In the first category are the five mahāyajnas (pañca-mahāyajñas).

Rites done to the chanting of mantras are more beneficial than those done without it — a sacrament involving mantras is a saṁskāra. The social service that a householder does is included among his daily pañca-mahāyajñas. The pañca-mahāyajñas are: brahmayajña, devayajña, pitṛyajña, manuṣyayajña and bhūtayajña. The chanting of the Vedas constitutes brahmayajña. Sacrifices and pūjā are devayajña. Tarpaṇa is pitṛyajña. Feeding guests is manuṣyayajña. And offering bali to various creatures is bhūtayajña.

Aupāsana and agnihotra are part of the daily religious routine. Though a pākayajña, aupāsana is not included in the group of seven pākayajñas mentioned above, while agnihotra is one of the seven haviryajñas. Darśa-pūrṇamāsa is a haviryajña to be performed once in fifteen days. The other five haviryajñas and the seven somayajñas are to be performed once a year or, at least, once in a lifetime. As if out of consideration for us, the Smṛtis have granted us this concession: that the difficult somayajñas need be undertaken only once in a lifetime.

But for the pārvaṇī-śrāddha which is to be performed once a month and the sthālīpāka every Prathamā[2], the other five pākayajñas are to be performed once a year.

To put it differently: the five mahāyajñas (brahmayajña, devayajña, pitṛyajña, manuṣyayajña and bhūtayajña) together with agnihotra and aupāsana are to be performed every day; darśa-pūrṇamāsa and sthālipāka once a fortnight; pārvāṇi śrāddha once a month. The other yajñas are to be conducted once a year or at least once in a lifetime.

On a plot of land growing one crop, harvesting is done once a year, while on another plot growing three crops the same is done once every four months. Some crops have to be watered every day, some on alternate days. Such jobs are saṁskāras. But there are differences in the saṁskāras for different crops. The same is the case with the saṁskāras meant for human beings.

Note & Reference

1 All these are explained in detail in subsequent chapters.

2 The first day of the lunar fortnight.

Chapter 9

Saṁskāras Performed by Parents

The saṁskāras begin with garbhādhāna, that is from the moment of conception [or, more correctly, impregnation]. The "śarīra-piṇḍa"[1] must be formed to the chanting of mantras. People mistakenly think that rites like puṁsavana[2] and sīmanta[3] are meant for the mother. Actually, they are for the life taking shape in her womb, the foetus, and are meant to purify it. The elders have a responsibility in this matter. One may not do the rites meant for oneself, but it is sinful to be negligent about those meant for another life. Nowadays people omit to perform garbhādhāna, sīmanta, etc, since they think that such rites are not fashionable.

Where there should be some delicacy in man-woman relationship people act without any sense of shame after the fashion in the West. But, when it comes to performing Vedic rites in which the well-being of the new life created is involved, they feel a sense of awkwardness. Such an attitude is not right.

Garbhādhāna, puṁsavana and sīmanta are performed before the child is born. The sexual union of man and wife must be sanctified by mantras. Instead of being an act of animal passion, it is raised to the level of a saṁskāra with the chanting of mantras: the purpose is the well-being of the life to be formed. It is madness to give up such rituals without realising the high principles inspiring them and, instead, thinking them to be "uncivilized". If there is any feeling of delicacy on your part about the garbhādhāna (ṛtuśānti) ceremony, you do not have to invite a crowd. But the rite itself must be gone through within the four walls of the home. It is no longer the custom to have a four-day wedding with the couple doing daily aupāsana. Nor is the rite of śeṣahoma[S] conducted following the day of the wedding. The couple have sexual intercourse on the same day as the marriage without any ceremony and the chanting of mantras. This is an evil practice and sinful. Since the intercourse takes place in an animal manner, the children born too will be likewise. Puṁsavana must be performed in the third month of pregnancy and sīmanta in the sixth or eighth. Nowadays both rites are gone through together anyhow.

On the birth of a child, its jātakarma must be performed. Gifts must be given away. Nāmakaraṇa is on the eleventh day. Even this, the naming ceremony, has a purificatory purpose according to the śāstras. There are rules regarding the name to be chosen for the child in accordance with the nakṣatra or asterism under which it is born. It must be one from the many names of the Lord and to call the child by such a name is itself a saṁskāra since it has a cleansing effect. We do not have the custom of "christening" our children as "Longfellow" or "Stone". But nowadays even in this land similar names are given to children. Also when the child's name is that of the Lord it is corrupted or twisted clumsily. The name given to a child during a Vedic ritual must be treated with some respect.

When the child is six months old it is time for its annaprāśana. The saṁskāras from garbhādhāna to nāmakaraṇa are performed by the parents on behalf of the child. In annaprāśana, even though the father chants the mantras, it is [obviously] the child that takes the anna or food.

If the mother takes medicine, the baby is nourished, is it not? In the same way the inner thoughts and feelings of the parents will affect the foetus and its character will be shaped accordingly. There is a difference between what you write when your mind is calm and what you write when you are in an angry mood: the first will be good to read while the second will not be so pleasant. The body too is subject to good and bad influences. The sexual union must take place when the couple are imbued with good thoughts: it will then lead to the creation of a blob of life (piṇḍa) that will have the potential to develop into a noble character. This is the reason why the marriage is consummated with the intonation of mantras.

There are people who have not altogether ceased to observe such rites, but sometimes they go through two or three rites together. There is a right time for every saṁskāra and there are mantras as well as dravyas (materials) appropriate to them.

Cauḷa comes after annaprāśana. It is meant for the "śikhā"[S] which is essential to the conduct of all good rites. The sannyāsin has no śikhā and is shaven-headed; in fact, the śikhā has to be removed with the recitation of mantras at the time one receives initiation into sannyāsa. It is worn in the cauḷa ceremony with the chanting of mantras and with a vow made to Parameśvara (as part of the saṁkalpa[S]). So it is wrong to remove it as we like in violation of this vow. Is it proper to remove this lock of hair as if it were just a handful of leafy vegetables? People install the Śivaliṅga or the sālagrāma[5] for worship. Would it be right on their part to discard them as they like. It would be a different matter if they were stolen or lost accidentally. Similarly, to wear a śikhā ceremonially and then remove it, as and when we like, and wear a crop is not proper.

The chanting of the Vedas, the performance of Vedic rituals and the dharma practised by the householder with his wife strengthen both body and mind (the latter through the vibrations in the nāḍis[S] produced by the mantras). The śikhā on the Brahmarandhra[6] is a protection and a means of obtaining such strength. It is like the tiles on the roof of a house. Only when you cease to perform Vedic rites is it not needed, that is when you are no longer a householder and become an ascetic. Today even as student-bachelors or as householders we have ceased to chant the Vedas and practise Vedic rites. So, naturally, we do not wear the śikhā also.

Upanayana[S] comes after cauḷa. It is the first saṁskāra that a boy performs, chanting the mantras himself. Those conduced until this ceremony are meant to protect the child from the evil influences arising from the sins committed by its parents. These are either "gārbhika" or "baijika" (belonging to the womb or to the seed or sperm). The saṁskāras performed by the parents are to remove the ills caused to the child by these harmful influences.

Any saṁskāra must be performed at the right time and by doing so we are absolved of our sins. To wash away the pāpa earned by us in the past we have to go through saṁskāras in which our body, mind and speech are applied.

We think evil with our mind, tell lies with our mouth, and sin with our body also. Indeed we practise all kinds of deception. The wrongs committed by mind, speech and body must be wiped away by applying mind, speech and body to virtuous purposes. With the mind, Parameśvara must be meditated upon; with the faculty of speech, mantras must be chanted; and with the body, noble deeds must be performed. It is from the time of the upanayana that one becomes mature enough to perform saṁskāras that bring together mind, speech and body.

I must speak about another matter. Apart from the saṁskāras that a father performs specifically for the sake of his child (from garbhādhāna to cauḷa), those (including other types of rites) he conducts otherwise also benefit the children. This is according to the saying, "The good done by mother and father goes to protect their children." Until recently the children of Vaidika Brahmins[7] were particularly bright, the reason being the impetus they received from the saṁskāras performed by their forefathers. What our ancestors did by way of good works served as the foundation of our moral and intellectual uplift for two or three generations. Children born afterwards have been so much embroiled in worldly affairs as to have become degraded.

Our fathers did not perform any saṁskāras. So we may feel sorry that we have been deprived of the benefits that would otherwise have come to us. Let us not give room for our children to make the same complaint about us. Let us perform saṁskāras for our sake and theirs.

Notes & References

[1] This term may be taken to mean the embryo, a blob of life; it also means a lump, a ball of rice, etc.

[2] This is a ceremony performed for the birth of a male child.

[3] Sīmanta or sīmantonnayana literally means "parting of the hair" (that is of the expectant mother).

[4] Also known as "cūḍā-karma", the first cutting of the hair on the child's head. "Cūḍa" means the "lock or tuft of hair" kept after the remaining part is shaved off.

[5] Stone found in the Gaṇḍakī river and worshipped as a symbol of Viṣṇu.

[6] Aperture in the crown of the head where the suṣumna-nāḍi terminates. This nāḍi is situated between the "iḍa" and the "piṅgala" of the spinal column.

[7] Brahmins who adhere to the Vedic dharma. In theory all Brahmins are expected to follow this dharma.

Chapter 10

Why not All Saṁskaras for All?

Jātakarma, nāmakaraṇa, annaprāśana and cauḷa are common to all jātis. Only Brahmins, Kṣatriyas and Vaiśyas have the upanayana ceremony. There is nothing discriminatory about this nor need there be any quarrel over the same. People belonging to the fourth varṇa do physical work to serve the world and in the process acquire inner purity. They will gain proficiency in their hereditary vocations only by learning them from their parents or grandparents. They do not require gurukulavāsa[S] over some twelve years [as is the case with Brahmins] nor do they have to learn the Vedas. If so their work will suffer.

Upanayana[S] is the first step taken towards gurukulavāsa. When a boy learns the Vedas he must have no ego-feeling. At home he has a lot of freedom. His father will not be able to discipline him because his affection will come in the way. That is why the child is to be brought under the care of a guru. Vocations that require physical effort are different from the pursuit of the Vedas. There is no room for intellectual arrogance in them or for the nursing of the ego. So such work may be taught at home by the father or some other elder in the family.

Those who serve by doing manual work do not require to go through upanayana or gurukulavāsa. Certain special skills or the finer aspects of an art or craft that cannot be taught at home may be learned from a Brahmin teacher. The Brahmin is expected to be proficient in all arts, all subjects, but none of these is meant to be a source of his livelihood. His vocation is teaching and the chanting of the Vedas and the performance of Vedic rites.

There is a relationship between the saṁskāras prescribed for a man and his vocation and mental outlook. So it would be wrong to think poorly of certain jātis who do not have to perform certain saṁskāras. You may think it strange, but it is my view that it is those who have to undergo more saṁskāras than others that must have been thought of poorly. The idea is that these people need more rites to be rendered pure. Others are not in need of so many to be cleansed within. The larger the dose of medicine taken by a patient the greater must be his affliction.

None excels the sages in impartiality. They do not talk glibly like us of equality but they are truly egalitarian in outlook since they look upon all as one with Īśvara. The conduct of the world's affairs is such that it requires people following different vocations, doing different jobs and with different mental qualities in keeping with them. It is in conformity with these differences and dissimilarities that the sages assigned the saṁskāras also differently to different people. There is no question of high or low among them.

It is in observance of the same principle that the śāstras lay down upanayana for the first three varṇas (Brahmins, Kṣatriyas and Vaiśyas) and also certain saṁskāras connected with it.

Part Seventeen

BRAHMACARYĀŚRAMA

Chapter 1

Upanayana

The upanayana of a boy is performed when he is old enough to understand things and to chant the mantras. During this ceremony he is asked to go begging for alms. "Bhikṣacaryam cara," he is told. "Bāḍham," he replies ("I will do so"). So, before his upanayana, the child must know enough Sanskrit to understand what is meant by "Bhikṣācaryam cara". When he starts learning at the age of five he will have a basic knowledge of Sanskrit by the time he is eight years old, the age fixed for the upanayana saṁskāra.

The world will stand to gain if eight-year-old children wear the sacred thread, have sufficient knowledge of Sanskrit and chant the Gāyatrī mantra. Today things have so changed that Godlessness is thrust into tender minds.

Upa = near; nayana = to take or lead (a child). Near whom or what is (the child) taken? Near the guru. That is what upanayana means. Who is a guru? One who has mastered the Vedas. There is one guru during the brahmacaryāśrama (student-bachelorhood) and another during the last āśrama of sannyāsa. The first guru is learned in the Vedas, Vedāngas and so on while the second is one who has forsaken all including the Vedas. In the first āśrama you acquire vidyā; in the last asrama you realise jñāna[1].

Upanayana is initiation into the brahmacaryāśrama while "samāvartana" is the completion of this stage of life. "Samāvartana" means "return". To repeat, from the upanayana to the samāvartana is student-bachelorhood or brahmacaryāśrama. Samāvartana thus denotes returning home on completing one's study of the Vedic discipline in the gurukula.

Upanayana is the "pūrvānga" of student-bachelorhood. Any "anga" must have something that gives it its distinctive character. This is called "angī". Thus for the anga called upanayana the angī is brahmacarya. The word "Brahma" has six different meanings. In the term "brahmacarya" it means the Vedas. An entire āśrama or stage in life is set apart for the study of the Vedas: this is brahmacarya. The minimum period for student-bachelorhood is twelve years which is the time taken to master the Vedas.

"Brahma" also means Viṣṇu as well as Śiva. The word, in addition, is also used to denote a Brahmin, tapas or austerities and the Paramātman. When you say Brahma with a long "a" at the end (Brahmā) it means the Creator.

At mealtime we do "pariṣecana"[S], that is we sprinkle water over our food, say, rice. It is the anga for the meal. The rice must be eaten only after it has ceremonially been made a prasāda[S] of Īśvara. This is the purpose of the pariṣecana. Is it not foolish to refuse the food after it has been made a prasāda of Īśvara. Not to learn the Vedas after one has had the upanayana is akin to refusing to eat the food placed before one after one has done the pariṣecana. In this sense the majority of people who have had their upanayana must be called foolish.

There are four "vratas"[S] between the pūrvānga called upanayana and the uttarānga called samāvartana. These are prājāpatya, saumya, āgneya and vaiśvadeva [see following para].

There are certain rules to be followed to master a mantra. The Vedas are replete with mantras that help you to go forward spiritually and find release from worldly existence. "Brahmacarya" may be described as the total discipline required to master the Vedas. There are also rules meant for the study of each part of these scriptures. Each Veda has four "kāṇḍas", each associated with a great sage. Brahmayajña is performed in honour of them. For each kāṇḍa there is also a separate vrata. During student-bachelorhood when a kāṇḍa is studied its vrata must also be observed. The kāṇḍas are prājāpatya, saumya, āgneya and vaiśvadeva. After completing the four kāṇḍas the pupil will have his samāvartana with the permission of his guru.

The four vratas mentioned above are for students of the Kṛṣṇa-Yajurveda. For students of the Ṛgveda there are the Mahānāmnī, Mahā, Upaniṣad and Godāna vratas. Thus each Veda has its own vratas. I mentioned those for the Kṛṣṇa-Yajurveda first since it is widely followed [in the South].

Samāvartana is also called "snāna" and one who has gone through it is a "snātaka". Everybody must learn his own Veda [the Veda that is his by birth] and other subjects in addition. When we perform upākarma[S] we must start learning a new part of the Vedas. Later, at the time of the utsarjanā[S], it must be discontinued and the study of the Vedāngas taken up. The Vedas, to repeat, must be studied during the six months roughly of Dakṣiṇāyana[2], from the month of Śrāvaṇa to Taiṣya[3]. The next six months must be devoted to the Vedāngas.

To master the mantras the student must strictly observe the rules pertaining to brahmacarya and to the particular part of the Veda that is being studied. Nowadays we do not observe anything, we do not even learn the Vedas or a part thereof. Before the wedding ceremony, we perform a rite called "vrata": in one hour we go through a number of saṁskāras without understanding what we are doing and why we are doing them. Perhaps, I find myself giving this discourse because so much at least survives of the Vedic tradition.

The importance of the upanayana ceremony lies in this: it makes a person fit to receive instruction in the Vedas and spread their divine power throughout the world. Parents must realise this fact and perform their sons' upanayana at the right time.

"Dvi-ja" (*"irupirappāḷan"* in Tamiḻ) is the name given to a Brahmin, Kṣatriya or Vaiśya. They merit the second birth only when they become qualified to learn the Vedas. Such a birth is meant, as mentioned earlier, to spread the divine power all over the world, and it is through the upanayana ceremony that they become qualified for it. Performing this ceremony at the right time is the responsibility of the parents. At present, in matters like this, no regard is paid to the canons. In contrast, in the old days, people had faith in the scriptures and acted according to their dictates.

Note & Reference

[1] All this is discussed in detail in *The Guru Tradition*.

[2] & [3] The six months from the day the sun turns from the tropic of Cancer. For Srāvaṇa and Taiṣya see Chapter 13, Part Six.

Chapter 2

The Śāstras and Popular Custom

It is to be regretted that, while the rules and injunctions of the dharmaśāstras are conveniently disregarded, certain popular customs prevalent in this or that part of the country are being followed as if they had śāstric validity. For instance, the belief has gained ground that the upanayana of a son must not be performed if he has an elder sister yet to be married. Another belief is that three brahmacārins must not stay together in a family at the same time. The upanayana of boys is delayed on this pretext. It is not right to go against the dharmaśāstras in preference to such popular customs and disregard the upper age limit fixed by them for the upanayana saṁskāra. The customs mentioned above must have originated as a matter of convenience or for some sentimental reason. Popular practices may be followed so long as they are not contrary to the dictates of the dharmaśāstras.

Let us quote here again what Āpastamba says concluding his dharmaśāstra: "What I have dealt with so far does not exhaust all the rules. There are still many more. These must have evolved according to the custom of the family or the region concerned and may be known from women and members of the fourth varṇa...." We must, however, remember that Āpastamba does not want us to go against the dharmaśāstras.

The upanayana saṁskāra must not be postponed on any pretext whatsoever. Sometimes the marriage of a girl is delayed because the parents do not have enough money to meet all the wedding expenses. This is also not justified and is against the śāstras. I will speak about it later when I deal with the vivāha (marriage) saṁskāra. There is a lot of "show" in our weddings and this has come to be accepted as inevitable. Even if we, for our part, do not like any lavish display at weddings we yield to the wishes of the groom's people. The marriage of a girl is delayed until her parents manage to raise the money needed to celebrate it in a big way. It is also held up because a suitable groom does not turn up. Then there is the problem of the groom's people giving approval to the alliance.

There are no such reasons for the "thread ceremony" to be delayed nor is there any compulsion to make it expensive. It is not like a marriage in which we have to take into consideration the views and wishes of the groom's people. So there can be no valid excuse for failure to perform the upanayana of a son at the right time. The delay is unforgivable on any count.

Chapter 3

Basic to the Vedic Tradition

When a child falls ill the parents take special care of it. How wrong would it be to neglect a sick child? If there is anything worse it is not to perform the upanayana of one's son at the proper age and fail to impart him the Gāyatrī mantra. This rite is for his Ātmic uplift as well as for the good of the world. It is sheer vanity that the "thread ceremony" is nowadays performed like a mini-wedding. This is one reason why it gets postponed since the parents have to find enough money to "celebrate" it on a lavish scale. Delaying this saṁskāra for such reasons must be condemned in the severest terms possible.

We in the Maṭha are ready to do anything [to help parents to perform the upanayana of their children at the proper age]. We arrange "mass upanayana" ceremonies. A number of other religious organisations also have similar arrangements. The Gāyatrī is common to all. Mass upanyana is conducted for boys belonging to different denominations, Smārta, Vaiṣṇava, Mādhva, etc, and is being done fairly satisfactorily. This practice must grow with more and more participants.

Well-to-do parents think that such mass ceremonies are meant for people without means. But, at the same time, they do not perform the upanayana of their children on their own at the right time. In this saṁskāra the importance of which is hard to exaggerate, there is no question of some being able to spend more on it than some others or some being able to afford the expense more than others. Money or property has nothing to do with it. It is sad that in the upanayana rite considerations that are not relevant to it are brought in with the result that the saṁskāra that is at the heart of the Vedic tradition is emptied of all its meaning.

It is the duty of parents to make sure that, after they are invested with the sacred thread, their sons chant the Gāyatrī every day without fail. Some boys discontinue chanting this mantra from the very first day after the upanayana ceremony. Parents must see to it that they don't. They must also make sure that the children perform the sandhyāvandana[S] without being distracted by cricket matches, cinema, party meetings, etc. I am not sure how far my urging is going to help, considering that parents nowadays are themselves more interested in clubs, films, meetings and the races than in matters concerning the Self. If there is any realisation on their part that their own lives have been lived in vain, they may perhaps want their children to do better. But will the boys listen to them? In all likelihood they will turn back to tell their parents: "Why do you ask us to perform sandhyāvandana and recite the Gāyatrī? What about you?"

In this unfortunate situation, if I am wasting your time by speaking about such matters, it is because I have a duty to remind you of your responsibility with regard to your children's Ātmic advancement.

I do not know whether you will do what I ask you to do, nor do I know how you will do it. I have to carry out the duty imposed on me by the Maṭha. The Maṭha bids me to see to it that the upanayana of children is performed when they are of the right age, all those children who are entitled to learn the Vedas. Further, the Maṭha also bids me to see to it that, once the boys are invested with the sacred thread, they perform the sandhyāvandana without fail every day and that they learn to chant the Vedas at least one hour a day.

Chapter 4

Qualities of a Brahmacārin

The celibate-student must perform samidādhana[S] every day, beg for his food and take no salt. If he is a Brahmin he must keep a staff (daṇḍa) of palāśa[S], if he is a Kṣatriya a staff of aśvattha[S]. The Vaiśya brahmacārin has a staff of uḍumbara[S]. The staff helps the pupil to retain his learning. It is similar to the lightning conductor or the aerial and is as scientifically valid as they are. It is needed to retain all the Vedic mantras in the student's memory. The daṇḍa has the capacity to "fix" these hymns. That is why it should be kept — to safeguard the treasure called the Vedas that the student has acquired. The brahmacārin must wear the skin of the black antelope (kṛṣṇājina) and must not wear any upper cloth. There are rules the electrician has to observe for his safety: he must stand on a wooden plank or wear rubber gloves during work. Similarly, there are rules prescribed by our great men of the past to protect the Ātmic electricity, the Ātmic energy.

Today we perform upākarma[S] as a one-day ceremony without keeping up the study of the Vedas. We do not go through the utsarjana[S] at all. For our failure to do it we mutter a mantra in expiation, the mantra called "Kamokārṣīt" which says, "I did not sin. Kāma (desire) did it. Anger did it..." There is no need to repeat this mantra if we perform the utsarjana.

Brahmacarya implies adherence to a number of rules with regard to food, the performance of rites and the observance of vratas[S]. If a brahmacārin makes any mistake in chanting the Vedas, in the matter of tone or enunciation, he must do penance for the same on upākarma day. On this occasion he eats no more than a few sesame seeds; otherwise he fasts the whole day; and on the following day he offers 1,008 sticks of the palāśa in the sacred fire chanting the Gāyatrī. He should do this every year. Nowadays brahmacārins perform this rite only on the day following the first upākarma after the upanayana. Actually, this is a rite all Brahmins are expected to perform, though we find today householders doing only Gāyatrī-japa[S]. When you merely mutter the mantra you feel sleepy and you may go wrong in the japa. But such will not be the case if you also perform a homa[S] as you chant the Gāyatrī. Sticks offered in the fire must be those of the palāśa, if not of the asvattha; darbha[S] grass may be used if the other two are not available.

At mealtime the student can have his fill. The only restriction is that he must not give free rein to his appetite. He must beg for his food for such a practice makes him humble. The śāstras do not require him to fast. The student must be nourished properly during his growing years. But he must, at the same time, learn to develop sāttvic[S] qualities and there must be nothing rude or rough about him. It is by serving his guru that these qualities are inculcated in him.

During the twelve years in the gurukula[S] the student must learn his recension of the Vedas and also the caturdaśa-vidyā. On completion of his stay in the gurukula he performs the samāvartana[S], returns home and marries.

Chapter 5

Naiṣṭhika Brahmacarya and Family Life

In the past, some students continued to reside with their guru without performing the samāvartana. Even after his passing, they remained brahmacārins and did so indeed all their life.

Our dharma takes into account the natural urges of man. The general rule is that, on his return home from the gurukula, the student must marry and settle down. It is difficult to go against the natural urges. But going along with nature does not mean being swept away in the flow of urges. After all, the goal of all our efforts is reaching the other shore — that is release from worldly existence. The householder must lead a life of dharma with his wife. But later he must become a forest recluse first and then, renouncing everything, a sannyāsin. This path to asceticism through stages is based on the fact that curbing the natural instincts forcibly is likely to be harmful. A person who decides in his youth to become a naiṣṭhika brahmacārin (lifelong student-bachelor) may later succumb to his natural passions. This would be an offence against the āśrama code of conduct and therefore sinful. As a householder he is not guilty of any offence if he goes by his natural urges within the constraints of dharma.

There are exceptions to any rule. Those who have firmness and maturity of mind and strength of character obtained from the saṁskāras performed in an earlier birth may become lifelong brahmacārins. We have the example of Samartha Rāmadāsa who lived more than 300 years ago. It was he who inspired Śivājī to uphold our dharma against the onslaught of Islam. Rāmadāsa, the naiṣṭhika brahmacārin, personified one aspect of Hanumān.

Śrī Śankara Bhagavatpāda was an incarnation of Parameśvara and his mission was re-establishment of the Vedic dharma. He went directly from brahmacarya to the ascetic's stage of life. His disciples too, with the exception of Sureśvarācārya, did the same. Śankara gave initiation into sannyāsa to Padmapāda, Hastāmalaka and Toṭaka. In the Śankara Maṭha also brahmacārins are initiated into sannyāsa because, according to the rule, only such sannyāsins can occupy the Pīṭha. All this points to the fact that everybody need not become a householder before donning the ascetic's garb. But it must be conceded that only a few will have the wisdom and mellowness necessary to skip two āśramas (that of the householder and of the forest recluse) to take to sannyāsa. Naiṣṭhika brahmacārins do not have to perform the following saṁskāras: marriage, the five mahāyajñas, the seven pākayajñas, the seven haviryajñas and the seven somayajñas. Their antaḥ-karana[S] must be sufficiently pure even without going through these rituals. So they are exceptional cases.

Dahana-kriyā (cremation) is the last saṁskāra according to the śāstras. It is argued, on the basis of this, that they (the śāstras) do not enjoin all, even the aged, to take to sannyāsa. If everybody were to live through all the four āśramas (that of bachelor-student, householder, forest recluse and ascetic) there would truly be no question of the cremation rite for anybody. Are not sannyāsins interred on their attaining siddhi[S], instead of being consigned to the flames? If we believe that asceticism is only for the mature, and not even for the aged among the rest, the above argument cannot be said to be wrong.

The view that the cremation rite applies only to those who die too young to become sannyāsins is unfounded. Indeed not only those who die prematurely but also the old are to be cremated [if they do not become sannyāsins]. So the inference is that the śāstras do accept aged people also not taking to sannyāsa.

A person who has the light of knowledge in him and is free from passion must live in the forest giving up family responsibilities and performing only Vedic rites. He must leave his children and property behind and take only his wife with him to the forest. The wife, however, is not meant for carnal pleasure but is a partner in the conduct of rites involving the sacred fire — sacrifices, aupāsana, etc. This is the meaning of vānaprastha. A person qualifies for this stage of life when he is mature enough to leave home and hearth, children and relatives. Later he gives up the Vedic karma itself and turns his mind exclusively to the quest of the Self. This is the time when he enters the sannyāsāśrama[S].

The man who has thus separated himself from his wife and given up Vedic works is initiated into sannyāsa by his guru. He must constantly meditate on the Paramātman and experience the Truth as an inward reality. Also, he must have the realisation that, "That Truth am I, all else is false play." Then he is by himself, beyond his body and mind, as the Ultimate Truth. This is mokṣa, liberation. Such a man will continue to dwell in his body until the fruits of his past karma are exhausted. But he will not be affected by such karma as a sannyāsin who has inward realisation. From the point of view of the outside world he may still dwell in his body; but even in this state he is liberated. He is now a "jīvanmukta". When the body perishes he becomes a "videhamukta" (liberated without the body). And he himself is now the unconditioned Ultimate Truth.

He who becomes a sannyāsin without having lived as a householder and he who becomes a sannyāsin after doing so, performing all the forty saṁskāras and acquiring all the eight Ātmic qualities, become alike the Ultimate Truth.

What is the fate of the man who does not become an ascetic but who keeps performing, until his death, all the saṁskāras and cultivates the eight Ātmic qualities? He is cremated on his death, is he not? After all, the majority of people belong to his category. What happens to such people after their death?

Śankara does not state that they will dissolve in the Ultimate Reality. They do not have the intense urge, the burning desire, to grasp the Brahman, abandoning everything. If they have the all-consuming desire for the Truth, no force can hold them back from their quest. It is because they do not possess such a desire that they do not obtain non-dualistic release. However, they have faith in the śāstras and perform works according to them and contribute to the well-being of mankind and they are also thereby rendered pure inwardly. So, though they are not united with the Paramātman, they go to the presence of Īśvara, Īśvara who is the Paramātman with attributes (Saguṇa Brahman) and is behind the affairs of the world.

This is called "Hiraṇyagarbha-sthāna" and it is the same as the Brahmaloka. In this there is no inseparable dissolution in the Paramātman, but the man who attains it remains in bliss "experiencing" Īśvara. Such a state is also to be described as mokṣa. There is nothing wanting, there is no sorrow, and there is the presence of the Lord. What more is wanted? This state is reached by those who perform all the saṁskāras even though they do not become ascetics.

But one day Īśvara (the Saguṇa Brahman) will put a stop to the activities of all worlds and dissolve them in the great deluge (mahā-pralaya). He will now become the Nirguṇa Brahman, the Paramātman without any attributes. At this time all those who reside by his side will unite with the Paramātman as the Paramātman, that is attain non-dualistic liberation.

In the great deluge all creatures — even those who have not performed any of the prescribed rituals, creatures like worms, reptiles and so on also — will merge in the Paramātman. Then what is special about the one who unites with the Supreme Being after having performed all the saṁskāras? When the Paramātman, as the Īśvara with attributes, creates the worlds again those who do not perform the saṁskāras will be born again according to the karma of their past lives. Only those who have properly gone through the saṁskāras and been rendered pure will be inseparably united with the Brahman.

I have come far from the subject of upanayana. I had sought an answer to the following questions: "Can a person remain a brahmacārin all his life? Can a brahmacārin become a sannyāsin without going through the stage of the householder?"

Chapter 6

Upanayana: When to Perform It?

A Brahmin child's upanayana must be performed when he is eight years old from conception, that is when he is seven years and two months old from birth. A Kṣatriya's is to be performed at the age of twelve. Kṛṣṇa Paramātman who belonged to the clan of Yadus (Yādavas) was invested with the sacred thread at that age. The corresponding age for a Vaiśya is sixteen.

According to the śāstras, the lower limit for Brahmin youngsters is eight years and the upper limit sixteen which means a grace of eight years. It is sinful in the extreme not to have performed the upanayana of a Brahmin boy before his passing the upper age limit.

Uttarāyaṇa is the right period to perform upanayana — from the Tamiḷ month *Tai* to *Āni*[1] when the sun journeys northwards. While this is the right time for marriages also, the season of spring (*Cittirai* and *Vaikāśi*)[2] is considered particularly auspicious. For upanayana the month specially favoured is *Māśi*[3]. Upanayana and marriage are not permitted during Dakṣiṇāyana (from the Tamiḷ month *Āḍi* to the end of *Mārgazhi*)[4].

Nowadays, for various reasons, the upanayana and marriage ceremonies are delayed for as long as possible and celebrated in any month other than *Mārgazhi*[5]. The results are there for you to see. But one must be happy perhaps that a function called marriage is still performed somehow. So long as people perform it, let them perform it at any time. If we take this attitude, marriages may be permitted in any season as a desperate step. But upanayana is a different matter. It should never be permitted in Dakṣiṇāyana. If it is for some reason celebrated during this period, I would ask for its performance again in Uttarāyaṇa. Money is the main problem in conducting an upanayana or a marriage. Parents postpone the upanayana because they want to perform it at the same time as the marriage of their daughter so as to minimise the expenses.

The upanayana is sometimes performed when the boy is only five years old. This is called "kāmyopanayana", "kāmya" meaning in pursuance of a desire. Such early upanayana is all right if you want the child to develop inwardly at an early age. But seven years is the proper age for a child to be invested with the sacred thread because by now he will have learned enough Sanskrit to chant the mantras clearly. Nowadays, the "thread ceremony" is conducted together with the marriage, that is when the "boy" is 30 or 35 years old. So to suggest that the upanayana needs to be performed only when the child is seven years old — and not at five — would be taken as a joke. Joke or no joke, it [the delay in performing the upanayana] should make you uneasy deep within if you have some concern for the Vedic dharma.

Ādi Śankara's upanayana, it is believed, was performed when he was five years old. If the child is extraordinarily intelligent and can articulate words properly, his upanayana may be performed at five years.

Notes

1 Mid-January to mid-July

2 Mid-April to mid-June

3 Mid-February to mid-March

4 Mid-July to mid-January

5 Mid-December to mid-January. The Paramaguru is speaking of the custom now obtaining in the South, particularly Tamiḷ Nāḍu.

Chapter 7
Models to Follow

It often occurs to me that two divine children demonstrate the purpose of their descent to earth through their very upanayana saṁskāra. One of the two is Śankara who gave new life to the Vedic religion and the other is Jñānasaṁbandhar[T]. The Tamiḷ *Periyapurāṇam*[T] mentions that Jñānasaṁbhandhar's upanayana was performed when he was a small child. From the fact that he calls himself "*Nānmarai*[1] *Jñānasaṁbandhan*" we know that he was conversant with all the four Vedas. Both the Ācārya and Jñānasaṁbandhar had to listen only once to grasp their lessons: that is why they were called "eka-santagrāhins". So they could learn the Vedas in one or two years. Indeed, there was no need to teach them, for they were capable of learning everything on their own. The one (Śankara) was an incarnation of Śiva and the other of Subrahmanya. If they had accomplished their respective missions only after their upanayana had been performed and after they had received instruction in Gāyatrī, it was only to show ordinary people like us the importance of that saṁskāra.

There was a poet called Rāmabhadra Dīkṣita who spoke about himself thus: "Before Gāyatrī came to me, Sarasvatī was already with me." Before he was eight years old, the usual age for imparting the Gāyatrī mantra, he had begun to compose poems. Jñānasaṁbandhar too sang his composition, *"Toḍuḍaya ceviyan"*[2], when he was only three years old. He had already been performing miracles. But even so he had his upanayana ceremony performed and was taught the Gāyatrī mantra. If he did so it was to show the world that he was able to accomplish his great mission in life only by upholding the Vedic dharma. He has opened our eyes to the significance of the upanayana saṁskāra and the Gāyatrī mantra.

Notes

[1] "*Nānmarai*" means the four Vedas.

[2] "One wearing ear-studs" (Śiva).

Chapter 8

Why Early Upanayana

Let us leave aside the question of a child being inspired by Sarasvatī before he is imbued with Gāyatrī. The more important thing is that before Kāma[S] takes hold of a boy he must be inspired by Gāyatrī. That is why the age of upanayana is fixed at eight. When one is possessed by Kāma one would be dragged away from one's ideal, that of acquiring the power of mantras. Even the power already acquired would be destroyed. That is why the upanayana ceremony is performed early so that the boy is helped to become perfect by constant repetition of the Gāyatrī mantra. After 16, he will not be able to do the same. If he somehow ascends one span spiritually, he will the next moment descend by one cubit. That is the reason why the upanayana saṁskāra must be performed early.

We do not take such saṁskāras seriously nowadays. We do things to no purpose, and at the same time we do not have the courage to give up such rites altogether. So we go through them "somehow" for a false sense of satisfaction. Far better it would be, instead, to have the courage to be an atheist. The atheist at least has some convictions, so it seems to me.

If the Gāyatrī mantra is learned in childhood itself it would be retained like a nail driven into a tender tree. Gāyatrī imparts in great measure mental strength, lustre and health. It will increase the child's power of concentration, sharpen his intelligence, make him physically strong. Later in life, when he feels the urge of Kāma, Gāyatrī will prevent him from being dragged downward and be a protective shield for his body and intelligence. When one learns to meditate on the Gāyatrī in childhood itself, it would be a great help, as one grows up, in not wasting one's seed, in acquiring Brāhmic lustre and qualities like studiousness, humility, devotion to God and interest in matters of the Self.

Parents nowadays deny their children the opportunity of being afforded such great benefits and for no reason.

A student spends the years of his gurukulavāsa[S] in Gāyatrī-japa[S]; study of the Vedas and the Vedāngas, begging for his food, serving his guru, observing various religious vows. When he completes his education thus, he will have become a young man ready for his samāvartana[S]. Later he must go to Kāśī and, on his return home, take a wife. He is called a "snātaka" between his samāvartana and his return from his journey to Kāśī. Samāvartana is equivalent to today's convocation ceremony. In present-day marriages there is a farcical procedure called "Kāśī-yātra"[1].

Marriage is one of the forty saṁskāras.

Note

[1] Again, the Paramaguru is referring to marriages in the South, particularly Tamiḷ Nāḍu.

Chapter 9

Domestic Life and the Carnal Desire

Great men have spoken in the past about the evil done by carnal desire. Remarkably enough, our Vedic dharma has turned the same into an instrument for the purification of the Self by means of a saṁskāra and by imparting to it an element of propriety. It is not easy for an ordinary man to go to the forest and live as a recluse there or become a sannyāsin. To become mellow, he has to go through all the rough and tumble of life, experience all the joys and sorrows of his worldly existence. In the years of tenderness he must taste bitter, in boyhood or student-bachelorhood he must taste astringent, as an unripe fruit [in youth] he must taste sour and as a mellow fruit [in old age] he must taste sweet[1]. Ordinary people must go through all these stages so as to become mellow finally and to be filled with sweetness. What has not ripened naturally, or by itself, cannot be ripened forcibly. In this context one is reminded of the words of Rāmaliṅgasvāmigal[T] who speaks of a "prematurely ripe and withered fruit dropping". The sages knew that such would be the result if a man were forced into maturity by going against nature. The duties of marriage and the life of a householder are intended to make a person mellow naturally. Besides, are there not many beings that are to be born again as a consequence of their past karma? How can they be reborn in the absence of the saṁskāra called marriage?

The householder has to continue to chant the Vedas he was taught as a brahmacārin. He has also to teach these scriptures, perform a number of sacrifices and rites like aupāsana and sandhyāvandana[S]. At present the conduct of sacrifices has become rare and not many learn the Vedas. But the tradition of sandhyāvandana[S] and Gāyatrī-japa is still followed though only to a very small extent. I will now speak about the Gāyatrī mantra.

Note

[1] The statement reads odd in English but it conveys the idea of a man naturally developing from immaturity to the stage of wisdom and enlightenment.

Chapter 10

Gāyatrī

"Whoever sings it is protected," that is "Gāyatrī". "Gāyantam trāyate yasmāt Gāyatrī'tyabhidhīyate."

"Sings" is not used here in the sense of singing a song. It means intoning or chanting (the mantra) with affection and devotion. People who chant the Gāyatrī in this manner are protected. While speaking about this mantra the Vedas use these words: "Gāyatrīm Chandasām mātā." "Chandas" means the Vedas. So Gāyatrī is the mother of all Vedic mantras (that is the Vedas themselves proclaim so.) It has twenty-four akṣaras (letters or syllables) and three feet, each foot of eight syllables. That is why the mantra is called "Tripadā Gāyatrī". Each foot is the essence of a Veda. Thus Gāyatrī is the essence of the Ṛgveda, Yajurveda and Sāmaveda. The Atharvaveda has its own Gāyatrī. To receive instruction in it you must have a second upanayana.

Says the *Manusmṛti:* "Tribhya eva tu Vedebhyaḥ pādam pādamadūduham". It means that each pāda of Gāyatrī is taken from one of the (three) Vedas. We have forsaken all else that is Vedic. What will be our fate if we give up the Gāyatrī mantra also?

Gāyatrī-japa is essential to all rites performed according to the śāstras.

(See also Chapter 12.)

Chapter 11

The Brahmin must keep his Body Pure

The Brahmin must keep his body chaste so that its impurities do not detract from the power of the mantras he chants. "Deho devālayaḥ prokto jīvaḥ prokto sanātanaḥ." (The body is a temple. The life enshrined in it is the eternal Lord.) You do not enter the precincts of a temple if you are unclean. Nothing impure should be taken in there. To carry meat, tobacco, etc, to a temple is to defile it. According to the Āgama[S] śāstras you must not go to a temple if you are not physically and ritually clean.

The temple called the body — it enshrines the power of the mantras — must not be defiled by any impurity. There is a difference between the home and the temple. In the home it is not necessary to observe such strict rules of cleanliness as in the temple. Some corner, some place, in the house is meant for the evacuation of bodily impurities, to wash the mouth, to segregate women during their periods. (In the flat system it is not possible to live according to the śāstras.) In the temple there is no such arrangement as in a house.

Wherever we live we require houses as well as temples. In the same way our body must serve as a house and as a temple for Ātmic work. The Brahmin's body is to be cared for like a temple since it is meant to preserve the Vedic mantras and no impure material is to be taken in. It is the duty of the Brahmin to protect the power of the mantras, the mantras that create universal well-being. That is why there are more restrictions in his life than in that of others. The Brahmin must refrain from all such acts and practices as make him unclean. Nor should he be tempted by the sort of pleasures that others enjoy with the body.

The Brahmin's body is not meant to experience sensual enjoyment but to preserve the Vedas for the good of mankind. It is for this purpose that he has to perform rites like upanayana. He has to care for his body only with the object of preserving the Vedic mantras and through them of protecting all creatures. Others may have comfortable occupations that bring in much money but that should be no cause for the Brahmin to feel tempted. He ought to think of his livelihood only after he has carried out his duties. In the past when he was loyal to his Brahminic dharma the ruler as well as society gave him land and money to sustain himself. Now conditions have changed and the Brahmin today has to make some effort to earn money. But he must on no account try to amass wealth nor must he adopt unśāstric means to earn money. Indeed he must live in poverty. It is only when he does not seek pleasure and practises self-denial that the light of Ātmic knowledge will shine in him. This light will make the world live. The Brahmin must not go abroad in search of a fortune, giving up the customs and practices he is heir to. His fundamental duty is to preserve the Vedic mantras and follow his own dharma. Earning money is secondary to him.

If the Brahmin keeps the fire of mantras always burning in him, there will be universal welfare. He must be able to help people in trouble with his māntric power and he lives in vain indeed if he turns away a man who seeks his help, excusing himself thus: "I do the same things that you do. I possess only such power as you have."

Today the fire of māntric power has been put out (or it is perhaps like dying embers). The body of the Brahmin has been subjected to undesirable changes and impure substances have found a place in it. But may be a spark of the old fire still gives off a dim light. It must be made to burn brighter. One day it may become a blaze. This spark is Gāyatrī. It has been handed down to us through the ages.

Chapter 12

Gāyatrī and Sandhyāvandana

If the Gāyatrī has not been chanted for three generations in the family of a Brahmin, its members lose caste (they cease to be Brahmins). The quarter where such Brahmins live cannot be called an "agrahāra"[S]. It is perhaps not yet three generations since Brahmins gave up the Gāyatrī. So they may still be called Brahmins.

In the same way, if a Brahmin family has not performed sacrifices for three generations its members are called "Durbrahmaṇas", degenerate Brahmins. Even though degenerate, the label "Brahmin" sticks to them. There are prāyaścittas (expiatory rites) by means of which the corrupted Brahmins will be remade true Brahmins. But there is no such hope for a Brahmin in whose family Gāyatrī has not been chanted for three generations. A member of such a family ceases altogether to be a Brahmin and cannot be made one again. He is just a "Brāhmaṇa-bandhu", a kin or friend of Brahmins. The same rule applies to Kṣatriyas and Vaiśyas with regard to the Gāyatrī mantra; they become "Kṣatriya-bandhus" and "Vaiśya-bandhus" respectively.

The spark I mentioned earlier must be built into a fire. The spark by itself does not serve any purpose. But it has in it the potential to grow into a bright flame or a radiant fire.

At least on Sundays, all those who wear the sacred thread must do Gāyatrī-japa a thousand times. They must not eat unclean food, go to unclean places and must atone for lapses in ritual observances and in maintaining ritual purity. Henceforth they must take every care to see that their body is kept chaste and fit for it to absorb māntric power.

Even in times of misfortune the Gāyatrī must be muttered at least ten times at dawn, midday and dusk. These are hours of tranquillity. At dawn all creatures including human beings rise and the mind is serene now. At dusk all must be restful after a day's hard work: that is also a time of calm. At noon the sun is at its height and people are at home and relaxed and their mind is calm. During these hours we must meditate on Gāyatrī, Sāvitrī and Sarasvatī. In the morning the dominant presence is that of Viṣṇu, at noon that of Brahmā and at sundown of Śiva. So we must meditate on Gāyatrī in the morning as Viṣṇu personified, at noon as Brahmā personified and at dusk as Śiva personified.

Gāyatrī contains in itself the spirit and energy of all the Vedic mantras. Indeed it imparts power to other mantras. Without Gāyatrī-japa, the chanting of all other mantras would be futile. We find hypnotism useful in many ways and we talk of "hypnotic power". Gāyatrī is the hypnotic means of liberating ourselves from worldly existence as well as of controlling desire and realising the goal of our birth. We must keep blowing on the spark that is the Gāyatrī and must take up Gāyatrī-japa as a vrata[S]. The spark will not be extinguished if we do not take to unśāstric ways of life and if we do not make our body unchaste.

Gāyatrī japa and "arghya" (offering libation) are the most important rites of sandhyāvandana[S]. The other parts of this rite are "angas" (limbs). The least a sick or weak person must do is to offer arghya and mutter the Gāyatrī ten times. "Oh, only these two are important, aren't they? So that's all we will do, offer arghya and mutter the Gāyatrī ten times." If this be our attitude, in due course we are likely to give up even these that are vital to sandhyāvandana. A learned man remarked in jest about people who perform arghya and mutter the Gāyatrī only ten times, thus applying to themselves the rule meant for the weak and the unfortunate: "They will always remain weak and will be victims of some calamity or other." Sandhyāvandana must be performed properly during the right hours. During the Mahābhārata war, when water was not readily available, the warriors gave arghya at the right time with dust as a substitute.

Arghya must be offered before sunrise, at noon and at sunset. Once there was a man called Iḍaikāṭṭu Siddha who grazed cattle. He said: *"Kāṇāmar koṇāmar kaṇḍu koḍu ādugān pohutu pār." "Kāṇāmal/r"* means before you see the sun rise and *"koṇāmal/r"* means when the sun is overhead and "*kaṇḍu*" is when you see the sun (before sunset). These are the three times when you ought to offer arghya. "*Āḍu*" means "*nīrāḍu*", bathe in the Gangā. "*Kāṇ*" here means "visit Setu" or "have darśana of Setu". "*Pohutu pār*" — by bathing in the Gangā and by visiting Setu your sins will be washed away. Here is mentioned the custom of going to Kāśī, collecting Gangā water there and going to (Setu) Rāmeśvaram to perform the abhiṣeka[S] of Rāmanāthasvāmin there.

Only by the intense repetition of Gāyatrī shall we be able to master the Vedic mantras. This japa[S] of Gāyatrī and the arghya must be performed every day without fail. At least once in our lifetime we must bathe in the Gangā and go on pilgrimage to Setu.

If a man has a high fever, people looking after him must pour into his mouth the water with which sandhyāvandana has been performed. Today it seems all of us are suffering all the time from a high fever! When you run a high temperature you have to take medicine; similarly the Gāyatrī is essential to the Self and its japa must not be given up at any time. It is more essential to your inner being than medicine is to your body. Sandhyāvandana must be performed without fail every day. Gāyatrī japa can be practised by all of us without much effort and without spending any money. All that you require is water. Sandhyāvandana is indeed an easy means to ensure your well-being. So long as there is life in you you must perform it.

Gāyatrī must be worshipped as a mother. The Lord appears in many forms to bestow his grace and compassion on his devotees. Mother loves us more than anybody else. We know no fear before her and talk to her freely. Of all the forms in which Bhagavān manifests himself that form in which he is revealed as the mother is liked most by us. The Vedas proclaim Gāyatrī to be such a mother.

This mantra is to be repeated only by men. Women benefit from the men performing the japa. Similarly, when the three varṇas practise Gāyatrī-japa all other jātis enjoy the benefits flowing from it. We may cease to perform a rite if the fruits yielded by them are enjoyed exclusively by us. But we cannot do so if others also share in them. Those entitled to the Gāyatrī mantra are to regard themselves as trustees who have to mutter it on behalf of others like women and the fourth varṇa who are not entitled to it. If they fail in their duty of trustees, it means they are committing an irremediable offence.

The mantras are numerous. Before we start chanting any of them, we say why we are doing so, mention the "fruit" that it will yield. The benefit we derive from the Gāyatrī mantra is the cleansing of the mind (cittaśuddhi). Even other mantras have this ultimate purpose, but cittaśuddhi is the *direct* result of Gāyatrī-japa.

Even in these days it is not difficult to perform sandhyāvandana both at dawn and dusk. Officegoers and other workers may not be at home during midday. They may perform the mādhyāhnika (the midday vandana) 2 hours 24 minutes after sunrise — this is called "sangava- kāla"[1].

We must never miss the daily sandhyāvandana unless we find it absolutely impossible to perform. When we fall ill, in our helplessness, we ask others for water or *kanji*[2]. In the same way, we must ask a relative or friend to perform sandhyāvandana on our behalf.

Let us all pray to the Lord that he will have mercy upon us so that the fire of the mantras is never extinguished in us and that it will keep burning brighter and brighter.

Notes

[1] If daytime is divided into five parts, this will be the second part.

[2] Gruel — in the South it is usually made of broken rice.

Chapter 13

Other Aspects of Sandhyāvandana

"Astra" and "śastra" are terms used in Dhanurveda (military science) to denote two types of weapons. Knife, arrow, spear, club and so on — real weapons — come under the term "śastra". "Astra" is what is energised by a mantra into a weapon. If you discharge just a darbha[S] or a blade of grass chanting or muttering the appropriate mantra it will be turned into a weapon. Śastras are also discharged similarly with mantras. If you hurl something at an object or person muttering the mantra proper to it, that object or person will be destroyed when hit.

The twice-born (Brahmins, Kṣatriyas and Vaiśyas) have the duty of discharging "astras" every day to destroy asuras or the evil forces besieging mankind. Does not "astra" mean that which is discharged, thrown or hurled? What is the "astra" which is to be thrown or discharged [by the twice-born]? We throw water so as to drive away or destroy the demons or evil forces that have taken hold of the minds of people. This water, the astra, is the same as the libation offered during sandhyāvandana. We must keep this purpose in mind when we offer arghya[S]: "May sinfulness and falsehood be annihilated. May the sun of knowledge shine brightly. May those obstacles that keep the sun of knowledge dim in us be demolished." Whatever you do or do not do, you must perform this arghya thrice a day. Do it somehow "holding your breath"[1].

When a person does a job earnestly and whole-heartedly, we say that he does it "holding his breath". As a matter of fact sandhyāvandana is to be performed "holding one's breath". If we do this all the evil forces will be destroyed. Nowadays all we do is to hold our nose with our fingers. The śāstras do not say, "Nāsikām āyamya", but say, "Prāṇān āyamya." It means, instead of merely holding the nose, control the vital breath, the prāṇa itself or the life force.

All work must be done with one-pointedness. There must be such one-pointedness of the mind to turn water into a weapon (astra). The breath is controlled for this purpose. You will ask: "How is it that if you control your breath the mind will be still?" We see that when the mind is still the breath also stops. When our wonder is aroused, when we are grief-stricken or when we are overjoyed, the mind becomes one-pointed. We exclaim "Ha" and the breath stops for a moment. But soon we breathe fast. We do not stop breathing with any effort on our part — the stopping is involuntary. The mind stops when it is enwrapped or absorbed in something. Then we heave a sigh — take a long breath — making up for the momentary stoppage of breathing. We learn from this that, when breathing momentarily stops, the mind becomes one-pointed. This is the reason why the breath is controlled when arghya, libation, is offered.

If we practise prāṇāyāma we will train ourselves to have mental concentration. This is important to yoga. Practising prāṇāyāma for long is difficult and it must be done under the guidance of a guru. In sandhyāvandana we do it only ten times. For some rites it is performed three times as a preliminary step. If we had practised prāṇāyāma regularly from the time of our upanayana we should have become yogīśvaras[2] by now. What we do we must do properly. When we practise prāṇāyāma as part of sandhyāvandana we must stop our breath for 30 seconds or so, not more. When the vital breath stops, the mind will become still. If the arghya is offered in this state the evil forces will truly be driven away. The water that we pour or throw when our mind is still will turn a weapon to destroy all evil.

After employing the arghya weapon against the evil forces, we must perform Gāyatrī-japa. Prāṇāyāma we must do according to our ability, holding the breath for a while, then releasing it: this process may be repeated without controlling the breath for too long a time. All the steps in sandhyāvandana — saṁkalpa, mārjana[S], arghya- pradāna[S], japa[S], stotra[S], abhivādana[S] — have for their purpose the blessings of Īśvara : this is stated in the saṁkalpa that we make at first. From beginning to end sandhyāvandana is dedicated to Parameśvara and prāṇāyāma is an important part of it.

According to the śāstras even the sick must do prāṇāyāma three times a day. This means that breath-control is not such as to cause trouble or discomfort. Indeed it could mean a cure for the illness and a prescription for long life.

Ṛṣayo dīrgha-sandhyatvād dīrghamāyuravāpnuyuḥ
Prajñām yaśaśca kīrtim ca brahmavarcasameva ca

— Manusmṛti, 4.94

In abhivādana we mention the name of the sage from whom we are descended. It is our duty to observe Vedic rituals at least for the fact that we belong to the gotra[S] of that sage. After him there have been so many ṛṣis in the line. We use the terms "trayārṣeyam", "pañcārṣeyam", "ekārṣeyam", meaning that, in the gotras concerned, there were three sages, five sages, one sage... . They must have lived long and secured knowledge, fame, Brāhmic lustre and spiritual eminence by performing sandhyāvandana. This is what the *Manusmṛti* stanza means.

By our neglect we should not sever the thread, the tradition, handed down to us uninterruptedly. We must perform sandhyāvandana as an offering to

Parameśvara and must do so understanding its meaning and with faith and devotion. There must be one-pointedness in it and no mantra must be left out.

We sin with our mind, speech and body. I told you that these sins must be washed away by performing rites with the same mind, speech and body. In sandhyāvandana we mutter the mantras with our mouth and, even as we repeat the Gāyatrī, we meditate on it with our mind and in such rites as mārjana (sprinkling of water) we acquire bodily purity. Sandhyāvandana is karmayoga, bhaktiyoga and jñānayoga combined [it unites the three paths of karma, devotion and knowledge].

Notes

1 This is a literal translation of the Tamiḷ idiom the meaning of which is explained in the first sentence of the following para. The English idiom "to hold one's breath" or "catch one's breath" means to stop breathing for a moment because of fear or shock. But when we further read the Paramaguru on one-pointedness of the mind we realise that the Tamiḷ idiom is not entirely different from the English.

2 Lords of yogins.

Chapter 14

What about Women?

I said that the twice-born must perform sandhyāvandana with the well-being of women and other jātis in mind. I also explained why all saṁskāras are not prescribed for the fourth varṇa. Now we must consider the question of women, why they do not have such rituals and saṁskāras.

Even though we perform the puṇyāha-vacana[1] and nāmakaraṇa of new-born girls and celebrate their first birthday, we do not conduct their cauḷa and upanayana nor the other saṁskāras or vows laid down for brahmacārins. Of course, they have the marriage saṁskāra. But in other rites like sacrifices the main part is that of the husband, though she (the wife) has to be by his side. In aupāsana alone does a woman have a part in making oblations in the sacred fire.

Why is it so?

The rites performed before a child is born are intended for the birth of a male child (niṣeka, puṁsavana, sīmanta). Does it mean, as present-day reformers and women's libbers say, that Hindu women were downgraded and kept in ḍarkness?

What reason did I mention for the fourth varṇa not having to perform many of the saṁskāras? That these were not necessary considering their vocations and the fact that they can work for the welfare of the world without the physical and mental benefits to be derived from the saṁskāras. If they also spend their time in Vedic learning and in sacrifices, what will happen to their duties? So most of the saṁskāras are not necessary for them. They reach the desired goal without these rites by carrying out their duties. "Svakarmaṇa tam abhyarcya siddhim vindati mānavaḥ"[2], so says the Gītā. I have spoken to you about this earlier.

Just as society is divided according to occupations and the saṁskāras are correspondingly different, so too there are differences between men and women in domestic life. Running a household means different types of work, cooking, keeping the house clean, bringing up the children, etc. By nature women can do these chores better than men. If they also take an active part in rituals, what will happen to such work? Each by serving her husband and by looking after her household becomes inwardly pure.

In truth there is no disparity between men and women, nor are women discriminated against as present-day reformers allege. Work is divided for the proper maintenance not only of the home but the nation on the whole; and care has been taken not to have any duplication. There is no intention of lowering the status of any section in this division of labour.

The body, in the case of certain people, is meant to preserve the mantras and there are saṁskāras which have the purpose of making it worthy of the same. Why should the same rituals be prescribed for those who do not have such tasks to carry out? Glassware to be sent by railway parcel is specially taken care of since it is fragile. Even greater care is taken in despatching kerosene or petrol. If the same precautions are not taken in transporting other goods, does it mean that they are poorly thought of? Astronauts are kept in isolation before being sent up in space and after their return. Mantras have their own radiation that is even more powerful than what is found in space. If you appreciate this fact, you will understand why Brahmins are separated from the rest and special saṁskāras prescribed for them.

The body of a Brahmin (male) is involved in the nurturing of mantras. So from the time of conception itself it is to be made pure through saṁskāras like puṁsavana, sīmanta,[3] and so on. There are saṁskāras with the same objective also after the boy child is born.

The vocations have to be properly divided for the welfare of mankind. If everybody paid attention to this fact, instead of talking of rights, it would be realised that the śāstras have not discriminated against women or any of the jātis.

Notes & References

[1] It is a declaration by the Brahmins present at a function that the rite about to be performed will prove to be auspicious.

[2] Bhagavadgītā, 18.46

[3] These terms are explained elsewhere in this part.

Chapter 15

The High Status of Our Women

Those who complain that women have no right to perform sacrifices on their own must remember that men too have no right to the same without a wife. If they knew this truth they would not make the allegation that Hindu śāstras look down upon women. A man can perform sacrifices only with his wife. He does them for the well- being of all mankind and for his own inner purity. It is for this purpose that, after the samāvartana[5] following the completion of his student-bachelorhood, he goes through the saṁskāra called marriage.

Marriage or vivāha is known as "saha-dharma-cāriṇi-saṁprayoga". It means (roughly) union with a wife together with whom a man practises dharma. The clear implication is that carnal pleasure is not its chief purpose, but the pursuit of dharma. The śāstras do not ask a man to pursue dharma all by himself but require him to take a helpmate for it. The wife is called "dharma-patnī", "saha-dharma-cāriṇī", thus underlining her connection with dharma, and not with kāma or sensual pleasure. Here is proof of the high esteem in which the śāstras hold women.

The celibate-student and the ascetic alike follow the dharma of their respective āśramas (stages of life) not in association with anyone else. The householder has to conduct the karma as well as the dharma of domestic life with his wife as a companion, such being the rule laid down in the śāstras. The dharma of domestic life is their common property. Only a householder with a wife may perform sacrifices, not student-bachelors and ascetics. If the wife were meant only for sensual gratification, would the dharmaśāstras have insisted that a man cannot perform sacrifices after her death? Women's libbers, who note that a woman cannot perform a sacrifice on her own, must also recognise the fact that the husband loses the right for the same without the wife and this is according to the Vedas themselves. ("Patnīvatasya agnihotram bhavati.") A great man lamented thus at the time of his wife's death: "You have taken away all my sacrifices as well as other rituals."

Our śāstras have thus given a high place to women in the matter of duties and works.

(See also Part Eighteen)

Part Eighteen

MARRIAGE

Chapter 1

For the Practice of Dharma

Dharma, artha, kāma and mokṣa are the four puruṣārthas, the four aims of life. The first of them, dharma, is a lifelong objective. The pursuit of artha (material welfare) and kāma (desire, love) must be given up at a certain stage in a man's life. But so long as such a pursuit lasts, it must be based on dharma. When a man renounces the world and becomes an ascetic, he transcends dharma, but he does not go contrary to it nor speak against it. Indeed, his life is governed by the dharma of sannyāsa.

I have already spoken about Pūrvamīmāṁsā (karmakāṇḍa) and Uttaramīmāṁsā (jñānakāṇḍa). The *Pūrvamīmāṁsā-sūtra* opens with "Athāto dharmajijñāsā," meaning "starting the inquiry into dharma". The *Uttaramīmāṁsā-sūtra*" (or *Brahmasūtra),* on the other hand, starts with "Athāto Brahmajijñāsā," meaning "starting the inquiry into the Brahman"[1].

When you inquire into the Brahman and meditate on It you are not conscious of dharma. Dharma is for the dualistic world of karma. Since the phenomenal world does not exist in non-dualistic jñāna there is no consideration of dharma in it. But this does not mean that it [non-dualistic jñāna] is contrary or opposed to dharma; and all that is meant is that it goes beyond dharma. Bhagavān declares in the Gītā[2]: "Sarvadharmān parityajya mām ekam śaraṇam vraja" (Forsaking all dharmas come to me alone for refuge). Are we to construe that the Lord asks us to go to him for refuge as perpetrators of adharma? The true meaning of the words of the Lord is this: "Give up all inquiry into dharma and adharma. Go beyond them and comprehend the Object that is the source of both." What is sought is an inward experience. The actions performed by jñānins who have this inner realisation will naturally be in conformity with dharma. The doings of high-souled ascetics may not be consciously based on dharma but, nevertheless, they would be nothing but dhārmic.

All told, dharma is always a part of a man's life. When he reaches a high spiritual state, he may not be conscious of it, but dharma will abide in him and will keep shining as a light in all that he does.

The pursuit of the second of the four aims of life, artha, must be based on dharma. The same applies to the third aim, that is kāma. Kālidāsa expresses the same thought in his *Raghuvaṁśam* when he speaks in praise of Dilīpa: "Abhyarthākamau tasyāstām dharma eva manīṣinaḥ" (With Dilīpa, the wise, even artha and kāma were of the nature of dharma). The householder's stage of life commences with marriage. In it both material well-being and desire have their source in dharma. The student-bachelor and the ascetic are not concerned with the acquisition of wealth or carnal pleasure. The householder's stage of life, or gṛhasthāśrama, is a bridge between the two and in it both are permitted [within the bounds of dharma].

A man needs money and material goods to live in this world. As for kāma or carnal desire, it is needed so that children may be born according to their past karma. Until we have lived out our karma we too will have to be in this world. In this way if we want to give a "chance"[2] to others, we have to earn money and experience kāma so that they [these others] may be born again. We need householders to feed sannyāsins who have given up karma. It would not be practical for all people in this world to become ascetics. The śāstras extol householders as the backbone of society since they live, or are expected to live, according to the dictates of dharma and fulfil the requirements of student-bachelors and ascetics.

After completing one's student-bachelorhood and acquiring learning and good qualities, one must marry so as to perform religious rites and live a life guided by dharma. Marriage is included among the forty saṁskāras, which fact shows that it is a sacred rite that sanctifies life. Just as upanayana is preliminary (pūrvānga) to the student-bachelor's stage of life, marriage is preliminary to that of the householder. Its purpose is disciplining the senses and the basis for the performance of various duties.

The householder's life is not to be taken to mean merely the enjoyment of sensual pleasure along with the carrying out of duties that mean good to the world. The fact is that the śāstras have formulated this stage of life in such a way as to make kāma itself instinct with dharma. "Dharma" means essentially bringing everything within certain limits, under a certain discipline and decorum. Kāma must be inspired by dharma, that is one must bridle one's passions in one's conjugal life, so that, step by step, the carnal urge will lose its keenness and eventually one will gain the mellowness to graduate to sannyāsa. That stage, though, comes later. But at first, even now, in the householder's stage of life, the passions have to be curbed, little by little, but not forcibly. In the gurukula[S] the celibate-student is brought under strict discipline. That saves him from being swept away by animal passion.

Though we talk of animal passion, we must note that animals mate only during a particular season. They have the sexual urge only when the female of the species is ready for pregnancy. Man is baser in such matters. Brahmacarya helps to control the carnal urge as it first shows up. Then, in the householder's life, since kāma is made subservient to dharma, the passions are kept under check.

What is the śāstric method to control the carnal urge? From the day of a woman's period there should be no intercourse for four days. Then it is permitted for twelve days. Again there should be no intercourse until the woman has her next period. Even during the twelve days mentioned above the couple should not meet during the new moon, on days conjoined by certain asterisms, etc. If such rules are followed the couple will remain healthy mentally as well as physically.

Notes & References

1 Literally, the words mean, "Now the desire to know the Brahman". Similarly, the opening words of the *Pūrvamīmāṁsā-sūtra* mean, "Now the desire to know dharma."

2 *Sarvardharmān parityajya mām ekam śaraṇaṁ vraja*
Ahaṁ tvā sarvapāpebhyo mokṣayiṣyāmi ma sućaḥ

— Bhagavadgita, 18.66

3 What the Paramaguru means here is that those who have not exhausted their karma too must be given the opportunity of living it out by being born again in this world.

Chapter 2

Upanayana for Girls

If brahmacarya prepares boys [or young men] to live according to dharma, what about girls? A girl has neither upanayana nor brahmacaryāśrama. Should not a woman's mind also be disciplined like a man's? If you echo the criticism of reformers and say that injustice has been done to women by denying them the brahmacaryāśrama[S] and upanayana, my answer is "No".

Men marry after their upanayana and student-bachelorhood. Now for women marriage itself is upanayana. Just as a boy dedicates himself to his guru, a girl must dedicate herself to her husband from her childhood until the start of their conjugal life and beyond. The *Manusmṛti* says: "Strīṇām upanayana-sthāne vivāham Manurabravīt" (Manu said that for women marriage is in place of upanayana). If you ask for an external sign of this like the sacred thread worn by the men, we may at once point to the married woman's maṅgalasūtra[S].

I said that "upanayana" means "taking near", taking a boy near his guru for his brahmacaryāśrama. A woman's guru is her husband. Being joined to him in wedlock is her upanayana.

According to the śāstras a boy's upanayana must be performed when he is seven years old. A girl must be married at the same age. If a boy is to be initiated into brahmacarya before his mind is disturbed by kāma, a girl is to be married before she feels the carnal urge. She must also accept her husband as her guru. According to the śāstras, the guru must be looked upon as Īśvara. In the same way the child bride must think of her husband as both guru and Īśvara and dedicate herself whole-heartedly to him. She will be able to adopt such an attitude only when she is married very young. Later she might start to reason about things, ask questions and develop egoistic feelings.

Laying oneself at the feet of the guru or Īśvara — in short surrender — is the best means of liberating oneself. This concept of surrender is proclaimed in the carama śloka of the Gītā, surrender to Īśvara, guru or husband: once you surrender to an individual or deity you no longer own anything. Īśvara will give you his grace through the one to whom you surrender.

According to the system devised by the sages, a boy is made to surrender to his guru at the time of his upanayana ceremony, while a girl does the same to her husband at the time of her marriage.

It is not that the girl is considered inferior and asked to surrender to a man, that is her husband. The boy too is asked to surrender as a child to the guru. It is the view of the śāstras that the age at which the girl is married and surrenders to her husband must be the same as that at which the boy surrenders to the guru.

Talking of the husband and the wife, the question whether the one is superior to the other or inferior is of no consequence. Equally unimportant is the question of rights and status. If this is realised surrender will be seen to be of the utmost importance. We must appreciate the fact that it is in keeping with this view that the concept of upanayana has taken shape in the case of boys and of marriage in the case of girls.

Chapter 3

The Age of Marriage and the Law

We saw that it would be best to perform a boy's upanayana when he is seven years old[1]. A girl must be married about the same age so that she too will develop the attitude of surrender. But you will ask: "Is it possible these days? Will it not be against the law?"

It would not be right on my part to ask you to disobey the law. Those who rule us today themselves resorted to civil disobedience once[2]. They justified their action thus: "Some people have enacted what are called laws. But we won't let them come in the way of our freedom." Why do I ask you not to defy the law that stipulates the minimum age for the bride? Not because people are not spirited enough to rise in protest against it, not because they are not ready to go to gaol or even die instead of accepting a law that has brought down the marriage saṁskāra with its high ideal of Ātmic well-being to the mundane level. I ask you not to disobey the law because the attitude of defiance, if extended to other matters, will jeopardise discipline and order in society itself. We must, however, keep impressing upon the government the śāstric view with regard to the age at which a girl ought to be married.

But it is not the government alone that has gone against the śāstras. More than 90 per cent of our people do not respect the śāstric view. The few conversant with the scriptures must keep enlightening the rest about this view. Without going against the law they must resolve themselves to do their best, in a peaceful manner, to restore a worthy custom, no matter whether it takes a hundred years or even more to yield results. Why, even if we do not live to see the results, even if it takes a thousand years, we must sow the seeds now. Nothing will be achieved without effort. The tree does not grow if the seed is not sown.

We must — in a persuasive manner — keep impressing upon the government and the public that the Dharmaśāstra itself is a great legal code.

Notes

[1] Reckoned as nearly eight years from the time of conception.

[2] When the Paramaguru said this the Congress was in power not only at the Centre but in most of the States. And, it will be remembered, civil disobedience was the weapon wielded by the Congress — under the leadership of Gāndhījī --- in the battle for freedom.

Chapter 4

Controversy about Age of Marriage

At the turn of the century, extremely influential people, among Hindus themselves, demanded the abolition of child marriage and advocated that girls ought to be married only after they attain puberty. They held meetings and passed resolutions against child marriages. Not that they were wanting in faith in the Vedas, most of them; indeed they claimed that their view had support in the scriptures themselves. Among them were distinguished men like M.Raṅgācāryār, Śivasvāmi Ayyar, Sundaramayyar and Kṛṣṇasvāmi Ayyar. Then there was the Rt Hon'ble Śrīnivāsa Śāstrī who was particularly vehement in his crititicism of the system of child marriage[1].

Vaiṣṇavas and Smārtas[S] learned in the śāstras held meetings at Kāñcīpuram and Tiruvaiyāru respectively and put forward the view that, according to the Vedas, girls in the past were married after they had attained puberty. They found an explanation for the origin of the custom of child marriages. Their view was this: After the advent of Islam in India, Hindu girls were abducted and dishonoured in large numbers. Girls already married were spared, they claimed. That is how the new custom of child marriage came into practice. The reformers now argued that we must go back to what they thought was the original Vedic practice and put an end to the uncivilized custom of pre-puberty marriages.

They cited their own evidence from the śāstras in support of their view. One piece of evidence they presented was drawn from the Vedas themselves, that is the mantras chanted during the marriage rite. The other was from the *Manusmṛti* which is respected by all as the foremost among the dharmaśāstras.

What do the marriage mantras say[2]? Before answering the question I must tell you another matter. Each part of our body has a deity associated with it ("adhidevatā" or tutelary deity). The sun god with the eye, Indra with the hand and so on — thus there are divine forces inwardly associated with us. Apart from this, during different stages of our life various deities hold sway over us. Thus, a girl is under the sway of Soma (the moon god) from birth until the time she is old enough to wear clothes herself. (The *dhoti* or *veṣṭi* that men wear is called "*soman*".) Then, until the girl has her menarche, she is under a gandharva. Thereafter, for three years, she is under Agni. When she is under the moon god as a little child she is cool like moonlight. Gandharvas are playful and beautiful, so when a girl is under the gandharva she is particularly attractive. Under Agni she has the fire that kindles kāma. This is a worldly interpretation of how certain deities have hold over a girl. But let that be.

What is the meaning of the Vedic mantras quoted by the reformers in support of their view? The mantras are chanted by the groom addressing the bride: "At first Soma had hold on you; then the gandharva became your guardian; thirdly Agni became your master. I, as a human being, have come as the fourth to hold sway over you. Soma passed you on to the gandharva and the gandharva to Agni. Agni has now given you over to me."

Are we not to construe from the Vedic mantras, which are chanted at the marriage ceremony, that at the time of the wedding the girl has already had her menarche, three years after being under the guardianship of Agni? The reformers maintain that their argument against child marriage is not contrary to the śāstras. The marriage custom, according to them, changed after the Muslim invasion and they want the original practice restored. No sanātanī[S], they argue, can cite any authority better than the Vedas.

The reformers also quote a stanza from the *Manusmṛti* in support of their argument:

Trīṇi varṣāṇyudīkṣeta kumārī ṛtumatī satī
ūrdhvam tu kālādetasmādvindeta sadṛśam patim

The śloka means: "A girl who has come of age must wait for three years for a groom to come seeking her hand. If no such groom turns up, she may herself go looking for a groom." Here too it is post- puberty marriage that is indicated. Not only that. Manu's code of conduct, it is argued, is "modern" in that it permits a girl to look for a husband herself without any need for her elders to do so. After Manu, the reformers contend, the orthodox Vedic scholars changed everything and made the marriage custom barbarous.

"In the light of these Vedic mantras and the dharmaśāstra quoted, are not the reformers right? What is your answer, *Svāmijī*?" I will give my answer.

Note & Reference

1 Most of the men mentioned here were lawyers of Madras. The Rt Hon'ble Śrīnivāsa Śāstrī headed the Servants of India Society after the death of Gopal Kṛṣṇa Gokhale and was an educationist and liberal politician, apart from being a widely reputed English orator.

2 *Somaḥ prathamo vivide*
Gandharvo vivida uttaraḥ
Tṛtīyo Agniṣṭepatih
Turīyastemanuṣyajāḥ

Controversy about Age of Marriage

Somo dadad gandharvāya
Gandharvo dadadagnaye
Rayiñcaputrāṁścādād
Agnirmahyamatho imām

—Ṛgveda, 10.85, 40-41

Chapter 5

Eight Forms of Marriage

The dharmaśāstras, including the *Manusmṛti,* mention eight forms of marriage.

Brāhmo-daivastathaivārṣaḥ
Prājāpatya-statha'suraḥ
Gāndharvo rākṣasaścaiva
Paiśacāṣṭamaḥ smṛtaḥ

— Manusmṛti, 3.21

The eight types are: brāhma, daiva, ārṣa, prājāpatya, āsura, gāndharva, rākṣasa and paiśāca.

After the student-bachelor has completed his gurukulavāsa[S], his parents approach the parents of a girl belonging to a good family and ask them to give away their daughter in marriage to their son — to make a gift of their daughter (kanyādāna) to him. A marriage arranged like this is brāhma. In it the girl's family does not give any dowry or jewellery to the boy's family. There is no "commercial transaction" and the goal of a brāhma marriage is the dhārmic advancement of the two families. Of the eight forms of marriage the dharmaśāstras regard this as the highest.

Marrying a girl to a ṛtvik (priest) during a sacrifice is called "daiva"[1]. The parents, in this type, after waiting in vain for a young man to turn up and ask for their daughter's hand, go looking for a groom for her in a place where a sacrifice is being conducted. This type of marriage is considered inferior to brāhma. In the śāstras womanhood is elevated in that it is the groom's family that has to go seeking a bride for their son.

The third form, "ārṣa" suggests that it is concerned with the ṛṣis, sages. It seems the marriage of Sukanyā to Cyavana Maharṣi was of this type. But from the dharmaśāstras we learn that in ārṣa the bride is given in exchange for two cows received from the groom[2]. If the term is taken to mean "giving away a girl in marriage to a ṛṣi", we must take it that the girl is married off to an old sage because the parents could not celebrate her marriage according to the brāhma rite at the right time. The fact that cows are taken in exchange for the bride shows that the groom does not possess any remarkable qualities. According to the śāstras, in marriages of a noble kind there is no place for money or anything smacking of a business transaction.

In prājāpatya there is no trading and kanyādāna is a part of it as in the brāhma ceremony. But from the name prājāpatya it must be inferred that the bride's menarche is imminent and that a child must be begotten soon after the marriage. For this reason the bride's father goes in search of a groom, unlike in the brāhma type. The brāhma is a better type of marriage than prājāpatya since, in it, the groom's people go seeking a bride who is to be the Gṛhalakṣmī of their household.

In the āsura type the groom is in no way a match for the girl, but her father or her relatives receive a good deal of money from the man who forces them to marry her to him[3]. In ārṣa in which cows are given in exchange for the bride there is no compulsion. Nor is the groom wealthy or powerful like his counterpart in the āsura type. Many rich men must have taken a second wife according to the āsura type of marriage.

The next is gāndharva. The very mention of it calls to mind Śakuntalā and Duṣyanta[4]. The gāndharva type is the "love marriage" that has such enthusiastic support these days.

In the rākṣasa form the groom battles with the girl's family, overcomes them and carries her away. It was in this manner that Kṛṣṇa Paramātman married Rukmiṇī.

The eighth and last is paiśāca. In āsura even though the girl's willingness to marry the man is of no consequence, at least her people are given money. In rākṣasa, though violence is done to the girl's family, the marriage itself is not against her wish. Rukmiṇī loved Kṛṣṇa, did she not? In paiśāca the girl's wish does not count, nor is any money or material given to her parents. She is seized against her wish and her family antagonised.

We have the brāhma type at one end and the paiśāca at the other. There cannot be the same system or the same arrangement for everybody. Our śāstras have taken into account the differences in temperament and attitude among various sections of people and it is in keeping with the same that they have assigned them different rites, vocations, etc. All our present trouble arises from the failure on the part of men, who advocate the same system for all, to recognise this fact.

There are tribals living in the forests who look fierce and have a harsh way of life. But at heart they may be more cultured than townspeople, not to speak of the fact that they are useful to society in many ways. They have frequent family feuds. In consideration of this rākṣasa and paiśāca marriages may have to be permitted in their case. After the marriage, they are likely to forget their quarrels and live in peace with each other. Kṣatriyas who are physically strong and are used to material pleasure are allowed the gāndharva form of marriage and their girls have even the right to choose their husbands as in the svayaṁvara ceremony.

It is for these reasons that the dharmaśāstras, which are based on the Vedas and which constitute Hindu law, permit eight forms of marriage. In all these eight, the bride and groom have the right to be united in wedlock with the chanting of mantras. But brāhma is the highest of the eight forms. In it the bride must not have attained puberty. "Pradānam prāk ṛtoḥ" — this statement is in the dharmaśāstras themselves. A girl's marriage, which has the same significance for her that the upanayana has for a boy, must be performed when she is seven years old (or eight years from conception).

Unfortunately, in the case of some girls, a groom does not turn up in time for a brāhma marriage to be performed. Meanwhile, they grow old and their marriage is conducted in the ārṣa, daiva, or prājāpatya way. Only these types are permitted for Brahmins. But for the rest other types are also allowed. They may marry a girl who has come of age either in the gāndharva way or in a svayaṁvara.

The marriage mantras are intended for all the eight forms. It means that they are employed even in the marriage rite of girls who have attained puberty. The two mantras quoted above[5] are recited in all the eight types of marriage. They are addressed by the groom to the bride who comes to him after she has attained puberty and after she has been under the guardianship successively of Soma, gandharva and Agni. The mantras are chanted not only in brāhma marriages but also in all other forms. The same are addressed by the groom to his child bride also. Though his marriage is being solemnised to the child bride now, he will start living with her only after she comes of age, after she becomes a young woman. He will bring her home to live with him only after she has come successively under Soma, gandharva and Agni. So he chants the mantras in advance.

Nowadays we sometimes perform a number of saṁskāras together long after they are due according to the śāstras. For example, we perform the jātakarma of a son as well as his nāmakaraṇa and caula[6] during his upanayana when he is 20 or 22 years old and not long before his marriage. Similarly, instead of such postponement of the rites, in the brāhma marriage the mantras mentioned above are chanted in advance.

I will give you an example in this context. When the brahmacārin performs the samidādhāna[S] he prays before Agni to grant him good children. How absurd would it be for our reformers to argue, on the basis of this prayer, that a young boy must have children when he is yet a celibate-student and that he may become a householder only later. The point to note is that the boy prays in advance for good children. The Vedic mantras cited by reformers must be seen in the same light.

The mantras [quoted by reformers] are appropriate for the marriage of a girl who has come of age also.

This is our reply to the school of opinion represented by the Rt Hon'ble Śrīnivāsa Śāstrī. If the mantras in question are chanted at the time of the marriage of girls who have come of age, it does not mean that all marriages are to be celebrated after the girls have attained puberty. According to the brāhma form of marriage, the girl must not have had her menarche. There is incontrovertible proof for this in the Vedic mantra chanted at the end of the marriage rite[7].

I told you that a girl is under the sway of a gandharva between the time she is able to wear her clothers without anybody's help and her menarche. His name is Viśvāvasu. The mantra I referred to is chanted by the groom addressing this demigod. "O Viśvāvasu," it says, " I bow to you. Leave this girl and go. Go to another girl child. Have I not become the husband of this girl? So give her over to me and go to another girl who is not married and lives with her father." During the wedding the groom performs a pūjā to this gandharva and prays to him to free the girl from his control. Here is proof that the bride is not yet under Agni and has not had her menarche.

The question now is about the verse (from the *Manusmṛti*) cited by the reformists. According to it, a girl may wait three years after her menarche and then seek her husband on her own.

There is an answer to this. The general rule according to the dharmaśāstras is that a girl must be married before she attains puberty: "Pradānam prak ṛtoḥ." What happens if this injunction is not followed? If a groom does not come on his own, seeking the girl's hand, her father or brother must look for a groom and marry her off. But if they turn out to be irresponsible or otherwise fail to find a groom? Or if the girl has no guardian, no one to care for her? The lines quoted by the reformers from the *Manusmṛti* apply to such a girl. She may look for a husband on her own if none of her relatives, neighbours or well-wishers take the trouble of finding her a groom even after she has attained puberty.

Though the reformists quote from the Vedas and the śāstras in support of their view, they fail to take into account the context in which the relevant passages occur. They see them in isolation. That is why they keep arguing that the customs followed by people steeped in our traditions are contrary to the śāstras.

In the *Chāndogya Upaniṣad* there is mention of a sage called Cākrāyaṇa Uṣasti whose wife had not come of age[8]. The reformists do not examine such references in our ancient texts with a cool head but are carried away by their emotions.

In the past the common people did not know how to counter the arguments of the reformists. Even so they did not accept their views thinking it best to follow the practices of their elders, of great men. That is why the bill brought twice by the Rt Hon'ble Śrinivāsa Śāstrī before the legislative council to amend the marriage act (with reference to the age of marriage) did not receive enough support. Later (Harbilās) Sārda introduced the bill which [on its passage] came to be called the Sārda Act. Many people (in the South) think Sārda was a woman and call the law named after him the "Śāradā Act". The Central legislative assembly was equally divided on the bill — 50 per cent for and 50 per cent against. Then the British asked one of the nominated members to vote in favour of the bill; and thus the minimum age of marriage for girls was raised by a legal enactment. The bill was passed not on the strength of public opinion but because of the government's intervention. The mind of our British rulers worked thus: "The Congress has been demanding *svarāj* but we have refused to grant it. Let us give it some satisfaction by being of help in inflicting an injury on the (Hindu) religion."

Now things have changed. There is no respect any longer for old customs and traditions. When the Sārda Act came into force in British India, some Sanskrit scholars returned the "Mahāmahopādhyāya" title conferred on them by the government. Among them were Pañcānana Tārkaratna Bhaṭṭācārya of Beṅgāḷ and Lakṣmaṇa Śāstrī Draviḍ. The latter was settled in Kāśī and had the "Draviḍ" tagged on to his name to make it known that he belonged to the land of the Tamiḷs. How many people today are inspired to rise in protest against the changes introduced by our government in our śāstric observances.

Our children must be taught the substance and meaning of the śāstras in a comprehensive manner. To speak to them about one aspect here and another there will lead to a haphazard and confused view. The half-baked research carried on in the Vedas has given rise to the opinion that the scriptures favour love marriage. The canonical texts must be seen in their entirety. When a subject is examined, its underlying meaning and purpose must be grasped. Also they must be seen in the light of other relevent passages occurring elsewhere. A conclusion must be arrived at only after a thorough inquiry into all points.

The brāhma marriage is for all castes. Other forms of marriage are also permitted for non-Brahmins, also post-puberty marriage. If the idea is to give importance to carnal pleasure these other forms may be permitted. But brāhma is the best if the purpose of the marriage saṁskāra is the advancement of the Self.

Notes & References

1 *Yajñasya ṛtvije daivaḥ.*

—Yajñavalkya Smṛti, 1.59

2 *Ādāryārṣastu godvayam.*

—Ibid, 1.59

3 *Āsuro draviṇādānat*

—Ibid, 1.61

4 Kālidāsa's world-famous dramatic work, *Abhijñana-Śākuntalam,* is based on their story.

5 See Note 2 appended to previous chapter.

6 These rites have already been explained.

7 *Udīrṣvāto Viśvāvaso namaseḍāmahe tvā / Anyāmicchạ prapharvyam sañjāyām patyā sṛja / Udīṣrvāto pativatī hyeṣā Visvāvasunnamasā gīrbhirīḍe / Anyāmichha pitṛṣadam vyaktām / sa te bhāgo januṣā tasya vidhi.*

8 *Maṭacīhateṣu kuruṣvāṭikyā saha jāyayoṣastirha Cākrāyaṇa ibhya-grāme pradrāṇaka uvāsa.*

—Chāndogya Upaniṣad, 1.10.1

Chapter 6
Why Child Marriage

The saṁskāra called marriage has a manifold purpose. One of its important ideals is to make women inwardly pure through their attachment to their husbands. With such attachment and devotion alone will they make their way to the Ultimate. The disciple cleanses his mind by surrendering to his guru. The wife must surrender to her husband for the same purpose.

Our karma and the cycle of births and deaths we are subject to stem from the unceasing activity of our mind. We sin by pandering to the desires of the mind and are born again and again. When the mind becomes still there will be neither karma nor janma (birth) — this state is liberation. Stilling the mind is extremely difficult. It may be possible to attain the eight great siddhis[S]; but it is impossible to still the mind and be oneself, so says the Tamiḷ saint-poet Tāyumānavar[T].

If we cannot control or still our mind on our own, the next best thing is to dedicate it to another person, not allowing it to sway according to our likes and dislikes. We shall not then be subject to the consequences of doing things on our own which means we shall not be subject either to sin or rebirth. If we lay our mind at the feet of another person we will absolve ourselves of the responsibility of being a "kartā" or doer. So we will not suffer the consequences that we will otherwise have to suffer for our actions like pāpa, puṇya or another birth. We are taught to dedicate ourselves to Īśvara in an attitude of surrender, implying that we do not do anything on our own. But only one in a million is disposed in this way. However, there are a large number of examples in the history of our religion of women who have shown that a wife can be liberated by looking upon her husband as Īśvara. The husband is the Lord in flesh and blood; even if he be a stone the husband is a husband. Total loyalty to him and the desire to die a "sumaṅgalī[S]" are the ideals that have inspired the dharma of our womanhood from time immemorial.

It is true that all countries have produced great women. All religions too have given birth to men and women of exemplary character. But it cannot be claimed that the qualities mentioned above are as much a characteristic of life in other countries as it is in our own, in our religion and in our culture. To think of changing all this in the name of civilization or modernity would be to cut at the very roots of our great cultural and religious heritage.

A girl must become attached to her husband [that is she must be married] before her mind is disturbed by thoughts of love and desire and before she begins to take an interest in her body. The innocent child that she is now, she will have the humility to regard her husband in an attitude of surrender in the thought that he alone is her guru and that he alone is her Īśvara.

Women in Āndhra Prades and Mahārāṣtra even today observe many vratas[S]. Unmarried girls in these parts of the country worship Śiva, looking upon him as their husband. When they get married they worship the husband as Śiva. First a girl, before her marriage, worships Śiva as her husband; later whoever comes into her life as her husband she looks upon as Śiva.

In childhood a girl does not ask questions. It is now that she will, out of her simple faith, look upon her husband as Parameśvara. This faith, formed in her innocence, will take firm root in her mind when she becomes older and begins to understand things. It is all the influence of our ages-old dharma of womanhood. A woman's devotion to her husband will now be enduring and she will always look upon him as Parameśvara. When a wife dedicates herself to her husband and does not nurse any feelings of honour or dishonour so far as she herself is concerned, her ego will become extinct. And that means cessation from worldly existence; in other words, liberation. Devotion, jñāna, austerities, worship, sacrifices, yoga — all these have for their goal the eradication of the ego. This a woman obtains naturally and with ease through devotion to her husband.

There are such examples of womanhood in our land, women who were totally dedicated to the husband. In the ethos of our nation they are exalted even above the gods. Among them are Nalāyanī, Anasūyā, Sītādevī who was Mahālakṣmī herself, Dakṣa's daughter Satī who was indeed Parāśakti (the Supreme Goddess), Sāvitrī, Kaṇṇagī, Vāsukī (wife of Tiruvaḷḷuvar[T]). To think of them is to feel ecstatic with a sense of pride. We bow to them in respect at the very mention of their names. Why it is so we cannot say.

We often hear critics of our traditions exclaim thus: "The husband is God to the wife? It's just babble. It's all superstition. It's suppression of women. An outrage." Whatever the criticism be, this is the custom of our land. In this land called Bhārata we have the Himālaya and the Gangā. If you ask why they should be here, is there any answer? It is the same with the women who were queens of chastity. Do Europeans think of the Alps as we think of Kailāsa? Do we think of the Gangā in the same way as the Americans think of the Mississippi? Don't we experience in our hearts the divinity of our mountains and our rivers? For people in other countries marriage is only a family arrangement. Our śāstras have inspired our conjugal life with the ideal of surrender to the husband as the supreme means for the wife to obtain purity of the Self. If the system of child marriage is opposed and changed on the pretext of bringing about the social advancement of women, it will only serve the purpose of causing injury to their Ātmic advancement. It would mean creating a small convenience for our women at the expense of the very great spiritual reward that is theirs as the inheritors of our traditions.

To say that child marriage is harmful to a woman's body is empty talk. Though the girl is married as a child she will be ready for conjugal life only after she becomes physically mature. Besides on many days like the full moon and the new moon the couple will have to practise continence. Now such restrictions are not observed. Physical weakness has become more common among people and neurophysicians prosper at their expense.

That the system of early marriage led to the existence of child widows is said to be a blot on the Hindu religion. But the number of children who become widows is exaggerated, and the implication is that their husbands must have died when they were in the age-group of 15-25. From what I have heard there are few deaths in this age-group. So the number of child widows cannot be many. I would not deny their existence altogether. It is painful to see even one child becoming a widow. But considering the great benefits that child marriage brings we must make an allowance for misfortunes like young girls being widowed.

Even now, if she is so fated, where is the assurance that a girl married at the age of 20 or more will not become a widow when she is still young? We hear reports of couples who have been married only for two or three months being killed in rail or plane accidents. Such tragedies do create anguish. If the reason for banning child marriage is the phenomenon of child widows, what is the guarantee that girls married when they are older in years will not become widows?

If, according to the custom of our land, women are to look upon the husband as the Lord in order to be released from worldly existence, the only way to accomplish it is by following the śāstras. "Our women receive high education, manage jobs, marry as they like. All this means progress," we often hear such talk. But that they are exposed to the gaze of all and sundry, become mentally and emotionally disturbed and are trapped in awkward situations is a matter of constant worry to me, even fear.

Reformists rise in protest against child marriages and cry angrily: "Women are suppressed and are subjected to cruelties like child marriage. They are denied their social rights." But I feel angrier when I think of the fact that conditions created in the name of social reform have put the great family treasure of women in jeopardy, I mean their prized possession of chastity. In fact I feel like shedding tears. Like Arjuna I too feel like crying that "when women are spoiled the family, the clan, declines. No, the whole world will go to rot. And all will go to hell (Strīṣu duṣṭāsu Vārṣṇeya jāyate varṇasaṁkaraḥ.... Saṁkaro narakāy'aiva)[1]."

That women agree to be exposed like this, that their parents look on this with approval, burns me with anguish.

Leave aside all talk of progress or advancement. My constant worry is that our girls must not be exposed to risks to their character. People try to console me with the assurance that nothing untoward happens to our women because they go to school or college or because they work in offices. I too have not lost faith in our women. But I see that they go about as they please and that they have many opportunities to go astray. Cinema, fiction, newspapers — all these diversions are such as are calculated to cause them injury. All such things fill me with fear.

Now and then I do hear reports of unpleasant happenings involving women. How can we right a wrong, what can we do after all the damage has been done? Can we allow even a single incident to happen in this land of ours that brings a taint to its womanhood? It makes my blood boil to think of what is happening to women in our society. I seem to suffer all the worry and all the fear that parents ought to suffer about their daughters. I do not believe that all women will go astray or will be corrupted. Reformists say that the presence of even one child widow is a blot on our society. I am afraid that even if one woman goes astray or is corrupted it should be a blot on our society that is a thousand times worse.

Vedam odiya Vediyarkkoru mazhai
Nīti mannar neriyinukkor mazhai
Mādar karpuḍai maṅgayarkkor mazhai
Mādam mūnru mazhaiyenappeyume

To ensure that the king or the government will rule justly ("*Nīti mannan neri*") is not in my jurisdiction. But it is my responsibility to see that the Brahmin chants the Vedas ("*Vedam odiya Vediyarkkoru...*"). It is also my duty to see that women are not afforded the "chance" to stray from the path of virtue and chastity and that before a girl feels the urge of kāma she will learn to look upon her husband as Īśvara. Yes, it is my responsibility to see that women do not deviate a bit from pātivratya[S]. I feel that I must do all I can for this and I keep drawing up plans for the same. The goal is far off and it is receding faster than the speed with which I try to reach it. But I will not give up the race. Nor will I nod in approval of what is happening in the name of modernity. I have not been installed on this Pīṭha to watch helplessly the world go by and cry in despair: "What is lost is lost. It is impossible to stem the tide of Kali and change things."

From the remote past the Vedic tradition has flourished in this land, so too strīdharma[S]. These have been nourished by this Maṭha for some two thousand years. I have the title of "Jagadguru" and bear the name of Śankara Bhagavatpāda. I cannot therefore keep my mouth shut as this heritage of ours is being destroyed. There will be no greater offence than it. As Bhagavān says in the Gītā I must do my work in the belief that victory or failure is in his hands. I will not retrace my steps and shall keep exerting myself to achieve the goal. The result will depend on my sincerity, on my inner purity and on the intensity of my austerities. If no appreciable results are seen so far, it means that I am lacking in sincerity of purpose, mental purity and austereness. I feel so however much I am applauded by the world.

Had we lost all, I would not have spoken on this subject. If all is lost where is the need to put in any effort? The Maṭha itself may be disbanded. But all is not lost. A spark still remains. Proof of it is the presence of so many of you here wanting to listen to me. It does not matter whether or not you will do what I ask you to do. The fact is you keep listening to me patiently. That is why I tell you that there is a spark still left. I am trying to find out whether it could be fanned into a bright flame. If I too go the way that people go — that is the new way — I should be disloyal to Śankara Bhagavatpāda.

It does good — does it not? — to speak my mind and unburden myself of my feelings. You will remain devoted to me and I shall keep giving you my blessings: this relationship between us will continue. But if I fail to bring you to the path for which the Maṭha exists and yet accept money from you, it means that I am guilty of extortion. That is why I gave candid expression to my feelings.

With the grace of the Supreme Goddess we have had some success in implementing the plans drawn up for the preservation of our Vedic heritage. True we are far from having achieved the goal of ensuring that the scriptures are chanted in every home. But the fear that we once had felt that Vedic learning might become extinct by the next generation or so no longer exists. Today all over the country many students are learning not only to chant the Vedas but also to understand their meaning.

The Child Marriage Act has my hands tied. According to the Dharmaśāstra, a girl must be entrusted in the hands of a man, that is her husband, before she starts feeling the urge of kāma. She will then become steeped in the belief that he is her Lord. And when she begins to feel the natural urges she will dedicate her body to him. This is the law of the Dharmaśāstra. But the law of the state is contrary to the law of the Dharmaśāstra. Even so I will not ask you to disobey it. However, we must keep speaking untiringly of the law of the Dharmaśāstra and wait and see whether the government changes its mind.

Reference

[1] *Adharmābhibhavāt Kṛṣṇa praduṣyanti kula-striyaḥ*
Strīṣu duṣṭāsu Vārṣṇeya jāyate varṇasamkaraḥ

Saṁkaro narakāy'aiva kulaghnānāṁ kulasya ca
Patanti pitaro hyeṣāṁ luptapiṇḍ'o'daka-kriyāḥ

— Bhagavadgītā, 1.41 & 42

Chapter 7

Our Duty Now

Let the authorities take their own time to change their mind. What is our immediate duty? If the limit fixed by the law for a girl's marriage is 14, 16, 18 or whatever, let us celebrate it immediately on her attaining this age. We must prepare for the day in advance, deciding on the groom and making all other arrangements for the wedding. It would be reprehensible on our part to prolong the period of waiting after a girl begins to feel the biological urge and the consequent emotional disturbance. It is one thing if the marriage gets postponed owing to circumstances beyond our control, but quite another if we do not exert ourselves sufficiently to conduct it in time.

Chapter 8

Make Marriages Simple

Girls today are sometimes married at the age of 25 or 30, far beyond the limit fixed by the law. The inability to raise the money required for the wedding is one reason for this. All the ostentation at weddings, the dowry and other gifts given to the groom's people have no sanction in the śāstras. To demand a suit for the groom or a pair of boots, an expensive wrist-watch or other luxury articles is nothing but extortion. It is as good as milking the bride's party dry. This kind of plunder is not approved by the śāstras. So too the procession called "*jānavāsam*"[T], with all its glitter, taken out on the eve of the wedding as though it were an essential part of the ceremonies.

In the past, when the bride and groom were very young, the wedding included functions to keep the couple in good cheer since they would perhaps have felt uncomfortable before the smoke of the sacred fire. There were elements of play like *nalaṅgu*[T] and also the procession.

"Kanyām kanaka-saṁpannām" (the bride adorned with gold): these words occur in the śāstras relating to the marriage rites. Gold symbolises the grace of Lakṣmī but a maṅgalasūtra[S] with a grain of gold as part of it is enough. There is no need for other types of expensive jewellery, diamond studs, and so on. No silks are required. A cotton *sārī* will serve the purpose of the *kūrapuḍavai.*[T] Above all the custom of dowry must be scrapped. There is also no justification in holding a lavish wedding dinner for the whole neighbourhood. Nor is a music or dance recital needed. A big *paṇḍāl* too is not necessary.

Chapter 9

Duty of Motherhood

Our women must give up their fondness for diamonds and silks. This will be of great help to our family and social life. Indeed womanhood itself will stand to gain and strīdharma will flourish. Women should think of the millions of silkworms killed to make the *sārī* with which they drape themselves. They claim that they are vegetarians. So should they not feel remorse about being indirectly responsible for the destruction of countless silkworms because of their love of silk *sārīs*. If women of well-to-do families realise this and stop wearing silk, they will no longer set a bad example to their less fortunate sisters. It is because of the example of the wealthy that the poor too hanker after silks and diamonds. Then the groom's people bring pressure on the bride's parents for silks and diamond studs. This is one reason for the marriage of girls being delayed.

It is a crime to have turned the marriage saṁskāra into an economic problem. After all, we too have our daughters. That being so, merely because we belong to the groom's family, we cannot take an arrogant attitude and dictate terms to the bride's family, demanding this and that. We should not lay down conditions like Shylock and tell the girl's parents: "Give us a big dowry, bring us expensive vessels, bring us diamonds and silks." Such behaviour is unpardonable: it is one reason why girls remain unmarried, pining away at home. If you happen to be the groom's parents you must satisfy yourself about the girl's character, family, etc. "This girl will be the Lakṣmī of our home and she will brighten it" : with such thoughts you must accept the bride, without laying down any conditions for the marriage and without insisting that you must receive gifts in the form of money, jewellery and so on.

In this matter women have a special responsibility. They must naturally have respect and sympathy for fellow women. When they celebrate their son's marriage they must conduct themselves in the manner I suggested earlier. The presents given by other parents to their sons-in-law must not be an example for them to make similar demands. On the contrary, they must set an example to the parents of other prospective grooms, telling themselves: "Why should we be guilty of the sort of wrongs that others have committed? We will try to bring about a change and set an example for others to follow." This is how our motherhood must be motivated.

"We gave a dowry to the groom's people when our daughter was married." Or: "My father gave a dowry to my in-laws when I was married, so there is nothing wrong if I accept the same now." You must be warned against taking such an attitude. This evil custom of dowry that undermines our very dharma must be done away with. Someone must take the first step [take the lead] in a spirit of sacrifice. People make sacrifices in this or that cause. If their village is included in a neighbouring district a hundred or a hundred thousand people rise in protest and court arrest. Some of the agitators set fire to themselves. Shouldn't we make a little sacrifice in the cause of preserving the great ideals of our womanhood?

Women come to see me and seek my blessings, saying: "We recite the *Saundaryalaharī,*[S] the *Abhirāmi Antādi*[T]." What they do is commendable. But they would deserve the compassion of Ambā better if they sincerely followed my advice in the matter of marriage. They must not dictate terms regarding dowry, jewellery, gifts, and so on, and must agree to the marriage alliance with their whole heart. There are girls like them, or rather women, who are getting on in years but still remain unmarried. They are emotionally disturbed and nurse a hurt to their sense of honour because of their sad predicament, but may be later they will become so hardened as to have no feelings whatsoever. You must try to change the system that is responsible for the fate of such women. If your hearts melt in sympathy for them Ambā will also look upon you with a kindly eye.

You cannot justify the acceptance of a dowry and other gifts on the pretext that they are given by the girl's parents on their own. This can lead to others also doing the same and cause a bad chain reaction. If the girl's parents give a dowry on their own, they will expect the same from the parents of their son's bride. You must refuse a dowry even when it is given voluntarily. If the girl's people are wealthy you may tell them: "Don't give us any money. If you wish you may give it to your daughter in the form of strīdhana[S]."

The groom's parents spend on clothes, travel, etc, and expect the expenses to be "reimbursed" by the girl's parents. This is not at all justified. They must tell themselves: "Our son is getting married. Why shouldn't we ourselves spend for it? It is shameful to take money from someone else to buy our own requirements. Will it not mean that we can't afford them ourselves?" Unfortunately, people think that they have certain rights and privileges as the groom's parents and fleece the bride's people by intimidating or browbeating them. Whether the dowry is given voluntarily or out of compulsion, it is money stolen. It is all a vicious circle that causes injury to society itself. We must somehow see to it that this evil system of dowry is scrapped.

Chapter 10

Duty of the Bridegroom

Young men who are contemplating marriage can also help in the matter. Ordinarily, no son should go against the wishes of his parents. It would not be proper for me to ask young men to defy their parents. In any case, nowadays they do not obey their parents as they used to in the past. So I should not [normally] encourage children to go against the wishes of their parents. I am not unaware of all this. However, I find that immense damage is being done to our ancient strīdharma[S] by the money factor brought into the conduct of marriages.

In this context, I must ask young men to lend me their support. They must clearly tell their parents that they will agree to marry and settle down only on condition that the usual dowry and other gifts are not taken from the bride's parents. I feel I should even ask them to offer satyagraha[S] against the system of dowry. But if they are to be true to the spirit of satyagraha, they must not marry on their own on the plea that their parents did not listen to them. Satyagraha implies an element of sacrifice. The young men offering it must tell their parents firmly: "You say that you will not celebrate my marriage without taking a dowry. All right, I will not marry and will remain a bachelor if you don't change your mind." If young men are so determined there will be a change of heart in any mother or father. The biggest reform young men can help in bringing about is to stand firm in their refusal to accept any dowry. To take pride in an intercaste marriage or a "love marriage" is not right because that would be going against the śāstras. The duty of sons is to try and put an end to the dowry system. There can be no greater reform than this.

The Vedas equate mother, father and guru with Īśvara. I must repeat what I stated earlier that no son shall act against the wishes of his parents. But as a guru I would ask him (I have the label of guru, haven't I?) to make an exception in the matter of dowry. So, acting on my advice — the advice of a guru — he must plead with his parents that they must not take any dowry since it is against the śāstras. If necessary he must offer satyagraha to convince them of his determination and sincerity of purpose.

This oppressive system called dowry is a canker eating into our society. By excising it our young men will be doing a great service to society, at the same time giving an impetus for it to blossom again. They must work for the eradication of this evil not only out of faith in our religion but also as a duty towards fellow men.

Duty of the Bridegroom

Marriage is an ancient institution, a guarantee for the future of mankind and a dhārmic protection for society. That being so, young men must marry the girls chosen by their elders. But the dowry system is undermining the very foundations of society and young people ought to have nothing to do with it. If they have a duty to their parents, they have also a duty to society, haven't they? Thus it becomes obligatory on their part to refuse firmly to marry if their parents insist on taking a dowry. Such refusal will be a service done not only to the family and society but also to womanhood and religion. Young men must take a vow to act in the manner I have suggested and help in putting an end to the malignant system called dowry.

Chapter 11

Arrangements made by the Maṭha

Girls must be married at least at the age permitted by the law if not at the age of seven or eight. Towards this purpose we have started the Kanyakādāna Trust. Daughters of poor parents must not remain unmarried after they have attained puberty merely because they have no money. The Trust extends help to conduct their marriage on a modest scale. Much merit will be earned by contributing towards such marriage expenses.

Other communities have not degenerated to the same extent as have Brahmins. Among non-Brahmins the dowry system is not as oppressive. Their women do not go to college in such large numbers as their Brahmin sisters do, nor do they, like the latter, go about as freely wherever fancy takes them.

The Trust was created to help daughters of poor families. In my opinion, donations for the Kanyakādāna Trust and the Veda Rakṣaṇa Nidhi Trust must be accepted from Brahmins alone. The reason is that others ought not to be made to pay a penalty for the wrongs perpetrated by the Brahmin. The biggest offence he has committed is that of forsaking Vedic learning. By not conducting the marriage of his daughter at the minimum age permitted by the law he commits an offence equally grave. So it is his responsibility to support the arrangements made to remedy the wrongs done by him. Other communities must not be made to pay for the same. To do so would be to add to the list of his sins. After all, he takes up any calling today, does any job so long as it brings him money. He spends lavishly on clubs, on entertainment, and so on. So is it not reasonable that he should be asked to contribute to the two Trusts?

The Kanyakādāna Trust meets the expenses of the *tiru-māṅgalyam* (maṅgalasūtra[S]), the 18-cubit *sārī*, the *dhoti* for the groom, etc. It is ready to help in conducting a simple, inexpensive wedding.

The arrangements made for the Kanyakādāna Trust have not yielded the same satisfactory results as those made for the Veda Rakṣaṇa Nidhi Trust. Not much has been done to solve the problem for which the former body was started. I say this with great regret. The little bit we have done for the corrupted Brahmin community is like administering a concoction made of dried ginger to a man who has swallowed a crowbar[1]. Parents do not in the least worry about damming the swollen stream of adharma. So not many come forward to make use of the Trust. They are no longer worried about their daughters not being married at the right time. They take it easy while their daughters work and earn. What do we do with the Trust? Instead of looking for a groom, parents look for a man who can recommend their daughter for a job. Things have become so bad in our land — it is all so unfortunate. We extend help at best to hold some 50 marriages. Every year 5,000 women go to work[2]. Ten times that number go looking for a job. So only some 50 girls come to us for help to be married at the minimum age according to the law. The only purpose served by the Trust is that of giving me some satisfaction that I have not failed in my duty.

I have spoken frankly, without mincing words, in the hope that, with their sense of self-respect and sense of urgency aroused, parents will take timely steps to celebrate the marriage of their daughters without losing a moment after the girls are old enough for the same according to the law.

Notes

[1] This is a literal translation of the very expressive Tamiḷ idiom.

[2] This figure presumably applies to Tamiḷ Brahmins: the number of Brahmin women working today must be far more.

Chapter 12
The Real Reform

The law has stipulated the minimum age for marriage. I wish it had also stipulated the maximum age considering the attitude of people today. We are not in the least justified in blaming the law if girls aged 25 or 30 remain unmarried. The reason is our own indifference. Take the upanayana saṁskāra. After all, it does not come under the Sārda Act. Why then do we perform our son's upanayana together with his marriage when he is 30 years or so? It is all due to our indifference to our śāstras, our dharma.

Apart from this general apathy, most parents want to celebrate the upanayana and marriage on a lavish scale, indeed like festivities. Both get postponed since the money has to be raised. That even a lifetime's earnings are not sufficient to meet the expenses of a daughter's marriage is preposterous. The result is the saṁskāras are not performed at the proper time as required by the śāstras.

According to our scriptures money has nothing to do with these saṁskāras. That today it has come to be so is a tragedy — and it is a tragedy that is of our own making. In none of the eight forms of marriage does the groom have to be given any money. Even in the āsura type it is the groom that pays money, that is in exchange for the bride. If such a transaction is considered demoniac, what would the ṛṣis who authored our śāstras have thought of the prevailing custom of dowry, of the groom's parents telling the bride's people: "Give us your daughter in marriage and also cash." They could not have even imagined that such a custom would ever crop up. There obtained the custom of "kanyā-śulka" — money offered to the bride or "bride price" — which has some support in the canons. But you cannot find an iota of justification in our scriptures for the present dowry system.

Putting an end to this custom — this evil — is the marriage reform that is the true need of the country. Instead of carrying out such a reform, what we have done is to stipulate — in the name of reform — the minimum age of marriage for girls. And this has played havoc with our family and social life. I am referring to the present phenomenon of girls going to work. When it became difficult to find the money for the dowry, for the gifts to be made to the groom's people and for the lavish celebration of the wedding, the Sārda Act[1] came in handy by obviating the need to be in a hurry to hold the function.

Note

[1] The Sārda Act has been superseded by the new marriage laws enacted by the goverment of free India. Dowry has been made illegal but the evil persists in a more vicious form than in the past. The passages here dealing with dowry, marriage expenses and strīdharma are both moving and eloquent and are as relevent today as they were when the Paramaguru first spoke on the subject.

Chapter 13

Working Women

When the marriage of girls got delayed and they had to stay at home doing nothing, the parents wondered why their daughters should not study, go to work and start earning. The money would also come in handy when the girls were to be married. Thus started the practice of women going to work. At first the parents felt a little embarrassment or a sense of shame about doing something they thought to be improper, that is depending on the daughter's own earnings for her marriage expenses. They were also worried and fearful about the girls being exposed to various risks and temptations. But, in due course, this worry and fear vanished. Also the parents came to think that there was no need to feel awkward about their daughters going to work.

According to the Purāṇas, even royal sages like Janaka were worried that their daughters stayed at home without being married. They felt so uncomfortable as if they were carrying fire inside them. At first we felt sheepish that our women went out to work. But, by and by, we learned to accept it. Now we take it as an advance, a step forward in our civilization. Parents have thrown all sense of responsibility to the winds and are not worried in the least about their daughters going out to work and, indeed, they take pride in it. Our dharma has sunk to such low depths. Working girls come to me seeking my blessings for promotion in their office. Turning a blind eye to everything — seeing and not seeing — I have earned the name of being a good *Svāmiyār*[T]...

"That women are receiving higher education and are working is a great step forward," proclaim the reformists. "A great injustice done to them in the past has been undone," they add. My own view is that no injustice was ever done to women in the past and I would go to the extent of saying that, if at all any injustice was done, it was to men. You may be amused by this remark. Let me explain[1]. A male, after his student-bachelorhood, graduates to the stage of the householder. He has now to perform many duties and rituals like aupāsana and a number of other saṁskāras with the ultimate object of finding release from worldly existence. A woman attains the same goal by dedicating herself to her husband and to do so is to go beyond all the saṁskāras performed by a man. Though reformists think this to be an injustice done to women, to me it appears that the śāstras favour women more than they do men. I tell you why. How does a man realise himself? He has to perform many religious works; he has to learn the Truth and feel it inwardly through nididhyāsana[S]. In this way alone does he erase his mind.

A pativratā[S] does not need such difficult sādhana[S], such ardent and intense practice, to reach the same goal and all she has to do is to surrender to her husband. By respecting the wishes of her husband such a wife obliterates not only her own wishes, but all feelings of honour and dishonour and all ego-sense. In this way she comes close to stilling her mind. When the mind is utterly dedicated to another person in an attitude of surrender, should it not be close to being blotted out? Is there any "promotion" for a woman higher than this?

A woman exalted by inner purity occupies a position far higher than another who earns a promotion in her office. This is how many a woman in the history of this land won powers far greater than those earned even by the sages. According to Tiruvaḷḷuvar[T], if such a woman says, "Let there be rain", it will rain, it must rain. If she says to the sun, "Don't rise", it will not rise. Such a woman can retrieve her husband from Yama. Our śāstras, our traditions, give these women a place more elevated than that accorded to any sage or deity. We see from the Purāṇas that a woman of lofty character can transform even gods into little children by sprinkling water on them. Our religious texts speak about how a woman may rise to true heights of glory and how she is enshrined in a temple and worshipped. They do not ever condemn her to an inferior position. It seems to me that it is the reformists who do so by preventing her from rising to the heights of glory.

If marriage is one of the many saṁskāras to render a man pure, for a woman it is the single saṁskāra that gives her the ultimate fruits of all saṁskāras. Now the essence of this saṁskāra is cast away and what remains, the refuse, is retained. Marriage and the householder's stage of life are not meant for carnal pleasure alone. They constitute a path for liberation. If this truth is understood people will appreciate that the role assigned to women by the śāstras is just and proper.

Few seem to have realised the undesirable economic consequences of women going to work. I am referring to the unemployment problem. Until some years ago parents had this excuse for their daughters going to work : "Let her work till she gets married. Otherwise she will have to stay at home brooding over things and being sorry for herself. Going to work will be a way of spending the time. Besides, the girl's earnings will come in handy for the dowry and other expenses of marriage." The idea then was to let the daughter work until her marriage and then ask her to resign her job. The groom and his people thought it demeaning for the bride to work after the marriage.

This attitude changed not before long. How? During the past one century or so, the Brahmin community has developed an increasing appetite for money. Owing to this greed that grew with the years, girls going to work even after their marriage became a more widely accepted practice. The result is that the noble duties of motherhood like child care are neglected. It is the same as in Western countries and there is no warmth and sincerity governing relationships involving parents and children and other family members.

On the economic front too the phenomenon of more and more women working has had an undesirable consequence. These days hundreds of thousands of young men are unemployed. At the same time, in some families both husband and wife work and earn. If the husband alone worked, the wife's job would go to a young man who is without work. Unfortunately, husbands no longer take pride in caring for the wife and family with their earnings alone; they want the wife also to earn. At first the parents reluctantly sent their daughters to work. Then the husband did the same perhaps half-heartedly. As for the wife, she is now proud to be working. In fact, she is so used to working outside that she does not like being confined to her home. When she earns on her own she wants to spend as she likes without being questioned by her husband.

To stay at home does not mean to be locked in. There is no shortage of śāstras and Purāṇas in Sanskrit and in other languages. If women develop a taste for them, they will keep reading them for a whole lifetime and find happiness. They may form satsanga[S] groups and read such books by turns at home. There is no need to form a club or some other organisation nor any board. The satsanga may be held at home without any office-bearers like president, secretary, committee members and so on. I suggest this to avoid contests and rivalry for positions. Women may also keep themselves occupied in making pure kumkuma from turmeric and in collecting unbroken rice grains ("akṣata") for use in maṭhas, temples and other religious establishments. To stay at home does not mean being caged in while doing such work. Besides, women will not lose their most precious possession, femininity. Work mentioned above will be a means for the freedom of their Self and for bliss.

For women, surely, this is far better than going to work out of greed and losing their femininity in the process, not to speak of earning the higher reward of Ātmic well-being. It is also in keeping with a woman's nature. For a woman to work in an office on the pretext that she is otherwise confined to the four walls of her home is the cause of so many problems, so many evils. Though there is much talk of women's liberation, what we actually see is that they have to work under so many people and have to be answerable to so many of them. Is there peace in such a life? In the liberation that is so much talked about, is there the bliss of domestic life? Are working women able to cook at leisure, eat in peace, and enjoy the warmth and affection of children?

What purpose is served by all such talk? Each man thinks of his own selfish interests and is least bothered about others. People never pause to wonder whether others suffer on their account. There is no feeling for others, no sense of justice. In some families there is "double income" because both husband and wife earn while in some others even one member does not have a job and so has no income. It is a sad state. If women decide not to work after their marriage it is possible that the vacancies thus created will be filled by the unemployed men. Families without any means so far will then benefit. Working women must think about this and those who try to bring equality between men and women ought to consider the logic behind my observations.

Nowadays people do not know where to apply the principle of equality and where not to. Each entity or aspect of life has its own way of being, its own character; that is how life in the universe is ordained. It is wrong to contend that there must be a sameness about everything, that all things must be equal. To insist on such sameness and equality is to wreck the natural order of life. Each finds its fulfilment and true happiness in being related to another as intended by nature and in promoting the common social life. To pursue an arbitrary kind of equality instead of this means not only the denial of happiness on the individual level but jeopardizing family and social life.

Nature has assigned the job of child-bearing to women. However much we fight for equality we cannot change this fact of life. It is the natural dharma of women to care for children and to be Gṛhalakṣmīs. They do not lose anything by doing so, nor do they become superior in any sense by refusing to do it. Equality in such matters has no meaning.

Note

[1] The Paramaguru is speaking of the duties of men according to the śāstras and not obviously referring to the present condition.

Chapter 14

Any Use Talking...?

Saṁskāras such as marriage are akin to making chillis less hot by tempering them with ghee: they serve to tame the natural urges. We add ghee to the chilli so that it does not inflame the intestines. Carnal pleasure and worldly enjoyment are part of the life of a householder but they are kept within certain limits so that he is not overcome by them. For a woman a life of chastity and loyalty to her husband, together with the care of the household, constitutes a saṁskāra that is equivalent to all the saṁskāras prescribed for her husband put together. All of us must recognise this fact.

The goal of this nation is Ātmic well-being. We must all pray with a pure heart to Īśvara that we remain true to this goal. As we pray, we must have also faith in the Lord's grace. If we keep speaking about the ideals of marriage and womanhood, one day perhaps people will see the light. As things stand now, I am afraid that one day our people will be pushed to the wall. That will be the time when they will realise how they brought disaster upon themselves. When they have such an awakening they will recognise the need to find a way out of their predicament. That is why I keep speaking about the path shown by the śāstras.

"What purpose is served today by speaking about varṇāśrama, child marriage and so on?" This is a natural question. "Three-quarters of it is all gone. Many aspects of our life are governed by the laws of the state and these are contrary to the ordinances of the śāstras." This is true. The laws are such as to have our hands tied.

We are called a "secular state". It means, we are told, a state that does not concern itself with matters of religion. It further means that the government can interfere only in social matters and not in religious affairs. But ours is a religion in which all aspects of life, individual and social, are woven together. So the laws enacted by the state to govern social life have an impact on our religion too. Our rulers do not recognise or accept this fact. They limit their view of religion to certain matters and think that all else belongs to the social sphere and are the concern of the government.

All religions contain features that relate to the social life of their followers. Does the government interfere with them as it does with the social foundations of Hinduism? No. It is this fact that causes us pain. Though our rulers swear by the principle of secularism, they do not apply the same standard or yardstick to all religions. The minorities rise in protest against measures affecting their religious life introduced by the government. "These are against the Qu'rān," the cry is raised. Or, if the people affected are Christians, they say: "These are not in keeping with Christian doctrines." Yielding to such pressure, the government exempts the minorities concerned from the scope of the measures.

In spite of its claim to being secular, the government thinks it fit to interfere with anything that has to do with the Hindu traditions. Representatives of the minority communities come forward to speak in protest against acts of interference. But what about the Hindus? Even if a couple of Hindus speak up they are dubbed "reactionaries" or "obscurantists" and the government goes ahead with its measures or laws brushing them aside. Our rulers often proclaim that "a secular state means a state that does not concern itself with any religion, that it does not mean that the government is opposed to religion as such, and that the prosperity of all religions is acceptable to the state." But in actual practice what do we see? The government's actions are not opposed to any religion barring Hinduism. The Hindu religion has become a no-man's land.

You will wonder why I am harping all the time on śāstric matters fully aware though I am of what is happening in the country.

My answer is that, whatever the present situation be, we cannot foresee how things will take shape in the future. In the previous generation we thought dollars grew in the American soil and that people there were not wanting in anything. But what is the situation there today? We now know that no other people experience the same lack, the same emptiness, in their lives as do the Americans. It is only after reaching the heights of worldly pleasure that the realisation has dawned on them that the very pursuit of pleasure has created a void in their lives, an emptiness in their very Self. They realise that, floating as they did in a sea of dollars, they were drawn to all kinds of evil like drinking, loot, murder and prostitution. Now as they have no peace of mind they come to our country in large numbers seeking peace in our yoga, in our philosophy and in our devotional music.

We learn from this that what seemed good two or three generations ago is now seen to be evil. When people realise this they go in quest of liberation. The government, however well intentioned it be, has introduced measures that are against the śāstras, thinking that they are good. But some day in the future people will realise that they are harmful. Even today we see signs of such realisation on the part of people here and there. There is a saying: "In the beginning it looked so good. It was like a colt but as the days passed...well, it was seen in its true form." The same could be said about some of the reforms introduced by the government, reforms contrary to the śāstras. They look fine now but eventually we will realise that they will lead to a hopeless situation in society. Bhagavān speaks of two types of happiness in the Gītā[1]. "Yad tad agre viṣamiva, pariṇāme'mṛtopamam." Here the first type is described. This type of happiness is like poison in the beginning but like ambrosia, amṛta, in the end. It is the sāttvika or the highest type of happiness, like "hālāhala", the terrible poison, emerging first and amṛta coming up later[2]. The śāstras may now seem to be bitter like poison because of the discipline they impose on the individual, the family and society, but in due course they will be seen to be sweet. Now all bonds, all shackles will break and the incomparable bliss of Ātmic freedom will be experienced. Here the poison is tasted momentarily but the amṛta will be everlasting.

"Yad tad agre'mṛtopamam pariṇāme viṣamiva," here the second type of happiness is referred to. In the beginning this type of happiness will taste sweet like ambrosia but, with the passage of time, it will turn bitter like poison. In America the dollar once tasted sweet like nectar but later turned bitter like poison. In India too, the reforms that are contrary to the śāstras "taste" good now but they will be found to be poison in the times to come, when both the individual and society will suffer in the absence of contentment as well as discipline. People will then seek the amṛta. Should they not know where they can find it? But by then the poison will have gone to their head and they will be in danger. So it is our duty to tell them where they can find the amṛta. It is for them, for future generations, that we must keep speaking about the śāstras instead of burying them deep in the earth.

Even though we ourselves do not imbibe the śāstric nectar today we must preserve the śāstras to help future generations when they will have become spiritually weak because of the poison going to their head. This lamp of the śāstras should show the way at least in the times to come.

Nothing can be done now because I have my hands tied. But if I keep speaking to you unceasingly about the śāstras it is because I am not yet gagged.

References

[1] *Yat tad agre viṣamiva pariṇāme'mṛtopamam*
Tat sukhaṁ sāttvikaṁ proktam Ātma-buddhi-prasādajam

Viṣayendriya-saṁyogād yat tad agre'mṛtopamam
Pariṇāme viṣamiva tat sukham rājasaṁ smṛtam

—Bhagavadgītā, 18.37&38

[2] The reference here is to the "Churning of the Ocean".

Chapter 15

Marriage Expenses and the Śāstras

Even if it is not possible for us to celebrate a marriage according to the śāstras in respect of the age of the bride, could we not be true to their tenets at least in the matter of expenses? As I have made it clear so often a marriage has nothing to do with questions of money in any sense. Even though we have neither the will nor the courage to act according to the śāstras in all matters, we could at least see to it that marriages are not turned into what may be called an economic problem; in other words we could follow the cononical texts at least in conducting weddings more economically.

The marriage ceremony is in fact almost as inexpensive a rite as sandhyāvandana[S]. How much is to be spent on it? The newly-weds have to be presented with new clothes (cotton will do), a *tirumāṅgalyam* (maṅgala-sūtra) with a piece of gold attached to it. Only a few close relatives need be fed. At the time of the muhūrta[S] an auspicious instrument must be played. This will cost you a small sum. The other expense is the dakṣiṇā paid to the priest. All this is fully in accord with the śāstras. Even a poorly paid clerk can perform his daughter's marriage in this simple manner.

If wealthy people make marriages a lavish or showy affair, it would be a bad example for others not so wealthy. The money they otherwise spend on a music or dance recital or on other items that add glitter to the wedding must be used for marriages in poor families. This means that money that is otherwise wasted is converted into dhārmic currency. It should be possible for every affluent man to celebrate the marriage of his daughter economically and save money with which a poor girl can be married and made happy. "Mass marriages" may be conducted in the same way as "mass upanayana".

The rent charged for the *paṇḍāl* itself [or the "hall" or maṇḍapa] takes up half the wedding expenses. You cannot hold a marriage ceremony in a flat even on a small scale. Philanthropists should join together to construct small maṇḍapas in various localities for the marriage of the daughters of less fortunate people.

There was a time when girls blushed when the very word marriage was mentioned. Then came a time when young women waiting to be married pined away at home, cried their hearts out, wondering whether they would be married at all. Now things have come to such a pass that women are on their own, not married and working like men[1] in offices. The very life-breath of our culture, strīdharma[S], is being stifled. We hear reports of unseemly incidents happening here and there.

What is particularly tragic is that no one seems to be concerned about finding a remedy for all the unhappy occurrences. What is worse, these happenings are sought to be justified in terms of psychology, this and that. Stories are written on the undesirable incidents and films produced based on them and encouragement given to wrong-doing. If we question the people who give such encouragement they turn back and speak to us about freedom of imagination, freedom of art, and so on. In this republican age there is freedom for everything except for the pursuit of the śāstras.

I started by saying that according to the scriptures questions of money have no place in the marriage ceremony. Talking of marriage expenses, I must consider the complaint that a wedding lasting four days (which is how it ought be celebrated) can be very expensive.

The śāstras do not ask you to perform rituals likely to impoverish you. The marriage proper, the solemnisation of the wedding, is a one-day affair. The groom must spend the following three days in his own house observing brahmacarya[S]. During these days there is no need for any music, nor any *nalangu*[T], or any other celebration. Let those who want to reform the marriage ceremony, think of changing it in this manner.

The groom's people must tell the bride's parents: "The marriage proper will be celebrated in your house. The remaining three days' functions will be held in our house without your having to spend anything." On the day following the marriage the householder (the young man just married) must bring the "aupāsanāgni" (the sacred fire in which the aupāsana is performed) to his home. There are mantras to be chanted as this fire is being brought, as it is placed on the cart, as the bullocks are yoked to the cart, etc. You may do the same nowadays if you go by car or train. In the old days marriage alliances were formed between families living in neighbouring villages. So it was easy to carry the auspicious fire from the bride's to the groom's house.

The four-day function may be performed in another way also. The place where the marriage is celebrated is to be treated as the groom's house. Or the three-day function may be conducted in the house of a relative. No one need be invited for food, not even the girl's family. (The śāstras do not permit the completion of the marriage rites in a single day.) The priest has to be paid a dakṣiṇā — this is the only expense.

Marriage Expenses and the Śāstras

According to the śāstras, the groom must observe what is called "saṁvatsara dīkṣā" from the day of marriage (dīkṣā for one year); he must practise brahmacarya during these months. The marriage is to be consummated only later. Such practices have however changed. Until the recent past, the groom observed dīkṣā at least for four days if not for a whole year. Now everything is performed on a single day. One is reminded of the saying: "The donkey is reduced to an ant and the ant itself eventually vanishes into thin air."

During the marriage, Āndhras wear cotton clothes dipped in turmeric water. However well-to-do they are they follow this simple custom. In the North too[2] women wear ordinary clothes at weddings. We must try to follow their practice.

One of the marriage rites is "praveśa homa"[S] which is performed when the groom returns to his house. He has to carry the sacred fire of the marriage with him and perform aupāsana in his home. It is for the sake of convenience — and with the approval of the śāstras —— that it is allowed to be done where the groom's party stays for the marriage. To perform a marriage in a temple as a one-day ceremony — and "be done with it" — is not right. Even rich people who spend lavishly on clubs and races follow this practice because of their reluctance to conduct the function according to the śāstras. Unfortunately, the poor are likely to follow their example. There is no extra expense involved in performing a marriage in the śāstric manner as a four-day function.

How are marriages celebrated today? The bride is one who has already attained puberty and the marriage is gone through in just one day. On the following day the bride is taken to the house of her in-laws. Another unśāstric practice is that of consummation on the same day as the marriage.

The groom is expected to observe brahmacarya at least for three nights after marriage. There are eight types of brahmacarya. Even though a man cannot be continent throughout, he must remain chaste at least on certain days. The least that is expected of him is celibacy for a minimum of three days after the marriage. This rule is no longer observed. Worse, the consummation, as mentioned before, is on the same day the wedding is solemnised.

The undesirable practices now associated with the marriage saṁskāra are due to the anxiety to curtail expenses. If all rites are performed on the same day there is a saving in the matter of feeding the guests, the music, etc. Curiously enough, despite such an anxiety to curtail expenses, there is a great deal of ostentation in our weddings. To obviate the expenses incurred thus, parents perform the upanayana of their son along with the marriage of their daugther.

We must try to reduce the unnecessary expenses incurred in performing Vedic saṁskāras. Friends and relatives can help much in this respect. They need not attend a marriage or upanayana even if invited. Instead, the money that they would otherwise spend in travel may be presented to the bride's [or the brahmacārin's] father. The fewer the invitees present at a wedding the less expensive will it be to feed them.

Notes

1 The term the Paramaguru uses here is "udyoga-puruṣīs": it is his own coinage and conveys sharply how unhappy he was about women going out to work. (Incidentally, the word "udyoga" here is used in the special sense in which it is popularly understood in the South, that is as a job.)

2 This seems no longer true today.

Chapter 16

Three Ways to Economy

I feel that the marriage expenses could be reduced in three ways. First, both men and women must discard silks and other costly wear and use clothing of the lowest quality. Second, coffee must be given up; instead wheat *kañji* or buttermilk may be taken as a substitute. I say this because coffee[1] has become a habit and a substitute may be needed for those who find it difficult to give it up. According to medical science buttermilk is as good as amṛta (ambrosia). Expenses will be reduced by 60 per cent in this way. If you check on the money you spend on rice and on milk and coffee, you will find that you spend more on the last two items than on the first. Third, you must refuse to take a dowry. If this advice of mine is taken there will be no room for ostentation or vanity in our life. At the same time, apart from better physical health, there will be inner advancement. Above all, śāstric life and traditions will be revived.

Note

[1] The Paramaguru refers here to the near compulsion in the South of entertaining guests with coffee.

Chapter 17

Ideals of Marriage

The Vedas are learned during the years of student-bachelorhood. Then the "theory" taught has to be put into practice; in other words the rites prescribed in the Vedas must be performed. For this purpose a man has to take a helpmate after he has completed his brahmacaryāśrama[S]. This helpmate is a "property" that can never be separated from him. She is meant not only to be a cook for him, not only one to give him sensual gratification. She is called "dharma-patnī" and also "yajña-patnī." She has to be with her husband in the pursuit of dharma and has also to be a source of encouragement in it. As a dharma-patnī, she has to be by his side during the performance of sacrifices; she must also play a supportive role in all those rituals that have the purpose of making the divine powers favourable to mankind.

It must be noted that a wife creates well-being for the world even as she does the work of cooking or as a source of sensual gratification for her husband. I will tell you how. It is not that she cooks for the husband alone. She has to provide food every day to the guests, to the sick and to birds and beasts and other creatures. This is how she serves the purpose of "ātithyam"[S] and "vaiśvadevam"[1]. The children born to her are not to be taken as the product of the pleasure she affords her husband. She gives birth to them to perpetuate the Vedic dharma. Yes, even the raising of sons is intended for the dhārmic life of the future. No other religion has before it such a goal for the marriage saṁskāra.

In our religion the man-wife relationship is not concerned with the mundane alone. It serves the Ātman as well as the good of mankind. In other religions too marriages are conducted, say, in a church with God as witness. But their ideal of marriage is not as lofty as ours. The purpose of marriage in our religion is to purify the husband further and to impart the wife fullness as his devoted and self-effacing companion. There is no such high purpose in the marriage of other religions. In other countries the man-woman relationship is akin to a family or social contract. Here it is an Ātmic connection. But this very *connection* is a means of *disconnection* also — of freeing the Ātman, the Self, from the bondage of worldly existence. There is no room for divorce in it. Even to think of it is sinful.

[To sum up and further explain] the three objectives of a saṁskāra of so elevated a character as marriage. The first is to unite a man with a helpmate after he has completed his study of the Vedas. This helpmate is expected not only to run his household but assist him in the practice of the Vedic dharma. The second is to bring forth into this world children of noble outlook and character who are to be heirs to the great Vedic tradition, citizens of the future who will be the source of happiness in this world. The third is to create a means for women to be freed from worldly existence. A man who is not yet fully mature inwardly is assisted in his karma by his wife. By doing so, by being totally devoted to her husband, she achieves maturity to a degree greater than he does. The fourth objective is the subordination of sensual gratification to the other three.

We have forgotten the first three important objectives. All that remains is the fourth, the enjoyment of carnal pleasure. If people take my advice in respect of the noble ideals of marriage as taught in the śāstras a way will open out to them for their inner advancement. May Candramaulīśvara bless them.

Reference

[1] That is manuṣyayajña and bhūtayajña — dealt with in Chapter 5, Part Nineteen.

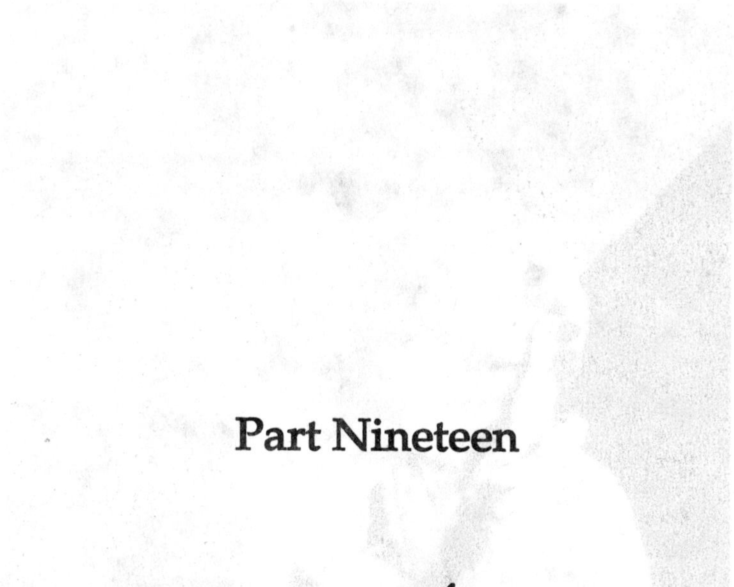

Part Nineteen

GṚHASTHĀŚRAMA

Chapter 1

Gṛhastha, Gṛhiṇī

After a young man has completed his gurukulavāsa[S] and performed the samāvartana[S], he has to wear a "double sacred thread"[1]. He must discard the marks of his student-bachelorhood — the staff, the antelope skin, the girdle — and wear the pañcakaccha[S] and an upper cloth. As a celibate-student he was not permitted to use any footwear; he could not also adorn himself with sandal-paste, ear-studs and flowers. He may now even darken his eyes with lampblack. Adorning himself and putting up his umbrella he must approach the king or a royal representative. The latter must be impressed by his learning and the quality of his brahmacarya. The young man now must acquire [from the king or the royal representative] money and material as a gift for his marriage, so say the śāstras.

One point that emerges from this is that the marriage expenses are to be borne by the groom or his parents. A second point is that a young man who has had his samāvartana must wear the "double sacred thread" and pañcakaccha even if he remains single. One's strength or potency is preserved by wearing a cloth whose ends are pleated, or made into folds, and tucked in. Muslims have the ends of their clothes sewn together. Even people who do not belong to the twice-born castes — except in Tamiḷ Nāḍu and Keraḷa — tuck in their *dhoti* or *veṣṭi,* not to speak of the pañcakaccha. (Today even when they come to see me people come in trousers. That being the case it is ridiculous or meaningless to speak of differences between the two types of wear.)

In these days there is neither gurukulavāsa nor samāvartana nor the pilgrimage to the Gaṅgā. But there is an extra "item" in weddings called "*Paradeśi-k-kolam*"[T] just to extort money or gifts from the bride's family. The groom is presented with an umbrella, a pair of sandals and a walking stick. A ceremony called "Kāśiyātra" (the pilgrimage or journey to Kāśī) is conducted in which the groom darkens his eyes with lampblack and wears a gold chain.

Those who do not marry and remain "naiṣṭhika brahmacārins" (lifelong brahmacārins) are exceptions to the rule that no man ought to remain even a single moment without belonging to one of the āśramas. That is after the proper conclusion of his student- bachelorhood he has to prepare to become a householder.

The Brahmin is born with three debts: he owes a debt to the sages, to the celestials and to the fathers. He repays the first by learning the Vedas as a student-bachelor; the second by taking a wife and performing sacrifices; and the third by begetting a son. So without marriage he cannot repay the second and third debts.

Sons are primarily intended for the repayment of the debt to the fathers. Performing the śrāddha[S] ceremony is not enough. Forefathers of the past three generations are to be made to ascend from the manes. So even after a man dies, for two generations the daily libations must be offered to him. That is why the birth of a son is considered important. (The case of the naiṣṭhika brahmacārin and the sannyāsin is different. Because of their inner purity and enlightenment, they can liberate, not just two generations, but twenty-one generations of fathers without performing any śrāddha ceremony.)

Pāṇigrahaṇa (the groom taking the hand of the bride in his), māṅgalya-dhārana[S], saptapadī (the bridal pair taking the seven steps round the sacrificial fire) are important rites of the marriage function. There is a controversy about whether or not māṅgalya- dhāraṇa is a Vedic rite. It is an unnecessary controversy. Māṅgalya- dhāraṇa is a custom that is thousands of years old and it is an essential part of the marriage saṁskāra.

As I said before, after completing his student-bachelorhood a young man must take a wife for the pursuit of dharma. The latter should dedicate herself to him so as to become pure within. The purpose of marriage is a life of harmony and the procreation of virtuous children.

Gṛhasthāśrama is called *illaram* in Tamiḷ and it is extolled by the wise in the Tamiḷ country also. "Gṛha" means a house. A young man who returns to his house from the guru's and practises dharma is a "gṛhastha". One who resides in a house, a gṛha, is a gṛhastha. The Tamiḷ wife calls her husband *"ahamudayān", "ahattukāran", "viṭṭukkāran"*: these terms have to do with the house or the home. Only the wife can refer to her husband thus, not others. She herself is called "gṛhiṇī", not "gṛhasthā". The latter would mean no more than "one who resides in a house". But "gṛihiṇī" means that the house belongs to her (the wife), that she manages the household. The husband is *illarattān* in Tamiḷ and it means one who performs the dhārmic rites in the house,*"il-arattān"*[1]. The wife is *"illāḷ"*, one who owns the house.

The husband is not called *illān* (*illān,* as it happens, means one who does not possess anything or one who is indigent). The wife is also called *illattaraśi* (queen of the house), *"manaivi"* (owner of the house), or *"manaiyāḷ"*; but the husband does not have similar appellations like *"illattaraśan"* (king of the house), *"maṇaivan"* or *"manaiyān"* (owner of the house). In Teḷugu the wife is called *"illu"* (corresponding to the *illāḷ* of Tamiḷ).

Notes

1 What is called the "sacred thread" or yajñopavīta has three strands that are knotted together. Two such sacred threads make a "double sacred thread".

2 "*Il-arattān*" : "*il*" means house and "*aram*" from which "*arattan*" is derived is dharma

Chapter 2

Aupāsana

Pāṇigrahaṇa, māṅgalya-dhāraṇa, saptapadī and other rites are performed on the day of the wedding. Aupāsana begins with marriage and is performed every day until one becomes a sannyāsin or until one's death. The sacred fire that is witness to the marriage is preserved throughout and aupāsana performed in it every day.

The sacred fire has an important place in the Vedic religion. The student-bachelor performs samidādhāna[S] twice a day offering samidhs (sticks of the flame of the forest or palāśa) in the fire. This rite is not continued after his marriage. When a person becomes a householder he has a number of rites to perform in the sacred fire. In place of the samidādhana he now has the aupāsana. The latter word is derived from "upāsana" which term is used in the sense of pūjā, chanting of mantras, meditation, etc. But, according to the Vedas, aupāsana is a rite performed in the sacred fire by all Hindus.

Though members of the fourth varṇa do not wear the sacred thread they have the marriage saṁskāra and, along with it, aupāsana. Dharmaśāstras like the *Vaidyanātha-Dīksitīyam* describe how Śūdras are to go through the jātakarma[S] and nāmakaraṇa[S] ceremonies. The work deals with how the fourth varṇa should perform pūjā, the śrāddha ceremony and apara-karma (obsequies). Reformers ignore all these and allege that members of the fourth varṇa have no "right" to any rituals. Instead they must try to persuade people of this varṇa to perform the rites they are enjoined upon. Aupāsana is one of the "rights" of this caste and it is to be conducted every day with the recitation of certain verses.

Chapter 3

Can a new Brahmin Caste be Created?

The fact that aupāsana is to be performed by all castes gives rise to the question: "Why only aupāsana? Why should not all castes have the right to learn the Vedas, chant the Gāyatrī and perform sacrifices?" On the one hand, we have atheists who want the Vedas to be consigned to the flames and the idols of gods like Gaṇeśa to be broken and, on the other, we have people calling themselves reformists who want to extend to all the right to perform Vedic rites.

Do I not lambaste Brahmins for having become a degenerated class? Taking a cue from this the reformers argue: "After all, it is the Brahmin who has become debased and it is he who has debased others also. Now, when new life is being breathed into the Vedic dharma, why should Brahmins alone be given the right to it, Brahmins who have failed in their duty? All those castes that believe that the Vedas and Vedic works are essential to the well-being of mankind must be enabled to learn the Vedas and perform Vedic rites. All of them must have the right to wear the sacred thread and learn the scriptures."

Organisations like the Ārya Samāj have accepted the right of all to learn the Vedas and perform sacrifices. Here and there a Subrahmaṇya Bhāratī[T] or someone like him imparts Brahmopadeśa[S] to a Pañcama[S]. The reformists ask why the Vedas cannot be made common to all.

This is not acceptable in the least. I am a representative and spokesman of the śāstras. It is my duty to state that this (making Vedic dharma common to all castes) is not permitted by the sages who created the śāstras and assigned the duties special to each caste. They (the sāges) were known for their spirit of sacrifice and impartiality and they had no interest other than the happiness of mankind.

A man sins in two ways. If he forsakes his hereditary karma, he commits one kind of sin — such a man is called a "karma-bhraṣṭa". But if he forsakes his karma and takes up the karma of another (that is if he practises the religious customs and duties of another caste) he becomes a "karmāntara-praviṣṭa". According to the śāstras he is guilty of a greater offence than the karma-bhraṣṭa.

Why? There are two reasons.

An individual who forsakes his karma because he believes that varṇa dharma itself is meaningless may be said to act out of conviction and he may be said to be obeying his conscience. In his action we may find some justification. But, in the matter of the śāstras, the question is not one of conscience. The question is: What about the man who opts for the customs and rites of another? He does so because he believes that the customs and rites to which he is born are not as good as those of the latter. To think that one vocation or one type of work is inferior to another, or superior to it, is not in keeping with modern ideas of socialism and the principle of dignity of labour. At the same time, it is not also in accord with the ancient śāstras. The karma-bhraṣṭa who discards all varṇa dharma believes that the sages created a system not suitable to the times. He does not, however, think that they were partial to some castes. But not so the karmāntara-praviṣṭa who thinks that the sages were partial. He chooses another man's dharma because he believes that it is better for his inner advancement than his hereditary calling and dharma. His action implies that the sages practised deception by creating the division of varṇas. So his offence is greater.

It is true that Brahmins have gone astray. But what is the meaning of creating a new class of Brahmins? It amounts to saying, "He (the Brahmin) has forsaken his dharma. Now I will take it over." To take up another man's dharma, apart from forsaking one's own, is a grave offence, worse than merely giving up one's own dharma. I have stated repeatedly that all karma has only one purpose, that of destroying one's ego-sense, ahaṁkāra[S]. What is the foundation of varṇa dharma? It is one's willingness to follow the vocation and dharma that belong to one by heredity without any consideration of one's likes and dislikes.

Such willingness is based on the realisation that the vocation and dharma that have come to us are according to the will of Īśvara, that they are manifested through the Vedas and śāstras and that to practise them is to destroy our ego.

What does it mean to create a new caste, to create new Brahmins? However good the intention behind such a process may be — even if it be the desire that Vedic works must be performed and that the sound of the Vedas must fill the air — the ego-consciousness will obtrude in it like the nut jutting out from a cashew fruit.

Apart from this, however much you may talk of equality and rationalism, the newly created Brahmins will suffer from an inferiority complex and will be racked by doubts as to whether they can practise their new dharma and whether they can chant the mantras and practise the rites in the same manner as people who are Brahmins by birth.

The Ārya Samāj and other reformist organisations have for their part abolished caste and given everybody the right to learn the Vedas. Then how is it that non-Brahmins have not joined these organisations in large numbers or taken to the study of the Vedas? One important reason is a certain hesitation in joining anything new. Another, equally important, is that people believe that it is one thing to become an atheist but quite another for the old Vedic customs to be changed.

So, though a couple of reformers may start a movement to throw open Vedic learning to everybody, only four or five per cent of the people will join them. The remaining 95 per cent or so will continue to be in the old Hindu set-up. Also the few who join the new caste will have at heart a sense of fear and a feeling of inferiority. They will keep doubting whether their actions will yield the desired results. If that be so, how will their minds be pure? It is not only the ego-sense that makes the mind impure but fear, the feeling of inferiority and being racked by doubts. Rites performed in such a frame of mind will not serve the purpose of creating happiness in the world. Besides, members of the new caste are likely to develop conceit thinking that they are doing what Brahmins by birth ceased to do or could not do — there will be a spirit of challenge in their action. When they practise what others were practising [or were expected to practise] there will naturally be a desire on their part to make an exhibition of it. There will be no sincerity in their actions. All told, neither they nor the world will benefit from their works.

We must recognise facts for facts and not be carried away by emotions. Have I not told you about the power of the sound of the Vedas? This sound is not produced easily by everybody in the right manner. What I say applies not only to the sound of the Vedas or the Vedic language but also to other languages and their sound. Take the case of German or Urdu. Some words in these two languages are tongue-twisting. Telugu is spoken in our neighbourhood[1] but we find it difficult to vocalise some of its sounds. Suppose a German child or a Muslim or Telugu child were to be born in Tamiḷ Nāḍu. These children would be able to pronounce such words easily — that is German, Urdu or Telugu as the case may be — because to them they would come naturally.

However vehemently you may deny the existence of hereditary factors, you find evidence of the same every day in all spheres. Those who have been the custodians of the Vedas all these centuries will find it easy to learn and chant the Vedas despite the present gap of two or three generations in their tradition. The same cannot be said of other communities. The mantras will serve no purpose if they are wrongly enunciated. However well-intentioned the new class of people studying the Vedas may be, their efforts will not be fruitful.

Another point. Here we have a class of people born into a dharma and practising it hereditarily for thousands of years and acquiring in the process certain qualities. If such people forsake that dharma, how would you expect others who are strangers to it to take their place especially in the present new circumstances?

There are today two unfortunate developments in the country. One is that of Brahmins giving up Vedic learning and Vedic works and the second that of other communities wanting to practise the Vedic dharma. It is difficult to say which of the two is worse. Not performing the duty that belongs to us by birth is an offence. But, as the Lord says in the Gītā, to take up the duty of another is a greater offence.

"Svadharme nidhanam śreyo paradharmo bhayāvahaḥ[2]". It is better to die within the sphere of one's own duty than take up another's duty. Perilous and fearful is the duty of other men. Since death is certain anyway, if we carry out the duty that is properly ours there will be no rebirth for us. What do we mean by saying that another man's dharma is fearful? If a person practises another man's dharma he will be pushed into hell. Suppose such a man does not believe in a place called hell, we may then take it that he will suffer infernal sorrow in this or the next birth. Apart from this, not being an atheist, he will be eaten up by the fear that he is perhaps committing a sin by pursuing another man's dharma. Were he a non-believer he would not have faith in the Vedas and śāstras and he would not in the first place take up the Brahmin's vocation. So the one who has faith in the Vedas would be constantly nagged by the worry: "The śāstras proclaim that the sound of the Vedas will bring good to the world. But the same śāstras proclaim, don't they, that the pursuit of another man's dharma is fearful?"

The point to be noted is that if you believe in the śāstras you must believe in them fully. If you are an atheist you could of course reject all of them. But to make a show of being very clever and twist the śāstras as you like, accepting some parts or rejecting or changing some others, is an offence more grave than that of being an atheist. To think that Mother Veda should dance to our tune is also a great offence. Learning the Vedas in such an attitude is tantamount to ridiculing them.

I am not angry with the reformists, nor do I suspect their motives. They go wrong because of their ignorance or thoughtlessness. If they wish to pull down the fence to go to the other side, they must think of the possibility of the few still remaining there walking over to this side.

If people truly feel that their present vocation is as honourable as the practice of Vedic dharma, they will not think of taking up some calling other than their own. "Brahmins have forsaken the Vedas. So the world is not filled with the sound of the Vedas which is sc essential to its well-being. To fill this vacuum a new Brahmin class must be created." Those who want to take the place of the Brahmins, who are traditionally duty-bound to follow the Vedic dharma, will have a feeling of conceit, not to speak of a spirit of challenge and a sense of inferiority also. If you really want to work for the goal of making the Vedas a living reality again, your efforts must be directed towards turning those who were engaged in the preservation of the Vedic heritage back to the dharma to which they hereditarily belong.

If I criticise Brahmins[3] it is not because I feel that they cannot be corrected or that I have washed my hands of them. Nor do I think that Brahmins alone as a caste are responsible for all the ills of today. If I administer them a reproof now and then for their having given up their dharma during Islamic and British rule and for being lured today by the glitter of modern civilization, it does not mean that they are to be wholly blamed for everything. Placed as they are in today's circumstances any caste or class would have done the same. Those who find them guilty now think that they would acquit themselves better if they were in their place. But they too would have been compelled to make the same mistakes by the force of circumstances. If people hereditarily engaged in intellectual pursuits find themselves unable to apply their minds to Ātmic matters and instead become involved in mundane affairs, it means a topsyturvy slide-down.

I do not justify such behaviour nor the descent into worldly affairs from the heights of spirituality. Nowadays reformists try to justify even prostitution on psychological grounds. Similarly, I wish to point out that there is a psychological explanation for the degeneration of Brahmins also. If I criticise Brahmins, it does not mean that others should join in the attack, thinking that they (the Brahmins) alone are worthless people. It is the duty of these others to make Brahmins worthy of their caste. After all, during the past forty or fifty years, Brahmins have been an easy target of attack and ridicule. How silently they have suffered all this, also the humiliation at the hands of their detractors. Until some four or five generations ago, Brahmins were the guardians of all our Ātmic wealth, all our arts. Considering this is it not the duty of others to bring them back to the practice of their true dharma? They must be tactfully reminded of the high dharma they had once pursued and the spirit of sacrifice for which they were known.

It is likely that in the past a few ignorant Brahmins treated other communities harshly. This is no reason why their descendants today should pay for it and be maligned and harassed in a spirit of vengefulness. It must also be borne in mind that Brahmins themselves have been in the forefront in the fight against "the old unjust practices" and in giving other communities a high place in society. So there is no point in fuelling the flames of hatred. Nor can it be claimed truthfully that such hatred is part of "Tamiḷ culture".

Unfortunately, what Brahmins did in the name of reforms resulted in the wrong kind of equality for, instead of raising people belonging to the lower strata to a higher level, it had the effect of bringing the upper classes downward. Equality can be of two types: in the first all occupy a high level in society; in the other all occupy a low level. To carry a load uphill is difficult but it is easy to push it down. Quality has suffered in the attempt to create equality. It is not desirable to have that kind of equality in which everybody does the same kind of work. Nor should it be thought that there is no equality in a system in which the various vocations, the various types of work, are divided among different groups of people. I have already spoken a great deal on the subject. Our endeavour must be to create unity in diversity, not uniformity.

It is important to remember that neither hatred of Brahmins nor dislike of Sanskrit has ever been a part of Tamiḷ culture and civilization. Sanskrit is the repository of Ātmic and religious śāstras, a storehouse of poetry and works on arts. Everyone must learn to regard it as "our own language". The need for the existence of "Brāhmaṇya" as a separate entity must be recognised. This is essential to the preservation of the Vedas, the performance of sacrifices, etc, whose purpose is the good of mankind. Today the Vedas, the Upaniṣads and so on are available in print. Anybody can read them and try to understand them. But everybody need not learn to chant the Vedas ; it takes many years to do so. Everybody need not also perform sacrifices.

There ought to be an element of humility on the part of those who wish to carry out reforms; there must also be sincerity of purpose. Then no need will arise to go contrary to the śāstras.

Notes & References

1 Āndhra Pradeś (Andhra Pradesh).

2 See notes appended to Chapter 6, Part Three.

3 For straying from the path of their dharma. See Chapter 6, Part Three.

Chapter 4

Aupāsana and Women

I said [in an earlier talk] that members of all castes must perform aupāsana. The husband and wife must do it together. Even when the husband is away the wife must perform it by offering unbroken rice grains in the sacrificial fire. The Vedas themselves have given women such a right.

Aupāsana is the only Vedic right that a woman is entitled to perform on her own. Of course, there are so many paurāṇic vratas[S] and pūjās that she can perform according to the śāstras, but these belong to a different category. Besides, she has naturally a share in all the works of her husband. Apart from caring for the household, she does not have to perform any rite (other than aupāsana). Even if she does, it will not yield any fruit, for such is the rule according to the Vedic dharmaśāstras.

We hear people talk of "rights". It is my wish to create an awareness among women about their right, the right to aupāsana. I should like every home to become bright with the sacred aupāsana fire. Women should fight for this right of theirs and impress upon their husbands the importance of performing aupāsana. "Even though you have given up all scriptural karma, you at least do the Gāyatrī japa[S] to retain your tenuous connection with the Vedic dharma. If you do not do this japa or even forget the mantra, one day you will feel repentant over it thinking of the upanayana saṁskāra you had," women should tell their husbands. "As for me I have had no upanayana, nor am I entitled to mutter the Gāyatrī. If at all I have any right according to the Vedas, which are the source not only of our religion but of this world and of creation itself, it is this aupāsana. If you refuse to perform it I will be denied my Vedic right." In this manner women must fight for this sacred right of theirs and make their husbands perform aupāsana. Aupāsana is indeed their one great Vedic "property".

Women must bear in mind the importance of aupāsana and agnihotra (like aupāsana agnihotra also must be performed twice a day). "So many fires are burning in the home", they must tell themselves. "We make coffee on the fire and cook food or make the water warm to bathe. By not performing aupāsana we will be extinguishing that fire which was witness to our marriage."

The sacred fire must be kept burning by adding rice husk to it now and then. In many ways it is advantageous to pound rice at home for, apart from the husk, we will have nutritious hand-pounded rice to eat. Also the poor labourer who does the pounding will get a little cash or a few handfuls of rice for his or her sustenance. (For the unbroken rice grains offered in the fire the housewife must pound the rice herself. This is a piece of work done to the accompaniment of mantras.)

It does not cost much to perform aupāsana nor does the rite take long to go through. All you need is the will to do it. Hand-pounded rice is also good for your health. Milled and polished rice is not good. Besides in hand-pounding there is something of the Gāndhian ideal too.

The aupāsana fire will keep away evil spirits and afflictions of all types. Many Brahmins today have exorcist rites performed by others with *neem* leaves or bamboo sticks. They go to a mosque for relief, or they come to me praying for help. Aupāsana is a remedy for all ills and wearing the aupāsana ashes is a great protection.

Chapter 5

Agni and the Vedic Religion

The householder has the duty of performing a number of rites in the sacred fire. Aupāsana is the first of them. Agni is of the utmost importance to the Vedic religion. This deity is called "Agni-Nārāyaṇa". The hymns to Rudra also show that he has a connection with the god of fire. In Tiruvaṇṇāmalai (in Tamiḷ Nāḍu) Īśvara revealed himself as a mountain of fire. In Keraḷa there is the custom of worshipping Ambā [the Mother Goddess] in the form of light (in the flame of the lamp); the idol or yantra[S] is not important. The goddess is invoked in the lamp itself. We speak of Subrahmaṇya who originated from Śiva's third eye as fire incarnate. Thus Agni is of great importance to us. According to researchers, the term Āryan means fire-worshipper. Fire worship is the dominant feature of the religion of Zoroastrianism which is a branch of Vedism.

The sacred fire should keep burning and glowing in home after home. Ghee, milk and other oblations offered in it will produce the aroma that will bring health and mental uplift to all.

I have already stated that whatever the deity invoked in a sacrifice, the oblation must be placed in the sacred fire.

Chapter 6
Sacrifices

(Part Five also contains chapters pertaining to this subject.)

Four hundred yajñas or sacrifices are said to be mentioned in the Vedas[1]. Of these, aupāsana alone is to be performed by all the four varṇas. Though the first three varṇas have the right to all the other sacrifices, in practice these were performed mostly by Brahmins and Kṣatriyas only. But later Kṣatriyas too neglected to perform them. There are yajñas to be conducted specially by them to earn physical strength, victory in war, and so on. Sacrifices like rājasūya and aśvamedha were performed by imperial rulers. There are yāgas that have to be performed by Vaiśyas for a good agricultural yield, for wealth, etc. As mentioned before, the yajamāna of a sacrifice may be a Kṣatriya or a Vaiśya but the four priests must be Brahmins. (The idea behind it is that if members of these two castes were to participate directly in the sacrifices their duties like protecting the country and looking after agriculture would suffer.)

Not all sacrifices need be performed by all Brahmins. A number of them are meant to serve one specific purpose or another. For instance, you must have heard of the putrakāmeṣṭi in the Rāmāyaṇa, the sacrifice performed to beget a son.

Any rite meant to fulfil a wish is "kāmya-karma" and it comes under the optional category. Then there are rites that are obligatory on your part to conduct for the good of your Ātman as well as of the world. They come under the category of "nitya-karma", but the word "nitya" here does not denote "daily".

In the category of nitya-karma there are 21 sacrifices. There is no compulsion with regard to the rest of the 400. But the 21, included in the forty saṁskāras, must be performed at least once in a lifetime. As we have seen, these are divided into groups of seven —pākayajñas, haviryajñas and somayajñas.

Marriage is conducted with offerings made in the fire, is it not? Aupāsana, which must be performed every day, is commenced in this fire and it must be preserved throughout one's life. The seven pākayajñas, rites like upanayana and śrāddha must be conducted in the aupāsana fire. The son lights his aupāsana fire during his marriage from his father's aupāsana fire. The son's aupāsana fire, like his father's, must be maintained throughout his life. Thus, without any break, the sacred fire is kept burning in the family generation after generation.

All rites in which the aupāsana fire is used and pertain to an individual and his family are "Gṛhyakarmas". The seven pākayajñas also belong to this category. They are related exclusively to the family and are not very elaborate. Even so they are conducive to the good of the world outside also. The Gṛhyasūtras deal with such rites. They belong to the Smṛtis and are called "Smārta-karmas".

The elaborate works that are especially meant for the well-being of mankind are called "Śrautakarmas". They are so called because their procedure is directly based on the authority of Śruti or the Vedas. The śāstras dealing with them are "Śrautasūtras".

I told you, do you remember, that there was no question of Śruti being superior to Smṛti or *vice versa*? Similarly, the Śrautasūtras and the Gṛhyasūtras are of equal importance. In the sanātana dharma[S] that goes under the name of Hinduism both are to be cared for like our two eyes.

The aupāsana fire (lighted at the time of marriage from that of the groom's father) is divided into two in a ceremony called "agniyādhāna". One part is called "gṛhyāgni" or "smārtāgni": it is meant for rites to be performed at home. The second part is śrautāgni and meant for śrauta rites. These two sacred fires must be preserved throughout.

Gṛhyāgni is also called aupāsanāgni since the daily rite of aupāsana is performed in it. This is the fire contained in one "kuṇḍa" and so it is called "ekāgni". Rites conducted in the family are included in the chapter called "Ekāgni-kāṇḍa" in the *Āpastamba-sūtra*. The saṁskāras and other rites I have so far mentioned are mostly in accordance with this work since the majority of Brahmins in the South are Kṛṣṇa-Yajurvedins following this sūtra. Ṛgvedins and Sāmavedins who constitute a minority follow the *Āśvalāyana* and *Gobhila-sūtras* respectively. These differences, however, relate only to the rites performed at home. There are no differences in the śrauta rites with regard to the different Vedas.

Śrautāgni meant for the śrauta rites is in the form of three fires burning in three mounds. So it is called tretāgni. The section in the *Āpastamba-sūtra* dealing with rites performed in it is called "Tretāgni-kāṇḍa". One who worships the three Agnis is called a "tretāgnin" or "śrautin" and, if he worships the śrauta and gṛhya fires, he is called an "āhitāgnin". One who performs an elaborate sacrifice like a somayajña is called a "yajvā", "dīkṣita" or "makhin". And one who conducts the greatest of the somayajñas, vājapeya, is known as a "vājapeyin". Sacrifices are called variously "kratu", "makha", "iṣṭi", "stoma", "samstā". There are some differences between these. Ancient Tamiḷ works contain references to "*muttī*" (tretāgni or śrautāgni).

One of the three sacred fires, one of the tretāgni, is called "gārhapatya" and it belongs to the master of the household. It must be kept burning in the gārhapatya mound which is circular in shape. In this no oblations are to be made directly. Fire must be taken from it and tended in another mound for the performance of rites relating to the fathers (this is different from the usual śrāddha[S] and is a ritual performed to the manes every new moon) and also for certain deities. This mound is in the south, so it is called "dakṣiṇāgni" and it is semicircular in shape. Offerings to deities are made generally in a third fire in the east called "āhavanīya" and it is also to be kindled from the gārhapatya fire. In the North any yāga or sacrificial rite is called a "*havan*", the word being derived from "āhavanīya". The āhavanīya mound is square in shape. Big sacrifices like somayajñas and others meant to propitiate deities are to be conducted in the fire taken from the āhavanīya mound to the yāgaśāla or the hall where a sacrifice is held.

If aupāsana is a gṛhyakarma, agnihotra is a śrauta ceremony and it too must be performed twice a day. Agniyādhāna mentioned before and agnihotra are the first two of the seven haviryajñas. Those who perform agnihotra are called agnihotrins. (Nowadays smoking is referred to as agnihotra and going to the races as aśvamedha. Such references are intended to be humorous but are indeed blasphemous.)

If the agnihotra fire is extinguished for whatever reason, it must be kindled again through a new ādhāna[2] (agniyādhāna) ceremony. The same applies to the aupāsana fire. Now in the majority of houses neither the aupāsana nor the agnihotra fire burns. I have mentioned here how these fires can be renewed since most of you perhaps must not have kept them after your marriage.

In aupāsana unbroken rice grains are offered in the fire and in agnihotra milk, ghee or unbroken rice grains. (It has become customary now to offer milk in the agnihotra.)

As already mentioned, the dakṣiṇāgni and the āhavanīyāgni are made from the gārhapatyāgni. When śrauta rites for the fathers have been performed in the dakṣiṇāgni and other śrauta rites in the āhavanīyagni, the two fires no longer have the exalted name of "śrautāgni" and are just like any other ordinary fire and they have to be extinguished. Only the gārhapatya and aupāsana fires are to be kept burning throughout.

On every Prathamā (first day of the lunar fortnight), a pākayajña and a haviryajña have to be performed in the gṛhyāgni and śrautāgni respectively. The first is called sthālīpāka. "Sthālī" is the pot in which rice is cooked and it must be placed on the aupāsana fire and the rice called "caru" cooked in it must be offered in the same fire. The rite that is the basis of many others (the archetype or model) is called "prakṛti". Those performed after it, but with some changes, are known as "vikṛti". For the sarpabali called śrāvaṇī and the pākayajña called āgrahāyaṇī, sthālīpāka is the prakṛti.

The haviryajña performed on every Prathamā is "darśa-pūrṇa-isti", "darśa" meaning the new moon and "pūrṇa" the full moon. So the "iṣṭis" or sacrifices conducted on the day following the new moon and the full moon (the two Prathamās) are together given the name of darśa-pūrṇa-iṣṭi. The two rituals are also referred to merely as "iṣṭi". This is the prakṛti for haviryajñas.

For soma sacrifices "agniṣṭoma" is the prakṛti, the word "stoma" also meaning a sacrifice. In conjunction with "agni", the "sto" becomes "ṣṭo" — "agniṣṭoma". "Sthāpita" becomes "establish" in English: here the "sta" of the first word becomes "ṣṭa" in the second. Some unlettered people pronounce "star" and "stamp" as "iṣṭar" and "iṣṭāmp". Such phonetic changes are accepted even in the Vedas.

I will now deal briefly with the remaining pāka, havir and soma sacrifices.

Pākayajñas are minor sacrifices and are performed at home. Even śrauta rites like the first four haviryajñas — ādhāna, agnihotra, darśa-pūrṇa-māsa and āgrayaṇa — are performed at home. The last three haviryajñas — cāturmāsya, nirūḍhapaśubandha and sautrāmaṇī — are performed in a yāgaśalā.

The yāgaśālā is also known as a "devayajana". The *Kalpa-sūtras* contain a description of it, not omitting minute details. There are altars called "cayanas"[S] to be built with bricks. (There are no cayanas for havir and pākayajñas.) As I said before there is the application of mathematics in all this. Several kinds of ladles are used in making offerings in the fire, "tarvi", "sruk" and "sruva". Their measurements are specified, also the materials out of which they are made. No detail is left out. In a nuclear or space research laboratory even the most insignificant job is carried out with the utmost care, so is the case with sacrifices which have the purpose of bringing forth supernatural powers into the world.

To repeat, pākayajñas are simple, "pāka" meaning "small", "like a child". Cooked food is also "pāka"; that is why the art of cooking is called "pākaśāstra" and the place where cooking is done is called "pākaśālā". Just as in sthālīpāka cooked rice is offered in the fire, so too in pākayajñas cooked grains are offered in the fire. The watery part is not to be drained off — this rite is called "caruhoma". But in aupāṣana unbroken rice (not cooked) is offered. In the pākayajña called "aṣṭaka" purodāśa[3] is offered in the fire. Aṣṭaka is performed for the fathers. The bright half of a month (waxing moon) is special to the celestials while it is the dark half (waning moon) for the fathers. The latter is called the "apara-pakṣa" since during this fortnight rites for the fathers are performed. The eighth day of the dark fortnight (Aṣṭamī) is particularly important for them. The aṣṭaka śrāddha must be performed on the eighth day of the fortnight during the Śiśira and Hemanta seasons (the first and second half of winter) — in the [Tamiḷ] months of *Mārgazhi, Tai, Māśi and Paṅguni.*[4] The aṣṭaka performed in *Māśi* is said to be particularly sacred. The rite gone through on the day following the aṣṭaka is "anvaṣṭaka".

"Pārvaṇī", one of the pākayajñas, is the prakṛti (or the archetype) for śrāddhas[5]. Since it is performed every month it is called "māsiśrāddha". (This is according to the *Āpastamba-sūtra.* According to the *Gautama-sūtra* "pārvaṇa" denotes the sthālīpāka performed during each "parva".)

The pākayajña "śrāvaṇī" is also called "sarpabali". On the full moon of the month of Śrāvaṇa caru rice and ghee are placed in the fire and flowers of the flame of the forest are offered similarly by both hands. Designs have to be drawn with rice flour over an anthill or some other place and offerings made to snakes with the chanting of mantras. This ceremony must be held every full-moon night up to *Mārgazhi* (mid-December to mid-January).

On the *Mārgazhi* full moon, apart from completing the sarpabali, the pākayajña called "āgrahāyaṇī" must be performed. Like "śrāvaṇī", the name "āgrahāyaṇī" is also derived from the name of the month of the same name — Āgrahāyaṇī is *Mārgazhi.* "Hayana" means "year" and the first month of the year is "Āgrahāyana". In ancient times the year started with this month. The first of January [of the Gregorian calendar] falls in mid-*Mārgazhi.* It was from us that Europe took this as their new year. Though we changed our calendar later, they stuck to theirs. There are two more pākayajñas called "caitrī" and "āśvayujī": these fall respectively, as their names suggest, in *Cittirai* and *Aippaśi*[5].

Caitrī is conducted where four roads meet. Since it is performed for Īśāna it is called "Īśānabali": Īśāna is Parameśvara (Śiva). In the other pākayajñas the deities worshipped are different but through them Parameśvara is pleased. It is like a tax paid to the ruler through the sub-collector. In Caitrī it is as if the tax is paid directly to the ruler.

In *Aippaśi, kuruvā*[6] rice is harvested [in Tamiḷ Nadu]. This is first offered to Īśvara in the rite called "āsvayujī" before it is taken by us. Similarly *samba*[7] rice is eaten only after āgrahāyanī is performed in *Mārgazhi.*

The haviryajñas are more elaborate, though not so large in scale as the somayajñas. Anything offered in the sacrificial fire is called "havis". In Tamiḷ works like the *Tirukkural*[T] it is referred to as "*avi*". However, ghee is specifically referred to as "havis". Sacrifices in which the soma juice is offered are called somayajñas and those that are not elaborate are categorised as pākayajñas. Now the other śrauta sacrifices among the forty saṁskāras are called haviryajñas.

When I spoke to you earlier about sacrifices I referred to the men who conduct them. The sacrificer is the yajamāna and those who perform the sacrifice for him are the ṛtviks (priests) who consist of the hotā, adhvaryu, udgātā and brahmā.

In pākayajñas there are no ṛtviks; the householder (as the yajamāna) performs the rites with his wife. In haviryajñas there are four ṛtviks and the yajamāna. But the udgātā's place is taken by the agnīdhra. The udgātā is the one who sings the Sāman. It is only in somayajñas that there is Sāmagāna, not in haviryajnas. In cāturmāsya and paśubandha there are more than the usual number of priests. But there is no need to deal with them here. I wanted to give you only a basic knowledge of the important sacrifices that had been conducted for ages until recently.

"Āgrayaṇa" is performed on the full moon of *Aippaśi*[8]. In this śyāmāka grains are offered in the fire. Cāturmāsya gives the impression that it includes a number of sacrifices. Some of you probably know that "cāturmāsya" is a term that refers to sannyāsins staying at the same place during the rainy season. But it is also the name of a haviryajña to be performed by householders once every four months, in *Karttigai, Panguni, Āḍi*[9]. From this onwards the sacrifices are to be performed in a yāgaśālā [built in a public place].

The haviryajña called nirūḍhapaśubandha (or simply "paśubandha") is the first yajña in which there is animal sacrifice, "mṛgabali". Though I have used the word "bali", technically speaking — or according to the śāstras — it is not strictly a bali. "Bali" means that which is offered directly — and not in the fire. What is offered in the fire is āhuti or havis. The flour offered in the anthill for the snakes is sarpabali. In what are called pañca-mahāyajñas there is a rite called "vaiśvadeva": in this offerings are made in the fire or they are thrown inside and outside the house with the chanting of mantras. The latter are meant for various creatures of the earth and are termed as bali.

When we make an offering to a deity with mantras we must say "svāhā". When it is made to the fathers we must say "svadhā". The corresponding word to be said when offerings are made to various creatures is "hantā". Here we have something like the gradation of authority: "your majesty", "your honour", and so on.

There are rules to determine which part of the sacrificial animal's body is to be offered in the sacrificial fire. This is not the same as bali. What is offered in the fire is "homa". In paśubandha only one animal is sacrificed.

In yajñas involving animals there is a yūpa-stambha or sacrificial post of bamboo or khadira[S] to which the animal is tethered.

In the last haviryajña called "sautrāmaṇī" surā (liquor or wine) is offered to appease certain inferior powers or deities for the welfare of the world. Our government, which otherwise strictly enforces prohibition[10], relaxes the rules to entertain foreigners with drink, considering the gains to be had from them. The oblation of liquor in sautrāmaṇi is to be justified on the same grounds. It is never offered in the sacrifices meant for higher deities. What is left over of the liquor — what is purified by mantras — is imbibed by the performers of the sacrifice, the quantity taken in being less than a quarter of an ounce. To say that Brahmins drank the soma juice and surā to their heart's content on the pretext of performing sacrifices is an outrageous charge. I have already spoken about the falsehood spread about the partaking of the meat left over from a sacrifice.

I will now deal briefly with somayajñas or somasaṁstās. What is a samstā? The conclusion of the Sāmavedic hymns chanted by the udgātā is called saṁstā. Compositions recited in praise of deities are generally known as stotras. But in the Vedic tradition the Ṛgvedic hymns are "śastras". In the Sāmaveda such hymns which suggest the seven notes or saptasvara are called stotras. In soma sacrifices it is this, singing of the stotras of the Sāmaveda, that is the major feature. Homa (placing oblations in the fire) is the dominant feature of pāka and haviryajñas while in somayajña it is the singing of stotras.

The name somayāga is derived from the fact that the essence of the soma plant, so much relished by the celestials, is made as an oblation. Apart from this, animals are also sacrificed. Even so the singing of the Sāman creates a mood of ecstasy. When a musician elaborates a rāga and touches the fifth svara of the higher octave the listeners are transported to the heights of joy. So in the singing of stotras of the Sāmaveda during the saṁstā all those assembled for the sacrifice feel as if heaven were upon earth . This is one reason why somayajña is also known as "somasamstā".

In such soma sacrifices there is the full complement of priests — the hotā, the adhvaryu, the udgātā and the brahmā. Each priest is assisted by three others. So in all there are sixteen priests in a soma sacrifice. Agniṣṭoma which is the first of the seven somayajñas is the prakṛti (archetype) and the other six are its vikṛti. These six are: atyagniṣṭoma, uktya, ṣodaśī, vājapeya, atirātra and aptoryāma.

Vājapeya is regarded as particularly important. When its yajamāna (sacrificer) comes after having had his ritual bath (avabhṛtha snāna) at the conclusion of the sacrifice, the king himself holds up a white umbrella for him. "Vāja" means rice (food) and "peya" means a drink. As the name suggests, the vājapeya sacrifice brings in a bountiful crop and plentiful water. The name is appropriate in another sense also. This sacrifice consists of soma-rasa homa, paśu-homa (23 animals) and anna - or vāja-homa. The sacrificer is "bathed" in the rice that is left over. Since the rice is "poured over" him like water the term "vājapeya" is apt.

In the old days a Brahmin used all his wealth in performing the soma sacrifice. Much of this was spent in dakṣiṇā[S] to the priests and the rest for materials used in the sacrifice. Now people are concerned only with their wealth and do not perform even sandhyāvandana[S] which does not cost them anything. Among Nampūtiris, until some forty or fifty years ago, at least one family out of ten performed the somayajña. Since only the eldest member of the family[11] could conduct the sacrifice he alone had the right to property.

There was also a time when even poor Brahmins performed this sacrifice every spring ("vasante vasante") by begging. A Brahmin who conducted the sacrifice every year was thus called "prati-vasanta- somayājin".

The Vedas will flourish in the world if at least the somayajña called agniṣṭoma or jyotiṣṭoma is performed.

Notes & References

1 A number of subjects dealt with in this chapter have been elucidated by Kuṁbhakoṇam Śrī Lakṣmī Kānta Śarmā Daṁpatī and Agnihotram Rāmānuja Tātācāriyār. —Ra. Ga.

2 "Ādhāna" literally means "placing" or "keeping".

3 It is an oblation made of ground rice.

4 Mid-December to mid-January; mid-January to mid-February; mid- February to mid-March; and mid-March to mid-April.

5 Mid-April to mid-May; mid-October to mid-November.

6&7 These are varieties of rice grown in Tamiḷ Nāḍu.

8 Mid-October to mid-November.

9 Mid-November to mid-December; mid-March to mid-April; mid-July to mid-August.

10 Prohibition was perhaps sought to be strictly enforced (particularly in Tamiḷ Nāḍu) at the time the Paramaguru gave this discourse.

11 Only the eldest son married among Nampūtiris.

Chapter 7
Other Saṁskāras

There are certain rites common to all Hindus though they are not included in the forty saṁskāras. The ears of a child must be pierced ceremonially ("karṇa-vedhanam")[1]. Initiating a child into the alphabet ("akṣarābhyāsa") is another saṁskāra[2].

Cremation is not included in the forty saṁskāras but, as already pointed out, it is also a sacrifice, the last one, antyeṣṭi, and performed to the chanting of mantras by the son or a close relative of the deceased

An āhitāgnin's cremation must be performed with the sacred fires he had tended, that is by bringing together his gṛhyāgni and tretāgni. The four fires will consume his body and transport his soul to a sacred world. If a man has not worshipped the tretāgni and kept only the aupāsanāgni, his cremation must be performed with that fire.

There is no cremation, of course, for a sannyāsin.

Since cremation is regarded as the last sacrifice, it follows that it is a rite that belongs to all except the inwardly mature and enlightened who take to sannyāsa. If sannyāsa were compulsory for all there would be no dahana-kriyā or cremation mentioned in the śāstras.

Notes

[1] The lobes of the ears of the child are pierced. In the case of boys the right ear first and in the case of girls the left ear.

[2] It is also called vidyārambha.

Chapter 8

Sahagamana

When people nowadays talk of "satī" or "sahagamana" they mean it to be a custom in which the widow is forcibly thrown into the funeral pyre of her husband. We do not know for sure whether such an act of cruelty was indeed committed at any time in the past in any part of our land, that of forcibly pushing a widow into the funeral pyre of her husband. In any case satī has never been a widely practised custom. Only women of exemplary chastity and devotion, who did not wish to live after the passing of their husband, resorted to sahagamana. I have heard stories of such pativratas[S] in my childhood. When the relatives lamented, "Oh, you are burning yourself alive," the widow exclaimed, "This fire does not burn me. I am dying in the warmth of my husband's embrace." Such noble women died with a smile on their lips.

When Hanumān set the aśoka[S] woods ablaze with his burning tail, Sītā remained unhurt because of her pātivratya. When Kumārilabhaṭṭa was being scorched in the burning heap of rice-husk, he felt it cool in the presence of Śankara. Because of her supreme devotion to her husband the funeral pyre was as comforting as sandal-paste to a woman immolating herself. It seems even the clothes of such women were not consumed by the fire and were removed from the burning body to be cherished with devotion.

A wife of exemplary pātivratya falls dead on the death of her husband. In the story of Kaṇṇagī[T] we come across such an example of devotion. When the Pāṇḍyan king dies owing to his profound feeling of guilt, his queen also dies with him. There is a similar story told of Padmāvatī, wife of Jayadeva, author of the *Gīta-Govindam.* In order to test her devotion for her husband, the queen light-heartedly tells her that Jayadeva, who had been out on a journey, was dead. Thereupon Padmāvatī falls dead. The queen is filled with remorse for her thoughtlessness and it is said that Jayadeva was able to restore his wife to life with the grace of Kṛṣṇa.

Only women highly devoted to their husbands resorted to sahagamana. They were not forcibly thrown into the fire and were indeed prevented from taking such an extreme step. When Pāṇḍu died, Mādrī, one of his two wives and mother of Nakula and Sahadeva, ascended the funeral pyre of her husband as expiation for her being the cause of his death. The great men who permitted this act of sacrifice prevented Kuntī, the second of the two wives, from taking a similar step. They said to her: "Desist from such an extreme act. Your duty now is to bring up your own children as well as Mādrī's."

When Pukazhanār, father of Apparsvāmigal[T] (he had not yet come to be called by that name — he was then Maruḷ Nīkkiyār), died his wife Mādiniyār immolated herself in her husband's funeral pyre. This story is told in the *Periyapurāṇam*[T]. The chastity of Mādiniyār's daughter was even of a higher order. Her name was Tilakavatī. She was young and not yet married. It was her devotion to her husband-to-be that makes her a memorable character. She had been betrothed to Kalippakayār who was commander-in-chief of the Pallava army. But at the same time as Pukazhanār died word came that the young Kalippakayār had been killed in battle. The young Tilakavatī decided at once to put an end to her life. "I became his (Kalippakayār's) wife the moment I was betrothed to him. I will not now look upon anybody else as my husband. Since he is gone I too will follow him in death." Then Appar, that is Maruḷ Nīkkiyār, said to his sister: "What will I do without my parents and without you? I am such a small boy. I too will accompany you to the other world." Tilakavatī had now no choice but to change her mind so that she could look after her young brother. (True to her name she has remained an ornament to womanhood.) Later her brother embraced Jainism with the new name of Dharmasena and it was she who weaned him from it. She was indeed instrumental in his becoming the poet-saint celebrated as Apparsvāmigal.

In Rājasthān there were so many noble women who earned a place in history by resorting to sahagamana.

I should like to emphasise here that there was no compulsion for a widow to ascend the funeral pyre of her husband. But women who voluntarily resorted to sahagamana were greatly revered and the śāstras supported their action. Even today we hear of rare cases of "satī", though the law does not permit it and the relatives dissuade such women from taking the extreme step. This seems to me particularly worthy of appreciation. In the old days the circumstances were favourable for a widow to perish in the fire with her husband. So, without being compelled by others and urged only by the desire to attain to a higher world, one or two widows immolated themselves. But today, in the age of Kali and of reforms, the circumstances are not favourable for such an act of sacrifice. So, despite this, if a woman decides to follow her husband in death it must be out of true devotion for him.

I have often impressed upon you the importance of gurukulavāsa. Like satī it is now a forgotten tradition. We find it difficult nowadays to run a gurukula. So if one or two boys come forward to study with a preceptor in his home and are prepared to observe bhikṣācarya (that is begging for their food) their example must be considered worthier than that of brahmacārins of the past.

Like sannyāsa sahagamana has never been compulsory. I will tell you an important reason for this. The dharmaśāstras deal extensively with the conduct of widows. If everybody was expected to be a sannyāsin there would be, as I said before, no need for cremation to be brought under the purview of the śāstras. Similarly, if every widow was expected to immolate herself in the funeral pyre of her husband, where would be the need for a separate code of conduct for them (that is for widows)?

Nobody can foretell when the hand of death will strike. It can come in one's childhood or during the time one is a householder. So everyone cannot be expected to die a sannyāsin. If the śāstras insist that on the death of a man his widow must also be cremated with him, then there will be no need for codifying "vidhavā dharma" (code of conduct for widows).

Chapter 9

Goal of Saṁskāras

I have dealt with a large number of saṁskāras, indeed more than forty of them. The Brahmin is expected to perform sacrifices almost all through his life, thereby making his life itself a sacrifice in the cause of mankind[1]. On his death his body is cremated with the chanting of mantras and this rite also brings good to the world. While the saṁskāras refine a man, purify him, the mantras chanted at the time create benign vibrations in the world. And, while each karma is apparently meant for the performer as an individual, it also brings benefits to the entire world. In truth there is no karma that does not benefit mankind in general. All rites begin with the prayer, "Jagat-hitāya Kṛṣṇāya". When we chant the Gāyatrī we do not say, "may the sun god quicken or inspire *my* intelligence", but "*our*" intelligence. So the Gāyatrī is a prayer made on behalf of all creatures. (It would be perverse to argue that it should be enough if *one* Brahmin did the Gāyatrī-japa for the benefit of all — the word "our" is not to be construed thus. Brahmins, Kṣatriyas and Vaiśyas must mutter the Gāyatrī not only for their own good but for that of all castes, all creatures including animals, birds, insects, all sentient beings.)

You must have seen that sacrifices constitute the major portion of the saṁskāras. There is a mantra in the *Bṛhadāraṇyaka Upaniṣad* (4.4.22)[2] which describes the benefits derived from their performance. It says that Brahmins endeavour to realise the Self through Vedic learning, through the performance of sacrifices, through charity, through austerities and through fasts. But when this purpose has been accomplished they renounce all (rites including sacrifices) and become sannyāsins. It follows that all the elaborate sacraments are performed for the cessation of these very sacraments. Of all the benefits derived from rituals like sacrifices this is the highest, the very abandonment of rituals. How does a big karma like a sacrifice prepare you for the renunciation of that very karma, that very sacrifice?

There are two types of karma. One is doing what we like. This, instead of purifying the mind, muddles it and makes our burden of karma heavier. The second is the performance of rites without any expectation of rewards, dedicating them to Īśvara in a spirit of sacrifice. In the second type we are cleansed inwardly and the burden of our karma is made lighter and ultimately we are taken to the point beyond which it is not necessary to perform any rites. A man who has renounced all works in this way may, with the compassion of Parāśakti, continue to work for the good of mankind. But even though he is a doer he will not be conscious of his "doership".

How is the impurity of the mind washed away? If you perform a big sacrifice without any desire in your heart, without any feelings of hatred against anybody and without any consideration of loss or gain, success or failure, your mind will be cleansed. The mind, body and speech must be totally involved in it and must remain fixed on a single goal. Then all the impurities will be burnt away. It is like the rays of the sun passing through a magnifying glass and converging on a piece of paper and burning it. There are a hundred thousand things to do in a sacrifice; there are so many mantras to be chanted; so many different materials to be collected. So the performer's mind will be fixed on a single goal.

If a king is to perform a horse sacrifice (aśvamedha), he has to look into so many different requirements. Different animals have to be brought to the place of sacrifice including even a tiger. If a man devotes himself for a number of years with single- minded purpose and devotion to some work or other his mind will be made pure and he will reach the stage when there will be no need for him to perform any more rites. To build a gopuram, to dig a large pond or to be engaged in some other public work is to make one's mind taintless. In fact the mental purity so achieved seems to my mind to be a reward greater than anything else.

Even if a man does not take to sannyāsa after performing sacrifices as a householder, he goes to a meritorious world. With the grace of Īśvara he becomes one with that very Īśvara. And, when Īśvara himself is absorbed in the Brahman as the Paramātman, he too becomes one with him. When Īśvara emerges to create the world he does not become trapped in it. Or there is another way of putting it. Kṛṣṇa Paramātman speaks of the "yoga-bhraṣṭa"[3], one who dies without realising the Self in spite of practising yoga. In his next birth such a man starts where he left off in the earlier birth and ascends to a higher state. What is said about people who practise yoga applies also to those who perform sacrifices. It means that a man who conducts sacrifices but dies before becoming a sannyāsin is born again with a greater sense of discrimination[4] in his next birth and with enough maturity to forsake all karma and become a sannyāsin.

Those who are not entitled to all the saṁskāras will reach a high state by doing their work properly, by being devoted to God, by reciting his praises, by performing aupāsana and by offering libations to their fathers.

Notes & References

[1] The Paramaguru is obviously speaking here of the ideal according to the śāstras.

[2] Sa vā eṣa mahānaja Ātma yo'yaṁ vijñānamayaḥ prāṇeṣu ya eṣo'ntarhṛdaya ākāśastasmiñcchete, sarvasya vāśī sarvasyeśānaḥ, sarvasyādhipatiḥ sa na sādhunā karmaṇā bhūyānno evāsādhunā kanīyāneṣa. sarveśvaraḥ, eṣa bhūtādhipatiḥ, eṣa bhūtapāla, eṣa setur vidhāraṇa eṣām lokānām asambhedāya. Tam etaṁ Vedānuvacanena Brāhmaṇā vividiṣanti, yajñena, dānena, tapasā'nāśakena; etameva viditvā munir bhavati, etam eva pravrājino lokam

icchantaḥ pravrajantiyetetaddhasma vai tat pūrve vidvāṁsaḥ prajāṁ na kāmayante: kim prajayā kariṣyāmaḥ; yeṣāṁ no'yam Ātmāyaṁ loka iti, te ha sma putraiṣaṇāyaśca vittaiśaṇayaśca lokaiṣanāyaśca vyutthāya, atha bhikṣacaryaṁ caranti; ya hyeva putraiṣaṇā sā vittaiṣaṇā, yā vittaiṣaṇā sā lokaiṣaṇā; ubhe hyete eṣaṇe eva bhavataḥ sa eṣa neti netyātmā; agṛyaḥ, na hi gṛhyate; aśiryah, na hi śiryate; asaṅgaḥ, na hi sajyate; asito na vyathate, na riṣyati; etam u haivaite na tarata iti, ataḥ pāpaṁ akaravam iti, ataḥ kalyāṇam akaravam iti; ubhe u haivaiṣa ete tarati, nainaṁ kṛtākṛte tapataḥ.

— Bṛhadāraynyaka Upaniṣad, 4.4.22

[3] Prāpya puṇya-kṛtāmllokān uṣitvā śāśvatīḥ samāḥ
Śucīnāṁ śrīmatāṁ gehe yoga-bhraṣṭo'bhijāyate

— Bhagavadgītā, 6.41

[4] Such a man will be a greater "vivekin".

Chapter 10

A Day in the Life of a Brahmin

"How can any Brahmin perform so many saṁskāras these days?" is perhaps a natural question. "What is the use of speaking about things that are not practicable?" Suppose I myself give two lists, the first containing the saṁskāras that are easy to perform these days and the second containing those that are not so easy. What will happen then? You will keep on adding items to the second from the first list and, eventually, I am afraid, nothing will be left for you to perform. So, on your retirement at least, you must perform all the religious rites imposed on you as Brahmins. You must not ask for an extension of service with your present employers nor look for a new job.

Let me now speak about a Brahmin's daily religious life according to the śāstras. It is indeed a harsh routine. A Brahmin must get up five nāḍikās[1], or two hours, before sunrise. "Pañca-pañca- uṣatkāle," so it is said. "Pañca-pañca" means "five x five" — "pañca-pañca-uṣatkāle" denotes "during the 25th nāḍikā". From sunset to sunrise is 30 nāḍikās. So a Brahmin must rise during the 25th nāḍikā — from this time to sunrise is "Brāhma muhūrta".

After getting up, he cleans his teeth, bathes in cold water and performs sandhyāvandana[S] and japa[S]. Next he goes through aupāsana and agnihotra. These rites come under "devayajña", sacrifices to the gods. Next is "Brahmayajña", the daily study and chanting of the Vedas. As part of this rite there are some tarpaṇas or libations to be offered. (For people following certain sūtras these come later.) If daytime is divided into eight parts, one part will have been over by now.

In the second part of daytime, the Brahmin must teach his disciples the Vedas — this is adhyāpana. Afterwards, he must gather flowers himself for the pūjā he is to perform. Since he is not expected to earn a salary — and if he does not own any land received as a gift — he must beg for his food and also for the materials for the conduct of various sacrifices. The Brahmin has the right to beg, but it is a restrictive right because it means that he can take only the minimum needed for his upkeep and what is required for the performance of rituals. A considerable part of what he receives as gifts is to be paid as dakṣiṇā to the priests officiating at the sacrifices he performs.

Of the six "occupations" of a Brahmin one is "pratigraha" or accepting gifts. Another is "dāna", making donations to others. It is asked why Brahmins alone have the right to receive gifts. The answer is that they are also enjoined to make gifts to others. Indeed, the Brahmin accepts gifts for the purpose of the charity he himself has to render. This apart, he has also to make gifts during the rites to be mentioned next, "ātithya" and "bhūtayajña".

After the second part of the day and a portion of the third have been spent thus, the Brahmin must bathe again and perform the mādhyāhnika. Next he does pitṛ-tarpaṇa, that is he offers libations to the fathers; and this rite is followed by homa and pūjā. In the latter rite he must dedicate to the deities all those objects that he perceives with his five senses (the five jñānendriyas)[2]. It must now be midday and the fourth part of daytime will have been over and the Brahmin must have completed the rites meant for the deities, the Vedas and the fathers.

Of the five great sacrifices or pañca-mahāyajñas, two remain —manuṣya-yajña" or honouring and feeding guests and "bhūtayajña" which includes bali to the creatures of the earth and feeding the poor (vaiśvadeva). Rice is offered in the sacrificial fire and also as bali (that is without being placed in the fire). In bali food is placed in different parts of the house to the chanting of mantras — food meant for outcastes, beggars, dogs, birds, etc[3]. In manuṣya-yajña, guests are entertained and it is also known as ātithya. The Brahmin has his mealtime only after going through these rites. Until then he must not take anything except perhaps some milk or buttermilk, but never coffee or any snacks. If he has any other sacrifices to conduct, pāka, havir or soma, his mealtime will be further delayed. If he has a śrāddha[S] to perform also he will have to eat later than usual. A śrāddha ceremony must be commenced only in the "aparāhna": I will tell you what it means.

Daytime, we have seen, is divided into eight parts. But it can also be divided into five, each of six nāḍikās. If the sun rises at 6, 6 to 8.24 is morning or "prātaḥ-kāla"; 8.24 to 10.48 is "sangava-kāla"; and 10.48 to 1.12 is "mādhyāhnika." From 1.12 to 3.36 it is "aparāhna"; and from 3.36 to 6 (or sunset) is "sāyam-kāla". (The time close to sunset is "pradoṣa". "Doṣa" means night, the prefix "pra" meaning "pre" or "before". The English "pre" is derived from "pra". Pradoṣa thus is the time before night.)

I said that the time for śrāddha is aparāhna. Rites meant for the gods may be performed only after the completion of the śrāddha. After his meal, the Brahmin must read the Purāṇas. Next he has the duty of teaching members of other castes their hereditary vocations, arts and crafts. He does not have a moment for rest or relaxation. For soon it will be time for his evening bath, sandhyāvandana, sacrifices and japa. Vaiśvadeva has to be performed at night also before the Brahmin has his meal and retires to bed. On most nights he takes only light food consisting of fruit, milk, etc. On Ekādaśī[S] he has to fast the whole day.

There is not a moment without work. It is clear that, if the Brahmin created the śāstras, it is not because he wanted to live a life of ease and comfort. On the contrary, the śāstras impose on him a life of hardship and austerity, a life of utter physical and mental discipline.

Even today Brahmins who work in offices or other establishments must try to live according to the śāstras. They must get up at 4 a.m. (Brāhma muhūrta), perform aupāsana, agnihotra, Brahmayajña, etc, in the traditional manner. They may perform pūjā and mādhyāhnika during the sangava time (8.24 a.m. to 10.48 a.m.). "Mādhyāhnika" as the name suggests is a midday rite but, making allowances for present-day life, it may be performed during the sangava-kāla. In the evening too the rites may be gone through in the śāstric manner. As they say, if there is a will there is a way. On holidays it must be possible for a Brahmin to perform all the rites expected of him.

Even those who are on the morning shift and have to rush to their places of work must perform the rites as best they can. In the evening the Gāyatrī-japa may be extended to compensate for non- performance in the morning. If it is morning shift for a week, will it not be mid-shift or night shift in the subsequent weeks? There could be adjustments made to suit these timings.

Brahmins must feel repentant if they fail to perform the rites they are duty-bound to perform. They must devote the years of their retirement to the pursuit of their dharma instead of feeling sorry for not going out to work. There are rare cases — perhaps one in a lakh — of people who have learned the Vedas during their retirement and lived the rest of their life according to the tenets of the śāstras.

The rites of our religion go back to a time when no other faith was prevalent. We must make every effort to ensure that they do not cease to be performed. They are not meant for our sake alone [as individuals] but for the welfare of all mankind.

(See also Chapter 5, Part Twenty)

Notes & References

1 A nāḍikā is 24 minutes.

2 In this rite there is grateful recognition of the fact that all those things that delight our five senses, the Lord has created for our sake.

3 One authority on our śāstras says that vaiśvadeva "is the outcome of the noble sentiment of universal kindliness and charity, the idea that One Spirit pervades and illumines the meanest of creatures and binds all together".

Part Twenty

VARṆA DHARMA FOR UNIVERSAL WELL-BEING

Chapter 1

Jātis — Why so many Differences?

There are four varṇas — Brahmins, Kṣatriyas, Vaiśyas and Sūdras. We identify "varṇas" with "jātis". In point of fact, varṇa and jāti are not the same. The varṇas are only the four mentioned above, that is Brahmins, Kṣatriyas, Vaiśyas and Śūdras. Within each there are many jātis. Among Brahmins there are Ayyars, Ayyaṅgars, Raos, and so on. In the fourth varṇa there are Mudaliars, Piḷḷais, Reḍḍis, Naikkars, Nāyuḍus, Gauṇḍars, Paḍayācis[1].

In common parlance jāti is used for varṇa. I am also using the two as interchangeable terms.

The śāstras lay down separate rites and practices for the four jātis (that is the four varṇas). This means that within the fold of the same religion, Hinduism, there are numerous differences. Food cooked by one caste is not to be eaten by another. A young man belonging to one jāti is not to marry a girl belonging to another. A vocation practised by one jāti is not to be practised by another. The differences are indeed far too many.

Apart from the large number of divisions in each varṇa already existing, more and more divisions (or jātis) are coming into being. Thus Hinduism appears to be a strange religion.

Hindus today feel ashamed of the fact that a religion of which they have otherwise reason to be proud (because it once belonged to the whole world) should have so many differences in it. Other religions too have their dos and don'ts. The Ten Commandments are meant for all Christians. So are the injunctions of the Qur'ān for all Muslims. But in Hinduism the dos and don'ts are not the same for all. What one man does as part of his dharma becomes adharma if done by another. For instance, it is dharma for one man to wear the sacred thread and chant the Vedas, while the same is adharma for another. If the person who chants the Vedas does not bathe and keep his stomach empty he will be guilty of adharma. Another, however, need not necessarily bathe nor observe fasts. When I see that our religion is still alive with all these differences, I am reminded of the words of a great man[2]: "That one day all of us will die is not to be wondered at. The real wonder is that we have nine openings (or gates) in our body but our life does not escape through any of them."

Navadvāre śarire'smin āyuḥ sravati santatam
Jivatītyadbhutam tatra gacchatīti kim adbhutam

Similarly, one must wonder at the fact that our religion is still alive in spite of all its differences and in spite of the fact that people are troubled by doubts about the same.

For some it is an offence to chant the Vedas, while for some others it is an offence not to chant the same. Why should there be so many differences in our religion and why should it seem to be discriminatory? Some feel that it is shameful even to speak about the differences and believe that they are a blot on our faith, which has otherwise many worthy features. While some Hindus try to satisfy themselves about these somehow, many find them to be a constant irritant. Then there are also people who feel angry about these differences and turn atheists as a reaction to the same.

Some are at heart proud of Hinduism but want the varṇa system to be scrapped and all Hindus to form a single class without any distinctions as is the case with the followers of other religions. "The Vedas must be thrown open to all and there must be one common form of worship for all," they declare. "We must do away with the system of separate religious rites and practices." Some go further and claim that such was the concept obtaining in our religion during the time of our forefathers. "The original thinkers of our religion who proclaimed the oneness of the individual self and the Pāramātman," they argue, "would not have believed in such differences among the individual souls. Kṛṣṇa Paramātman says in the Gītā that the vocations are assigned to people according to differences in their nature, not according to their birth." So they hold caste to be a blot on our religion and believe that the system of hereditary occupations did not originally obtain but was a later invention.

We must examine these views in some detail.

Note & Reference

[1] These are jātis of the South.

[2] There is a reference to this in Chapter 2, Part Three.

Chapter 2

Caste according to the Vedas and the Gītā

Let us first consider the view that according to the Vedas themselves caste is not based on birth. (After all, the Vedas are the source of our religion. So it is essential to be clear on this point.) Earlier I sought to counter the view that there was Vedic sanction for post-puberty marriages. The present contention about what the Vedas say about caste is similar, being based on a passage read out of context. What is mentioned as an exception to the rule is being interpreted as the rule itself. I will give firm proof in support of the view that caste is based on birth and not on the nature or qualities of individuals. The cauḷa[S] of children belonging to a particular caste is performed at the age of three, the upanayana at five or seven. These are saṁskāras based on birth and performed in childhood. So it would be absurd to claim that one's vocation is based on one's nature or qualities. Is it possible to determine one's qualities or nature in early childhood?

Let us now come to the Gītā. It is true that the Gītā speaks of "samadarśana"[1], "seeing the selfsame thing in everything and everybody". But it would be perverse to argue on this basis that the Gītā does not recognize any caste distinctions. When, according to Kṛṣṇa, do we attain the stage of samatva, the stage when we will look upon all as equal? We must consider the context : The Lord speaks of the samadarśana of the wise man who is absorbed in the Ātman and for whom there exists nothing [other than the Ātman] including creation — and even the fact that Īśvara is the creator is of no consequence to him. The Lord says that all are equal for a man when he renounces karma entirely to become an ascetic and attains the final stage of enlightenment. The Vedas and the Upaniṣads say the same thing. Only an individual belonging to the highest plane can see all things as One [as one Reality]. Samadarśana is not of this phenomenal world of plurality nor is it for us who are engaged in works. The Lord speaks in the Gītā of samadarśana, samacitta and samabuddhi from the yogin's point of view, but by no means does he refer to "samakāryatva" as applied to our worldly existence.

Some concede that Bhagavān does not deny caste differences, but however argue that, according to the Lord, caste is not based on birth but on the individual qualities of people. In support they quote this line from the Gītā[2]: "Cāturvarṇyam mayāsṛṣṭam guṇa-karma- vibhāgaśaḥ."

When do we come to know the qualities that distinguish an individual? At what age does he reveal his nature? How are we to determine this and impart him the education and training necessary for the vocation that will be in keeping with his qualities? Take, for instance, the calling of the Brahmin who has to join the gurukula[S] when he is seven or eight years old. His education covers a period of twelve years; after this alone will he be qualified for his vocation which includes, among other things, teaching. If a man's occupation were to be fixed until after his character and qualities are formed, it would mean a waste of his youthful years. Even if he were to learn a job or trade thus at a late age it would mean a loss not only to himself but also to society. The Lord speaks again and again that we must be constantly engaged in work and that we must not remain idle even a moment. How then would he approve of an arrangement in which every individual has to be without any work until his vocation is determined according to his character?

Does this mean that the Lord lends his support in theory alone to the system of vocations according to the differing qualities of people and that in actual practice he wants occupations to be based on birth? But he is not like a politician [of these days] speaking one thing and doing something entirely different[3].

What do we see in Kṛṣṇa's own life as a divine incarnation? When Arjuna refuses to fight saying that it is better to become a mendicant than spill the blood of friends and relatives even if it be to rule over an empire, what does the Lord tell him? He urges Arjuna to fight. "You are born a Kṣatriya and you are duty-bound to wage war. Take up your bow and fight."

Here too it may be argued thus: "Arjuna was a great warrior and a great hero. His reluctance to take up arms against friends and relatives must have been a momentary affair. His inner quality and temperament were that of a man of valour. So the Lord enthuses him to go to war. What he refers to as Arjuna's svadharma (own duty) cannot be the same as his jāti dharma (caste duty). The Lord must be referring to Arjuna's natural character as his svadharma."

If such an argument is correct, what about the character of Dharmaputra (Yudhiṣṭhira)? From the very beginning he is averse to war and anxious to make peace with the Kauravas. Does he not go so far as to say that he would not insist on half the kingdom but would be satisfied with just five houses? Kṛṣṇa goes to the Kauravas as his envoy [of peace] but is himself dragged into war by them. Earlier he encouraged Yudhiṣṭhira to subjugate all his neighbouring kingdoms to become an imperial ruler and perform the rājasūya[S]. Does Dharmaputra desire such glory? His inner character and temperament show that he is not warlike by nature nor do they suggest that he desires the status of a mighty imperial ruler. Śrī Kṛṣṇa Paramātman makes such a man practise his dharma of a Kṣatriya. All this shows that by svadharma it is jāti dharma that the Lord means. Men like Droṇācārya were born Brahmins but they took up the duty of Kṣatriyas. Bhagavān does not deprecate them since they were otherwise great men, but all the same he does not show any displeasure when Bhīma taunts Droṇācārya for having forsaken the dharma of his birth. Thus we have confirmation that by svadharma the Lord means the jāti dharma of birth.

Then why does he use the phrase "guṇa-karma-vibhāgaśaḥ" in the Gītā?

Notes & References

1 *Vidyā-vinaya-saṁpanne Brāhmaṇe gavi hastini*
Śuni cai'va śvapāke ca paṇḍitāḥ samadarśinaḥ

— Bhagavadgītā, 5.18

2 *Cāturvarṇyaṁ mayāsṛṣṭaṁ guṇa-karma-vibhāgaśaḥ*
Tasya kartāram api māṁ viddhyakartāram avyayam

— Ibid, 4.13

3 In other words the Lord's precept is not at variance with his practice.

Chapter 3

Character and Vocation by Birth

It is jātidharma that goes to make the inner guṇa (inner quality or nature) of an individual. So Śrī Kṛṣṇa's dictum in the Gītā that the caturvarṇa division is in accord with guṇas and the idea that caste is based on birth are one and the same. There is no conflict between the two. You cannot find fault with Śrī Kṛṣṇa for his practice being at variance with his precept.

Paraśurāma and Droṇācārya were Brahmins but they were Kṣatriyas by nature. On the other hand, Viśvāmitra, a valorous Kṣatriya king known for his violent and passionate temperament, became a Brahmin ṛṣi. Cases like these are extremely rare, and are exceptions to the rule of jāti dharma. On the whole we see that the Lord functions on the basis that, whatever be the outward qualities of individuals, their inner quality is in keeping with their hereditary vocations.

How can birth be the basis of the quality on which one's occupation is based? Before a man's individual character develops, he grows in a certain environment, the environment evolved through the vocation practised in his family from generation to generation. He adopts this vocation and receives training in it from his people. It is in this manner that his guṇa is formed, and it is in keeping with his work. Everybody must have the conviction that he is benefited by the occupation to which he is born. When people in the past had this attitude they were free from greed and feelings of rivalry. Besides, though they were divided on the basis of their vocations, there was harmony among them. Children born in such a set-up naturally develop a liking and aptitude for the family vocation. So what is practised according to birth came to be the same as that practised according to guṇa. Whatever the view of reformers today, in the old days an individual's ability to do a job was in accord with his guṇa; and in the dharma obtaining in the past a man practised his calling according to his guṇa. Now it has become topsyturvy.

What is the view of psychologists on this question? According to them, heredity and environment play a crucial part in determining a man's character, abilities and attitudes. In the past all vocations were handed down from grandfather to father and from father to son. Besides, each group practising a particular occupation or trade lived in a separate area in the village. The Brahmins, for instance, lived in the agrahāra[S] and, similarly, each of the other jātis had its own quarter. So the environment also helped each section to develop its special skills and character. These two factors — heredity and environment — were greatly instrumental in shaping a person's guṇa and vocation.

Instead of speaking about the subject myself, I will cite the views of Gāndhījī who is much respected by the reformists: "The Gītā does talk of varṇa being according to guṇa and karma, but guṇa and karma are inherited by birth." So the fact that Kṛṣṇa Paramātman's practice is not at variance with his doctrine is confirmed by Gāndhījī. Modernists should not twist and distort the Vedas and śāstras and the pronouncements of Kṛṣṇa Paramātman to suit their own contentions.

Kṛṣṇa is usually imperative in his utterances. "I speak, you listen," such is his manner. But when he speaks of people and their duties, he does not impose himself saying "I speak thus", but instead he points to what is laid down in the śāstras to be the authority. During Kṛṣṇa's own time the various castes were divided according to birth: we learn this, without any room for doubt, from the Mahābhārata, the *Bhāgavata* and the *Viṣṇu Purāṇa.* I mention this because some research scholars today are likely to put forward the view that caste based on birth evolved after the time of Kṛṣṇa. The epic and the Purāṇas mentioned above declare categorically that during the age of Śrī Kṛṣṇa Paramātman the śāstras dealing with varṇāśrama were the authority for dharma. It was at such a time, when an individual's vocation was determined by birth, that the Lord declared in clear terms:

Yaḥ śāstra-vidhim utsṛjya vartate kāma-kārataḥ
Na sa siddhim avāpnoti na sukhaṁ na parām gatim

Tasmācchāstraṁ pramāṇaṁ te kāryākāryavyavasthitau
Jñātvā śāstravidhān'oktaṁ karma kartum ihā'rhasi

— Bhagavadgītā, 16.23 & 24

Whoso forsakes the injunctions of the śāstras and lives according to his own desires does not obtain liberation, finds no happiness. (The śāstras determine your work, what is right and what is wrong. You must know the way shown by the śāstras and pursue the work — vocation — according to them.)

Śrī Kṛṣṇa establishes that an individual owes his caste to his birth. There should not be the slightest doubt about it.

Chapter 4

Vocations according to Guṇa - not in Practice

Critics of varṇa dharma will perhaps argue thus: "Let the pronouncements of the Vedas and of Kṛṣṇa be whatever on the subject of jāti dharma. We do not accept them because they represent a partisan view. We must devise a system in which vocations are determined according to one's guṇa or quality and mental proclivity and not according to birth. Caste distinctions must be done away with."

What is the relationship between a man's vocation on the one hand and his guṇa — his character and natural inclination — on the other? If you pause to think about the question, you will realise that this relationship is highly exaggerated these days. Everybody suffers from a sense of self-importance and wants a great measure of freedom for himself in all things. That is the reason why people insist that their feelings and thoughts must be respected. They do not pause for a moment to consider whether such feelings are helpful to society, whether they are good or harmful for it. And, if they are harmful, should they not be checked for the sake of the community? Freedom is demanded for everything without such questions being taken into consideration.

If we examine how far the natural inclination and character of a man have to do with the work he likes to do, we will discover that in 90 out of 100 cases there is no connection at all between the two. A person of vairāgya (that is one who is detached and without any passion) would not like to stick to any job. Another who is full of energy and enthusiasm and who does his work after careful planning would be averse to any job of a routine nature. Some are keen to join the army and some the navy and, in contrast, there are some others who would turn their face against either even if compelled to do so. Those with a flair for writing, music or painting would discountenance any type of drab work.

But how many get the job for which they think they are fitted and for which they have a natural aptitude? Not even 10 per cent.

All sorts of people come to the Maṭha to see me. They pay their respects and tell me about what they want to do in life. I gather the impression that most of them are in jobs that are not in keeping with their interests or aptitude. A father comes and tells me: "My son has applied for admission to the engineering college as well as to the commerce college. If he fails to get admission to the first he will join the second. If he joins the engineering college there is nothing like it. I seek your blessings." Is there any connection between the job of an engineer and that of a commerce graduate? Even so the boy in question is prepared to do the work of an engineer (like surveying) or of a commerce graduate (like auditing). A young man tells me: "I have passed my Intermediate[1]. "I am not sure whether I should join the medical college or prepare for the IAS examination." Again, what is the connection between the work of a doctor and that of a collector perhaps? If one's profession is based on one's qualities, how is it that a young man who wants to become a doctor also contemplates a career in the IAS?

What would you say of a lawyer or an industrialist joining a political party and eventually becoming a minister? Among ministers today we see not only lawyers and industrialists but also ex- officials, professors, doctors, and so on. Are the qualities required for a minister the same as those required for a doctor, lawyer or professor?

There being no compatibility between a man's job and his qualities and natural inclination is a phenomenon not confined to the "higher" levels. Sometimes a devotee comes to tell me: "I was a counter clerk in a cinema. Now I have joined the army. Please bless me." Another says: "I was a waiter in a restaurant but now I manage a kiosk." What is the connection between the job of a cinema assistant and a soldier or between that of a waiter and that of a wayside shopkeeper?

Today the government professes to be "socialistic". Its view is that appointments are to be made not on the basis of caste but on the basis of the character and educational qualifications of the candidates. But when it conducts examinations for big positions, some are selected for the IAS and some for the IPS from the same group of candidates. Now from the point of view of natural inclination what is the relation, say, between a collector and a police superintendent? So long as no technical work is involved, employees of one department are transferred to another where the work is entirely different. In these instances there is nothing to support the theory of quality and mental proclivity in the allotment of work.

The majority of people do not choose their jobs according to their inborn character. They somehow learn to adjust themselves to their work whatever it happens to be. On the whole there is competition for such jobs as are very paying. To talk of inborn nature, quality or mental outlook is all bunkum. Would it not be ridiculous if "svadharma" comes to mean the job or vocation that brings the maximum money for the minimum of work.?

Note

[1] The equivalent of today's "Plus Two".

Chapter 5

A Wrong Notion

A wrong notion has gained currency that in the varṇāśrama system the Brahmin enjoys more comforts than others, that he has more income, that he has to exert himself less than others[1].

In the order created by our śāstras the Brahmin has to make as much physical effort as the peasant. Since, at present, there is ignorance about the rites he has to perform, people erroneously believe that he makes others work hard and himself lazes about and enjoys himself. The Brahmin has to wake up at four in the morning and bathe in cold water, rain or shine, warm or cold. Then, without a break, he has to perform one rite after another: sandhyāvandana, Brahmayajña, aupāsana, pūjā, vaiśvadeva and one of the 21 sacrifices. If you sit before the sacrificial fire for four days you will realise how difficult it is with all the heat and smoke. How many are the vows and fasts that the Brahmin has to keep and how many are the ritual baths.

Other castes do not have to go through such hardships. A Brahmin cannot eat "cold rice"[2] in the morning like a peasant — he has no "right" to it. The dharmaśāstras are not created for his convenience or benefit, nor to ensure that he has a comfortable life. He would not have otherwise imposed on himself the performance of so many rites and a life of such rigorous discipline. When he has his daytime meal it will be 1 or 2. (On the day of a śrāddha[S] it will be 3 or 4.) This is the time the peasant will have his rest after his meal under a tree out in the field where he works. And the Brahmin's meal, mind you, is as simple as the peasant's. There is no difference between the humble dwelling of the peasant and that of the Brahmin. Both alike wear cotton. The peasant may save money for the future but not the Brahmin. He has no right either to borrow money or to live in style.

In the "Yakṣa-praśna" of the Mahābhārata the simple life of the Brahmin is referred to:

Pañcame'hani ṣaṣṭe va śākam pacati svegṛhe
Anṛṇī cā'pravāsī ca sa vāricara modate

If daytime is divided into eight parts, the Brahmin may have his food only in the fifth or sixth part after performing all his rites. Before that he has neither any breakfast nor any snacks. And what does he eat? Not any rich food, no sweets like almonds crushed in sweetened milk. "Śākam pacati" — the Brahmin eats leafy vegetables growing on the banks of rivers, such areas being no one's property. Why is he asked to live by the riverside? It is for his frequent baths and for the leafy vegetables growing free there and for which he does not have to beg. He should not borrow money: that is the meaning of the word "anṛṇī", because if he developed the habit of borrowing he would be tempted to lead a life of luxury. Poverty and non-acquisitiveness (aparigraha) are his ideals. A Brahmin ought not to keep even a blade of grass in excess of his needs.

Now even the government and big industrialists are in debt. If there are any people who live according to the śāstras, without being indebted to anybody and without bowing to anybody and at the same time maintaining their dharma, it is the tribe called *narikuravas*.

"Apravāsam" (mentioned in the verse) means that a Brahmin must not leave his birthplace and settle elsewhere. Honour or dishonour, profit or loss, he must live in his birthplace practising his dharma. Nowadays, for the sake of money, people settle in England or America abandoning their motherland and their traditional way of life — and they are proud of it. Such a practice is condemned severely by the śāstras.

If all castes worked hard and lived a simple life there would be no ill-will among people and there would then be no cry that caste must be done away with. One reason for the "reformist view" is that today one caste is well-to-do and comfortable while another is poor and has to toil. Simplicity and hard work bring satisfaction and inward purity. Such a state of simple and happy life prevailed in our country for a thousand, ten thousand years.

I said that in these days too vocations are not chosen on the basis of a man's qualities or natural inclinations. The only considerations are income and comforts. All people are on the lookout for all kinds of jobs and this has resulted in increasing rivalry and jealousy, not to speak of growing unemployment.

In the beginning, when vocations were determined on the basis of birth, everyone developed an aptitude for the work allotted to him as well as the capacity to learn it easily. This is no longer the case now. In the past a man's vocation was like a paternal legacy and he was naturally very proficient in it. Now there is universal inefficiency and incompetence.

Note & Reference

[1] See "A Day in the Life of a Brahmin", Chapter 10, Part Nineteen. Here again the Paramaguru is speaking of how the Brahmin's life is ordered according to the śāstras.

[2] This is cooked rice kept overnight in water, called *"pazhaiyadu"* (literally "old") in Tamiḷ.

Chapter 6

Equal Opportunities

As we have already seen, we cannot sustain the claim that vocations are determined today according to the qualities of individuals and their inclinations or aptitudes. Also untenable is the demand for equal opportunities for all. To take an example: there are a certain number of seats in medical and engineering colleges. For highly specialised and new subjects like nuclear science the seats are very few. When candidates possessing the same qualifications (or merit) apply for admission to the colleges teaching these subjects only a fixed number are selected. Naturally, it is not practicable to choose all. Would it be right to contend that all candidates, even though equally qualified, who want to do research in a new science like atomic physics, should be given an opportunity? All those who apply for high positions in the government will not be selected for appointment even though they possess more or less the same qualifications. The government decides that we need so many doctors in the country, so many scientists, so many specialists and so many officials. In choosing them, a number of candidates are naturally rejected. This system is accepted by all.

It is in the same way as candidates are selected for seats in colleges or for appointments in the government that a certain percentage of people are thought to be sufficient for the purpose of conducting the rites meant to invoke the heavenly powers for the happiness of mankind — and these few function on a hereditary basis. Not more are needed for such a task since all the other work required for the proper functioning of society will otherwise suffer. This is the principle on which vocations are divided. People agitate for the application of the principle of equality (a product of the French Revolution) to scriptural matters without realising that it has hardly any place even in worldly affairs.

Chapter 7

Strength of Unity

When there are so many jātis and each lives separately from the rest, how can the community remain united as a whole? But the fact is unity did exist in the past. Indeed it is now that our society is divided because of ill-will among the various groups. The binding factor in the past was faith in our religion and its scriptures. The temple strengthened this faith and the sense of unity, the temple which belongs to the whole village or town and which is situated at its centre. People had the feeling of togetherness in the presence of Īśvara as his children. In festivals all jātis took part contributing to their success in various ways.

In the rathotsava (car festival) of a temple, all sections, including Harijans, pulled the chariot together. On returning home they did not bathe before eating. This practice has the sanction of the śāstras. [Talking of the past] it was a time when people were divided in their callings but were of one heart. Though stories are concocted that there was no unity since society was divided into a number of jātis, the fact is people then had faith in the śāstras and in the temples and this faith was a great unifying force. Today, ironically enough, hatred and enmity are spread between the various jātis in the name of unity. That is the reason why nowadays the cry against caste has become a cry against the Vedic dharma and temples.

The Vedas themselves proclaim that when a man attains to the highest state [that is jñāna] he does not need either the Vedas themselves or the temples. The Upaniṣads too have it that in the state of jñāna or supreme awareness the Vedas are not Vedas, the Brahmin is not a Brahmin, the untouchable is not an untouchable. It is to reach this state — a state in which the Vedas and all the differences in society cease to be — that you need the very Vedas, temples and caste differences. The condition of utter non-difference, may it be noted, is realised through these very means.

He who constantly strives to be free from worldly existence ultimately discovers that everything is one, so proclaim the Vedas. Kṛṣṇa Paramātman pronounces the same truth when he says that in the end there is worklessness — "Tasya kāryam na vidyate"[1].

In the phenomenal world with its works and day-to-day affairs, it does not make sense to claim that there are no differences. The śāstras, however, teach us that even in such a world we must be filled with love for all castes, for all creatures and that we must look upon all as the same without regarding one as inferior to the rest or superior. It means that the attitude of non-difference is in love, not in karma. "We must always feel inwardly that all are one and we must be permeated with love for all. But in karma, in action, there must be differences," such is the teaching of the śāstras.

"Bhāvādvaitam sadā kuryāt, kriyādvaitam na kārayet," so it is said. Oneness must be a matter of our feelings, not of our actions. Unless differences are maintained outwardly the affairs of the world will be conducted neither in a disciplined nor in a proper manner. It is only then that Ātmic inquiry can be practised without confusion and without being mentally agitated. In sanātana dharma[S] worldly life has been systematised as though it were real for the very purpose of its being recognised and experienced as unreal.

In this worldly life, the four varṇas developed branches and many jātis came into being. From the saptasvaras (the seven notes) are formed the 72 meḷakartā rāgas[2]. And from them have developed countless musical modes called janya rāgas. In the same way, from the four varṇas the numerous jātis were born. Separate dharmas, separate customs and rites, evolved for these jātis.

Notes & References

1 *Yas tvātma-ratir eva syād Ātmatṛpataś ca mānavaḥ*
Ātmanyeva ca saṁtuṣṭastasya kāryaṁ na vidyate.

—Bhagavadgītā, 3.17

2 Meḷakartā or janaka rāgas are parental scales. The division into 72 basic scales was the work of Venkaṭamakhī (17th century). The Paramaguru's mother, it may be noted, was a descendant of Govinda Dīkṣita, father of Venkaṭamakhi. The Dīkṣita was a minister to the Nāyaka rulers of Tañjāvūr and was himself a musicologist. (Janya rāgas are derived from the 72 janaka rāgas.)

Chapter 8

Hinduism and Other Religions

We feel apologetic about the differences in Hindu society especially since we think that the followers of other religions are not divided in the same way as we are. The latter are scornful of Hinduism on this score and some Hindus themselves feel that the differences in our society are unjust. But, if you pause to reflect on the subject, you will realise that if our civilization has survived from prehistoric times until today it is only because of these very differences in our society, the differences according to varṇa dharma.

In other religions too, even if there is no caste according to their scriptures, the communities are divided. Some of the divisions are almost like jātis and they do not intermarry. Muslims are divided into Ṣias (Shias), Suṇṇis and Ahmadiyās. In the South the Paṭṭāṇis (Paṭhāns) and Labbai Muslims do not intermarry. Among Christians there are Catholics, Protestants and followers of the (Greek) Orthodox Church. Hindus are divided on the basis of labour or work, but are united on another level. But followers of other religions, though themselves divided, speak ill of us. Yet we do not respond properly to their criticism.

Chapter 9

The Eternal Religion

The moral and ethical ordinances in other religions are applicable to all their followers. In Hinduism too there is a code of conduct meant for all varṇas and all jātis. But, in addition to this, there are separate dharmas for jātis with different vocations. There is no intermingling of these vocations and their corresponding dharmas. This fact is central to Hinduism and to its eternal character.

This religion has flourished for countless eons. What is the reason for its extraordinarily long history. If Hinduism has survived so long it must be due to some quality unique to it, something that gives it support and keeps it going. No other religion is known to have lasted so long. When I think of our religion I am reminded of our temples. They are not kept as clean as the churches or mosques. The latter are frequently whitewashed. There are so many plants sprouting from the gopurams and our temples support all of them. The places of worship of other religions have to be repaired every two or three years. Our sanctuaries are different because they are built of granite. Their foundations, laid thousands of years ago, still remain sturdy. That is why our temples have lasted so long without the need for frequent repair. We do so much to damage them and are even guilty of acts of sacrilege against them, but they withstand all the abuses. All are agreed that India has the most ancient temples. People come from abroad to take photographs of them. These temples still stand as great monuments to our civilization in spite of our neglect of them and our indifference. It is not easy to pull them down. Perhaps it is more difficult to demolish these edifices than it must have been to build them.

Our religion, to repeat, is like these temples. It is being supported by something that we do not seem to know, something that is not present in other faiths. It is because of this "something" that, in spite of all the differences, it is still alive.

This something is varṇāśrama dharma. In other religions there is a common dharma for all and we think that that is the reason for their greatness. These religions seem to touch the heights of glory at one time but at other times they are laid low. Christianity supplanted Buddhism in some countries. Islam replaced Christianity or Christianity replaced Islam. We know these developments as historical facts. The civilizations and religions that evolved in ancient Greece and China no longer exist today. Hinduism is witness to all such changes in other religions and it is subject to attacks from inside and outside. Yet it lives — it refuses to die.

There was a palm-tree round which a creeper entwined itself. The creeper grew fast and within months it entwined the entire tree. "This palm has not grown a bit all these months," the creeper said laughing. The palm-tree retorted: "I have seen ten thousand creepers in my life. Each creeper before you said the same thing as you have now said. I don't know what to say to you." Our religion is like this tree in relation to other faiths.

Although there are separate duties and religious rites for the different castes in our religion, the fruits of the rites are the same for all.

Chapter 10

Brahmins are not a Privileged Caste

It is alleged that Brahmins created the dharmaśāstras for their own benefit. You will realise that this charge is utterly baseless if you appreciate the fact that these śāstras impose on them the most stringent rules of life. There is also proof of the impartiality of the dharmaśāstras in that the Brahmin who is expected to be proficient in all the arts and all branches of learning can only give instruction in them but cannot take up any for his livelihood however lucrative it be and however less demanding than the pursuit of the Vedic dharma.

Now it is claimed that all people are equal in all spheres, that all are equal before the law. But members of legislative bodies, judges, etc, enjoy certain privileges and cannot be treated on the same footing as the common man. These privileges have indeed been codified. If anyone criticises a judge he will be charged with contempt of court. Even I may be hauled up for contempt for my remarks. People who call themselves democrats and socialists have managed for themselves special allowances, special railway passes, etc, that the common people are not entitled to. In contrast, the Brahmins who have preserved the dharmaśāstras have bound themselves to a rigorous discipline, roasted themselves, as it were, in the oven of ritual practices. If the Brahmin's purity is affected by someone he punishes himself by bathing and fasting.

The Brahmin must be conversant with the fourteen branches of Vedic lore. He must be proficient even in Gāndharva-veda or music and must be acquainted with agricultural science, construction of houses, etc. At the same time he must give instruction in these subjects to pupils from the appropriate castes. His own vocation is the study of the Vedas and he must have no other source of income.

Viśvāmitra was a master of Dhanurveda (military science). When he performed sacrifices, the demons Subāhu and Mārica tried to play havoc with them. Though a great warrior himself, he did not try to drive away the demons himself. Instead, he brought Rāma and Lakṣmaṇa for the purpose. Viśvāmitra thereafter gave instruction to the two in the use of astras and śastras[1].

If the Brahmin is asked, "Do you know how to wield a knife?" he must be able to answer, "Yes, I know." If he is asked, "Do you know to draw and paint?" again he must say, "Yes." But he cannot wield the knife or become an artist to earn his livelihood. All he can do is to learn these arts and teach others the same according to their caste. He is permitted to receive a dakṣiṇā[S] to maintain himself and he must be contented with it however small the sum may be. The Brahmin's speciality, his true vocation, is Vedic learning.

If members of certain castes are seen to enjoy certain privileges there must be a reason for the same. The man selling tickets has a room to himself and those who buy them have to stand outside and cannot complain about it saying that the practice offends against the principle of equality. If everybody gets in on the pretext of equality how can the ticket seller function? Will the man be able to sell the tickets properly? Everybody needs some special convenience to carry out his duties. A member of a joint family who falls ill has to be afforded certain special comforts — other members are not justified in demanding the same. In our religion there are many duties and rites that are common to all. But to carry out one's special duties certain conveniences are needed: as a matter of fact what are called conveniences are actually not conveniences or privileges, and also they are necessary to carry out the duties of the caste concerned for the welfare of society as a whole. It is important to accept this truth: the special dharma of any jāti is meant not only for those who constitute that jāti but for society as a whole.

Love must spring from the heart, so too a sense of unity. Unity is not achieved by all jātis becoming one. What do we see in Western countries where intermarriage is not prohibited and where all people mix together? There is much rivalry and jealousy among people there. According to our śāstras, everyone in the past performed his duty and helped others to perform theirs and this was how they remained united. The daughter-in-law does not speak to the father-in-law out of respect for him. Would you call such respect ill-will? If someone close to us and belonging to our own caste has some "pollution"[2], we do not touch him. Does it mean that we dislike him? It seems we are all mentally confused and do not have a proper appreciation of our different dharmas.

Note & Reference

[1] The terms astra and śastra are defined in Chapter 13, Part Seventeen.

[2] This is caused by the death of a relative or a birth in the family. There are elaborate rules governing pollution.

Chapter 11

Universal Well-being

According to the canonical texts, the Brahmin must perform vaiśvadeva every day in front of his house — the offering of bali[S] to the Pañcama is a part of this rite. The goal of Vedic works is the happiness of all mankind, indeed the happiness of all the worlds ("Lokāḥ samastāḥ sukhino bhavantu"). The sound of the Vedas creates universal well-being, so too Vedic sacrifices.

As a ruler, the Kṣatriya wages wars and does policing work for the security of all citizens. The Vaiśya too serves society — to think that he takes home all the profit he makes is unfair. The Lord speaks of the dharma of Vaiśyas in the Gītā[1]: "Kṛṣi-gaurakṣya-vāṇijyam Vaiśya-karma svabhāvajam." The third varṇa has three duties — the raising of crops, cow protection and trading — and it carries them out for the welfare of all people. The Vaiśya ploughs the field and grows crops for the benefit of the entire community. Similarly, the milk yielded by his cows is meant for general consumption and for sacrifices. A Vaiśya must also take care to see that the calves have their feed of milk. As a trader he procures commodities from other places to be sold locally.

However rich a man may be, he cannot sustain himself with his money alone. He has to depend on traders for essential goods. Trading is the dharma of Vaiśyas and it is an offence on their part not to practise it. Similarly, Brahmins would be committing a sin if they gave up Vedic rituals and earned money by doing other types of work. It is wrong to think that the trader carries on his trade for his good alone. Just imagine what would happen if there were a *hartal* and all shops were closed for a week. Surely people would suffer when essential goods are not readily available. Vaiśyas must conduct their business in the belief that their vocation is one that is ordained by the Lord and that it is for the good of the entire community.

Reference

1 *Kṛṣi-gaurakṣya-vāṇijyam Vaiśya-karma svabhāvajam*
Paricary'ātmakaṁ karma Śūdrasyā'pi svabhāvajam

——Bhagavadgītā, 18.44

Chapter 12

The Fourth Varṇa has its own Advantages

The dharma of the fourth varṇa involves much physical exertion and effort in its practice. Outwardly it may seem that its members do not enjoy the same status and comforts as others do. But we must note that they are comparatively free from the discipline and rituals to which the rest are tied down. In the past, they knew more contentment than the other castes, living as they did by the side of the Lord. Vyāsa himself says: "Kaliḥ sādhuḥ, Śūdraḥ sādhuḥ" (The age of Kali is in no way inferior to the other ages nor are Śūdras inferior to the other castes. Kali is indeed elevated and Śūdras exalted.) In other yugas or ages Bhagavān is attained to with difficulty by meditation, austerities and pūjā, but in Kali he is reached by the mere singing of his names. The Brahmin, the Kṣatriya and the Vaiśya are likely to have self-pride, so they cannot earn Ātmic liberation easily. The Brahmin is likely to be vain about his intellectual superiority, the Kṣatriya about his power as a ruler and the Vaiśya about his wealth. So these three varṇas will tend to stray from the path of dharma. A member of the fourth varṇa, on the contrary, is humble.

Has not Vaḷḷuvar[T] said, "Humility raises one to the gods"? This is the reason why the Śūdra, being humble, resides by the side of the Lord. One must not be subject to one's ahaṁkāra or ego-sense. It is as a means of effacing their ego and of making them deserve the grace of Īśvara that the first three castes are authorised to learn the Vedas and to perform Vedic rites. Performing Vedic rites implies a number of restrictions in the matter of food, habits, etc. It is only with the pathya[S] of this discipline that the medicine called the Vedic dharma will be efficacious. Any lapse in the observance of the rules of personal conduct and religious life will be a serious offence and it will have to be paid for by suffering. So the first three castes must be ever careful about their religious practices. The fourth varṇa is free from most of these restraints. The labour put in by the Śūdra will cleanse him inwardly: it is his Vedic observance; it is his God; and through it he easily achieves perfection. That is why Vyāsa proclaimed, raising both hands, "Śūdraḥ sādhuḥ."

If a Śūdra does not have enough food to fill his belly, if he does not have enough clothing, and if he has no roof over his head to shelter him from rain and sun, the whole community and the government must be held responsible — and both must be held guilty.

I repeat that the Brahmin's means of livelihood was in no way better than the Śūdra's, nor did he enjoy more comforts than members of the fourth varṇa.

Chapter 13

Removal of Ego

"All that is fine. But what about the question of self-respect?" ask reformers who profess to be socialists. For them, however, to raise such a question is to remain untrue to their own ideals. They talk a great deal, don't they, about dignity of labour? They proclaim that no job, no work, is degrading. Gāndhijī cleaned his toilet himself. Rājagopālācāri[1] washed his clothes himself when he was premier. To demonstrate the principle of dignity of labour VIPs like the mayor sweep the streets one day in a year. Photographs of important men doing such work are published in the newspapers. If the reformists think that manual work is degrading it means that they are opposed to the ideals they themselves uphold.

If you ask me, "ahaṁkāra" or ego-feeling is a cover for all such ideas as "status", "self-respect", etc. If you look at the question from the angle that the Śūdra does not have the self-pride associated with the Brahmin, the Kṣatriya and the Vaiśya, you will realise the truth of Vyāsa's dictum, "Śūdraḥ sādhuḥ". The śāstras are one with the socialists in proclaiming that all types of work are equally noble. If the socialists say so from the worldly or material point of view, the śāstras say the same from the spiritual point of view. To explain, since the well-being of mankind is dependent on the performance of a variety of jobs, there is no question of one job being inferior to another job or superior to it. If everybody does the work allotted to him thinking it to be an offering to Īśvara, all will be rewarded with inner purity, so say the śāstras. When work is accomplished in a spirit of dedication to God, the consciousness will be cleansed. And this, inner purity, is a means to becoming aware of the Self.

You may look at your work from two angles. One is from that of dignity of labour according to which principle no work is degrading. The second is from that of consecrating your work, whatever it be, to God. In either case "self-respect" has no place in it. If there is neither vanity nor ego-sense in doing one's duty or work, there will be no cause for anger, no reason to feel that one is assigned a particular set of religious practices that is humiliating. One should then be willing to accept the religious ordinances prescribed according to one's vocation. It must be noted that if a Brahmin enjoys bodily comforts in the same manner as a Kṣatriya or a Vaiśya, his mantras will cease to be efficacious. If a labourer keeps fasts like a Brahmin he will not be able to do his duty, that is he will not be able to do physical work satisfactorily.

"According to the śāstras," once a learned man told me, "the Brahmin must wear white, the Kṣatriya red, the Vaiśya yellow and the Śūdra blue. At first, I wondered whether in this order one caste was regarded as inferior to another. On reflection, I saw the reason behind it." Until then I myself had not given any thought to the subject. So I asked the paṇḍita to explain the principle behind the arrangement he had spoken about. He said: "Even the slightest stain will be visible on white. When a Brahmin performs a sacrifice he has to be careful that he does not spill anything or waste anything. If he does, his white clothes will show it. He has necessarily to be frugal since he must not bother others for money or material. The Kṣatriya, as a warrior, spills blood, but the bloodstains on his dress should not show, nor should it be a cause of fear for others — that is why he wears red. A Vaiśya handles a variety of commodities in the *bāzār* but it is yellow that sticks to his clothes the most. That is why the Vaiśya must wear yellow so that the yellow stains will not show easily. Blue is most suitable for those who work in dust and grime. Even in modern times workers wear blue uniforms. So blue is the most suitable colour for Śūdras." You will thus appreciate the reason behind each type of wear. The śāstras are indeed mindful of the conveniences and comforts of each jāti. If you realise this, you will understand the meaning of the saying, "Śāstrāya ca sukhāya ca." You will thus also appreciate the reason behind many a śāstric rule and realise that there must be an inner meaning to those rules the significance of which you have yet to grasp.

Today even intelligent people do not know the meaning behind different caste duties. "How can the work done by one man be according to dharma and meritorious while the same done by another is contrary to dharma and sinful?" they ask. In the old days, even unlettered people knew that it was a sin to adopt the vocation and duties of another jāti because it was injurious to society. They worked together during temple festivals and in carrying out public duties but in matters like food and so on they did not mix together since such mixing, they knew, was harmful to their traditional vocations. The mingling of castes, they realised, would damage the system of vocations, the system that was devised for the good of all society. For thousands of years all castes have lived according to this system, finding happiness and fulfilment in it. If they had not found such happiness and fulfilment, they would have surely rebelled against the system.

After the inception of British rule, Brahmins lost the royal grants of land but got jobs in the government. With the introduction of machines and increased urbanisation, the handicrafts were destroyed and village life received a setback. While other communities found it difficult to get jobs, Brahmins were able to earn their upkeep without any physical exertion. This shook the very foundations of the system of four varṇas and the British now used the opportunity to introduce the new principle of egalitarianism and the race theory. People lost their faith in the śāstras and with it there was a change of outlook. If, by the grace of Īśvara, the old system is restored, the work done by every individual — from the Brahmin to the Pañcama[S] — will bring inward purity to all. Besides, there will be the realisation that each, according to his hereditary occupation, will contribute to the general welfare of mankind. If we pause to reflect on the subject, we will feel proud of varṇa dharma instead of being ashamed of it — and we will also develop a deep respect for those who created it.

Note

1 Śrī Cakravartī Rājagopālācāri (Rājājī) became premier of Madrās Presidency in July 1937 when provincial autonomy was introduced by the British according to the Government of India Act of 1935. After India became independent in 1947, with the status of a Dominion, he was appointed Governor-General. ("Premier" is the equivalent of the "chief minister" of today.)

Chapter 14

The Ultimate Purpose of Varṇa Dharma

When factories took the place of handicrafts and cottage industries, the small village communities became urbanised. The needs of people multiplied, so too the number of occupations. Today when the old way of life is gone, it seems impossible to revive the system of hereditary vocations. Is it any longer practicable now to insist that only Kṣatriyas ought to man the defence services, that only Vaiśyas can transact trade and business, that the members of the fourth varṇa must continue to remain labourers? Is it at all possible to revive the old system? I am not unaware of the state of affairs now prevailing. If so why do I keep extolling varṇa dharma? There are two reasons.

Whatever be the situation today — and whether or not we can return to the old order — it is not right to claim as people nowadays do that the old order was utterly unjust, that it was created by the vested interests for their own good and convenience. We must be able to convince the critics that the old order was not unjust at all and that there is nothing like varṇa dharma to help people to attain inner purity. They must also be made to realise that this dharma, apart from helping society to function in a disciplined and harmonious manner, will bring well-being to all and give an impetus to culture.

There is an even more important reason. Today the functions of Kṣatriyas, Vaiśyas and Śūdras have changed and become mixed. Even so the work of the government goes on somehow. Defence, the manufacture of various articles, trade, labour — all these go on somehow. But, unlike in the past, there is jealousy as well as rivalry in all fields. Even so, the duties of the three castes are carried out despite the fact that varṇa dharma has broken up. They are a practical necessity for day-to-day life as well as for the functioning of the government. So they are performed, albeit unsatisfactorily.

There is, however, a function higher than all these. It is that of taking all of them — all these functions — to their ultimate point. And this function belongs to the Brahminic way of life and it has become almost extinct. To teach dharma by precept and practice, the dharma that is the foundation of all activities, to invoke the divine powers through the Vedic chant for the good of all mankind, to create high ideals through their own austere life, to nurture the Ātmic strength of the community, to promote the arts, to nourish culture -- these embrace the dharma of Brahmins and it is now on the verge of extinction.

The need for the Brahminic dharma is not widely recognised because of its subtle and intangible character. There is no realisation of the fact that it is as much essential to life as that of the other three varṇas. Indeed, it is this dharma that gives meaning to life and creates a path for the fulfilment of that life. We ignore it and devote ourselves solely to the functions of the other three varṇas. If any improvement is made in them we are happy. But what use is material prosperity without Ātmic and cultural advancement? Material progress is no progress at all. Americans have realised this truth — we ought also to realise the same. So however confusedly the functions of the other castes are carried out, the Brahmin must function in the right manner as a pathfinder for others by living a life of simplicity and sacrifice, performing Vedic rites and creating worldly and Ātmic well-being for mankind. In this way the soul of India will be kept alive.

If the Brahmin caste is restored to order, it might well be the beginning of the end of the confused state of the other castes. In this land alone has there existed — and existed for ages — a jāti for the protection of dharma and the Ātmic uplift of all. If this jāti becomes extinct there will be all-round decay. If I have spoken at length I have this purpose in view, that this jāti must be revived in its true form so as to prevent the general decline of the nation. The Brahmin jāti must not live a life of self-indulgence. On the contrary it must perform rites all through the day for the welfare of society. Brahmins must live austerely, with love for all in their hearts. If they are restored to their dharma our society in its entirety will be brought to the path of dharma and will be saved.

Chapter 15

The Universal Remedy

In the past, though people were divided on the basis of caste, they were free from hatred and ill-will. It is now that we see ill-will and hatred everywhere in the country. One state is at loggerheads with another; one state has a dispute with another over the sharing of river waters; and again one state has a quarrel with another on the question of boundaries. In the past, the Ceṭṭiars [of the South] built dharmaśālās [free boarding and lodging houses] for pilgrims from Kāśī. Correspondingly, the Seṭhjīs constructed *dharamśālās* for pilgrims going to Kāśī and Badarīnāth. People then were united as devotees of the Lord. Everything has gone awry today because of increased political activity and empty talk. So, as a medicine for our ills, as a sovereign remedy, we must pray that people become more devoted to the Lord.

The incessant cry that "Caste must go" has resulted in an aggravation of hatred between one jāti and another. Though the propaganda against caste has been going on for 30 or 40 years, the caste factor comes to the fore even today during elections. Caste feelings run so high that violent clashes between communities are not infrequent. Here it is not hatred between Brahmins and non-Brahmins. Fortunately, the Brahmin has been made to distance himself from politics[1]. It is a matter for some comfort that, even though they have not quit politics on their own, others have pushed them out of it. So the present quarrels are between other castes. In Āndhra Pradeś the Khammas and the Reḍḍis are quarrelling between themselves; in Karṇāṭaka the Liṅgāyats are at war with some other community. Ironically enough, it is in these days when the cry of equality is the loudest that we witness so many caste wars. This phenomenon is something unknown to the śāstric tradition. Here [in Tamiḻ Nāḍu] candidates are chosen for elections on the basis of jātis. Paḍayācis in one district, Gauṇḍars in another, Tevars in a third, Mukkulattārs in a fourth, and so on. Elections are fought not on the basis of ideology but on that of caste.

Note

[1] This is particularly true of the South and to some extent of Mahārāṣṭra.

Chapter 16

Śankara and Sanātana Dharma

There is a saying in English: "Give a dog a bad name and hang him." The dog is a faithful animal and full of gratitude for its master. Few would relish the idea of a dog being hanged. So if any dog is to be hanged, it has perhaps to be given a bad name.

Reformers who claim to be modern do the same with our dharmaśāstras. For ages these śāstras have done this nation nothing but good. But the reformers want to sentence them to the noose on the plea that they have given rise to many an evil. Some feel that there is no need for the division of society based on our ancient and eternal śāstras. So they invent outrages ostensibly perpetrated in pursuance of the tenets of the dharmaśāstras. "In our country there is a stipulation about who can do what," they say opposing the varṇa system. "As a result, the people have become divided. There is no unity among Hindus. This is the cause of our having frequently come under the heel of foreign powers." There is not an iota of truth in this allegation.

It may be that when a common adversary confronted us there was no unity among the rājās. But there is nothing to support the view that, because of differences arising out of caste, this or that section of the people helped the invader. Ironically enough, it is today that there is so much disunity and hatred with all the clamour for the abolition of caste differences. In the past, on the contrary, there was nothing but happiness in society when caste distinctions were maintained. When there were disputes between two villages over a plot of land, boundary or canal, the inhabitants of either village remained united as one man — from the Brahmin to the untouchable. If it was the example of unity provided by a village, you could very well imagine how the country on the whole would have remained united.

People divided into small communities were enabled and encouraged to live together in a well-knit manner and the members of each community were proud of belonging to it. And these had also their headmen. If anybody was proved guilty of an offence he was excommunicated. Such a punishment was considered a disgrace since people were greatly attached to their respective communities apart from being proud of belonging to them. And this acted as a deterrent to crime. Now there is no institution to unite people together in this manner on a heart-to-heart basis. Perhaps it is not possible also to cement people together today since they are all part of a larger system which is not easy to control. What is the result? The incidence of crime is on the increase and correspondingly the responsibilities of the police. Those who are opposed to the śāstras must pause to think about such developments.

There is bound to be opposition to any idea, any system and it is indeed to be welcomed. It is by respecting the views of the opposition that we discover our own drawbacks and prepare to remedy them. But it is quite another matter to oppose a system for its imaginary defects because the only consequence then would be that its good features would come under threat.

I will give you an example of criticism that is totally unfounded or imaginary. Some people think it "uncivilized" to wear any sacred mark on the forehead. It is given a bad name as a "caste mark". As a matter of fact the sacred ashes (bhasma or vibhūti)[S], for example, are worn by all castes, from the Brahmin to the Harijan. So is the case with the Vaiṣṇava *nāmam*[T] (made of *Tiruman*[T] or the sacred earth): it stands for the truth that everything is of the earth and mingles with the earth, that all is Viṣṇu. The ashes are a symbol of the Paramātman. When the body is cremated all that remains is the ashes which are the symbol of the eternal Brahman. Is it right to condemn the use of such symbols that stand for great truths?

All old dhārmic traditions must be protected and kept alive. Śrī Śankara Bhagavatpāda has commanded us to do so. I bear his name. So it is my duty to remind you of his injunction. Whether or not you will heed it, I should impress upon you that the śāstric customs have the purpose of ensuring the good of all mankind.

Chapter 17

Cry "Grow" — Don't Cry "Perish"

To speak on the one hand of the glory of Tamiḷ culture, constantly recalling the words of Tiruvaḷḷuvar[T] and others who extol love and divine grace, and to raise on the other hand the cry of hatred against a certain community—with the display of posters everywhere proclaiming such hatred—does not seem to me right. It goes against the very spirit of the Tamiḷ land and causes me great anguish. If you cry "Grow", instead of crying "Perish", all the hatred and all the quarrels will vanish. Instead of agitating for the abolition of the caste system, people must start a movement to build more and more temples and spread devotion.

If everybody joins in this endeavour, the devotion that brought all of us together in the past as one family will again become a powerful force to reunite us and create a sense of universal well-being. If there is devotion, there will be no caste hatred. Such was the case during all these centuries. There was caste in the old days but it did not cause bitterness among the communities.It is not caste itself that is to be faulted but the hatred arising from it. So to attempt to destroy this institution is like burning a house to kill a rat. The movement to put an end to the caste system has disrupted the old division of labour and together with it caused discontent,disquiet and jealousy among the people. Hatred among the different communities has grown like a big tree with many branches.

It is time that we opened our eyes to the evil and started making an effort to substitute the campaign with its cry of destruction with a movement to bring all classes and castes together so as to promote devotion to Īśvara and service to humanity. It will be one way of ignoring caste hatred. Countering caste hatred as such might have the effect of refuelling it. If we ignore it and turn our minds to other matters — other noble matters — bitterness due to caste will cease by itself. Suppose you are admonished not to think of the monkey while taking medicine, you will perhaps be tempted to do the opposite (that is to think of the monkey). Similarly, when we keep all the while speaking against caste hatred, the effect will be the opposite, that of reminding people of caste differences and of arousing feelings of inferiority among some sections and of superiority among some others.

It is important for all to become involved in a good cause, like the construction of a temple, or some public welfare scheme. Good feelings like love will surely spring in the hearts of people; at the same time much good will be done to society in general. Today, it is because people are not involved together in such [constructive] work that they turn their minds to destructive ideas, to argumentativeness and to gossip and quarrels. Unfortunately, some people think that if they inflame hatred between the communities or instigate quarrels or disputes, they will be able to gather a crowd of admirers round them. If we are all the time engaged in constructive work there will be fewer opportunities for trouble-making; indeed people will not find the time to do evil.

People go in procession until their legs ache, raising cries against this and that. Would there not be all-round growth and prosperity if all this manpower were employed to good work, if all the energies of people were turned to some constructive task? There is one type of "growth" that is higher than all others, it is the love that springs in the hearts of people. I think there must be a "tight" time-table for all: performing religious rites; worshipping at temples; listening to religious discourses; all castes working together for a divine cause or being engaged in social service. Adhering to such a time-table would mean universal happiness and prosperity. Besides, it would obviate the necessity of raising the cry of hatred against any caste.

There are certainly no differences between one jāti and another so far as "status" is considered; that is one jāti is not inferior to another or superior to it. All jātis have produced great men — Appar, Nammāzhvār, Śekkizhār, Nandanār and Kaṇṇappar[T] to name a few. The Ācārya himself has sung the praises of Kaṇṇappar in his *Śivānandalaharī.* The śāstras declare that it is a sin for anybody to regard himself as superior to others. Great men have shown us the way in this matter. They have spoken, abasing themselves, "*Nāyinum kaḍaiyen*"; "*nāyaḍiyen*"[1]. People do not share this kind of humility in the present age of freedom— and that indeed is the cause of much of our trouble. We must regain the old sense of humility and modesty. If so, jāti will be confined to work, functions, and will not in the least be a cause of any feelings of differences. If all people adopt the same style of living that is simple and virtuous, there will be no cause for jealousy or heart-burning.

Whether or not we have the courage or the spirit of sacrifice to work towards this ideal, a way will open out for us if we at least recognise the ideal. May we have success in achieving this ideal with the blessings of Ambā.

Note

[1] "I am inferior to a dog..." "I, your humble servant, am a dog."

Part Twenty-One

FROM WORK TO WORKLESSNESS

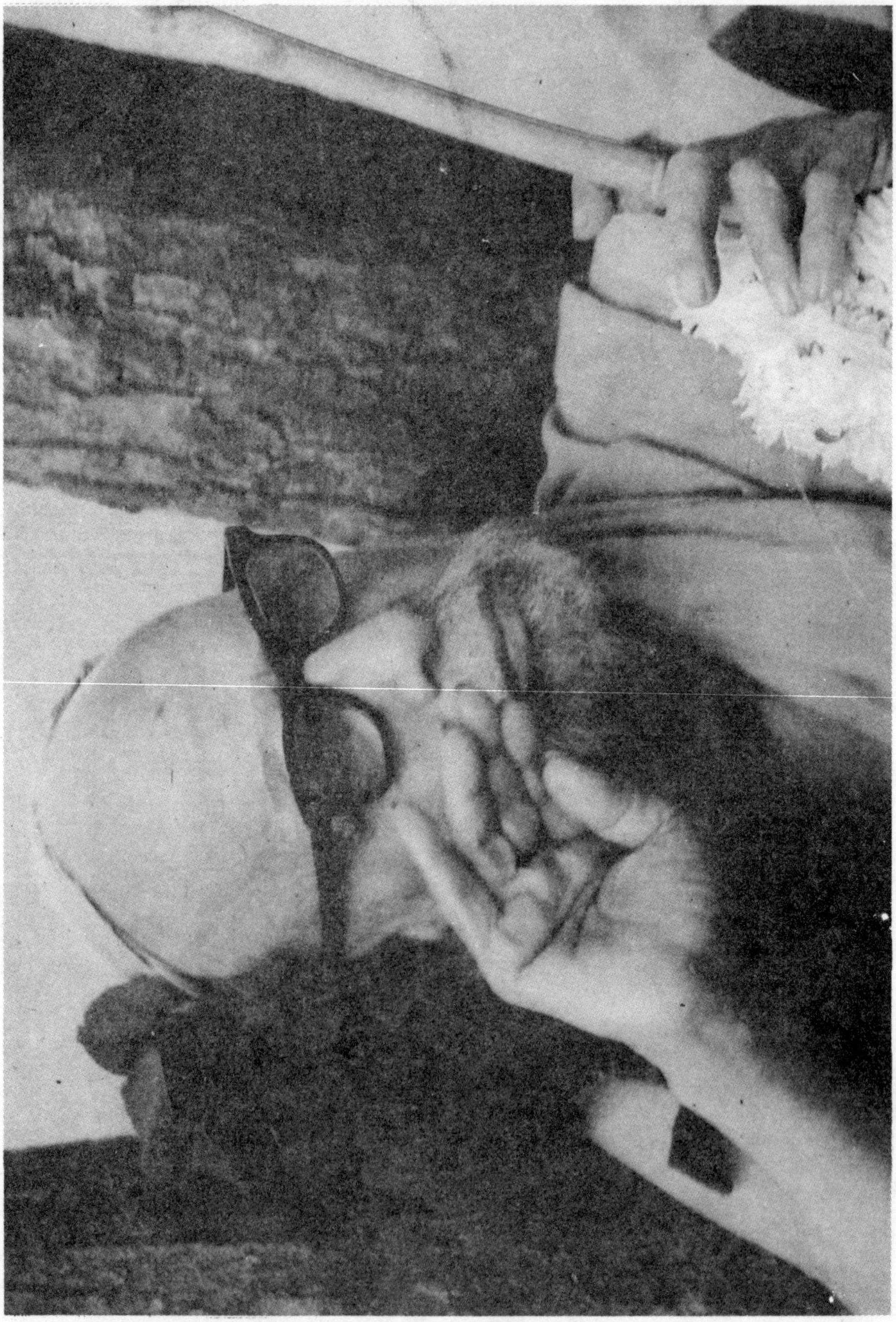

Chapter 1

Outward Karma — Inward Meditation

I have, in the course of my talks, dealt with a large number of religious rites. It may seem that the rituals, the pūjā to Parameśvara and the service done to fellow men are meant for "others". But in truth they are meant for ourselves. By helping others, by serving them, by worshipping the Lord, we are rewarded with a sense of fullness. Others may really benefit from our help or may not. But when we serve them we experience inward peace and happiness — about this there is no doubt. What is called "paropakāra" (helping others) is indeed upakāra done to oneself (helping oneself).

In serving others we may have to undergo hardships, make sacrifices and exert ourselves physically. But the happiness and sense of fullness we obtain is far greater compared to the trouble taken by us. The Lord does not have to gain anything from the pūjā we perform. In worshipping him, in reading the sacred texts, in going on pilgrimages we find inward joy. Why do we perform pūjā and why do we help others? It is all for our own satisfaction.

Our affection for our wife, children and others is in fact affection for ourselves. According to the Upaniṣadic teaching of Yājñavalkya, it is for our own inner contentment that we love others. We perform pūjā to the Lord purportedly because of our devotion for him and we do social service persumably because of our love of mankind. But in truth the reason is we like ourselves and find happiness in such acts. For the sake of such happiness we do not mind encountering difficulties or making sacrifices.

If we spend money on ourselves or go seeking sensual pleasure, we do not obtain the same inner satisfaction. Work done for our own sake leads to disquiet and sorrow. We see our face in the mirror and note that there is no tilaka[S] on our forehead. What happens if we apply a tilaka of dark unguent to the mirror [to the image]? It will be blackened. To apply a tilaka to the image means applying it to the one who is in front of the mirror. Doing things for ourselves [serving ourselves] is indeed like applying a dark spot to our mind—it is blackening ourselves. We take the image of the Paramātman reflected in the Māyā mirror that is the mind to be ourselves. To bedeck the image in reality means adorning the Paramātman. This is the reason why serving humanity gives us a sense of fulfilment because humanity is a manifestation of the Paramātman. Worshipping the Supreme Being is the same. Only then will the black spot that we apply to ourselves will become an ornament. We decorate Ambā to decorate ourselves. If we adorn ourselves we only enlarge our ego and feed our arrogance. When Ambā is bedecked everybody will be happy about it. When we wear a well-laundered *dupaṭṭa* and preen ourselves, do others feel happy about it? They will speak scornfully of us: "See, how well-ironed he looks."

All of you give me heaps of garlands. You do so because you think I am great and want to express your devotion for me. You also feel that instead of wearing them yourselves the garlands would be an ornament for me. If I decorated myself with them thinking myself to be a great man, it would mean that I am satisfying my ego. But you bring me garlands with devotion and would it be right for me to spurn them? So just as you want to see me decorated I want to see Ambā adorned and so I offer the garlands to her[1].

To go in search of money, fame and sensual pleasure, thinking them to be good, is to blacken our minds. What is it that is good for us? That which is good for the world — and it is but a form of the Paramātman. This truth is known to our inner being; we realise it deep in our mind. That is why we find greater fulfilment in doing good to others, unmindful of all the difficulties, than in finding comforts for ourselves.

The world is a manifestation of the Paramātman and so must be we too. We must remove the mirror called the mind and experience the truth within us that we are none other than the Paramātman. This is what is called meditation. All the work we do ought to lead finally to worklessness, to the meditation of the Ātman. The goal of all the sacraments I speak about is this.

Our actions make us happy in many ways. But in none of these actions do we find the peace that we enjoy during sleep. How we suffer if we lose even a single night's sleep? There is so much happiness in sleep[2]. Do we not realise from this that the supreme "comfort" or happiness is worklessness. Dhyāna or meditation is the state of being absorbed in the Paramātman, a state of non-doing.

In sleep we are not conscious that we are happy. It is only when we are awake that we realise that we were happy when we were asleep. The ultimate goal of meditation is samādhi[S] in which we are fully conscious of the great bliss experienced by us. If we teach ourselves to remain in a state of non-doing within (inside ourselves) we will experience tranquillity even though we keep working outwardly. The inner peace will never be disturbed.

The quietude of Dakṣiṇāmūrti is the bliss of knowingness. It is not the same as the stilling of the mind during sleep. In sleep there is no voluntary control of the mind; the mind becomes still because of exhaustion. Such stillness we are not capable of sustaining on our own. What becomes still during sleep, without being subject to our control, returns on our awakening again without being subject to our control.

Death too is a kind of sleep. In it, too, the mind is stilled. But with rebirth when the individual self becomes incarnate the mind starts to be active again. If we learn to control the mind voluntarily it will be able to remain in that state. Though Dakṣiṇāmūrti remains still without doing anything he is full of awareness. It is because he is inwardly a non-doer that he is able to do so much in an outward sense. The Dakṣiṇāmūrti who remains still is the one who dances the dance of bliss, who destroys the demon Tripura and who keeps roaming as a mendicant. After granting boons to his devotees he goes from place to place. He is still inwardly but is in a frenzy outwardly. If we manage to still ourselves inwardly we will be able to do so much outwardly.

We are the opposite of Dakṣiṇāmūrti. We don the disguise of non-detachment in order to make others believe that we are at peace with ourselves, but inside we remain all the time agitated.

Outward calm is the first step towards inward stillness—and this stillness is to be brought about in degrees and will not be gained all at once. That is why the wise tell us: "Reduce all your sensual activities. Do not join the crowd. Try to disengage yourself from all work including that of doing good to the world. Keep away from money and dwell in the forest." But do we listen to such advice? We shall do so only when our mind is cleansed.

That is why so many rituals are prescribed to purify the mind, the consciousness. It means that, instead of asking us *not to do* this and that, we are asked *to do* (perform) this and that rite. It is natural for us to be involved in some work or other. So, without any regard for our personal likes and dislikes, we perform the rites laid down in the śāstras. Even here our personal likes and dislikes will intrude but, unlike in the matter of meditation, we succeed to some extent at least in curbing them during the conduct of the rites. In due course, with the grace of the Lord, we will be able to perform good works without minding the discomfort and ignoring our personal likes and dislikes. Desire and hatred will be reduced and the mind will become pure. With the mind cleansed we will be able to perform one-pointed meditation. This is the time when we will be mature enough to forsake all works and become a forest recluse and practise meditation. If we are able to meditate with utter one-pointedness then everything will acquire the character of the Paramātman. There will be no need to leave everything and depart for the forest. Nor will it be necessary to speak of any religious discipline and remain holding the nose with the hand. The forest, the village, solitude and crowd—they are all the Paramātman. Both work and meditation are the Paramātman. Our inner peace will not be shaken by anything. Like Dakṣiṇāmūrti we can remain still and tranquil and yet be all bustle outwardly.

In the Gītā, the Lord exhorts Arjuna to practise svadharma—in the case of Arjuna it means waging war. The Lord also propounds the yoga of meditation in which there is no "doing". He refers to the example of Janaka[3] who was all the time working for the welfare of his people but at the same time remained in the ultimate meditation called Brahma-niṣṭhā. He himself, says the Lord, is like Janaka. There is apparently a contradiction in all this. But in reality no. The one arises from the other. In the beginning when it is not easy to control the mind and meditate on the Ātman, perform rituals. Then gaining mental purity through them, that is the rituals, forsake karma and practise meditation, yoga, etc. Once perfection is attained in meditation and yoga, nothing will affect us. In this all is still inwardly and yet outwardly there will be much activity.

Briefly put, this is the concept of Bhagavatpāda: ultimately everything (the phenomenal world) will be seen to be Māyā. The One Object, the One and Only Reality, is the Brahman. We must be one with It, non-dualistically, without our having to do anything in the same way as the Brahman. I, who bear the name of Śrī Śankara, keep speaking about many rites, about pūjā, japa[S], service to fellow men, etc. It is because in our present predicament we have to make a start with rites. In this way, step by step, we will proceed to the liberation that is non- dualistic. It is this method of final release that is taught us by Śrī Kṛṣṇa Paramātman and by our Bhagavatpāda. At first karma, works, then upāsana[S] or devotion and, finally, the enlightenment called jñāna.

If we advance in this way, by degrees, with faith and devotion, we will obtain the wisdom and mellowness for Ātmic meditation and inner control. Afterwards, we may keep doing any kind of work outwardly for the good of mankind.

What is the best means of practising Ātmic meditation? We must be imbued with the tranquillity that is Parāśakti incarnate and remember every day Dakṣiṇāmūrti in his quiescence. Let alone the idea of forsaking all works and becoming plunged in meditation. Let us also leave aside, for the time being, karma which itself is transformed into the high state of meditation. These are conditions to which we must rise at a later stage in our inward journey. But right now — at the beginning — let us train ourselves in the midst of our work to remain at peace and learn to meditate a little.

To start with, let karma, devotion and meditation be practised together. These are not opposed to one another but are complementary. In the end all will drop off one by one and the samādhi of dhyāna alone will remain. When we start our inward journey we must keep this goal of samādhi before us. So every day, leaving aside all other work, we must practise meditation for some time. But all the same we must not dismiss rituals as meaningless or as part of superstition. We must keep performing them. It is only when our impurities are washed away thus that we will realise the self-luminous Reality in us.

Notes & References

[1] The Paramaguru was like a priceless treasure-chest of humility. In this discourse when he speaks about the garlands, he reveals a great truth. It is well known that instead of wearing the garlands offered to him round his neck, he would wear them on his head. Here he speaks of offering the garlands to Ambā. The guru's feet are held by his disciple. So we must realise that our Ācārya's guru was Ambā herself. — Ra. Ga.

[2] See next para. When we are asleep we are not actually aware of our happiness

[3] *Karmaṇa'iva hi saṁsiddhim āsthitā Janakādayaḥ*
Loka-saṁgraham evā'pi saṁpaśyan kartum arhasi

Na me Pārthā'sti kārtavyaṁ trīṣu lokeṣu kiñcana
Nā'navāptam avāptavyaṁ varta eva ca karmaṇi

— Bhagavadgītā, 3.20 & 22

Chapter 2

How to Cultivate Character and Good Conduct

How do we acquire character, how do we come to possess good qualities? By living according to the precepts of the Vedas and śāstras and by following the good customs practised by our forefathers as well as by performing the rites that have been passed down to us. Good conduct springs from a good mind. So the mind must be free from evil.

Everybody does not possess a good mind. Look at your child. It is all the time up to some mischief or other. It cuts paper with scissors or cuts down little plants and shrubs. It is naughty all the time. When the same child is sent to school it is brought under a certain discipline. It has fixed timings to go to school and return home, to read its lessons, etc. It is no longer found to be wayward.

In the same way if we have no opportunity of being involved in evil thoughts and activities, we will also come under a certain discipline. That is why the śāstras lay down rules to keep us involved in good works. When we are conducting religious rites we must have no ego- feeling. The preceptors of the Vedic way have shown us the path to consecrate our karma to Īśvara. The Lord has given us not only the strength to perform them but also the intelligence and the means. Even a little ego-sense would be ruinous because it is capable of taking many disguises and of seizing us at an unwary moment.

Are we able to see ourselves in a soiled mirror? If we dust it and clean it well, we can see our reflection clearly. Even a clean mirror cannot produce a proper image if it keeps shaking. The mirror must be both clean and steady; only then will the reflection be true and clear. The mind, the consciousness, is like a mirror. The Supreme Being is the only Truth. When there are no evil thoughts in us, the mind-mirror will also be clean. If it is fixed on a single object it will remain steady—like a mirror that does not shake. Only then will the Paramātman be reflected in it.

Who created this world? Who gives us our food, clothing and comforts? Who is an ocean of grace? If we wish to know who it is we must keep our mind steady and free from impurities.

Suppose a copper pot has remained immersed in a well for ten years or so.

How much rubbing will it have to take before it becomes clean? The more we rub it the cleaner and brighter it will be. If our mind has been made impure with evil actions over many years it can be made chaste only by the performance of many a good deed, many a good work.

Is it enough to keep the copper vessel clean for today? What will happen to it tomorrow or the day after? It will become dirty again if it is not rubbed. Similarly, we must keep our mind ever pure by the daily performance of good works. In due course, a time will come when the citta, the consciousness, will vanish and the Self alone will remain. Thereafter, there will be no need to cleanse the mind for the simple reason that there will be no mind to be cleansed. Until then we have to keep our mind pure through good actions and good conduct.

Chapter 3
"Saṁsāre Kim Sāram?"

In his *Praśnottara-Ratnamālikā*, our Ācārya asks: "Saṁsāre kim sāram?" (What is the meaning of worldly existence?) He responds to the question himself: "You asked the question thus. Keep asking it again and again. That is the meaning of saṁsāra." ("Bahuśaḥ abhi vicintyamānam idam eva.")[1]

"What is the purpose of my birth? Why was I born?" You must ask yourself this question again and again. You must also have some concern about whether you will reach the goal of your birth. "Why do we keep sinning?" is a problem that always worries us. "Why do we get angry? And why do we desire this and that? Can't we remain always happy without sinning, without anger and desire?" We do not seem to know the answers to these questions.

The fruit is formed from the flower, first in the tender unripe form and finally in the mellow form. The flower smells fragrant to the nose and the ripe fruit tastes sweet to the palate. The mellow or ripe fruit is full of sweetness. How did the fruit taste before it became ripe and sweet? The flower was bitter, the tender fruit was astringent, the unripe fruit was sour and the fruit that is mellow now is sweet. Peace means sweetness. When there is peace all attachments sever themselves. When the heart is all sweetness all attachments disappear. There is attachment only so long as there is sourness. When you pluck an unripe fruit from a tree there is sap in the stem as well as in the fruit. It means that the tree is not willing to part from the fruit and *vice versa.*

But when the sweetness is full, all the ties will be snapped and the fruit will drop to earth by itself. The tree releases the fruit or the fruit frees itself from the tree. The separation is without any tears and happy [there is no sap]. Similarly, step by step, a man must become wholly sweet like a mellow fruit and free himself happily from the tree of saṁsāra, the cycle of births and deaths. Desire, anger, and so on, are necessary stages in our development like bitterness, astringency, sourness and sweetness in the growth of a fruit.

When we are subject to urges like desire and anger we will not be able to free ourselves fully from them. But we must keep asking ourselves why we become subject to these urges and passions. We must constantly wonder whether they serve any purpose. If we do not remain vigilant about them we will become victims of their deception.

There must be astringency when it is time for astringency and sourness when it is time for sourness. But neither astringency nor sourness must remain a permanent state. Just as a tender fruit becomes mellow, we too must become mellow and sweet. If we do so there is no need to seek liberation on our own. If we are as we should be in the different stages of our life, liberation shall come in the natural process. On the other hand, if we make an effort at an inappropriate time [if we force ourselves] it will be like making the fruit prematurely ripe. Such a fruit will not taste sweet.

We should not, however, remain always in the same state as the one in which we find ourselves today, indifferent to everything. At the same time, when our bag of sins is still to be emptied, we cannot thirst for the supreme knowledge. Instead, let us keep doing our duty hoping that we will realise the supreme knowledge, if not now, after many a birth. Let us adhere to the dharma prescribed by the Vedas. If we do so, we will proceed gradually to the supreme jñāna. Now we are aware only of outward matters and outward disguises. So let us start with the outward rites of our religion and the outward symbols and signs. By degrees then let us go to the inner reality through the different stages—from that of the tender fruit to the fruit that is mellow and sweet.

Note

1 You will find the answer to the problem of existence in this manner.

Chapter 4
Inward and Outward

I have stated again and again that people must perform the rites handed down to them from their forefathers, that they must adhere to the practices pertaining to the tradition to which they belong and that they must wear the symbols appropriate to the same, like the holy ashes or *Tiruman*[T], the rudrākṣa[S], etc. Some people hold the view that all that is needed is conduct and character, that conduct is a matter of the mind, that religious customs are but part of the external life.

In truth, however, your outward actions and the symbols worn by you outwardly have an impact on the inner life. There is a relationship between bodily work and inner feelings. Let me illustrate this truth. One day, unexpectedly, a man comes to know that he has won a prize in a lottery, say, one lakh rupees. His joy knows no bounds, but it makes its own impact on his body. He becomes so excited that his breathing itself stops for a moment and he faints. "A particular feeling creates a specific change in the process of breathing." From this practical observation yoga develops lessons in breathing to create healthy and noble feelings and urges. Often the outward appearance reflects the inner feelings. When you are angry your eyes become red, your lips quiver. When you are sorrowful your eyes become moist and you shed tears. If you are happy you are agape, showing all your teeth. Thus there is a definite connection between the body and the mind, between the body and the inner feelings. Based on this fact, the wise have devised yogic postures that are calculated to nurture particular Ātmic qualities.

Will soldiers be less valorous if they do not wear their uniforms? All over the world members of the defence services wear uniforms and it is claimed that they keep them fighting fit and inspire courage in them.

The symbols worn outside, the saṁskāras performed outwardly, are inwardly beneficial. If you think that it is all a disguise so it will be. You must resolve to wear the symbols in all sincerity and perform the rites too. Then they will truly cause purity within. Outward action helps you inwardly.

It is perhaps natural that I should give importance to saṁskāras, to the custom of wearing symbols like the sacred ashes, rudrākṣa, etc. After all, I am the head of a Maṭha and you will come to me only if I wear all these. You will give me money for the conduct of the Maṭha. So all these symbols that I wear serve a purpose in my case. But your case is different. You have your own means of livelihood and you may be able to perform saṁskāras even more sincerely than I do and make yourself pure by wearing the symbols of our religion.

Let us wear the signs that remind us of the Supreme Truth. Let us perform the rites that keep us away from evil. Let us be of good conduct and character and cleanse our consciousness. And let us meditate on the Ultimate Reality, experience It inwardly, realise bliss.

Chapter 5

Do We Need Rituals?

Some ask me whether religious functions, pūjā, etc, are not "mere" rituals. Ātmic awareness is an inward experience. As for rituals they are outward actions. The question is how rituals will help in experiencing the Self.

Rituals are indeed not necessary for one who has realised the Self. But we must put the question to ourselves whether we have truly realised It, whether we are mature enough for realisation, whether we have become inwardly pure. Were we honest we would admit that we are far from having become mature for awareness of the Self. By taking many births, by performing many works and by the vāsanā[1] of previous lives, we have concealed the bliss of knowing the Self. By conducting good rites, and by associating ourselves with noble objects, we have to banish the evil habits sticking to us from our past lives. Then there will be an end to karma itself and we will embark on Ātmic inquiry. Until then we have to perform what are called "mere" rituals.

The proper thing for ordinary people is to conduct all the rites mentioned in the śāstras. The benefits obtained from them may be seen in practice. When a person takes care to go through the rites strictly in the manner prescribed in the canonical texts, he will gain one-pointedness of mind. This should be of immense help to him in contemplating the Self later. And the desire to follow the śāstras in all aspects of life will mean that he will be brought under a certain discipline. When we conduct rites according to the śāstras our determination and will power will be strengthened. Since we subordinate our views to the injunctions of the scriptures, we will cultivate the qualities of humility and simplicity.

So what do we gain by performing "mere" rituals? We will acquire one-pointedness of mind, discipline, non-attachment, will power, humility. On the whole it will help us to live a moral life. Without moral conduct there can never be Ātmic inquiry and Ātmic experience.

The Buddha did not prescribe any Vedic rites. But he too laid stress on morality and discipline. The Pañcaśīla that Nehru often spoke about is of the utmost importance to the Buddhists. The Buddha points to the value of morality without the performance of Vedic rites. What about the Pūrvamīmāṁsakas? They believe that Vedic rites are of the utmost importance and that there is no need to worry about God. In our sanātana dharma[S], however, there is a weaving together of rites, the good conduct and discipline arising out of them, devotion to Īśvara and finally knowledge of the Self.

Morality does not arise by itself. If you want milk you must keep a cow. If you keep a cow you will get not only milk but also cowdung. Then there will come up a haystack. When you keep the cow called karma you will derive not only morality and good conduct from it but also something that you feel is not wanted, that is cowdung. When you keep a cow you must keep the place free from cowdung—that is part of common sense or wisdom. It is in this manner that you must obtain the real benefits from religious rites.

If rituals are not necessary for true Ātmic knowledge, even the mūrti called Īśvara is not necessary for the same. But we can dispense with rituals and Īśvara only when we reach a high plane of knowledge. At first Īśvara is very much necessary for our inward journey and there are so many reasons for it. I will tell you one. We need an entity that exemplifies all that is good. Have we not for ages together thought of Īśvara as such a one, one who represents all virtues and all auspicious qualities. When we mention the word "Īśvara" we at once think of him as one without any evil. If anything or anyone combines beauty, compassion, power and enlightenment to the full it must be Īśvara. It is a psychological principle that we become that which we keep thinking of. By meditating on Īśvara's manifold auspicious qualities our own undesirable qualities will give place to good ones.

There are many benefits that flow from rituals, pūja, etc. One of them is that they help to make us good. They are also of value in taking us to the path of workless yoga and the inward quest.

Reference

[1] See notes appended to Chapter 2, Part One.

Chapter 6

Karma is the Starting Point of Yoga

People usually think that yoga means no more than controlling the breath and sitting stone-like. The literal meaning of the word is "joining", "uniting". All through our life's journey we have to join ourselves to various objects. But such joining is not permanent. That is why the mind remains unsteady. If we are joined to an object without the least possibility of being separated from it, it is yoga in the true sense. The root of the minds of all of us is the one Paramātman. Yogins control their breath to turn their mind to this prime root object. The root that gives rise to thoughts is the same as the root that gives rise to the breath. So if the breath is fixed on the root, the mind too will be absorbed in it.

The opposite of yoga is "viyoga". When a man dies we say that he has attained viyoga. The Lord says in the Gītā that a particular kind of viyoga is itself yoga. What is it? If you keep away sorrow, that is if sorrow does not attach itself to you, you have the yoga of disconnection.[1] (Tam vidyād duḥkha-saṁyoga-viyogaṁ yoga-saṁjñitam.)

What we normally understand to be pleasure in a worldly sense is truly sorrow. All experiences that create separation from the Paramātman are sorrow. It is because the citta or consciousness is unstill that we undergo sorrow and happiness. These disappear when the mind is still. To make the mind pure is to train it in one-pointedness. This is the means of yogic perfection. To start with, all will not be able to control their breath like yogins. If we are absorbed in a worthy subject, in some good work, our mind will remain untainted to some extent. If we try to control our mind in one go, so to speak, it will free itself and wander in all directions. If we keep doing some noble work or take an interest in some noble subject the mind is less likely to become unstill.

In the old days they used to wear what is called an *arikaṇḍam,* that is an iron ring, round the neck to keep themselves disciplined and live according to the śāstras. In the same way we must wear an *arikaṇḍam* to keep the mind from going astray. To be involved in good actions is itself a kind of *arikaṇḍam.*

Performing sacrifices, observing fasts and vows, building great temple towers, digging ponds, etc, were a means in the past to cleanse the mind by making it one-pointed. In the midst of such good work also one experiences difficulties, even humiliation, but one should not be daunted by criticism or obstacles. This itself becomes the means of mental purification. Then come prāṇāyāma[S], meditation, etc.

The *kazhakkoḍi*[T] keeps rolling without gathering any dirt. If you smear some ashes on it they will not stick to it. Like the *kazhakkoḍi* we too must not be affected by pain or pleasure and keep journeying towards the Paramātman and becoming one with It. Such union is called yoga — it is our original as well as ultimate state. In between we somehow become different. That is why we do not understand that ultimate and original state now. To reach that state we must make a beginning with the performance of rites.

Reference

[1] *Tam vidyād duḥkha-saṁyoga-viyogaṁ yoga-saṁjñitam*
Sa niścayena yoktavyo yogo'nirviṇṇa - cetasā

— Bhagavadgītā, 6.23

Chapter 7

Karmayoga

Arjuna asks [Kṛṣṇa] whether it is not a sin to wage war and slay friends and relatives in battle. It seems to us a natural and reasonable question. Srī Kṛṣṇa Paramātman gives an answer in the Bhagavadgītā. An action that outwardly seems to be bad and cruel need not neccessarily be sinful. Acts that apparently cause pain to others may have to be committed for the good of the world and there is no sin in them. Then what action is sinful and what is meritorious? The Lord answers this question also. Only such deeds as are motivated by desire and hatred can be sin. Those performed for the well-being of the world without being impelled by desire and hatred are meritorious even though they may seem to be cruel.

The question arises: Is there any action that does not spring from desire or hatred? I will give an example. When a judge awards punishment to a man found guilty of a crime is he driven by desire or hatred? His sentence may seem cruel but it is indeed for the Ātmic well-being of the accused himself. If one's son is suffering from advanced insanity does one not keep him in chains? Is that sinful? It is for the son's good as well as for the good of others who might come to harm by him.

It is in this manner that the śāstras have kept us bound, ordering us to do this and that. It is for our benefit as well as the world's, says Śrī Kṛṣṇa, that we must live according to the tenets of the śāstras: "Tasmātcchāstram pramāṇam te kāryākārya-vyvasthitau (the śāstras are the authority as to what you must do and must not).[1] The Gītā today enjoys wide esteem. Even people who have no respect for our religious customs and traditions—researchers, Western scholars, etc—speak in praise of it. They interpret variously the Gītā's teaching on svadharma. There is no room for doubt about what the Gītā says about svadharma: it is the karma allotted to a man by the śāstras.

When there is neither selfish desire nor hatred, there will be nothing unpleasant about any kind of work. One can then be always happy doing one's allotted work.

The reason for desire and hatred is ego-feeling, ahaṁkāra. When there is no ego-sense, considerations of high and low, or inferior or superior, will be found to be meaningless. We will keep doing our work happily as a matter of duty and thus also contribute to the world's happiness. The karmayoga taught by the Gītā is doing one's work without ahaṁkāra, in a spirit of dedication to the Lord. This tradition of desireless action that purifies our inner being has existed in this land from the Vedic period. Śrī Kṛṣṇa Paramātman presents it to us as a boon encased in a handy casket.

We must keep applying this teaching with ardour in every work or action of our life. Every time we do a work we must ask ourselves: "How do we benefit from this work? Will it bring us fame? Are we moved by desire or hatred? Are we being partial to somebody in carrying it out?" If there is any of these elements associated with our action it must be considered sinful even if it seems exalted to the outside world. If we do something on our own, dictated by our own desire, there will be much wrong-doing in accomplishing it. So, as Śrī Kṛṣṇa says, all our actions must be founded on the śāstras. If everybody acts with equal love for all and with a pure heart there will be neither any rivalry nor any quarrel in society. The world then will be filled with joy.

Reference

[1] See śloka quoted on page 651.

Part Twenty-Two

DHARMAS COMMON TO ALL

Paying homage to a Jīvanmukta. 1993-1994 was observed as the śatābadi or birth centenary year of Pūjyaśrī Candraśekharendra Sarasvatī Svāmī. Picture shows Pūjyaśrī Jayendra Sarasvatī Svāmī (right) and Pūjyaśrī Śankara Vijayendra Sarasvatī Svāmī performing the kanakābhiṣeka of the Great Ācārya. Standing, at extreme left, is Śrī A. Kuppuswāmi.

Chapter 1

How to Control the Mind

What is the obstacle to one-pointed meditation? The answer is the unstill mind. All problems are caused by the mind, by the desires arising in it. It is not easy to control the mind and keep it away effectively from desire. If we ask the mind to think of an object, it seems to obey us for a moment, but soon it takes its own course, wandering off. When I speak to you about meditation and tranquillity, for a moment your mind will perhaps become still and you will be happy. But in a trice it will go astray and the calm you experienced for a few seconds will give place to unquietness.

If you bid your mouth to keep shut, it obeys you for a brief moment. Similarly, if you close your eyes asking them not to see anything, they shut themselves off from the outside world for some moments. But try as you might to tell your mind not to think of anything, it will not listen to you.

The mind must be kept under control. Thinking and non-thinking must be governed by your will. Only then can we claim that it is under our control, that we are masters of our consciousness.

Lunatics are usually referred to as people with no control over their minds. In fact none of us has any control over the mind. A madman keeps blabbering. But what about us? We let the mind go freely to keep blabbering *inwardly*.

Do you know what it means to have mental control? Suppose you are suffering from a severe pain. If you ask your mind not to feel the pain, it shall not feel it in obedience to you [that is *you* will not feel the pain]. Even if a tiger comes face to face with you and growls you will feel no fear if you ask your mind not to be afraid of the beast. Now we keep crying for no reason. If the mind is under control we will keep smiling even if there is cause for much sorrow. And under the gravest of provocations it will not be roused to anger and will remain calm.

First we must train our mind not to keep wandering. One way of doing it is to apply it to good activities. When oil falls in a steady flow, without spraying, it is called "tailadhārā". The mind must be gathered together and made steady. It must be accustomed to think of noble and exalted objects like the Lord. Eventually, the very act of "thinking" will cease and we will dissolve in Īśvara to become Īśvara.

Yoga is controlling the mind in this manner.

Before we pass on, we must find a way to control the mind. Otherwise, we will be born again and we will be subject to the constant unquietness of the mind again. So we must use the opportunity of this birth itself to subdue the mind even while we are in the midst of so much that can rouse our desire or anger. A man who has succeeded in bridling his mind thus is called a "yukta" by the yogins. He is a "sukhin", one who truly experiences bliss, so says Śrī Kṛṣṇa[1].

You must not turn away from yoga thinking that it is meant only for people like the sages. Who needs medicine? The sick. We suffer from manovyādhi, mental sickness. So we must take the medicine that cures it.

There are two different ways of mastering the mind—the first is outward (bahiranga) and the second is inward (antaranga). We must have recourse to both. The Maṭha has a cartman and a cook. Their work is outward in nature. Then there are those who prepare the wicks of the lamps, gather flowers for the pūjā—they are "inward" workers. Both types are needed for the functioning of the Maṭha. By employing both the outward and inward means, the mind must first be applied to good things one-pointedly and eventually led to a state in which it does not think of anything at all.

The outward means consists, for example, of sandhyāvandana[S], sacrifices, charity and so on. The best inward means is meditation. There are five inward (or antaranga) means to aid meditation. They are ahimsā (non-violence), satya (truthfulness), asteyam (non- stealing), śauca (cleanliness) and indriya-nigraha [subduing the senses, if not obliterating them]. To practise ahimsā is to imbue the mind with love for all and not even think of harming others. Asteyam means not coveting other people's goods. For satya, or truthfulness, to be complete one's entire being, including body, mind and speech, must be involved in its practice. Śauca is hygiene, observing cleanliness by bathing, maintaining ritual purity, etc. Indriya-nigraha implies limits placed on sensual enjoyment. "The eyes must not see certain things, the ears must not hear certain things and the mouth must not eat certain things" —restrictions with regard to what you can see, listen to, eat and do with your body. The body is meant for sādhanā, for Ātmic discipline. The senses must be "fed" only to the extent necessary to keep the body alive. These five dharmas are to be practised by all Hindus without any distinction of caste or community.

Reference

[1] *Yato-yato niścarati manaścañcalam asthiram*
Tatastato niyamyai'tad Ātmanyeva vaśaṁ nayet

Praśāntamanasṁ hyenaṁ yoginaṁ sukham uttamam
Upaiti śānta-rajasaṁ Brahma-bhūtam akalmaṣam.

How to Control the Mind

Yuñjannevam sadā'tmānam yogī vigata-kalmaṣaḥ
Sukhena Brahma-saṁsparśam atyantaṁ sukham aśnute

Sarvabhūtastham Ātmānaṁ sarvabhūtāni cā'tmani
Īkṣate yogayuktātmā sarvatra samadarśanaḥ

— Bhagavadgītā, 6. 26,27, 28 & 29

Chapter 2
Ahimsā

According to the *Manusmṛti,* ahimsā is the foremost among the dharmas that are common to all. It is included in the yoga of mind control. Ahimsā means much more than what is meant by non-injury; it implies not doing harm to others even by thought or word.

By nature none of us wants to cause any hurt to other people. But if others do us harm we want to retaliate in anger. Suppose one of our own children sets fire to our house in all innocence. We do not punish it but try to extinguish the fire and thereafter take care to see that the child is kept away from fire and other dangerous objects. We must learn to think that all those who cause us pain are like this child. If a person tries to hurt us, we must lovingly prevent him from doing so. We must not bear any ill-will against him nor think of retaliating. This is true ahimsā.

The practice of ahimsā contributes greatly to the yoga of mind control. The mind is like a demon. But see what wonders the demon — the vetāḷa — accomplished for Vikramāditya after he had been brought under control. The mind will do us unlimited good if it is made subservient to us. Āñjaneya [Hanumān] acquired his immense strength and was able to perform so many great and good deeds only because he had conquered his mind. The mind's power is immeasurable. All the cosmos is the work of the Supreme Goddess and in this creation of hers even the mind of a tiny ant pervades the entire universe.

Many great men, many yogins, have stated that they were able to control their minds by adhering to true ahimsā. When we practise ahimsā, anger will naturally give way, the mind will become clear and will easily be controlled.

Though the chief aim of non-violence is the control of the mind, there is another unexpected benefit that it brings. It is called "avāntara prayojana". All of you came to the Maṭha to see the pūjā. But with that you listened to the *nāgasvaram* music and saw persons whom you had not seen for long—and now you listen to my discourse. All these belong to the category of avāntara prayojana. Thus if a man practises true non-violence (by body, mind and speech), he will be rewarded with a benefit that he had not expected. In his presence all creatures will forget their ill-will and cease to cause hurt to any other creature.

Ahimsā

Ahimsā- pratiṣṭhāyām
tatsannidhau vairatyāgaḥ

— Yogasūtra, 2.35

The minds of even cruel people will be transformed in the presence of men practising utter ahimsā: in other words when a man is full of love he can make other people also loving and this is an avāntara prayojana.

A sannyāsin must observe total non-violence. He must not even pluck a leaf from a tree and must not do violence to plants by cooking them. It is because of the rule of absolute non-violence enjoined on him that there is an interdiction on his performing rites in the sacred fire. Tending a fire for the conduct of a ritual might unwittingly make us responsible for the destruction of some insects. It is because the sannyāsin has no Agni ceremony that when he dies his body is not cremated but interred. When he is initiated into sannyāsa he takes a vow that he shall never be the cause of fear to any creature.

"Ahimsā paramo dharmaḥ" (Non-violence is the supreme dharma). Buddhism and Jainism impose total non-violence on their followers. Not so our religion except in the case of ascetics. In Hinduism an exception to the general dharma of non-violence is made in the case of a righteous or just war and in a sacrifice in which sometimes animals are killed. It is to fetch the divine powers to earth and to appease them that animals are sacrificed in yajñas. It is our belief that the animals so sacrificed will attain to a high state that they cannot otherwise through their own efforts. Altogether it means the good of the animals and the welfare of the world.

In a war, heroes of the army sacrifice themselves in the cause of their nation. Is it not better to lay down one's life for the sake of others than fatten oneself doing nothing?

It is easy to claim oral allegiance to the principle of non-injury but difficult to practise the same. Quarrels and disputes are inevitable in the workaday world. In dealing with them action that is apparently violent may have to be taken. In reality such action is not to be regarded as violent. The intention or purpose is important here, not the action itself. Certain types of violence are justified according to the śāstras and not considered sinful, because such violence is committed not for our personal delight but in pursuance of our duty towards society: the offering of an animal in sacrifice, sentencing a murderer to death, killing an enemy in war.

If a religion makes the practice of non-violence universally applicable, there will be problems. Obviously, all cannot practise it at all times. So those who find it not practicable to follow the rule of ahimsā are made liable to sin. Our religion has taken a more realistic view on the question. As we have seen, Buddhism imposes total non-violence on its followers. But what do we see in practice? In all those lands where Buddhism has a hold there are armies that take part in fighting. Besides, almost without exception, everybody is a meat-eater there.

If a great dharma or principle is made common to all, in the end it is likely to lead to a situation in which no one will respect it in practice. In our religion — to repeat — the rule of absolute non-violence is menat only for sannyāsins. Following their example, Brahmins, Vaiṣṇavas in regions like Gujarat and Śaivas in the South like Veḷḷaḷas and Komuṭṭi Ceṭṭis practise ahimsā. Without being bound by any śāstric injunction they have voluntarily adopted the principle and practised it from generation to generation. Influenced by the example of the sattva guṇa[S] of ascetics these communities have become vegetarians on their own. And, following their example and without being compelled to do so, other castes too abstain from meat on days like the new moon, on the day of a śrāddha[S], and days sacred to the various deities. When a principle is imposed only on a few, since it is difficult to make it universal, it becomes an ideal for others to whom it may not formally apply: they try to practise it as far as they can. Non-violence is a sāmānya dharma (a dharma common to all) in Hinduism. It is kept as an ideal though, on occasion, adherence to it is not practicable.

In the Vedic dharma the definition of ahimsā is the absence of ill-feeling in all action.

Chapter 3

Truthfulness

Truthfulness means mind and speech being well integrated. The wise say that speech being at variance with the mind is untruthfulness.

Vāṅgmanasyoḥ aikarūpyam satyam

God has given man the gift of speech so that he may give expression to his thoughts and feelings. If what we speak is at variance with what we think (with our mind) God will take away the faculty of speech from us in our next birth—that is we will be born in the animal kingdom.

There are, as we have seen before, exceptions made in our śāstras to the rule of absolute non-violence: in waging a war to preserve dharma, in offering animals in sacrifice. Are there similar exceptions to the rule of truthfulness? You will perhaps say none. But, as a matter of fact, there are.

In any locality there must be a number of undesirable characters. Let us suppose that a certain citizen is annoyed with such characters and gives open expression to his anger. "He committed this outrage. That other man is guilty of such and such a crime," he keeps recounting the misdeeds of the bad elements. In doing so he is being truthful, that is his speech and mind are in accord. But by giving expression to his feelings no purpose is served for neither he nor the community is benefited. It is a futile kind of accord -- that of his speech and mind -- and it cannot be called truthfulness.

Take the example of another person. He is full of evil thoughts and, if he gives expression to them, can he be called truthful? No.

So truthfulness, now we see, is not merely accord between mind and speech. It means voicing good thoughts, thoughts that are beneficial and are liked by people: "Satyam bhūtahitam priyam."

Doing good through thought, word and deed is truthfulness. All that does ill is untruthfulness. It is not enough that you speak to a man what is good for him. You must speak with affection and the one to whom your words are addressed must find them acceptable. If you speak harshly nobody will listen to you even if you mean well. Thus words that serve no purpose do not constitute a truth. Your speech must be beneficial and, at the same time, capable of bringing happiness to the man to whom it is addressed. This is truthfulness.

The wise say: "May he speak the truth. May his speech be pleasing. May he not speak the truth that is unpleasing. And may he not speak an untruth that is pleasing."

> [1]*Satyam brūyātpriyam brūyan-*
> *Na brūyatsatyamapriyam*
> *Priyam ca nanṛtam brūyād—*

A mind that is subject to desire and anger will not give rise to words that bespeak affection and cause well-being. Truthful words that create good are the product of a mind free from desire and anger.

What is truth then? Thought and speech must be in accord; the mind must be serene; and the words spoken must be pleasing, that is what is spoken must do good to the speaker as well as the listener.

For a man rooted in truth there is an avāntara prayojana, an incidental benefit, gained from his speech. Since such a person habitually speaks the truth, his words *will become the truth*. Such a man will never deliberately utter a lie. But, if unwittingly or out of ignorance, he commits an error while speaking, that error will turn out to be the truth. I will tell you a story to illustrate this.

In Tirukkaḍavūr, in Tañjāvūr district, there was a great devotee of Ambā called Abhirāmibhaṭṭa.[T] He would often go into an ecstasy of devotion to the goddess. During such times he would speak like one mad. Someone poisoned the ears of the rājā Śarabhoji[T] against him. "Abhirāmibhaṭṭa is a drunkard," he told the ruler. "His devotion is a mere pretence." Śarabhoji wanted to find out the truth. So he went to see Abhirāmibhaṭṭa in Tirukkaḍavūr and asked him: "What day of the moon is it today?" The Bhaṭṭa was then lost in devotional joy and, thinking only of the radiant face of Ambā which was like the moon, said that it was a full moon day. Actually it was the new moon. The rājā concluded that what he had heard about the Bhaṭṭa must be true and said scornfully: "Is that so? Let us look up and see whether the full moon has risen."

At that very moment the full moon did appear in the sky. Abhirāmibhaṭṭa was steeped in truthfulness. By mistake he had spoken an untruth but Ambā made it the truth by hurling her earstud into the sky and causing it to shine like the full moon.

The blessings as well as the curses of great men come true because of the force of their innate and habitual truthfulness. This is the "incidental benefit" they derive from their habit of truthfulness. But truthfulness must not be practised with the deliberate intention that what one speaks must come true. Power such as this is earned unintentionally and unconsciously.

A man will purify himself completely if he performs the forty saṁskāras[2] and adheres to principles like non-violence, truthfulness, non-covetousness, cleanliness and also controls his senses. He will then develop the maturity and wisdom to find out who in truth he is, who Īśvara is and what the Ultimate Reality is.

References

[1] The last line of the stanza: "*Eṣa dharmaḥ sanātanaḥ.*" (Manusmṛti)

[2] See Part Sixteen.

Chapter 4

Sesame and Water: Where do they Go?

All human beings must express their gratitude to their fathers (pitṛs) and to the gods—they have a debt to pay their fathers, rites to perform for the gods. We must serve our fellow creatures to the best of our ability and extend hospitality at least to one guest a day. This is ātithya or what Tiruvaḷḷuvar[T] calls "*virundu*", also known as manuṣyayajña. Then there is Brahmayajña to perform, the word "Brahma" here denoting the Vedas. Brahmayajña means chanting the Vedas and making others chant them. This is a duty carried out by a few on behalf of all. One of the rites common to all is bhūtayajña, demonstrating our love to all creatures, feeding them, etc. Pitṛyajña, devayajña, manuṣyayajña, bhūtayajña are rites all are duty- bound to perform in one way or another[1]. If each individual does his work according to the Vedic dharma and does it in a spirit of dedication to Īśvara he may be said to be performing Brahmayajña. Tiruvaḷḷuvar has said more or less the same thing as the Vedas say:

Tenpulattār, deivam, virundu, okkal, tān enru āṅgu
aimbulattāru ombal talai

Tenpulattār are the pitṛs, the fathers. All are duty-bound to pay their debt to them. Mother Veda says: "Mātṛ-devo bhava, pitṛ-devo bhava." (Be one to whom the mother is a deity. Be one to whom the father is a deity.) Auvvai[T], who brings us the essence of the Vedas, observes: *Annayum pitāvum munnari deivam*" [Mother and father are the deities first known.]

We must treat our parents with respect and do all we can to keep them in comfort. We cannot make sufficient recompense for all the sacrifices they make on our behalf. After they depart from this world we must without fail offer libations to them and perform the śrāddha[S] ceremony, all in the śāstric manner. Though they ridicule the idea of performing śraddha, even reformers are agreed that we must care for our parents.

"The sesame you offer, the water, the balls of rice, the plantains and other items of food remain here," point out the reformists. "Or we see someone removing them before our own eyes, or eating them. You say that the departed parents are born again in this world. If that is true, is it not madness to claim that what is offered here will reach them?" Some of you must be harbouring similar doubts.

Sesame and Water: Where do they Go?

Let me tell you a story.

A certain man had sent his son to college in a distant town. One day the boy woke up to the fact that he had to pay his examination fee in a few days. So he wrote to his father: "Please send such and such a sum by telegraphic money order." The father was a little perplexed. All the same he went to the telegraph office and handed the clerk at the counter the money that had to be sent to his son. "Please send it by telegraphic money order," he told the clerk. He had thought that the clerk would make holes in the notes, put a length of wire through them and send the whole thing to his son. Moments later the clerk said to the man: "Your son will get your money. It has already been sent." The villager was again puzzled. He saw the money still in the cash box without the notes strung together. He told the clerk: "My money is still here. You haven't made holes in the notes yet..." The clerk assured him: "It will reach your son." Now he turned to his work of sending messages: "*Ka-ṭu-kaṭu-kaṭu...*" The poor villager was still not satisfied.

But the money of course reached his son.

Offering libations to one's fathers is similar. If this rite is performed according to the śāstras, the deities concerned will convey them to those for whom they are meant. If the fathers are reborn as cows the offering made to them will be taken to them in the form of grass or hay. The deities in charge carry out the orders of the Paramātman. So the father or the mother whose śrāddha is performed need not personally come to receive the offering.

Does not the telegraphic money order reach the addressee? If the addressee resides in a foreign country our currency will not be valid there. If rupees are paid here arrangements are made to pay the money in dollars, pounds, or whatever. The things offered to the fathers according to the śāstras are conveyed in a form suitable to them.

What is important is a sense a gratitude to our fathers and faith in the śāstras. At parties a toast is proposed to somebody and all the guests drink or eat to his health. They do so in the belief that by virtue of their mental power the man toasted will become healthy. Śrāddha means that which is done in faith. Faith is of the utmost importance. If we do something we must do it according to the rules laid down for it. When you write a letter how do you make sure that it reaches the addressee? "I will write the address as I like. Why should I drop the letter in that letterbox over there? I have a better box at home," would you speak thus?

In the state of worklessness, love, devotion and jñāna are not bound by any rules. But when an action has a purpose behind it you have to respect the rules pertaining to it.

Reference

[1] These have been dealt with in earlier chapters.

Chapter 5

Pūjā

Every family must perform pūjā to Īśvara. Those who find it convenient to do so may conduct elaborate types of pūjā after receiving proper initiation into them. Others need perform only a brief pūjā, not lasting more than ten minutes or so. Officegoers must offer at least this brief worship. The sacred bell must ring in every home.

Images must be installed to worship Śiva, Ambā, Viṣṇu, Vināyaka and Sūrya. This is called "pañcāyatana pūjā". According to one custom, no graven images [images with limbs] are used but instead natural objects to represent the five deities. The "bāṇa-liṅga" for Śiva is obtained from the Omkāra-kuṇḍa of the Narmadā river. The svarṇamukhī stone for Ambikā (it has a golden streak on it) is to be taken from the bed of the Svarṇamukhī river in Āndhra Pradeś. The symbol of Viṣṇu, sāḷagrāma, is obtained from the Gaṇḍakī river in Nepāl. The crystal stone for Sūrya is got from Vaḷḷam, near Tañjāvūr. The śoṇabhadra stone for Vināyaka is obtained from the Sone river, a tributary of the Gangā. These five stones are symbolic of the unity of India.

None of these five stones has eyes, nose, ears, etc. Since they have no corners that become untidy, they are easy to bathe and dry. Being small they do not occupy much space. No big pūjā hall or room is necessary. A small casket is enough.

Pañcāyatana pūjā was revived by Śankara Bhagavatpāda. As the creator of the Ṣanmata system (the worship of six deities) he added Subrahmaṇya to the five. So with the five stones we may add a small spear to represent Velāyudha (Subrahmaṇya) who bears the spear.

Not much effort is needed for the pūjā. If you have the will, it could be performed wherever you happen to be.

At home when you do the pūjā you have to present to the deities cooked rice called "mahā-naivedya"[S]. The Lord has created the entire cosmos for our sake. Our sense organs take delight in the various objects in creation. All that gives us joy, all that is beneficial in creation, must be first offered to the Lord [symbolically] before being partaken of by us. When we offer any food as naivedya to him, do we really give it away to him? We just place it before him and then partake of it ourselves.

Some ask, scornfully, whether the Lord himself eats what is offered to him. "Nivedana" does not mean making the Lord really "eat" what is offered. He does not have to eat. Pūjā is meant to make us inwardly pure and the Lord does not have to gain anything from it. "Nivedayāmi" means "I am making it known to you (informing you)" and does not mean "I am feeding you." You must speak thus to Īśvara: "O Lord, in your compassion you have given us this food." Then you must eat the food thus offered, thinking of him. Without his grace how does the rice grow? Experts may conduct research and write big tomes on rice. But are they capable of making one grain of rice? What is called synthetic rice is made out of materials already created by Īśvara. So all that seems to be made by man must be finally traced to God's creation. To enjoy what he has given us without first presenting it to him would be tantamount to thieving.

He who is present everywhere must be present where we want him to be present so that he may be grasped by us. Whatever the material out of which his image or symbol is made—stone, earth, copper—he will come to us in that material and in that image or symbol. He will do so out of his compassion and he has the power to do so. We would have no need for him otherwise.

The Lord must be worshipped in every home. He must be invoked and it must be made known to him that we are using nothing but what he has made over as a gift to us. If we keep doing so, we will in due course have the wisdom not to use in pūjā things not fit to be offered to him. We ourselves will come to possess good qualities.

Chapter 6

Philanthropy

[In the chapter entitled, "Sesame and Water: Where do They Go?", the Paramaguru spoke of the debt to be paid to our fathers,our duty to worship Parameśvara as well as to feed the creatures of the earth. He stated that Tiruvaḷḷuvar also spoke of the same dharma in his "Kural" : "Tenpulattār deivam, virundu, okkal tān enru āṅgu aimbulattāru ombal talai."]

Here (in the foregoing quotation) is one good proof that Tiruvaḷḷuvar respected the authority of the Vedas. Some suggest that he did not belong to the Vedic religion and that he was a Jaina or a Buddhist. And some claim that he transcended all religions. It is also suggested that he openly condemned sacrifices in which animals are killed. In support of their view they quote a stanza from the *Kural.*

[The Paramaguru's comment on the Kural *passage is contained in Chapter 23, Part Five.]*

Tiruvaḷḷuvar who composed his *Kural,* with its universal appeal, was not an atheist opposed to the Vedic dharma. What he refers to as *virundu* is the same as the Vedic manuṣyayajña.

Every morning a handful of rice (uncooked) must be set apart for the poor. All families must do this without fail every day. The rice thus kept must be collected from house to house, from quarter to quarter, cooked, offered to the deity of the local temple as naivedya[S] and then distributed among the poor. With the handful of rice set apart for the poor, keep just one paisa also. The paisa collected from each family would be sufficient to buy salt, chilli powder, etc, to mix with the rice to make it more palatable. It would also serve to buy firewood and to pay the rent for the vessels. To carry out such a scheme is to do a great service to the poor — and to the Lord. Charity like this should encourage templegoing, not to speak of devotion. Since the food is first offered as naivedya, it would mean that the poor will take it as prasāda[S] which will impart them inner purity.

Annadāna or the gift of food is one kind of service or paropakāra. We talk of service to the poor, social service and so on. Today all this is done with much fanfare and publicity. In the past the needy were served naturally, without making any noise. Service comes under "pūrta-dharma" and it includes digging wells and ponds for the public, feeding the poor, building temples for the spiritual well-being of people, laying out gardens. Excavating wells and ponds has been mentioned first. The importance of this work may be gauged from such remarks in ordinary conversation: "What's he doing? Digging a well or something?" It is extremely meritorious to excavate a pond outside the village to slake the thirst of cattle. All people in a village or locality must join together in such work without distinction of poor and rich, high and low — work involving physical effort. It will incidentally contribute to greater social harmony.

With education we purify our intelligence, with meditation we cleanse our mind, with śloka or poetry we clarify our speech. How do we purify our body? By exerting ourselves in the service of others. As we keep serving people in this way we will obtain inward purity. When all take part in the work of digging a pond or well, without any differences, without one man feeling superior to another or inferior to him, our ego too will be dug away. More important than the water welling up in the pond is the love welling up up from our hearts. No outward show is needed in social service; we must not make an exhibition of our work. Collect pieces of glass scattered on the footpath and keep them away in a safe place: even this is service to people and a means of cleansing ourselves. We must try to please the Lord with the very hands and feet that he has given us — we must do so by serving others and by looking upon all as himself.

Chapter 7

To Serve Others is to Feel Blessed

A man can be fortunate in many ways. But there is nothing that makes him more fortunate than the opportunity he has of serving others.

When we serve our family we are not conscious of how we help it. We must learn to help people who are not our kin — other families, our village or home town, our nation, indeed all mankind. We have so many problems ourselves, we suffer so many hardships, and we have so many worries and cares. We must not, however, mind serving others in the midst of all our difficulties. We will forget our problems when we are immersed in the work of helping others. There is a saying: "Feed milk to your neighbour's child, your child will be nourished." The Lord will raise us up from our troubles as we do good to others. However, it is not with such considerations of profit that we must try to help people in difficulties. We must not worry about how others will benefit from our work, but consider how we will become naturally pure. Also, we must think of the happiness we will experience by serving our fellow men.

Service should not be confined to mankind but must be extended to the animal kingdom. In the old days ponds were dug exclusively for cattle and stone pillars were installed here and there for them to scratch themselves. Everyone must feed at least one cow every day with a handful of grass. This is called "go-grāsam" and this act is extolled in the śāstras. "Grasam" means a mouthful and the English word "grass" is derived from it.

Conducting sacrifices, offering oblations to the fathers and performing śrāddha[S] must be regarded as an extension of the service we do in this world to the denizens of other worlds. These rites must be gone through with the intoning of mantras.

There must be many others like us, many groups, who want to be engaged in social work. It should be ideal if the efforts of all were brought together under one body of like-minded members. Care must be taken that associations so formed do not break up; they must be managed honestly with a proper enforcement of discipline. Those who do philanthropic work must be men of courage and enthusiasm who take praise and blame equally.

You ought not to waste your time in eating places displaying appetising fare nor in establishments where alluring objects are exhibited. Instead, you must spend your time in helping others. You will ask whether it is wrong to spend a little time in gaiety in the midst of life's worries and hardships. I should like to impress on you that the happiness you find in helping others is not to be found in anything else.

Kṛṣṇa Paramātman was playful, wasn't he? But all his playfulness was an outward phenomenon for inwardly he served others all the time. How sportingly did he save people from trouble and how many were the men who were helped by him. To protect the cowherds the child Kṛṣṇa lifted up the big Govardhana mountain. And, again, as a little child he danced on the hoods of the dreaded Kāliṅga (Kāliya) that poisoned the Yamunā. It all seemed play, all the heroic acts he performed to save the people of Gokula. Nobody sported like Kṛṣṇa but at the same time nobody served mankind like him. It was not worldly service alone that he did. He served mankind by imparting jñāna. As a preceptor of Arjuna and Uddhava alike he taught great truths. All this he did with a smile, spreading serenity everywhere. What he did he did with the utmost ease. Those who have taken up the work of serving humanity must be inspired by his example.

Among the various incarnations of the Lord, the service rendered to humanity was the greatest in that of Kṛṣṇa. During the avatāra of Rāma, Āñjaneya appeared as seva (service) personified. We must be inspired by their example [of Kṛṣṇa and Hanumān] as we work for others; we must be unselfish like them and shun publicity.

We keep aloof from the outside world when we are ritually impure. We must regard any day on which we fail to do any service to others as a day of impurity. Parameśvara is the father of all creatures. By serving our fellow men we serve the Lord. This is the message of Tirumūlar[T] in his *Tirumantiram*[T]:

Naḍamāḍa-k-koyil naṁbar-k-konrīyil
Padamāḍa-k-koyil Bhagavarkadāme

It means: Serving people is worshipping the Lord.

Chapter 8

Making all Creatures Happy

We must not fail to perform sacrifices to the celestials, offer libations to our fathers and perform śrāddha. In the past, apart from these, our ancestors did pūjā to the gods, fed guests and performed vaiśvadeva which rite is meant for all creatures. You must have some idea of these rites even if you do not perform them. I will speak to you about vaiśvadeva[1].

To sustain ourselves, we cause hurt to so many creatures, don't we? We take pride in keeping our house clean but we forget that every household is a butchery. According to the dharmaśāstras it is not one butchery but five butcheries together. What are these five?

Pañcasūnā gṛhasthasya vartante'harahaḥ sadā
Khaṇḍanī peṣanī cullī jalakumbha upaskaraḥ

Khaṇḍanī is used to cut vegetables—it stands for one type of butchery. Vegetables also do have life. The second butchery is represented by the grinding or pounding stone. We mercilessly grind corn, pulses, etc, in it.

Here an answer must be given to objections raised by meat-eaters about vegetarian food. They tell us: "Like the goats, cows and fowl that we eat, vegetables and cereals also have life." True. Though there is no difference in kind between them, there is a difference in the degree of violence done to vegetables and animals. Plants have life and feelings like humans but they do not have the sensation of pain to the same degree as animals and birds have. This has been scientifically established. Also, but for certain leafy vegetables which we uproot to be prepared as food, most other vegetables are obtained from plants without killing them: it is like removing our nails or hair. The plants suffer only a little pain. Pain even to this degree will not be caused if we eat the fruits of these plants after they drop ripe. As for the cereals they are harvested only after the crop is ripe and dry.

There is one more argument in favour of vegetarianism. Now only certain types of meat like beef are eaten. Horsemeat is not usually eaten. During World War I or II, when the question arose as to whether the soldiers could be fed horsemeat, the non-vegetarians themselves opposed the idea. People who think it civilized to eat birds and animals condemn tribes in some remote land who eat human flesh as barbarous and call them cannibals. We must tell meat-eaters who remind us that vegetables also have life: "Yes, but when it comes to violence, are all creatures the same? Why do you make a distinction between animal flesh and human flesh? Similarly, we make a distinction between plants and animals. Vegetarianism also promotes sāttvic[S] qualities." Unavoidably, for the sake of existence, we have to keep at home instruments of butchery like the khaṇḍanī, peṣanī, etc.

The third butchery is represented by the cullī or the kitchen fire. Many insects perish in the cooking fire. An ant crawls about the oven or fireplace and is burnt. Sometimes when we keep a pot on the floor or the shelf an insect or two get crushed. In the summer insects come seeking wet places, places for example where vessels are kept. The water-pot is also included among the objects of butchery. Then there is the upaskara, the broomstick. Aren't many tiny insects killed as we sweep the floor? Thus there are five instruments or objects of butchery in our home.

We must not cause harm even to those creatures that hurt us. But what do we do? We cause pain to, or kill, even harmless creatures. It is sad to think that to live, to sustain ourselves, we have to keep hurting so many living things. But it all seems unavoidable. We do not kill deliberately. There is an expiation for the sin committed unwittingly. It is the prāyaścitta of "vaiśvadeva". We perform this function to ask the Lord to forgive us our sin of having caused the destruction of various creatures and to pray for their happiness in afterlife. Vaiśvadeva is meant for the excommunicated and for all creatures of earth like dogs, crows, insects, all. This rite absolves us of many a sin.

The pañca-mahāyajñas[1] were conducted for eons by the sages, by the children of Brahmā. All performed them from the hoary past until the time of our grandfathers. The five great sacrifices are to be performed uninterruptedly until the deluge. But we have had the "good fortune" of having broken this tradition. Worse, we have deprived future generations of the benefits to be derived from them.

I have dealt with a variety of rites. Perform at least those you can without prejudice to your office or professional work. If you fail to do so you must be regretful about it and make amends for the same.

Reference

[1 & 2] The "pañca-mahāyajñas", including vaiśvadeva, are dealt with in earlier chapters.

Chapter 9

Towards Mental Purity

There are a number of simple rites the performance of which will free you from inner impurities. From generation to generation our forefathers performed them and earned happiness and contentment. We must follow in their footsteps. We do not have to go in search of any new way of life, any new doctrine or belief.

We can learn from the great men of our past who have left us lessons not only in Ātmic matters but in the conduct of family and social life. For instance, kinship and friendship in their time were based on high principles. When there was a marriage or obsequial ceremony all friends and relatives came forward to help. It was cultured behaviour at its best and it was not based on any empty outward show. People then were truly and sincerely interested in helping the needy and the poor. At weddings they gave a little cash to the bride's parents, five or ten rupees, and the burden of those who conducted the marriage was lightened.

When everybody pays a little to the needy, the donor does not feel the pinch but the donee has a tidy sum with which to celebrate a marriage or perform an obsequial ceremony. Among relatives in the past there was not much gap between the rich and the poor. And the rich man helped his poor relatives. All this is part of dharma. The man who helps purifies himself more than the man who is helped.

Now things have changed. The well-to-do do not help their poor relatives. Annadāna (gift of food) was part of the noble tradition of the past. How is it today? At present too the well-to-do feed people, but with this difference that those fed are also well-to-do like them. When they give parties, banquets, etc, a great deal of money and material is spent in this manner. Where is the room for dharma or mental purity in all this? A party is given not with any noble intention but to promote one's selfish interests. The man who gives it thinks that he is practising deception on the invitees. But the invitees, however, know that the host has no true feelings of affection for them. The host and the guest thus deceive one another. Altogether parties and toasts are nothing but part of the modern art of deception and have nothing to do with the cleansing of the mind.

If you help a poor man with food or material, you and he are equally happy: there is affection on both sides. In parties, on the contrary, there is even ill-will. Hatred and resentment are caused in the hearts of have-nots by the parties given by the haves [for the haves]. Among relatives there should be no distinction between rich and poor.

You must not think that only the affluent can help the poor and earn merit. If you are not well off you may serve others by helping them physically. All of you in a locality may join together to dig a pond. All this contributes to inner purity. How do you deserve the grace of Iśvara? By constantly serving others, by being compassionate to all creatures. Your mind, your consciousness, will also become clear. In this pure consciousness of yours, in this pure citta, you will see the image of the Lord. Do you see any image in turbid water? We have made our minds muddy with impurities. We must make them limpid by being devoted to the Lord and by serving mankind. Then Iśvara will be within our grasp.

Chapter 10

Fault-finding

To live a life inspired by dharma means coming under a certain discipline and following certain rules of conduct. It is important for people to acquaint themselves with these rules. It would be ideal if they lived according to them on their own because to abide by them out of compulsion is not a matter of pride. "Saṁpradāya" or tradition is something that has evolved naturally and it is naturally that people adhere to them. The customs and rules making up a saṁpradāya are not all of them written down in the śāstras. Anything laid down as a law becomes a matter of compulsion. Nowadays everywhere people are aksed to, "Do this" and "not to do that." Notices are displayed about this and that. They are displayed even where I perform the pūjā (in the Maṭha), notices that say, "Don't keep talking", "Don't wear shirts", etc.

When I speak thus and ask you not to do this or to do that, I myself am guilty of offending against the good rule I just spoke about. When I say, "Don't do...", it becomes a law. I should speak to you thus: "You think about it yourselves whether it is right to have such notices."

"Do not magnify the faults of others," say the wise. "But if there is something good about a man speak appreciatively about it." I myself, however, am bringing your faults into the open. But, to repeat, you must not bring to light the drawbacks of others but only their good qualities. See, even the crescent moon is cool and radiant. That is why Śiva wears it in his matted hair, makes its beauty known to the world. The same Śiva swallowed the terrible hālāhala poison concealing it from everyone, so says Daṇḍin[S] in one of his poems.

Pointing a finger at the faults of others or exaggerating them in speech and writing has become the practice today. The more learned a man is, the more eager he is to find fault with others. "Finding fault is indeed the work of a vidvān," it is said. "The word vidvān itself is said to mean a doṣajña." But a doṣajña is one who knows the faults of something or somebody, not one who reveals them to the world or exaggerates them. If you think a person has any drawbacks you must speak to him about them in a friendly manner [so that he may correct himself] but not constantly harp on them and expose them to the outside world.

We must be worthy enough to speak about the faults of others and we cannot take upon ourselves the role of an adviser when we need to correct ourselves. Advice given by us then would be counterproductive. If we tell a man what is wrong about him he might even feel boastful about it. When are we fit to advise others? When we are worthy enough and when we know that our word will have the desired effect.

If we praise a person for his good qualities he will have greater enthusiasm to cultivate them further. But there should be restraint in praise too — praise indeed is a tricky thing. That is why the wise say: "Īśvara and the guru alone may be praised directly. Friends and relatives, instead of being praised to their face, must be spoken of well to others. You may praise a servant only after he has carried out the job entrusted to him. (It is like patting a horse after a ride.) You may never praise your son."

Pratyakṣe guravaḥ stutyāḥ
Parokṣe mitrabāndhavāḥ
Kāryānte dāsabhṛtyāśca
Na svaputrāḥ kadācana

I have been finding fault with you all the while. As I said fault-finding is not an exercise to be welcomed but the stanza just quoted frees me from any blame because it says that children should not be praised and that you must tell them what is wrong with them. So no fault can be ascribed to me for my having found fault with you.

Chapter 11

Anger

It is customary to speak of kāma (desire) and krodha (anger) together. Kṛṣṇa Paramātman says in the Gītā[1] that desire and anger goad a man into sinful action.

When we intensely desire an object we try to get it by fair means or foul. It is a deadly enemy, desire: it eggs us on to commit sin. Equally deadly is anger. When we fail to get the object of our desire we turn our anger against the man who, we believe, was an obstacle. Unfulfilled desire becomes anger.

If we throw a rubber ball against the wall, it bounces — in other words it returns to us. The ball thrown is desire and it is the same ball that becomes anger as it bounces. The attack we believe we make on others in our anger is actually an attack we make on ourselves — and we are hurt more than those we wanted to hurt. When we are angry our whole body shakes. Anger indeed causes pain both to the body and the mind and we make ourselves ugly when we are angry. You will know the truth of this if you see a photograph taken when you are in a foul mood.

Hunger is appeased by eating. But is fire assuaged in the same way? You keep feeding it and it keeps devouring everything. Fire is bright but it chars all that it consumes. Or, in other words, it turns everything black. That is why it is called "kṛṣṇavartman". Kāma or desire is similar. It flares up like fire. The more it is fed the more it becomes hungry. Indeed kāma blackens our mind. When a desire is gratified there is joy for the moment, but soon it goes in search of more "food" and in the process we lose our peace of mind and happiness and become victims of sorrow and anger.

Sorrow and anger are two forms of unrequited desire. If we think that those who are a hindrance to the gratification of our desire are inferior to us, we turn our anger against them, and if we think that they are superior, all we do is to grieve within ourselves. Anger is packed with more evil power than even desire. *Naiṣadham*[S], the story of Nala, illustrates this truth beautifully. As King Kali makes his appearance, desire and anger (kāma and krodha) accompany him as his two army commanders. The herald sings their praises. "There is no place that kāma cannot gain entry to. No, there is a place he cannot enter. It is the fortress in which anger resides. This fortress is the heart of Durvāsas." Durvāsas does not know desire but he is subject to fits of anger.

We must be extremely wary of this terrible sinner called anger. A little thought will convince us that we are not in the least qualified to be angry with anybody or to shout at anybody. We are even more guilty than those against whom we turn in our anger. We know this in our heart of hearts. Even if we are guiltless, before we rush to find fault with someone, we must ask ourselves whether we would not have committed the offence we think he is guilty of were we placed in the same circumstances as he.

We must try our best to keep anger always at a distance.

Reference

[1] *Dhyāyato viṣayān puṁsaḥ saṅgasteṣū'pajāyate*
Saṅgāt saṁjāyate kāmaḥ kamāt krodho'bhijāyate

Krodhādbhavati sammohaḥ sammohāt smṛti-vibhramaḥ
Smṛtibhraṁśād buddhinaśo buddhināśāt praṇaśyati

— Bhagavadgītā, 2.62 & 63

Chapter 12

Are We Worthy of being Angry?

Often we find ourselves angry with some person or other. Anger is provoked in two ways. When we see a man guilty of an offence we lose our temper. But we do not pause to think whether we too are not like him. Even if we have not been guilty of sinful deeds we must have had sinful thoughts. Perhaps we have reason to think that we have sinned less than others. This must be because we are a little more mature. Even so, how difficult do we find it to correct ourselves. Would it not be more difficult for a habitual sinner to retrieve himself? We need not associate ourselves with him. The śāstras proclaim that the first step towards Ātmic improvement is to sever ourselves from evil people and to seek the company of virtuous men. But there is no point in looking upon sinners with hatred or anger. All we can and must do is to pray that they turn to the path of virtue. If, by the grace of the Lord, we acquire a little grace ourselves we must use it to take them to the right path.

Our opponent is not likely to change his attitude towards us simply because we are angry with him. Instead, he might turn against us with greater venom. Hatred thus will be kept fuelled on either side. One must realise one's mistakes and try to reform oneself. We cannot congratulate ourselves if a person corrects himself fearing our anger. Also the change thus brought about in him will not be enduring. If we think that there is something wrong with a man we must try to correct him with love.

Why do people sin? The reason must be their mental condition and the circumstances in which they are placed. If we happen to be free from any guilt, it must be because we are more favoured by circumstances. When you see a sinner you must pray: "O Ambikā, I too might have sinned like him. But in your mercy you did not give me the occasion to do so. Be merciful to him in the same way."

We must not be angry with a man even if he bears ill-will against us. Our innermost mind knows how far we deserve to be spoken ill of. It may be that the man who nurses bad feelings against us is doing so not because of any wrong done by us. We know, however, in our heart of hearts that the sins we have committed are indeed great. Such is our predicament that we must shed tears before Ambā, atone for our sins and pray that they are washed away. In what way are we qualified to point an accusing finger at others?

The question arises: may we direct our anger against others when we are free from all sin? Were we truly sinless, we would be all love and affection. Where is then the question of our being angry with anyone? Even towards a sinner we should have then no feeling other than that of love. On the other hand, if we are guilty of wrongs ourselves we have no right to be angry with those we think are sinners. In the state of utter sinlessness we realise it all to be the sport of Ambā. In her sport who merits praise, who deserves blame? Anger, in any case, has no place in our life.

As I said earlier, according to Kṛṣṇa Paramātman the two great forces inciting man to sin are desire and anger. In other words we hurt ourselves with our anger. Our opponent may ignore our anger but then we hurt ourselves with it — both our body and mind suffer. The natural dharma of man is to be loving and affectionate. And to be loving and affectionate is to be ever in bliss. Love is Śivam, it is said. We must always learn to attain the condition of love that is Śivam.

Chapter 13

Love and Sorrow

The purpose of human birth is to live a life full of love for all. No joy is greater than that of loving others. Amassing wealth, acquiring property, earning fame, bedecking oneself give but transient pleasure, not any sense of fullness. The happiness that permeates our inner being is the happiness of loving others. When we love others we are not conscious of our suffering the physical exertion we make and the money we spend: indeed the joy of loving gives us a transcendent feeling. A life in which there is no love for others is a life lived in vain.

I said that when we love a person we forget our sorrows. But one day, at last, it may be that the object of our love itself becomes the cause of great sorrow. One day the person we love leaves us for ever—or one day we will leave him for ever. "O he has left me for ever"—"O I am leaving him for ever": we lament in this manner. We feel disturbed when we realise that all the happiness that love gave us has at last proved to be a lie and ended in sorrow. "Is the final outcome of love then sorrow?" we ask ourselves in our agitation. The greater our love for a person the more intense our grief when he or she is separated from us for ever. We may then even wonder whether a life without love, a life of selfishness or a life of insensibility would be better. One leading such a life will not be affected by being separated from the object of his affection.

A selfish or self-centred man, however, gathers only sin. Is it not a life lived without joy—a life lived without a sense of fullness—a life lived in vain, a life like that of a log of wood or stone?

[The problem then is]: Our love for others ends in sorrow. However, if there is no love there is no meaning in life. What is the solution to this problem? We must create such love as will never change, love that will be enduring. The object of our love must never become separated from us, never desert us. If there were such an object and if we devoted all our love to it we would never be separated from one another—there would be eternal bliss, everlasting fullness.

To explain, we must love the One Object that never changes. What is that Object? The Paramātman. The Paramātman will never be separated from us. Even if our life departs it will dissolve in the Paramātman and become one with him. Only that love is everlasting which is dedicated to him.

The question arises: If one is to love the Paramātman that never perishes, does it mean that we must not love anyone else, that we must not love others because they will perish one day? If our love for the Supreme Being keeps growing the truth will dawn on us that there is no one or nothing other than He. All those whom we loved, all those who caused us sorrow by being separated from us, they too will seem to us the imperishable Supreme Being. We must learn to look upon the entire universe as the Paramātman and love it as such. Our love then shall never be a cause of sorrow.

Even if it be that our love is not such as to embrace the universe with all its creatures as an expression of the Paramātman, we can learn to love with ease all those great men of Ātmic qualities as the Paramātman, so also our sadguru who is full of wisdom and grace. Sufficient it would be to love them and surrender to them. Through them the Paramātman will give us his blessings. When someone we love dies we should not grieve for him. We must console ourselves that only the body which was the disguise of the Paramātman has perished, that the one who was in that disguise has become united with the Paramātman. Our love then will be everlasting. We must first learn to have such love for Īśvara and for people of goodness, for men of God. Then, step by step, we must enlarge it to embrace all creation. In this way the purpose of our life will be fulfilled.

Chapter 14

Love

What is called love may be divided into three categories. We love great men for their high qualities, I mean distinguished men, men of truth, philanthropists, jñānins, men of grace. We mix with our friends and relatives intimately and affection develops between them and us. Then we love people — love them ostensibly for a specific purpose, for the reason that we stand to gain from them. For instance, we may seem to love a rich man hoping that he would help us in our business or some other enterprise. We may love our employer because he pays us our wages.

These three types of love are neither true nor everlasting. If our employer sacks us we will cease to have either respect or affection for him. If people with whom we have had close contacts leave for a distant place or die or if we lose touch with them, we are likely in due course to forget them. All the sorrow we felt in the beginning because of being separated from them will eventually be forgotten. Were it true love the grief also should be enduring. Even our love for a great man is not lasting. If there happens to be a diminution in his qualities — or if he seems to us not as great as we thought he was — we will love him in correspondingly lesser measure.

All three categories of love have some reason [or motive] behind them. That is why they are not everlasting. We love great men because they possess certain qualities: there is an element of selfish interest in our feelings for them: because we think they will be helpful in our advancement.

True love knows neither reason nor motive. When do we love a man truly? When our affection for him is unchanging and unwavering — we love him even if he does not apparently move closely with us or does not seem to possess inward qualities or the capacity to bless us; we love him even when we do not have any selfish interest to be served by him. Does anyone possess such love? Yes, only One. It is Īśvara — he alone has such love.

God loves us for no reason. If he needed a reason he would not give us even a morsel of food. It is Parameśvara who forgives us all our misdeeds and protects us — and he is all love. It is his love that is manifested in the three categories mentioned earlier.

We must learn to have such love as is revealed through Parameśvara; that is love that is universal, love that is not based on any reason or interest. Why should we dislike a man because we think he is guilty of certain wrongs? Are we not similarly guilty ourselves? Do we then discard ourselves? We must have the same attitude towards others as we have towards ourselves. There is nothing remarkable about our love for a great man; the remarkable thing is to love a sinner also. If you ask me, you must have greater concern and affection for him. "He commits wrongs like us," we must tell ourselves. "His mind goads him into doing them. We must have sympathy for him and try to correct him." There may be a few whom Īśvara, out of his compassion, has given the gift of blessing others. Such men must take it upon themselves the task of freeing others from sinful actions.

We must, to start with, learn to have disinterested love for an individual, that is love that is not tainted by self-interest. Eventually, this love will permeate us, inspire our inner being, and we will then be able to enlarge it to embrace all. It is the teaching of the wise that we must have such love for our guru, love without any consideration of the fruits thereof. We must not look for any reason to love our preceptor. If we constantly "practise" to have such love for our guru we will be the recipients of his blessings. Our love for him will eventually grow into love that will encompass all. If our love is manifested in this manner there will be fullness, tranquillity and bliss.

Appendices

Appendix 1

Vedic Dharma and Tamiḷ Nāḍu

[The first volume of Deivattin Kural *includes the text of a brief discourse by the Paramaguru on Vedic dharma and Tamiḷ Nāḍu. The second volume contains a lengthier discourse on the same subject. The two lectures appear in a combined and abridged form in this translation. The subject dealt with is of paramount importance to any student of religion and history. The Paramaguru was a great unifying force and was of the firm view that the people of India belong to one family. Here, with his profound knowledge of history and mastery of languages, he establishes that the Vedas were at no time alien to the Tamiḷ land or to the South, that the Vedic dharma was an integral part of Tamiḷ life from time immemorial and that it was not an import from the North as claimed by some historians and misguided politicians.]*

I believe that the Vedas are essential for the good of mankind as well as for the Ātmic well-being of all. At present this great wealth, this capital asset [the Vedas], is going to waste. I am anxious that this deplorable state must change and that the Vedic dharma must grow again like a spreading tree. That is why I am drawing up schemes to preserve the Vedic tradition — to keep alive the Vedas — with the offer of stipends to students. However, preserving the Vedic dharma is not the responsibility of one monastic institution alone or of a few establishments. Everybody must feel that he has a part in it; everybody must work for it as a matter of duty, and not out of compulsion but out of the conviction that the Vedic dharma must be sustained in this Vedabhūmi [land of the Vedas]. I am addressing these words specially to the people of Tamiḷ Nāḍu.

The Tamiḷ soil has nurtured the Vedic tree with its numerous aerial roots. "Tamiḷ Nāḍu where the air was filled with the chanting of the Vedas," so sings Subrahmaṇya Bhārati[T]. And there is no exaggeration in the statement.

From the time of the Saṁgam[T] period, Vedic sacrifices have been extolled all over the Tamiḷ country. The Pāṇḍyan kings who fostered the Saṁgam earned many a title by performing Vedic sacrifices. Their capital Madurai had two distinctions. There they used elephants instead of bullocks to thresh grain — proof of the plentiful yield in their kingdom. The second distinction of Madurai may be referred to as "Ātmic prosperity". Citizens of the Pāṇḍyan capital said with pride: "In our city dawn breaks with the sound of Vedic chanting. In the Cera capital Vañji and the Cola capital Kozhi (Uraiyūr), people wake to the crowing of cocks. We in the Pāṇḍyan capital have reason to be proud about how we rise in the morning. We waken to the sound of Vedic chanting every dawn." This is mentioned in a Saṁgam work entitled the *Paripāḍal*[T].

There is an edict of Karikāla Coḷa[T] in the form of a stone inscription in Sanskrit. It includes these lines:

Pātrākālita Vedānām śāstramārgānusāriṇām
Tadetu arikālasya Karikālasya śāsanam

Karikāla describes himself here as "Karikāla the arikāla". "Ari" means foe. The Cola is thus the Kāla (Yama or death) of his foes. But who are the enemies of Karikāla himself? Those who do not adhere to the path of the Vedas and śāstras. People who follow the Vedic and śāstric way must be protected and those who do not must be punished. This is the purport of the edict.

Here is proof that the rulers of Tamiḷ Nāḍu, famed in history, wholeheartedly fostered the Vedic religion. A Pāṇḍyan king belonging to the Saṁgam period is called "*pal yāgaśālai mudukudumipperuvazhuti*". "*Vazhuti*" means a Pāṇḍyan monarch. In the stone inscriptions of later times also we see that the rulers of the Tamiḷ region donated tax-free (*iraiyili*) lands to Vedic scholars. There are a number of villages called "Caturvedi-maṅgalam" here, places made over as gifts to Brahmins to promote the Vedic dharma.

There are usually no equivalents in our regional languages to denote anything new or foreign introduced into our country. For instance, there are no words of our own for the radio, telephone, bus, and so on. Now we keep coining Tamiḷ equivalents for such words, equivalents that are neither easily understood nor well adapted for popular usage.

Some people believe that the Vedas, yāgas (sacrifices), etc, do not belong to the original civilization of Tamiḷ Nāḍu and that they were introduced from outside. If this belief were true there could be no authentic Tamiḷ words for the "Vedas", "yāgas", etc. But the fact is that even in very ancient Tamiḷ works the Vedas and the Vedic sacrifices are extolled and they are referred to as "*Marai*" and "*veḷvi*" respectively. In the same way, there are Tamiḷ words for "yajanam" (performing a sacrifice) and "yajñam" (sacrifice) —"*veṭṭal*" and "*veḷvi*". The sacrificial altar, "cayana", is called "*parappu*".

There cannot be such independent words in any language to describe what belongs to an alien culture or civilization. We [in the South] call the Bible the *Kristuva Veda* (Christian Veda) but the term does not independently belong to Tamiḷ like *veḷvi* or *Marai*. The Bible is still Bible in our country. That apart, in calling it "Veda" we are not using a separate independent word but applying a term already existing for a religious work. The Vedic sacrifice is called *veḷvi* in Tamiḷ but there is no rite called *veḷvi* that is unique to Tamiḷ Nāḍu. In the same way, there was nothing called *Marai* unique to that region and later applied to the Vedas.

Words like *Marai, veḷvi,* etc, are extremely meaningful as will be conceded by both Sanskrit and Tamiḷ scholars. *Veḷvi* is from "*veṭṭal*". The Vedas are the root of all dharmas. The root is hidden in the earth, not seen outside. Similarly, the Vedas are not exposed to all but *concealed* among a few who sustain them, living a life of severe moral and religious discipline. The word *Marai* implies so much. Were Tamiḷ Nāḍu not steeped in the Vedic ethos with its sacrifices, it could not have given rise to such beautiful words (*Marai, veḷvi, etc*) in its own language to reflect that ethos or culture.

To further illustrate the profound significance of the word *Marai.* There are passages of esoteric significance in the Vedas that are described as "rahasyam" in these scriptures themselves. In the Upaniṣads such passages are called "Upaniṣat". The Vedas and the Upaniṣads themselves refer only to a few passages that Brahmins have to keep concealed. Tamiḷ has gone one step further by describing the entire Vedic corpus as concealed (*Marai*): that is the meaning of the word *Marai,* that which is to be kept secret.

The Vedas contain this instruction to those entitled to chant them: "Keep such and such passages secret." If, according to the Vedas, some passages must be kept secret among Brahmins themselves, the Tamiḷ tradition goes further by taking into account all varṇas and proclaiming that those who are entitled to learn the Vedas must keep these scriptures concealed from all others who are not entitled to learn them. The secrecy thus is not confined to some passages alone but to the entire Vedas. We must infer from the use of the word *Marai* that the Tamiḷ tradition is against "democratising" the Vedas.

From another angle also the word *Marai* is apt. The benefits derived from the Vedas are not immediately apparent. The Ātmic fruits yielded by them remain hidden now and are revealed later. So it is usually said that the rewards of practising the Vedic dharma are "adṛṣṭa" (that is "adṛṣṭa phala" or "unseen fruits"). The Tamiḷ for adṛṣṭa, unseen or concealed, is *marai,* is that not so? The Vedas are the root of our religion, the root of devotion, temples, meditation, jñāna and so on. If temples, devotion, worship, etc, are the trunk, branches, flowers and fruit, the visible outward parts of the tree, the Vedas are its root. The root is hidden in the earth but from it has sprung the trunk and the branches. In this sense also *Marai* is a happy equivalent for the Vedas.

The Vedas are also called "*Ottu*" in Tamiḷ. The word is beautiful as well as meaningful and signifies that which is chanted and taught in the oral tradition. It occurs in the *Tirukkural*[T]. There is a place called Tiruvottūr in North Arcot district (Tamiḷ Nāḍu) and it figures in the story of Jñānasaṁbandhar[T]. Tiruvottur —Tiru-ottu-ur—is the place where the Vedas worshipped Parameśvara. In Sanskrit it is called Vedapuri. Another Tamiḷ name for the Vedas is "*Āraṇam*".

I have, in the course of my talks, told you about popular Tamiḷ usages like "*Veda vākko?*"; the custom of referring to a dharmaśālā as a *cattiram*[1], using words like "*yajamān*" (employer) and "sāngopāngam" (thorough, covering all parts including "anga" and "upānga"). All these terms and usages are evidence of how deep-rooted the Vedic dharma is in Tamiḷ Nāḍu.

[The Paramaguru explains once again why the Vedas are known as "Śruti" and how they came to be called "*ezhutāta kiḷavi*" (unwritten old text).] Since Śruti means what is heard, the inference is that the Vedas must not be written down. But the Tamiḷ term *ezhutata kiḷavi* shows explicitly that the Vedas must not be written down. In the Tamiḷ land every care was taken to ensure that our scripture was preserved according to the prescribed rules.

Any religious rite is called *caḍangu (śaḍangu)* in Tamiḷ—it has reference to the Ṣaḍanga of the Vedas. Here again there is proof that from the dim past Tamiḷ Nāḍu has adhered to the Vedic dharma.

In my opinion, the *Tirukkural,* which is called the Tamiḷ *Marai,* is wholly Vedic in character. In the Vedic religion, the first place is given to the fathers (pitṛs), then only to the sacrificial offering made to the gods. The deities are to be worshipped only after offering libations to the fathers and performing śrāddha[S]. Tiruvaḷḷuvar has followed this order of rites in his *Tirukkural*:

Tenpulattār, deivam, virundu, okkal, tān enrāngu aimbulattāru ombal talai.

The fathers, deities, guests, neighbours, oneself: all these five categories are to be nourished, says Tiruvaḷḷuvar. He mentions God or the deities after mentioning the *tenpulattār,* the manes. Incidentally, he uses the term *tenpulattār* following the Vedic belief that the fathers reside in the abode of Yama which is the south.

The share of the offerings we make to each of the five categories mentioned above is decided by ourselves. Apart from this, by royal command [or according to the state order] one-sixth of the yield of the land owned by us is to be paid as tax. The rest of the yield is to be divided into five parts as mentioned above. One part goes as food to those taking part in the ceremony intended for the fathers. The second goes to the temple (that is to the deities). The third is used to feed guests; and the fourth given to one's needy relatives. The remaining fifth is the share of one's family. There is no greater socialism than the dharma taught by the Vedas and by Tiruvaḷḷuvar. The principle on which the Vedic religion is founded is that a man must not live for himself alone but serve all mankind. Tiruvaḷḷuvar proclaims the same idea. *Kural,* that is the Tamiḷ *Marai* or Tamiḷ Veda, and other Tamiḷ works on law and ethics are products of the Vedic tradition.

There are many passages in the *Tirukkural* that reflect Tiruvalluvar's high regard for the Vedic dharma. In the line quoted above (*Tenpulattār, deivam,* etc) he refers to the Vedic pañca- mahāyajñas[2].

That cows and Brahmins will suffer if the royal [or state] policy goes wrong is an important Vedic concept. Why are cows and Brahmins specially mentioned? It is the cow that provides sacrificial materials like milk, ghee and cowdung. As for Brahmins it is they that are entitled to perform sacrifices. Tiruvaḷḷuvar refers to them and observes that, if the ruler is guilty of lapses or in other words is guilty of following a wrong policy, the nation stands to lose the benefits to be derived from cows and Brahmins.

Brahmins are called "ṣaṭ-karma-niraṭas" in Sanskrit, meaning those intently engaged in six "occupations" or works. Tiruvaḷḷuvar translates the term into Tamil literally—"*ārutozhilor*" is his word. What are these six karmas or *tozhils*? Adhyayana-adhyāpana (chanting the Vedas and teaching pupils to chant the same); yajanam-yājanam (performing sacrifices on one's own and performing them for others); dānam-pragrahaṇam (giving dakṣiṇā[S] to priests during sacrifices and receiving the same from others for giving them instruction in the Vedas and the Vedic dharma). It is ṭhe dakṣiṇā thus received that enables a Brahmin to conduct sacrifices and pay dakṣiṇā himself to the priests. These six "occupations" are mentioned in the *Manusmṛti.* Another dharmaśāstra, the *Parāśarasmṛti,* lists six other duties as part of a Brahmin's daily routine:

Sandhyā snānam japo homam devatānam ca pūjanam
Ātithyam vaiśvadevam ca ṣaṭkarmāṇi dine dine

Sandhyāvandana must be performed after bathing. A Brahmin must never be afraid of taking a dip in cold water. He has to bathe so often, twice or thrice a day, at dawn, midday and dusk (prātaḥ-snāna, mādhyāhnika-snāna and sāyaṁkāla-snāna). Sandhyāvandana must be performed after the bath in the morning and evening respectively and mādhyāhnika after the midday bath. Though the verse says "sandhyā snānam" you should not construe it perversely to mean bath after performing sandhyāvandana.

(Nowadays people tend to be argumentative about everything and speak irreverently about matters that deserve the highest respect. In one of his last teachings, the *Sopāna-Pañcaka,* the Ācārya specifically condemns peevish argumentativeness in religious matters. He accepts sound reasoning in Vedāntic discussions and has spoken only against "dustarka" or wayward or peevish arguments. It is not wrong to conduct any inquiry into the Vedas to the extent permitted by human reasoning. What is wrong is the refusal to recognize the limits to human understanding.)

Sandhyāvandana is the most important rite for the Brahmin. That is why it has been mentioned before bath. Of the six duties according to Parāśara, the first is constituted by sandhyāvandana and bathing. The second is japa, the muttering of great mantras, especially those pertaining to one's family deity (or one's chosen deity). The third is homa, offering oblations in the sacred fire, in other words, yajña. The fourth is deva-pūjana, worshipping the Lord with flowers, incense, light, food articles, etc. The fifth is ātithya, honouring and feeding guests, and the sixth and last is vaiśvadeva, offering bali[S] to outcastes, animals, birds, etc.

Such a great man as Vaḷḷuvar describes people who are charged with these six duties as "*ārutozhilor*". He states that in a country that has gone to rot the Brahmins will not chant the Vedas, that, indeed, they will even forget the scripture. We learn from this that the ideal nation or kingdom according to Vaḷḷuvar is one in which the Brahmins keep intoning the Vedas.

Subrahmaṇya is called the god of Tamiḷs. He has six faces and, while describing them, the Saṁgam work *Tirumurugarṟupaḍai*[T] mentions that one of the faces is meant to protect sacrifices performed by Brahmins, to ensure that the Brahmins adhere to the rules laid down in the Vedas for their conduct.

The five great Tamiḷ epic poems consist of Jaina and Buddhist works and they have passages extolling the Vedic dharma. Of them, *Śilappadikāram*[T] has many references to varṇāśrama. Vedic chanting by Brahmins is specially mentioned. There is considerable evidence to show that Kovalan, the hero of *Śilappadikāram,* was a Vaiśya who performed many Vedic rites.

If the mantras are the life-breath of the Vedas, the life-breath of the mantras themselves is the purity or clarity of their sound, their proper intonation. I have spoken about how by altering the sound or tone of the mantras the vibration in space as well as in our nādis[S] will change and how the fruit yielded by the chanting will not be what is desired. The Śikṣā śāstra deals in a scientific manner with how the sound of syllables originating in different parts of the body are revealed[3].

The sound we hear with our ears is called "vaikharī" and its source is within us and called "parā". Vaikharī originates in the lips and parā is the sound present in the mūlādhāra[4] below the navel. Before it is revealed as vaikharī through the mouth it goes through two stages, "paśyantī" and "madhyamā". It is only when we go higher and higher on the path of yogic perfection that we shall be able to hear the sounds paśyantī, madhyamā and parā. The seers who are masters of yoga are capable of hearing the parā sounds. There are certain parā sounds originating in the mūlādhāra which, on being transformed into vaikharī, can be heard by men. Such sounds please the deities, create good to the world and bring Ātmic uplift. It is such parā sounds that the seers have grasped from the transcendent space and given us as the Veda mantras. That the Tamiḷ work *Tolkāppiyam* mentions these truths and has a clear understanding of them came to light recently.

It had been known for some time that the words parā and paśyantī occur in old Tamiḷ works as *parai* and *paiśanti.* But it came to our knowledge only recently that the very first Tamiḷ work [extant], the *Tolkāppiyam,* mentions profound matters like, for instance, the fact that the sounds of the mūlādhāra are created by the upward passage of udāna, one of the five vital breaths. Apart from containing references to mantrayoga, this ancient Tamiḷ work also reveals a knowledge of Vedic intonation.

Recently, there was a controversy as to why the mantras recited in temples must be Sanskrit and not Tamiḷ. Tamiḷ scholars themselves gave the reasons: "It is totally wrong to raise questions about the language in which mantras are couched. The language and the meaning are of secondary importance. The special quality, or the special significance of mantras, is their sound and the fruits they yield. Tolkāppiyar has himself stated that the Veda mantras have a special quality and power arising from their sound."

While on the subject, I must speak about another matter. Many of you might find what I am going to say to be strange. You must be thinking, don't you, that the Vedas are in the Sanskrit language? If you do so you are wrong. The Vedic language is not Sanskrit but "Chandas". "Chandas" means not only metre but also the Vedas which are metrically composed as well as the language of the Vedas. The language used in ordinary speech, poetry, the Purāṇas, the epics, other writings is Sanskrit. The Vedic language alone is Chandas. When Pāṇini makes a reference to the Vedas he says, "Iti Chandasi", and when he refers to any question relating to Sanskrit he says, "Iti loke".

Sanskrit, which evolved through a constant process of saṁskāra or refinement, contains many words drawn from the Vedic language. But if there is a language that is based entirely on sounds meant for the well-being of mankind it is Chandas (the Vedic language). "Kṛtam" means created; "Saṁskṛtam" (Sanskrit) means well created. It would thus mean that the language called Sanskrit was created with great effort and care. The Vedic language is different. Have I not told you so often that the Vedic language (the mantras) occurred to the seers in a flash. Grammar is not important to it. The celestial race used the Vedic language as a base—that is the sounds of that language that emanated for the good of mankind—and created Sanskrit out of it and made it their own speech. The Vedas have their own grammar and prosody. Since Sanskrit was created out of the Vedas it follows that the Vedas are not Sanskrit. Sanskrit grew on its own, spreading all over the world and absorbing new words. But there has been no addition to the Vedas or to the Vedic language.

Some people are displeased with the fact that their mother tongue is not given the same place as Sanskrit and for that reason they refuse to have any respect for Vedic learning. It would be a matter of comfort for them to learn now that the Vedas are not Sanskrit. The vibrations of the sound of the Vedic language are beneficial to all orders of creation including bipeds and quadrupeds; so too the language in which all mantras belonging to the mantraśāstra are couched. This is not a language in the sense we understand the term in ordinary usage and is not the property of one jāti or of one race, but of the entire world. Is not moonlight pleasant and cool to people all over the world? And does not the sun bring life and sustenance to the entire planet? It would be ridiculous to exclaim: "What moon? The moon of which country? Whose sun are you talking about? We don't want either."

Tolkāppiyar stated that he would not deal with the Vedic sounds since they had their source in parā and were of great import. "I will deal with the sounds that are within the reach of ordinary people, vaikharī," he said. "The other sounds belong to the inner mysterious world..." Tamiḷ scholars have pointed out that there is the authority of the *Tolkāppiyam* itself for not changing the mantras used in temples.

It does not stand to reason to claim that what is present in one's own language is of high value and that what exists in another tongue is worthless. If we believe that our language represents all the wisdom in the world, would it not be natural for others also to take a similar view of their respective languages? So it is not rational to take pride in one's own language to the exclusion of those of others. People are scornful of accepting certain ideas as a matter of faith but at the same time they reveal an inability to think rationally when it comes to the question of language. *"Yādum mūre; yāvarum keḷir"*[5], it is proudly proclaimed. It is said to be part of the Tamiḷ tradition. But people who speak thus want to destroy certain traditions that have come down in this land from very ancient times.

The mantras have nothing to lose if we spurn them. The loss indeed will be ours. The Kāverī flows into Tamiḷ Nāḍu from Karṇāṭaka. A life-saving drug is imported from abroad. Does it make sense to say, "I will drink only water springing from our own land and I will take only medicine manufactured by us"? It is equally senseless to reject mantras that are meant for our protection for the reason that they are not couched in our language, or more correctly, for the reason *we think* that they are not in our language. As a matter of fact the mantras are not alien to us, have never been so. They have been with us as an integral part of our life from time immemorial.

In the old days there was no such feeling of separateness as now between speakers of one language and those of another.

In a Tamiḷ work as ancient as the *Puranānūru*[T] there is a reference to God with his long matted hair chanting the Vedas all the time, the Vedas with their six limbs (Ṣaḍanga). I read this in an article recently. The following appears in another *Puranānūru* passage: The rulers of the three Tamil kingdoms — Cera, Coḷa and Pāṇḍya — were always at war. But on one occasion the three were seen together as friends in the same place. The old lady Auvvai[T] saw the three kings together and was immensely delighted. She wished to compare the scene to something worthy. And how did she express her idea? "The three of you," she said, "seen together remind me of the three sacred fires in a Brahmin's household, gārhapatyāgni, āhavanīyāgni and dakṣiṇāgni."[6]

Even after the Saṁgam period, the Tamiḷ rulers (Cera, Coḷa, Pāṇḍya and Pallava) continued to give away gifts of land free of tax to Brahmins. They promoted scriptural learning by establishing Vedic schools (pāṭhaśālās and ghaṭikās) throughout the land.

In the Tamiḷ Vedas—the Śaiva *Tirumurai*[T] and the Vaiṣṇava *Divyaprabandham*[T]—there are as many passages dealing with the Vedas as there are those devoted to the Lord. Even though we think that devotion has a greater place in Tamiḷ Śaiva and Vaiṣṇava literature than karma or works, in actual fact we see that they speak more about Vedic sacrifices than about worship of Śiva or Viṣṇu as the case may be.

I said that the language of the Vedas is not Sanskrit. What I am going to tell you now will sound equally strange. Most of us think that the term "nāstika" means one who does not believe in God. This is wrong. It is possible to be an āstika even without believing in a God. There were many such āstikas in the past. Then what does the word āstika mean? An āstika is one who has faith in the Vedas. Even if a man does not believe in God but has faith in the power of the Vedic sounds and performs rites like sacrifices he is an āstika. "The Vedas do not speak of one God. They speak of many gods who are like human beings, not aspects of the Paramātman. If they are propitiated we will be happy." If a man performs Vedic rites even with such a half-baked knowledge of the truth of our scripture he will be called an āstika.

We include mīmāṁsakas among the āstikas, mīmāṁsakas who perform Vedic rites not consecrating them to the Supreme Being but merely for the sake of the fruits they yield. Let their view of the Vedas be wrong, but they believe that the Vedas are the authority for dharma and hence they are included among āstikas. Take followers of the Śaiva and Vaiṣṇava systems, called Pāśupata and Pāñcarātra respectively; they may be very much devoted to Śiva or Viṣṇu, but if some of their practices are opposed to the Vedic dharma they will be described as nāstikas — so it is mentioned in the old texts. Similarly, the Śāktas will make themselves liable to be called nāstikas if there are elements in their system contrary to the Vedic dharma.

Jñānasaṁbandhar[T] too regarded anyone opposed to the Vedic tradition as a nāstika: it was not devotion to the Lord that necessarily made one an āstika.

Jñānasaṁbandhar was one of the preceptors of the Śaiva system. His word was law in the Tamiḷ country. In his childhood he visited many a place and performed miracles there. At Paṭṭīśvaram he received the gift of a palanquin made of pearls from Īśvara himself and was taken in it from place to place, his entourage consisting of 5,000 devotees who kept singing the praises of Śiva.

That was a time when Jainism and Buddhism (both opposed to the Vedas) had a following in the South. The Jainas became powerful in the Pāṇḍyan kingdom and converted the king to their faith. The queen Maṅgayarkkaraśi and the minister Kulaccirai were extremely devoted Śaivas and very much regretted the king's conversion to Jainism. They had heard of the greatness of Jñānasaṁbandhar and sought his help in their predicament. They brought the saint to Madurai, the Pāṇḍyan capital, hoping that he would be able to bring the king back to the Śaiva faith.

Soon after Jñānasaṁbandhar had arrived in Madurai, the Śramaṇas (that is the Jainas) came to him for a religious disputation. The queen and the minister were afraid that the saint might come to harm at the hands of the Jainas. When we have the grace of Īśvara we can be without fear in the face of any threat. In the end it will overcome everything. A man is always protected and has nothing to fear if he is the recipient of the blessings of the Lord in full measure. Even dreadful weapons like cannons will not hurt and will fall at his feet. When there is a decline in devotion as well as in the grace of the Lord, there will be decay of both the nation and its religion. If there is but one individual who is the recipient of the grace of the Blessed Lord, he can bring welfare to the whole country. It will then have nothing to fear from any quarter.

Jñānasaṁbandhar had Īśvara's grace in full measure and it was with courage that he faced the Jainas in debate. Before the discussion started he recited songs composed by himself as a prayer to the deity Sundareśvara of Madurai. He prayed for victory in his debate with the Jainas and for success in upholding the glory of Śiva (that is Sundareśvara).

Why did Jñānasaṁbandhar want to triumph over the Jainas? Was it because the latter did not worship at Śiva temples? Was it because they did not wear the sacred ashes, that they did not put on the rudrākṣa[S] or that they spoke ill of devotion to Śiva? It would have been natural for the saint, who wanted the glory of Śiva to spread all over the world, to think on these lines. But his prayer was that he must have success in his debate with the Jainas and Buddhists because they were opposed to the Vedic dharma, not because they were not devoted to Śiva.

In the *Pattupāṭṭu*[T] the Jainas are first criticised for forsaking the Vedic dharma and then only for having no devotion to Īśvara. In many of the Tamiḷ works the utmost importance is given to the Vedas.

In the *Tevāram*[T] and *Divyaprabandham*[T], Brahmins are praised for being proficient in performing sacrifices and other rites. Jñānasaṁbandhar refers to Cidambaram as a place where Brahmins drive away the Kali Puruṣa [the evil age of Kali personified] by learning and chanting the Vedas, tending the sacred fires and performing sacrifices. It would be wrong to think that Jñānasaṁbandhar speaks in praise of sacrifices because he was a Brahmin. Apparsvāmigal[T] was not a Brahmin but he adores the Lord associating him with Vedic sacrifices. He says that Īśvara himself intones the Vedas.

Appar has sung a *Tevāram* hymn at Omapuliyūr. In it he says that Omapuliyūr is filled with *omam* (homa) and refers to the three sacred fires tended by Brahmins, gārhapatya, āhavanīya and dakṣiṇāgni. In his poems he reveals a precise understanding of a Brahmin's religious life.

When you read the *Divyaprabandham* you note that, if there is a description of a place with its temple to Perumāḷ[T], there is also a reference to the smoke of the sacrificial fire there rising high like the clouds and covering the whole sky. Without betraying any bias against any caste, non-Brahmin Āzhvārs[T] have also sung the praises of the Vedas. Tirumaṅgaiyāzhvār was not a Brahmin, but he adores the Lord mentioning the names of the Vedic recensions. If Appar refers to the three sacred fires kept by Brahmins, Tirumaṅgaiyāzhvār goes further by mentioning the two additional fires (sabhyam and āvasthyam). We saw that Omapuliyūr is mentioned in the *Tevāram;* Tirumaṅgaiyāzhvār refers to places like Tirunaṅgūr, Tirunaraiyūr and so on describing them as places known for Brahmins living strictly according to the Vedic dharma.

The *Tolkāppiyam* is the creation of Tiruṇadūmakkini, a disciple of the sage Agastya. In the excellent preface (*pāyiram*) to it, written by Paraṁparanār, occurs this line, "*Araṅgarai nāvin nānmarai muṟṟiya adangoṭṭu āśan.*" In his commentary on this, Naccinārkkiṇiyār says: "Here by *nānmarai* (the four Vedas) is not meant the Ṛg, Yajur, Sāma and Atharva Vedas because the *Tolkāppiyam* was composed before the Vedas had been divided into four by Vedavyāsa." He further observes that at the time of this work on grammar the four Vedas were known as "Taittirīyam", *"Pauḍikam"*, "Talavakāram" and "Sāmam". In the *Divyaprabandham* occurs the term, *"Pauzhīya Chandoga"*. "Chandoga" refers to the Sāmaveda. The *Kauṣītaki Brāhmaṇa* belongs to one of the Ṛgvedic recensions and it is this, "Pauṣyam", that is known as *"Pauzhīyam"* or *"Pauḍīkam"*. "Talavakāram", "Taittirīyam" and *"Pauzhīyam"* are the recensions of the Sāmaveda, the Kṛṣṇa-Yajurveda and the Ṛgveda respectively. "Sāmam" is the only full-fledged Veda mentioned in the above reference.

All Nampūtiri Brahmins of what is called "Malayāḷam" (Keraḷa) do adhyayana[S]. Even those engaged in the affairs of the world must have been taught to chant the Vedas in their boyhood — for instance, E.M.S. Naṁboodiripāḍ, the communist leader who was chief minister [of Keraḷa]. Until recently, the brahmacārins in Keraḷa wore the kaupina[7], the skin of the black antelope and the staff. They performed samidādhāna[S] and other rites without fail. Today there is a change in their life too. When members of a caste known for their exemplary conduct and loyalty to great ideals fall from their heights, they plunge indeed to low depths. Ṛgvedins predominate among Nampūtiris. In one of their palm-leaf manuscripts we find that the Ṛgveda is referred to as *"Pauzhīyam"*. We know from this conclusively that *"Pauzhīyam"* is the name of the Ṛgveda: it is the same as the *"Pauḍīkam"* mentioned by the commentator of the *Tolkāppiyam.*

The Nampūtiris, among whom Bhagavatpāda was born [as an incarnation of Śiva], have still the distinction of not entirely abandoning the Vedic dharma. It is said that at a time when many faiths were wildly contending against one another for dominance in the country, Parameśvara, who wanted to re-establish the Vedic dharma, looked for a place where Vedic learning and the Vedic way of life flourished. He found Kālaṭi in Keraḷa to be such a place and took birth there in a Nampūtiri family.

During the time of Śankara the language called Malayāḷam had not yet evolved. Tamiḷ was then spoken in Keraḷa. Even during the time of Ceramān

Perumāl Nāyanār, who was an intimate friend of Sundaramūrtisvāmin's[T], the land called "Malayāḷam" was still Tamiḷ-speaking. It was in Tamiḷ that he composed his *Tirukkailāyajñāna-ulā.* He ruled from Tiruvañjaikkuḷam. Kulaśekhara Perumāḷ, who composed the *pāsurams*[T] called *Perumāḷ Tirumozhi* of the *Divyaprabandham*[T], had his capital at Tiruvanantapuram. During this time too Tamiḷ was the language of his kingdom. Before all this, more than two thousand years ago, when the Lord descended to earth as Śankara, Keraḷa was part of the Tamiḷ country. Śankara chose to be born there because in all Bhārata it was in that region that the Vedas flourished with vigour. This is a pointer to the fact that the Tamiḷ land was specially attached to the Vedic dharma.

If the Vedic tradition was kept alive in Keraḷa more than elsewhere, the reason must be that this region was once part of the Tamiḷ land. Today the Vedas are learnt more widely in Āndhra than in Tamiḷ Nāḍu. The reason for this is that in the old days there were marital alliances between the Āndhra rulers and the Coḷas and the former fostered the Vedic dharma by settling in their kingdom a large number of Vedic scholars from Tamiḷ Nāḍu. What does it mean? Though today there is greater opposition to the Vedic dharma in Tamiḷ Nāḍu than in the other Draviḍian states, in the past it was from here (Tamiḷ Nāḍu) that Vedic learning spread to other parts. The Brahmins in Āndhra who call themselves "Drāviḍalu" are descendants of those who had been brought from Tamiḷ Nāḍu.

All religious and philosophical systems known to Tamiḷ Nāḍu, including the religion that existed there in the hoary past and the Śaiva, Vaiṣṇava and Śākta faiths (that is the Ṣaṇmata), Sānkhya, Yoga, Nyāya and Vaiśeṣika, and the mantra and tantra āgamas[S] are based on the Vedas. All these systems respect the authority of the Vedas.

Researchers in modern times propagate the view that the Vedas came to the South from the North, that the South had another religion and religious texts. This view of theirs, along with the theory that Northerners are Āryans and Southerners Dravīḍians, has created a conflict among the people. But if you truly examine Sanskrit and ancient Tamil texts you will find no basis for such a view or for the race theory. The researchers say that one should not be deceived by placing blind faith in the śāstras. But, in the end, what obtains today? Many people have come to accept the view of these researchers without examining it properly, merely because the research scholars concerned claim that their view is "rational" and "scientific."

In the Vedas and śāstras there are indeed matters that have to be accepted in faith. But there are also scriptural aspects that can be examined rationally. If we inquire into such texts together with the ancient works in Tamiḷ we will realise that the race theory is baseless. The fact that there was such a thing as a Tamiḷ religion will also seen to be totally unfounded. It is a matter for regret that wrong notions have arisen with regard to subjects of great value, along with lack of faith in the śāstras. All these must go and the Vedic culture flourish again, a culture that brings good to all the worlds and all creatures. This is the prayer we must always make to the Lord.

Notes & References

[1] From "sattram", a type of sacrifice. See Chapter 26, Part Five.

[2] See Chapter 6, Part Nineteen.

[3] Part Six for Śikṣā śāstra.

[4] See notes appended to Chapter 2, Part Six.

[5] See note appended to Part Nine.

[6] These sacred fires are referred to in Chapter 6, Part Nineteen.

[7] Undergarment.

Appendix 2

Steps to Promote Vedic Learning

[Among the varied and remarkable contributions the Paramaguru made to the Ātmic, religious and cultural resurgence of the nation was the work he did to promote Vedic learning. He breathed new life into an ages-old tradition at a time it seemed alarmingly on the decline.]

In 1954 devotees approached me for permission to celebrate my ṣaṣṭyabdapūrti (60th birthday). I told them then: "I don't need any celebration for myself. I should like to be saved from the ill fame that I am likely to earn if the Vedic dharma becomes extinct in this country in my own lifetime. To be saved thus would be celebration enough for me. If I am unable to keep the Vedic dharma alive I shall not be worthy of any celebration conducted in my honour."

It was after this that the Ṣaṣṭyabdapūrti Trust was created. Its objective was to encourage the study of the Veda-bhāṣya. Veda-bhāṣya deals with the meaning of scriptural passages and expounds the principles and truths underlying them. It is to be studied after one has learned to chant the mantras. When the Trust was created there were still a small number of students who learned to chant the Vedas but the study of the Veda-bhāṣya had ceased altogether. That is the reason why the Trust was established to revive the study of the bhāṣya.

Later (in 1957) devotees expressed a desire to celebrate the 50th anniversary of my installation on the Pīṭha[1]. It was then that the Kaḷavai Bṛndāvana Trust was formed to run Vedic pāṭhaśālās (schools) apart from teaching the Veda-bhāṣya. It was at Kaḷavai[2] that my guru and paramaguru [guru's guru] attained siddhi[S]. Their Bṛndāvana is at this place. The Kaḷavai Bṛndāvana Trust is dedicated to their memory.

Some time earlier, in 1942, the Veda-Dharmaśāstra Paripālana Sabhā had been formed and arrangements made to conduct Vedic assemblies and to honour Vedic scholars.

In 1960 was created the Veda Rakṣaṇa Nidhi Trust, with the objective of carrying out the work of the above bodies in an integrated manner. This Trust has implemented many a scheme, taking upon itself the responsibility of running Vedic schools all over the country and honouring Vedic scholars everywhere.

According to one scheme of the Trust, examinations are held once a year at various centres in the country for students studying at Vedic schools or at the residences of Vedic scholars.

It takes eight years to learn — memorise — one recension of a Veda. Every year examinations are conducted and, on conclusion of the course of study, successful candidates are presented titles. I spoke in one of my earlier talks about different methods of Vedic chanting[3] like "pada" and "krama". We award titles to students proficient in such methods, titles like "Padānta Svādhyāyi" and "Kramapāṭhi".

Leave aside the question of titles. After all, it is with monetary or material help to pupils that Vedic learning has to be encouraged. During the course of study both teacher and taught are paid donations on a graduated scale. The teacher is paid every month but the pupil is paid only after he finishes his course so that he does not drop out in between with a half-baked knowledge of the Vedic recension he is taught.

A teacher earns from Rs 100 to Rs 150 per student every year. For instance, if he has ten students under him he earns a minimum of Rs 1,500 a year. As for the pupil he will receive at the end of his course of study a lumpsum of between Rs 2,000 and Rs 4,000.

A student who, after completing his Vedic studies, does a course in poetry, the śāstras, etc, and acquires proficiency in Sanskrit, receives a donation ranging between Rs 1,500 and Rs 3,000. Out of the sum the student receives he has to give one-fourth to his guru [as dakṣiṇā].

We have observed from experience that, after completing his normal course in Vedic chanting, a student takes three years to qualify for the title of "Salakṣaṇa Ghanapāṭhin".

It is the duty of every brahmacārin to perform samidādhāna[S] with the offering of sticks (samidhs) in the sacred fire. Another duty of his is to go begging from house to house for his food (this is bhikṣācarya). A student who — apart from learning to intone the Vedas — performs samidādhāna and does bhikṣācarya receives twice the normal donation he is otherwise entitled to.

It is only after a student becomes a Saḷakṣaṇa Ghanapāṭhin that he can enrol for the study of the Veda-bhāṣya, and this takes seven to eight years. In all, a pupil takes about 20 years to complete his Vedic learning—eight years to qualify for the "Kramapāṭhi" title, four years to become a "Salakṣana Ghanapāṭhin" and seven years to study the Veda-bhāṣya. Does it not take 17 or 18 years to qualify for the M.A. degree [that is from the first standard onwards]? Vedic learning is more

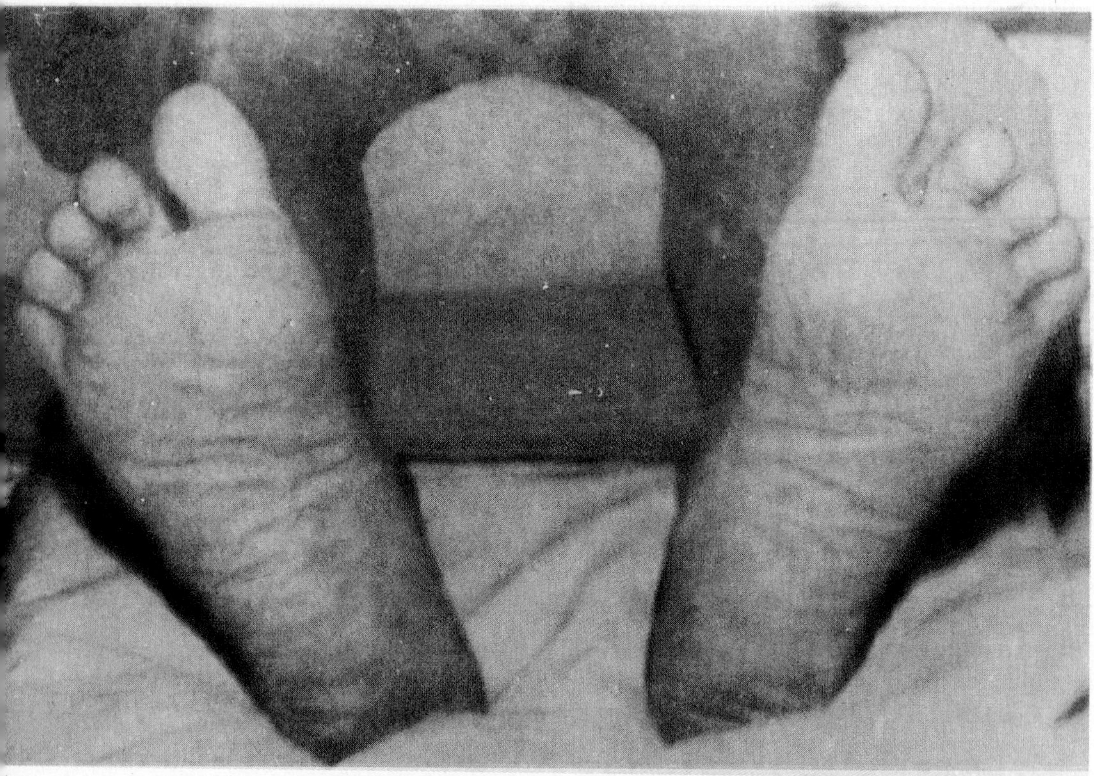

The sacred lotus feet of the Sage of Kāñcī.

प्रकाशात्मिकया शक्त्या प्रकाशानां प्रभाकरः ।
प्रकाशयति यो विश्वं प्रकाशोयं प्रकाशताम् ॥

useful, more beneficial to mankind [than university education] and capable of conferring greater Ātmic well-being.

When a student graduates to the Veda-bhāṣya class he will be of an age when others, the same years as he is, usually go for jobs. We thought that, to turn him away from jobs and encourage him to continue his Vedic education, we must give him a stipend. So, during the seven-year bhāṣya course, 13 tests are held for the students and cash gifts given to those who are successful : for those who pass in the first class Rs 60, in the second class Rs 40 and in the third class Rs 30. Apart from this, a student who has appeared for the second test is paid Rs 100 until he appears for the third test, Rs 200 until he appears for the fourth, and above that Rs 250. Even if a student fails twice he receives the payment. I am anxious that young boys must somehow be persuaded to continue their study and not drop out. Hence this arrangement. The idea is that every student of Veda-bhāṣya must receive about Rs 600 every year.

After 20 years of study, is it right to abandon a student to his fate with the final year's cash gift or donation? We thought his Vedic learning must enable him to obtain at least a starvation diet. So we decided to give a donation to students who complete the entire course of Vedic studies: Rs 7,000 who pass in the first class; Rs 5,000 who pass in the second; and Rs 3,000 who pass in the third. They also receive a title: "Bhāṣyaratna" for the first category; "Bhāṣyamaṇi" for the second; and "Bhāṣyajña" for the third.

We have also a "Pāraṁparīya Niyamādhyayana Scheme". With the change in the old system of gurukulavāsa[S], it has now become customary for a brahmacārin to study under his father instead of a guru outside the family. For some generations Vedic learning has been maintained in the father to son line. Those who study the Vedas at home like this—and their number is not many—have to be given an incentive. The purpose of the Niyamādhyayana scheme is to encourage a Brahmin proficient in the Vedas and śāstras to impart his knowledge to his sons. A sum of Rs 12,500 is deposited in the name of any student who comes under this scheme. During the years of his study he receives Rs 40 every month as stipend. When he finishes Rs 9,000 is paid as a lumpsum. Apart from this he will receive throughout his life 80 per cent of the interest from the capital of Rs 12,500 originally invested in his name.

Notes & References

[1] The Paramaguru was installed as the Śankarācārya of Kāñcī Kāmakoṭi Pīṭha in 1907 when he was hardly 13 years old.

[2] Kaḷavai is 60 kilometers from Kāñcī.

[3] See Chapter 10, Part Five.

Notes & References

Sanskrit Glossary

Listed here are words marked with a superior "S" in the main text (for example, "AdhyāpanaS", "ŚrīharṣaS", "UpadeśaS").

The translator is indebted to Principal Vāman Shivarām Āpte's The Practical Sanskrit-English Dictionary *in the preparation of this glossary. He has also relied on Mahāmahopādhyāya P.V. Kāṇe's* History of Dharmaśāstra, *M. Krishṇamāchāriār's* History of Classical Sanskrit Literature, *and the works of a couple of other indologists.*

Abhicāra: Exorcism; practice of black magic; using spells with an evil intent.

Abhivādana: Reverential salutation of a superior like a teacher or any elder.

Abhiṣeka: Sprinkling; showering; bathing a deity or a guru.

Ācāra: Matters of custom and tradition that serve as a general discipline. Vyavahāra is applying them to the performance of outward rites.

Adhikaraṇa: Placing at the head of; appointing; in Pūrvamīmāṁsā the word means a topic or a "unit" of argument.

Adhyāpana: Imparting instruction in the Vedas; it is one of the six duties of a Brahmin.

Adhyāya: A chapter or division of a work; a lesson or lecture; also study of the Vedas.

Adhyayana: Learning the Vedas, chanting them; also one of the six duties of a Brahmin.

Ādi Śankara: See under "Śankara".

Advaita: Non-dualism or monism; the doctrine that declares that there is but One Reality, that the individual self and the Brahman are one.

Āgama: Traditional doctrine, science or knowledge; the āgama śāstras deal with ritual, iconography, the construction of temples, yantras and so on.

Agrahāra: The Brahmin quarter in a village or town; land granted to Brahmins for their sustenance.

Ahaṁkāra: Ego-sense; "I-feeling"; self-conceit.

Āhitāgnin: One who tends the sacred śrauta and gṛhya fires.

Āhuti: Oblation made in the sacrificial fire.

Airāvata: The celestial elephant.

Ajñāna: Ignorance; nescience.

Akṣata: Whole, uninjured; unbroken rice grains used in various rites.

Angas: Limbs; the six limbs of the Vedas—Śikṣā, Vyākaraṇa, Chandas, Nirukta, Jyotiṣa, Kalpa; the Upāngas are Mīmāṁsā, Nyāya, Purāṇa and Dharmaśāstra.

Antaḥ-karaṇa: The internal organs or faculties: the mind, the intellect, the consciousness and the ego; according to another reckoning, the heart, the soul, the seat of thought and feelings, the mind and conscience.

Anudātta: See under "Udātta".

Anumāna: Inference in Nyāya.

Anusvāra: Literally means "after-sound"; one authority describes it as the unmodified nasal following a vowel.

Apavarga: Liberation according to Vaiśeṣika.

Appayya Dīkṣita: Various dates are ascribed to this medieval polymath. According to one authority Appayya Dikṣita lived between 1554 and 1626. He belonged to a family of distinguished scholars and was the author of 104 works on subjects like poetics and Vedānta and on Śaiva themes. His work in the first-mentioned category, *Kuvalayānanda,* is particularly famous. He was patronised by King Venkaṭadeva of Vijayanagara and Tirumala Nāyaka of Madurai.

Apsaras: Celestial damsel. Among the apsarases are Rambhā, Menakā, Urvaśī and Tilottamā. These damsels were often employed by the celestials to distract sages from their ascetic endeavour.

Aparā-vidyā: Lower type of knowledge.

Āratī: The conclusion of a ceremony; presenting lights before a deity at the conclusion of worship.

Arghya: Libation to the gods, ṛṣis or fathers; an important part of sandhyāvandana (qv) is arghya-pradāna, the offering of arghya. Arghya also means valuable or venerable.

Aśoka: *Saraca indica.*

Āśrama: Hermitage; one of the four stages of life, these being brahmacaryāśrama, gṛhasthāśrama, vānaprastha and sannyāsa. Āśrama-dharma denotes the duties and code of conduct for each of these stages in life.

Āśrama-dharma: See under "Āśrama".

Aṣṭākṣarī: An eight-syllable mantra like "Om Namo Nārāyaṇāya".

Astra: That which is energised by a mantra and turned into a weapon.

Aśvamedha: Horse-sacrifice performed by an imperial ruler or a "sārvabhauma" (literally a "universal monarch").

Aśvattha: *Pīpal, Ficus religiosa.*

Ātithya: Pertaining to a guest; one of the "pañca-mahāyajñas" (or five great sacrifices) to be performed every day, it means honouring guests and offering them food. It is also called manuṣya-yajña.

Ātman: The soul; the individual self or the Self. In Advaita the Ātman is identified with the Brahman or the Paramātman.

Ātmavidyā: Science of the Self; it is learning that imparts the highest wisdom and enlightenment.

Bali: This is also one of the "pañca-mahāyajñas" and forms part of the vaiśvadeva or bhūtayajña rite to be performed by the householder. In this rite food is offered with the chanting of mantras to birds and beasts and outcastes. Bali is what is directly offered while "āhuti" is what is offered in the fire.

Bāṇa: A great master of Sanskrit prose, he flourished in the court of Harṣavardhana of Kānyakubja (A.D. 606-647). His *Harṣacaritam* is based on the life of his patron. His *Kādambarī* is a landmark in the genre called "gadyakāvya".

Bhartṛhari: One of the oft-quoted poets, he is author of the *Nītiśatakam* (on policy), *Śṛṅgāraśatakam* (on love) and *Vairāgyaśatakam* (on renunciation). Bhartṛhari was also a grammarian. According to some historians he belonged to the 7th century.

Bhasma: Ashes of cowdung smeared on the forehead and body.

Bhāṣya: Commentary or exposition, especially of sūtras.

Bhavabhūti: As a poet and dramatist, his place is second only to that of Kālidāsa. He is believed to have lived in the 8th century in Kānyakubja. Among his dramatic works are the *Uttararāmacaritam, Mālatīmādhavam* and *Mahāvīracaritam.*

Bhūtayajña: See under "Bali".

Bilhaṇa: Kāśmīrī poet (10th-11th centuries); *Caurapañcāśikā, Karṇasundarī* and *Vikramānkadevacaritam* are among his major works. He has also written a hymn to Siva.

Bilva: *Aegle marmelos*

Bodhendra Sarasvatī Svāmin: The 59th Śankarācārya of Kāñcī Kāmakoṭī Pīṭha (1638-1692), he was known as "Bhagavannāma Bodhendra". He and Tiruviśanallūr Ayyāvāḷ (qv) were foremost among those who propagated devotion through "nāma japa". Śrī Bodhendra Svāmigaḷ spread the glory of Rāma and Govinda while Śrī Ayyāval propagated devotion to Śiva. (See Chapter 10, Part Fourteen.)

Brahmacārin: One who has had his upanayana, that is a student who lives with his ācārya to learn the Vedas and other subjects; celibate.

Brahmacarya: Total discipline required to master the Vedas and other branches of learning. "Brahma" has the meaning of the Vedas here. Brahmacarya also denotes strict chastity; so a bramacārin has also come to mean a celibate.

Brahmacaryāśrama: The first stage of life, that of the brahmacārin.

Brahman: The Supreme Godhead, the Ultimate Reality. Saguṇa Brahman is the Brahman with attributes and Nirguṇa Brahman is the Brahman that is unconditioned, without any attributes.

Brahmarandhra : Aperture in the crown of the head where the suṣumna nāḍi terminates.

Brahmopadeśa: Instruction in the Vedas or sacred knowledge. It usually means the imparting of the Gāyatrī mantra during the upanayana ceremony, Gāyatrī being the essence of the Vedas.

Bṛndāvana: Forest near Gokula, the word bṛnda (or vṛnda) itself meaning the tulaśī. It is also understood as the place where a sannyāsin lies interred and where tulasi, bilva and other sacred plants are grown.

Caitanya: Spirit, life, vitality.

Caturdaśa-vidyā: The foruteen branches of Vedic learning: the four Vedas, the six Angas (Śikṣā, Vyākaraṇa, Chandas, Nirukta, Jyotiṣa and Kalpa), Mīmāṁsā, Nyāya, Purāṇa and Dharmaśāstra.

Caula (or cūdākarma): The first cutting of the hair on the head of a child, leaving a cūda or lock of hair (śikhā), the remaining part being shaved.

Cayana: Literally collecting or piling; piling of the fire-altar, the character of the yajñabhūmi.

Chandas: The Vedas; prosody.

Citta: The consciousness, mind.

Dakṣiṇā: A present, gift or fee paid to a priest or to a guru; the daughter of Prajāpati; also regarded as the wife of Sacrifice personified.

Dakṣiṇāyana: The six months from the time the sun turns from the tropic of Cancer. Mid-July to mid-January is the period traditionally regarded as Dakṣiṇāyana. Uttarāyaṇa, in the same manner, consists of the six months from mid-January to mid-July.

Dāna: Giving, donation, charity.

Daṇḍin: Daṇḍin belonged to Kāñcī and lived during the reign of the Pallava king Narasimhavarman I (630-668). He was a junior contemporary of Bāṇa and is remembered today for his picaresque prose romance *Daśakumāracaritam* and *Kāvyādarśa,* a work on poetics.

Darbha: A kind of sacred grass used in religious rites.

Dhanurveda: The art of warfare or weaponry; military science.

Dhāraṇa: Concentration; fixing one's mind or inner faculties on an object, on the One Reality.

Dharma: That which supports; religion in general; code of conduct; set of duties as, for example, included in the varṇa or jati system; the divine moral order; duties to God and to mankind. Dharma is the means to attain the ultimate good that is liberation.

Dīkṣā: Initiation in general; consecration for a religious ceremony; dedicating oneself to some work or ideal. Dīkṣita is one who is initiated, one who has performed an elaborate sacrifice like a somayāga.

Dīkṣita: See under "Dīkṣā".

Dīrgha-sumaṇgalī: Long-lived sumaṅgalī (qv).

Dravya : Material; material for a sacrificial rite. Dravya-śuddhi is purifying material meant for a sacrifice.

Dravya-śuddhi: See under "Dravya".

Dhyāna: Meditation or contemplation; undistracted focusing of the mind on a particular idea, object or deity.

Dvaita: System of Vedānta according to which the individual self and the Brahman are two separate entities.

Ekādaśī: Eleventh day of the lunar fortnight that is sacred to Viṣṇu. It is a day of fasting and devotion. There is a great deal of literature on the Ekādaśī-vrata.

Gandharva: Celestial musician; one of a class of demigods. The art or science of music is called Gāndharva-veda. Gāndharva-vivāha is one of the eight forms of marriage.

Garbhādhāna (or niṣeka) : Saṁskāra in which marriage is consummated; impregnation.

Gāyatrī: Mantra held in great esteem and regarded as the essence of the Vedas; it is imparted to the brahmacārin during his investiture with the sacred thread. Also a Vedic metre of 24 syllable.

Gāyatrī-japa: Muttering, repeating, the Gāyatrī mantra.

Ghanapāṭhin: One who can chant the Vedas according to the ghana method. (See Chapter 10, Part Five.)

Gotra: Family, lineage, descendants of a great sage; literally cowpen or a herd of cows.

Graha: A celestial body. The grahas are the sun and the moon, Mars, Mercury, Jupiter, Venus, Saturn, Rāhu and Ketu (navagraha).

Grantha: A literary work or treatise. The Grantha script consists of a mixture of Tamil characters and symbols to represent phonemes of Sanskrit.

Guṇas: Qualities or constituents. There are three guṇas in the phenomenal world: sattva-guṇa, rajo-guṇa and tamo-guṇa (sattva, rajas and tamas). Sattva-guṇa is purity, virtue, goodness, clarity (it is the highest state); rajo-guṇa is impurity, action, passion, violence; and tamo-guṇa denotes darkness, inertia, sloth.

Gṛhastha: Householder. Gṛhasthāśrama is the second stage in a man's life, that of the householder.

Gṛhasthāśrama: See under "Gṛhastha".

Guru: Preceptor, any person worthy of veneration; weighty; Jupiter. The true function of a guru is explained in *The Guru Tradition*. Gurukula is the household or residence of a preceptor. A brahmacārin stays with his guru to be taught the Vedas, the Vedāngas and other subjects: this is gurukulavāsa.

Gurukula: See under "Guru".

Gurukulavāsa: See under "Guru".

Havis: An oblation or burnt offering.

Homa: Offering oblations in the consecrated fire.

Indrāṇī: The consort of Indra, the king of the celestials.

Iṣṭadevatā: One's chosen deity; the deity one particularly likes to adore.

Jambu: *Eugenia jambolana.*

Japa: The meditative muttering of the names of the Lord or a mantra.

Jātakarma : A saṁskāra performed for the well-being of a new-born son.

Jāti: One of the many subdivisions of a varṇa.

Jñāna: Knowing or understanding. Though usually translated into English as "knowledge", "jñāna" does not mean proficiency in a subject like history or physics. It is not mere learning but inward *experience* or awareness of a truth. In Advaita it is the realisation that one is inseparably united with the Supreme.

Jñānendriyas: Organs of perception or "faculties of apprehending": the eyes, the ears, the nose, the tongue and the skin.

Kālidāsa: The most celebrated poet and dramatist of the "classical" period of Sanskrit. Among his works: plays — *Abhijñāna-Śākuntalam, Vikramorvaśīyam* and *Mālavikāgnimitram*; long poems — *Raghuvamśam, Kumārasaṁbhavam, Meghadūtam* and *Ṛtusamhāram*(?). We still do not know for sure when he flourished — some historians believe that he belonged to the 1st century B.C.

Kalpa: One of the six Vedāngas dealt with in Part Eleven; it is usually referred to as a "manual of rituals". In the Hindu reckoning of time a kalpa is one-seventh of the life-span of Brahmā (see Chapter 8, Part Ten).

Kalpavṛkṣa: Celestial tree that yields all desires:

Kāma: Desire; one of the puruṣārthas (see Chapter 3, Part One); god of love.

Kāmadhenu: Celestial cow that grants all desires.

Karmendriyas: Organs of action: the tongue, the hands, the legs, the anus, the genitals.

Kartā: Creator, God; one who performs a religious function.

Ketakī: The screwpine flower.

Khadira: *Acacia catechu.*

Kumārilabhaṭṭa: Great mīmāṁsaka and senior contemporary of Śankara Bhagavatpāda. He is believed to have immolated himself in expiation of the sin of not revealing his true identity to his Buddhist guru. During his last days Śankara was able to convince him of the truth of Advaita.

Kuṁbhābhiṣeka: Sanctifying ceremony connected with the building, renovation or reconstruction of a temple and the installation of a deity.

Lagna: The moment of the sun's entrance into a zodiacal sign; auspicious hour for a marriage or other rites.

Lakṣaṇa: Quality, property or distinguishing characteristic.

Madhvācarya (Madhva): Founder of the Dvaita or dualistic school of Vedānta. He was born in a village near Udupi, Karnāṭaka, in 1199.

Mahā-naivedya: See under "Naivedya".

Mahāvākyas: Great dicta, formulae, or pronouncements found in the Upaniṣads (like, for example, "Tattvam asi") on which the seeker has to meditate with one-pointedness.

Maṅgala-sūtra (māṅgalya-sūtra): The auspicious string worn by the bride at her wedding. In the South it is called a *tāli.* A married woman prizes it more than any other ornament and is divested of it only on the death of her husband.

Māṇgalya-dhāraṇa: Wearing of the maṇgala-sūtra (or māṅgalya-sūtra) during the marriage ceremony.

Mantra: Variously defined as an incantation, formula or "word-sound". Mantra is that which protects you by being turned over in the mind again and again.

Mantrākṣata: Simply stated, unbroken rice grains that are imbued with the power of mantras are mantrākṣata. Such rice grains (mixed with turmeric and kumkuma) are received with the blessings of Vedic paṇḍitas to the chanting of mantras.

Mantrapuṣpa: There are 16 different constituents in the worship of any deity: these are called the ṣoḍaśopacāra. The 15th upacāra is mantrapuṣpa. In this flowers are offered to the Lord with the chanting of mantras. There is also the mantrapuṣpa associated with the honouring of an ascetic.

Mantravādin: One who recites mantras; one who tries to cure diseases with the chanting of mantras; an exorcist or sorcerer. Māntrika means the same.

Māntrika: See under "Mantravādin".

Manvantara: The regnal period of a Manu. One thousand mahāyugas constitute the regnal period of the 14 Manus put together (See Chapter 8, Part Ten.)

Mārjana: Sprinkling.

Maṭha: The dwelling of an ascetic. The term refers particularly to any of the monastic institutions established by Ādi Śankara; for example, the Kāñcī Maṭha.

Mātra: A measure; a measure in prosody; time taken to intone a syllable; time interval.

Māyā: The term is usually understood as illusion; it is what we perceive of the phenomenal world or the phenomenal world itself. Māyā can also mean creative power.

Menakā: See under "Apsaras."

Muhūrta: A period of 48 minutes; an instant; auspicious time for the performance of a rite.

Mūrti: Anything that has a definite shape; an image or idol; personification.

Nāḍi: Blood vessel or nerve.

Nāḍikā: Known as *nazhikai* in Tamil, it is 24 minutes.

Nāgasvaram: Musical instrument of the South — a double-reed pipe.

Naiṣadham: See under "Srīharṣa".

Naivedya: What is presented or offered to a deity. Mahā-naivedya is cooked rice offered to a devatā.

Nāma-japa: Repeating the names of the Lord in an undertone. See under "Japa".

Nāmakaraṇa: The naming ceremony.

Nididhyāsana (nididhyāsa): Deep and constant meditation. Heinrich Zimmer defines it as "an intense focusing on a long-enduring, one-pointed inner vision; a fervent concentration". He adds: "This step leads beyond the sphere of argument and cogitation. The restlessness of the mind is put at rest because all of its energies have been brought to a single point."

Nīlakaṇṭha Dīkṣita: Great-nephew of Appayya Dīkṣita (qv) who is best remembered for his poetic works, *Śivalīlārṇava* and *Śivatattvarahasya*.

Nirguṇa-Brahman: See under "Brahman".

Om (Aum): Mystic syllable symbolising the Supreme Godhead. The *Māṇḍūkya Upaniṣad* declares that past, present, future, all this is Om, and even what is beyond the threefold time. Also called Praṇava.

Padārtha: The meaning of a word; in Nyāya Padārthas mean categories.

Palāśa: The flame of the forest; *Butea frondosa.*

Pālikā: The custom of germinating seeds is observed in ceremonies like caula, upanayana and marriage. Five earthen pots are filled with sand (or earth) — these are meant for the five deities, Brahmā, Indra, Yama, Varuṇa and Soma. The one for Brahmā is kept in the centre while the other four are kept at the four points of the compass (the pots for Indra, Yama, Varuṇa and Soma being kept in east, south, west and north respectively). Seeds of rice, black gram, green gram, sesame and mustard are soaked in milk and sown in the five different pots by five suhāsinīs. On the fourth day of the marriage when the seeds have germinated the pots are immersed in a sacred river or pond. This custom, called pañcapālikā, is meant for the protection and prosperity of the family or the individuals for whom the function is performed.

Pañcakaccha: Style of wearing the *dhoti* in which the ends are made into pleats and tucked in.

Pañcākṣara: Five-syllable mantra, "Namaḥ Śivāya". Also Śiva-Pañcākṣara.

Pañcama: One who is outside the four varṇas.

Pāṇigrahaṇa: Marriage rite in which the groom takes the right hand of the bride in his.

Parā-vidyā: Higher learning; learning related to the Self or the Ultimate Truth.

Pariṣecana: Sprinkling water; this is done at mealtime — water is sprinkled round the food before it is eaten.

Paropakāra: Philanthropy; serving others; humanitarian work.

Pāṭhaśālā: A Vedic school.

Pathya: What is suitable or what is liked; diet regimen during medical treatment.

Patita-pāvana: The Lord who sanctifies the sinner or raises him up.

Pativratā: The chaste, devoted and loyal wife.

Pātivratya: Total and unquestioning devotion to the husband.

Paurāṇika: One who is learned in the Purāṇas and gives discourses on them.

Pragrahaṇa: Receiving gifts.

Pramāṇa: Authority; source of knowledge; a measure or standard; perception.

Praṇava: See under "Om".

Prāṇāyāma: Control of breath so as to master prāṇa, the vital breath. It consists of pūraka (filling in), kuṁbhaka (retention) and recaka (exhaling) in a measured manner.

Prasāda: Literally radiance or happiness. The word is usually applied to what has been offered or presented to a deity and it symbolises the grace of the deity worshipped.

Prathamā: First day of the lunar fortnight.

Prātiśākhya: Related to Śikṣā and the study of the śabda-śāstra of the various Vedic recensions, it examines Vedic sounds.

Pratyakṣa: Directly perceptible to the eye.

Praveśa-homa: The rite performed soon after the groom returns to (or "enters") his house with his bride.

Prāyaścitta: Expiatory rites; atonement.

Prayoga: Procedure for the application of mantras to various religious rites.

Puṁsavana: Rite for the birth of a male child usually performed in the third month of pregnancy.

Puṇḍra: According to the Paramaguru, the mark worn on the forehead, "puṇḍra", is derived from "puṇḍarīka", meaning a lotus or a lotus petal. Somehow the ashes worn on the forehead also came to be called "tripuṇḍra" and the Vaiṣṇava mark came to be known as "ūrdhva-puṇḍra".

Puroḍāśa: A sacrificial oblation made of ground rice.

Puruṣārthas: The four aims of a man's life. (See Chapter 3, Part One.)

Pūrva-śikhā: See under "Śikhā."

Rāga: Colour; passion; emotion; a melodic mode.

Rājasūya: A great sacrifice performed by a universal monarch.

Rajoguṇa: See under "Guṇas"

Rāmānujācārya (Rāmānuja): Founder of the Viśiṣṭādvaita school of Vedānta (qualified non-dualism) was born in Śrīperumbudūr, Tamil Nāḍu, in 1027.

Rambhā: See under "Apsaras."

Ṛtvik: Priest, especially one associated with sacrifices.

Rudrākṣa: *Elaeocarpus ganitrus.*

Śabda: Sound, word, logos.

Śabda-pramāṇa: Verbal authority like that of the Vedas; the words of sages and other great men.

Śabda-Brahman: The Brahman as sound.

Sadāśiva Brahmendra: A great saint, yogin and mystic, he was a disciple of the 57th Śankarācārya of Kāñcī Kāmakoti Pīṭha (1539-1586). He has composed a number of hymns which are still sung today all over the South. He is also the author of works on Advaita Vedānta like *Ātmavidyāvilāsa, Siddhāntakalpavallī* and *Brahmasūtravṛtti.*

Sādhanā: Accomplishment, fulfilment; any means employed in worship and the attainment of the Supreme Being.

Saguṇa-Brahman: See under "Brahman".

Sahagamana: A widow ascending the funeral pyre of her husband; what is known as *satī.*

Samacitta: Even-minded, equable.

Samādhi: The final step in yogic practice; absorption in the Infinite; state of mystical experience or enstasy; some call it super-consciousness.

Samāvartana: Return; a brahmacārin's return home after finishing his gurukulavāsa: it is one of the saṁskāras.

Samidādhāna: The offering of samidhs (fuelsticks) morning and evening by the brahmacārin in the sacred fire. He does so chanting mantras.

Samidhs: See under "Samidādhāna".

Saṁkalpa: Resolve; concept; will or volition; determination.

Saṁsāra: The phenomenal world; worldly existence; the cycle of births and deaths.

Sanātana Dharma: The immemorial religion that is Hinduism; the ancient or timeless religion. Sanātanī or sanātanist is one who is a staunch believer in sanatāna dharma.

Sanātanī (sanātanist): See under "Sanātana Dharma".

Sandhi: The coalescence of the final and initial letters of words; the euphonic combination of syllables.

Sandhyāvandana: Morning and evening prayers to be performed by the twice-born every day. These consist mainly of ācamana (sipping of water), prāṇāyāma, mārjana (sprinkling oneself), offering of water to the sun (arghya), Gāyatrī-japa and upasthāna (reciting of mantras by way of worship of the sun in the morning and of Varuna in the evening). Similar prayers are performed at midday called Mādhyāhnika.

Sangava-kāla: The second of the five periods into which the day is divided.

Śankara Bhagavatpāda (Ādi Śankara, Śankarācārya, Śankara or simply "Ācārya): Among the foremost creative thinkers and religious leaders of the world, Śrī Śankarācārya is venerated as an incarnation of Śiva. He was born in Kālaṭi., in Keraḷa, and, during his all too brief life (509-477 B.C.), he made a profound and lasting impact on the life of the nation. He not only established Advaita Vedanta on an unshakable foundation but also breathed new life into the Vedic religion. The glory of sanātana dharma is inseparably linked with his name.

Ṣanmata: The worship of the six deities established by Śankara Bhagavatpāda. The six deities are Sūrya, Gaṇapati, Kumāra, Śiva, Viṣṇu and Śakti.

Sannyāsa: Renunciation of the world and its attachments. A sannyāsin is an ascetic, one who has renounced the world. Sannyāsāśrama is the last of the four stages in a man's life.

Sannyāsin: See under "Sannyāsa".

Sannyāsāśrama: See under "Sannyāsa".

Śastra: A weapon like a knife, sword, arrow.

Śāstra: A scripture or treatise written by a sage; traditional authority, canonical text; a science; a rule, order or commandment or a treatise containing commandments.

Sārvabhauma: Universal monarch; imperial ruler.

Satsanga: The company of virtuous and devout people.

Sattva-guṇa: See under "Guṇas".

Satyagraha: Holding on to the truth at all costs; satyāgraha is desire for truth.

Saundaryalaharī: Famous poetical work of Śankara Bhagavatpāda dedicated to Ambā.

Śeṣahoma: Homa conducted on the fourth day of marriage. It is also called "angahoma".

Siddha: One who has attained perfection; accomplished adept; liberated person; an inspired sage; one who has acquired the eight siddhis. Siddha-puruṣa is a master who possesses all the siddhis.

Siddhi: Accomplishment, fulfilment; one of the eight superhuman faculties like "aṇimā" "mahimā" and īśitva"; liberation.

Siddhānta: A doctrine or philosophical system; the established end or conclusion.

Śikhā: Lock of hair on the head. Urdhva-śikhā is lock of hair on the crown of the head, while pūrva-śikhā is lock of hair on the forepart of the head.

Śikhara: Top or summit; spire; tower surmounting the sanctum of a temple.

Sīmanta (sīmantonnayana): Parting of a woman's hair upwards. This is a rite for the pregnant woman but meant for the protection of the child she is carrying.

Śiva-Pañcakṣara: See under "Pañcākṣara".

Smārta: Literally one who adheres to the Smṛtis. Smārtas are followers of the traditions established by Ādi Śankara.

Śraddhā: Faith; confidence.

Śrāddha: Rite performed in honour of the pitṛs or fathers.

Śrīdhara Ayyāvāl (Tiruviśanallūr Ayyāvāl): Śrīdhara Venkaṭeśvara Ayyāvāḷ belonged to an Āndhra Brahmin family and was a contemporary of Śrī Bodhendra Svāmigaḷ (qv). While Śrī Bodhendra Svāmigaḷ propagated the glory of Rāma and Govinda, Ayyāvāḷ spread the glory of Śiva. He is the author of a number of devotional works. (See Chapter 10, Part Fourteen, for the story told by the Paramaguru of how Ayyāval made the Gangā well up in Tiruviśanallūr on a Kārtika new moon. Even today pilgrims flock to this place to have their bath here on Kārtika amāvāsya.)

Śrīharṣa: This famous poet is said to have belonged to the latter half of the 12th century. *Naiṣadham* or *Naiṣadhīyacaritam* is his best-known work and it is regarded as a mahākāvya. It tells the story of Nala and reveals the poet's erudition and mastery of Sanskrit. "Naiṣadham vidvadauṣadham," it is said. (*Naiṣadham* is medicine for the learned.)

Śrotriya: A Brahmin who has mastered at least one Vedic recension with the six Angas and performs the six duties of his varṇa.

Stotra: Hymn of praise; Sāmavedic hymns intoned during soma sacrifices are particularly referred to as stotras.

Strīdhana: Woman's property which is to be distinguished from dowry. One jurist observes: "Nowhere were property rights of women recognised so early as in India; and in very few ancient systems of law have these rights been so largely conceded as in ours."

Strīdharma: The duties of women; the code of conduct of womanhood.

Sūkta: Well spoken; a Vedic hymn.

Sumaṅgalī: A married woman whose husband is still living. She symbolises or represents all that is auspicious.

Sureśvarācārya: After he was converted by Ādi Śankara to Advaita Vedānta, Maṇḍanamiśra was given initiation into sannyāsa by Śankara with the new name of Sureśvarācārya. Sureśvara has written a gloss on some of his master's commentaries.

Sūtra: Literally rope or string; what is expressed in the least possible number of words to convey an idea or a truth; an aphorism.

Svara: Sound; a note of the musical scale; accent in Vedic intonation.

Tamo-guṇa: See under "Guṇas".

Tāṇḍava: Dance, particularly, with masculine aspects, as contrasted with lāsya; the frenetic dance of Śiva-Naṭarāja.

Tapas: Austerity; intense mental concentration; literally warmth, fire; self-denial; ascetic endeavour; keeping the mind one-pointed in the search of truth or an ideal.

Tāraka-Rāma: Rāma who takes one across worldly existence; Rāma who liberates.

Tarpaṇa: Pleasing or satisfying; offering libations to the fathers, seers and celestials.

Tilaka: Ornament; a mark applied to the forehead with sandalwood paste, kumkuma or any unguent. The word "tilaka" is derived from "tila" or sesame; so the mark on the forehead is shaped like a sesame or is sesamoid — it resembles a mini lotus petal. (See "Puṇḍra" in this Glossary).

Tīrtha: A ford; a place of pilgrimage especially one situated on a river, lake or the shores of the sea; a preceptor or holy personage; the word is also used to denote the sacred water used in the worship of a deity or in any other ceremony.

Tretāgnin: One who worships the three śrauta fires.

Tulasī: *Ocium basilicum.*

Udātta: Raised tone in Vedic chanting; anudātta is the lowered tone; while svarita is the falling tone, or the one between the two.

Uḍumbara: *Ficus glomerata.*

Upadeśa: Instruction; teaching. The word is derived from upa + diś. The Paramaguru says, explaining the significance of the word "upadeśa": "The guru does not merely ask his disciple to perform a task; he helps him by remaining by his side and directing him, indeed remaining close to his heart, and showing the pupil the path he must follow in this life. The guru does more: the student is helped to go beyond this impermanent life to take the path of the life eternal to realise the Brahman."

Upākarma: Commencing the term for Vedic studies. Utsarjana is the cessation of such studies and commencing the study of the Vedāngas. The two rites are nowadays performed on the same day since the majority of those who perform them do not know their significance. Ṛgvedins, Yajurvedins and Sāmavedins have different days for upākarma (See page 77, *The Guru Tradition.*)

Upanayana: Taking a child near his guru. It is a saṁskāra in which the child is invested with the sacred thread and imparted the Gāyatrī mantra. According to the Paramaguru, "leading a child to his guru is leading him ultimately to the Brahman."

Upāngas: See under "Angas".

Ūrdhva Śikhā: See under "Śikhā".

Utsarjana: See under "upākarma".

Uttarāyaṇa: See under "Dakṣiṇāyana".

Vaiśvadeva: See under "Bali".

Vājapeya: A somayajña, biggest of the sacrifices performed by Brahmins. (See Chapter 6, Part Nineteen.) One who has performed it is a "vājapeyin."

Vākya: An utterance or pronouncement; a group of words forming a sentence and conveying a message.

Vānaprastha: The third stage in a man's life, that of the forest recluse.

Vapā: Fat or marrow of the animal sacrificed.

Vārtika: An explanatory text often regarded as subsidiary to a bhāṣya (qv); the literal meaning of the word is "relating to news".

Vibhūti: Might, power, prosperity and splendour; ashes of cowdung.

Vihāra: Garden; removing; walking for pleasure; Buddhist temple.

Vidyā: Knowledge; learning, particularly that which leads to inner wisdom.

Viśiṣṭādvaita: System of theistic philosophy that teaches qualified non-dualism, founded by Śrī Rāmānujācārya (qv).

Vrata: A vow; religious act of devotion. There are vratas observed according to the Vedas and the Purāṇas.

Vṛndāvana: See under "Bṛndāvana".

Vyavahāra: See under "Ācāra".

Yāgaśālā: Sacrificial hall.

Yajamāna: One who performs a sacrifice and pays the expenses or one on whose behalf a sacrifice is conducted; a host or patron; one who employs priests.

Yantra: Diagrams used in worship.

Yupa : Ṣacrificial post

Tamiḷ Glossary

According to the C.O.D., "glossary" means "list and explanations of abstruse, obsolete, dialectal or technical terms". Extending the scope, we include here — apart from a number of Tamiḷ words and their meanings — brief notes on figures from the Tamiḷ religious, literary and political history and on Tamiḷ works. The words listed are marked in the main text of the book with a superior "T" : for example, "Jñānasaṁbandhar[T]", "Tevāram[T]", "Āzhvār[T]", "Nalangu[T]".

The words (by which we mean also the names of the figures and the titles of works) are transliterated more or less according to how they are pronounced and not necessarily according to how they are written in the original Tamil.

The dates of a number of saint-poets as well as of religious and other texts are not finally determined. According to the Paramaguru, however, the hymnodists of the Śaiva Tevāram *and the Vaiṣṇava* Nālāyira-Divyaprabandham *belonged to a period not later than A.D. 500.*

Abhirāmibhaṭṭar (Abhirāmibhaṭṭa): His real name was Subrahmaṇya and he was a contemporary of the Marāṭhā rājā of Tañjāvūr, Śarabhoji II (1798-1832). He belonged to Tirukkaḍavūr, Tañjāvūr district, where there is a temple to Amṛtaghaṭeśvara and his consort Abhirāmī. (Amṛtaghaṭeśvara is another name of Śiva who freed Mārkaṇḍeya from Yama, the god of death, and made him a cirañjīvi, long-lived one.) Subrahmaṇya came to be called Abhirāmibhaṭṭa because of his graet devotion for Abhirāmī (Ambā) which finds expression in his famous *Abhirāmi Antādi*. In this work each succeeding stanza begins with the last word of the preceding one. For the story told on the Bhaṭṭa by the Paramaguru see Chapter 3, Part Twenty-two.

Abhirāmi Antādi: See under "Abhirāmi Bhaṭṭa".

Aiyanār: Almost all villages of Tamiḷ Nāḍu have a guardian deity (grāma devatā) called Aiyanār, also known as Śāstā. This god is a symbol of Śaiva-Vaiṣṇava unity: he is believed to be the son born to Viṣṇu (when he took the guise of Mohinī) by Śiva. Aiyanār is the same as Ayyappa of Keraḷa, among the temples to whom the one at Śabarimala in the Western Ghats is the most famous.

Āṇḍāḷ: Daughter of Viṣṇucitta who belonged to Śrivilliputtūr in Tirunelveli district. The story goes that Viṣṇucitta found Āṇḍāḷ on a bed of tulasī in his garden. The girl grew up to be a great devotee of Viṣṇu (her original name was Goda or Kodai). Her compositions exemplify bridal mysticism and include the *Tiruppāvai* and the *Nācciyār-Tirumozhi* which form part of the *Nālāyira-*

Divyaprabandham. Both daughter and father are included among the twelve Āzhvārs (qv): the father came to be called Periyāzhvār.

Appar (Apparsvāmin, Apparsvāmigaḷ, Tirunāvukkaraśu): A celebrated Śaiva saint-poet whose hymns are included in the *Tevāram* (qv). It was under his influence that the Pallava king Mahendravarman II was brought back to the Śaiva faith from Jainism. As a boy Appar himself had embraced Jainism and it was his sister Tilakavatī who was responsible for his return to the Śaiva fold.

Araṅgeṟṟu (araṅgeṟṟam) : Presenting a literary work, dance recital or dramatic performance for the first time.

Aruṇagirināthar: After the Āzhvārs and Nāyanmārs his is one of the truly great names in Tamiḷ devotional poetry. Aruṇagirināthar belonged to the 15th century and his hymns in praise of Kanda or Muruga (Skanda, Subrahmaṇya or Kumāra), the *Tiruppugazh* and the *Kandar Anubhūti,* are still extremely popular.

Auvvai (Auvvaiyār): Great saint-poetess who is often referred to as "Auvvai-pāṭṭi" (the Grand Old Lady Auvvai). Her compositions combine devotion, moral instruction and practical wisdom. *Ātticūdi* and *Vināyagar Agaval* are among her works. (It is said that there was an earlier Auvvai who lived in the Saṁgam period, 2,000 years ago.)

Āzhvār: The word means "immersed in the Lord". The Āzhvārs, numbering twelve, are Vaiṣṇava saint-poets. Their compositions constitute the *Nālāyira-Divyaprabandham* (also known in short as the *Divyaprabandham*). For the Vaiṣṇavas of the South, this work is almost as sacred as the Vedas. The twelve Āzhvārs: Poigai, Bhūtattāzhvār, Pey, Tirumazhiśai, Kulaśekhara, Periyāzhvār, Āṇḍāḷ, Toṇḍaraḍippoḍi, Tiruppan, Tirumaṅgai, Nammāzhvār and Madhurakavi.

Bhāratī: See under Subrahmaṇya Bhāratī.

Divyaprabandham: See under "Āzhāvār".

Ilango Aḍigal: Cera prince, author of the *Śilappadikaram.* See under Kaṇṇagī.

Jñānasaṁbandhar (Tirujñānasaṁbandhar, Saṁbandhar, Saṁbandha-mūrti): One of the great figures of Southern Śaivism, he is believed to have been blessed with jñāna by Ambā herself who, it is said, suckled him as a child. His compositions form part of the *Tevāram* (qv) and, together with those of Appar and Sundarar, constitute the first seven works of the *Tirumurai* which to the Śaivas of Tamiḷ Nāḍu is almost as sacred as the Vedas. Jñānasaṁbandhar, who is believed to have performed a number of miracles, played a notable role in restoring the glory of the Vedic religion, especially in the South.

Jānavāsam: The word is probably derived from "janavāsa" which in Sanskrit means an assembly or place fit for all people to live. Probably the word was later used in Tamiḷ Nāḍu as the place where the bridegroom and his people were accommodated on the eve of marriage. *Jānavāsam* is now used in the sense of the procession in which the groom is taken through the streets on the eve of the wedding.

Kaṇṇagī: She is much revered among Tamiḷs and her story is told in the *Śilappadikāram,* one of the five great Tamiḷ poetic works. *Śilappadikāram* is by Ilango Aḍigaḷ, a Cera prince who is ascribed by some historians to the 2nd century A.D. Kaṇṇagi's husband, Kovalan, is unjustly accused of having stolen the anklet of the Pāṇḍyan queen and put to death. She proves his innocence and in her wrath plucks out one of her breasts and hurls it over Madurai. The city is engulfed in flames. To Tamiḷs Kaṇṇagi is the "wife goddess", a model of chastity. The story of *Śilappadikāram* links the three kingdoms of the ancient Tamiḷ land, Cola, Cera and Pāṇḍya.

Kaṇṇappa (Kaṇṇappar): One of the 63 Nāyanmārs (qv), his story is told to illustrate unqualified love for the Lord. Kaṇṇappar was a hunter who dug out one of his eyes to be offered to Śiva at Kālahasti.

Kamban (Kambar): Called the "emperor of poets", he is the author of the Tamiḷ Rāmāyaṇa (or *Rāmāvatāram*). It is one of the great works of Tamiḷ literature and is as much the delight of the *paṇḍit* as of the ordinary reader. Kambar lived during the time of Kulottunga Cola III who reigned in the latter part of the 12th century.

Karikāla Cola : One of the builders of the Cola empire (2nd century A.D.), he was "as great in war as in peace." He was master of the South and his kingdom carried on trade with a number of foreign countries.

Kazhakkodi: It is a grey-coloured seed that resembles a marble, the sort used by children in games.

Koccenkot Cola : A Cola king who was a builder of temples and is regarded as a Nāyanār. According to legend, as a spider in his previous birth, he was devoted to the deity of Tiruvānaikkā (Tiruci) and made a canopy out of his web for the god. There happened to be another devotee, an elephant, who pulled down the canopy. In a rage the spider crept into the trunk of the elephant who, unable to bear the consequent pain, dashed his trunk against the jambu tree. Both elephant and spider perished. The spider was reborn the son of the Cola queen Kamalāvatī and came to be called Koccengaṇṇan (Koccenkot), one with red eyes.

Kovalan: See under "Kaṇṇagī".

Kūn Pāṇḍyan: Jñānasaṁbandhar (qv) is said to have removed the hunch (*kūn*) of this Pāṇḍyan ruler and made him upright. It was also this saint who weaned the king from Jainism.

Kural (Tirukkural): One of the most widely known Tamil classics, it consists of 1,330 stanzas and deals with ethics and morality (the aims of life in general like dharma, artha, kāma and mokṣa or their equivalents, *aram, porul, inbam* and *vīḍu).* Tiruvaḷḷuvar (Vaḷḷuvar), the author, expounds the same values as the Vedic religion. K.A. Nīlakanṭ(h)a Śāstrī ascribes *Kural* to the 5th century A.D., while some other authorities place it between the first century B.C. and the first century A.D.

Kūrapuḍavai: The 18-cubit *sārī* worn by the Tamiḷ Brahmin bride (particularly during the māṅgalya-dhāraṇa ceremony). *Kūrapuḍavai* means new *sāri* (*kūra* meaning new and *puḍavai* meaning *sāri*). It is also believed that *kūra* denotes the place where such *sārīs* were once made, that is "Kuranāḍu" (Koranāḍu), near Māyūram in Tañjāvūr district. In keeping with the expensive marriages of our times, the *kūrapuḍavai,* usually a Kāñcīpuram silk *sāri,* costs anything between Rs 2,000 and Rs 10,000.

Mahendravarman I: Great Pallava ruler (7th century). He has an enduring place in the history of Indian architecture. He excavated temples from living rock and for his great interest in art earned the title of "Vicitracitta". His son Narasimhavarman I took up his architectural work at Māmallapuram. Mahendravarman is also remembered for his two Sanskrit plays (prahasanas or comedies), *Mattavilāsam* and *Bhagavadajjukam.*

Maṅgaiyarkkaraśī: Pāṇḍyan queen who humbled herself, along with her minister Kulacciraiyār, in the service of Śiva. The king Kūn Pāṇḍyan had embraced Jainism and it was in response to their entreaties that Tirujñānasaṁbandhar came to Madurai and brought the rājā back to the Śaiva fold.

Maṅgalā-śāsanam: There are Vaiṣṇava centres of worship in Tamiḷ Nāḍu and beyond (108 divya deśams or divine places) that have received the "maṅgalā-śāsanam" of the various Āzhvārs (qv) which means these places have been sung by the Vaiṣṇava hymnodists and been made specially sacred by their words with their grace and power of creating auspiciousness.

Māṇikkavācakar: A highly regarded Śaiva saint who spent some of his early years as minister to a Paṇḍyan king. The compositions of this saint are extremely moving and are also characterised by bridal mysticism. He is among the foremost figures of Southern Śaivism and his *Tiruvācakam* and *Tirukovaiyār* form the eighth part of the *Tirumurai.* His *Tiruvembāvai* was specially composed for the worship of the Lord by young women in the early hours of the morning.

Manu-nīti-Cola (Manu-nītī-kaṇḍa-Cola) : An ancient king of legendary fame held up as an ideal in dispensing justice. The Paramaguru speaks about him in Chapter 5, Part Five.

Mastān Sāhib (1800-1847) : His real name was Sultan Abdul Qadir Labbai.

He was a man of great devotion and one of the first to translate the Qur'ān into Tamiḷ. His songs are simple but profound and reflect the spirit of resignation and Vedāntic thought. Mastān Sāhib spent the last years of his life in austerities. He had disciples among both Muslims and Hindus.

Mīnākṣisundaram Piḷḷai (1815-1876) : He was a man of great erudition and was justly called "Mahāvidvān". The Tamiḷ world is indebted to him for his profound knowledge of the Tamiḷ heritage. He was the guru of Dr U.V. Svāminātha Ayyar (qv) and, apart from being the author of a number of works, including Purāṇas, he was a gifted speaker.

Murugan (Muruga) : The god whom the Tamiḷs regard as their own, he is the same as Subrahmaṇya, Skanda (Kanda), Kārttikeya or Kumāra. (The name means beautiful.) There are many temples to Muruga in the South, some of them built on hills like Pazhani (Paḷni) and Tiruttaṇi. A considerable section of Tamiḷ hymnal literature is devoted to him of which the *Tiruppugazh* is particularly famous.

Mūvar : The three great Śaiva saint-poets, Tirujñānasaṁbandhar, Appar and Sundarar.

Mūvendar: The rulers of the three Tamiḷ kingdoms, Cera, Cola and Pāṇḍya.

Naccinārkiṇiyār: A Śaiva who was vastly erudite in Tamiḷ and probably also in Sanskrit. He is famous for his commentaries on the *Pattupāṭṭu, Kalittogai* and *Tolkāppiyam.* It is said that works like the *Pattupāṭṭu* would be hard to understand without his annotation.

Nakkīrar: Author of the famous *Tirumurugāṟṟupaḍai* which forms the first part of the Saṁgam classic, *Pattupāṭṭu. Tirumurugāṟṟupaḍai* sings the glory of Muruga and is remarkable for its beauty of expression and profundity of thought.

Nalaṅgu: On the afternoon of a Tamil wedding, the bride and groom keep rolling a coconut (real or one made of brass or bell-metal) between them. This is called *nalangu* and it adds an element of fun to the marriage proceedings. People gather round the bridal pair and it is an occasion for women belonging to the two families to display their musical talent. The original idea of *nalaṅgu* must have been to keep the bridal pair in good cheer when they were still children.

Nālāyira-Divyaprabandham: The collected hymns of the twelve Āzhvārs ("the Divine Four Thousand"). See under "Āzhvār".

Nālvar: The four great Śaiva saints, Jñānasaṁbandhar, Appar, Sundarar and Māṇikkavācakar.

Nāmam: When Vaiṣṇavas in the South wear the Tirumaṇ (qv), they do so chanting the names of Viṣṇu: hence the term "nāmam". Apart from the whitish mark of the Tiruman, the nāmam also consists of the "Śrīcūrṇam".

Nammāzhvār: The greatest of the Āzhvārs, he is regarded as an incarnation of Senai Mudaliar or Viṣvaksena (chief of the Lord's hosts). His real name was Māran and he is also known as Śaṭhakopan and Pārānkuśan. His hymnal works are *Tiruviruttam, Tiruvāśiriyam, Periya Tiruvantādi* and *Tiruvāymozhi*. Vedāntadeśika describes the *Tiruvāymozhi* as "Dramiḍopaniṣad". Nammāzhvār's songs are among the chief sources of the Vaiṣṇava siddhānta.

Nāyanār (Nāyanmār): The word means a leader or chieftain. The Nāyanmārs are devotees of Śiva and are 63 in number, including members of all jātis like Brahmins, hunters, untouchables. Their lives are told in Sundarar's *Tiruttoṇḍarttogai*, Nambi Āṇdar Nambi's *Tiruvantādi* and Śekkizhār's *Periyapurānam*. Names of some Nāyanmārs: Tirujñānasaṁbandhar, Appar, Sundarar, Māṇikkavācakar, Kaṇṇappar, Nandanār, Kāraikkāl Aṁmayār, Ceramān Perumāḷ.

Oṭṭakūttar (Oṭṭakūttan) : Like Kambar he too had the title of "kavicakravartī" or "emperor of poets". He was patronised by three successive Cola monarchs, Vikrama, Kulottunga II and Rājarāja II. Oṭṭakūttar has composed two *paraṇis*, the *Kalingattu-paraṇi* and the *Dakkayāga-paraṇi*. (A *paraṇi* is a war-poem, by definition one that celebrates the victory of a hero who destroys a thousand elephants of the enemy's forces and an equal number of horses and chariots.) Oṭṭakūttar was a great devotee of Sarasvatī and one of the rare temples to this goddess is said to have been built by him at Kūttanūr.

Paccai: This word refers to a custom followed in Southern (or Tamil) weddings in which a paste of kuṁkuma and oil is applied to the bride's face as well as to the groom's. The word *paccai* means "green" and the application of the paste must be intended not only to ward off the evil eye but also to express the wish and prayer that the bridal pair may remain ever fresh.

Paṅguni-Uttram Tirukkalyāṇam: In March-April when the full moon is (usually) conjoined with the asterism Uttara-Phālguni, the marriage of Āṇḍāḷ (qv) and Ranganātha (Viṣṇu) is ceremonially conducted at her birthplace, Śrivilliputtūr. It is also a festive day in Śiva temples where the marraige of Śiva and Pārvatī is performed.

Paradeśikkolam: It is the same as Kāśīyātra which (in Tamiḷ Brahmin marriages) simulates the groom's journey to Kāśī. As the groom sets out on the mock journey to Kāśī, he is approached by the bride's father and asked not to proceed and promised the hand of his daughter. Paradeśikkolam or Kāśiyātra must be a re-enactment of the old custom according to which the brahmacārin, after his gurukulavāsa and samāvartana (see Part Nineteen), journeyed to Kāśī.

Paripāḍal: It is part of the *Eṭṭutogai* ("Eight Anthologies) and contains not only the praises of Viṣṇu and Skanda but also descriptions of the Vaigai river and Madurai.

Pāsuram: A devotional or mystic poem, particularly applied to the Vaiṣṇava *Divyaprabandham.*

Patigam: A poem consisting of ten (or sometimes eleven) stanzas.

Paṭṭiṇattār : A great siddha whose hymns are included in the eleventh *Tirumurai* (qv). His real name was Tiruvengaḍar but came to be called Paṭṭiṇattār since he was born in Kāveripūmpaṭṭiṇam. *Nānmaṇimalai, Mummaṇikkovai* and *Tiruvenbamuḍaya-Tiruvantādi* are some of his works.

Pattupāṭṭu: It is a collection of Ten Songs and includes the *Tirumurugāṟṟupaḍai* by Nakkīrar, the *Āṟṟupaḍai* and *Porunāraṟṟupaḍai.*

Periyapurāṇam: This 12th - century work of Śekkizhār (qv) forms the concluding part of the *Tirumurai. Periyapurāṇam,* the Great Story, also known as the *Tiruttoṇḍar-Purāṇam,* narrates the lives of Śaiva saints and is a landmark in the bhakti movement. Śekkizhār's contribution to hagiography is considered so significant that he is spoken of as the 64th Nāyanār.

Perumāḷ: The term *usually* refers to Viṣṇu or any Vaiṣṇava deity. It also denotes an eminent personage, one invested with greatness. Cera rulers assumed the title of "Perumāl", whether they were Śaiva or Vaiṣṇava. Aruṇagirināthar addresses the Śaiva deity Murugan as "Perumāḷ". Śiva himself is sometimes called "Śiva Perumān".

Peyarccol: Noun.

Puhazhendi Pulavar: A Vaiṣṇava poet belonging to the 12th century and a contemporary of Kulottunga II. His work, *Nalavemba,* has brought him undying fame.

Puranānūru: An anthology belonging to the third Saṁgam period (*c.* 300 B.C. to A.D. 200) and forming part of the *Eṭṭutogai.* It contains 400 songs and sheds light on Tamil life during the Saṁgam period in fields such as politics, religion, trade and society. It also tells the story of seven *vallalārgal,* that is philanthropists.

Pūśāri: Priest (usually non-Brahmin) of a small temple like that of Māriyamman (known as Śitaḷādevi in Mahārāṣṭra). He plays the role of an exorcist as well as that of a story-teller.

Rājarāja I: Cola emperor (985-1014) who must rank as one of the great rulers in the history of India. His empire included most parts of South India. As a conqueror he brought the Māladives and northern Simhala (Śrī Lanka) under him. The Bṛhadīśvara temple of Tañjāvūr was built by him. Rājarāja created an administrative system that was remarkable for his time.

Rāmaliṅgar (Rāmaliṅgasvāmī (1823 - 1874): A mystic devoted to Śiva and Muruga, he preached universal brotherhood. "Deathless life" is the goal of his "Samarasa Śuddha Sanmārgam". At Vaḍalūr he built the "Hall of Universal Worship". Ramālinga Vallalār often spoke of *"arul jyoti"*, the "light of grace": indeed light had a special place in his worship.

Rāmānujācārya, C.: The Rāmakṛṣṇa Home in Maḍrās was started by Rāmasvāmi Ayyangār and C. Rāmānujācārya was his cousin. On Śrī Ayyangār's death, Rāmānujācārya took over his work. He dedicated himself totally to the cause of the Rāmakṛṣṇa Maṭh and used all his energies to raise funds for the institution.

Saṁbandhamūrti (Saṁbandhar, Tirujñānasaṁbandhar): See under Jñānasaṁbandhar.

Saṁgam: Tamiḷ assembly of the learned or academy which was, according to tradition, presided over by Śiva himself and was located at the Pāṇḍyan capital, Madurai. There were three Saṁgams and of the first two which belong to the dim past we know precious little. The earliest extant poetry is traced to the third Saṁgam.

Śarabhoji: Marāṭhā ruler of Tañjāvūr between 1798 and 1832. He was a great patron of learning and the arts. He himself was a man of erudition and the author of a number of Sanskrit works. The Sarasvatī Mahaḷ in Tañjāvūr which has a vast collection of manuscripts and other records in various languages and on various subjects is a monument to his wide-ranging scholarly interests.

Śekkizhār: Author of the important Śaiva hagiographic and canonical text called the *Periyapurāṇam*. He is said to have composed this work at the request of Kulottunga Cola (1130-50) and it is based on earlier works like those of Sundaramūrti and Nambi Āṇḍār Nambi.

Śilappadikāram: See under Kaṇṇagī.

Subrahmaṇya Ayyar, N.: He was headmaster of the Rāmakṛṣṇa High School in Māmbalam, Maḍrās, and was a Sanskrit and Tamiḷ scholar. Ayyar, who wrote a commentary on the Upaniṣads, was popularly known as "Aṇṇā" and it was the Paramaguru who described him as *"Āstika-ulagattin-Aṇṇā"* ("Elder Brother of the World of Believers).

Subrahmaṇya Bhāratī (1882-1921): He was perhaps the greatest of modern Tamiḷ poets. Indeed, he was the poet of freedom, an extremist who also preached social reform. He was hounded by the British and for some years lived in Pondicerri. Bhāratī, who was a devotee of Parāśakti, brought his people the message of flaming petriotism and fearlessness. He influenced not only Tamiḷ poetry but also Tamiḷ prose. He was a humanist and his love extended to all creatures of earth. Bhārati was one of the few major poets of our country to have written poems for children. Among his works are *Kuyil Pāṭṭu, Kaṇṇan Pāṭṭu, Pāñcāli Sabatam* and *Pudiya Āttícūḍi.*

Sundaramūrti (Sundarar) : Śaiva saint-poet whose compositions form part of the *Tevāram* along with those of Jñānasaṁbandhar and Appar. It is believed that he had a unique relationship with Śiva — the god was both his master and companion. See Page 211, *The Guru Tradition.*

Svāminātha Ayyar, Dr U.V.: A savant who brought to light a number of Tamiḷ classics. It was under Mahāvidvān Mīnākṣisundaram Piḷḷai that he found the inspiration for his lifelong work for Tamiḷ. *U Ve* (his Tamil initials) Svāminātha Ayyar travelled all over Tamiḷ Nāḍu, went from village to village, house to house, in search of palm-leaf manuscripts of ancient and medieval Tamil works. His prodigious labours were rewarded with the discovery of a number of manuscripts which he edited and published. He has also written a lengthy autobiography. Dr Ayyar who died in 1942 at the age of 87 was fondly called "Tamil Tātta" ("Grand Old Man of Tamil").

Svāmigaḷ (Svāmiyār): Honorific Tamiḷ plural of svāmī.

Svāmiyār: See under "Svāmigaḷ"

Tāyumānavar: Śaiva saint-poet (1705-42) was in his early years in the employ of the Nāyakas of Madurai. He lived during a time of political and spiritual turmoil caused partly by the impact of European colonialism. Tāyumānavar nourished the eternal values of the land and attempted a synthesis of Śaiva Siddhānta and Advaitic Vedānta. *Ānandakkaṇṇi* and *Parāparakkaṇṇi* are among his works.

Tevāram: One of the basic scriptures of Southern Śaivism and part of the *Tirumurai.* It includes compositions of Tirujñānasaṁbandhar, Appar and Sundaramūrti. The term *"Tevāram"* means the garland adorning a deity.

Tirujñānasaṁbandhar: See under "Jñānasaṁbandhar".

Tirukkural : See under "Kural".

Tirumaṇ: Sacred earth worn by Vaiṣṇavas. It is purified white clay obtained from Tirunārāyaṇapuram in Karṇāṭaka, Śrīrangam, Śrimūṣaṇam and Madurāntakam in Tamiḷ Nāḍu, Śrikākulam in Āndhra Prадеś and Puṣpaka in Rājasthān. *Tiruman* stands for the truth that everything is of the earth and mingles with it.

Tirumaṅgaiyāzhvār: One of the twelve Vaiṣṇava saint-poets whose compositions are included in the *Nālāyira-Divyaprabandham.*

Tirumāngalyam: Same as "maṅgala-sūtra". See Sanskrit Glossary.

Tirumūlar: A great siddha and mystic who must have been the forerunner of Sundaramūrti and other Śaiva saints. His *Tirumantiram,* a recondite work dealing with authentic spiritual experience, forms part of the *Tirumurai.*

Tirumurai: It is regarded as the *Marai* or Veda of Tamiḷ Śaivism and comprises the *Tevāram,* the *Tiruvācakam,* the *Tirumantiram* and the *Periyapurāṇam.* It is believed that these texts were "discovered" and brought together by Nambi Aṇḍār Nambi at the behest of the 11th-century Cola monarch "Apayakulasekaran."

Tirumurugaṟṟupaḍai: The first part of the Saṁgam classic *Pattupāṭṭu,* this work by Nakkīrar sings the glory of Muruga (qv).

Tiruppugazh: See under "Aruṇagirināthar".

Tiruvaḷḷuvar: See under "Kural".

Tiruvāymozhi: See under "Nammāzhvār".

Tolkāppiyam: Treatise on Tamil grammar, it is perhaps the oldest extant work in that language. Its author, Tolkāppiyanār, was one of the twelve students of Agastya to whom is attributed the origin of the Tamil language itself. *Tolkāppiyam,* which deals with the written as well as the spoken word, has lessons on aspects of human life.

Vaḷḷuvar: See under "Kural".

Vedanāyagam Piḷḷai (1826-1889): He wrote the first Tamiḷ novel, *Pratāpa Mudaliāṟ Caritram.* A Christian, he was influenced by Vedāntic thought and was a philanthropist. He has translated into Tamiḷ Edwin Arnold's *Light of Asia.*

Vinaiccol: Verb.

INDEX

Ābhāsa, 53.
Abhāva, 405, 413, 417-18.
Abhicali (author of a Śikṣā śāstra), 287.
Abhicāra, 86.
Abhijñāna-Śākuntalam, 577.
Abhirāmī Antādī, 587.
Abhirāmibhaṭṭa, 706.
Abhivādana, 374.
Abhyāsa, 240-41.
Abodes of knowledge (caturdaśa-vidyā), 132.
Acanas (author of a Smṛti), 492.
Ācāra, 496.
Ācārya (meaning Ādi Śankara), accepts the karma that Mīmāṁsā asks us to perform and bids us finally to give up that very karma as suggested by Buddhism 390; apāna-śakti of earth referred to in one of his commentaries 361; aśarīratvam is liberation 222; *Brahmasūtra* : in it, he says, the flowers that are the Upaniṣads are strung together as a garland 204; Buddhism, very few references to it in his works 386; condemns peevish argumentativeness in his *Sopāna Pañcaka* 738; connection with temples 480; creation: Brahman with Māyā appears in the disguises of creation 425; criticism of Sānkhya and Mīmāṁsā 386; exhortation to chant the Vedas 105; harmonises Buddhism, Mīmāṁsā, Sānkhya and Vedānta into a single whole truth in his Advaita 390; how he countered non-Advaitic systems 248; joy experienced by Indra a droplet in the ocean of Ātmic bliss, so he says in his *Mānīṣa Pañcaka* 509; Kaṇṇappar, he praises 675; Kumārilabhaṭṭa, debate with 395; liberation, shows the practical path 392; Maṇḍanamiśra, debate with 395; Maṭha (Kāñcī) established by him for the sake of the Vedas 270; Paramaguru installed in the Maṭha to make people perform rites — according to the command of the Ācārya 498; *Praśnottara-Ratnamālikā*: in it he inquires into the meaning of existence or saṁsāra 686; sacrifices, importance of performing them 172; *Saundaryalaharī* and *Śivānandalaharī* among his devotional hymns 168; *Sopāna Pañcaka* contains essence of his teachings 201; tarka should not become dustarka 419; tolerance, he exemplified it 484; uses "tvam" as a pun in *Saundaryalaharī* 243; Vedic karma, bids us to perform them 201; Vedic religion, re-established it 384; Vedic works renounced in the last āśrama to devote oneself to meditation and metaphysical inquiry 390; *Viṣṇu-Sahasranāma*, his commentary on it 446.
(See also under "Ādi Śankara", "Śankara" and "Śankara Bhagavatpāda".)
Acyutarāya, 441, 442, 443.
Adam, 32, 33, 34.
Adharma, God does not plunge the world in it 37.
Adhikaraṇa, 382.
Adhvaryu, 190, 629.
Adhyāpana, 80, 88, 639.
Adhyayana, 80, 88.
Ādikāvya, 338.
Ādi Śankara, incarnation of Śiva 39; instituted Ṣaṇmata 46; people drawn to him 21; when he held sway non-Vedic religions declined 20; his

Brahman, jñāna, mokṣa, etc 403; one of the fourteen abodes of knowledge 132; one of the six śāstras according to one reckoning 317; our duty to perform Vedic works 398; Prabhākara school 418; six ways of determining meaning of a Vedic vākya 240; some authorities in the South 408; term explained 381; term usually denotes Pūrvamīmāṁsā 381; Vaidyanātha Dīkṣita follows it in determining the meaning of Vedic texts 494.
Mīmāṁsakas, adherents of Pūrvamīmāṁsā 384; āstikas even if they don't consecrate their works to the Supreme Being 742; do not favour sannyāsa 401; giving up works sinful — also looking at a sannyāsin 401; Īśvara not Kartā 384, 385.
Mīnākṣisundaram Pillai, Mahāvidvān 481.
Mind, all problems caused by it 699.
Mishra, P.S., xii, xx.
Mississippi, 579.
Mitākṣara, 375, 492.
Mitra, 30, 46.
Mitrā-Varuṇa, 138.
Moghul, influence mainly in the North 61.
Mohammedan Veda (Qur'ān), 137.
Mokṣa, how it may be attained — chief purpose of religion 10; state of supreme bliss 9; the ultimate quest 9.
Money, one should not run after it 114; not essential to the performance of rites 114.
Monotheism, a Vedic tenet 171.
Mortimer Wheeler, 149, 151.
Motherhood, its duty 586-87.
Mother Veda, 618.
Mṛgabali, 629.
Mudalāḷi, 189.
Mūka-Pañcaśatī, composed in Śārdūlavikrīditam and Śikhariṇī 339.
Mūlādhāra, 283, 284, 739.
Mūlavarman of Kotei, 30.
Muṇḍakopaniṣad, arrow of the Ātman, 224; belongs to the Atharvaveda 223, 261; bow of Oṁkāra 224; how to be one with the Brahman 224, 233; motto of the Union of India, "Satyameva Jayate", taken from it 224, 234; only sannyāsins with a high degree of maturity are qualified to study it 224; on sannyāsins who are videhamuktas 224, 234; on the jñānin 224, 234; speaks of the Akṣarabrahman 224; account of the two birds, source of the biblical story of Adam and Eve, occurs in it 224, 233-34.
Munshi, K.M. (Kulapati), xiii.
Muruga, 39, 44, 46.
Mussolini, 435.
Muttī (tretāgni or śrautāgni), 625.
Muvendar, 304.

Naccinārkkiṇiyār, 305, 744.
Naciketas, 493.
Nādabrahman, 322, 329.
Nāda, 148.
Nāḍis, changing sound or tone of mantras will mean their harmful vibrations 738; beneficial vibrations of 164; breath that passes through them 144; control over nāḍis through Rājayoga 163; different emotions and urges created by different vibrations of the nāḍis 163, 283; sounds of Sanskrit cause beneficial nāḍī vibrations 328; their vibrations

Hindu Dharma
The Universal Way of Life

Extracts from Press Reviews

...The Jagadguru of Kanchi whose pilgrimage on earth ended in his 100th year, on January 8, 1994, personified the everlasting Moral Force. He was the living embodiment of the highest aspirations of mankind, the noblest instincts of humanity, the loftiest attributes of the divine spirit in earthly garb. His was not a life to be described in words or measured in years. He lived in eternity....

...The book brings out the essential message of Indian dharma — the message of universal brotherhood and mutual respect...

...The book presents the Vedic vision of universality and harmony. It presents a panorama of the Dharma of this ancient land. In the words of Will Durant, India can teach the world the tolerance and gentleness of the mature mind, the quiet content of the unacquisitive soul, the calm of the understanding spirit and a unifying, pacifying love for all living things...

...The book contains a fund of wisdom which is not only for Hindus, not merely for the various communities of India, but for the whole world...

He delivered his discourses over the decades in Tamil. Extracts from his discourses, selected and translated into English by the well-known writer RGK, have now been published by the Bhavan. A more meritorious job of translation has never been done.

— N.A. Palkhivala
The Times of India

...The topics covered, in the twenty-two sections of the book, are wide-ranging. They cover the Vedas, the Shadangas, the Dharmasastras, the Puranas, Varna dharma, the forty Samskaras, ashrama dharma, etc. With the encyclopaedic amplitude of his mind, the Acharya's discourses, reveal to us, his astonishingly wide range and the quenchless vitality of his spiritual voyage through the ocean of Hindu Dharma. Calm, unaggressive and persuasive in tone, he is resolutely firm and uncompromising in the tenor of his discourse...

...The book is excellently produced. The translation is both elegant and fruitful...

S.R.
— *The Hindu*

...As I read the book, I kept marvelling at the ease with which the sage has made abstruse thoughts sound so simple...

If I say that I could not put the book down, I would be telling the literal truth. I read this book deep into the night, and picked it up first thing in the morning.

...The aim is not to frighten the reader with massive scholarship, but to engage his attention with homely language. Even as I read the book, I kept thinking that the sage was talking specifically to me. The book would appeal to a high school student as much as to a professor of philosophy...

— M.V. Kamath
Mid-Day

...Befittingly, Bharatiya Vidya Bhavan by publishing this book has 'immortalised' India in every sense of the word. This book is a must for one and all, cutting across all man-made barriers. Indeed, the Paramacharya was a pipeline to Godhood, who gave a new dimension to Hinduism as a Universal Way of Life...

V.H. Desai
— *Sunday Chronicle*

...The Kanchi Mahasvami was a saint extraordinary. Combined with the purity of his saintliness was his clarity of thought. To his intellectual stature attained through arduous study he added spiritual splendour through tapas. As the head of a Matha founded by Adi Sankara, he was looked upon as the custodian of Hindu Dharma. Thus, in more than one respect, his right to speak on our faith is unassailable. His words carry the weight of authority and his exhortations to us the quality of a divine command...

V.S.R.K.
— *Dilip*

...The more I read *Hindu Dharma* the more I realised what a great soul the guru was. Though he spoke in Tamil, one of our richest languages, his utterances have been rendered into English by RGK...

...*Hindu Dharma* is a monumental work of deep thinking. It strikes at the root of most of our ills.

It must be read by all those who want to understand India in all her varied manifestations. It should be prescribed as a textbook in all our universities and commended as subsidiary reading in centres of higher learning abroad.

— Dr Rafiq Zakaria
— *Mid-Day*